OLD TESTAMENT
SURVEY

OLD TESTAMENT
SURVEY

*The Message,
Form, and Background
of the Old Testament*

WILLIAM SANFORD LASOR
DAVID ALLAN HUBBARD
FREDERIC WM. BUSH

WILLIAM B. EERDMANS PUBLISHING COMPANY
GRAND RAPIDS, MICHIGAN

THE PATERNOSTER PRESS
CARLISLE

Copyright © 1982 by Wm. B. Eerdmans Publishing Co.
255 Jefferson Ave. SE, Grand Rapids, Mich. 49503
All rights reserved

First published 1982 by
Wm. B. Eerdmans Publishing Co.

This edition published jointly by
Wm. B. Eerdmans and
The Paternoster Press
P.O. Box 300
Carlisle, Cumbria CA3 0QS UK

Printed in the United States of America

Reprinted 1994

Library of Congress Cataloging in Publication Data
La Sor, William Sanford.
Old Testament survey.
Bibliography: p. 675
Includes index.
1. Bible. O.T.—Introductions.   I. Hubbard, David Allan.
II. Bush, Frederic William.   III. Title.
BS1140.2.L25   221.6′1   81-12630
ISBN 0-8028-3556-2   AACR2

CONTENTS

PREFACE

THIS book has been in the making for some years. The plan for it developed when one of us taught Old Testament survey courses at the collegiate level and was frustrated by the lack of an adequate text. Though teachers of Scripture have been blessed amply with specialized works like histories, theologies, and introductions, no one volume was available that combined those elements in a framework whose theological and scholarly approaches we found congenial. For more than fifteen years now the three of us have taught together as a team at Fuller Theological Seminary, sharing the Old Testament core courses and testing these chapters with hundreds of students along the way. Their suggestions and criticisms we have tried to incorporate into the various drafts, and their fingerprints are on every page.

We have approached our materials with both college and seminary students in mind. Our aim has been to pitch the text at a level that most college students can handle and then to meet some of the more technical needs of seminary instruction with the footnotes and bibliographies. (Works cited in the annotated chapter bibliographies—labeled "For Further Reading"—are representative studies chosen to supplement those cited in the chapter notes. For more comprehensive works see the General Bibliography.) Though each of us has drafted certain chapters, we have all read, reviewed, and revised each other's work so thoroughly that the book is a joint effort in every sense.

Our purpose is straightforward: to introduce the reader to the background, content, literary quality, and message of the Old Testament as a whole and of its various books. To do this we have not followed a rigid outline for each biblical book but have sought to let the contents and style of each book dictate the way we have studied it. The basic sequence of the later prophets has been altered to fit our understanding of their approximate chronological order. In no way is our design to substitute for the Bible. What book can? Our hope is that it will be read as a guide and supplement to the biblical text itself and that, as such, it will enhance the devotion and obedience of its readers to Scripture and to Scripture's Lord.

We venture to state succinctly here what we have tried to make apparent throughout the book: we are committed to the inspiration and the authority of the Bible, including every part of the Old Testament, and seek to honor it as Holy Scripture in all we say about it. Beyond that, we have written of the Old Testament as those who understand that its fulfillment is in the New Testament and in Jesus of Nazareth, whom we believe to be the Messiah and the incarnation of the living God. Though at every point we have sought to approach the Old Testament text from the vantage of Israel's sons and daughters to whom it was first given, yet we have been constrained not to stop there but to suggest the relationships of the Old Testament themes to the New Testament, the creedal affirmations of the early Church, and the evangelical confessions of the Reformation—all of which govern and express what we believe and teach.

Out of that commitment to the reality and authority of divine revelation flows a concern to take with full seriousness the historical, cultural, and social setting of Scripture together with the literary and linguistic means by which it was recorded. That concern necessarily entails the reverent use of the tools of textual, literary, and form criticism in order to hear the nuances with which God spoke to the first hearers of his word. We do the Bible no honor to revere it without making every effort, with every available scholarly means, to understand it. Obedience to God and worship of his holy name are our ultimate aim as God's people. Such obedience and worship will be best informed where we have grasped the how, why, when, where, and by whom of his sacred revelations. Both piety and study are essential to sound discipleship. To combine them has been the goal of our ministries and of this book.

WILLIAM SANFORD LASOR
DAVID ALLAN HUBBARD
FREDERIC WM. BUSH

September 1981

ACKNOWLEDGMENTS

UNLESS otherwise stated, the Scripture quotations in this book are from the Revised Standard Version of the Holy Bible, copyright 1946, 1952, and © 1971, 1973 by the Division of Christian Education, National Council of the Churches of Christ in the U.S.A., and used by permission.

Special thanks for help goes to our graduate assistants Eugene Carpenter, Ph.D., Edward M. Cook, Marianne Meye Thompson, and Marguerite Schuster, Ph.D. Inez T. Smith coordinated the typing and collating of the various drafts. Phyllis Jarvis of Wm. B. Eerdmans Publishing Co. retyped the entire edited manuscript, which was revised for style and checked for accuracy by Allen Myers.

LIST OF MAPS

ABBREVIATIONS

AASOR   *Annual of the American Schools of Oriental Research*

AJA   *American Journal of Archaeology*

AJSL   *The American Journal of Semitic Languages and Literature*

ANEP   J.B. Pritchard, *The Ancient Near East in Pictures*, 2nd ed. (Princeton: 1969)

ANET   J.B. Pritchard, ed., *Ancient Near Eastern Texts*, 3rd ed. (Princeton: 1969)

Ant.   Josephus, *Antiquities of the Jews*

ARAB   D.D. Luckenbill, ed., *Ancient Records of Assyria and Babylonia*, 2 vols. (Chicago: 1926-27)

BA   *Biblical Archaeologist*

BANE   G.E. Wright, ed., *The Bible and the Ancient Near East* (1961; repr. Winona Lake: 1979)

BASOR   *Bulletin of the American Schools of Oriental Research*

BDB   F. Brown, S.R. Driver, and C.A. Briggs, *A Hebrew and English Lexicon of the Old Testament* (Oxford: 1907)

BDPT   R.G. Turnbull, ed., *Baker's Dictionary of Practical Theology* (Grand Rapids: 1967)

Bibl   *Biblica*

BJRL   *Bulletin of the John Rylands Library*

BKAT   M. Noth and H.W. Wolff, eds., *Biblischer Kommentar Alten Testament* (Neukirchen)

BWANT   *Beiträge zur Wissenschaft von Alten und Neuen Testament*

BZAW   *Beihefte zur Zeitschrift für die Alttestamentliche Wissenschaft*

CAH   I.E.S. Edwards et al., eds., *Cambridge Ancient History*, 3rd ed., 2 vols. in 4 parts (Cambridge: 1970—)

CBQ   *Catholic Biblical Quarterly*

CCHS   B. Orchard, ed., *A Catholic Commentary on Holy Scripture* (New York: 1953)

CTM	*Concordia Theological Monthly*
DJD	*Discoveries in the Judaean Desert of Jordan* (Oxford: 1955—)
DOTT	D.W. Thomas, ed., *Documents from Old Testament Times* (New York: 1961)
HAT	O. Eissfeldt, ed., *Handbuch zum Alten Testament* (Tübingen)
HDB	J. Hastings, ed., *Dictionary of the Bible,* 4 vols. (New York: 1898-1902); supplement (1904); rev. ed., 1 vol. (1963)
HKAT	*Handkommentar zum Alten Testament* (Göttingen)
HSAT	E. Kautzsch and A. Bertholet, eds., *Die heilige Schrift des Alten Testament,* 4th ed. (Tübingen: 1922-23)
HSM	*Harvard Semitic Monographs*
HTR	*Harvard Theological Review*
HUCA	*Hebrew Union College Annual*
IB	G.A. Buttrick, ed., *The Interpreter's Bible,* 12 vols. (Nashville: 1952-57).
IBD	N. Hillyer, ed., *The Illustrated Bible Dictionary* (Wheaton: 1980)
ICC	*The International Critical Commentary* (Edinburgh)
IDB	G.A. Buttrick, ed., *The Interpreter's Dictionary of the Bible,* 4 vols. (Nashville: 1962)
IDBS	K. Crim, ed., *The Interpreter's Dictionary of the Bible, Supplement* (Nashville: 1976)
IEJ	*Israel Exploration Journal*
Interp	*Interpretation*
ISBE	J. Orr, ed., *The International Standard Bible Encyclopedia,* 5 vols. (Grand Rapids: 1939); rev. ed., 4 vols., G.W. Bromiley et al., eds. (1979—)
JAOS	*Journal of the American Oriental Society*
JB	*The Jerusalem Bible*
JBL	*Journal of Biblical Literature*
JJS	*Journal of Jewish Studies*
JNES	*Journal of Near Eastern Studies*
JPOS	*Journal of the Palestine Oriental Society*
JQR	*Jewish Quarterly Review*
JSOT	*Journal for the Study of the Old Testament*
JSOTS	*Journal for the Study of the Old Testament, Supplement Series*
JSS	*Journal of Semitic Studies*
KAT	E. Sellin and J. Herrmann, eds., *Kommentar zum Alten Testament* (Leipzig, Gütersloh)
KJV	*King James Version*
LXX	Septuagint
MT	Masoretic Text
NASB	*New American Standard Bible*
NBC	D. Guthrie and J.A. Motyer, eds., *The New Bible Commentary Revised* (Grand Rapids: 1970)

NCBC	R.E. Clements and M. Black, eds., *The New Century Bible Commentary* (Grand Rapids)
NEB	*New English Bible*
NICOT	R.K. Harrison, ed., *The New International Commentary on the Old Testament* (Grand Rapids)
NIV	*New International Version*
OBS	J.J. Finkelstein and M. Greenberg, eds., *Oriental and Biblical Studies* (Philadelphia: 1967)
OTL	*The Old Testament Library* (Philadelphia)
OTMS	H.H. Rowley, ed., *The Old Testament and Modern Study* (Oxford: 1951)
OTS	*Oudtestamentische Studiën*
PEQ	*Palestine Exploration Quarterly*
RSV	*Revised Standard Version*
RV	*Revised Version*
SBT	*Studies in Biblical Theology*
SJT	*Scottish Journal of Theology*
SOTS	The Society for Old Testament Study
TCERK	L. Loetscher, ed., *Twentieth-Century Encyclopedia of Religious Knowledge*, 2 vols. (Grand Rapids: 1949)
TDNT	G. Kittel and G. Friedrich, eds., *Theological Dictionary of the New Testament*, 10 vols. (Grand Rapids: 1964-1976)
USQR	*Union Seminary Quarterly Review*
UUÅ	*Uppsala Universitets Årsskrift*
VT	*Vetus Testamentum*
VTS	*Vetus Testamentum, Supplements*
WMANT	*Wissenschaftliche Monographien zum Alten und Neuen Testament*
WTJ	*Westminster Theological Journal*
ZAW	*Zeitschrift für die Alttestamentliche Wissenschaft*
ZNW	*Zeitschrift für die Neutestamentliche Wissenschaft*
ZPBD	M.C. Tenney, ed., *The Zondervan Pictorial Bible Dictionary* (Grand Rapids: 1963)
ZPEB	M.C. Tenney, ed., *The Zondervan Pictorial Encyclopedia of the Bible*, 5 vols. (Grand Rapids: 1975)

CHAPTER 1

THE AUTHORITY OF
THE OLD TESTAMENT

THE Old Testament was the Bible used by Christ and the apostles. Almost uniformly (2 Pet. 3:16 is an exception) the words "Scripture" or "Scriptures" in the New Testament refer to the Old Testament (e.g., John 5:39; 10:35; Acts 8:32; Gal. 3:8; 2 Tim. 3:16). For about two decades after Christ the only parts of the New Testament in existence were fragmentary accounts of his life and teachings. During this period when a vital Church was extending its influence into Syria, Asia Minor, and North Africa, the basis for preaching and teaching was the Old Testament as reinterpreted by Christ himself.

JESUS AND THE OLD TESTAMENT

You search the scriptures . . . and it is they that bear witness to me. (John 5:39)

Christ recognized the full authority, the binding nature, of Scripture while reserving for himself the right to be its true interpreter. Although he crossed swords with Jewish leaders at many points, Christ gives no evidence in the New Testament of conflict over the inspiration or authority of the Old Testament. On the contrary, Christ frequently appealed to the Scriptures as the ground for his claims and teachings. This is illustrated in the threefold use of "it is written" in the temptation story (Matt. 4:1-11), which is clear testimony to his personal reliance on the authority of the Old Testament, and in his argument with the Jews concerning the right to call himself God's Son (John 10:31-36), which hinges on the complete reliability of the Scriptures.

In thus relying on the Old Testament as the word of God in writing, Jesus followed his Jewish kinsmen, who centuries before had begun the practice in response to their unique experiences as God's people. God's words and acts of revelation had spoken to them with such power and clarity that they preserved and treasured them in written record. Stage by stage a body of authoritative literature had grown among the Israelites: laws, narratives of their past, oracles

1

of their prophets, teachings of their wise men, and hymns and prayers of their worship. In these documents, which shaped the understanding of their life, faith, and destiny, they recognized the word of the one Lord whom they knew to be the only true God.

Though sharing his Jewish contemporaries' attitude toward the authority of the Old Testament, Christ's interpretation of it differs sharply on at least two points. First, like the prophets, Christ sensed the emptiness of much of Jewish legalism in which routine and ritual had become a worthless substitute for purity of heart, integrity, and social concern (e.g., Mark 7:1-13; Matt. 9:13; 12:7, which quote Hos. 6:6). As the true prophet, the new Moses, Christ interpreted the law in the Sermon on the Mount (Matt. 5–7). Renouncing the prevalent Jewish interpretation of the law and emphasizing love, forgiveness, and inward piety, Christ brought fresh import to some major prophetic themes, which many Jews had neglected in magnifying the letter of the law.

Second, an even sharper distinction, is Jesus' insistence that as the personal fulfillment of the Old Testament, he is its major theme. His declaration in the synagogue in his home town—"Today this scripture has been fulfilled in your hearing" (Luke 4:21)—may be seen as the epitome of his claims. This sense of fulfillment both sparked his conflict with the Jewish officialdom (John 5:46) and shaped his followers' attitude toward the Scriptures (Luke 24:44f.).

Christ revolutionized Old Testament interpretation by drawing together various strands of teaching and braiding them into a single cord in himself. He was the great prophet like Moses who taught the new law from the mountain; the peerless priest who made the whole temple system obsolete (cf. Matt. 12:6; John 2:13-15); the wise king, the "greater than Solomon" (Matt. 12:42); David's son and Lord, rightful heir to Israel's throne (Mark 12:35-37; 15:2); the triumphant Son of man (Dan. 7:13ff.; Mark 13:26); and the suffering servant (Isa. 53; Mark 10:45). The great themes of prophetic expectation found their consummation in him.

Compared to the viewpoint of most of his Jewish contemporaries, Christ's approach to the Old Testament is dynamic, not static. He looked upon the Old Testament not as a catalogue of fixed principles regulating religious conduct, but as the inspired and authoritative record of God's activity in history, an activity which presses toward its denouement in his coming kingdom. As Jesus' words are spirit and life (John 6:63), so the Old Testament when viewed with his insights becomes a guide to life (John 5:39).

In highlighting the prophets as legitimate interpreters of the law and in focusing the Old Testament revelation on himself, Christ shaped the patterns of biblical interpretation adopted by the evangelists and apostolic writers. For example, Matthew's constant concern is the correspondence between events in his Messiah's life and Old Testament prophecy, evidenced in his oft-repeated "to fulfill what was spoken" (e.g., 1:22; 2:15, 17, 23; 4:14; 12:17; 13:35; 21:4; 27:9), and John makes frequent explicit and implicit comparisons of Moses and Christ (e.g., 1:17; 3:14; 5:45-47; 6:32; 7:19).

PAUL AND THE OLD TESTAMENT

As a Jew and a rabbi, Saul of Tarsus knew the Old Testament well; as a Christian and an apostle, Paul found the familiar text pregnant with fresh meaning. Like Jesus he accepted the full inspiration and authority of the Scripture (2 Tim. 3:16) and found its deepest significance in its anticipation of and preparation for the New Testament. The similarities between Christ's approach and Paul's are not accidental. Undoubtedly Christ singled out relevant Old Testament passages and taught his disciples the principles by which they were to be interpreted.[1]

In his four pillar epistles—Romans, 1–2 Corinthians, and Galatians—Paul's heavy dependence on the Old Testament shows most clearly. A large percentage of his more than ninety quotations are found in them, while his great theological themes and frequently his means of argumentation in these key doctrinal letters are drawn from the Old Testament. Paul's willingness to bow to the authority of Scripture, his use of it to clinch his arguments, his regard for its verdicts, and his reverence for its sanctity set the pattern for all who follow him in handling the oracles of God.

So drastic was the transformation of Paul's understanding of the Old Testament that the Christ whose followers he had doggedly vowed to stamp out became for him the very heart of Old Testament revelation:

> For Paul, Christ was not only a factor giving added meaning to the OT but the only means whereby the OT could be rightly understood; it was not merely that he saw Christ in the OT but that he viewed the whole scope of OT prophecy and history from the standpoint of the Messianic Age in which the OT stood open, fulfilled in Jesus Christ and in His new creation.[2]

The extent to which Paul grounds his doctrinal instruction in Old Testament soil is indicated by a score of topics held to reflect either explicitly or implicitly its influence. These include the fall of man and its effects (Rom. 5:12-21), the universality of sin (3:10-20), the obedience and sufferings of Christ (15:3), justification by faith (1:17; 4:1ff.; 10:5ff.), and the final salvation of the Jews (11:26).[3]

Typology plays no small part in the Pauline epistles.[4] Studies of New Testament typology[5] have stressed the continuity between Paul's and Christ's uses

---

1. So, among others, C.H. Dodd, *According to the Scriptures* (London: 1952), pp. 108ff. Cf. E.E. Ellis, *Paul's Use of the Old Testament* (Grand Rapids: 1957), p. 113.
2. Ellis, *ibid.*, pp. 115f.
3. *Ibid.*, p. 116.
4. Typology has been defined as "the establishment of historical connections between certain events, persons or things in the Old Testament and similar events, persons or things in the New Testament." See. G.W.H. Lampe and K.J. Woollcombe, *Essays in Typology* (London: 1957), pp. 147ff.
5. E.g., *ibid.*

of Old Testament types and have contrasted both with the exegetical methods of Philo of Alexandria and Jewish rabbinical writers. The contemporary revival of interest in typology is sparked, in part at least, by a renewed regard for the unity of the Bible and the ways in which the New Testament writers depend upon the Old. An increasing awareness that the unity of the Bible is a dynamic one, based on the continuity of God's activity in both Testaments, has helped explain the historical character of biblical typology.[6] For Paul the same God was working in both ages, and the patterns of his past activity were prototypes of his present and future acts. In their use of God's past activity to illustrate his present and future works, both Christ and Paul follow the example of the Old Testament itself, in which, for instance, the Exodus from Egypt sets the pattern for the return from captivity—the New Exodus (cf. Isa. 43:16-20). The Old Testament is significant for Paul not for hidden mystical, spiritual meanings but for its inspired record of God's creative, elective, and redemptive activity, consummated in the New Age ushered in by the incarnation of Jesus Christ.

Those who have placed their emphasis on the historical continuity within the Bible have not always pointed out the moral or ethical relationship between the Testaments. Though the New Testament certainly transcends the Old in ethical insights, the earlier revelation has much to say about themes most fully presented in the teachings of Christ and the apostles: doing God's will is the highest good; immorality, idolatry, inhumanity, and spiritual rebellion are to be shunned; honesty, integrity, diligence, and concern for the rights and needs of others are valued as sterling and admirable qualities. Paul noted the importance of the Old Testament's ethical and moral instruction (2 Tim. 3:16f.), and his writings reflect its illustrative use by the early Christians (1 Cor. 10:1-11).

The freedom with which Paul and other New Testament writers (especially Matthew) sometimes handled the Old Testament has been puzzling. At times they followed no known Greek or Hebrew textual tradition. That the apostolic authors sometimes wove interpretative strands into their quotations has been recognized increasingly. However, these interpretative glosses are usually not arbitrary or capricious but should be classed as quotation expositions which neither follow the text with slavish literalism nor alter its meaning with haphazard interpretation.[7] In interpreting the Scriptures, Paul paid close attention to their historical setting and their grammatical structure. Yet he interpreted historical events not so much in their past significance as in their significance for later fulfillment; and he moved beyond the *prima facie* grammatical structure to a meaning which is grammatically possible and which also fits an overall interpretation of the Old Testament revelation.[8]

---

6. *Ibid.*, pp. 147ff.

7. F.F. Bruce compares the arbitrary interpretations of a passage from Amos in the Zadokite Admonition and Stephen's sympathetic, sensitive rendering of another prophetic passage in Amos 7:42f.; *Biblical Exegesis in the Qumran Texts* (Grand Rapids: 1959), p. 73.

8. Ellis, *Paul's Use of the Old Testament*, pp. 147f.

CONCLUSION

The pattern of authority and the principles of interpretation discussed could easily be applied to other New Testament writings such as Hebrews, James, and Revelation. Laced with Old Testament allusions and quotations, each has its own way of employing them. James, for instance, depends heavily upon Israel's wisdom literature and particularly upon both the teaching techniques and the thought of Christ, the Master Sage. The author of Hebrews employed Old Testament proof texts and types to demonstrate the marked superiority of Christ and his new covenant. John in the Revelation, convinced that Christ is the Alpha and Omega, constantly described the cosmic climax of history in terms borrowed from Old Testament descriptions of God's acts in mercy and judgment; by so doing, his book suggests that this climax is what was spoken of and longed for by the prophets—the triumph of the kingdom of God.

Following their Lord's example in yielding to the authority of the Scriptures, the New Testament writers found in them not the letter which kills but the inspired witness to God's redemptive activity, which alone brings life. They read the Scriptures not as lifeless collections of enslaving laws but as the earlier acts in a great drama of salvation, a drama whose central actor was their Lord. Modern readers are no less in need of the earlier acts, for in them may still be seen the activity of God and the various responses of surrender and rebellion which his activity sparked. What was important, authoritative, and crucial to the Lord and the early Church cannot be any less so today (1 Cor. 10:11).

In study as in worship humankind needs the entire revelation, the whole Bible. The Old Testament belongs not to the Jewish people alone but to all. It is the account of the ways in which God has worked; it is the summary of what he has demanded; it is the record of his preparation for Christ's coming; it is the best canvas on which to catch the picture of his dealings with the human family through the centuries. In short, it is the indispensable foundation on which the New Testament is built. To understand the Old Testament as Christian scripture, one must see it through the eyes of Jesus and his apostles. They were especially inspired by God's Spirit to grasp the meaning of his revelatory words and deeds and the directions in which they were moving.

Yet at the same time, the modern reader must try to see the Old Testament passages on their own terms. The reader must ask: "What was the Old Testament author saying to his own times?" He or she must sit with the hearers in the marketplace, city gate, temple, or synagogue and try to understand his words as they heard them. He or she must see God through their eyes and discern his purposes in their lives.

In other words, one must be sensitive to the original context of an Old Testament passage. Why was it written and when? What problems called it into being? What question was it initially intended to answer? What did it tell the people about God's will and ways or about their responsibilities that they would not otherwise have known? Only when one understands the intent of a passage for the author's own times, can he then catch the full significance of the passage for Christian faith and life. The Old Testament context will not tell all one needs to know about the meaning of the passage. But unless one starts there, it becomes easy to twist the Scriptures to one's own purpose. Rather, the sense of the individual authors must be grasped in order to capture the meaning put there by the overall Author, the Spirit of God, who speaks through all of Scripture and whose speaking gives the whole Bible its authority for his people.[9]

FOR FURTHER READING

Barr, J. "The Authority of the Bible: A Study Outline." *Ecumenical Review* 21 (1969): 135-166. (Historically a "Western problem.")

Bright, J. *The Authority of the Old Testament*. Nashville: 1967. (Focuses on interpretation for preaching.)

Coats, G.W., and Long, B.O., eds. *Canon and Authority*. Philadelphia: 1977. (Esp. essays by Long on prophetic authority, W.S. Towner on wisdom.)

Cunliffe-Jones, H. *The Authority of the Biblical Revelation*. Boston: 1948. (Distinguishes between historical and theological study of the Bible.)

Dodd, C.H. *The Authority of the Bible*. Rev. ed. New York: 1938.

Forstman, H.J. *Word and Spirit: Calvin's Doctrine of Biblical Authority*. Stanford: 1962.

Fullerton, K. *Prophecy and Authority*. New York: 1919. (Study in history of the doctrine and interpretation of Scripture.)

Hebert, A.G. *The Authority of the Old Testament*. London: 1947. (Esp. sections on literal and spiritual interpretation.)

Hesse, F. "The Evaluation and the Authority of Old Testament Texts." Trans. J.A. Wharton. Pp. 285-313 in C. Westermann, ed., *Essays on Old Testament Hermeneutics*. Ed. J.L. Mays. Richmond: 1963.

Johnson, R.C. *Authority in Protestant Theology*. Philadelphia: 1959.

Marsh, J. "Authority." *IDB* 1:319f.

Kelsey, D.H. *The Uses of Scripture in Recent Theology*. Philadelphia: 1975.

Ramm, B.L. *Protestant Biblical Interpretation*. 3rd ed. Grand Rapids: 1970. (Textbook of hermeneutics for conservative Protestants.)

Reid, J.K.S. *The Authority of Scripture: A Study of the Reformation and Post-Reformation Understanding of the Bible*. New York: 1957.

Richardson, A., and Schweitzer, W. *Biblical Authority for Today*. Philadelphia: 1951. (Esp. pp. 17-126, a variety of mainline Protestant perspectives.)

---

9. On the relationship between the Testaments, see D. Moody Smith, Jr., "The Use of the Old Testament in the New," in J.M. Efird, ed., *The Use of the Old Testament in the New and Other Essays* (Durham, N.C.: 1972), pp. 3-65.

CHAPTER 2

REVELATION AND INSPIRATION

THE BASIC PROBLEM

ONE can approach the Bible from either of two directions. As a product of the ancient Near East, it can be studied together with similar types of other literature from approximately the same period. One value of this method is the realization that the biblical people were real people, with more purpose in life than just to receive revelations from God and worship him by various cultic acts. The view that they were an isolated people is contradicted by the biblical evidence, in which many nations and several religious systems came constantly in contact with the people of Yahweh. At the same time, this comparative approach has several disadvantages. Perhaps most important of these is the fact that noting the similarities between the people of Yahweh and the surrounding peoples tends to obscure the significant differences.[1] The hard fact is that the other ancient Near Eastern religions have disappeared while the biblical religion remains—a survival most likely explained by the distinctive qualities of biblical religion.

The second approach begins with what the Bible says about itself. This does not mean ignoring ancient Near Eastern history and geography or the religions and culture of that world, for the Bible itself does not do so. But certain characteristics of biblical religion are either unique or markedly dissimilar from the religions of the surrounding peoples. One of these is the biblical concept that Yahweh, as God is called in the Old Testament,[2] desires and maintains communication with his people.

The Bible opens with an account of the God who created the heavens and earth, created a human family[3] in his own image (Gen. 1:26), and communi-

---

1. For a critical evaluation of this approach, see H.F. Hahn, *The Old Testament in Modern Research*, rev. ed. (Philadelphia: 1966), pp. 83-118.
2. This does not imply a different God than is found in the New Testament, although the name Yahweh does not occur there.
3. Heb. *'ādām* is a generic term encompassing both male and female.

7

cated with them (vv. 28-30). That primal fellowship was broken by disobedience (3:23), but in spite of that rebellion against God's authority God continued to communicate with humankind throughout the Old Testament. Therefore in the Old Testament (and in the New) a basic concept occurs, accepted in faith by the people of the Bible, that God made people for fellowship with him. To maintain this fellowship, God revealed his will to his creatures, and, after their fall, made known his desire and intention to restore this fellowship by continuing to make known his will and his person.

REVELATION

God revealed himself to Abraham, Moses, Samuel, and many other persons. The prophet Amos, setting forth the authority for his message, said: "Surely the Lord God does nothing, without revealing his secret to his servants the prophets" (Amos 3:7). This concept of revelation recurs with noteworthy frequency throughout the Old Testament.

Meaning of the Term. "Revelation" can be active or passive in meaning, referring either to the act of revealing or uncovering or to that which has been revealed or uncovered. Formerly, stress was placed on the active meaning: revelation was to be found in the communications of God to persons—through the visions he gave, the words he spoke, and the deeds he performed. According to the more recent emphasis, revelation is to be found in certain events of history which people have perceived as the acts of God. The biblical viewpoint includes both elements. As one scholar has stated it, one "*sees* in the historical event and *understands* from the word of Yahweh."[4]

Act Revelation and Word Revelation. It is certainly true that God reveals himself by his activity. The deliverance of Israel from Egyptian bondage, including the mighty acts that accompanied the Exodus, is one of the greatest revelatory acts of Yahweh in the Old Testament. But alongside this activity is a word of revelation. Yahweh revealed himself and his purpose before the deliverance (Exod. 3:2-10), in connection with the Exodus (cf. 12:12f.), and after the event (cf. 20:2; Ezek. 20:6-10). In fact, the Old Testament has been described as a rehearsal of the mighty acts of God, for he repeatedly reminds his people of what he has done on their behalf. The inference is clear: without the revelatory word, the act would have had revelatory significance to very few, if any. Even when God explained his acts, the people often forgot their revelatory and redemptive significance.

Revelation, by act or word, does not exist for itself but is intended to produce an effect upon those to whom it is given. They are to observe it, learn

---

4. B.D. Napier, *From Faith to Faith* (New York: 1955), p. 157.

Jebel Musa, traditionally identified with Mt. Sinai, where the Lord spoke to Moses (Exod. 19:3). (W.S. LaSor)

from it, and respond to it. Because God's continuing purpose in the Bible is redemptive—to undo the result of the fall in Eden and to restore human beings to the original creation image—biblical revelation is often called "redemptive." From the biblical viewpoint every revelation of God probably can be sustained as redemptive in purpose, for even his negative (i.e., judicial or punitive) acts contribute to the establishment of his beneficent will.

The principal word used to express this concept in Hebrew is *gālâ* "to uncover, lay bare" (cf. New Testament Gk. *apokalýptō* "lay bare, uncover," and *apokálypsis* "uncovering, laying bare, revelation"). In the Old Testament, the word can be used not only for God's revelation, but also with reference to human events. For example, Nebuchadnezzar "laid bare" the land of Judah (cf. Esth. 2:6; RSV "carried away"). By contrast, the New Testament words are used only of God's revelation to the Israelites and the Church.

Necessity of Revelation. Two reasons can be given for the need for revelation. First, Yahweh is a being who transcends the space-time system perceived by human sense. The first Russian astronaut to return from outer space reported that he did not find God up there. From the nature of God as revealed in the Bible, one should not expect to perceive him directly by any sensory method. It is necessary for him to reveal himself, to "uncover" himself, to communicate in ways that can be perceived. In the Bible he is presented as using audible, visible, and other sensory means of communication, so that mankind "heard" his "voice," "saw" some appearance, or "felt" the earth quake at his presence. Second, mankind is represented as a fallen race whose rebellion against God and slavery to sin make it unable to hear or see or understand what is clearly revealed.

General and Special Revelation. According to the biblical view, God has revealed himself in creation and continues to reveal himself in the works of his providence. "The heavens are telling the glory of God; and the firmament proclaims his handiwork" (Ps. 19:1 [MT2]). Since this revelation is through nature, it sometimes is called "natural" revelation. Since it is to all people— even if all are not capable of comprehending it—it is also called "general" revelation.

In contrast, "special" revelations are not given in general ways to all people, but in specific ways to selected individuals or groups chosen by God to receive particular revelations of his person or will. God revealed himself to Abraham, Isaac, and Jacob, and to Moses and the Israelites. He parted the waters of the Red Sea so that the Israelites could pass through safely and let the waters close on the Egyptians. He led his people into the promised land and drove out the inhabitants of that land, and, in the fullness of time, God sent his Son into the world.

Means of Revelation. In addition to his acts in creation and history, God also revealed himself to individuals through dreams and visions and by verbal communications. This last means is sometimes called "propositional revelation."

Strictly speaking, propositional revelation implies that God communicates by ordinary means, making statements that can be understood by ordinary people. But how such a thing can happen never is explained fully in the Bible. Experience shows that communicating by spoken word entails certain physiological and physical events that constitute both speaking and hearing. However, to suggest that God, who is spirit, must use these physical means of speaking is clearly ludicrous. Nevertheless, in human terminology, God does "speak." The Bible clearly implies that people received communications from God in the same way as from other people through the spoken word. The prophets' strongest conviction was that God had spoken to them in words they could understand and which they could communicate to others in obedience to God's revealed will.

The ultimate revelation of God was given in the incarnation of his Son, Jesus Christ. Biblical doctrine holds that the fulfillment of all previous revelations occurred in the person, works, and especially the words of Jesus Christ (Heb. 1:1-3).

Progressive Revelation. Reading through the Old Testament, one becomes aware that God did not reveal all of himself or his purpose at one time. Rather, he made a sequence of revelations, each of which added to earlier revelations. For example, God revealed his will that Abram (Abraham) go to Canaan (Gen. 12:1), which he promised to give his descendants (12:7). Later, God revealed that Abram's descendants would inhabit that land only after they had been oppressed in a foreign country for four hundred years (15:13). Traced through the Old Testament, this theme becomes more elaborate and its extent more fully defined, finally becoming a central motif in the prophecies of a future day of glory. In much the same way the unfolding revelation of other themes can be traced. This concept has been given the name "progressive revelation."

This concept, however, is more than the simple addition of communicated data, for there is a qualitative as well as a quantitative difference in the revelation. Thus, for example, Jesus Christ specifically stated that he did not come into the world to destroy the law and the prophets, but to fulfill them (Matt. 5:17). This fulfillment, or bringing to fullness of God's intended purpose, does not destroy the law and the prophets (the Old Testament) but adds a "newness" that renders them "old." Thus the author of Hebrews can speak of the "new covenant" as having made the first covenant "obsolete" (Heb. 8:13). Therefore, the Old Testament remains the word of God,[5] but it must be understood in the light of the completed revelation of the two Testaments.

Redemptive Purpose. According to the Bible, God reveals the truth concerning himself and his will not merely to satisfy human curiosity but to accomplish his purpose, which is primarily redemptive. God's purpose is to restore fallen humanity to its original created nature and to lead beyond that into the perfect understanding of God and the perfect fellowship that is redemption's proper culmination.

Such a revelation demands trust in and obedience to what is revealed. For the revelation to Abraham to achieve its redemptive purpose, it required of Abram first faith in God and then obedience to the revealed word. The same can be said of revelation at any point in Scripture. Many men and women heard the words of Jesus and saw the great works he did during his lifetime. Revelation of truth occurred, but for those who had no faith, who failed to obey his words, the revelation did not achieve its redemptive purpose. Likewise, God's revelation in Jesus Christ requires faith in him and obedience to his words today in order to accomplish its purpose. In a sense, then, to those who do not

---

5. The Church correctly rejected the Marcionite view and therefore rejects any similar view that would render the Old Testament as less than the word of God.

(and did not) receive the revelation in faith and obedience God has not really revealed himself.[6]

Even when the prophets were asked questions with seemingly only ephemeral relevance, their replies had deeper revelatory significance. For instance, in the story of Saul's asking the prophet to locate his father's lost asses, the significant task of the prophet was not to answer Saul's question, but to reveal God's will concerning him (1 Sam. 9:3–10:8). In a number of accounts in which kings seek prophetic advice on the eve of battle, the replies consistently show that the prophet's office was not to demonstrate clairvoyance but rather to make known God's sovereignty over Israel's history (cf. 1 Kgs. 22:1-28).

Inscripturation. The Bible nowhere suggests that all of God's revelations were committed to writing. On the contrary, the Gospels clearly indicate that Jesus Christ did and said many things which are not recorded—and these were part of God's revelation to that generation (cf. John 20:30). But for the sake of future generations and in the light of his ongoing redemptive purpose, God did will that some of his revelation be written down so that his redemptive acts in former generations might serve as examples to those who came later. The result of this inscripturation is the Bible.

According to biblical teachings, God ordered redemptive history so there would be a sequence of events ultimately leading to the completion of his perfect will. He interpreted these events by revelations to his servants, who are described as "men moved by the Holy Spirit" (2 Pet. 1:21). He inspired these servants (or in some cases other holy persons to whom the original revelations frequently were communicated) to write down a record of these events and their interpretation to be passed on to future generations. Furthermore, by his Spirit he enlightens people in all ages to recognize the authority of these writings, to receive them by faith as the word of God, and to respond in faith and obedience.

Relationship of Inspiration to Revelation. Inspiration, in the biblical view, is the action of God's Spirit on "holy men of old time" to present the revelation with accuracy in its spoken and inscripturated forms. Revelation is God's act of making himself and his will known. Inspiration is God's work to assure that the revelation will be transmitted accurately to others, and ultimately inscripturated.

"God-breathed." "Inspiration" is not a biblical word, although the concept is biblical. The New Testament Greek word translated "inspired" is *theópneu-*

---

6. This leaves aside the problem of the complex nature of God's will. According to certain biblical statements, even God's revelation to those who do not receive it achieves his purpose. See Isa. 6:9 and its use in the New Testament (Matt. 13:14f.; Mark 4:12; Luke 8:10; John 12:39-41; Acts 28:26f.).

stos,[7] which means "breathed out by God." It refers to the fact that the Scriptures ultimately have God as their source and thereby have an inherent quality intended to have certain effects upon the person who reads or hears them. It is in this sense that Scripture may be called "inspired."

Logically, if God has revealed himself to former generations, not merely for their sake but for that of succeeding generations as well, then the revelation must be accurately received, preserved, and transmitted. Several steps or stages constitute the process. First, the revelation was received by the chosen person or persons in one of several forms discussed above. Then, that revelation was transmitted, usually by spoken proclamation. The process of preservation down to the time of writing has not been uniform, for the word may have been dictated by the recipient to a scribe (e.g., Jer. 36:4, 18, 32) or gathered by the writer from several transmitted forms (e.g., Luke 1:1-4). Next, various copies of the written word were transmitted in the original language and subsequently in translations. Finally, God's revelation through the Scriptures comes to the person who hears or reads.

To how many of these stages the word "inspiration" should be applied is a matter of theological discussion. To insist that God's inspiration was uniformly effective at each stage, so that, for example, the books of Jashar (Josh. 10:13) and Enoch (Jude 14) also were inspired is claiming too much. Yet, to restrict inspiration to the final act of "inscripturation,"[8] so that Jeremiah was inspired only when dictating to Baruch and not when preaching, for example, is far too narrow. Inspiration was simply the work of God's Spirit in whatever form, at whatever stage, by whatever means, and to whatever extent necessary to ensure that the redemptive purpose of his revelation was made effectually available.

The Spirit of God. The principal agent in inspiration is the Spirit of God. The Old and New Testament words for "spirit" also can be translated "wind" or "breath." The close connection between the idea of God "breathing out" the Scriptures and the "in-spiring" of the human agent or agents involved in the process is apparent. In scriptural language, the holy ones of old were inspired by the Spirit of God. Any attempt to define the activity of the Spirit more precisely runs up against the truth that the Spirit, like the wind, is uncontrollable, manifesting only its effects (John 3:8).

Human Agent. Both divine and human agency are present in the process of the inspired inscripturation of God's revelation. A direct inscripturation in which God himself writes on pages, tablets, or plates is exceedingly rare in the

---

7. Used only in reference to Scripture; 2 Tim. 3:16.
8. The scriptural author sometimes is viewed as led by the Spirit to correct his sources or select from them that which God wanted included in his word.

Bible (Exod. 31:18; Deut. 9:10).[9] Otherwise, and possibly even in the cases noted, a human agent was an active participant in the process.

The personality and culture of the inspired human agent is clearly evident through words, style, and interests, in the historical and social setting of the work, and in many other ways. The Psalmist writes in poetry, the author of Proverbs uses proverbial sayings, while the language and ideas of Isaiah differ markedly from Hosea or Amos. In the process of inspiration the Spirit worked upon a human mind in such a way that the personality was in no way diminished or altered, yet the resulting Scripture is the word of God.[10]

However, inspiration in the biblical sense is not to be understood as equiv-alent to the inspiration of an artist in the production of his art. One may say that Shakespeare, for example, was "inspired" when he wrote one of his plays or sonnets, and literary genius may be perceived in the writings of the book of Esther and the gospel of Luke. One might even conclude that, since Shake-speare shows greater signs of genius, he was "more inspired" than either of the other authors mentioned. But this is in no way the meaning of "inspiration" as it applies to the Scriptures. The biblical concept of inspiration does not mean that the writer of Scripture was inspired to produce an artistic product. Rather, it means clearly and simply that the human author was so influenced by God's Spirit that what was written was God's word. This understanding of the term is implicit in the continual equation of the human word with the word of God and the alternation of such expressions as "Moses said" with "God said."

Levels of Inspiration. Are there "inspired" and "uninspired" portions of Scrip-ture? There are portions in the Bible not dependent on direct revelation—for example, quotations from profane writings such as court records, the decree of Cyrus, and Greek poets. But the Bible never suggests that these were revealed by God. Portions of the Bible are more *inspiring* than others. The Psalms, for example, are more "inspiring" than a list of "begats" or the levitical regulations for worship in ancient Israel. Some portions of Scripture are much more likely to bring the reader to salvation than others, as the accounts of the crucifixion of Christ or Paul's letter to the Romans when compared with the accounts of the deeds of the kings of Israel and Judah or the writings of the Preacher (Ecclesiastes).

Nevertheless, the biblical position is that all Scripture is inspired. Thus, God's Spirit led the original authors and editors to include both the divine revelations and the purely human deeds and sayings, because in God's redemp-tive purpose the total is necessary for the understanding of the parts: Satan's

---

9. Even here one must be careful in interpretation. In Exod. 32:16; 34:1, it is said that God wrote the tablets of the law on Sinai, but in 34:28 it would appear that Moses was the writer. God and his human agent are identified very closely in inspiration.

10. Some compare Scripture to the Incarnation, with two natures, divine and human, each distinct yet present at every point.

lies and the truth of Jesus Christ, the levitical sacrifices and that of Christ. The same God is the focus, with the same purpose throughout, and even the seemingly less significant portions of his word are essential to comprehend the total revelation.[11]

Verbal Inspiration. "Verbal inspiration" means that the inspiration of Scripture extends to the very words. To some, this means that God dictated the words and the authors wrote them down.[12] Now, if this means that the words are exactly those of God only, then no difference should be apparent on the basis of vocabulary, style, or literary genre among the individual human authors, declaring in human language the revelation which they received.

But for communication to be meaningful, the statements must be meaningful and composed of words that are meaningful. According to the consensus of modern scholarship, the most certain way of arriving at a correct understanding of a passage is by using all of the grammatical rules that (so far as can be determined) governed the author's writing and all of the available historical data. This involves words. Music or art can be said to "communicate" a message, but precision is only possible in verbal communication. To assure verbal precision God, in communicating his revelation, must be verbally precise, and inspiration must extend even to the words. This does not mean that God dictated every word. Rather, his Spirit so pervaded the mind of the human writer that he chose out of his own vocabulary and experience precisely those words, thoughts, and expressions that conveyed God's message with precision. In this sense the words of the human authors of Scripture can be viewed as the word of God.

FOR FURTHER READING

Barr, J. *Old and New in Interpretation*. London: 1966.

Benoit, P. *Aspects of Biblical Inspiration*. Trans. J. Murphy-O'Connor and S.K. Ashe. Chicago: 1965. (Roman Catholic perspective.)

Brunner, H.E. *Revelation and Reason: The Christian Doctrine of Faith and Knowledge*. Trans. O. Wyon. Philadelphia: 1946. (Seeks to separate genuinely biblical understanding of revelation from later additions and accretions.)

Burtchaell, J.T. *Catholic Theories of Biblical Interpretation Since 1810*. Cambridge: 1969. (Review and critique.)

Clifford, J. *The Inspiration and Authority of the Bible*. 3rd ed. London: 1899. (Classic.)

---

11. Cautiously following the analogy of Scripture to the Incarnation, one might say that as every part of the body is essential, so every part of Scripture is necessary for the functioning of the whole; see 1 Cor. 12:12-27.

12. Such is the doctrine of Islam concerning the Qur'ân: Allah dictated the words, which the prophet Mohammed wrote down exactly, even to the punctuation.

Geisler, N.L., and Nix, W.E. *A General Introduction to the Bible*. Chicago: 1968. (Esp. pp. 17-87.)

Henry, C.F.H., ed. *Revelation and the Bible*. Grand Rapids: 1958.

_____.*God, Revelation and Authority* 3-4. Waco: 1979. (Compendious evangelical statement on the Bible.)

Lampe, G.W.H. "Inspiration and Revelation." *IDB* 2:713-18.

Mowinckel, S. *The Old Testament as Word of God*. Trans. R.B. Bjornard. Nashville: 1959. (Divine revelation through a human book.)

Pannenberg, W. et al., eds. *Revelation as History*. Trans. D. Granskou. New York: 1968. (Seeks to bridge gulf between exegesis and systematic theology.)

Pinnock, C.H. *Biblical Revelation: The Foundation of Christian Theology*. Chicago: 1971.

Robinson, H.W. *Inspiration and Revelation in the Old Testament*. Oxford: 1946.

Rogers, J., and McKim, D. *The Authority and Interpretation of the Bible: An Historical Approach*. San Francisco: 1979.

Seeberg, R. *Revelation and Inspiration*. London: 1909. (Revision of the doctrine in light of historical criticism.)

Snaith, N.H. *The Inspiration and Authority of the Bible*. London: 1956.

CHAPTER 3

CANON

THE CONCEPT OF CANON

THE Christian church was born with a canon in its hands.[1] The apostolic community never knew what it was not to have authoritative writings.[2] Their roots in Judaism guaranteed this; inspired writings had been part of the Hebrew heritage from the days of Moses. Moreover, from Jesus' temptation to his crucifixion, he punctuated his ministry by citing the Old Testament (see Matt. 4:4, 7, 10; 5:18; John 10:35)—a persuasive witness to his regard for the sacred writings of his Jewish inheritance. Even his opponents never fault his loyalty to the holy oracles. Sharp conflict may arise over interpretation of Scripture, but no battle is joined over its authority. Furthermore, Jesus not only salutes the authority of the Old Testament; he offers himself as its fulfillment: "everything written about me in the law of Moses and the prophets and the psalms must be fulfilled" (Luke 24:44). As Peter's sermon from the prophet Joel indicates (Acts 2:16-21, 32f.), the combination of Old Testament writings and Christ's teachings was the canon of the Church the day it came to birth at Pentecost.

---

1. The word "canon," borrowed by the Greeks from the Semites who themselves had borrowed it from the Sumerians, originally meant "reed." Because reeds often were used as measuring sticks, the word has come to have a variety of meanings related to measurement, including "rule," "standard," "law," "boundary," "list," "index."

2. B.S. Childs sees the "growth" of the canon as a body of authoritative literature as intrinsically related to the life of the community which treasured it: "The authoritative Word gave the community its form and content in obedience to the divine imperative, yet conversely the reception of the authoritative tradition by its hearers gave shape to the same writings through a historical and theological process of selecting, collecting, and ordering. The formation of the canon was not a late extrinsic validation of a corpus of writings, but involved a series of decisions deeply affecting the shape of the books. Although it is possible to distinguish different phases within the canonical process . . . the earlier decisions were not qualitatively different from the later. When scripture and canon are too sharply distinguished, the essential element in the process is easily lost"; *Introduction to the Old Testament as Scripture* (Philadelphia: 1979), pp. 58f.

17

God's revelation through the centuries came in a combination of words and deeds. The Egyptian plagues might have been viewed merely as vexing accidents of nature had not Moses given their meaning. David's rise to the throne of Israel and his capture of Jerusalem might have been written off as minor tides in the ebb and flow of Middle Eastern politics had not Samuel and Nathan laid bare their true significance. Jesus' crucifixion might have seemed another vengeful Roman execution had he not revealed that he would give his life as a ransom for many.

All this affirms that a canon of Scripture—an authoritative collection of writings, the teachings of which are binding on believers—is not a luxury which the Church has taken to itself. It is an utter necessity arising from the essential nature of God's revelatory process. God made himself known by speaking and acting in history. All along he saw to it that the precise nature of his actions and an accurate account of his words were preserved for his people. These records comprise the canon.

FORMATION OF THE OLD TESTAMENT CANON

Four closely related yet readily distinguishable steps were involved in the formation of the Old Testament canon: authoritative utterances; documents; collections of writings; and a fixed canon.

Authoritative Utterances. For the people of Israel, the principle of canonicity began when they received the law through Moses at Mt. Sinai. God gave strong words, the people pledged themselves to abide by them, and Moses put them in writing (Exod. 24:3f.). The seeds of canonicity were present even earlier, when the people, becoming increasingly aware of Israel's peculiar role in God's program of redemption, treasured the commands and the promises affirmed to the patriarchs as sacred words from which to draw strength and comfort.

Authoritative Documents. In Deut. 31:24-26, Moses "finished writing the words of this law in a book" and commanded the Levites to "put it by the side of the ark of the covenant . . . that it may be there for a witness against you."[3] The binding authority of this book was reaffirmed to Joshua: "This book of the law shall not depart out of your mouth, but you shall meditate on it day and night . . ." (Josh. 1:8).

The rediscovery of the book of the law in the eighteenth year of Josiah's reign (621 B.C.) was a landmark in the development of the Old Testament

---

3. Systems of writing were developed in both Mesopotamia and Egypt more than a millennium before Abraham's time. By Moses' day they had reached a high state of refinement in Canaan, as the Ugaritic literature from the Syrian coast suggests. Hittite treaties, which show some similarity in form to Old Testament covenantal agreements, provided for the preservation of the document in case disputes arose between the parties.

canon (2 Kgs. 22). In contrast to the kings of Egypt and Assyria, who tended to equate their will with law, Josiah surrendered to the scroll's authority, acknowledging the written law of God as an inescapable mandate (2 Kgs. 23:3). That people heard and obeyed a book, convinced that God was speaking through it, is the essence of canonicity.

Authoritative Collections of Writings. The traditional threefold division of the Hebrew scriptures into Law, Prophets, and Writings probably indicates stages in the formation of the canon as well as differences in subject matter.

The five books of Moses, also called the "Law" ("Torah") or "Pentateuch," probably were completed in substantially their present form by about the time of David (1000). It is possible that modest amounts of revision continued through the centuries until about the time of Ezra (*ca.* 400).

The Prophets customarily were divided into two groups, Former and Latter. The Former Prophets are the historical books: Joshua, Judges, Samuel, and Kings. The Latter Prophets are the great preachers of Israel: Isaiah, Jeremiah, Ezekiel, and the prophets included in the Book of the Twelve. Sometimes called "minor" because of their comparatively brief writings, these twelve often were contained in a single scroll.

Final editing of the Former Prophets, which relate Israel's covenant history from the conquest of Canaan to the Babylonian captivity (1250-550), cannot have taken place until the Exile. However, the narratives are virtually contemporary with the events recorded.

As the continuation of the story of God's dealings with Israel, the books of the Former Prophets were readily revered by the covenant people. Their names, which linked them to Israel's great leaders, especially Joshua and Samuel, added to their repute. Furthermore, the fact that these writings told of prophets such as Elijah and Elisha and also reflected an interpretation of Israel's history akin to that of the great prophets contributed to their prestige.

How long after the time of Malachi (450) the Latter Prophets were gathered into a collection is not certain. Probably many of the preexilic prophetic writings like Amos, Hosea, Micah, Isaiah, Zephaniah, Jeremiah, Nahum, and Habakkuk had been drawn into an authoritative collection during the Exile, when destruction and captivity had stunned the people of Judah into realizing that God himself had spoken through those prophets and their warnings of disaster.

The situation with the Writings is even more complex because of the diverse character of the books. Psalms, Proverbs, and Job are books of poetry and devotion. Five of the books, written on individual scrolls, were read separately at annual feasts: Song of Solomon at Passover; Ruth at Pentecost; Lamentations on the ninth of Ab, the day Jerusalem was destroyed in 586; Ecclesiastes at the Feast of Tabernacles; Esther at Purim. Daniel is the lone prophet, and the Writings conclude in the Hebrew Bible with the historical narratives of Ezra, Nehemiah, and Chronicles.

Nash papyrus (first or second century B.C.), containing the Ten Commandments and the Shema (Deut. 6:4f.). (Cambridge University Library)

Reasons for including these books are varied. Psalms and, indirectly, Ruth were connected with David, Ruth's great grandson. Proverbs, Song of Solomon, and Ecclesiastes were linked to Solomon, and Lamentations to Jeremiah. Job's wisdom and Daniel's visions were seen as the direct gifts of God. Ezra, Nehemiah, and Chronicles were connected with the distinguished leaders (note the prominent place given David and his family in Chronicles) and recorded the later stages of the covenant history.

Most of the Writings were written or collected during and after the Exile, i.e., after 550, although some material, especially in Psalms and Proverbs, dates from the Monarchy (1000-587). That the whole collection was put together by 150 is virtually certain, although evidence for the use of Esther is scanty.

The people of Judah were keenly conscious of their past during the immediate postexilic period. Rocked to the foundations by their captivity, they sought both to ground themselves again in their ancient heritage and to fortify themselves against another disastrous judgment. Ezra and Nehemiah, key figures in the rebuilding process, rightly emphasized the importance and authority of the sacred writings (Ezra 7; Neh. 8–10), and probably were significant in the formation of the canon (cf. Josephus *Contra Apionem* i.8; Talmud B. *Bat.* 14b; 2 Macc. 2:13-15; 2 Esdr. 14).

Fixed Canon. Evidence for the threefold catalog of sacred writings is found prior to 150 B.C. The book of Ecclesiasticus, an apocryphal wisdom book also known as Ben Sirach, was provided with a preface by the author's grandson, who translated the work into Greek *ca.* 132 B.C. In this preface the author refers to "the Law and the Prophets" as well as "the other (books) that follow after them." From this it seems likely that Ben Sirach himself (*ca.* 190) recognized the threefold division of the Old Testament canon. The precise contents of the "other books," i.e., the Writings, unfortunately are not mentioned. The most important Jewish reference to the canon occurs in the Talmudic tractate *Baba Bathra*, the pertinent section of which probably dates to the first or second century B.C. Here the threefold division is implied clearly, and authors are listed for most books, all of which are in the present Protestant canon. In the New Testament Jesus alludes to "the law of Moses and the prophets and the psalms" (Luke 24:44), but the Old Testament is more often called "the law and the prophets" (e.g., Matt. 5:17; Luke 16:16), undoubtedly including the Writings with the Prophets. The New Testament authors never cite apocryphal writings directly, and it is probably safe to assume that the Old Testament they used was identical with that known today. Similarly, though the exact contents of their canon cannot be determined, no evidence suggests that either Philo (*On the Contemplative Life* ii.475) or Josephus (*Contra Apionem* i.8), both contemporary with the New Testament, included books not in the present Old Testament.[4]

There were, of course, differing approaches to the canon in antiquity. The

Samaritans, who had broken with the Jews as early as Nehemiah's day (*ca.* 450) and established their own religious rites, included only the Pentateuch, omitting the Prophets—often critical of the northern kingdom with its capital at Samaria—and the Writings—so closely tied to the Jerusalem temple.

The relationship between the most popular Greek version of the Old Testament (the Septuagint or LXX) and the Hebrew canon is difficult to assess. To say that Greek-speaking or other Dispersion Jews had a larger canon which included the apocryphal writings is probably an oversimplification. Manuscripts of the LXX, which date from the fourth century A.D. at the earliest, were transmitted through Christian rather than Jewish hands, and the lists of books contained in various manuscripts may differ, making it difficult to draw precise inferences regarding the canon.

Jewish speculation about the canon continued into the Christian era. But the nature of the speculation seems to be limited to questions of whether Esther (which does not mention God), Ecclesiastes (with its bursts of skepticism and hints of hedonism), Song of Solomon (with its passionate expressions of love), Proverbs (with its supposed contradictions), and Ezekiel (which some held to conflict with the Torah) should be kept in the canon. The issue was not whether new books should be included but whether all the books then recognized were sacred enough to merit continued inclusion.

Their temple lost with the destruction of Jerusalem in A.D. 70 and their faith contested by the rise of Christianity, the Jews clung to their Scriptures for security and unity, for their very religious identity was in jeopardy. This attention to Scripture led to the recognition of the Hebrew canon as now known. The Jewish religious headquarters at Jamnia (Jabneel or Jabneh; Josh. 15:11; 2 Chr. 26:6) in southwestern Judah became the hub of discussions about the canon. The exact process by which the rabbis came to a final verdict about A.D. 90 is shrouded by the passing of time. Probably the verdict came through a general consensus reached by common usage rather than out of an official discussion at a so-called "council of Jamnia."[5]

The consensus of the rabbis and the affirmations of the apostles both support the judgment that the Old Testament which Jesus knew comprised the present thirty-nine books. They, in a way the apocryphal books do not, give the events and meaning of redemptive history. They reach beyond themselves to speak of a day and a deliverance that lie beyond their scope. According to their own witness, the history of redemption marches through their pages to a future fulfillment.

---

4. At Qumran, neither the apparent absence of the book of Esther nor the presence of fragments of apocryphal writings can be used as positive evidence of a different canon. In any case, since this was a sectarian group, their views cannot be assumed normative for the rest of Judaism.

5. A. Bentzen, *Introduction to the Old Testament* (Copenhagen: 1948) 1:20-41, offers a helpful discussion.

DEUTEROCANONICAL OR APOCRYPHAL BOOKS

Roman Catholics call the books found in the Hebrew Bible "protocanonical" and the additional books and portions of protocanonical books found only in the Greek Old Testament "deuterocanonical,"[6] terms equivalent to canonical and apocryphal as used by Protestants and Jews. Both protocanonical and deuterocanonical books were deemed inspired and authoritative by the Catholic Church at the councils of Trent (A.D. 1546) and the Vatican (1870).

Anglican and some other recent Protestant Bibles include the noncanonical portions, inserted between the Old and New Testament as the "Apocrypha," which means "hidden." Roman Catholics understand this term to mean that a work is "neither inspired nor authentic,"[7] so they avoid using the word.

The Greek Orthodox position is less well-defined. Prior to the Reformation, the tendency was to use the full Greek canon without distinction. Although not supported by the decision of any church council, the post-Reformation distinction between the first and second canons generally obtains today.[8]

Limiting canonicity to the books of the Hebrew Bible, as mentioned by Jerome[9] and others, led to the inference that only Scriptures written in Hebrew were canonical, and sometimes also to the inference that all Scriptures written in Hebrew were canonical. But the latter idea was set aside by Origen, who noted that 1 Maccabees was outside the canon even though written in Hebrew.[10]

Ultimately, canonicity is not based on the language of writing but on the testimony that the believing community has heard the voice of God in the canonical books. To the Jews, to Catholic scholars like Jerome and Gregory the Great, and to the Reformers, only the writings of the Hebrew canon spoke with an authority worthy of inclusion in the Old Testament.[11]

---

6. Terms first used by Sixtus of Sienna in 1566; R.J. Forster, "The Formation and History of the Canon," CCHS §13b; J.E. Steinmueller, A Companion to Scripture Studies (New York: 1941) 1:47.

7. Forster, CCHS §13b: "I.e., it is not the work of the author to whom it is ascribed, or, if it is anonymous, does not belong to the date to which it is assigned." Works by recent Catholic scholars (for example, works on "Deutero-Isaiah") suggest that this definition of "neither inspired nor authentic" would have to be modified.

8. Patriarch Cyril Lucan's 1629 confession favoring the distinction in canonicity as expressed by the Reformers was rejected by his successors and by the synod of Constantinople and Jerusalem in 1672; cf. A. Fortesque, The Orthodox Eastern Church, 3rd ed. (London: 1929), pp. 264ff. Nevertheless, most scholars of the Greek Church seem to adhere to the shorter canon containing only the protocanonical works.

9. Prologus galeatus, which he placed at the beginning of his Latin translation (later known as the Vulgate).

10. Eusebius Ecclesiastical History vi.25. Note that the Hebrew fragments of Sirach (2Q18 [2QSir] = Sir. 6:14; 20:31) and Tobit (4QTob, fragments of one Hebrew and 3 Aramaic MSS) were found among the Dead Sea scrolls; cf. W.S. LaSor, Amazing Dead Sea Scrolls (Chicago: 1956), pp. 242f.

11. To press this statement further, Christ and the apostles, by not quoting the deuterocanonical works, likewise seemed to consider them of lesser authority. This argument, however, could be extended to a few of the protocanonical works, which are not cited in the New Testament.

CANON OF THE OLD TESTAMENT

HEBREW BIBLE (24)	ENGLISH BIBLE (39) (Protestant)	ENGLISH BIBLE (46) (Catholic)
TORAH (5)	LAW (5)	LAW (5)
Genesis	Genesis	Genesis
Exodus	Exodus	Exodus
Leviticus	Leviticus	Leviticus
Numbers	Numbers	Numbers
Deuteronomy	Deuteronomy	Deuteronomy
PROPHETS (8)	HISTORY (12)	HISTORY (14)
Former Prophets (4)	Joshua	Josue (Joshua)*
Joshua	Judges	Judges
Judges	Ruth	Ruth
1–2 Samuel	1 Samuel	1 Kings (1 Samuel)
1–2 Kings	2 Samuel	2 Kings (2 Samuel)
Latter Prophets	1 Kings	3 Kings (1 Kings)
Isaiah	2 Kings	4 Kings (2 Kings)
Jeremiah	1 Chronicles	1 Paralipomenon (1 Chr.)
Ezekiel	2 Chronicles	2 Paralipomenon (2 Chr.)
The Twelve	Ezra	Esdras-Nehemias (Ezra, Neh.)
Hosea	Nehemiah	Tobias (Tobit)
Joel	Esther	Judith
Amos		Esther
Obadiah	POETRY (5)	
Jonah	Job	POETICAL AND WISDOM (7)
Micah	Psalms	Job
Nahum	Proverbs	Psalms
Habakkuk	Ecclesiastes	Proverbs
Zephaniah	Song of Solomon	Ecclesiastes
Haggai		Canticle of Canticles
Zechariah	MAJOR PROPHETS (5)	Wisdom of Solomon
Malachi	Isaiah	Ecclesiasticus (Sirach)
	Jeremiah	
WRITINGS (11)	Lamentations	PROPHETICAL LITERATURE (20)
'Emeth (Truth) (3)	Ezekiel	Isaias (Isaiah)
Psalms	Daniel	Jeremias (Jeremiah)
Proverbs		Lamentations
Job	MINOR PROPHETS (12)	Baruch
Megilloth (Scrolls) (5)	Hosea	Ezechiel (Ezekiel)
Song of Solomon	Joel	Daniel
Ruth	Amos	Osee (Hosea)
Lamentations	Obadiah	Joel
Ecclesiastes	Jonah	Amos
Esther	Micah	Abdias (Obadiah)
Daniel	Nahum	Jonas (Jonah)
Ezra-Nehemiah	Habakkuk	Micheas (Micah)
1–2 Chronicles		

Zephaniah	Nahum
Haggai	Habacuc (Habakkuk)
Zechariah	Sophonias (Zephaniah)
Malachi	Aggeus (Haggai)
	Zecharias (Zechariah)
	Malachias (Malachi)
	1 Machabees (1 Maccabees)
	2 Machabees (2 Maccabees)

*Recent editions of the Catholic Bible and some recent Roman Catholic writers have conformed to the names as used in the RSV.

Canonicity and inspiration cannot be separated. The ultimate basis for canonicity is simply this: if the writing is inspired (God-breathed) it is canonical. If it is not inspired, it is not canonical. This side of the New Testament such questions are settled by the words of Jesus and the apostles, who ratified the inspiration and authority of the Old Testament (cf. 2 Tim. 3:16f.).

FOR FURTHER READING

Ackroyd, P.R. "Original Text and Canonical Text." *Union Seminary Quarterly Review* 32 (1977): 166-172. (Distinction between "inspired" text and "read" or "redactional" form.)

Geisler, N.L. "The Extent of the Old Testament Canon." Pp. 31-46 in G.F. Hawthorne, ed., *Current Issues in Biblical and Patristic Interpretation*. Grand Rapids: 1975. (Esp. regarding apocryphal books.)

Hubbard, D.A. "The Formation of the Canon." Pp. 5-7 in *The Holy Bible*. Philadelphia: 1970. (Parts of the preceding discussion were adapted from this article.)

Katz, P. "The Old Testament Canon in Palestine and Alexandria." *ZNW* 47 (1956): 191-217.

Metzger, B.M. *An Introduction to the Apocrypha*. New York: 1957.

Newman, R.C. "The Council of Jamnia and the Old Testament Canon." *WTJ* 38 (1975/76): 319-349. (Consensus preceded Council.)

Pfeiffer, R.H. "Canon of the OT." *IDB* 1:498-520.

Sanders, J.A. *Torah and Canon*. Philadelphia: 1972. (Holistic approach to Scripture.)

Skehan, P.W. "The Qumran Manuscripts and Textual Criticism." *VTS* 4 (1957): 148-160.

Sundberg, A.C., Jr. *The Old Testament of the Early Church*. Harvard Theological Studies 20. Cambridge, Mass.: 1964.

Young, E.J. "The Canon of the Old Testament." Pp. 153-185 in C.F.H. Henry, ed., *Revelation and the Bible*.

CHAPTER 4

FORMATION OF THE OLD TESTAMENT

THE printed Old Testament has a lengthy history. A product of a distant time and place, it has come through a centuries-long process of editing, collecting, copying, and translating. Documents from a score or more of authors spanning almost a millennium have been combined and transmitted by devoted but fallible hands. In what languages did the biblical writers speak and write? Are present Bibles accurate representations of the original documents? How important are the ancient translations in helping to recover the meaning of passages obscured by careless copyists? On what basis were the Old Testament books chosen? Have recent discoveries like the Dead Sea scrolls forced changes in attitudes toward the accuracy or authority of the Bible? These and many other questions arise as one considers the complex process through which God's providence allowed the Old Testament to pass before reaching the present.

LANGUAGES

The two languages of the Old Testament, Hebrew and Aramaic, are members of the family of kindred languages called "Semitic," a word derived from the name of Noah's son Shem.[1] The original Semites seem to have come from the Arabian peninsula. Countless migrations to Mesopotamia, Syria, Palestine, and parts of Africa allowed gradual changes to take place in their speech, and hence separate though related languages developed. Although any classification has its pitfalls, grouping them geographically is sometimes helpful, as in this representative list:

---

1. Not all of Shem's descendants spoke Semitic languages. Elam and Lud, for instance, used non-Semitic languages (Gen. 10:22), while a few descendants of Ham (e.g., Canaan, v. 6, and the sons of Cush mentioned in v. 7) spoke Semitic rather than Hamitic languages.

East Semitic	North Semitic	West Semitic	South Semitic
Babylonian	Aramaic	Canaanite	Arabic
Assyrian[2]	Amorite	Moabite	Ethiopic
		Phoenician	Old South
		Ugaritic	Arabic
		Hebrew	

The olympian achievements among linguists and philologists of the past century or so have placed scholars today in a better position to interpret the Scriptures in terms of their language and cultural setting than any previous generation in the history of the Church.

Hebrew. The affinities between Hebrew and the other Canaanite languages are recognized by the Old Testament itself, for one of the names applied to it is literally "lip of Canaan" (Isa. 19:18). The patriarchal narratives in Genesis seem to suggest that Abraham's family spoke Aramaic and that the patriarch and his descendants learned a Canaanite dialect when they settled in Canaan; Jacob called the stonepile in Gen. 31:47 by a Hebrew name, while Laban used Aramaic. Particularly helpful for understanding the Hebrew language have been numerous Phoenician inscriptions from the time of the Hebrew monarchy (tenth to sixth centuries B.C.), the Moabite stone (an excellent illustration of the kinship between Hebrew and Moabite), and the Ugaritic tablets from Ras Shamra on the northern Syrian coast. Though linguistically farther removed from Hebrew than Phoenician or Moabite and written in a cuneiform alphabet, Ugaritic has made a more substantial contribution to the knowledge of Hebrew and of Old Testament life and literature than the other languages mentioned because of both the quality and the quantity of its literature. The importance of these kindred languages is heightened by the discouraging paucity of Hebrew texts contemporary with the Old Testament.[3]

The earliest Hebrew manuscripts undoubtedly were written in the Phoenician alphabet, which has been preserved in the Phoenician and Moabite inscriptions mentioned above. This script apparently gave way to the square type of writing about 200, although the ancient style is found on occasion in the Dead Sea scrolls, particularly in the divine name Yahweh. Early manuscripts contained consonants only, the vocalic pronunciation being supplied by the reader.[4]

---

2. Babylonian and Assyrian are called collectively "Akkadian."

3. The Gezer calendar, apparently a school boy's exercise tablet (*ca*. 1000); the Samaritan ostraca, about seventy-five brief inscriptions on potsherds (*ca*. 750); the Siloam inscription telling of the completion of Hezekiah's water tunnel (*ca*. 700); and the Lachish letters, about one hundred lines of legible Hebrew (*ca*. 589) are the most important of the nonbiblical Hebrew documents dating from the Old Testament period.

4. Vowels in postbiblical Hebrew are written above or below the consonants by a system of dots and dashes called points. "Unpointed" Hebrew is the consonantal text without these vowel indications.

The written vowels (or vowel points) which appear in printed Hebrew Bibles were added shortly after A.D. 500 by the Masoretes, a group of Jewish scholars who were able to stabilize the pronunciation of Biblical Hebrew as they understood it. However, ancient translations of the Old Testament, together with nonbiblical evidence such as Canaanite words in the Amarna letters,[5] suggest that the traditional pronunciation of the Masoretes differs at many points from the original biblical language. As a matter of fact, it is probable that dialect variations originally existed in Biblical Hebrew but have been obscured by the Masoretic attempts at standardization.

Hebrew words, like those of other Semitic languages, usually are based on roots containing three consonants. Various vowel patterns together with the addition of prefixes and suffixes determine the semantic significance of the word. For example, some words based on the root *mlk* are *melek* "king," *malkâ* "queen," *malkût* "rulership," *mālak* "he ruled," and *mamlākâ* "kingdom."

The verbal system has some basic differences from other more familiar languages. For instance, there are two basic tenses, which actually denote kind of action (i.e., whether completed or not completed) rather than time distinctions (usually determined from the context). Hebrew grammar tends to be direct and simple, especially in sentence structure. For instance, coordinate clauses are found far more commonly than the subordination familiar in English.

The relationship between Hebrew language and distinctive Hebrew forms of thought is a vexing question. Linguists are by no means in agreement on the relationship between a given people's language and their view of reality. Could biblical truths have been expressed as well in any other language? Too strong a negative answer may suggest that only a knowledge of the Hebrew can guarantee an accurate understanding of the Old Testament's meaning. Too strong an affirmative may minimize the fact that God did choose to record his revelation in this language—and the biblical God does not do things accidentally.[6]

Aramaic. When the Assyrian empire began to push west in the middle of the eighth century, Aramaic was adopted as the official language of diplomacy and commerce. During the heyday of the Persian empire (*ca.* 500) it was the second, if not the first, tongue of the peoples of the Near East from Egypt to Persia. The hellenizing conquests of Alexander spread Greek throughout this area, but it supplanted Aramaic only partially and gradually, as the New Testament suggests.[7]

---

5. Akkadian diplomatic correspondences between officials in Canaan (among others) and their Egyptian superiors, dating from the fourteenth century and discovered at Tell el-Amarna in Egypt.

6. For a discussion of the problem, see J. Barr, *The Semantics of Biblical Language* (London: 1961).

7. Aramaic was quite likely the native tongue of Jesus and most New Testament authors (e.g., the evangelists, except Luke); cf. Mark 5:41; 7:34; 15:34. Compare also Jesus' use of *mammon* (Matt. 6:24), *Raca* (5:22; RSV mg.), *Ephphatha* (Mark 7:34),

Hebrew ostracon (seventh century B.C.) from Yavneh Yam. (Israel Department of Antiquities)

Inkwells from the scriptorium at Qumran (first century A.D.). (Israel Department of Antiquities)

Despite its relatively late ascendancy, Aramaic had a lengthy history before becoming the lingua franca of the Middle East. For this reason scholars have become increasingly cautious about branding passages in the Hebrew Bible as "late" on the basis of Aramaic words occurring in them. Indeed, some scholars point to an Aramaic word (i.e., the word translated "repeat" in the RSV, Judg. 5:11) in one of the earliest poems in the Bible, the Song of Deborah (ca. 1150).

The book of Genesis testifies to the close relationship between Hebrew- and Aramaic-speaking peoples (e.g., Gen. 31:47). In the midst of an oracle against idolatry directed to the people of Judah, Jeremiah inserts in Aramaic a verse of judgment against false gods:

> Thus shall you say to them: "The gods who did not make the heavens and the earth shall perish from the earth and from under the heavens." (Jer. 10:11)

Perhaps he chose this device to make his indictment of gentile gods more graphic by denouncing them in a gentile language—Aramaic.

Though Aramaic was known to Judah's court officers well before the Exile (note the conversation between Hezekiah's delegation and the Assyrian Rab-shakeh, ca. 701; 2 Kgs. 18:17-37), it was adopted as the first language of many commoners during the Captivity and afterwards. Thus, the authors of Ezra and Daniel felt no need to furnish translations of the lengthy Aramaic passages in their writings.

TEXT

A chief problem of biblical scholarship has been to determine as nearly as possible the exact form of the original writings (sometimes called the *autographa*) of Scripture. Centuries of copying and sometimes even editing have allowed changes in vocabulary and phrasing and possibly, on occasion, in the order of verses or sections. Slight omissions and additions have crept in, as well as errors in spelling and word division. The scribes hardly played fast and loose with the text, but as human beings they were bound to commit errors despite their concern and care. The task of textual or lower criticism is to spot these errors and restore the Hebrew and Aramaic texts to a form as close to the original as possible.

Materials and Methods of Writing. The scroll or roll was the standard form in which the Scriptures were preserved in Old Testament times.[8] The Dead Sea

---

Talitha cumi (Mark 5:41), *Eloi, lama sabachthani* (Mark 15:34), and *Abba* (Mark 14:36), all of which seem to represent Aramaic originals. For Aramaic influence on the Gospels and Acts, particularly on the Greek sentence structure, see M. Black, *An Aramaic Approach to the Gospels and Acts*, 3rd ed. (London: 1967). However, see also the references in Ch. 51 regarding the book of Daniel.

8. See Ps. 40:7 (MT 6); Jer. 36:2ff. (the best Old Testament account of methods of writing Scripture); Ezek. 2:9–3:3; Zech. 5:1f.

scrolls are a good indication of the nature of ancient rolls and the methods of writing employed. Made of carefully prepared leather (parchment), the scrolls are composed of many pieces sewn together and carefully scraped. The Isaiah scroll (1QIsa^a), for instance, comprises seventeen leaves sewn together to make a roll about 24 feet long. The scribe took pains to mark both horizontal and perpendicular lines on the leather to serve as guides for the lines and columns (cf. Jer. 36:23) and to assure neatness.

However, the earliest biblical documents probably were written on papyrus, which was used in Egypt as early as the third millennium and was exported to Phoenicia by at least 1100. The material for these rolls was prepared by splitting the papyrus reeds and laying one layer of reeds on top of another at right angles. The natural gum of the papyrus served as glue for the crossed strips of each section and for the number of sections joined together to make a scroll. The scribes wrote only on the inside of the scroll, using the horizontal strips as guide lines. Although the Harris papyrus measures more than 120 feet, scrolls longer than about 30 feet were difficult to make and awkward to handle. This may help to account for the length of some Old Testament books.

Though the more formal writing was on papyrus, many other materials were used, generally for shorter messages: tablets of wood, wax, or clay, and fragments of broken pottery (ostraca). The perishability of papyrus makes exceedingly unlikely any substantial discoveries of papyrus scrolls in Israel or Jordan, where the climate, in contrast with Egypt, is too moist to allow their survival. The transition from papyrus to leather apparently took place in the late pre-Christian centuries, while the use of codices (books) instead of scrolls dates from about the first century A.D. The introduction of book form greatly facilitated the circulation of the Scriptures because, for the first time, all the writings could be contained in a manageable volume.

The instruments of writing in antiquity varied greatly and were determined largely by the system of writing employed. Cuneiform, for instance, was either carved in stone with a chisel (for many permanent or public documents) or inscribed on clay tablets with a stylus. The customary implements in Israel were apparently the reed pen, whose point probably was sharpened and split with a pen knife, although Jeremiah mentions an iron pen with a diamond point (17:1), which may have been used for writing on harder materials. The ink used with the reed pens was made from the lampblack of olive oil lamps and, much later, from various metallic powders. The amazing durability of nonmetallic ink is demonstrated by the Qumran scrolls and, even earlier, the Lachish letters.

Standardization of the Text. The ancient translations of the Old Testament and the Dead Sea scrolls indicate that a certain amount of freedom must have prevailed among the scribes who copied and recopied the biblical documents in the pre-Christian centuries. Both the Old Phoenician script and the square alphabet contain letters which can be confused because they look alike. Furthermore, evidence shows that brief sections may have been omitted by hom-oioteleuton (Greek for "similar ending"), when a scribe's eye skipped from one phrase to another with a similar ending, omitting the intervening material. Other common mistakes occurred when a scribe unwittingly repeated a letter, word, or phrase (dittography) or failed to repeat one which the original text had repeated (haplography). Complicating the matter is the fact that earlier manuscripts apparently contained no spaces or markers between words, leaving the scribe to make the proper divisions with the eye. Also, as the Hebrew letters *yodh*, *waw*, and *he* gradually were added as vowel markers, the possibility of errors in spelling increased.

At times, as in the case of Jeremiah's book (see Ch. 31), two or more separate editions seem to have existed simultaneously. Explanatory notes or other marginal comments by one scribe may have been included with the text by another, while one scribe's textual omissions crowded into the margin or between the lines may have been regarded as glosses and left out by his suc-cessor. Theological prejudice accounts for a few changes, such as the substitu-tion of *bōšeṭ* ("shame") for the element *ba'al* ("Baal" or "lord") in some proper names in the books of Samuel.[9] Another possible source of variation is oral tradition. Sections of the various writings may have been transmitted orally in forms somewhat different from the written text. In other cases two or more oral forms may have been preserved in the text when reduced to writing.[10]

After the destruction of Jerusalem in A.D. 70, Judaism, threatened by decentralization due to the loss of the temple and by Christian opposition throughout the Mediterranean world, took definite steps to standardize the text for study and worship. Christian use of the LXX, cherished for years by Jews in the Diaspora, sparked Jewish opposition to it and increased Jewish loyalty to every word of the Hebrew text. In about the second century A.D., a grand venture of textual criticism was launched which not only affected the Scriptures but resulted eventually in the standardization of other Jewish texts, notably the Mishnah (extrabiblical laws) and the Talmuds (collections of these laws with rabbinic comments). The miscarriage of a number of revolts against Rome brought renewed Roman repercussions and forced many Jewish sages to flee to Babylonia, where they avidly pursued their grammatical and textual studies. During the tenth century, the center of Jewish learning shifted to Tiberias in Galilee, where scribes and rabbis had congregated soon after the seventh-century Muslim conquest of Palestine.

A driving force behind the movement to standardize the text was Rabbi Akiba (died *ca.* A.D. 135), a vigorous opponent of Christianity and a metic-ulous scholar of the Hebrew scriptures. The exact results of Akiba's textual

---

9. Ishbosheth in 2 Sam. 2:8 is Eshbaal in 1 Chr. 8:33; Jerubbesheth of 2 Sam. 11:21 is Jerubbaal in Judg. 6:32.

10. Some of the duplications among the proverbs and psalms may be accounted for in this fashion. E.g., Pss. 14, 53 are well known to be identical except that Ps. 14 uses the divine name Yahweh and 53 uses Elohim. See also Pss. 40:13-17; 70.

endeavors are shrouded in antiquity, but he likely established a text which, with considerable modification in details, has persisted until today.

While the scribes edited and transmitted the text, the Masoretes insured its careful preservation. Appearing about A.D. 500, they carried on the scribal practice of making textual notes in the manuscript margins. The letters, words, and verses of each book were counted carefully, and a note was added at the close of each book to summarize the totals for the book. This final *masora* (lit. "tradition") contained mnemonic devices by which each new copy of the scroll could be checked for accuracy. It is to the Masoretes that the present system of pronunciation in the Hebrew Bible can be attributed, for they preserved the traditional pronunciation by a system of vowel marks.

In printed Hebrew Bibles the basic text is that of ben Asher, who flourished in Tiberias during the tenth century.[11] Thanks to the millennium-long process of standardization, the variations among the available manuscripts, including the Qumran scrolls, are minimal and have no bearing on the theological teachings of the Old Testament.

The Practice of Textual Criticism. Few disciplines in Old Testament studies call for as much discernment as textual criticism. In contrast with the New Testament, for which manuscripts are both more abundant and closer to the date of origin, the Old Testament presents severe problems to the textual critic. The chief problem is to get behind the attempted standardization which began in the early Christian centuries. Such efforts have been frustrated frequently by the paucity of early manuscripts (before the discovery of the Dead Sea scrolls the earliest complete Hebrew manuscripts dated from the tenth century A.D.) and by the difficulties which obscure Hebrew words and phrases posed for the early translators into Greek, Syriac, and Latin. Although these and other ancient translations offer considerable help in tracing the earliest Hebrew text, they sometimes fail just at those points where help with an obscure passage is needed most. In other words the ancient translators on occasion were as baffled as their modern counterparts by the Old Testament text.

In the light of these difficulties, how does a textual critic recover the original reading where Hebrew manuscripts of ancient translations offer variant readings or where the MT is itself obscure? A working rule generally accepted by contemporary scholars is "follow the MT unless it makes no sense or overwhelming evidence favors another reading."[12] At all points one must assume

---

11. R. Kittel's *Biblia Hebraica*, revised by K. Elliger and W. Rudolph as *Biblia Hebraica Stuttgartensia* (Stuttgart: 1968-1977), gives an accurate reproduction of ben Asher's text, even though the variant readings in the critical apparatus are not always accurate and the suggested emendations are not always happily chosen; see B.J. Roberts, "The Textual Transmission of the Old Testament," pp. 1-30 in G.W. Anderson, ed., *Tradition and Interpretation* (Oxford: 1979).

12. This is in line with what A. Bentzen calls "the modern higher evaluation of the Masoretic text"; *Introduction* 1:96.

that what the author of a given passage wrote originally made sense. Having used every available tool to understand the MT as it is, yet still without success, one would then examine the evidence of other manuscripts and the ancient versions.

Not all the versions, however, carry the same weight. A version dependent on another (sometimes called a "secondary" or "daughter" version) is not of equal authority with the primary versions based on the Hebrew text. Furthermore, each version has its own textual problems: parts may have been translated more accurately or based on more reliable Hebrew manuscripts. When confronted with several reasonably reliable readings, one may employ certain rules of thumb. First, the more difficult reading is usually to be preferred because scribes and translators tend to smooth out rough passages. Similarly, the shorter reading frequently is preferable, since copyists are more apt to add glosses to the text than omit authentic phrases or sentences. A third, and extremely important, principle is to accept that reading as authentic which best accounts for all the other variants. Only when all attempts to restore the text based on the evidence of variant readings have led to an impasse is one justified in guessing what the text must have said. Even then one must admit the high degree of tentativeness of such conjectures. Happily, the day is past when biblical scholars emended the text in ruthless, roughshod fashion. Caution is more and more the watchword. Readings are adopted and emendations suggested only on the basis of careful textual and linguistic analyses.

A word of reassurance may be in order. At no point is the basic teaching of the Old Testament in question. Readers of the various Hebrew texts and the ancient versions heard and responded to the word of God just as moderns do to their translations. The precise meanings of some words are in doubt (several hundred Hebrew words are difficult to define with confidence because they occur only once or twice in the Bible), and the exact form of the Hebrew text is questionable in many passages. Nevertheless, biblical scholars are able to reconstruct the probable meaning in a vast majority of the difficult passages, and the message of virtually every section of the Old Testament is clear. The Old Testament, which God has seen fit to preserve, can be relied upon as his word in all its truth and authenticity.

ANCIENT VERSIONS

The term "ancient versions" refers to a number of translations of the Old Testament made during the late pre-Christian and early Christian centuries. The scarcity of ancient Hebrew manuscripts makes these versions exceedingly important as witnesses to early textual traditions, and their roles in aiding the spread of the Jewish and Christian faiths should not be underestimated.

Samaritan Pentateuch. The sparks of tension between the Samaritans who had infiltrated Judah during the Exile and the Jews who returned to their homes after the edict of Cyrus (*ca.* 538) broke into open flames at the time of Ezra and Nehemiah (between 450 and 400). These ancient hostilities, dating from before Jeroboam's disruption (*ca.* 931), had continued to flare and still were smoldering steadily in the New Testament period (cf. John 4:7-42). Though the details of the final breach are hazy, a complete cleavage between Jews and Samaritans certainly had developed by *ca.* 350. That the Hagiographa (or "Writings," the third section of the Hebrew Bible) were being assembled during the period of dissension and that the prophetic writings frequently were disparaging of the northern kingdom with its capital at Samaria no doubt helped to restrict the Samaritan canon to the Pentateuch.

Although not strictly a version, the Samaritan Pentateuch (which still is treasured by the tiny community at Nablus, near ancient Shechem) preserves an ancient and independent form of the Hebrew text. Most of the approximately six thousand variations from the MT are matters of spelling or grammar. Both Jews and Samaritans may have made slight alterations in the text to refute the claims of the other. For example, in Deut. 27:4 MT *Ebal* is, in the Samaritan, *Gerizim*, the sacred mountain of Samaria; cf. John 4:20. Similarly, in more than a score of passages in Deuteronomy (e.g., 12:5, 11, 14, 18; 14:23-25), MT "the place which the Lord your God *will choose*" is altered to "*has chosen*" to show that the sacred mountain is Gerizim, not Zion (which did not fall into Israelite hands until David's time).

Although no really accurate critical edition survives, the Samaritan text is extremely valuable as a confirmation of certain ancient readings in the versions, notably the LXX, with which it agrees against the MT in nearly two thousand instances. Many of these involve a correction in spelling. For example, MT *Dodanim* should be *Rodanim* in Gen. 10:4; cf. LXX and 1 Chr. 1:7. In Gen. 22:13, MT "and behold a ram behind" should read "and behold one ram"; cf. LXX. These alterations involve a change in one Hebrew word from *r* to *d*, in letters which resemble each other closely in both the Phoenician and the square script. Others imply the omission of a word. For example, Gen. 15:21, with LXX, probably should be read "and the Girgashite, *and the Hivite,* and the Jebusite." Occasionally an entire phrase has been omitted from the MT and may be restored from the Samaritan and the LXX, as with Cain's statement "Let us go out to the field" in Gen. 4:8, RSV.[13]

Aramaic Targums. The inroads which Aramaic made on Hebrew as the spoken language after the return from exile made necessary an Aramaic translation to accompany the synagogue readings. Originally oral, these targums probably began to assume written form shortly before the Christian era. While their history is difficult to trace, the major problems that impede use of the written targums in textual studies are the lack of good critical editions and the

---

13. See R.H. Pfeiffer, *Introduction to the Old Testament*, rev. ed. (New York: 1948), p. 103.

fact that at times they become paraphrases or commentaries rather than translations.[14]

The most important and most faithful translation is the Targum of Onkelos,[15] the official synagogue rendering of the Pentateuch. Of some use in textual criticism in corroborating other versions, Onkelos is more important as a witness to the Jewish attitude toward the Old Testament. Its lengthy history—portions from the beginning of the Christian period, final editing probably in fourth or fifth century A.D. Babylonia—has permitted insertion of brief comments or interpretative glosses, which illuminate the growth of Judaism but are of little value in textual criticism.

Contrasted with Onkelos is the Jerusalem Targum, written in a Palestinian dialect of Aramaic and completed about the seventh century A.D. Though it contains some earlier material, its translation of the Law is cluttered with Jewish traditions and legal instructions, making it of more interest to the student of Judaism than to the textual critic.[16]

The official Aramaic translation of the prophets, the Targum of Jonathan[17] took shape in Babylonia in about the fifth century A.D., after first undergoing a Palestinian revision. It takes greater liberties with the text than Onkelos, particularly in the Latter Prophets, and does not seem to have been held in such high esteem in Judaism.

The targums to the Writings are many and varied. Most are paraphrases rather than translations, and their late date (seventh century A.D. and later) curtails their usefulness for textual studies.

The Samaritans also produced a targum to their Pentateuch. Its survival in several different forms, with no official edition yet discovered, is a witness to the textual fluidity of the early targums before an official form was produced and to the freedom with which early translators sometimes handled biblical texts.

Septuagint (LXX). The history of the LXX is not only shrouded in antiquity but also clouded by Jewish and Christian legends which stress its miraculous origin. According to these legends the translators worked in isolation from each

---

14. The need for a reliable critical text is being met currently by A. Sperber, ed., *The Bible in Aramaic*, 4 vols. (Leiden: 1959-1973).

15. Apparently a Babylonian corruption of "Aquila," whose name also graces an ancient Greek version of the Bible.

16. Two ancient targums found only in fragmentary form, the Palestinian targum on the Pentateuch and the Jerusalem II targum (or Fragment Targum), are witnesses to the didactic and interpretative nature of the targums, containing a lavish amount of extrabiblical commentary.

17. Jewish tradition attributes this targum to Jonathan ben Uzziel, a pupil of the famous Rabbi Hillel in the first century A.D. Some modern scholars, however, associate the name with its Greek equivalent "Theodotion," the name of the one responsible for one of the Greek versions. However, the official targum texts were hardly the work of individuals, but more probably were derived by groups of scholars from the numerous targumic traditions in circulation.

other and yet produced translations which agreed verbatim. Named after the traditional number of translators (Lat. *septuaginta* "seventy," thus LXX), it seems to have originated among the Jewish community in Alexandria between 250 and 100 B.C. Its development has been likened to that of the targums: various unofficial translations were made as need arose, with the text somewhat standardized in early Christian times,[18] when it became the Church's authoritative Old Testament.

The LXX exhibits considerable variety in theological outlook and in literalness and accuracy of translation, so its readings cannot be accepted haphazardly. Nevertheless, it is of crucial significance in textual studies, since it represents a form of the Hebrew text prior to the standardizing which took place in the early Christian centuries. In connection with the Samaritan Pentateuch and the Dead Sea manuscripts, it is the most valuable witness to the pre-Masoretic forms of the Hebrew text.

Other Greek Versions. As Christians used the LXX more and more, Jewish communities in the Diaspora turned to other Greek translations. Early in the second century A.D., Aquila, a gentile convert to Judaism and perhaps a disciple of Rabbi Akiba, produced a wooden, literal rendering which rigidly adhered to the text and so was rapidly and avidly embraced by many Jews. Unfortunately, only fragments of his work have survived.

Toward the end of the same century, Theodotion, apparently also a proselyte, revised an older translation, producing a version which proved more popular with Christians than with Jews. Apart from his translation of Daniel, which has virtually replaced the LXX, only fragments remain. These works, as well as Symmachus' superior translation, are known through the surviving fragments of Origen's Hexapla (*ca.* A.D. 220), a monumental attempt at textual criticism in which the Hebrew text and various versions were recorded carefully in parallel columns for comparison.

Syriac Version. Usually called Peshitta (or Peshitto; interpreted as "simple," i.e., the accepted version of the "common" people), the translation into Syriac (a dialect of Aramaic) apparently took place in the early centuries of the Christian era. Its value for textual studies is curtailed by several considerations. First, parts of the Pentateuch seem to be dependent on the Palestinian targum. Also, the influence of the LXX is apparent in some passages, so agreements between the two sometimes may be considered only a single witness to an ancient reading. Our ability to assess the Peshitta's contribution to Old Testament studies

---

18. P. Kahle (*The Cairo Genizah*, 2nd ed. [London: 1959]) and others (e.g., Bentzen, *Introduction* 1:80-85; E. Würthwein, *The Text of the Old Testament*, trans. E.F. Rhodes [Grand Rapids: 1979]) hold this view, while H.S. Gehman ("Septuagint," *TCERK* 2:1015-17) and H.M. Orlinsky ("On the Present State of Proto-Septuagint Studies," *JAOS* 61 [1941]: 81-91) favor an archetypal or original LXX which developed in various ways through editors and copyists.

should be considerably enhanced by the publication of a critical edition now underway.[19]

Latin Versions. Latin translations were necessary first not in Rome (where the learned used Greek) but in North Africa and southern Gaul. Based on the LXX, the Old Latin translations (*ca.* A.D. 150) are more valuable as witnesses to the Greek text than as aids in clarifying the Hebrew. Knowledge of the Old Latin tradition is limited to quotations by the Latin Church Fathers, some liturgical books, and brief manuscripts.[20]

The variety of the many Old Latin translations posed for the Latin Church the problem of which text to use in liturgy and theological conversation. Pope Damasus I (*ca.* A.D. 382) commissioned the gifted scholar Jerome to produce an authoritative version. Substantial parts of Jerome's translation are based on the Hebrew text, although other sections, notably the Psalms, rely on the Greek versions. His use of the Hebrew made his translation suspect for some time, even by his friend Augustine, but the suspicion was ill-founded. Jerome worked cautiously and, in perplexing passages, leaned heavily upon the LXX, Aquila, Theodotion, and Symmachus, as well as the accepted Old Latin.

The composite origin of Jerome's "Vulgate" ("accepted by the common people" or "popular") limits it for textual criticism, since occasional departures from the MT may reflect the influence of Greek or Latin translations rather than a pre-Masoretic tradition. Furthermore, because Jerome's version was not accepted as authoritative for centuries (not officially until the council of Trent in 1546) it was susceptible to editorial alteration influenced by the other Latin translations. So the Vulgate—still the authorized Roman Catholic version[21]—requires a great deal of caution when using its readings to correct the MT.

Other Secondary Versions. The other main Old Testament translations are important testimonies to the widespread outreach of Christianity and the zeal of missionaries to transmit the word of God in the vernacular. All of these secondary versions are more important for reconstructing the histories of the texts on which they were based than in correcting the Hebrew text.

Based on the LXX, the Coptic translations were produced in about the third and fourth centuries A.D. for the peasant population of Egypt. Though written in a form of the Greek alphabet and employing many Greek loanwords, Coptic is the latest stage of the Egyptian language. The diverse dialects called for several translations, particularly Sahidic ("Upper," i.e., Southern Egyptian), Akhmimic, and Bohairic ("Lower," i.e., Northern Egyptian). Many fourth-

---

19. P.A.H. de Boer, ed., *Vetus Testamentum Syriace iuxta simplicem Syrorum versionem* 1 (Leiden: 1972).

20. A modern edition of the Old Latin texts is in process: B. Fischer, ed., *Vetus Latina: Die Reste der altlateinischen Bibel* (Freiburg: 1949–).

21. Modern Catholic scholars, nevertheless, avidly and productively are studying the Scriptures in Hebrew, Aramaic, and Greek, as shown by the JB.

and perhaps even third-century manuscripts have been preserved by the dry Egyptian climate.

By contrast, manuscripts of the Ethiopic translation date from the thirteenth century and later, although translating may have begun by the end of the fourth century. Most extant manuscripts seem to depend on the LXX but have been altered under the influence of medieval Arabic versions. Apart from individual books or sections, no reliable, critical edition exists.

Even later are the Armenian and Arabic versions. The Armenian dates from the fifth century and seems to be based on both the Peshitta and the LXX. Rather than one standard translation, the Arabic represents a rash of versions which sprang up in Egypt, Babylon, and Palestine, drawn from an assortment of accessible versions—Hebrew or Samaritan, LXX, Peshitta, and Coptic. The earliest may be pre-Islamic (*ca.* A.D. 600), but most are later by several centuries.[22]

FOR FURTHER READING

Bruce, F.F. *The Books and the Parchments*. 3rd ed. Westwood, N.J.: 1963. (Esp. pp. 114-162; includes examples in English of versional differences.)

Deist, F.E. *Towards the Text of the Old Testament*. Trans. W.K. Winckler. Pretoria: 1978.

Driver, G.R. "Hebrew Language"; "Semitic Language." *Encyclopaedia Britannica*. Chicago: 1970.

Roberts, B.J. *The Old Testament Text and Versions*. Cardiff: 1951. (Good bibliography.)

Rowley, H.H. *The Aramaic of the Old Testament*. London: 1929. (Grammatical and lexical study of relationship of biblical and other early Aramaic dialects.)

---

22. For other versions, e.g., Gothic, Georgian, Old Slavic, Anglo-Saxon, consult TCERK and J.D. Douglas, ed., *The New International Dictionary of the Christian Church* (Grand Rapids: 1974).

CHAPTER 5

GEOGRAPHY

THE hundreds of place names in the Old Testament—cities and countries, mountains and valleys, rivers and seas, and other geographical features[1]—make it unique among religious literature. According to the Bible, God's revelation took place in space and time, so correct interpretation requires attention to geographical and historical data in the text.

THE BIBLE WORLD

That region where Europe, Asia, and Africa converge is marked by several significant features of physical geography. From the Atlantic Ocean to southeastern Asia runs an almost continuous belt of mountains—the Pyrenees, Alps, Balkans, Caucasus, Elburz, Hindu Kush, and Himalayan ranges. Because they held back the cold winter winds, these mountains gave the lands to the south a climate favorable for the development of civilizations in ancient times. They also deterred invasions from the north. There is also a natural southern boundary, which is principally desert (the Sahara and the Syrian and Arabian deserts). This not only served as a barrier to invasion from the south, but, with the northern barrier, held the peoples of the region between the mountains and the desert within that area. As a result, the Mediterranean world, Mesopotamian region, foothills of the Iranian plateu, and Indus river valley became the "cradle of civilization"—the area in which mankind progressed from savage hunter-fisher to civilized food producer. Once able to stay home and produce their food, people could turn their energies to the arts and crafts and build cities, make pottery, invent musical instruments, discover processes for metallurgy,

---

1. About 622 place names west of Jordan are recorded in the Bible; J.M. Houston, "Palestine," *IBD*, p. 1138.

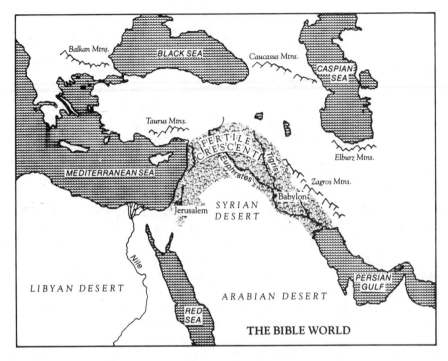

THE BIBLE WORLD

invent writing, and the other elements generally included in the broad term "civilization."[2]

The region between the mountains and deserts may be identified as "the Bible world" (see Map). All events recorded in the Bible took place in or involved peoples of this region.[3] The central Old Testament characters lived principally in Palestine, but at certain points were in Mesopotamia or Egypt. Occasionally, other peoples come into the story from Persia, South Arabia, Ethiopia (Cush, possibly Nubia), Asia Minor, the Mediterranean islands (Cyprus, Crete), Greece, and other areas.

PALESTINE

Name. In the early twelfth century B.C., "Sea Peoples" from somewhere around Crete or Greece attempted to invade Egypt. Thwarted in their attempt,

---

2. Anthropologists continue to debate the location of this "Neolithic revolution." Many place its origin in the piedmonts (foothills) of the Zagros range between Mesopotamia and the Iranian plateau; others place it in Africa. The available evidence, however, seems to favor the former.

3. E.g., the "Table of Nations" in Gen. 10 lists Noah's descendants, generally understood to be all the peoples of the world after the Flood. However, every name that can be positively identified refers to some nation or tribe that lived in the "Bible world." No central European, Asiatic, or African people beyond these limits is mentioned. Nevertheless, with the westward expansion of the Old Testament period, the Bible world indeed spreads over most of the territory mentioned.

some of them, including peoples known as Philistines,[4] landed on the coast of southern Palestine. In the fifth century Herodotus, the "father of history," referred to the area as "Philistine Syria,"[5] and subsequently the Greeks distinguished between "Philistine Syria" and "Coele Syria."[6] From the Greek word *Palaistina* came the Latin *Palestina* and English "Palestine."

The name Palestine, which came into use only after the fifth century B.C., is not used in the Old Testament.[7] Rather, the land often is called "the land of Canaan," because its principal inhabitants were the Canaanites.[8] It is known also as "the land of promise," a promise God made to Abraham (Gen. 17:7f.) and repeated to his descendants. After the Israelite occupation, it is called "Israel" or "the land of Israel" (1 Sam. 13:19, etc.). The term Holy Land (cf. Zech. 2:12) came into common use in the Middle Ages.

Extent and Significance. In popular usage, Palestine refers to the land "from Dan to Beersheba" (Judg. 20:1, etc.). This territory extends from the southern slopes of Mt. Hermon to the edge of the southern desert (the Negeb), bounded on the west by the Mediterranean (or Western) Sea and on the east by the Jordan valley. In Greek and Roman times, the term included territory east of the Jordan, or Transjordan.[9]

God's "promise" to Abraham included much more than Palestine. Genesis 17:8 mentions simply "all the land of Canaan," but in other places, the land of the promise extends north as far as "the entrance of Hamath" (in modern Syria) and south to "the river of Egypt" (Wâdī[10] el-'Arîsh in northern Sinai) (cf. Num. 34:1-12).[11] Under David and Solomon, Israel reached its greatest extent, occupying most of the territory described plus much of Transjordan, even though the promise excluded it (Num. 34:12).

---

4. In his eighth year (*ca.* 1190 B.C.), Ramesses III records repulsing an invasion of Sea Peoples, naming the *prst* (Philistines) and four other peoples.

5. Herodotus i.105, *en tē Palaistinē Suriē*.

6. Strictly speaking, the valley between the Lebanon and the Anti-lebanon. The name, however, was used of various portions of the region beyond Palestine, as far as the Euphrates, including Damascus, parts of Transjordan, and even Scythopolis (Beth-shan). Cf. Josephus *Ant.* xiii.13.2 §355.

7. "Palestine" occurs in Joel 3:4 of the KJV, and "Palestina" in Exod. 15:14 and Isa. 14:29, but this is an accident of translation. The RSV correctly renders the word "Philistia."

8. In the Amarna letters (EA 8:17; 137:76, etc.) the region is called *kinaḫni* or *kinaḫḫi*, which is quite likely cognate with the Hebrew word for "Canaan." Nuzi evidence suggests that the word may mean "purple"; if so, it has the same origin as the Greek word for the region, "Phoenicia," from the dye produced from the murex shellfish found along the coast of Palestine.

9. "Palestine" does not occur in the New Testament. Transjordan is called "Perea," a name with approximately the same meaning (Greek for "[the land] over there"): the land on "this" side is sometimes called "Cisjordan." The present discussion will distinguish between Palestine and Transjordan.

10. A seasonal water course, dry except in the time of rain.

11. This is in no way intended as applying to the modern State of Israel. For places named in Num. 34, see Y. Aharoni, *The Land of the Bible*, 2nd ed. (Philadelphia: 1979, pp. 69f.)

Jordan river as it winds through the flood plain of the Zor, the thick jungle oasis along its shore. (A.D. Baly)

J.H. Breasted gave the name "the Fertile Crescent" to the arable strip of land bordering the Syrian desert, those lands along the Tigris-Euphrates system in Mesopotamia, and the coastal lands of the eastern Mediterranean (the Levant). The southwestern end of this crescent includes Palestine, and stretches to the Nile valley. (See Map.)

Long before historical records appeared, judging from natural objects and man-made artifacts found hundreds and even thousands of miles from their origin, people traveled back and forth through Palestine, "the land-bridge of history" connecting Europe, Asia, and Africa. Merchants, migrants, pilgrims, and armies have traveled its roads, climbed its hills, and forded its rivers. God chose this land for Abraham and his descendants, and most of his redemptive revelation was given in it.

North-South Divisions. Political divisions alter with relative ease, but physical features remain almost unchanged for millennia. Palestine is part of a land formation stretching several hundred miles along the Levant. D. Baly has shown convincingly that the geological structure of this Levantine region is mainly

northeast-southwest,[12] but it is more important here to note the more obvious
north-south features. These five features, clearly observable for most of the
Levant, are from west to east: the coastal plain, the western mountain range
(in Palestine, the "central" mountain range), the rift valley system, the eastern
mountain range or plateau, and the desert.

Palestine is considerably wider (from east to west) at its southern end,[13]
so some variations in this general pattern may be expected. The coastal plain
is narrow in the north, becoming nonexistent at the Ladder of Tyre (the present
Israeli-Lebanese boundary) and the foot of Mt. Carmel. At its southern end,
the coastal plain is very broad. Accordingly, this maritime plain has been
divided into regions, known in Old Testament times as the Plain of Asher
(between the Ladder of Tyre and Carmel), the Plain of Sharon (south of Carmel
to Joppa or Tel Aviv), and the Philistine plain (south to Gaza). Of the few
natural seaports along the Palestinian coastal plain, Acco (Acre), Dor, and
Joppa were principal in antiquity. A major north-south highway followed the

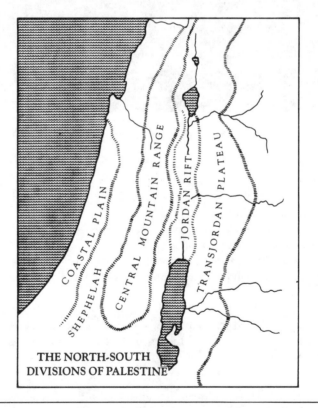

THE NORTH-SOUTH
DIVISIONS OF PALESTINE

12. *Geography of the Bible*, 2nd ed. (New York: 1974), pp. 28-41.
13. Palestine at its northern end, from the sea to the Upper Jordan, is about 32 mi.
(52 km.) wide; at its southern end, from Gaza to Sodom, about 65 mi. (105 km.).

coast, usually several miles inland because of the marshes and sand dunes characteristic of the coastal plain.

In the south, between the coastal plain and the mountain range, is a broad and fertile piedmont area, the Shephelah.[14] Under the Judges and the early Monarchy this area was a major focus of almost constant warfare between the Israelites (in the mountain range) and the Philistines (along the coastal plain).

The western mountain range (in Palestine, more descriptively called the central range) forms the backbone of the land. It is broken only at the plain of Jezreel (Esdraelon)[15] in lower Galilee, where a spur of the central range juts northwest to the sea to form the Carmel range. The major trunk road paralleling the coast turned inland just south of Carmel, traversing the narrow pass of Wâdī 'Ara alongside Megiddo, crossing the valley of Jezreel, through Lower Galilee and ultimately to Damascus. This part of the highway was known as "the way of the sea" (*Via Maris*; cf. Isa. 9:1). A shorter but more difficult north-south road followed the ridge of the central range, winding through the valleys between the mountain peaks.

The Plain of Esdraelon clearly separates the hilly region to the north from the mountains to the south. The northern region is best known as Galilee. The region to the south does not have a clear-cut natural boundary before the steppe or Negeb. Following political division of the land during the Israelite kingdom, the northern part may be called Samaria and the southern, Judea. South of the Negeb is the Sinai peninsula.

(1) Galilee. The natural boundary north of Galilee is the gorge of the Litani river to the northwest and Mt. Hermon to the northeast. The southern boundary is formed by the Carmel range to the southwest and Gilboa to the southeast. Upper Galilee to the north is mountainous, with elevations often above 3000 ft. (914 m.). Lower Galilee to the south is composed of rolling hills and broad valleys, sloping south to the broad Esdraelon plain.[16]

Galilee is from a Hebrew word meaning "the region of," and clearly is only part of a phrase such as "regions of the Philistines" (Josh. 13:2) and "regions of the Jordan" (22:10). Possibly the original name was "the region of the Gentiles" (Isa. 9:1).

(2) Samaria. The northern boundary of Samaria is marked clearly by the Plain of Esdraelon. The eastern boundary is the Jordan, and the Mediterranean forms the western limits, although the coastal plain was rarely under Israelite control. Samaria has no clear natural southern boundary, but Bethel is known to have been near the southern limits (1 Kgs. 12:29f.). Most of Samaria is mountainous, with elevations generally around 2000 ft. (610 m.). The broad valleys were watered principally by the seasonal rains. Western Samaria sloped

---

14. Hebrew for "lowlands," obviously named by those on the mountain ridge. Piedmont ("foot of the mountain") is a name devised by those on the plain.

15. The names Esdraelon (from Greek) and Jezreel (Hebrew) are interchangeable.

16. A very useful map is *Lands of the Bible Today* (Washington: 1967), by the National Geographic Society.

down to the maritime plain, until recently largely dunes and marshes. The arid eastern part drops off quickly to the Jordan.

The name Samaria is derived from the hill where Omri located his capital during the divided kingdom (1 Kgs. 16:24). Following their policy, after the Assyrians conquered Samaria, they carried off the most likely Israelite revolutionaries—the religious and political leaders—while at the same time settling captives from other nations in Samaria. From the intermingling of these captives with the Israelites left in the land came the mixed postexilic population, those to whom the name Samaritan came to apply (cf. 2 Kgs. 17:6, 24; Neh. 4:2). In New Testament times, the Jews had no dealings with the Samaritans (John 4:9).

(3) Judah. The region from the southern border of Samaria to the Negeb is generally called Judea, although this name properly belongs to the New Testament period. It is derived from Judah, the principal tribe, from which came the Davidic dynasty.

The mountainous portion is somewhat higher, as a rule, and more rocky than the mountains of Samaria; the valleys are narrow, often arid, and covered with large stones. The region to the east, dropping off suddenly to the Dead Sea, is "the wilderness of Judah." To the west, however, is a gradual slope of piedmont, the Shephelah, with hills and valleys that supply an abundance of fruit and vegetables. Beyond the Shephelah is the broad maritime plain.

(4) The Negeb. The biblical Negeb generally is limited to the region just south of Beersheba.[17] The Negeb is a high region of steppe, land receiving scarcely enough rainfall to support any vegetation. By digging wells and by careful rock-mulching, peoples actually did settle in the Negeb, as the Nabateans (ca. 5th cent. B.C.–2nd cent. A.D.) and, to a lesser extent, the tribes of the patriarchal narratives.[18]

(5) Sinai. The peninsula, with its great wilderness and its massive mountains, was never considered part of Palestine. Because it is prominent in the early narrative (particularly Exodus, Leviticus, and Numbers), three features deserve mention: (a) The "wilderness of Zin" is a barren region in northern Sinai. Its most important sites are Khirbet el-Qudeirât and 'Ain Qedeis, both suggested as the location of Kadesh-barnea, where the Israelites encamped for much of their thirty-eight years in the wilderness.[19] (b) The "river of Egypt" is Wâdî el-'Arîsh (not the Nile), formed by the drainage of the Sinai mountains. It flows approximately north and enters the Mediterranean at modern el-'Arîsh. (c) The great mountain massif in the southern end of the peninsula, where Sinai (or Horeb) was most likely located, is a region of rugged peaks rising to more than 7000 ft. (2134 m.).

---

17. The traditional southern boundary of Judah was Beersheba, although the tribal boundary was considerably further south (Josh. 15:1-4). In the Old Testament the Negeb is generally of little significance and considered outside the land.

18. See N. Glueck, *Rivers in the Desert*, rev. ed. (Philadelphia: 1968).

19. See Deut. 1:19; Num. 13:26; 14:26-35.

TRANSJORDAN

Names for the Region. The region between the Jordan rift and the Syrian desert seems never to have had a real name. That most common in the Old Testament, *'ēber hayyardēn*, means, literally, "across the Jordan," the approximate equivalent of "Transjordan." Obviously, it was given to the region by those west of the Jordan.[20] The New Testament Perea means the same. In the Persian period, the satrapy that included Syria, Palestine, and Transjordan was known as Beyond the River, referring to the Euphrates.

General Description. Transjordan is a plateau, which might be described as the southern extension of the rift system's eastern mountain range. It rises suddenly from the Jordan rift about 2000 ft. (610 m.) above sea level, then slopes gently to the Syrian and Arabian deserts. Well watered by a complex system of rivers and streams, it has long been noted for its produce. The drainage systems form a number of rivers that have cut deep gorges as they flow toward the Jordan valley, forming natural boundaries.

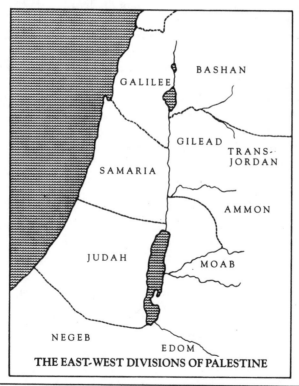

THE EAST-WEST DIVISIONS OF PALESTINE

---

20. This is the name given the region in stories describing the region prior to the Israelite entry into Canaan, i.e., while they were still in Moab. Some scholars have argued this as proof of the stories' later date. However, a well-established name can be used even when technically inaccurate. In modern times, people east of the Jordan have referred to their region as "Transjordan."

Regions of Transjordan. (1) North of the Yarmuk gorge and east of the Upper Jordan and Sea of Galilee was Bashan, a region formed largely by decomposed volcanic rock and therefore exceptionally fertile.[21] In Roman times the area was known as Gaulanitis (cf. modern Golan heights), and was an important source of wheat for the Roman empire.

(2) Gilead, south of the Yarmuk, was a land of numerous valleys with good grazing, land, and rugged hills with forests of oak and other trees. The proverbial "balm of Gilead" (Jer. 8:22; 46:11), noted for medicinal and cosmetic properties, was exported to Tyre and to Egypt. Jacob wrestled with the angel (Gen. 32:24-32) and was reconciled with Esau (33:1-17) in Gilead, and Elijah the prophet came from Tishbe (1 Kgs. 17:1). The southern boundary of Gilead is not clearly specified. Some scholars believe it was the Arnon (Wâdī el-Môjib), but the Jabbok gorge (Wâdī Zerqa) is more commonly accepted.

(3) Ammon was situated roughly between the Jabbok and Arnon gorges, more specifically on the tributaries of the Jabbok, well east of the Jordan. Its capital, Rabbath-amman, is the site of modern Amman. The thirteenth-century kingdom of Sihon lay between Ammon and the Jordan.

(4) Moab was situated mostly between the Arnon and the Zered (Wâdī el-Ḥesā), but at times it extended north beyond the Arnon. The "plains of Moab," between Wâdī Nimrîn and the Dead Sea, stretch up the gentle slope toward Heshbon (Ḥesbân) and Madeba. Ruth, Naomi's daughter-in-law and ancestress of David, was a Moabitess. Moses viewed the promised land from the mountains of Moab, and died there (Deut. 34:1-5). A significant archaeological discovery, the Mesha inscription, is written in Moabite.

(5) Edom generally is identified with the region east of the Arabah between the Zered and the head of the Gulf of Aqaba. During most of the Old Testament period, however, Edom spread across both sides of the Arabah. The high mountain range called Mt. Seir was the center of the Edomites' territory, whose capital was at Sela (Greek Petra; 2 Kgs. 14:7).

(6) Midian, not included in Transjordan, lay south of Edom, east of the Gulf of Aqaba and opposite Sinai. Jethro, Moses' father-in-law, was a Midianite. Some scholars contend the mountain where Moses received the law was in Midian, but biblical descriptions of the Israelites' journey do not support this view.

JORDAN RIFT

The Jordan rift is part of the Great Rift, a geological phenomenon extending from the Kara Su valley in Turkey to Victoria Falls at the southern end of Zambia. The deepest part of the Great Rift is the Dead Sea. The Jordan rift

---

21. Note the fat "cows of Bashan" (Amos 4:1) and the "strong bulls of Bashan" (Ps. 22:12 [MT 13]).

includes the tributaries of the Upper Jordan, the Sea of Galilee, Jordan river, Dead Sea, and the Arabah.

Upper Jordan. Copious springs gush from the slopes of Mt. Hermon to form the tributaries of the Upper Jordan. In biblical times, they formed a marshy region which drained into Lake Huleh, a turnip-shaped lake about 4 mi. (6.4 km.) long. Today, the marshes and lake have been drained, and the Upper Jordan continues in the "Middle Jordan," a gorge about 10 mi. (16 km.) long in the course of which the river drops from about 200 ft. (70 m.) above sea level to empty into the Sea of Galilee, 684 ft. (208 m.) below sea level.

Sea of Galilee. Of importance mostly in the New Testament, the Sea of Galilee is called Chinnereth ("harp") in Num. 34:11, and later Gennesaret (Luke 5:1) and Tiberias (John 21:1). The harp-shaped lake is 13 mi. (21 km.) long and 8 mi. (13 km.) wide. Situated between the hills of Galilee and the Golan heights of the Transjordan plateau, it enjoys a subtropical climate, but is subject to sudden and severe storms. The northwestern shore, the fabulous plain of Gennesaret,[22] was incredibly fertile.

Jordan River. From the Sea of Galilee to the Dead Sea, the airline distance is about 60 mi. (97 km.). As a result of the river's meandering, however, its length is about 200 mi. (325 km.). Because of the saline soil in the Jordan valley, the river carries a considerable quantity of salt into the Dead Sea.

A cross section of the Jordan valley shows that it is actually a valley within a valley. The largest valley, which extends from the hills of Samaria to the edge of the Transjordan plateau, is known by the Arabic name Ghôr. The Ghôr is about 5 mi. (8 km.) wide just south of the Sea of Galilee, but more than 12 mi. (20 km.) wide at Jericho. Within the Ghôr is the Zôr, the "jungle" or "pride" of the Jordan (Zech. 11:3), a valley 10 or 20 ft. (3 or 6 m.) deep and as much as 150 ft. (50 m.) wide, with almost perpendicular banks. Within the Zôr lies the actual Jordan watercourse, a river 15 to 25 ft. (5 to 8 m.) wide. Because the Jordan overflows its banks in flood season and spreads out in the Zôr, dense vegetation is found in the Zôr (see diagram).[23]

Some scholars have suggested that the stopping-up of the Jordan as the Israelites were to cross from Moab to Gilgal resulted when an earthquake tumbled the steep marl banks into the Zôr at Adam (modern Damiyeh; cf. Josh. 3:13, 16). This did happen in A.D. 1267, when the Jordan was dammed for several hours, and again in connection with the 1927 earthquake.[24]

---

22. Thus one of its names, according to Josephus, who calls it "the ambition of nature"; *War* iii.10.8 §518.

23. For a good aerial picture, see L.H. Grollenberg, *Atlas of the Bible*, trans. J.M.H. Reid and H.H. Rowley (London: 1956), Plate 26.

24. N. Glueck, *The River Jordan* (Philadelphia: 1946), p. 118.

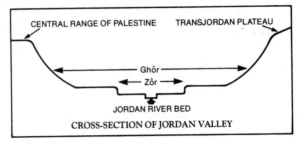

CENTRAL RANGE OF PALESTINE   TRANSJORDAN PLATEAU

Ghôr

Zôr

JORDAN RIVER BED

CROSS-SECTION OF JORDAN VALLEY

Dead Sea. The lowest body of water on earth is the Dead Sea, about 1290 ft. (395 m.) below sea level; its bottom at the deepest point is about 2500 ft. (765 m.) below sea level. The sea is 48 mi. (77 km.) long, and 9 mi. (14 km.) wide at its widest point. It is called the "salt sea" (Gen. 14:3), "sea of the Arabah" (Josh. 3:16), and "east sea" (Zech. 14:8). Josephus called it the "sea of asphalt" (*War* iv.8.4 §476), and the Arabs today call it the "Sea of Lot." It is not mentioned in the New Testament. Because evaporation is the only means of escape for the six million tons of water the Jordan pours into the Dead Sea each day, its concentration of salts is about 26 per cent. Nothing can live in it, hence the name, first applied by the Greeks.

Arabah. South of the Dead Sea, an arid valley, rising to 656 ft. (200 m.) above sea level and then descending to the sea, stretches to the Gulf of Aqaba, 185 mi. (298 km.) south. The Hebrew name "Arabah" is used for this valley today and is approximately equivalent to Arabic Ghôr. In the Old Testament Arabah is used also for the valley of the Dead Sea and for the Jordan river valley.

Gulf of Aqaba. The extension of the Jordan rift toward the Red Sea is known as the Gulf of Aqaba. In antiquity, "Red Sea" meant not only that body of water but also the Gulf of Aqaba, Gulf of Suez, and even the Arabian Sea and Indian ocean. The Red Sea through which the Israelites passed in the Exodus (Exod. 13:18; 15:22) is certainly none of these.[25]

General Description. The entire eastern Mediterranean is influenced largely by the Etesian winds, which in the winter bring moisture generally from the northwest, and in the summer dry weather principally from the southwest. Occasionally these are interrupted by desert winds from the east or south, the hamsîn[26] or sirocco, which bring stiflingly hot, dry weather a few days at a time.

---

25. "Sea of Reeds, the literal rendering of the Hebrew phrase usually translated "Red Sea," describes neither the Gulf of Suez nor the Red Sea, and most likely applies to reed-filled marshes in the vicinity of Lake Timsah or the Bitter lakes.

26. Arabic "fifty." About fifty days of such weather occur each year—but not a seven-week season, for the hamsîn rarely lasts more than three or four days at a time.

Seasons. As a result, there are two seasons: rainy (approximately December to March) and dry (May to September). At the end of the dry season in some years are showers, "the former rains" of the Old Testament. Likewise, in some years the rainy season extends into a few weeks of "latter rains."[27] Both "rains" were viewed by the Israelites as special blessings.

Rainfall. Since the winds blow mainly from the west, any moisture they bring is deposited as rain on the western slopes of both the central mountain range in Palestine and the Transjordan plateau. Accordingly, these slopes are usually well watered and quite fertile. The eastern slopes, however, are arid, and the hot winds from the east or south can quickly desiccate trees and plants, causing much damage. Periodically they also bring huge swarms of locusts which strip the vegetation bare in a matter of hours (cf. Joel 1–2).

Climatic Change. According to one theory, the climate has changed significantly between patriarchal times and the present, drying up much of the land, and causing deforestation and other results. But available records do not appear to support this theory. The amount of rainfall, average temperature, and other climatic matters seem to have remained relatively constant in Palestine and the surrounding regions for the past six thousand years. Changes in the amount of vegetation probably are explained better as the result of two common elements unusually hostile to a region's ecology: men and goats. Between them, hills have been stripped of trees and soil eroded away by rains, with an apparent change of climate. This is man-made, not a natural phenomenon.

SIGNIFICANCE OF GEOGRAPHY

Political Significance. Palestine was a land bridge between the civilizations of Europe, southwestern Asia, and northern Africa. Accordingly, the merchants and military forces of the ancient Near East frequently appear in the Old Testament. But this is only part of the story. Armies only march when one ruler is convinced of his forces' superiority to their opponent(s). There were periods of military balance, usually the result of weakness among all the surrounding nations. During such periods of power vacuum, Palestine was a buffer zone. Such was the state of affairs when the Israelites entered Canaan, and this continued during much of the monarchy and until the rise of the Assyrian empire. There were, of course, times when the Egyptians maintained outer lines of defense in Palestine or entered a marriage alliance with an Israelite king, and other times when the bordering small nations, such as the Philistines, Ammonites, Moabites, or Edomites, felt free to conduct raids on Israelite cities.

Physical characteristics also account for the "splendid isolation" of the

---

27. The occasional statement that Palestine had two rainy seasons arises from a misunderstanding of these terms.

Israelites for much of their history. The principal north-south highways that armies and merchants traveled lay either along the coastal plain to the west or on the edge of the Transjordan plateau to the east. Israel, however, was situated in the mountainous region of the central range. A foreign ruler might mock Israel's God as "a god of the mountains but not of the valleys" (1 Kgs. 20:28), but this only says that the Israelites were relatively secure in their "mountain fastness." This was more true of Judah, with narrow valleys filled with great rocks, than of Samaria, marked by broad plains. Hence the Assyrians were able to conquer the northern kingdom with relative ease, while Jerusalem was more difficult to take.

The physical features also help explain the frequent Israelite disunity. The land was designed more for tribal possessions or city-states than a strongly united nation. In this respect, ancient Israel resembled Greece. The Aramean city-states, on the other hand, were more like oases in the desert.

Because it is landlocked, Israel did not develop as a maritime people. Mediterranean shipping in the Levant was controlled almost exclusively by the Phoenicians,[28] and the best ports were from Acco north. Israel never controlled the coastal plain. Their only maritime development centered at Ezion-geber on the Gulf of Aqaba, providing trade with ports on the Red Sea (and possibly the east coast of Africa).

Theological Significance. Throughout the Bible physical features have theological overtones. The Lord established the land and held back the seas. He caused the land to yield its fruits, or he sent famine. He sent or withheld the rains. If he did not send the early rain, the soil was not ready for planting, and if he withheld the latter rain, the fruits did not ripen. God sent the blasting east wind or the devastating locust swarm. He determined the natural boundaries. The rivers ran to the seas, but the seas were not full. The Lord established the mountains. He moved the nations from place to place, bringing Israel from Egypt, the Philistines from Caphtor, and the Syrians from Kir (Amos 9:2).

Perhaps the theological understanding of the geographical features is best seen as the prophets of Yahweh struggled with Baal-worship. When the Israelites entered the land, they came into contact with Canaanite religion, a form of nature religion centered on Baal. Its basic beliefs conflicted with the concept of the natural world inherent in Yahwism, whereby not Baal but Yahweh gave the fruit, oil, wine, and increase of flocks (cf. Hos. 2:8). Baal was a very "earthy" god, and Baal worship included sexual prostitution to induce the land to yield its fruit. Therefore the prophets of Yahweh strenuously opposed Baal worship, insisting that Yahweh is the God who created the world and who gives or withholds its yield. The geographical and climatic features became a common

---

28. Even when his fleet was at its prime, Solomon's sailors were Phoenicians. The Hebrews' desert origins are evident, particularly in the place given the sea in Hebrew thought.

and essential part of the prophetic message. To understand the word of God as proclaimed by his servants the prophets, therefore, basic knowledge of the land's physical geography is necessary, for details of the geographical and climatic elements are part of the language of revelation.

FOR FURTHER READING

Aharoni, Y., and Avi-Yonah, M. *Macmillan Bible Atlas*. Rev. ed. New York: 1977. (264 maps of biblical events, showing geographical influences and historical processes.)

Cleave, R.L.W. *Student Map Manual.* Jerusalem: n.d.

Eichholz, G. *Landscapes of the Bible.* Trans. J.W. Doberstein. New York: 1963. (Magnificent photographs of biblical sites.)

Frank, H.T. *Discovering the Biblical World.* Maplewood, N.J.: 1975. (Stereographic physical maps; illustrated.)

Smith, G.A. *Historical Geography of the Holy Land.* 25th ed. New York: 1931. (A classic; descriptive aspects particularly useful.)

CHAPTER 6

THE PENTATEUCH

T HE first five books of the Old Testament—Genesis, Exodus, Leviticus, Numbers, and Deuteronomy—are called the "Pentateuch." The word derives from Gk. *pentáteuchos* "five-volumed (book)," following the Jewish designation, "the five-fifths of the law." Jews call it the "Torah" (i.e., "instruction"), often rendered in English, "Law," as it is called in the New Testament (Gk. *nómos*; e.g., Matt. 5:17; Luke 16:17; Acts 7:53; 1 Cor. 9:8). This was the most important division of the Jewish canon, with an authority and sanctity far exceeding that attributed to the Prophets and Writings.

The books of the Pentateuch are not "books" in the modern sense of independent, self-contained entities, but were purposefully structured and intended as part of a larger unity; therefore the term "Pentateuch" is not only convenient but necessary. However, granted this fact of the unity of the larger corpus, the conventional fivefold division into Genesis through Deuteronomy is important not simply as a convenient means of reference to the material, but because there is clear editorial evidence establishing just these five "books" as genuine subdivisions of the material.[1]

UNITY

Despite marks of real disparity and complexity in structure and origins, far more primary and important is the overarching unity which the Pentateuch evidences. This is created by and inheres in the historical narrative forming the Pentateuch's backbone and framework and into which the blocks of legal texts

---

1. For a succinct but thorough discussion of the editorial evidence for the independence of the fivefold division, together with the evidence for their intentional structuring into a purposeful whole, see B.S. Childs, *Old Testament as Scripture,* pp. 128-131. Of course, the division into smaller units was also prompted by the physical problem of length if written as one scroll.

have been placed. A clue to this narrative's central role and importance is the fact that the Old Testament events most frequently cited in the New Testament as the background and preparation for God's work in Christ are precisely that sequence of divine acts from Abraham's call through the kingship of David.[2]

Summaries or "confessions" (so G. von Rad) of this sequence of divine acts play a central role in scripture, e.g., Paul's address to the Jews in the synagogue at Antioch of Pisidia (Acts 13:17-41). The beginning of his address (vv. 17-23) is a confessional summary of what God has done from Abraham through David, after which the narrative passes directly to Jesus Christ. Paul thus implies that the stream of history from the patriarchs to David is the most significant part of the Old Testament story and affirms that Christ is the culmination and fulfillment of God's redemptive purposes begun there. In this light, it is instructive to note several very similar summaries in the Old Testament, especially in the Pentateuch. Consider, for example, the confession prescribed in the ritual of firstfruits (Deut. 26:5-10). Very similar are Moses' words in answering the question Israel's children will one day ask regarding the meaning of the law (Deut. 6:20-24). Similar also is Joshua's historical prologue to the covenant renewal ceremony at Shechem (Josh. 24:2-13).

Note the different uses of this summary and its variant forms. Yet it contains the same basic details confessing God's saving acts on behalf of his people:

(1) God chose Abraham and his descendants (Acts 13:17; Josh. 24:3) and promised them the land of Canaan (Deut. 6:23).

(2) Israel went down into Egypt (Acts 13:17; Josh. 24:4) and fell into slavery (Deut. 6:21; 26:5), from which the Lord delivered them (Acts 13:17; Josh. 24:5-7; Deut. 6:21f.; 26:8).

(3) God brought Israel into Canaan as promised (Acts 13:19; Josh. 24:11-13; Deut. 6:23; 26:9).

This is but the narrative backbone of the Pentateuch in miniature! Here is the plan that unifies the different elements forming the building blocks of the Pentateuch: promise, election, deliverance, covenant, law, and land.[3]

The one element universally present and central to these credos or confessions of faith is the Exodus, representing Yahweh's deliverance and the historical realization of his election of Israel as his people. It is Yahweh's first saving deed in Israel's history and becomes the model to which other saving deeds are likened (cf. Amos 2:4-10; 3:1f.; Jer. 2:2-7; Ps. 77:13-19 [MT 14-20]; 78:12-55).

---

2. So G.E. Wright, God Who Acts: Biblical Theology as Recital. SBT 8 (Chicago: 1952), pp. 69ff. He notes that, despite numerous citations of and allusions to the Psalms and Prophets, the events most often alluded to are in the Pentateuch. Almost surprisingly, Jerusalem's destruction, the Exile, and restoration are not used in the same way at all.

3. This historical base reveals that these "theological" terms do not deal with abstract ideas. They do not describe timeless universal truths but rather specific historical events that happened to a particular people.

As such, it forms the central core and pivotal event of the Pentateuch, showing how Yahweh *chose* Israel as "his own possession among all peoples" (Exod. 19:5) by his dramatic *deliverance* at the Red Sea; bound them to him in his *covenant* as their God, using his gracious, unmerited deliverance as the grounds for their accepting it; and bequeathed to them his *law* as their constitution. This is all recorded in Exodus through Deuteronomy. Gen. 12–50, the patriarchal pro- logue, sets forth the *promise* which the *deliverance* from Egypt and giving of the *land* fulfills. The promise to Abraham of land and nationhood stands at the very beginning of the patriarchal history, indicating the central theme and purpose of that history:

> Now the Lord said to Abram, "Go from your country and your kindred and your father's house to the land that I will show you. And I will make of you a great nation, and I will bless you, and make your name great, so that you will be a blessing." (Gen. 12:1f.)

This dual theme is repeated again and again in the Abrahamic cycle of stories (cf. Gen. 13:14-17; 15:2-5, 18-21; 17:7f., 15-19) and is renewed with each patriarchal generation (Isaac, Gen. 26:2-4; Jacob/Israel, 28:13; 35:11-13; Jo- seph and his sons, 48:1-6). It then is specifically set forth as fulfilled in the deliverance begun at the Exodus (Exod. 6:6-8), and at the end of the Penta- teuch in God's words to Moses (Deut. 34:1-4).

The purpose of this narrative is set forth by the fact that it does not stand alone. The whole story is given special historical and theological meaning by the relationship it sustains to its preface, the Primeval Prologue (Gen. 1–11).[4] Not concerned with the particularism of promise and election central to Gen. 12 through Deut. 34, the focus of concern of Gen. 1–11 is universal. It goes back to ultimate origins, to the creation of all things, especially man and woman. It then sets forth, in theological terms, how man and woman came to be the way they have been since ancient times: at war with themselves, alienated and separated from God and their fellows in a broken, disorderly world with nation pitted against nation, social element against social element, individual against individual. The author paints this dark picture by tracing the origin and rise of sin from the disobedience of the first man and woman in the Garden of Eden (Gen. 1–3); through the fratricide of Cain (4:1-16); the murderous vengeance expressed in Lamech's boastful song (vv. 17-23); the general corruption of man- kind, heinous enough to warrant the Flood (ch. 6); to the dissolution of man- kind's primal unity in which they are scattered into the disorder of the world, expressed in the story of the Tower of Babel (ch. 11).

The author of Gen. 1–11 intended by the whole plan of the primeval history to pose in all severity at its end the question of God's future relationship

---

4. This relationship is set forth by G. von Rad in *Genesis*, trans. J. Marks. OTL (Philadelphia: 1972), pp. 152-55, to which the following exposition is indebted.

to his scattered, broken, and alienated humanity. Is God's patient endurance exhausted? Has he dismissed the nations in wrath forever? Only in light of this introduction can one understand the significance and meaning of the election and blessing of Abraham (immediately following the genealogy separating the primeval and patriarchal prologues), which stands like a rubric at the beginning of the patriarchal story.

The contrast, then, between Gen. 1–11 and the particularistic history of promise, election, deliverance, and covenant that follows is dramatic and strik-ing; the latter is deliberately and consciously set forth as the answer to the former. In God's special dealings with Abraham and his descendants lies the answer to the anguish of the whole human family.

The Pentateuch thus has two major divisions: Gen. 1–11 and Gen. 12–Deut. 34. The relation between them is one of question and answer, problem and solution; the clue is Gen. 12:3.[5]

This structure not only elucidates the binding unity of the Pentateuch; it also reveals that the structure here begun stretches far beyond the Pentateuch itself. Only the *beginning* of the process of redemptive history is found within it. The end and fulfillment lie beyond Deut. 34—indeed, beyond the whole Old Testament! Nowhere does the Old Testament set forth an ultimate solution to the universal problem which Gen. 1–11 so poignantly portrays. The Old Testament indeed does present a redemptive history, but an incomplete one that does not arrive at full redemption. When the Old Testament ends, Israel still is looking for the final consummation when hope shall be fulfilled and promise become fact. So the juncture of Gen. 1–11 and chs. 12ff. is not only one of the most important places in the whole Old Testament but one of the most important in the entire Bible. Here begins the redemptive history that awaits the proclamation of the good news of God's new redemptive act in Jesus Christ; only then will be found the way in which the blessing of Abraham will bless all the families of the earth. The Pentateuch is truly open-ended, for the salvation history there begun awaits its consummation in the Son of Abraham (Matt. 1:1), who draws all people to him (John 12:32), ending the alienation of humanity from God and from one another so poignantly portrayed in the primeval prologue.

COMPLEXITY

A careful reading of the Pentateuch will reveal, beside a definite unity of purpose, plan, and arrangement, a diversity—a complexity—that is equally

---

5. For a similar analysis, carried out in great detail, that sees the theme of the Pentateuch as the partial fulfillment of the divine promise to the patriarchs of posterity, divine-human relationship, and land, see D.J.A. Clines, *The Theme of the Pentateuch.* JSOTS 10 (Sheffield: 1979).

striking. This has given rise to many and varied theories as to the Pentateuch's origin. Many of these theories, unfortunately, offer views of its origin, date, and authorship which evaluate its historical and theological worth very negatively. Often it is regarded as originating many centuries later than the Mosaic period, thus preserving little genuine historical information; the religious and theological ideas and practices recorded are said to be those held centuries later. For example, J. Wellhausen, one of the most eloquent proponents of these theories, viewed the Pentateuch as the product of the exilic and postexilic periods and thus the starting-point for the history of Judaism only, not that of ancient Israel.[6]

Although the Wellhausenian view has been so modified subsequently as to be well-nigh abandoned, this has not everywhere resulted in a more sympathetic evaluation of the Pentateuch. In fact, in the considered judgment of one of the most important of the recent schools of Old Testament thought, represented by scholars of such repute as M. Noth, hardly a single positive historical statement can be made on the basis of the pentateuchal traditions. Noth holds it as quite erroneous to refer to Moses as the founder of a religion, or even to speak of a Mosaic religion at all! But as noted above, the unity of the Pentateuch consists in the affirmation that God has acted in history on behalf of the human family in the events of the patriarchal and Mosaic story. If so, views such as Noth's remove the very heart and core of the biblical proclamation, reducing the Pentateuch to irrelevancy at best and to fraud and deceit at worst.

Reaction against such extreme and exaggerated criticism is the only possible approach for those committed to the truth of the Bible. Error must be combatted. However, conservative scholars have reacted all too often by going to the other extreme without producing a thorough introduction to the Pentateuch—one that takes seriously both the evidence for the Law's basic unity and the diversity on which negative theories are based. Consequently, a word must be said about the literary evidences of complexity in the text of the Pentateuch and about their implications for its origin, development, and literary nature.

Literary Evidence for Complexity. As soon as one begins to wrestle with the literary nature of the Pentateuch, an obvious question arises that would be difficult if it were not so familiar: Is the Pentateuch a book of law or history? No other law code, ancient or modern, knows anything like it: the historical narrative constantly cuts across and interrupts the legislation, while the narratives of the primeval prologue, the patriarchs, and Moses form an introduction to the Mosaic law. This dual character must be recognized in seeking the origin of the Pentateuch. God did not just promulgate a law code or redeem a people through a special series of saving acts. He did both: he chose a people whom

---

6. *Prolegomena to the History of Ancient Israel*, trans. J.S. Black and A. Menzies (1885; repr. Magnolia, Mass.: 1973), p. 1.

he bound to himself by a law. The Pentateuch then has a twofold character: a narrative interspersed with blocks of legal material.[7]

Other literary complexities also become obvious upon careful analysis of the text.[8]

(1) Both the narrative and legal division have a certain and striking lack of close continuity and order in their subject matter. Thus there is no sequence between Gen. 4:26 and 5:1; in fact, Gen. 2:4b–4:26 breaks the thread of the account of 1:1–2:4a; 5:1ff. Again Gen. 19:38; 20:1 show a definite discontinuity. So do Exod. 19:25; 20:1; in fact the decalogue account in 20:1-17 is clearly a discontinuity in the narrative represented by 19:1-25; 20:18-21. Finally, the legal codes themselves are not grouped in any logical arrangement.

(2) With these facts in mind, it is not surprising to find significant differences in vocabulary, syntax, and style and general composition of the various sections of the work. Such differences are seen clearly, for example, in comparing the codes of Leviticus and Deuteronomy.

(3) Further evidence of complexity is the variable use of the divine names Yahweh ("Lord") and Elohim ("God"). The evidence can be stated thus: even though these names often occur without any discernible reason for using a particular name, a number of chapters, or sections of chapters, especially in Genesis, use exclusively or predominately one name or the other and a correlation can be seen between the name chosen and the theological concepts and literary characteristics of the passages.[9]

(4) Duplications and triplications of material do occur in the Pentateuch. Of concern is not the simple repetition of identical material, but repetition of the same basic subject matter, replete with common features, yet with certain marked divergences. This phenomenon has been debated, affirmed, and denied at length. Zealous exponents of the documentary source theory have identified

---

7. Note that it is in the genre of the suzerain-vassal treaty form, whose comparison with the Mosaic covenant has been so fruitful (see p. 145), that one finds precisely this combination of history (in the historical prologue) and law (in the stipulations). Surely the correlation between this striking feature of the Pentateuch's form and the structure of one of its most important constituents, the Mosaic covenant, cannot be accidental!

8. See A. Robert and A. Tricot, eds., *Guide to the Bible*, 2nd ed. trans. E.P. Arbez and M.R.P. McGuire (New York: 1960), pp. 160f.

9. This phenomenon is striking and undeniable, particularly from Gen. 1:1 through Exod. 6, at which point God reveals himself by his name Yahweh. From this point on the distinction is not nearly so clear, since the name Yahweh predominates. Thus, according to statistics cited by J.B. Harford, the MT contains 178 examples of Elohim and 146 of Yahweh from Gen. 1:1–Exod. 3:15, but 44 examples of Elohim and 393 of Yahweh from Exod. 3:16 to the end; *Since Wellhausen* (London: 1926). Examples of sections that use Elohim include Gen. 1:1–2:3; 5; 17; 23; 25:7-17; sections that use Yahweh include 11:1-9; 12; 18. See the discussion in J. Orr, *The Problem of the Old Testament* (London: 1907), pp. 196ff.

as doublets passages that are far more easily explained in other ways.[10] But the fact remains that a number of such duplications cannot be so resolved. For example:

In two accounts, Abraham risks Sarah's honor by passing her off as his sister (Gen. 12; 20); note also Isaac's surprisingly similar episode (26:6-11). The name Beersheba ("Well of the Oath") commemorates not only a covenant between Abraham and Abimelech (Gen. 21:22-31), but also an alliance between Isaac and Abimelech (26:26-33). In Gen. 28:19; 35:7 Jacob changes the name of Luz to Bethel; but in 28:10-19 he does so on his way *to* Paddan-aram when Yahweh *appears* to him, whereas in 35:9-15 he does so on the way *from* Paddan-aram when Yahweh *speaks* to him (35:13, 15). The passage on the clean and the unclean in Lev. 11:1-47 is duplicated by Deut. 14:3-21; and the passage on slaves occurs in triplicate (Exod. 21:1-11; Lev. 25:39-55; Deut. 15:12-18).[11]

Additional evidences in the text suggest a long history of transmission and development. A striking number of passages clearly suggest an age later than that of Moses.[12] Representative examples can be cited. Statements such as "at that time the Canaanites were in the land" (Gen. 12:6; 13:7) and "the people of Israel ate the manna . . . till they came to the border of the land of Canaan" (Exod. 16:35) imply that Israel already occupied Canaan. Gen. 14:14 indicates that Abram pursued Lot's captors as far as Dan, yet the place did not receive this name until the Danites captured it following the Conquest (Josh. 19:47; Judg. 18:29). Gen. 36:31, at the beginning of a list of Edomite kings, states that they all ruled "before any king reigned over the Israelites." Obviously the writer's viewpoint can only be sometime after Saul.[13]

---

10. E.g., it often is claimed that Gen. 37:27, 28a differ as to who bought Joseph— Ishmaelites (v. 27) or Midianites (v. 28a)—and who sold him to Egypt—Ishmaelites (v. 28b; 39:1) or Midianites (37:36). When this ambiguity is combined with the similar roles of Reuben in 37:21f., 29f. and Judah in vv. 26f., it often is alleged that duplicate stories are conflated here: in one Judah rescues Joseph by arranging his sale to Ishmaelites who take him to Egypt; in the other Reuben saves him from death by having him cast into the pit from which, unknown to the brothers, Midianites draw him out and take him to Egypt. However, comparison of Judg. 6:1-3 and 8:24 shows "Ishmaelites" and "Midianites" as overlapping terms; Ishmaelites means something like "nomads" or "Bedouin," and Midianites, a particular tribe, as the Amalekites and "people of the East" (Judg. 6:3). With this in mind, the roles of Reuben and Judah can be fitted into a consistent narrative.

11. This list could be expanded at length. For a very illuminating example of divergent parallelism in the Pentateuch narrative, consider the two accounts of the second giving of tables of the law to Moses after he broke the first set (Exod. 34; Deut. 10). See W. Wegner, "Creation and Salvation," CTM 37 (1966): 522.

12. Most were noted in antiquity. For summaries, see G. Aalders, *Short Introduction to the Pentateuch* (London: 1949), pp. 105-8; H.H. Rowley, *The Growth of the Old Testament* (New York: 1963), p. 17.

13. For other examples, see Aalders, *ibid.*; Rowley, *ibid.* These phenomena can be explained by hypothesizing that they are all later editorial additions (see O.T. Allis, *The Five Books of Moses* [Nutley, N.J.: 1943], p. 13) but this conclusion will follow necessarily only if it can be demonstrated that all that surrounds them must come, in its present form, from the Mosaic age. The indications of diversity discussed above strongly suggest that it does not.

These examples of complexities in the text vary rather widely in extent of clarity or ambiguity. Some are simply literary *facts*; others are more ambiguous and their assessment more subjective and dependent on the interpreter's views. One cannot, however, hope to assess correctly the literary nature and origin of the Pentateuch without wrestling seriously with these complexities.

Positive Evidence for Authorship and Origin. To begin with, the Pentateuch is an anonymous work. It nowhere gives any indication of authorship. Moses is not so mentioned, nor is anyone else. It is worth noting that such anonymity is in keeping with Old Testament practice in particular and with ancient literary works in general.[14] In the ancient Near East an "author" was not the creative artist as in modern culture. He was primarily a preserver of the past and was bound by traditional material and methodology. "Literature" was far more community than individual property.[15]

Nevertheless, even though anonymous, the Pentateuch does give indications of literary activity by its principal figure Moses. He is described, in passing, as ordered to write or actually writing historical facts (Exod. 17:14; Num. 33:2), laws or sections of law codes (Exod. 24:4; 34:27f.), and one poem (Deut. 31:22). Thus Scripture refers to Moses' narrative, legislative, and poetical literary activity. However, his contribution is not limited strictly to the portions of the Pentateuch specifically attributed to him. Rather, there is every reason to presume that his involvement extends beyond these portions.

Moses' literary activity is corroborated by scattered but significant references in the rest of the preexilic literature. The exilic and postexilic references are far more numerous. In fact, careful examination yields a striking pattern:[16]

(1) Postexilic books (Chronicles, Ezra, Nehemiah, Daniel, etc.) refer quite frequently to the Pentateuch as a written text with authority; they draw on all the codes of the Pentateuch. Here the expression "book of Moses" occurs for the first time.

(2) Middle books (i.e., the preexilic historical books, Joshua, 1–2 Samuel,

---

14. Thus, no indication is given as to who wrote Joshua, Judges, Samuel, Kings, Chronicles, Ezra, Nehemiah, etc. Even though the prophetic books bear the names of those who spoke the oracles, usually no indication is given of who preserved them; the third-person biographical sections (e.g., Isa. 7, as opposed to chs. 6–8; Amos 7:10-17) clearly come from another hand than the prophet's.

15. In all the many thousands of Akkadian literary compositions, only three (two Akkadian and one Sumerian) incorporate explicit references to authorship. Even in these references and others found in lists of literary compositions, the term "author" is not to be taken in the modern sense; it is expressed with the formula ša pi "in (of) the mouth of," which identifies either the oral source or the redactor. Thus, the "author" built on earlier versions and was in part simply an adaptor. See W.W. Hallo, "New Viewpoints on Cuneiform Literature," *IEJ* 12 (1962): 14f.

16. For this analysis, see R.J. Thompson, *Moses and the Law in a Century of Criticism Since Graf* (Leiden: 1970), pp. 2ff.

1–2 Kings) refer very rarely to Moses' literary activity; all such references are to Deuteronomy.[17]

(3) Earlier books (i.e., the preexilic prophets) have no such references.[18] This evidence indicates that the tradition is a growing one, with the connection to Moses extended from some laws, to Deuteronomy, to all laws, to the whole Pentateuch.[19] The tradition's continued growth is further seen in the frequent New Testament references to the whole Pentateuch as the "law" or "book of Moses" (Mark 12:26; Luke 2:22; Acts 13:39) or simply "Moses" (Luke 24:27), and to the whole Old Testament as "Moses and the prophets" (16:29). In addition, the testimony to Moses as author of the whole Pentateuch is voluminous and unanimous in the Talmud and Church Fathers.

Implications of These Facts. What conclusions can be drawn from these data for the origin and development of the Pentateuch? Here, one must be radically biblical, letting the Bible speak and not imposing upon it preconceived concepts of the kind of literature it must be, any more than one can impose upon it the theology it must teach. At the same time, theories of its origin and development must be recognized as theories, to be held tentatively, with an openness to change and modification as more understanding is gained.

Upon examining the evidence of text and tradition, two things need to be stressed. First, the biblical sources and various streams of tradition concur that Moses wrote narrative, legislative, and poetic literature.[20] Abundant evidence now exists that such diverse abilities in one author were by no means unique in the ancient Near East, even centuries earlier than Moses.[21] Hence Moses' role in the formation of the Pentateuch must be affirmed as highly original. The tradition is certainly credible in assigning to him authorship of the Pentateuch, at least in the sense that the core of both the narrative framework and

---

17. There are only seven such occurrences. 1 Kgs. 2:3 draws on Deut. 17:18-20; 29:9; 2 Kgs. 14:6 cites Deut. 24:16; 2 Kgs. 18:6 uses phraseology common in Deuteronomy (e.g., 10:20; 11:22; 13:4; 17:11, 20); and 2 Kgs. 23:25 draws on Deut. 6:4. 2 Kgs. 21:8 is taken best as referring to Deuteronomy since the whole surrounding passage alludes to that book (cf. Deut. 17:3; 18:9-14; 12:5; chs. 29ff.), while Josh. 8:30-35 clearly refers to Deut. 27:4ff. Josh. 23:6 simply refers to the "book of the law of Moses," but the surrounding passage draws heavily on Deut. 7.

18. See R.J. Thompson, *Moses and the Law in a Century of Criticism since Graf*, pp. 2ff.

19. Thompson, *ibid.*, p. 3, notes that the process can be observed in a comparison between Kings and Chronicles, where "the book of the law of Moses" in 2 Kgs. 14:6 becomes "the law, in the book of Moses" in 2 Chr. 25:4. Further evidence can be drawn from the frequency of the mention of Moses: twice each in 1 Samuel and Daniel; 5 times in the prophets; 8 in Psalms; 10 in 1–2 Kings; but 31 in Ezra-Nehemiah-Chronicles. Cf. J.L. McKenzie, "Moses," pp. 589f. in *Dictionary of the Bible* (Milwaukee: 1965).

20. As P. Benoit observes (*Guide to the Bible* [New York: 1960], p. 160), such uniform testimony is a fact that, with due respect to certain radical critics, cannot be set aside a priori, but requires adequate explanation.

21. See R.K. Harrison, *Introduction to the Old Testament* (Grand Rapids: 1969), p. 538.

legislative material goes back to his literary instigation and authentically reflects both the circumstances and events of the epic there related. Although it is unlikely that Moses wrote the Pentateuch *as it exists in its final form*, the connectedness and uniformity of the evidence certainly affirms that he is the originator, instigator, and most important figure in the stream of literary activity that produced it.

Second, the complexities of the text and the distribution and growth of the evidence for its origin must be taken into account. These literary phenomena reveal that the Pentateuch is a composite, complex work with a long and involved history of transmission and growth. Faith affirms that this development was superintended by the same Spirit of God that prompted Moses to write and speak in the first place. Although this process is difficult to trace in detail with certainty, its main outlines are reasonably sure. The narratives of the patriarchs were preserved, primarily by oral means, during the period of slavery in Egypt and probably first put in writing in the Mosaic period.[22] To these were added the poetic and prose accounts of the Exodus and wanderings, probably first written down in the early Davidic period. Faced with the new shape of life as a monarchy and nation-state, the preservation of the events and meaning of Israel's formative period would have become of prime importance. Gathered together in various compilations, the documents of the Mosaic age may have been finally formed into a single collection by Ezra in the period of restoration after the Exile (fifth century). This suggestion is based on the following considerations. The biblical text itself presents Ezra as scribe par excellence, learned in the law of Moses (Ezra 7:6, 11f.), whose task was to teach the Torah and regulate its observance in Judah and Jerusalem (vv. 14, 25f.). Jewish tradition unites in attributing the final inscripturation of the Torah to him.[23] Furthermore, this juncture in Israel's history when the Babylonian battering rams had laid all their previous institutions and forms of life in ruins and thrust the Jews into exile logically represents the precise moment and indeed instigation for collecting and fixing the written remains of their life and service. Finally, whatever the details of this process, one must affirm with W. F. Albright:

> The contents of our Pentateuch are, in general, very much older than the date at which they were finally edited; new discoveries continue to confirm the historical accuracy of the literary antiquity of detail after detail in it. Even when it is necessary to assume later additions to the original nucleus of Mosaic tradition, these additions reflect the normal growth of ancient institutions and practices, or the effort made by later scribes to save as much as possible of extant traditions about

---

22. W.F. Albright, *The Archeology of Palestine*, p. 225.
23. The actual statement is that Ezra copied the Scriptures in "Assyrian" (Syrian) characters, i.e., the square Hebrew or "Aramaic" script, not the Old Hebrew characters; Talmud *Sanh.* 21b–22a. He presided over the Great Synagogue, to whom is ascribed the final collection of sacred books; *B. Bat.* 15a.

Moses. It is, accordingly, sheer hypercriticism to deny the substantially Mosaic character of the Pentateuchal tradition.[24]

In attempting to explain and understand the implications of the literary complexities, Old Testament scholars over the last two centuries have developed the "documentary theory," a hypothesis which seeks to separate out the various "sources" behind the present text of the Pentateuch.[25]

The documentary theory seeks to identify four main documents as the sources behind the present text of the Pentateuch. It does this by studying blocks of text that can be set apart on the basis of the lack of close continuity and order in subject matter, the use of the divine names Yahweh and Elohim, and the duplications of material. On this basis it seeks to bring together larger textual corpora that are marked by similarity of vocabulary and style and by uniformity of theological outlook, and that, to a variable extent, present parallel accounts of the basic pentateuchal story. Thus, four "sources" are established. (1) The Yahwist's narrative (J, from German *Jahweh*) stems from Judah, 950-850, and runs from Genesis through Numbers. (2) The Elohist's narrative (E) stems from the northern kingdom of Israel *ca.* 850-750 and also runs from Genesis through Numbers. J and E usually are held to have been combined into a composite narrative (JE) sometime after the fall of the northern kingdom in 721. (3) The Deuteronomist's document (D) comprises roughly the book of Deuteronomy plus many portions of the "framework" of the historical account that runs from Joshua through 2 Kings. D usually is regarded as having reached final form under Josiah and as the book of law then found in the temple (2 Kgs. 22:3–23:25; 621 B.C.). It was added to JE, producing JED. (4) The priestly document (P) stems from the exile or shortly after (sixth to fifth centuries) and contains portions of narrative, genealogies, and matters pertaining to ritual and cult in Genesis through Numbers. But primarily it draws together the great collections of law in the Pentateuch stemming from various periods of Israel's history. This was joined to the others to form JEDP, and the priestly school gave the Pentateuch its present form.

Basically accepting the documentary framework, H. Gunkel gave new impetus to critical studies *ca.* 1900 by introducing *Formgeschichte* (history of literary forms) or *Gattungsgeschichte* (history of literary genres).[26] Not concerned to analyze the text by grouping basic units into larger literary corpora or sources, this method isolates and studies the individual literary units themselves to de-

---

24. Albright, *The Archeology of Palestine*, p. 225.
25. A number of excellent surveys and studies, from various points of view, are available. Noteworthy are the following: (1) short summaries: D.A. Hubbard, "Pentateuch," *IBD*, pp. 1181-1187; D.N. Freedman, "Pentateuch," *IDB* 3:711-726; (2) longer treatments: Harrison, *Introduction*, pp. 3-82; Thompson, *Moses and the Law*; A. Robert and A. Feuillet, *Introduction to the Old Testament* (New York: 1968), pp. 67-128; and especially Childs, *Old Testament as Scripture*, pp. 112-127.
26. For an excellent introduction to the subject, see G.M. Tucker, *Form Criticism of the Old Testament* (Philadelphia: 1971). For a comprehensive treatment, see K. Koch, *The Growth of the Biblical Tradition*, trans. S.M. Cupitt (New York: 1969).

termine what kind of literature they are and particularly to determine and study their *Sitz im Leben*, the "setting in life" which produced them and from which perspective they speak. While this approach has resulted in extremely radical views, when used judiciously it has aided greatly in understanding the Pentateuch. It has been particularly fruitful in the study of the Psalms and Gospels.

Much of the old source criticism and of the hypotheses it produced remains conjectural and problematic. That there are sources is hard to doubt; that they can be extirpated so certainly from the closely-knit corpus that finally emerged is another matter. Of much more importance for interpretation is the final result of this long process, produced by the inspired authors, editors, and traditionalists of God's chosen people.

PRIOR IMPORTANCE OF STRUCTURAL UNITY

Although this study has revealed the Pentateuch as a complex literary production, a composite work with a long and complex history of transmission and growth, the fact that it represents a structural unity is of far greater importance. Whatever the process of transmission and growth or the date at which it finally reached its present form, whoever the writer or writers who finally put it together as the grand historical narrative that it is, surely far more important is the final creation itself. The overarching unity so creatively and powerfully formed out of its component parts is surely far more important than the existence of whatever sources its complexities may require positing. The real danger of literary analysis and criticism is not that it necessarily denies the reality of the biblical affirmation that these words and deeds are from God himself, or that it necessarily denies the spiritual values of the Old Testament revelation. The danger is rather that, when such analysis becomes the concern of biblical scholarship to the exclusion of more comprehensive, overall considerations, it tends to reduce the Pentateuch to unrelated fragments and hence to result in the loss of any real grasp of the unity really present in it.

Recent trends in Old Testament scholarship increasingly recognize this fact. On the one hand is the recognition that Old Testament study has devoted itself overwhelmingly to diachronic literary concerns, i.e., to the historical setting of the text and to the reconstruction of its origin and process of transmission, rather than to synchronic analysis, i.e., to the interpretation and meaning of the text itself. In fact it is probably fair to say that much, if not most, Old Testament scholarship has operated on the principle that the text (the only objective data available) can only be correctly interpreted and understood after and on the grounds of an investigation into the process by which it came into being, which process will always remain hypothetical.[27] Increasingly, Old Tes-

---

27. Much Old Testament study of the Pentateuch has not only worked on the premise that a particular diachronic hypothesis (i.e., the classical theory of the sources labelled JEDP) is necessary before the text can be interpreted, but has regularly broken the text into divisions on the basis of this hypothesis and then almost exclusively based its interpretation on these hypothetical sections alone.

tament research is turning to analysis, description, and evaluation of the text as an end in itself, not only as a means to ascertaining its genetic history.[28] On the other hand is the development of canonical studies, the study of the form and function of the text in the shape which the community of faith gave it as its canonical scripture.[29] This field of study argues for a "post-critical alternative"[30] which, while taking seriously the results of historical critical scholarship, nevertheless seeks to determine the role that the canonical form of the text played in Israel's faith. In this view the

> . . . formation of a Pentateuch established the parameters of Israel's understanding of its faith as Torah. For the biblical editors the first five books constituted the grounds of Israel's life under God and provided a critical norm of how the Mosaic tradition was to be understood by the covenant people.[31]

Consequently, the basic method and procedure here will be to allow the Pentateuch to stand as it is, the final creation of Israel's witness to what God has done on their behalf in the age of the patriarchs and Moses, the great formative, creative period of their life and service.

FOR FURTHER READING

Bright, J. *Early Israel in Recent History Writing*. Naperville: 1956.
————. "Modern Study of Old Testament Literature." Pp. 13-31 in *BANE*. (Argues for new approach.)
Cassuto, U. *Documentary Hypothesis*. Trans. I. Abrahams. Jerusalem: 1961. (Critical challenge.)
Childs, B.S. *Introduction to the Old Testament as Scripture*. Philadelphia: 1979. (Esp. pp. 109-135.)
Clements, R.E. "Pentateuchal Problems." Pp. 96-124 in G.W. Anderson, ed., *Tradition and Interpretation*. Oxford: 1979. (Thorough survey of recent trends.)
Driver, S.R. *Introduction to the Literature of the Old Testament*. 9th ed. 1913; repr. Magnolia, Mass.: 1972. (Esp. pp. 1-159; still indispensable for the older viewpoint.)
Eissfeldt, O. *The Old Testament: An Introduction*. Trans. P.R. Ackroyd. New York: 1965. (Comprehensive survey of scholarship, thorough bibliography.)

---

28. Diachronic study, such as investigation into origins, is, of course, a valid, worthwhile, and often indispensable avenue of research in and of itself; it is the question of evaluation and priority that is addressed here. For a succinct and insightful discussion, see the introduction to J.P. Fokkelman, *Narrative Art in Genesis* (Assen: 1975), pp. 1-8, and Clines, *The Theme of the Pentateuch*, pp. 7-15.
29. See Childs, *Old Testament as Scripture*, pp. 109-135. For the method see also J.A. Sanders, *Torah and Canon* (Philadelphia: 1972).
30. The phrase is that of Childs, *Old Testament as Scripture*, p. 127.
31. *Ibid.*, pp. 131f.

Livingston, G.H. *The Pentateuch in Its Cultural Environment*. Grand Rapids: 1974. (Esp.
    pp. 184-283; applies recent archaeological and manuscript discoveries.)
McKenzie, J.L. *The Two-Edged Sword*. Garden City: 1966. (Roman Catholic perspective.)
Robert, A. "The Law (Pentateuch)." Pp. 157-170 in A. Robert and A. Tricot, eds.,
    Guide to the Bible. 2nd ed. Paris: 1963.
Sawyer, J.F.A. *From Moses to Patmos: New Perspectives in Old Testament Study*. London:
    1977.
Soggin, J.A. *Introduction to the Old Testament*. OTL. Philadelphia: 1976.
Wright, G.E. *The Old Testament Against Its Environment*. Naperville: 1950.

CHAPTER 7

GENESIS:
PRIMEVAL PROLOGUE

NAME, CONTENTS, AND STRUCTURE

THE name "Genesis" is a transliteration of the Greek word meaning "source, origin," the name given the book by the LXX. The Hebrew name is $b^e r\bar{e}'\hat{s}\hat{i}\underline{t}$ "in the beginning," the book's opening word. Both are excellent names, for Genesis tells the beginnings of all things connected with biblical faith.

On the basis of content the book divides into two clearly separable sections: chs. 1–11, the primeval history, and chs. 12–50, the patriarchal history. (Technically the two sections are 1:1–11:26 and 11:27–50:26.) Gen. 1–11 is an introduction to salvation history, setting forth the origin of the world, humanity, and sin; 12–50 sets forth the origins of redemptive history in God's election of the patriarchs and his covenantal promise of land and posterity. As such, Genesis is complete in itself. These two prologues are an introduction to the account of the chosen people, formed through God's gracious deliverance at the Red Sea and his granting of the Mosaic covenant at Sinai.

On the basis of literary structure the book divides into ten sections. The clue to this external form is the "*toledoth* formula": "And these are (this is) the descendants (or story; Heb. $t\hat{o}l^e\underline{d}\hat{o}\underline{t}$) of. . . ." The contents that are so set off can be diagrammed as in the Table.[1]

CONTENTS

The first five *toledoth* structure the primeval prologue, with the major divisions set off by and clustered around them. Thus, ch. 1 is closed by 2:4a and the next unit—Eden and the Fall—is concluded by 5:1, which introduces the roll of Adam's descendants, setting off 2:4b–4:26 as a unit. In 6:9 the formula introduces the narrative of Noah, separating the story of the sons of God and

---

1. See H.T. Kuist, *Old Testament Book Studies* (Princeton: n.d.). Whether $t\hat{o}l^e\underline{d}\hat{o}\underline{t}$ is translated "descendants" or "story" depends upon whether it is affixed to a genealogy (e.g., 5:1; 10:1) or a narrative (e.g., 6:9; 25:19).

CONTENTS OF GENESIS

	I PRIMEVAL PROLOGUE					II PATRIARCHAL HISTORY		
Subject:	Creation	Eden and the Fall	Patriarchs before the Flood	The Flood and its Aftermath	Patriarchs after the Flood	Abraham and his Family	Jacob and his Sons	Joseph and his Brothers
Division:	1:1–2:4a	2:4b–4:26	5:1:32	6:1–11:9	11:10-26	11:27–25:18	25:19–37:1	37:2–50:26
Clue:		" .... These are the descendants/story (*toledoth*) of ...."						
Genealogies:			5:1 Adam and his descendants	10:1 Sons of Noah	11:10 Shem and his descendants	25:12 Ishmael and his descendants		36:1, 9 Esau and his descendants
Narratives:	2:4a the heavens and the earth			6:9 Noah and the Flood		11:27 Terah and his family (Abraham)	25:19 Isaac and his family (Jacob and Esau)	37:2 Jacob and his family (Joseph and his brothers)

the daughters of men (6:1-4) and the sketch of man's sin (vv. 5-8), both expressing the extent of the corruption leading to the Flood. Gen. 10:1 begins the Table of Nations, setting off this repeopling of the earth from the flood story of 6:9–9:29; 11:10 introduces the roll of patriarchs after the Flood, setting off the Tower of Babel story in vv. 1-9. These, then, are the natural divisions of the primeval prologue, imposed upon the material by the sacred author himself. An examination of these passages and the way in which they are linked together will reveal what the author intended by so arranging his story.

LITERARY GENRE

In order to interpret the primeval prologue with the same intent and purpose as the ancient author, one must examine its literary genre. What kind of literature is this? How does the author intend himself to be understood? These questions must be asked to avoid giving the author's words a meaning that was not in his mind. Let us, then, look at (1) the literary nature of Gen. 1–11, (2) the ancient Near Eastern material upon which Israel drew to tell the primeval story, and (3) their implications for Gen. 1–11.

   Literary Nature. When the material content and composition of chs. 1–11 are examined carefully, much can be observed that will help us determine the nature of the genre employed, even if many problems still remain. First, these chapters are strongly characterized by literary artifice and convention of two markedly different types. One set of texts (including chs. 1; 5; 10; 11:10-26) is set apart by a schematic, almost formulaic, character and careful logical arrangement. Ch. 1, for example, consists of a highly structured series of succinct, almost formulaic, sentences whose components can easily be separated out and outlined. Each creative command consists of:[2]
   —an introductory word of announcement, "God said . . ." (1:3, 6, 9, 11, 14, 20, 24, 26).
   —a creative word of command, "let there be . . ." (1:3, 6, 9, 11, 14f., 20, 24, 25).
   —a summary word of accomplishment, "and it was so" (1:3, 7, 9, 11, 15, 24, 30).
   —a descriptive word of accomplishment, "God made . . . ," "the earth brought forth . . ." (1:4, 7, 12, 16-18, 21, 25, 27).
   —a descriptive word of naming or blessing, "God called . . . ," "God blessed . . ." (1:5, 8, 10, 22, 28-30).

---

   2. See C. Westermann, *The Genesis Accounts of Creation.* Facet Books. Biblical Series 7 (Philadelphia: 1964). For further discussion of the literary characteristics of the Primeval Prologue, see A. Robert and A. Tricot, *Guide to the Bible*, pp. 480f.

—an evaluative word of approval, "God saw that it was good" (1:4, 10, 12, 18, 21, 25, 31).

—a concluding word of temporal framework, "It was evening and it was morning, day . . ." (1:5, 8, 13, 19, 23, 31).

Although each creative command follows a conscious and uniform scheme using the same stereotyped expressions, the effect is not mechanical or stultifying because of the way the order, length, and presence of these components is varied.[3] The arrangement of the commands follows a strict order, consciously separated into two periods of time: the creation and separation of the elements of the cosmos, proceeding from the general to the particular (first four commands, vv. 1-13), and the adornment of the cosmos, from the imperfect to the most perfect (second four commands, vv. 14-31). The account rises to a noticeable crescendo in the eighth command, the creation of mankind. The whole chapter is not really a "narrative" or story, but a carefully constructed report of a series of commands. Similarly, ch. 5 and 11:10-32 are carefully constructed genealogies with the same structure repeated for each generation, and ch. 10 is an ethno-geographical list, also marked by its schematic character.

The second set of passages (chs. 2–3, 4, 6–9; 11:1-9) is markedly different. Here also are order and progression, but the story form is used. Thus, for example, chs. 2–3 form an exquisite narrative, a literary creation, almost a drama. Each scene is drawn with a few bold strokes and a profusion of images. The author revels in naive but expressive anthropomorphisms. Yahweh appears as one of the dramatis personae. He is a potter (2:7, 19), gardener (v. 8), surgeon (v. 21), and peaceful landowner (3:8).[4]

Differences in conception and literary convention between chs. 1 and 2 also are found in the strikingly different ways of expressing creation. Both accounts use the generic term 'āśâ "to make," but ch. 1 is characterized by bārā' "to create," a verb used only with God as subject and never connected with a material from which an object is "created." Ch. 2, however, uses yāṣar "to form, fashion, shape," the technical term for the activity of the potter, who "shapes" clay into the desired form.[5] These two verbs play an important role in the different ways that creation is conceived: ch. 1 laconically states, "God *created* man in his image, . . . male and female he *created* them" (v. 27), but in ch. 2 God is the potter who "shapes" man out of soil, "breathes" life into his nostrils, and "builds" woman out of his "rib." In ch. 1 God creates by his *word*; in ch. 2, by divine *act*. The first might be termed "fiat creation"; the second "action creation." Given the Hebrew conception and world view, in which "word" and "deed" are not carefully distinguished or mutually exclusive, this difference involves no inherent contradiction (both are anthropomorphic

---

3. For a detailed study of these elements, see W. Wegner, CTM 37 (1966) 526ff.
4. See Robert and Tricot, *Guide to the Bible*, pp. 480f.
5. Hebrew for "potter" is yôṣēr, the participle of the verb yāṣar, i.e., "shaper, fashioner."

representations), but the two accounts stress in marked degree the complementary sides of God's creative activity.

Literary device also is found in the names used. The correspondence of the name with the person's function or role is striking in several instances. Adam means "mankind"[6] and Eve is "(she who gives) life."[7] Surely, when an author of a story names the principal characters Mankind and Life, something is conveyed about the degree of literalness intended! Similarly Cain means "forger (of metals)"; Enoch is connected with "dedication, consecration" (4:17; 5:18); Jubal with horn and trumpet (4:21); while Cain, condemned to be a nāḏ, a "wanderer," goes to live in the land of Nod, a name transparently derived from the same Hebrew root, thus the land of wandering! This suggests that the author is writing as an artist, a storyteller, who uses literary device and artifice. One must endeavor to distinguish what he intends to teach from the literary means employed.

Ancient Near Eastern Background. In understanding the literary genre of Gen. 1–11, one must take into account the numerous and clear resemblances

Fragments of Enuma Elish, the Assyrian creation epic. (British Museum)

6. Heb. *'āḏām* means "man, mankind," not man the individual. To indicate the individual, Hebrew uses other formulations, such as *ben-'āḏām* "son of *'āḏām*," or "one belonging to the category *'āḏām*," or an entirely different word, such as *'îš*, "man (not woman)."

7. The connection between *ḥawwâ* "Eve" and the verbal root *ḥāyâ* "to live" is, linguistically speaking, obscure. Nonetheless, Gen. 3:20 clearly shows that the name was understood so by the scriptural author.

and parallels between scriptural and Near Eastern, especially Mesopotamian, accounts. Quite simply the inspired author(s) of the primeval prologue drew on the material and manner of speaking about origins that was part of their culture and literary traditions. First, ch. 1 speaks against a background of Mesopotamian creation literature. Although the detailed comparisons are relatively few, they are enough to reveal that ch. 1 speaks from that perspective. Three basic parallels exist: both picture the primeval state as a watery chaos; both have the same basic order of creation; and both conclude with the divine rest.[8] Similarly, chs. 2–3 speak against a background of Semitic, and specifically Mesopotamian, literature. The paradise story as a whole, however, finds no ancient Near Eastern parallel; commonalities are only in individual elements, symbols, and conceptions.[9] Parallels even extend to technical terminology. The 'ēḏ in 2:6, usually translated "mist," is understood best as an Akkadian loanword meaning "flow of water from underground."[10] The geographical location of the garden, "in Eden" (2:8), also is understood best as a borrowing of Sumerian, and later Akkadian, edinu "plain," which quite fits the context.[11] Note that both borrowed terms are for phenomena not indigenous to Palestine.

As is now well known, the most striking resemblances between Mesopotamian literature and the primeval prologue occur in correspondences between the two flood accounts. Here are not only basic similarities but also detailed correspondences. The flood is willed by the gods and revealed to the hero by divine agency. He is instructed to build an unusual boat, caulked with pitch. Animals are taken along, the flood is universal, all people are destroyed, the hero releases a number of birds,[12] and the ship comes to rest on a mountain. On leaving the ark, sacrifice is offered and the sweet odor smelled by the gods.[13]

Finally, perhaps the clearest connection to Mesopotamia is the Tower of Babel story in 11:1-9. The story is specifically located in Babylonia (v. 2). The building material is that used in Mesopotamia, and the author somewhat scornfully comments on its uniqueness (v. 3). The tower is a clear reference to the

---

8. See A. Heidel, *Babylonian Genesis*, 2nd ed. (Chicago: 1963), for full discussion and balanced, judicious conclusions.

9. These more-or-less precisely parallel data are drawn from a number of sources, e.g., a terrestrial paradise inhabited by a single pair, marvelous gardens, sacred trees, a plant of life guarded by the gods and stolen by a serpent, a tree of life or truth, man formed from clay, often mixed with a divine element.

10. As a Hebrew word, 'ēḏ is virtually inexplicable, the only other possible occurrence being Job 36:27 where it is also obscure in meaning. The word is most likely a borrowing of Akk. edū "flow of water from underground," which in turn was borrowed from Sumerian. See E.A. Speiser, "'Ed in the Story of Creation," pp. 19-22 in J. Finkelstein and M. Greenberg, eds., *Oriental and Biblical Studies* (Philadelphia: 1967).

11. In 2:8, as well as 2:10; 4:16, "Eden" is a geographical location, not a proper name as elsewhere (2:15; 3:23; cf. Isa. 51:3; Ezek. 31:9).

12. Here the two accounts differ markedly in detail. The Babylonian hero sends out three birds—a dove, a swallow, and a raven, while Noah releases four, a raven and three doves.

13. For an excellent and detailed study of these similarities, see Heidel, *Gilgamesh Epic and Old Testament Parallels*, 2nd ed. (Chicago: 1949), pp. 244-260.

most characteristic Mesopotamian form of temple, the ziggurat, an artificial, stepped mountain of clay (v. 4). The city is named Babel, reflecting the Babylonian name Bâb-ili "the Gate of God" (v. 9).

These resemblances and parallels prove nothing beyond a genetic relationship between the biblical and Mesopotamian accounts. Quite certainly the evidence excludes direct dependence. The Genesis stories in their present form do not go back ultimately to the Babylonian traditions. On the contrary, all the evidence, even where the resemblances are as close as in the flood story, merely suggests a diffuse influence or common cultural atmosphere. It proves only that the biblical narrative moves in the same circle of ideas and that the inspired authors of the primeval prologue knew and drew on the material and manner of speaking about origins that was part of their culture and literary traditions.

Implications for Gen. 1–11. Recognizing the literary technique and form and noting the literary background of chs. 1–11 does not constitute a challenge to the reality, the "eventness," of the facts portrayed. One need not regard this account as myth; however, it is not "history" in the modern sense of eyewitness, objective reporting. Rather, it conveys theological truths about events, portrayed in a largely symbolic, pictorial literary genre. This is not to say that Gen. 1–11 conveys historical falsehood. That conclusion would follow only if it purported to contain objective descriptions. The clear evidence already reviewed shows that such was not the intent. On the other hand, the view that the truths taught in these chapters have no objective basis is mistaken. They affirm fundamental truths: creation of all things by God; special divine intervention in the production of the first man and woman; unity of the human race; pristine goodness of the created world, including humanity; entrance of sin through the disobedience of the first pair; depravity and rampant sin after the Fall. All these truths are facts, and their certainty implies the reality of the facts.[14]

Put another way, the biblical author uses such literary traditions to describe unique primeval events that have no time-conditioned, human-conditioned, experience-based historical analogy and hence can be described only by symbol. The same problem arises at the end time: the biblical author there, in the book of Revelation, adopts the esoteric imagery and involved literary artifice of apocalyptic.

Far more evident than the similarities are the dissimilarities and differences of these narratives from Mesopotamian literary traditions. Simply noting simi-

---

14. Cf. B.S. Childs, *Old Testament as Scripture*, p. 158: "The Genesis material is unique because of an understanding of reality which has subordinated common mythopoeic tradition to a theology of absolute divine sovereignty. . . . Regardless of terminology—whether myth, history, or saga—the canonical shape of Genesis serves the community of faith and practice as a truthful witness to God's activity on its behalf in creation and blessing, judgment and forgiveness, redemption and promise."

larities stresses them in a misleading way, leaving the impression that they are the most distinctive feature of the Genesis accounts. In point of fact, the situation is just the opposite. The unique features of biblical literature, which differentiate it from its world and from the closest exemplars of Israel's neighbors, are so strikingly obvious, so compellingly clear, as to be all that the ordinary reader can discern. It takes an eye trained to make literary judgments and note the unobtrusive features of literary form to see the similarities. Although this perhaps overstates the case with such pericopes as the flood story, it is in general true and serves to stress that what separates Gen. 1–11 from Mesopotamian literary traditions is far more significant and obvious than what joins them. Mesopotamian literature is steeped in polytheism. Its gods, personifications of natural forces, know no moral principle; they lie, steal, fornicate, and kill. Mankind enjoys no special role as the highest created earthly being, made in the Creator's image; man is rather the lowly servant of his divine overlords, made to provide them with food and offerings.

In absolute contrast, the biblical narratives present one, true, all holy and omnipotent God, who as Creator stands prior to and independent of the world. He but speaks and the elements come into being. His work is good, harmonious, and whole. Although the human family rebels, God tempers his judgment with mercy, supporting and maintaining them with grace and forbearance. The divine sublimity and perfection of the ultimate Author, albeit refracted by the human writer, so infuses Scripture with its own character and charm as to make it unique, even where it most closely touches contemporary thought forms.

How then, finally, is the unique literary genre of Gen. 1–11 to be understood? One may suppose that the inspired author, informed by God's revelation to Israel of the nature of the world and humanity and the fact of sin which resulted in mankind's alienation from God and one another, was led to true understanding about the nature of beginnings and stated them in contemporary language. Even more, the author marshalled current literary traditions to teach the true theological facts of humanity's primeval history. The author of Gen. 1–11 was not interested in satisfying biological and geological curiosity. Rather, he wanted to tell who and what human beings are by virtue of where they came from: they are of divine origin, made in the image of the Creator, yet marred materially by the sin that so soon disfigured God's good work.

THEOLOGY

Having briefly determined the literary genre of Gen. 1–11 and having observed that the section's primary purposes are theological, more explicit attention shall be given to its teaching. The author weaves into his account four major theological themes, often in a continuously recurring pattern: first, the nature and implications of the fact that God is Creator; second, the radical seriousness of sin; third, the way in which God's judgment meets human sin at each point;

and fourth, the presence, nonetheless and almost surprisingly, of his preserving, sustaining grace.[15]

God as Creator. At the very beginning of his work, in Gen. 1:1–2:4a the sacred author marshals the Hebrew language with wondrous beauty to affirm that all that exists came forth simply and solely at the free and sovereign command of God. In so doing he is combatting the erroneous world view of his own time which was radically different from that of today.

The world view out of which and to which the author spoke was radically different from today's. Ancient man personalized nature and its forces as divine beings. Humanity and nature were not grasped by different ways of knowing, but rather, natural phenomena were conceived in terms of human experience. Today the phenomenal world is regarded as an "it"; ancient people regarded it as a "thou." They lived in the midst of a highly personal world where there was no such thing as the inanimate.[16] Therefore, the divine was multipersonal, normally ordered and in balance, but at times capricious, unstable, and desperately threatening. It is this view of God that the author of ch. 1 seeks to combat by asserting: "In the beginning God created the heavens and the earth" (v. 1). In his conception nature comes forth at the simple command of God, who is prior to and independent of it. The sun, moon, stars, and planets, conceived by the Babylonians as individualized deities ruling the course of human affairs, are not even named; they are simply lights to shine on the earth (vv. 16-18). The sea and the earth are no longer primeval mother deities which procreate others, but are reduced to their natural reality (v. 10). He despiritualizes the cosmos, since its deification had led to polytheism.[17]

Greek thought also broke away from this polytheistic conception. Greek philosophers conceived of the primacy of the rational and speculative over the intuitional and inarticulate, thereby raising to autonomy the processes of reason. Replacing the mythological gods is nature manifested in the various realities of the world. As a result, for the average person God has been removed fully from nature and has disappeared from the horizon of reality altogether. To such

---

15. This analysis follows the perceptive treatment of G. von Rad, *Genesis*, pp. 152ff. For an insightful recent discussion of the theme of Gen. 1–11, see D.J.A. Clines, *The Theme of the Pentateuch*, pp. 61-79. Clines extends von Rad's treatment, which was based only on the narratives, to the rest of the material of Gen. 1–11 as well. Here he finds von Rad's general theme set forth also. After seeking to show that the theme "creation-uncreation-recreation" is also deeply imbedded in the material, he concludes that the proper reading of Gen. 1–11 is as follows: "No matter how drastic man's sin becomes, . . . God's grace never fails to deliver man from the consequences of his sin. Even when man responds to a fresh start with the old pattern of sin, . . . (he) experiences the favour of God as well as his righteous judgement"; p. 76. This analysis includes the three elements adopted above.

16. See H. Frankfort et al., *Before Philosophy* (Baltimore: 1949), pp. 11-36.

17. See J. Daniélou, *In the Beginning . . . Genesis I–III* (Baltimore: 1965), pp. 30ff.

a world view the author of Genesis also speaks by affirming that God is the Creator, who stands prior to and over against his creation and is the one upon whom all creation is dependent and to whom all creation will answer.[18]

The author of ch. 1 uses Heb. *bārā'* "to create," a word that expresses an activity predicated in the Old Testament of God alone and which never occurs with any reference to the material out of which the object is created. It describes a way of acting that is without human analogy, and cannot be translated by such terms as "manufacture" or "construct." This chapter thus depicts a category of works capable of being performed by God alone. Only God creates, as only God saves.

A central element in ch. 1, almost a refrain, is the affirmation that God's created world is good (vv. 4, 10, 12, 18, 21, 25, 31). The final summary (v. 31), "And God saw everything that he had made, and behold, it was very good," stands out markedly within the terse, impassive, and unsuperlative language of the chapter. No evil was laid upon the world by God's hand. It has ultimate value, but only because God made it. This teaching of the pristine goodness of creation, including mankind, is of utmost theological importance. First, it prepares the way for the question of the origin of that which has disturbed this good order—sin. Second, it prepares the way for the biblical affirmation, much later, that all will one day be restored in like manner at the conclusion of all things, when God will again see everything he has made as very good, for it will once again be a "new heaven and a new earth" (Rev. 21:1).

Finally, the conscious apex of this creative activity is humanity (Gen. 1:26-28). The monotone of formulas is broken here: the text introduces the creation of humankind by announcing a divine resolution, "Let us make man." Only here does the author leave his repetitive, ponderous, and carefully framed prose for the full beauty and power of the parallelism of Hebrew poetry:

> God created man in his own image,
> In the image of God he created him,
> Male and female he created them. (v. 27)

The threefold use of *bārā'* "to create" and the literary contrast signal that this is the climax toward which the chapter has moved in ever ascending stages as each creative command has been given and carried out.

Mankind's relationship to God, unique among created beings, is expressed by the deliberately ambiguous phrase "the image of God." Part of the background for such choice of words is surely the uniform Old Testament distaste for and specific prohibition against representation of God in any form. This phrase is thus the closest the author can come to ranging humankind alongside

---

18. For the implications of the biblical doctrine of creation, see J.M. Houston, *I Believe in the Creator* (Grand Rapids: 1980).

God in distinction to the rest of creation, especially since ṣelem "image" is explained more closely and made precise by dᵉmût "similarity" (1:26). The Hebrew has no connective "and" between the phrases, so the latter more explicitly defines the former, and the two words together mean "according to a similar but not identical representation." Against this and the common ancient Near Eastern literary background in which a deity formed mankind in divine shape, those interpretations limiting the "image" too exclusively to the "spiritual" side or moral capacity of mankind must be rejected. In point of fact, the author's purpose in using this concept seems to be far more functional than conceptual. He is more interested in what the gift entails than in its nature. The resemblance is dynamic, in that the human beings ('āḏām) in their personal relationships with other creatures, become God's representative, with the natural right to explore, subdue, and use everything around them. This is demonstrated most explicitly in the following clause, "and let them have dominion over. . . ." As a consequence of being in God's image, man and woman are to rule the world in God's name. The idea is that of an emperor appointing administrators over his domain and erecting his own statue so the inhabitants will know whose will it is that rules them.

Ch. 2 also describes the creation, but with a style markedly different from that of ch. 1. Ch. 1 reports a series of commands, but in chs. 2–3 the author tells a story, painting sublimely beautiful word pictures, full of symbol and imagery, to set forth his theological truth. Sometimes the differences in the accounts are pressed, as though these suggested two separate "creation accounts," mutually contradictory. But, besides ignoring the marked differences in genre, this suggests that ch. 2 purports to be a "creation account" in the same sense as ch. 1. Such is not the case. The purpose of ch. 1 is to relate that all that exists came into being through God's express creative activity. Ch. 2, however, was written for no such purpose. It is not an independent literary unit, but is closely related to ch. 3. Not intended as a second creation narrative at all, it rather gives an account of the origin of man and the Garden of Eden and hence sets the stage for the drama of ch. 3. Nevertheless, one cannot totally disregard the difference in literary genre. There is a considerable amount of material in ch. 2 that belongs in a creation narrative, material that presents marked differences from ch. 1. For example, the order of the creation of humanity in the two chapters is very different. But whether man is created first or last among animate creation is not of the essence of either account. What is essential is the fact of the crowning position of mankind as the apex of God's creation. This ch. 1 accomplishes by making man and woman the climax of God's creative activity, whereas ch. 2 accomplishes the same by naming their creation first.

In this very graphic, anthropomorphic story, Yahweh is pictured as the potter who "fashions" mankind out of "dust" from the ground. As 3:19 shows, this choice of words is determined by its use in the common expression for "to die," i.e., "to return to the dust" (cf. Job 10:9; 34:15; Ps. 104:29). The imagery employed thus stresses not only the bond between humanity and the earth but also man's frailty, his mortality; he is made of the soil, to which he must inevitably return. Into this lifeless form that he has shaped, Yahweh breathes the "breath of life," and man becomes a "living being." The word translated "breath" is technically that, so the text says that man is "body and life," not "body and soul."[19] He has a dual nature. He is of the earth, earthy, but also is endued with a life principle that comes from God. Although this composite nature does not in and of itself set man and woman apart from the animals (they are also called "living beings" [1:20; 2:19], and distinguished by the breath of life [6:17; 7:22; Job 34:14]), man is portrayed here very graphically as the object of God's special and solicitous attention. The author thus presents God's relationship to mankind as very personal and immediate. Pictographically he says the same thing as Gen. 1's clearer, more theologically articulate phrase "the image of God." His emphasis is on the frailty, mortality, and utter dependence of humanity on God. Only in this light can one see how unmerited was man's privileged position in Eden and how monstrous his desire to be like God.

Gen. 2:18-25 describes the creation of woman, who plays such an important role in ch. 3. The account begins with the basic statement of man's essential corporate nature—his sociability: "It is not good that man should be alone" (v. 18). He was not made to be an entity totally without need of others, but was created as a pair of beings ("male and female he created them"; 1:27)—two beings who cannot exist apart from each other. True human life is life together, and a life of isolation is a perversion of human nature as divinely created. God's answer to man's aloneness is to make for him a "help as one over against him," his "counterpart," corresponding to him, suitable to him. God first brings the animals to Adam, but having named them and so learned their essence, man finds no "help suitable for him" there.[20] So God fashions (lit. "builds") woman out of the body of the man himself and brings her to him. Adam's joyful "at last" (v. 23) signals the recognition of one of his own essence and being. With exquisite artistry, the author has man recognize the fullness of their correspondence by having him name her also. To do so he plays upon the assonance between 'îš "man" and 'iššâ "woman."

So in v. 24 it is concluded, in the narrator's summarizing word, that woman's creation explains why a man severs the close bond to his parents to become one flesh with his wife, as was their origin. Although "flesh" here does not refer to one part of man's physical makeup ("body" would be a better translation)

---

19. This follows also from the fact that the phrase *nepeš ḥayyâ* "living being" does *not* mean "living soul," as usually understood in English. In fact, in no other place is the expression used of man; everywhere else it refers to the animals (Gen. 1:20, 24, 30; 2:19; 9:12, 15f.). See von Rad, *Genesis*, p.77.

20. Here a secondary teaching is introduced, the relationship between mankind and the animal world. To the ancient Israelites, surrounded by religions which had raised the animal world to the status of divinity, this teaches that no animal is the equal of man, let alone his superior.

but to man as a whole, it does stress the visible and physical side, so here the physical side of marriage comes into its own (cf. Eph. 5:31).

Thus the sacred author begins with the meaning and significance of creation. The emphasis has been upon the wholesomeness and good order of that created world.

Problem of Sin. After the refrain of Gen. 1: "God saw that it was good," the way has been prepared to tell what corrupted that world. This is set forth primarily in chs. 2–3.[21] In contrast to ch. 1, which teaches theological truths about why the world exists at all, chs. 2–3 address the question of why things exist thus, in a ruined condition, subject to physical and moral evil. This corruption is a fact of experience brutally brought home as one matures, faces life on one's own, and wrestles with the evil of the physical cataclysm, man's inhumanity to man, the easy duplicity in one's own breast, and that ultimate specter, death. Chs. 2–3 are completely dominated by this problem. How can it be reconciled with God's goodness, righteousness, and love, and with the truth that all originates with God? According to the author, there is not complete continuity with the world as experienced and as originally created. The world was good as God made it, but man corrupted it by willful disobedience. Chs. 2–3, then, picture man as above all a sinner.

The author begins by picturing an ideal world, fully in accord with his understanding of God as revealed throughout Israel's history. This is the point of the garden of Eden in ch. 2. Then, in ch. 3 he sets alongside this the world of human experience, fractured and broken, alienated and in turmoil. Mankind, not God, is to blame for the difference. In Eden (2:8-17), man lives in a well-watered garden of trees and marvelous fruitfulness. All is in complete harmony, from the highest forms of life to the lowest. Man and animals use only plants for food. Although there are tasks to perform (v. 15), there is no struggle or pain to wrest a living from a recalcitrant earth. Thorns and thistles do not grow. Thus there seems a certain unreality about Eden, for the author does not attempt to describe the world of human experience. Rather, he describes an ideal world, the reflection and concomitant of the spiritual condition in which man lived: he is at peace with and in fellowship with God. The author accomplishes this by taking the world of human experience and removing from it all evil, physical as well as moral, and all unpleasantness. All of this brings home powerfully the fact of human innocence. Sin as yet does not exist.

In the midst of the garden are two trees, the tree of life and the tree of the knowledge of good and evil. The second tree has been much discussed, undoubtedly because the passage and subsequent narrative do not make its meaning clear. The author is consciously vague. However, from usage in the rest of the passage (2:16f.; 3:3-7, 22), the tree must symbolize the right of complete freedom of choice over good and evil. The first human pair, by eating of the

---

21. The following analysis is indebted to H. Renckens, *Israel's Concept of the Beginning* (New York: 1964), pp. 156ff.

tree, aim at being "as God" (3:5, 22) by determining for themselves what is good and bad, establishing moral autonomy over good and evil, thus usurping the divine prerogative.

That very moral autonomy is declared in ch. 3 through the serpent's obviously malevolent machinations. His subtle wiles induce the woman to doubt first God's word (v. 1) and then his goodness (vv. 4f.). Seeing the tree now in an entirely different light (v. 6), she takes of its fruit and eats, and the man follows suit. So simple the act: "she took . . . and she ate"; so drastic the results: humanity has lost the state of innocence forever; so hard the undoing: God himself will taste poverty and death before "take and eat" become verbs of salvation. [22]

In the sequel the author depicts very graphically the new dimensions of man's relationship to God: where before all had been harmony and intimacy, there is now shame at his nakedness (v. 7) and flight from the presence of God in fear (v. 8). In the ensuing interrogation, the primal unity of the human community disintegrates. The new togetherness in sin does not unite but divides. Man seeks to clear himself by placing the guilt on the woman and God ("the woman whom thou gavest to be with me . . . ," v. 12). The narrative closes with Adam as he is now known. Willfully a sinner, he has lost free and open fellowship with God and must wrestle with evil and temptation at all levels of his existence.

In the narratives that follow, the author piles story upon story as if to show the radical seriousness of sin by the sheer volume of the evidence. Once introduced into the world, sin rapidly reaches avalanche proportions. Humanity's second generation experiences fratricide, and the account of the succeeding generations ends with Lamech's brutal "Song of the Sword" (4:23f.). These two passages differ widely in literary form. Gen. 4:1-16 adopts the story form of chs. 2-3 to continue the narrative of Eden and the Fall, playing upon themes and ideas familiar from those chapters. On the other hand, 4:17-24 is basically a genealogical tree, modified with annotations and comments that communicate the author's intent. His primary interest is not who Cain's descendants were, but their kind and style of life. This information is given both at the beginning of the seven-member genealogy (v. 17) and the end, where it broadens into three branches and, indeed, is hardly a genealogy at all.

The details of the story of Cain and Abel are doubtless familiar. In a jealous rage over the rejection of his offering in favor of Abel's, Cain kills his brother, even though warned by God (4:3-8). God is immediately on the scene as interrogator; only now the question to the guilty man is not "Where are you?" as in the garden, but "Where is your brother?" Cain responds with an impertinent witticism: "Am I my brother's keeper?" Sin not only moves in ever widening circles; its manifestation grows more blatant and heinous.

In the annotated genealogy of 4:17-24, the virulence and violence of sin are underscored again. Here the author pictures the rise of civilization. Cain

---

22. D. Kidner, Genesis. Tyndale Old Testament Commentaries (Downers Grove: 1967), p. 68.

is the first builder of a city (v. 17), with its organized community life. With Lamech and his sons comes the rise of arts and crafts, metalworkers and musicians, together with shepherds (vv. 19-22). The author sketches mankind's cultural history in bold brush strokes, unrelieved by detail. His purpose is to get to vv. 23f., the Song of the Sword, where a new literary element is incorporated, the lyric poem. This is a brutal song of vengeance, a "boasting song." Having murdered a youth for striking him, Lamech boasts to his wives, who honor and esteem his cruel and barbaric valor. With powerful effect the author notes the change in attitude that has accompanied the rise of culture. First the Fall, then fratricide, now brutal and bloody vengeance, a cause for boasting! After the Song of Lamech, God's judgment set forth in 6:5 ("the wickedness óf man was great in the earth, and . . . every imagination of the thoughts of his heart was only evil continually") requires no further documentation.

The same point is made in 6:1-4, the account of the sons of God and daughters of men. The interpretation of this difficult and obscure passage is most problematical. Two main views have been adopted since antiquity: (1) "sons of God" refers in an ethical sense to the pious descendants of Seth's line, in opposition to the ungodly descendants of Cain ("the daughters of men"); or (2) it refers to angelic beings. As Kidner puts it, "if the second view defies the normalities of experience, the first defies those of language."[23] The normal meaning of "sons of God" is angels,[24] and nothing in the text remotely suggests that "daughters" and "men" can have any different sense in v. 2 than in v. 1, where they clearly refer to mankind in general. In this interpretation, which seems most faithful to the plain intent of the language, God's bounds have been overstepped anew: even decrees separating the divine and human worlds are broken by sin, and demonic powers are now loose that humanity cannot control. But whether the descendants of Seth have become corrupt or something demonic has entered the world, the point is that a new level has been reached in the rampant spread of evil.

After this interlude, the text directly introduces the flood story through a passage (6:5-8) that is very different in origin and form. In all the previous passages the author has drawn on existing traditions. Although freely adapting, modifying, and transforming them and frequently speaking against the views of God and humanity contained therein, he nonetheless has used traditional material.[25] The situation in 6:5-8 is quite different, as can be seen by a glance at the material. Heretofore the author simply has described the fact of rapidly spreading sin, but now, under divine inspiration, he presents a theological judgment from God himself about the sad and sordid story of mankind and sin

---

23. *Ibid.*, p. 84.

24. See Job 1:6; 2:1; Pss. 29:1; 89:6; Dan. 3:25, etc.

25. This means that the author has not created *de novo* in the details, symbols, and images he has used to tell the story. He has used the literary traditions about origins that are his by virtue of his own cultural situation in the ancient Near East.

thus far presented. This passage, then, shows that the main theological theme of the stories is the radical nature of the problem of sin. Thus it is also one of the main points of the long flood story. Human sin is so severe and heinous that God has no recourse but to wipe out his creatures and start again with Noah, a man of integrity in his generation.

Finally, the author closes the primeval prologue with the story of the Tower of Babel (11:1-9). Here he pictures human beings in their corporate life, no longer migratory but settling down in a civilized state. They build a city and a tower, but their purposes are motivated by a lust for fame and power: "let us make a name for ourselves, lest we be scattered abroad upon the face of the whole earth" (v. 4). God's assessment of the situation (v. 6) recognizes the evil propensities in this corporate human endeavor. Here the author depicts human society rising in rebellion against God. Sin not only radically corrupts the individual, but it invades corporate structures and entities, which become bent on power and control. The primary theme, then, woven through Gen. 1–11, is the radical seriousness of the sin which, from the beginning of the rebellion of mankind, has marred and stained God's good work.

God's Judgment on Human Sin. In each of these narratives God's judgment meets human sin. In the story of Eden, first the serpent (3:14f.), then the woman (v. 16), then the man (vv. 17-24) are judged by God. For each the judgment is the state in which he or she must live in the sinful, fallen condition that now characterizes the world. The serpent becomes the despicable, crawling creature that mankind finds so repulsive and fearful. In v. 15 the age-long battle between man and reptile symbolizes in stark, clear terms that relentless and mortal struggle between humanity and the force of evil in the world which has been the status quo from that time to this. This verse is properly a judgment on the serpent alone, as can be seen by a comparison of the three pairs of antagonisms set forth in the two main clauses of the verse. The first half of v. 15a places the serpent over against the woman, and the second half places the serpent's descendants over against the woman's descendants; but 15b places her descendants, viewed collectively in the pronoun "he," in opposition to the serpent itself, not its descendants. Thus, the real antagonist is the paradisal serpent, envisaged as a permanently present spiritual power ranged in opposition to the woman's descendants, viewed collectively.

Thus the author clearly indicates that the woman's descendants will struggle ceaselessly against the enslaving power of evil symbolized by the serpent. In broad terms he hints of the victory that will one day be theirs. That this will come about through an individual who represents the race is not expressly stated, but the idea is clearly there potentially in the collective designation of the descendants by the pronoun "he." Christians rightly interpret his unformulated hope as having found its realization in Christ's victory over sin and death (cf. Luke 10:17-20).

An important point should be noted about the judgments on the man and the woman. The woman and man are penalized but not cursed; only the serpent is cursed. However, as with the serpent, the judgment that falls upon the man and woman is the state in which they must live in the fallen order. Woman is to bear children in pain and have desire for her husband, her master. Man must gain his bread in toil and sweat from a recalcitrant earth and in the end return in death to the soil from which he was taken. These judgments show a certain amount of cultural conditioning; they reflect the social milieu and institutions of ancient Israel through which vehicle, under divine inspiration, they were formulated and set down. This is reflected especially with regard to the status of the woman, who was little more in the ancient world than a chattel of her husband. In this light one should no more argue on the basis of v. 16 that the wife slavishly should be subject to her husband than, on the basis of vv. 17-19, that man should scrap his tractors and air conditioners, grub the earth with a hoe, and sweat profusely![26]

As a further judgment upon the sin of the man and the woman, God expels both from the garden, and the way is barred from their ever returning. For humanity on its own there is no way back to fellowship with God.

Severe as was the judgment upon Adam and Eve, that upon Cain (ch. 4) was more severe still. Since the soil has drunk his brother's blood at his hand, it will no longer yield to Cain its produce, and he is doomed to be a fugitive and a wanderer in the earth. He leaves the Lord's presence to live in the land of ceaseless wandering in the far distant East.

The supreme example and paradigm of God's judgment on human sin, however, is the flood story. Through this story the author seeks to express in a most terrifying way that human sin brings God's judgment. Part of the problem here is that the path of understanding is bestrewn with the stumbling blocks of familiarity, which make it so hard to hear the story in its full force. The innocence of childhood and the ethos in which most people learn the story make it into a delightful tale of ancient adventure—a tale of the venerable and good-hearted Noah; boat building on the colossal scale; lighthearted and quick-footed animals of all shapes and sizes gaily tripping over a gangplank into a cavernous interior, two by two; the bursting of the fountains of the great deep and the opening of the windows of heaven; of ark and comic contents bobbing about in safety on wild waters while Noah's nasty neighbors (with whom one never once identifies) sink from view. But the account's original context is far removed from the bedtime story. For the ancient Mesopotamians the story was concerned with nature and the forces of nature—that realm of reality that so deeply affected the ancients' very life and existence. As noted for Gen. 1, these forces were personalized as divine beings. Nature was not an "it," but a whole series of divine "thou's." The biblical view of God cut diametrically across this

---

26. Especially is this so since the state described has been produced by sin, not by God's original intentions for creation. In seeking to overcome sin, it surely is mistaken to establish as a norm the evil effects sin has produced in the world.

view of nature. The God of Israel stood outside nature and its forces as their Creator, using them as the instruments of his purpose. But even though nature was God's creation, it was nonetheless of a personal order to the ancient Israelite, throbbing with the mysterious and immediate personal presence of the Lord's power and divinity. Viewed against this background, the awesome power and terror of the storm and the cataclysmic destruction of the Flood are raised to almost unutterable proportions as the expression of God's judgment on human sin. Here is the setting proper to that fearful judgment of God that comes upon humanity when "the imaginations of his heart are only evil continually" (6:5). This passage is the paradigm of divine judgment on that sin.

So, too, God's judgment confronts the sin of corporate humanity in the Tower of Babel story. To meet the threat of the evil propensities inherent in collective existence, God scatters mankind by confusing their language, breaking them into countless nations and states. So at the end of the primeval prologue mankind is in the state it has known since those times, alienated and separated by sin from God and from one another in a broken world of enmity and death. Individual is pitted against individual, social element against social element, nation against nation.

God's Sustaining Grace. But there is a fourth theological theme that, almost surprisingly, winds through the primeval prologue: God's supporting, sustaining grace. That grace is present in and along with each judgment except the last. In the Eden story, the penalty prescribed for eating the forbidden fruit is death that very day (2:17), yet God shows his forbearance in that death, though certain, is postponed to an unspecified time in the future (3:19). Further, God himself clothes the guilty pair, enabling them to live with their shame. Moreover, the story of Cain does not stop when the guilty Cain, merely contemplating his punishment, cries out in despair at his lot. In signal evidence of unmerited mercy, God responds to this bitter complaint by decreeing a sevenfold vengeance upon anyone who takes Cain's life, placing a mark upon him to make this protective relationship obvious to all.

The flood story, although the supreme example of God's judgment on human sin, also evidences in subtle ways his preserving grace. At the end of the flood story is another word from the Lord that is independent of ancient tradition, as was 6:5-8. Gen. 8:21f. is again a glimpse into the immediacy of God's own heart. Here the flood story is a measure of the grace of the living God as well as of his judgment. This contrast, which pervades the whole Bible, is presented here in all its unrelieved starkness: the same condition set forth as the grounds for God's terrible judgment ("every imagination of the thoughts of his heart was only evil continually," 6:5) is shown here as the grounds for his grace and providence ("for the imagination of man's heart is evil from his youth," 8:21). This is a paradoxical measure of God's supporting grace, known in the incomprehensible persistence of the natural orders despite the ongoing human sin: "while the earth remains, seedtime and harvest, cold and heat, summer and winter, day and night, shall not cease" (v. 22). Human corruption unchanged, God yet transfers humanity to a newly ordered world whose natural course of events solemnly is guaranteed to endure.

This theme of God's supporting, sustaining grace is missing, however, at one point in the account—the very end:

> The story about the Tower of Babel concludes with God's judgment on mankind; there is no word of grace. The whole primeval history, therefore, seems to break off in shrill dissonance, and the question . . . now arises even more urgently: Is God's relationship to the nations now finally broken; is God's gracious forbearance now exhausted; has God rejected the nations in wrath forever? That is the burdensome question which no thoughtful reader of ch. 11 can avoid; indeed, one can say that our narrator intended by means of the whole plan of his primeval history to raise precisely this question and to pose it in all its severity. Only then is the reader properly prepared to take up the strangely new thing that now follows the comfortless story about the building of the tower: the election and blessing of Abraham. We stand here, therefore, at the point where primeval history and sacred history dovetail, and thus at one of the most important places in the entire Old Testament.[27]

In a carefully constructed yet unobtrusive way, the author brings together the primeval prologue and the history of redemption in a relationship of problem and solution which is of utmost importance for understanding all of Scripture. The desperate problem of human sin so poignantly portrayed in Gen. 1–11 is solved by God's gracious action and initiative that begins with the promise to Abraham of land and posterity. But the redemptive history that begins there will not come to fruition until its consummation in the Son of Abraham (Matt. 1:1), whose death and resurrection will provide the ultimate victory over the sin and death that so soon disfigured God's good work.

FOR FURTHER READING

Clines, D.J.A. The Theme of the Pentateuch, 61-79.
Kaiser, W.C. "The Literary Form of Genesis I–II." In J.B. Payne, ed., New Perspectives on the Old Testament. Waco: 1970.
McKenzie, J.L. Myths and Realities: Studies in Biblical Theology. Milwaukee: 1963.
Renckens, H. Israels's Concept of the Beginning: The Theology of Genesis 1–3. New York: 1964.

---

27. G. von Rad, Genesis, trans. J.H. Marks. OTL, 2nd ed. (Philadelphia: 1972), p. 153.

Richardson, A. *Genesis I–XI*. 3rd ed. Torch Bible Commentary. London: 1959.
Thielicke, H. *How the World Began: Man in the First Chapters of the Bible*. Philadelphia: 1961.
Westermann, C. *The Genesis Accounts of Creation*. Trans. N.E. Wagner. Philadelphia: 1964.

CHAPTER 8

GENESIS: PATRIARCHAL HISTORY

CONTENTS OF GENESIS 11:27—50:26

As noted in the preceding chapter, the patriarchal history (Gen. 11:27–50:26) is divided into five sections by the same literary device used in ch. 1–11, the so-called *toledoth* formula (p. 68). In three instances this literary structure corresponds with major divisions clearly discernible on the basis of content. These are the cycles of stories about Abraham (11:27–25:18) and Jacob (25:19–37:1) and the long narrative about Joseph (37:2–50:26).[1] The remaining two instances of the *toledoth* formula introduce short genealogical sections following the first two major divisions. Each of these genealogical sections completes the contents of that section, for each concerns the secondary character of those stories, Ishmael at the end of the Abraham cycle (25:12-18) and Esau at the end of the Jacob cycle (36:1-43). Note how this reveals the secondary importance of Isaac's role in the patriarchal traditions, for no separate cycle deals with him.

HISTORICAL BACKGROUND

The call and blessing of Abraham represent a radical new development. Here God acts in history to begin a series of events that will heal the breach that sin has placed between him and his world. Therefore it is necessary to look briefly

---

1. The peculiar fact often has been noted that each of the major cycles of patriarchal stories is introduced by a *toledoth* formula naming the *father* of the principal character of that section. Terah (11:27) introduces the Abraham cycle, Isaac (25:19) introduces the cycle about Esau and Jacob, while the Joseph cycle is introduced by an abrupt reference to Jacob (37:2). The reference to Terah is easily explained because it actually introduces the short expanded genealogy in 11:27-32 linking the primeval prologue and story of Abraham. The other two may be explained by the highly patriarchal nature of Israelite society. Even though the major content centers in the sons, the patriarch is still alive and functioning as head of the family. Hence, in the Israelite conception it is his story because it is his family.

at the historical background of this redemptive history and to locate the biblical events within this general framework as accurately as possible.

With the apparent triumph of Wellhausenian views of literary criticism at the close of the last century, the evaluation of the historical worth of the patriarchal narratives was negative in the extreme. Their religious content was viewed as reflecting the beliefs of the period in which they were written—either the early Monarchy (ninth-eighth centuries B.C.) or the postexilic period (sixth-fifth centuries).[2] The patriarchs themselves were regarded as figures of astral mythology, Canaanite deities, heroes drawn from pre-Israelite folklore, or personifications of tribes whose history is reflected in their movements and relationships.[3] When these views were developed, the history and culture of the third and second millenniums were virtually unknown. Since then a wealth of material has been discovered, including hundreds of sites excavated in Palestine, Syria, and Mesopotamia[4] and literally hundreds of thousands of texts.[5] This material permits a fairly detailed reconstruction of early Near Eastern history, at least for the major centers of civilization, Egypt and Mesopotamia. Although many gaps and many questions remain unanswered, these discoveries have so transformed knowledge of the period that it is no longer a dark age.[6] A brief outline of the major events of the period follows.[7]

---

2. In his major work on the subject Wellhausen wrote: "It is true, we attain to no historical knowledge of the patriarchs, but only of the time when the stories about them arose in the Israelite people; this later age is here unconsciously projected, in its inner and its outward features, into hoary antiquity, and is reflected there like a glorified mirage"; *Prolegomena*, pp. 318f.

3. These views are discussed briefly with bibliography by H.H. Rowley, "Recent Discovery and the Patriarchal Age," in *The Servant of the Lord and Other Essays on the Old Testament*, 2nd ed. (Oxford: 1965), p. 283; and A. Parrot, *Abraham and His Times*, trans. J.H. Farley (Philadelphia: 1968), p. 3. The history and development of these views is set forth in detail in H. Weidmann, *Die Patriarchen und ihre Religion im Licht der Forschung seit Julius Wellhausen* (Göttingen: 1968).

4. For a brief description of relevant sites with bibliography, see I. Hunt, *World of the Patriarchs* (Englewood Cliffs, N.J.: 1967), pp. 2-11.

5. The important textual finds relevant to the patriarchal period are (1) the Mari documents, eighteenth century (*ANET*, pp. 482f.); (2) Nuzi texts, fifteenth century (*ANET*, pp. 219f.); (3) Cappadocian texts, nineteenth century; (4) Alalakh tablets, seventeenth and fifteenth centuries; (5) various legal corpora; e.g., the Code of Hammurabi (eighteenth century), Middle Assyrian laws (thirteenth century), Hittite laws (fifteenth century); (6) documents from the First Dynasty of Babylon, nineteenth–sixteenth centuries; (7) Ugaritic texts, fourteenth century (*ANET*, pp. 129-149); (8) Egyptian Execration texts, nineteenth–eighteenth centuries (*ANET*, pp. 328f.); (9) Amarna tablets, fourteenth century (*ANET*, pp. 483-490).

6. Thus the first two volumes of the *Cambridge Ancient History* (ed. I. E. Edwards et al., 3rd ed. [New York: 1975]) (the history of the ancient Near East from prehistorical times to 1000 B.C.) have been rewritten completely (see the preface to Vol. I, Pt. I, p. xix). These now appear as four volumes with more than twice the pages as the 1927 edition, and the interval between the two is but forty-five years.

7. For a thorough treatment with full bibliography, see J. Bright, *A History of Israel*, 3rd ed. (Philadelphia: 1981), pp. 23-66. For an excellent one-volume general history of the ancient Near East, see W.W. Hallo and W.K. Simpson, *The Ancient Near East: A History* (New York: 1971).

Prehistoric period. History in the proper sense[8] began shortly after 3000 in the ancient Near East. By that time, a rich and advanced culture already had arisen in the great river valleys of both Mesopotamia and Egypt. In Mesopotamia agriculture was advanced, with elaborate drainage and irrigation. Cities were founded, and the cooperative effort necessitated by large irrigation projects required the establishment of city-states with a complex administrative system. Technology was advanced, and writing already had been developed. The same is true in Egypt. With the first light of history Egypt was a united land with a pharaoh at its head. Evidence suggests that in the prehistoric period the numerous local districts had formed two large kingdoms, one in the northern delta region and the other in the south. Hieroglyphic script already had advanced beyond primitive stages. Demonstrative of this development, very early in the historical period the fourth-dynasty kings (*ca.* 2600) were able to mobilize and supply the vast resources of men and means necessary to build the great pyramids at Giza. Furthermore, Egypt and Mesopotamia, situated close to the extremities of the biblical world, were already in contact, producing significant cultural interchange. As history dawned, some 1500 years before Israel was to appear, the Near East already had seen the rise of all the essential elements of its two major civilizations.

Ancient Near East, Third Millennium. (1) Mesopotamia. The Sumerians were the creators of the civilization that already existed full-flowered when history dawned in Mesopotamia. The origin and development of their civilization cannot be traced. Politically it consisted of independent city-states (Early Dynastic Age, *ca.* 2800-2360). Sumerian life was organized about the temple, with religious and political authority closely integrated. The temple scribes already had

*West-Semitic (Amorite or "Asiatic") caravan, from tomb painting (*ca. 1890 B.C.*) at Beni Hasan, Egypt. (Oriental Institute, University of Chicago)*

----

8. I.e., that period for which contemporary inscriptions exist that can be translated and interpreted.

invented cuneiform writing, and most of the epics and myths of later Assyrian and Babylonian literature were written first in this period. Trade, commerce, and economic life flourished.

Although the Sumerians were predominant, Semites also inhabited lower Mesopotamia in this period. These people were called Akkadians after the city-state of Akkad, where they first gained ascendancy. They were deeply influenced by Sumerian culture and religion, and adapted the cuneiform syllabic script to their own language. Eventually a Semitic ruler, Sargon, seized power and founded an empire that lasted for 180 years (2360-2180). His dynasty controlled all Mesopotamia, a domain at times extending to Elam in the east and the Mediterranean in the west.[9]

The Akkadian empire was ended by barbarian tribes called the Guti, who swept in from the Zagros mountains to the east ca. 2180. Very little is known about the following century, but ca. 2050 the Sumerian city-states of the south broke the Gutian power. Under the third dynasty of the city of Ur (Ur III, 2060-1950), Sumerian civilization burned itself out in a last glorious revival. Ur-nammu, founder of the dynasty, is noted especially for his law code. During this period Sumerians and Akkadians lived side by side in racial and cultural harmony, while Akkadian language and culture slowly replaced the Sumerian. Although Sumerian continued as a sacred and traditional vehicle in the scribal schools, its vernacular use ceased. By the time God called Abraham from Ur of the Chaldees, Sumerian civilization had emerged, flowered, and faded from the scene, although deeply influencing the Akkadians and their successors. Ur III collapsed shortly after 2000, weakened by the influx of new peoples, notably the Amorites, who were to shape the history of Mesopotamia, south and north, for the next several hundred years.

(2) Egypt. Egypt continued for some seven hundred years as a unified nation enjoying a high state of civilization. The most impressive remains of this remarkable civilization are the pyramids—those massive monuments to its cult of the dead that still amaze observers 4500 years later. This advanced cultural flowering was the Old Kingdom (ca. 2900-2300), established by kings from the south and reaching its golden age under the Third and Fourth Dynasties (ca. 2600-2400). During this period all the features forever characteristic of Egypt's unique culture were firmly established. By accident of discovery, the work of the pharaohs of the Fifth and Sixth Dynasties, but pale reflections of the glorious Third and Fourth Dynasties, is better known. They covered the

---

9. The almost incredible discoveries at Tell Mardikh in northwestern Syria will force additions to and revisions of many statements about this period. It has been claimed that Ibrum, King of Ebla (the site's ancient name), was contemporary with Sargon of Akkad (however, the epigrapher, G. Pettinato, has since claimed that the name "Sargon" was misread in the texts) and controlled a large empire in the area. City-states as far away as Palestine (including Jerusalem) were tributary to him. The local culture was highly developed, including bilingual dictionaries giving the meanings of Sumerian words in the local language (presently termed Eblaic). Portions of a law code have been found, antedating the code of Ur-nammu by at least four hundred years.

walls of their pyramids with carefully carved and painted magic spells and hymns—the Pyramid texts, the oldest known religious compositions.

In the twenty-third century the state's unity was destroyed by rival provincial governors in the absence of a strong central power, and Egypt fell into a period of social chaos and economic ruin known as the First Intermediate Period (ca. 2200-2050). The literature of the period strongly reflects the difficulty of life and the national malaise.[10] Finally, in the mid-twenty-first century, a dynasty from Thebes, the Eleventh, reunited the land and ushered in the Middle Kingdom, Egypt's second period of stability and greatness. Long before Abraham, Egypt already had experienced a millennium of progress and civilization.

(3) Syria-Palestine. Knowledge of Syria and Palestine in the third millennium is shrouded by the mists of prehistory. The discovery in 1975-76 of nearly twenty thousand clay tablets at Tell Mardikh (Ebla), near modern Aleppo, has led scholars to believe that a vast empire was centered here in the mid-third millennium, with vassal cities as far away as Cyprus, Sinai, Anatolia, and the Mesopotamian highlands. Decipherment and publication of the cuneiform texts and analysis of the archaeological remains have not progressed extensively enough to permit adequate interpretation of this Early Bronze Age civilization and its impact upon biblical studies.

In the early third millennium Palestine itself was characterized by the development of small but well-built and heavily fortified cities, as shown by excavations at Jericho, Megiddo, Beth-shean, and Lachish. The inhabitants are usually known as Canaanites, from the name of the region in later texts. Archaeological evidence reveals that, late in the third millennium, every Canaanite city known thus far was destroyed, bringing to an end the Early Bronze civilization. The agents of this destruction are not known, although it is frequently hypothesized that they belonged to the Amorite groups who were just beginning to infiltrate Mesopotamia.[11]

Patriarchal Age, ca. 2000–ca. 1500. (1) Mesopotamia. Approximately 1950 Ur III was just falling from power, partly due to the influx of West Semitic peoples usually referred to as Amorites. This decline produced two centuries of inconclusive rivalry between the city-states of Lower Mesopotamia, by the end of which nearly every city-state in Upper and Lower Mesopotamia was ruled by an Amorite dynasty. Although the basic population in southern Mesopotamia remained Akkadian, in the northwest the Amorites completely displaced them. The period was one of political and economic chaos, but not a dark age. Two law codes have been found, one in Akkadian from Eshnunna, the other from Isin, codified by Lipit-Ishtar. Both evidence considerable similarities to the Covenant Code (Exod. 21–23).

---

10. *ANET*, pp. 405-410.
11. See the discussion of Middle Bronze I and the Amorites in notes 13 and 16 below.

In this period Assyria and Babylonia, which dominated Akkadian history in the next millennium, first play roles of historical significance. About 1900 Assyria, ruled by an Akkadian dynasty, established a commercial colony far to the northwest at the ancient Anatolian town of Kanish (modern Kültepe near Turkish Kayseri). This colony is known from the Cappadocian texts—several thousand tablets discovered at Kanish which throw considerable light on the area's culture and ethnic composition. This Akkadian dynasty continued in power until ca. 1750, when it was replaced by an Amorite dynasty founded by Shamshi-adad, who briefly dominated Upper Mesopotamia. His principal rival was the city of Mari, which threw off the Assyrian yoke ca. 1730.

Extensive excavations at Mari have brought to light a brilliant civilization, documented by more than twenty thousand tablets, of utmost importance for patriarchal backgrounds. For a brief period Mari was a major power of the day.

But neither Mari nor Assyria was to emerge victorious in the struggle for power. That distinction went to Babylon under Hammurabi (1728-1686), whose Amorite dynasty had ruled Babylonia since 1830. When he came to the throne, Hammurabi faced not only Mari and Assyria but also Larsa which, under an Elamite dynasty, ruled all Mesopotamia south of Babylon. In a series of brilliant campaigns Hammurabi defeated his rivals and came to rule a modest empire from Nineveh to the Persian gulf. The civilization that this First Dynasty of Babylon developed changed it from an insignificant town to the greatest cultural center of the day. A wealth of texts reveals a literature and learning seldom achieved in ancient times. Most important is Hammurabi's law code, based on a legal tradition stretching back centuries (as the codes of Ur-nammu, Lipit-Ishtar and Eshnunna show), and having numerous and striking parallels with the laws of the Pentateuch. Despite his achievements, Hammurabi's empire ended with him. Under his immediate successors most tributary states broke away and, although independent for more than a century longer, toward the end of that period Babylon struggled for its existence against the Kassites, a new people sweeping in from the Zagros mountains to the east.

Part of the reason for Babylon's decline and eventual fall was a virtual flood of new peoples into the area, especially from the north. The ethnic movements thus set off were so disruptive that much manuscript evidence has disappeared leaving yet undocumented almost two centuries of events that created new states and empires. Most important among the new peoples were the Hurrians, non-Semites who had settled in northwestern Mesopotamia since the late third millennium but who now moved in force into the area. When documentary evidence resumes ca. 1500, the Hurrians control the empire of Mitanni, stretching from Alalakh, at the bend of the Orontes river near the Mediterranean in the west, to the foothills of the Zagros, across the Tigris to the east. The proud state of Assyria lay under their control, and for a time in the early fifteenth century the Hurrians vied with Egypt for world empire. Moving with the Hurrians, but in far smaller numbers, were Indo-Europeans, who seem to have been mostly a ruling aristocracy. Most names of kings of the Mitanni empire are Indo-European.

In Asia Minor the Hittites, a people speaking an Indo-European language, now came to prominence. During the late third millennium they had moved into central Asia Minor, where they began to gain ascendancy among the city states. By *ca.* 1550 they had created a kingdom in central and eastern Asia Minor, with the capital at Hattusas (modern Boghazköy), and soon came into conflict with the Hurrian kingdom of Mitanni. It was indeed a sign of things to come that the end of the First Dynasty of Babylon in 1530 came not from a Mesopotamian power but from a lightning-like raid of Mursilis I, an early ruler of the Hittite Old Kingdom. However, the Hittites did not yet control Asia Minor, and were not able to take the path of empire for another century. Thus, shortly after 1500, Mesopotamia was just emerging from a period of disruption and chaos, with a new political alignment taking shape that would soon bring a struggle for world empire. The confusion caused by these ethnic movements did not leave even Egypt unscathed.

(2) Egypt. The Middle Kingdom, Egypt's second period of cultural flowering and stability, reached its zenith with the Twelfth Dynasty, which, with its capital at Memphis, ruled Egypt for over two hundred years (*ca.* 1991-1786). This was a period of great prosperity and brilliance. Literature and the arts reached heights seldom achieved again, with wisdom literature and narrative tales abounding. From this period come the Execration texts, magic spells against Egypt's Palestinian enemies written on bowls, which were smashed to effect the curse. The names in these texts indicate that Egypt exercised loose control over most of Palestine.

In the latter half of the eighteenth century, however, rival dynasties (the Thirteenth and Fourteenth) signaled the decline of the Middle Kingdom. The country became so weakened that foreign peoples from Palestine and southern Syria infiltrated and eventually seized power. Called Hyksos, an Egyptian term meaning "foreign chiefs," their exact identity still is much debated, but the majority were certainly West Semites (Canaanites or Amorites). They placed their capital at Avaris in the northeastern Delta region and for nearly a century (*ca.* 1650-1542) ruled Egypt and parts of Palestine. It is not unlikely that during this period Joseph and his brothers came down into Egypt.

The struggle for Egyptian independence from this foreign control began in the south, in Upper Egypt. Ahmosis, founder of the Eighteenth Dynasty, took Avaris and pursued the Hyksos into Palestine, capturing Sharuhen, their main center there, after a three-year siege. Free again, Egypt determined that the best defense was a good offense and embarked on the path of empire in Asia for the first time. This strategy led to direct conflict with the new powers already centered there, precipitating a struggle for world empire. This struggle introduced what J.H. Breasted termed "the First Internationalism," a period best described in connection with the Exodus.

(3) Syria-Palestine. By comparison with the evidence for this period in the major cultural centers of Egypt and Mesopotamia, that for the area of Syria-

Palestine is miniscule. Part of the reason for this is the "accidents" of discovery, of course, but much of it is due to the inherent nature of the history and physical culture of Palestine itself. As W.G. Dever puts it:

> Now that we have a more representative view of Palestine in the context of the entire ancient Near East, it is clear that the country was always a cultural backwater, impoverished artistically as well as economically. Furthermore, its stormy political history has led to frequent pillage, destruction, and rebuilding by a long succession of peoples of various cultures, which has rendered the stratification of its mounds complex and has left its material remains in a poor state of preservation. Finally, the damp climate of central Palestine and the choice of papyrus and parchment as writing materials have combined to rob us of all but a handful of epigraphic remains (the Bible being a notable exception). Even if we are fortunate enough to turn up literary remains, they are usually so fragmentary as to be enigmatic, and thus their correlation with the artifactual remains often poses severe difficulties. In short, in contrast to neighbouring cultures, much of the archaeology of Palestine before the Israelite era is really "prehistory."[12]

Consequently, a history of Palestine in this period cannot really be written at all, and very general statements must suffice.

After an obscure interim period at the end of the third millennium, usually known as Middle Bronze I (MB I),[13] a new cultural synthesis took place that

---

12. "The Patriarchal Traditions," in J.H. Hayes and J.M. Miller, eds., *Israelite and Judaean History*. OTL (Philadelphia: 1977), pp. 74f.

13. MB I is one of the most debated periods archaeologically in the whole era of early Palestine. Not even the nomenclature for the period is fixed. W.F. Albright's designation MB I indicates that he understood the period as separate from EB and connected to MB II which followed. On the basis of her excavations at Jericho, however, K.M. Kenyon posited a complete cultural break between "MB I" and both the preceding EB and succeeding MB II periods, and thus posited an "Intermediate EB/MB period." Others demurred and opted for a designation "EB IV" since the closest connections seemed to be with the preceding period. The present state of interpretation is described by Dever as follows: "In conclusion, there has been a virtual explosion in MB I studies in the past two decades, brought about by a wealth of newly excavated material as well as by a burst of creative theorizing. Yet we must caution that archaeologists still cannot draw a comprehensive picture of the MB I culture as a whole, let alone account for its origins or identify the ethnic movements which may be connected with its appearance in Palestine. The material at our disposal is too scant and too unrepresentative. There is an agreement only on the links of MB I with the Early Bronze rather than the Middle Bronze period; the tendency to stress its semi-sedentary character rather than its nomadic aspects; and the preference for dates about a century higher than Albright's dates, i.e., about 2200-2000 BCE"; *Israelite and Judaean History*, p. 84. Dever argues, as Albright, de Vaux, and Kenyon had before him, that this culture was introduced in Syria-Palestine by the Amorites. For a detailed discussion of the period, interpreting the evidence as suggesting a more sedentary than nomadic culture that arose from developments within Palestine itself rather than invasions from Syria, see T.L. Thompson, *The Historicity of the Patriarchal Narratives: The Quest for the Historical Abraham*. BZAW 133 (1974): 144-171. For a critique of Thompson which supports the Amorite view, see J.E. Huesman, "Archeology and Early Israel: The Scene Today," CBQ 37 (1975): 1-16.

produced an increasingly developed and urban civilization. For lack of written materials, this civilization is better referred to by its archaeological designation Middle Bronze II, though it is often dubbed "Canaanite" from the name of the area in later texts.[14] This period is divided on the basis of pottery styles into two subperiods, MB II A (dated 2000/1950-1800), the formative phase of the culture, and MB II B-C[15] (1800-1550/1500[16]). This last period, representing a continuous development from MB II A, forms the full flowering of the "Canaanite" civilization which produced the powerful and prosperous city-states of Syria-Palestine found in the later part of the period, after 1600. On the basis of the archaeological data scholars have concluded that Palestine in this period forms a cultural continuum with greater Syria. There is now little doubt that this urban civilization contributed the major portion of the so-called Hyksos peoples who controlled Egypt during the Second Intermediate Period. It also formed the major opposition to the creation of the Egyptian empire in Asia under the Eighteenth-Dynasty Pharaohs at the end of the Hyksos interlude.

Since no texts from Palestine are available from this period, the identity of the people who created this culture remains an open question. However, basing their conclusions on the apparent similarity between the pottery of this culture and that of contemporaneous Syria,[17] and on a posited identity between the personal names from Palestine in this period occurring in the Egyptian

---

14. For a succinct but full discussion, replete with bibliography, see Dever, *Israelite and Judaean History*, pp. 84-89.

15. The designation MB II B-C is given to accommodate a break in the period suggested by the ceramics and stratigraphy of certain excavations. This is a minor matter not pertinent here.

16. These dates follow Dever in *Israelite and Judaean History*, esp. p. 89, and R. de Vaux, *The Early History of Israel*, trans. D. Smith (Philadelphia: 1978), p. 68.

17. Dever summarizes the current state of interpretation of the archaeological data as follows: "The most intriguing question about this period concerns the origin of the MB IIA material culture and the possibility of identifying its appearance with ethnic movements. The question cannot yet be resolved, but already there is agreement on the main lines of future research. Although attempts have been made to relate the pottery to the preceding period . . . , it is clear that the material culture of MB IIA as a whole cannot be derived from MB I. The striking thing about this culture is that it appeared suddenly in Palestine, without local antecedents . . . . Furthermore, although detailed comparisons are difficult due to the lack of reliable materials, it may be argued that the pottery of Palestine is more closely related to that of Syria in the MB IIA period than in any other in the country's history. These observations suggest that after the disruption of life in Palestine at the end of the third millennium BCE (EB IV–MB I) there was a fresh cultural impetus from Syria, resulting in the emergence of a homogeneous and vigorous urban culture which came to dominate the entire Syro-Palestinian area in the Middle Bronze Age. Since this period in Upper Mesopotamia and Syria is marked by the Amorite expansion, nearly all scholars today equate MB IIA in Palestine with the arrival and establishment of the Amorites. . . ."; *Israelite and Judaean History*, pp. 85f.

The problematic nature of the present state of interpretation is revealed by the fact that the Amorites are regarded as the peoples responsible for the strikingly different material cultures of both MB I and MB IIA. Attempts to explain this as different stages in the cultural evolution of these people (as, e.g., Dever does, p. 869) hardly seem adequate. Cf. also de Vaux, *Early History*, pp. 63f.

Execration texts[18] and the Amorite names found in contemporary texts from Syria and Mesopotamia, most scholars attribute the MB II culture in Palestine to the arrival of the Amorites,[19] many of them positing a large-scale ethnic migration from north-central Syria into Palestine.[20] This general conclusion is not demanded by the evidence available at present.[21] First, the archaeological evidence is, by its very nature, mute and, although suggestive, not conclusive.[22] It is quite possible that the pottery styles that appear so suddenly in Palestine in MB II A and seem to have such close connections with Syria arose through the spread and borrowing of pottery styles through trade and other contacts, i.e., by cultural diffusion, rather than ethnic migration.[23]

Secondly, regarding the relationship between the names from Palestine and those of the Amorites from Mesopotamia, the posited identity is a premature conclusion.[24] Further, even if this basic identity could be established, it would

---

18. These texts consist of three groups of imprecations against the enemies of Pharaoh written in Egyptian hieroglyphics on bowls and statuettes which were then broken to effect the curse. A significant number name enemies of the pharaoh in Palestine and date somewhere in the period between 1875-1750. On these texts in general and particularly their relationship to the Amorite names from Mesopotamia, see Thompson, *Historicity*, pp. 89-117.

19. See Dever, note 17 above; also see G. Posener, J. Bottéro, and Kenyon, "Syria and Palestine c. 2160-1780 B.C.," CAH I/2: 532-594; de Vaux, *Early History*, pp. 66-71.

20. This is the view widely disseminated by J. Bright, *A History of Israel*, 3rd ed. (Philadelphia: 1981), pp. 55f., 96.

21. It is fair to say that the very choice of the term "Amorite" for these peoples has tended to foster a much more unified view of their history and ethnic identity than the evidence warrants. A far better, less prejudicial term would be "Early West Semites." In addition, the only ethnic migrations that the texts thus far support are (1) from the northern Syro-Arabian desert east and south into Babylonia in the Ur III period (2060-1950) and (2) from the same area north across the Euphrates into northwest Mesopotamia in the Old Babylonian period about two centuries later. There is certainly no textual evidence whatsoever for a migration of "Amorites" from southern Babylonia to northwest Mesopotamia or from northwest Mesopotamia to Palestine. See Thompson, *Historicity*, pp. 67-165.

22. Note the tenuous nature of the conclusions voiced by Dever, note 17 above. He indicates that detailed comparisons between the pottery of Palestine and that of Syria are difficult (since few sites in Syria have produced pottery dating to this period).

23. On the problem of equating marked changes in pottery styles and repertoire with changes in population without corroborating evidence in connection with the interpretation of MB I, see Thompson, *Historicity*, pp. 145f. The same remarks are cogent for MB II.

24. This identity is based on the apparent similarity of the two name fonts (see, for example, W.F. Albright, *From the Stone Age to Christianity*, 2nd ed. [Garden City: 1957], p. 164), which has not been substantiated by further study. Thus, in "The Early History of the West Semitic Peoples," JCS 15 (1961): 39, I.J. Gelb wrote: "As far as I can judge the situation, it is impossible at the present time to decide between two conclusions, one, that the language of the names in the Execration Texts preserves the characteristics of the older West Semitic language, namely Amorite, and the other, that it shows the innovating features of Canaanite." In addition, some evidence that the two name fonts represent two distinct dialects has been adduced, but there is too much ambiguity for any conclusion. See W.L. Moran, "The Hebrew Language in Its Northwest Semitic Background," BANE, p. 78 note 29; and esp. Thompson, *Historicity*, pp. 91-97.

not demonstrate an ethnic migration from Mesopotamia to Palestine. There is good evidence that early West Semites were present in Palestine and the Phoenician coast long before they penetrated Syria (and northwest Mesopotamia), so that identifying West Semitic newcomers amidst an already existent West Semitic population becomes highly problematic.[25] It is certain at least that no data at present can be construed to support the hypothesis of a large-scale ethnic migration of Amorites from north-central Syria. Further, if the hypothesis of a migration of West Semites to Palestine should be required by the archaeological and linguistic data, it is far more likely that they would have come either from the regions of southwest Syria to the immediate north[26] or the Syrian steppe-land to the northeast.

Finally, toward the end of the era of MB II Hurrian and Indo-European names appear in texts from the area and it is referred to as "Hurru land" by the Egyptians of the Eighteenth and Nineteenth Dynasties, revealing that Palestine was influenced by the same movement of these ethnic groups that was described above for northwest Mesopotamia. How deeply this influence was felt and how early is still disputed, but it seems very unlikely that the date could have significantly preceded the fifteenth century.[27]

DATE AND HISTORICITY OF THE PATRIARCHAL NARRATIVES

The voices of all the Old Testament traditions are unanimous in placing the patriarchal era prior to the exodus from Egypt,[28] hence somewhere in the period just briefly rehearsed. As the family history of a group whose life style was, in all probability, that of the pastoral nomad, the patriarchal tradition has recorded no data that relates either the persons or events to the political history of contemporary states and peoples, apart from the account of the attack of the

---

25. Geographical names are notoriously conservative and usually preserve an ethnic picture far older than the period in which they occur. (Compare the way in which present-day Arabic names for sites in Palestine frequently preserve pre-Arabic period names, many frequently going back to the Old Testament period and earlier.) In this light it is significant that almost all geographical names from Palestine from the early second millennium are West Semitic, in contrast to Syria, where the earliest geographical names are non-Semitic. See Gelb, JCS 15 (1961): 41; Thompson, Historicity, pp. 92, 319. In addition, the Ebla texts from Tell Mardikh may throw considerable light on the picture, for it has been claimed that the local language is a West Semitic dialect with its closest analogues being the Canaanite languages of the first millennium including Hebrew! This, however, waits to be demonstrated; see Gelb, "Thoughts about Ibla: A Preliminary Evaluation, March, 1977," Syro-Mesopotamian Studies 1 (1977): 17-27.

26. So also de Vaux, Early History, p. 68.

27. For a discussion of the Hurrian penetration of Syria and Palestine, see F.W. Bush, "Hurrians," IDBS, pp. 423f. For a more detailed treatment of the date and extent of their penetration of Palestine, see de Vaux, "Les Hurrites de l'histoire et les Horites de la Bible," Revue biblique 74 (1967): 481-503.

28. On this point see D.J. Wiseman, "Abraham Reassessed," pp. 149ff. in A.R. Millard and Wiseman, eds., Essays on the Patriarchal Narratives (Leicester: 1980).

four kings in Gen. 14, a pericope that thus far has defied attempts to relate it to extrabiblical events. Adding to this the fact that almost all the events of the patriarchal narratives take place within Palestine itself and, as noted, knowledge of that area in this period is exceedingly limited (and by the nature of the evidence likely to remain so[29]), it is antecedently extremely difficult to locate the patriarchs within this period. As a result, the struggle of scholars to do so has been a long, complicated, and often heated one that can only be reviewed here very briefly.

The brilliant light thrown on the history of the major cultural areas of the Near East in the second millennium resulted in a far more positive assessment of the historical worth of the patriarchal narratives than the prevailing view at the beginning of this century (see p. 89 above). A number of studies have summarized the evidence for this widespread consensus.[30] The ablest exponent of this view was W.F. Albright,[31] while the classical formulation has been that of J. Bright.[32] Despite many differences in details between the views of various scholars regarding the historicity of the patriarchs and their dating in this period, the general view adopted, at least in the English-speaking world,[33] is well summarized by Albright:

---

29. See the preceding section and especially the quotation from Dever, p. 95.

30. The best summaries are those of de Vaux: "Les Patriarches hébreux et les découvertes modernes," *RB* 53 (1946): 321-348; "The Hebrew Patriarchs and History," pp. 111-121 in de Vaux, *The Bible and the Ancient Near East* (London: 1971); and H.H. Rowley, "Recent Discovery and the Patriarchal Age," pp. 281-318 in *The Servant of the Lord.*

31. His most important treatment has been the chapter "Hebrew Beginnings," pp. 1-9 in *The Biblical Period from Abraham to Ezra* (New York: 1963). Others are "The Hebrew Background of Israelite Origins," pp. 236-249 in *From the Stone Age to Christianity*; "Abram the Hebrew: A New Archaeological Interpretation," *BASOR* 163 (1961): 36-54; "The Patriarchal Backgrounds of Israel's Faith," pp. 53-110 in *Yahweh and the Gods of Canaan* (1968; repr. Winona Lake: 1978); and, published shortly after his death, "From the Patriarchs to Moses: I. From Abraham to Joseph," *BA* 36 (1973): 5-33.

32. *History*, pp. 77-103.

33. In Germany A. Alt and M. Noth espoused a much less positive assessment of the historical worth of Gen. 12-50. In *The History of Israel*, Noth wrote: ". . . we have no evidence, beyond what has been said already, for making any definite historical assertions about the time and place, presuppositions and circumstances of the lives of the patriarchs as human beings. Even the original tradition of the patriarchs was not, however, much concerned with their human personalities, but rather with the divine promises that had been made to them"; 2nd ed., trans. P.R. Ackroyd (New York: 1960), p. 123. Alt and Noth, of course, while not ignoring the results of archaeology, were interested primarily in the study of the preliterary history of the narratives, and of the oral traditions from which they emerged, using the literary techniques of *Gattungsgeschichte* and *Redaktionsgeschichte*. Albright and his followers, while not eschewing the methodology and results of literary criticism, laid far greater weight on the parallels between the biblical texts and the nonbiblical materials. The two approaches came into open conflict in a series of journal articles and reviews. In *Early Israel in Recent History Writing*, Bright criticized Noth's methodology, in particular his negative conclusions regarding the validity of the traditions, his disregard for the archaeological evidence, and the inability of his views to explain adequately either the birth of Israel or its faith. Noth addressed the use of archaeology more directly in "Hat die Bibel doch recht?" pp. 7-22 in *Festschrift für Günther Dehn* (Neukirchen: 1957); and "Der Beitrag der Ar-

. . . as a whole the picture in Genesis is historical, and there is no reason to doubt the general accuracy of the biographical details and the sketches of personality which make the Patriarchs come alive with a vividness unknown to a single extrabiblical character in the whole vast literature of the ancient Near East.[34]

Although Albright never gave up his attempt to see the Middle Bronze I period as the age of the patriarchs,[35] the majority of scholars have placed them early in the general era of MB II (i.e., the early centuries of the second millennium) and connected them with the presumed Amorite migration.[36] This is the view that is carefully and persuasively argued by R. de Vaux.[37] Almost every line of evidence and argumentation used to establish this consensus has been seriously challenged in recent years,[38] so much so that an increasing number of scholars

---

chäologie zur Geschichte Israels," *VTS* 7 (1960): 262-282; cf. *Der Ursprunge Israels im Lichte neuer Quellen* (Cologne: 1961).

These exchanges led to some moderation of the two positions, as de Vaux has summarized: "Method in the Study of Early Hebrew History," pp. 15-29 in J.P. Hyatt, ed., *The Bible in Modern Scholarship* (Nashville: 1965); *The Bible and the Ancient Near East*, pp. 111-121; and "On Right and Wrong Uses of Archaeology," pp. 64-80 in J.A. Sanders, ed., *Near Eastern Archaeology in the Twentieth Century* (Garden City: 1970). See also J.A. Soggin, "Ancient Biblical Traditions and Modern Archaeological Discoveries," *BA* 23 (1960): 95-100.

De Vaux concludes that "in the end, it seems Noth accepts everything that Bright accepts with regard to the history of the Patriarchs"; *The Bible and the Ancient Near East*, p. 119. Such as assessment is doubtless overstated and somewhat misleading, for one gets the impression that Noth's statements are almost reluctant admissions of the parallels and connections claimed. He posits a very general historicity to these narratives in the sense that the patriarchs did exist, but feels nothing more specific can be said. Nevertheless, Noth had so modified his position that he could say: "It seems certain to me that the origins of Israel are rooted in historical conditions which are proved by archaeological discoveries to be located in the middle of the second millennium"; "Der Beitrag der Archäeologie zur Geschichte Israels," *VTS* 7 (1960): 269. To this significant extent one could say that the consensus included the German school as well.

34. *Biblical Period*, p. 5.

35. This was predicated on his view of this period as a nomadic interlude between the urban cultures of EB III and MB II, and on his dating of it as late as 1800. Both contentions have been given up. See above, note 13; also Thompson, *Historicity*, pp. 144-186; and esp. Dever, *Israelite and Judaean History*, pp. 82f., 93-95.

36. E.g., Bright, *History*, p. 85; E.A. Speiser, "The Patriarchs and Their Social Background," in B. Mazar, ed., *The Patriarchs and Judges*. The World History of the Jewish People, 1st ser. 2 (Brunswick, N.J.: 1971); S. Yeivin, "The Patriarchs in the Land of Canaan," *ibid.*; G.E. Mendenhall, "Biblical History in Transition," pp. 36-38 in *BANE*; D.N. Freedman, "Archaeology and the Future of Biblical Studies: The Biblical Languages," p. 297 in Hyatt, *The Bible in Modern Scholarship*. For a very helpful summary of the major positions and their arguments, see de Vaux, *Early History*, pp. 259-263.

37. *Early History*, pp. 257-266.

38. Although there had always been scholars who had dissented from the majority position (e.g., Mazar, "The Historical Background of the Book of Genesis," *JNES* 28 [1969]: 73-83), the major assault, questioning virtually every line of evidence on which historicity has been based, has been that of Thompson, *Historicity*, and J. Van Seters, *Abraham in History and Tradition* (New Haven: 1975). Both volumes seek to show that the majority consensus is without any validity whatsoever. Thompson observes: "The

regard the view as no longer valid.[39] Although these challenges have shown that some of the lines of evidence used to establish the historicity of the patriarchal traditions are invalid, there is still more than sufficient evidence from the Bible and extrabiblical texts to show that, on the contrary, this historicity is a warrantable conclusion.

First, both a surface reading and a literary study of the patriarchal narratives reveal both their historiographical nature and intent.[40] Granted, they are neither autobiographical nor biographical; their primary interests and message are theological; and they have come down through a long, complex process of oral and written transmission, so that neither in basic message nor form are they history in the modern sense (see below).[41] Nevertheless, their form and intent are clearly (and obviously) determined by literary and theological motives rooted in the experienced past of the community, in historically-based traditions.[42] Further, a comparison with other ancient Near Eastern narrative works will show

---

results of my own investigations, if they are for the most part acceptable, seem sufficient to require a complete reappraisal of the current position on the historical character of the patriarchal narratives. These results support the minority position that the text of Genesis is not a historical document"; *Historicity*, p. 2.

Although Thompson's primary judgment as to the historicity of the patriarchs is based on the literary judgment that the texts do not purport to be historiographical (p. 3), the great bulk of the book is devoted to a detailed and carefully argued attempt to demonstrate that the major lines of argumentation from the archaeological, epigraphical, and socio-juridical data for the historicity of the patriarchal narratives are not valid. He considers these texts as having no historical validity and dates the traditions they contain to the ninth–eighth century.

Van Seters also regards the patriarchal narratives as completely unhistorical. Using a radical "history of redaction" methodology, he critiques the literary arguments for dating them to the ninth–eighth century, and dates them instead to the exilic and post-exilic period. As further evidence for this date he attempts to show that the arguments from social customs, nomadism, etc. have a better historical setting in the later first millennium than the early second.

Also, in Hayes and Miller, eds., *Israelite and Judaean History*, Dever gives a thorough and heavily documented treatment of the archaeological background in the second millennium while W.M. Clark discusses the biblical traditions themselves (pp. 70-148). Both accept the judgment that little, if any, historicity can now be accorded the patriarchal narratives.

For useful discussions of the works of Thompson and Van Seters, see M.J. Selman, "Comparative Customs and the Patriarchal Age," pp. 99-108 in Millard and Wiseman, eds., *Essays on the Patriarchal Narratives*; and J.T. Luke, "Abraham and the Iron Age: Reflections on the New Patriarchal Studies," *JSOT* 4 (1977): 35-47.

39. Dever dismisses the whole case in one sentence: ". . . Albright's MB I date, along with all other second millennium BCE dates suggested by archaeological evidence, has been ruled out by the recent treatments of Thompson and Van Seters"; *Israelite and Judaean History*, pp. 94f.

40. For helpful discussions of the historical nature and intent of the patriarchal narratives, see Selman, *Essays on the Patriarchal Narratives*, pp. 103-5; K.A. Kitchen, *The Bible in Its World* (London: 1978), pp. 61-65; Luke, *JSOT* (1977): 35-38; and W.W. Hallo, "Biblical History in Its Near Eastern Setting: The Contextual Approach," pp. 1-26 in C.D. Evans, Hallo, and J.B. White, eds., *Scripture in Context: Essays on the Comparative Method* (Pittsburgh: 1980).

41. See Bright, *History*, pp. 75f.

42. See Luke, *JSOT* 4 (1977): 36.

that they stand closest in literary type to historically-based narratives.[43] In this light, then, it is important to stress that the biblical traditions unanimously place the patriarchs significantly prior to the Exodus, and two separate traditions give the interval as on the order of four hundred years.[44] Since the Merneptah stele (see below, p. 121) dates Israel's presence in Palestine *ca.* 1220[45] and the Exodus must have occurred significantly before that date, this biblical datum places the end of the patriarchal period *ca.* 1700 at the latest.

Second, and significant in the light of its correlation with this biblically derived chronology,[46] there is significant evidence that the patriarchal narratives reflect authentically the conditions pertaining in the ancient Near East in the early second millennium. The main lines of evidence are as follows:

(1) The font of patriarchal names is abundantly exemplified among the Amorite population of the period[47] and can be identified as Early West Semitic,[48] i.e., as belonging to the languages of the West Semitic family extant in the second millennium in contradistinction to the first.[49] Further, an examination of names of this type that do occur in the first millennium texts reveals a most significant chronological gap in attestation in both the biblical and non-biblical materials. Thus, names of this type are found among the extrabiblical

---

43. See Kitchen, *The Bible in Its World*, pp. 61ff.

44. Gen. 15:13; Exod. 12:40.

45. The Merneptah stele dates to the fifth year of that Pharaoh; this year must date between 1220 and 1209; see Kitchen, *The Bible in Its World*, p. 144 note 46.

46. Obviously, this *terminus ad quem* of 1700 assumes that the Israel mentioned in the Merneptah stele refers to the Israelite tribes that came out of Egypt. This of course cannot be demonstrated, but it is a widely held assumption and provides the latest viable date for the end of the patriarchal period based on the biblical data. Of course, if the 480 years of 2 Kgs. 6:1 is taken literally, then the biblical data places the Exodus *ca.* 1450 and the end of the patriarchal period is *ca.* 1850. In any case the date in question belongs to the early centuries of the second millennium.

47. See Bright, *History*, pp. 77ff.; de Vaux, *Early History*, pp. 193-200, 264; Kitchen, *The Bible in Its World*, p. 68.

48. On this designation for the West Semitic language distribution of the second millennium, prior to the ethnic movements at its end that brought into existence the "classical" and well-known West Semitic languages of the first millennium and later (notably Hebrew and Aramaic), see Thompson, *Historicity*, pp. 70-75. The adoption of this far less prejudicial terminology would provide a welcome clarification in the discussion.

49. Thompson, *ibid.*, pp. 17-51, has given the occurrences of ancient Near Eastern names parallel to those of the patriarchal narratives an exhaustive study in an attempt to show that they are not characteristic of the second millennium alone but occur throughout the first millennium also, and, indeed, "can be expected to appear wherever we find names from West Semitic peoples"; p. 318. The chronological gap discussed below seriously modifies this claim. Further, Thompson does not give sufficient weight to the observation that these names can "be classified typologically as Early West Semitic" (p. 317), particularly in light of his discussion on terminology (pp. 72ff.), where he favors "Early West Semitic" in order to distinguish "these groups [i.e., the Amorites] from the later, better-known West Semitic languages and peoples" (p. 72), obviously referring to the Canaanite, Aramaic, and Arabic language groups of the first millennium. This seems a much more significant phenomenon than the fact that parallels can be found from Aramaic and South Arabic names from the second half of the first millennium!

Early West Semites down to the end of the second millennium[50] and among the biblical names from the patriarchal period through the Mosaic era down to the time of David.[51] They then do not reappear in either corpus of texts until the period of classical Aramaic dominance beginning in the late eighth–early seventh century.[52] In this light it is striking to note that this type of name is not found among the Aramaic names that occur in texts from the tenth to the seventh century,[53] although they occur with some frequency in later Aramaic dialects. Finally, it can scarcely be accidental that these names are exceedingly rare among the Canaanite peoples of the first millennium, and the period of the gap in their attestation (the tenth–seventh centuries) is the period of Canaanite dominance (i.e., the period of the Israelite and Phoenician "empires" and ascendancy). This chronological distribution argues most strongly that the patriarchal period is to be dated to the second millennium.[54]

(2) Abraham's journey from northwest Mesopotamia (Haran) to Canaan accords well with a number of the conditions known to pertain during MB II A (2000/1950-1800). In this era a new, stable, peaceful, and prosperous period was in its developmental stages, whether its creators came from Syria or were indigenous to Palestine itself and only influenced by the major culture to the north.[55] In particular, the roads were open between Canaan and northwest Mesopotamia.[56] In this period most of the cities mentioned in the patriarchal narratives were founded or in existence, e.g., Shechem, Bethel, Hebron, Dothan, and Jerusalem (if it is the Salem of Gen. 14).[57] A major problem with this view is the fact that the Negeb, one of the major areas of Abraham's travel, has thus far revealed no evidence of occupation in MB II, but is extensively occupied in MB I.[58]

---

50. Names similar to Abram, Israel, and Jacob can be exampled from the Mari texts (eighteenth century) to the Ahiram sarcophagus (thirteenth/tenth century).

51. See the remarks of Noth. *Die israelitischen Personennamen im Rahmen der gemeinsemitischen Namengebung.* BWANT 10 (Stuttgart: 1928): 28. Compare the similar remarks on the name Isaac by de Vaux, *Early History*, p. 198 note 80.

52. A careful analysis of Thompson's study (see above, note 49) will show that for the name Abram after ca. 1000 he can refer to only four formally similar names from Assyrian texts of the late eighth and early seventh centuries (pp. 30-35); for the names Israel and Jacob, he can only note examples of similar names from the Aramaic dialects of Palmyra and Elephantine, from Epigraphic South Arabic, and from Jewish names in texts from Babylon, dating to the fifth century, taken from Noth, *Die israelitischen Personennamen*. See also de Vaux, *Early History*, p. 206.

53. Some fifty of these are known; see M. Liverani, "Antecedenti dell' onomastica aramaica antica," *Rivista degli Studi Orientali* 37 (1962): 65-76. See de Vaux, *Early History*, p. 206.

54. It makes it very difficult to date them to the period which Thompson posits, the Iron Age, more specifically, the end of the tenth or during the ninth century; see *Historicity*, pp. 316, 324-326.

55. See the historical survey above, p. 92.

56. See de Vaux, *Early History*, p. 265.

57. See Dever, *Israelite and Judaean History*, pp. 99-101.

58. For a detailed review of the archaeological evidence and a suggestion from the lack of occupation of the Negeb in MB II that Abraham should be dated to the end of MB I and Jacob to MB II, see J.J. Bimson, "Archaeological Data and the Dating of the Patriarchs," pp. 59-92 in Millard and Wiseman, eds., *Essays on the Patriarchal Narratives*.

It is important to note that this view does not posit an ethnic migration of Amorites from northwest Mesopotamia to Canaan in either MB I or MB II as a historical context within which to place Abraham's migration from Haran to Canaan. Apart from the fact that the evidence for such an Amorite migration is of extremely doubtful validity (see the historical survey above, p. 98), such an ethnic migration provides no verisimilitude for the biblical narrative simply because the biblical text knows nothing of a massive migration of peoples of which Abraham and his entourage are a part.[59] Abraham's move is not even that of a tribe (let alone a people!), but of one family.[60] The clear implication of the whole succession of narratives is that Abraham's people and his whole extended family are still living in northwest Mesopotamia[61] while he traverses Canaan as a resident alien (Heb. gēr).

(3) The pastoral nomadic lifestyle of the patriarchs fits the cultural milieu of the early second millennium. Understanding of nomadism in the ancient Near East has been radically transformed by recent studies implemented by modern anthropological research into the nature of nomadism.[62] No longer can one uncritically adopt as a model the pattern of life of the much later camel-mounted Arab Bedouin, with their ceaseless raids on the sedentary peoples of the civilized lands.[63] On the contrary, the pastoral "nomads" of the semi-arid steppe zone between the desert and the cultivable land[64] were in constant contact with the village farming areas, forming a dual society in which villagers and pastoralists were mutually dependent and integrated parts of the same tribal community.[65] Movement back and forth between the lifestyle of the settled agricultural community and that of the pastoralists moving seasonally into the

---

59. See the remarks of N.M. Sarna, Biblical Archaeology Review 4 (1978): 52.

60. Gen. 12:1 reads "Leave your country, your kindred [i.e., the tribal or subtribal group, related by blood], and your father's house [i.e., the extended family]. . . ."

61. Thus, Abraham sends his servant there to obtain a wife for his son Isaac (Gen. 24), and Rebekah sends Jacob to Laban his uncle in Aram Naharaim (Northwest Mesopotamia) to escape the vengeance of Esau whose birthright he has surreptitiously obtained (27:41ff.).

62. See the thorough review, with excellent bibliography, in Dever, Israelite and Judaean History, pp. 102-117.

63. Arab Bedouin nomadism is based upon the camel, which alone can survive and traverse the Nefud, the central Syro-Arabian desert. The domestication of the camel did not take place in the ancient Near East earlier than ca. 1200; see Luke, Pastoralism and Politics in the Mari Period (Unpublished Ph.D. diss., University of Michigan, 1965), pp. 42f.

64. In Mesopotamia, Syria, and Palestine, this zone of about 4-10 in. of annual rainfall lies between the desert and the cultivable regions with a higher rainfall and moves in a great semicircle up the Mesopotamian valley, across south-central Syria, and down the Palestinian coastal area. See the map in Dever, Israelite and Judaean History, p. 728.

65. The view that nomadism and village agriculturalism are mutually exclusive lifestyles must be corrected. In point of fact, archaeological evidence from prehistoric villages strongly suggests that the cultural evolution of the village proceeded from general food-collecting to incipient cultivation to primary village farming communities without any nomadic interludes. It is also likely that sheep and goats were domesticated in the village agricultural setting and that pastoralism developed from the village. See R.J. Braidwood, Prehistoric Investigations in Iraqi Kurdestan. Studies in Ancient Oriental Civilization 31 (Chicago: 1960): 170-184; and Luke, Pastoralism and Politics, pp. 22ff.

steppes seeking pasturage was endemic, depending on the rainfall in the semi-arid steppe zone. The conflict which continually occurred was not so much between pastoralist and villager as a struggle for political authority between the organized city-states with their powerful urban centers and these autonomous tribal chiefdoms.

Although detailed study of this concept of nomadism and comparison with the biblical texts remains to be done, the patriarchal lifestyle seems to reflect this same "dimorphic" society.[66] The patriarchs camp in the vicinity of towns (e.g., Gen. 12:6-9; 33:18-20) and even live as "resident aliens" in certain towns (e.g., 20:1ff.). They sporadically practice agriculture (26:12f.); Lot settles "among the towns of the plain, . . . on the outskirts of Sodom" (13:12); and the contrasting vocations of Jacob and Esau (25:27-34) possibly reflect this same dichotomy. Yet, as at Mari, the patriarchs are sheepbreeders, moving with their flocks over considerable distances; e.g., Jacob, while residing at Hebron, sends Joseph to visit his brothers at Shechem, and he finds them further north at Dothan (37:12-17). Parallel technical vocabulary has been observed in the usage of both the Mari society and Israel in the areas of tribal kinship terms and pastoral encampments.[67] It is quite clear that the patriarchal mode of life has numerous similarities to the pastoral nomadism of the Mari texts and that their mode of life fits well in the cultural milieu of the early second millennium.[68]

(4) Various social and legal customs occurring in the patriarchal narratives can be compared with a wide range of socio-juridical customs from both the second and first millennia, showing that these narratives authentically reflect the long-standing usage of the ancient Near East.[69] These socio-juridical parallels must be used with great care. On these grounds it has often been attempted to date the patriarchs to the first half of the second millennium by noting parallels from texts dating to that period, particularly the Nuzi texts.[70] More recent studies have shown that this methodology is unsound, for the simple reason that the customs, when they have been valid,[71] have been shown to be

---

66. See Dever, *Israelite and Judaean History*, pp. 112-117; de Vaux, *Early History*, pp. 229-233; and N.K. Gottwald, "Were the Early Israelites Pastoral Nomads?" pp. 223-225 in J.J. Jackson and M. Kessler, eds., *Rhetorical Criticism* (Pittsburgh: 1974).

67. De Vaux, *Early History*, pp. 230f.; Dever, *Israelite and Judaean History*, pp. 115f.

68. Much further study and clarification is needed, however. Thus, note Thompson's objections to an uncritical adoption of the model of the pastoral nomadism of the Mesopotamian steppe regions for the very different environmental topography of Palestine; "The Background of the Patriarchs: A Reply to William Dever and Malcolm Clark," *JSOT* 9 (1978): 2-43, esp. pp. 8-12.

69. See Bright, *History*, pp. 78ff.; de Vaux, *Early History*, pp. 241ff. For a thorough and critical analysis, see Selman, *Essays on the Patriarchal Narratives*, pp. 93-138.

70. For a fully documented account of the development of this methodology, see Selman, *ibid.*, pp. 93-99.

71. This whole procedure has been notoriously open to mistaken conclusions based upon surface similarities. The parallels involved have often been based upon the exegesis of complicated and difficult texts without carrying out the careful studies necessary to establish sound interpretations of the texts in their own literary and cultural setting, both biblical and extrabiblical, before attempting to establish parallels. This criticism is especially true of the treatments involving the Nuzi texts.

insufficiently precise chronologically to be used for dating purposes. A custom can only be chronologically significant if it can be shown to belong to a fixed period, but socio-juridical customs in the ancient Near East were most often of long duration. In particular, the special connection between the patriarchal narratives and a specifically Hurrian socio-juridical milieu based on the Nuzi texts, a connection which often loomed very large in the argument for the historicity of the patriarchs,[72] must be given up.[73] The Nuzi customs used for comparison were drawn from only a half a dozen of the approximately three hundred family law texts found at the site, so that they can hardly be said to be representative even of Nuzi society.[74] Secondly, the Nuzi customs show much greater similarity to the socio-juridical practices of the Mesopotamian world at large than originally thought, and consequently the whole question of a specifically Hurrian pattern of family law is extremely suspect.[75] Nevertheless, a sufficient number of valid parallels between patriarchal customs and those of the ancient Near East have been established to show that the patriarchal narratives accurately reflect the social and historical setting in which the Bible places them.[76]

(5) The general picture of patriarchal religion is early and authentic.[77] In particular, the portrayal of God as the personal God of the patriarchal father and his clan (rather than as a God of places and sanctuaries as among the Canaanites), who grants a unilateral covenant and promises of divine protection, is most authentic. Further, patriarchal religion is clearly not a retrojection into the past of later Israelite belief. Several features, such as the regular use of the divine name El instead of Yahweh, the complete absence of references to or use of the name Baal, the directness of the relationship between God and the patriarch, without the mediation of priest, prophet, or cultus, and the complete lack of any mention or reference to Jerusalem,[78] clearly indicate this.

---

72. These Nuzi parallels were often deemed important on the hypothesis that they explained features not found later in the Old Testament or else misunderstood by the later editors of the Pentateuch. Further, the Nuzi customs were regularly identified as Hurrian on the basis of a presumed difference between the Nuzi customs and those of the general Assyro-Babylonian culture which otherwise formed the fabric of Nuzi society. This presumed Hurrian background of the patriarchal customs gained significance since the Hurrians' main presence in Mesopotamia was located in the very area in which the Bible placed the origin of the patriarchs, the vicinity of Harran.

73. See especially Selman, "The Social Environment of the Patriarchs," *Tyndale Bulletin* 27 (1976): 114-136; de Vaux, *Early History*, pp. 241-256; and Thompson, *Historicity*, pp. 196-297.

74. See Selman, *Tyndale Bulletin* 27 (1976): 116.

75. *Ibid.*, p. 118.

76. For a list of such customs based on sound comparative methodology, see Selman, *Essays on The Patriarchal Narratives*, pp. 125-129.

77. See the discussion of Bright, *History*, pp. 100-103; de Vaux, *Early History*, pp. 267-287; and esp. G.J. Wenham, "The Religion of the Patriarchs," pp. 157-188 in Millard and Wiseman, eds., *Essays on the Patriarchal Narratives*.

78. See Wenham, *ibid.*, pp. 184f.

Other lines of evidence are less certain.[79] What has been presented is sufficient to permit the conclusion that the patriarchs are indeed historical figures. This does not imply that a single person or event in the patriarchal stories has been found in extrabiblical sources—nor is it likely that one of them will be, simply because the patriarchal narratives are a family history. The patriarchs themselves were chiefs of seminomadic clans, whose lives affected little outside their own family circle.

LITERARY GENRE OF THE PATRIARCHAL NARRATIVES

Although rediscovery of the ancient world has demonstrated that the patriarchal narratives authentically reflect the period in which the Bible places them, does this mean that they are "history" in the modern sense? Behind all history writing lie the actual events in space and time. Two major problems interpose themselves between these events and what is called "history." The first is the problem of knowledge. What are the facts and how have they been preserved? If the historian possesses documentary evidence, what is the interval between the event and when it was recorded? If this interval was spanned by oral tradition, did conditions exist to preserve the facts faithfully, such as a cohesive social group with historical continuity? Much will depend upon how the historian comes to know about the events he records.

The second problem is significance. To record all that happened is impossible. Furthermore, many events are insignificant or meaningless for particular purposes or interests. To the political historian a marriage contract between common people is of little interest, whereas to the social historian it is primary. In addition, history writing is much more than the bare chronicling of events, but involves a selecting of events, relating them to one another, and determining cause and effect. Therefore, the question of the writer's purpose, on the basis of which he selects his data, becomes of paramount importance.

The biblical writers were not exempt from either of these considerations. Their writing under divine inspiration (see above, Ch. 2) does not imply anything different about their human, material knowledge of the past. Inspiration did not give them new information or make the obscure clear, as may be discerned from the biblical texts. They frequently mention sources (Num. 21:14; Josh. 10:12f.; 1 Kgs. 14:19), and comparison of passages reveals vast differences

---

79. The only passage in Gen. 12–50 that could possibly relate to general world history is the account of the attack of the four kings in ch. 14. Although no connections with known events have been found, the kings' names fit the nomenclature of the second millennium well. Amraphel can be plausibly interpreted as Amorite; Arioch is very possibly Hurrian (Arriyuk or Arriwuk at Nuzi); Tidal is the Hebrew form of Tudhalias, the name of four Hittite kings; and Chedorlaomer clearly contains two Elamite name elements not yet found together elsewhere. On the "proto-Aramean" background of the patriarchal narratives and the vexed question of their relationship to the Hapiru/Apiru, see Bright, History, pp. 90-95; de Vaux, Early History, pp. 200-209.

in their knowledge of the past.[80] Further, the biblical authors' purposes are predominantly theological and their selection and presentation of events is dominated by their religious viewpoint. Their primary interest is God's action in human events, not the events themselves. They recount history so as to inculcate theology, whether the facts of redemptive history or some theological truth less closely related to history. They do not distort or falsify history, but are often highly selective in light of their purposes.[81]

In this light what can be said about the historical genre of the patriarchal narratives? First, they are family history, with little interest in relating their story to contemporary events. As such, they certainly were handed down primarily by oral tradition. Pastoral nomads normally do not keep written records, and the stories themselves give abundant indication that such is the case. They are grouped in three "cycles" (stemming from three of the patriarchal generations), marked off by the editorial *toledoth* formula. They often give only the most general indications of chronological relationship; and if the chronology is pressed, difficult problems result. For instance, in Gen. 21:14 Abraham placed Ishmael on Hagar's shoulder and sent her off into the desert. If the chronology is carried from chapter to chapter as history, Ishmael was sixteen years old (16:16; 21:5). Again, Jacob was born when Isaac was sixty (25:26), and Isaac died at 180 (35:28). If this chronology is forced across the intervening chapters, then Rebekah is deeply disturbed about a wife for Jacob (27:46) when he is between eighty and one hundred years old!

Interpreting the chapters as history in the modern sense raises other problems. In ch. 20 Sarah is such a beautiful woman at ninety that Abraham, fearing for his life, passes her off as his sister; and she ends up in the harem of Abimelech, king of Gerar. Yet in ch. 18, when Sarah had laughed when told she would bear a son, the story relates that she was old and "it had ceased to be with Sarah after the manner of women" (v. 11). The point is not just the high figure given for her age but that one series of stories acknowledges her as very old. Similarly, Abraham is presented as advanced in age at one hundred (18:11; cf. 24:1); he laughs at the prospect of having a son (17:17), yet miraculously fathers one (21:7). However, 25:1-6 laconically relates that after Sarah's

---

80. The account of Solomon's succession (2 Sam. 9–20 and 1 Kgs. 1–2) is recognized by nearly all scholars as virtually an eyewitness account; most of the material is contemporaneous, or nearly so, with the events described. Further, it comes from a period in Israel's history, the Monarchy, when the social institutions possessed the personnel, techniques, and materials for preserving records of events. With the book of Judges the situation is quite different. The author lived long after the events related, as Judg. 21:25 reveals. It was further a period of struggle and transition with great social upheaval and, at times, virtual anarchy. Under such conditions knowledge of the past is preserved only in scattered, almost haphazard, fashion. The author of Judges, perforce, resorts to a schematization (2:11-19) and shapes all his historical data by this theological framework. See H. Renckens, *Israel's Concept of the Beginning*, pp. 20-31.

81. To others with differing purposes, it may seem at times as if they have distorted, but this is a matter of viewpoint. See further J.R. Porter, "Old Testament Historiography," pp. 125ff. in G.W. Anderson, ed., *Tradition and Interpretation*.

death (ch. 23) he took another wife who bore numerous sons, and then he died at 175.

Some traditions are exceedingly difficult to harmonize with history. Both Midian and Ishmael are Joseph's great-uncles, yet the Midianites and Ishmaelites appear in his boyhood as caravan merchants plying their trade between Transjordan and Egypt (37:26-28). Amalek is the grandson of Esau (36:12), Abraham's grandson, yet in Abraham's day the Amalekites were settled in southern Palestine (14:7).

These data are a problem only if these cycles are interpreted as history as currently defined. Rather, their primary purpose is theological, as demonstrated by their very opening statement, which places God's promises in bold relief through the call of Abraham (12:1-3). The succeeding chapters are dominated by these promises and are intended to show how God brought them to pass in spite of Abraham's lack of an heir (see below, p. 112). This kind of "history writing" must be recognized as the "remembered past"—the folk memory of a people. The distinction between this and the history writing of Israel's monarchy is not in the event's historical reality but in the manner of its transmission. The centuries have been bridged by oral tradition.[82] In unsophisticated societies and among largely illiterate people, oral tradition is far more precise and tenacious than can be imagined by the modern western reader.[83] Furthermore, the patriarchal culture provided an ideal situation for the trustworthy and accurate transmission of tradition: it was characterized by a closed social sphere bound by ties of blood and religion (originally a single family, later a numerous people) and held together continually by forces of isolation and oppression from without. The patriarchal narratives, then, are popular tradition, kept alive over centuries by the collective memory of the people of Israel and the strands then woven together by the gifted artistry of a few master storytellers.

RELIGION OF THE PATRIARCHS

It is not possible to gather from the narratives of Gen. 12–50 a complete picture of the religious beliefs and practices of the patriarchs. Nonetheless, enough information can be gathered to give a general description and set their religion in its cultural context, given the rediscovery of the historical and cultural background of the patriarchal age.[84]

---

82. There seems to be nothing against the hypothesis that these traditions were first put into writing in Moses' time (and likely at his instigation). In view of the fact that various contracts, particularly marriage contracts, are of great antiquity, it is not unreasonable to suppose some written documents. Further, the widespread use of patronymics (Abram ben Terah, etc.) makes the recording of genealogical lists relatively easy.

83. On the tenacity of oral tradition, see Albright, *From the Stone Age to Christianity*, pp. 64-76, esp. 72ff.

84. For a short but thorough recent treatment, see Wenham, *Essays on the Patriarchal Narratives*, pp. 157-188. See also de Vaux, *Early History*, pp. 267-287.

The Bible clearly indicates that the heritage Abraham received from his immediate ancestors was polytheism. Josh. 24:2f. reads:

> "Your fathers lived of old beyond the Euphrates, Terah, the father of Abraham and of Nahor; and they served other gods"

(cf. also Josh. 24:14; Gen. 31:19-35, 53; 35:2). Abraham's religious experience cannot be traced, for the Bible tells almost nothing about his early beliefs. It does stress the new intervention in human affairs that God's call of Abraham in 12:1-3 represents. Although Abraham still moved in the religious milieu of his day, his departure for Canaan at God's bidding was also a departure from his polytheistic past to single-minded devotion to the one God who revealed himself to him. The patriarchs each worshiped a God who appeared to them, chose them, and promised to be with them (12:1-3; 15:1-6, 17; 28:11-15). Each in turn chose this God as his family's patron and called him by a special name indicating a close personal tie between the clan father and his God: "the God of Abraham," "the God of Isaac," and "the God of Jacob" (24:12; 28:13; 31:42, 53; cf. Exod. 3:6), and, as well, "the God of Nahor" (31:53).[85] He is called also "the Kinsman [usually translated "Fear"] of Isaac" (31:42, 53) and "the Mighty One of Jacob" (49:24). This close personal tie is revealed by the title "the God of my/your father" (26:24; 31:42, 53; 32:9; 49:25; and esp. Exod. 3:6). God was patron deity of the patriarch's clan, as clearly seen in Gen. 31:36-55, where Jacob swears by the Kinsman (or Fear) of Isaac, and Laban by the God of Nahor. This terminology has close parallels in the Cappadocian and Mari texts[86] as well as in Arabic and Aramean texts from the early Christian centuries.[87] This God of the clan blesses the patriarch (12:1-3; 26:3f.) with the promise of the land of Canaan and innumerable descendants (12:2, 7; 13:14-17; 15:4f., 18; 26:3f.; 28:13f.). He protects and saves (19:29), and can be called by name and petitioned (18:22-33): he punishes evil (38:7) yet has regard for the just (18:25).

The chief means by which God sets up and normalizes such a relationship is through his covenant. God first established his covenant with Abraham in ch. 15, sealing and ratifying it in a solemn and mysterious ceremony (vv. 7-21) in which he placed himself under oath by passing between the halves of the slain animals in the form of a firebrand and smoking furnace, ominous symbols

---

85. The fact that God is also called the "God of Nahor" should help those so familiar with the biblical terminology that they do not recognize "God of Abraham, Isaac, and Jacob" as a special title.

86. See Bright, *History*, p. 98. The phrase also occurs in the Amarna letters (fourteenth century); see de Vaux, "El et Baal, le dieu des pères et Yahweh," *Ugaritica VI* (1969): 504.

87. Another measure of this personal relationship can be seen in a class of "sentence names" where kinship terms, such as *'ab* "father" and *'aḥ* "brother," serve as epithets for the divine being (e.g., *Abiram* equals "My [Divine] Father is Exalted"). See Bright, *History*, p. 99.

borrowed from magical ritual.[88] God here symbolically brought himself under a curse should he violate his promise.[89]

This means that God is a personal God, whose nature it is to associate with persons. This is doubly significant since the Canaanite gods were primarily associated with places. But whether or not patriarchal belief can be called monotheism is a debate foreign to Old Testament thought. God certainly was conceived by the patriarchs as one God; Isaac worshiped the God of his father (26:23ff.), as did Jacob (31:5, 42, 53). Thus the same conception was transmitted from generation to generation. This God is unique, without colleagues or consort, so Jacob's family put away the strange gods they brought from Mesopotamia (35:2). Patriarchal belief is much more explicit in what it affirms than in what it denies, so perhaps with H.H. Rowley it may be called a "practical monotheism."[90]

About patriarchal religious life and worship the texts give only sparse information. They prayed (25:21), often prostrating themselves in the common Near Eastern manner (17:3; 24:52). They built altars and made sacrifices (12:7; 22:13; 31:54), but at no special place and with no official priesthood. Worship was less a matter of precise format and ceremony than a relation between God and human beings. Thus the patriarchs' religion did not differ so much from that of their contemporaries in outward form but rather in the conception of God and in the close personal relationship between God and those whom he called.

THEOLOGY OF THE NARRATIVES

Patriarchal history proper begins with the call and election of Abraham in 12:1-3. The call is abrupt and terse, as it is intended to be. It catches Abraham in mid-course, with no indication of time, place, or means of communication, and with no identification of Abraham beyond the few brief genealogical and familial facts of the preceding verses. This abrupt new beginning throws the call itself into stark relief, showing that here is a passage of programmatic significance for the whole of the patriarchal history.

Yahweh said to Abram:
"Go forth from your native land
And from your father's home
To a land that I will show you.

---

88. See Speiser, Genesis, Anchor Bible (Garden City: 1964), pp. 113f.

89. See the parallel passage in Jer. 34:19ff. The literal meaning of the Hebrew phrase "to make a covenant" is "to *cut* a covenant." The same idiom is found in a fifteenth-century text from Qatna. Slaying an animal to effect a covenant was common among the Amorites from Mari, where "to slay a donkey" was idiomatic for "to enter into a covenant."

90. *Worship in Ancient Israel* (Philadelphia: 1967), p. 21.

I will make of you a great nation,
   Bless you, and make great your name,
So be a blessing.

I will bless those who bless you,
   And curse him who curses you;
And through you shall bless themselves
   All the communities on earth." (12:1-3, lit.)[91]

This universal promise stands as the missing word of grace at the end of the primeval prologue and the answer to the disturbing questions about God's relationship to his scattered humanity raised thereby. The choice and blessing of Abraham and the unconditional promises of land and nationhood in vv. 1f. have as their ultimate goal v. 3, the great prospect that all communities of earth will gain blessing through him. Here at the beginning of redemptive history is already a word about the end of its course: the salvation promised Abraham ultimately will embrace all mankind. God has not dismissed the human family in wrath forever but now acts anew to heal the breach that sin has placed between him and his world. Thus, in a carefully constructed and unobtrusive way, the author brings together the primeval prologue and the history of redemption in a relationship of problem and solution of utmost importance for understanding all of Scripture.

But the passage is also of programmatic significance for understanding the stories of the patriarchs that follow. It reveals that their theme throughout is the progress, vicissitudes, and ultimate victorious fulfillment of those promises which here stand like a rubric at their beginning. The author does not give a biography; he teaches theology, with various themes woven through his stories.

Election and Promises of God. When the significance of Abraham's call is seen, the point of the narrative flow becomes transparent. Abraham is to be a great nation (12:2) but Sarah is barren (11:30); the land belongs to his descendants (12:7), but the Canaanites occupy it (v. 6). At the beginning the narrator consciously juxtaposes God's promise and Abraham's circumstances; this problem is the overarching, all-consuming interest of chs. 12–21. The promise is stated in the most extravagant way—Abraham's descendants are to be "as the dust of the earth" (13:16) and as numerous as the stars in heaven (15:5). And Abraham, childless, follows stratagem after stratagem. He adopts a slave born in his own house (15:2f.). Sarah, to protect her position as his wife, provides her maid Hagar as a secondary wife, through which union Ishmael is born (ch. 16). But neither attempt fulfills God's promise of a son through Sarah (15:4; 17:18f.). Finally, when old age makes the promise seem impossible in human terms, "the Lord visited Sarah as he had said, and the Lord did to Sarah as he had promised" (21:1). Isaac is born.

---

91. The translation is that of Speiser, *Genesis*, the strophic structure follows that of J. Muilenburg, "Abraham and the Nations," *Interp* 19 (1965): 391.

The same promise is reaffirmed to each of the patriarchal generations thereafter: to Isaac (26:2-4); to Jacob at Bethel as he leaves Canaan for fear of Esau, having stolen his birthright (28:13f.); again to Jacob at Bethel upon his return (35:11f.); and to Joseph and his sons (48:1-6).

That this is the major, overarching theme can also be seen in the way it is set forth as fulfilled in God's deliverance of Israel from Egypt:

> I also established my covenant with them [the patriarchs], to give them the land of Canaan, . . . and I have remembered my covenant. . . . I will redeem you with an outstretched arm. . . . And I will bring you into the land which I swore to give to Abraham, to Isaac, and to Jacob. (Exod. 6:4-8)

Thus the patriarchal period of redemptive history is the time of God's choice (election) of Abraham and his line and of the promise. Fulfillment of that promise seems strangely postponed, however, for the land was possessed by the Canaanites.[92] All the land Abraham and his immediate descendants ever possessed was the field and cave of Machpelah (Gen. 23), where Abraham (25:7-10), Isaac (35:27-29), and Jacob (49:29-31) were buried. Only in death were they sojourners no longer. And at the end of the patriarchal period, they were no longer even sojourners in the land, but had removed to Egypt.

The story of Joseph provides the first stage in the transition from a semi-nomadic, patriarchal family to an independent nation, in keeping with the promise. The favorite son, badly spoiled, is hated by his brothers, sold into slavery, and taken to Egypt. There his virtue, wisdom, and grace quickly establish him, then get him in trouble (chs. 37–39). A God-given ability to interpret dreams brings Joseph to Pharaoh's attention, and his interpretation of the famine dreams and his wise counsel lead to high position (chs. 40–41). This, in turn, opens the way for Joseph to provide for his own family and bring them to Egypt (chs. 42–47). This carefully-constructed story, so different in form from the Abraham and Jacob story cycles, is one long lesson—God's providence brings to nought the plots of men and turns their evil intent to his own ends. This lesson is explicitly stated in 50:20.

The result of Joseph's betrayal is the first step in the creation of the chosen people. The "children of Israel" are now an isolated and protected community, dwelling in the land of Goshen (generally identified as the northeastern Nile delta). This theme of "salvation" (the "survival of a numerous people," 50:20) looks forward to the Exodus (and ultimately to God's final deliverance through Christ). But now Israel, for a long time, has the opportunity to grow in number while retaining its identity. The promise of land and nationhood will wait to be fulfilled specifically through God's dramatic redemption from slavery in Egypt and the taking of Canaan under Joshua.

---

92. A favorite phrase for the land is "the land of your sojourning," Gen. 17:8; 28:4; 37:1; 47:9. The verb translated "sojourning" comes from the same root as gēr "resident alien."

But beyond these most general terms, the cycles of stories, coming from many different backgrounds, are used to teach numerous other theological truths. Only two of the more important can be touched upon here.

Faith and Righteousness. In the stories of Abraham, as noted, the promise of innumerable descendants is reduced to the single, absorbing question of one son, and that fulfillment is strangely, almost perversely, postponed. Very clearly the point of the stories is Abraham's faith, as seen in the account of his call. The summons to Abraham is radical: he is to abandon all his roots—land, kindred, and immediate family (12:1)[93]—for a most uncertain destination, "a land that I will show you." After the call, the narrator presents Abraham's response in terse and utter simplicity: "So Abraham went as the Lord told him" (v. 4). Abraham is presented as a paradigm of faith; the first thing said about him is his obedience and trust in the God who called him. That the author wrestles with the question of faith (and its relationship to righteousness) can be seen also in 15:6: "And he [Abraham] put his faith in the Lord; and he reckoned it to him as righteousness." The importance of this verse is signaled in that it is not part of the narrative of what happened between God and Abraham (vv. 1-5), but is the narrator's summarizing word that Abraham's righteousness consisted in his trusting—having faith in—God's promise.

The high point in the account of Abraham's faith is ch. 22, the so-called sacrifice of Isaac. Although the story once may have proscribed child sacrifice in Israel, that is not its present purpose. It is not the story of the "sacrifice of Isaac" but the "testing of Abraham," as the narrator himself indicates (v. 1). Told with consummate skill, it is a haunting and mysterious story of a situation which demands of Abraham almost incredible trust: he is called to an obedience which jeopardizes the patriarchal promise, not only should he prove unfaithful but also should he obey the demand for the life of his only son. The reader is cast back and forth between Abraham the father, who faces unspeakable tragedy, and Abraham the monster, who raises the knife over Isaac's prostrate form.[94] Abraham can meet the test in only one way—total and complete faith in the God who promised him Isaac and fulfilled the promise when it was beyond human means. Abraham does meet the test and becomes the model of the faith that God asks of his people.

As noted in 15:6, Abraham's righteousness consisted in the fact of his faith in God's promise. If righteousness is conceived, as in modern western society, as conformity to an abstract moral code, this equation is indeed hard to understand. However, righteousness in the Bible is not a norm-prescribing ethics,

---

93. Modern westerners, who live in a mobile society where the bonds of family and family residence are broken so easily, need to recall that such mobility was almost impossible for ancient peoples, firmly rooted in a patriarchal and patrilocal culture. A text at Nuzi tells of a man who totally disinherits two of his sons because they moved to another town!

94. See G.W. Coats, "Abraham's Sacrifice of Faith," *Interp* 27 (1973): 387-400.

but faithfulness to a relationship. The righteous man is faithful to the claims of all his relationships.[95] Therefore the significance of the passage is that a person's righteousness in relation to God is fulfilled when that relationship is characterized by faith (see Rom. 1:16f.; 4; Gal. 3:6-9).

The transition from sovereign election to the historical realization of God's covenant people, however, is not simple, historically or theologically, as the Genesis account affirms. Tensions arise out of the nature of humankind vis-à-vis the sovereign God. While evident in all biblical characters, these tensions are most dramatic in the life of Jacob. If the Abraham narratives present a picture of the man of faith scaling the heights of trust in God who called him, those about Jacob present a man of very "worldly" character—the paradigm of guile and self-reliance. A supplanter from birth (25:26), he is a crafty, scheming individual, remarkably like his mother (27:5-17, 41-45). His twenty-year service with his uncle Laban is a continual struggle between two crafty men, each scheming to get the better of the other. Finally, at the Jabbok on his return to Canaan, Jacob meets his match when he struggles with the "man" he later recognizes as a divine visitation. Only by God's direct action, elsewhere hidden in these stories in the "unedifying manifestations of human nature,"[96] does Jacob the Supplanter become Israel the Prevailer (32:28).

The accounts of Jacob reconciled with Esau (33:1-11), chagrined by his sons' behavior (34:30), revealed as faithful by the discarding of the idols (35:2-5), heartbroken by the loss of his favorite son, Joseph (37:33-35), and finally, obtaining the Lord's permission to go down into Egypt (46:1-5) are vignettes of the person who is mastered by God.[97] His dying request (49:29-32) that his body be buried in the cave of Machpelah completes the story, assuring that Jacob places himself within the promise God made long before to Abraham.

Covenant. Another element of great theological importance in Gen. 12–50 is the covenant God makes with Abraham in chs. 15 and 17. Covenant is one of the primary ideas in all of Scripture. In the ancient world it brought into being a relationship or arrangement that did not exist by normal ties of blood or social requirements; it is used in the same way when adapted to the divine-human covenants of Scripture. Covenant, then, is the establishment of a particular relationship or the commitment to a particular course of action, not naturally existing, which is sanctioned by an oath normally sworn in a solemn ceremony of ratification.[98] In ch. 15 God condescends to place himself

---

95. These include conformity to norms or laws, since faithfulness to one's relationship to the community to which he or she belongs demands basic obedience to that society's moral and legal codes. On the concept of righteousness, see G. von Rad, *Old Testament Theology*, trans. D.M.G. Stalker, 1 (New York: 1962) 370ff.

96. *Ibid.*, 1:171.

97. The biblical account indicates that Jacob "prevailed" (32:28). It is clear, however, that God really prevailed, not only in the change in Jacob's life, but in the very name "Israel"—"God shall prevail."

98. See M.G. Kline, *By Oath Consigned* (Grand Rapids: 1968), pp. 16ff.

symbolically under a curse in order to affirm to Abraham the certainty of his promises. It is God who takes the oath; nothing is required of Abraham (except the rite of circumcision [ch. 17] as a sign of the covenant). In this way the covenant with Abraham differs from that with Moses (see below, pp. 143f.). In the Abrahamic covenant God lays himself under obligation; in the Mosaic covenant, Israel, recipient of the covenant, is required to take the oath and thereby is placed under stringent stipulations. These two covenants are radically different in their results. Since God solemnly puts himself on oath to provide land and nationhood to Abraham's descendants, this is a covenant of promise, a divine dispensation of grace and blessing that depends only on the unchangeable character of the One who makes it.

Thus in Gen. 12–50 are presented the basic facts of the beginning of redemptive history: God has freely chosen one man and his descendants through whom "all the families of the earth shall find blessing" (12:3), and he solemnly promises him land and nationhood. How this is to be effected and in what terms it will come, however, waits to be disclosed. But these chapters also say much about the style of life that must characterize those who respond to God's call and belong by commitment to his covenant people: it is to be a life of trust and faith in him who calls. Indeed, the book ends with the scene set for the next act in the drama of redemption, deliverance from slavery in Egypt.

FOR FURTHER READING

Bailey, L. *The Pentateuch*. Nashville: 1981.

Delitzsch, F. *A New Commentary on Genesis*. 2 vols. 5th ed. Edinburgh: 1899. (Outdated in literary treatment and Near Eastern background, but a profound theological study.)

Hillers, D.R. *Covenant: The History of a Biblical Idea*. Baltimore: 1969. (Contrasts and compares Abrahamic and Mosaic covenants.)

Kidner, D. *Genesis: An Introduction and commentary*. Chicago: 1967.

LaSor, W.S. "Egypt." *ISBE* 2 (1982): 29-47. (Succinct presentation of historical background.)

Millard, A.R., and Wiseman, D.J., eds. *Essays on the Patriarchal Narratives*. Leicester: 1980. (Helpful discussion of recent issues relative to historicity, literary nature, and interpretation.)

Skinner, J. *A Critical and Exegetical Commentary on the Book of Genesis*. 2nd ed. ICC. Edinburgh: 1930. (A thorough technical presentation of the classical literary-critical position.)

Thompson, J. Arthur. "Covenant (OT)." *ISBE* 1 (1979): 790-793.

Von Rad, G. *Genesis*. OTL. Philadelphia: 1972.

Wiseman, D.J. "Assyria." *ISBE* 1 (1979): 332-341. (Succinct presentation of historical background.)

_____. "Babylonia." *ISBE* 1 (1979): 391-402. (Succinct presentation of historical background.)

CHAPTER 9

EXODUS:
HISTORICAL BACKGROUND

THE Exodus is the primary event of Old Testament redemptive history, the means by which God brought to historical fulfillment his promises to the patriarchs of land and nationhood. But for all its importance, to fix it in place and time is a difficult task, due in part to the book's literary nature. It never names the Pharaoh with whom Moses contended, nor is any other person or event recorded to connect it with certainty to the known history of Egypt and Palestine for the period within which it must lie. Because the evidence is all indirect, the historical question must be dealt with before turning to the contents and theology of the book.

HISTORICAL BACKGROUND OF THE PERIOD

To fix the Exodus in time and place one must first become familiar with the history of the period within which it took place—the heyday of the Egyptian empire. For continuity and completeness the following review will begin with the end of the "patriarchal age," *ca.* 1550 B.C., and continue until *ca.* 1200, when Israel already had entered Palestine. During this period, roughly coinciding with the Late Bronze Age in Palestine, Egypt dominated the ancient world and Palestine lay within the bounds of that empire.

Rise of the Egyptian Empire. In the middle of the second millennium, a whole series of relatively new states and empires was developing in the ancient Near East.[1] By *ca.* 1550 the Hurrian state of Mitanni lay stretched across northwest Mesopotamia, from western Syria to the foothills of the Zagros mountains in the east. It was apparently this alliance of Hurrian peoples and the Indo-Europeans who ruled them that revolutionized ancient warfare by developing the chariot and the composite bow. Northwest of Mitanni, in the eastern

---

1. See Ch. 8.

reaches of Asia Minor, were the Hittites, slowly recovering from the period of weakness into which they had fallen after their raid on Babylon. To the east of Mitanni lay Assyria, totally under Mitannian control, their capital despoiled by the Mitannian kings—for which they were later to exact a brutal revenge. The principal role in the drama about to unfold, however, was to go to Egypt, just emerging from the dominance of the Hyksos. When the Eighteenth Dynasty, under Ahmosis, threw off the Hyksos yoke, Egypt determined to secure its borders by defeating the enemy in his own territory, and embarked on the subjugation of Asia.

Even though they reached the Euphrates under Thutmosis I, the early Eighteenth-Dynasty pharaohs led mostly punitive expeditions, since Egypt initially was engrossed in reconstruction at home and the subjugation of Nubia and the Sudan in the south. However, the situation changed under Thutmosis III (1490-1436), one of Egypt's ablest rulers. In a famous battle at Megiddo, *ca.* 1468, he defeated the Hyksos, centered at Kadesh on the Orontes in southern Syria. In subsequent campaigns he crushed all resistance and extended an empire as far north as Aleppo. Inevitably this expansion brought Egypt into conflict with Mitanni over control of Syria. War between the two states continued intermittently for nearly fifty years until, under Thutmosis IV (*ca.* 1412-1403), a treaty was concluded. Without doubt both sides were motivated by the resurgent Hittites, now pressing into northern Syria.

Nonetheless, for some fifty years the arrangement worked well, particularly for Egypt, now at the zenith of power. Amenophis III (1403-1364), finding annual campaigns no longer necessary to secure the empire, turned to the pursuit of pleasure and luxury. He engaged in a building program aimed at self-glorification of a sort previously unsurpassed, and an age of imperial magnificence ensued.

A remarkable revolution occurred under Amenophis IV (1364-1317), a worshiper of Aten (the Solar Disk), whom he proclaimed the only god. (The Aten cult, if not a strict monotheism, does seem to have approached it.) To extricate himself from the growing power of the priests of Amon, and for religious reasons, he changed his name to Akhenaten (the Splendor of Aten), left Thebes, and built a new capital, Akhetaten, at modern Tell el-Amarna. It was there that the Amarna letters were found in 1887. Part of the official court archives apparently brought from Thebes to the new capital, the tablets include letters to Amenophis III and IV from most of the important states of the day, including Babylon, Assyria, Mitanni, and the Hittites; but the correspondence is principally from Egyptian vassals in Palestine, including Byblos, Megiddo, Shechem, and Jerusalem. These letters throw a brilliant light on the history and society of the "Amarna Age" and reveal that Palestine was organized into administrative districts with resident commissioners in garrison towns, such as Gaza, which were also centers of provisions and supplies for the Egyptian troops. Yet the city-states were allowed considerable local control and autonomy. By the mid-fourteenth century, Palestine could be held by small garrisons of Egyptian soldiers stationed in the administrative centers.

Egypto-Hittite War. Amenophis III's magnificence and Akhenaten's religious interests boded ill, however, for the Egyptian empire in Asia. The Amarna letters show Palestine in virtual anarchy, with individual rulers vying for power and often in open revolt against Egyptian authority. Loyal vassals appeal eloquently to Pharaoh for aid, apparently in vain. But if disorder reigned in Palestine, Egyptian control in Syria ceased altogether, and Mitanni was left to face the resurgent Hittites alone. About 1375 Suppiluliuma came to the Hittite throne and proceeded to carve out an empire in Syria. In a lightning attack he crossed the Euphrates and totally defeated the Hurrian state, placing a vassal on the throne. The northeastern part of the empire was taken by Assyria, now reviving under Assur-uballit I (*ca.* 1356-1321), who inflicted fearful vengeance on the Hurrian cities. By 1350 Mitanni was no more, and the Hittites controlled sections of Syria that brought them into direct contact with Egyptian territory.

In Egypt the once proud Eighteenth Dynasty was utterly ineffective. Although a measure of control at home was effected by Horemheb, last of the dynasty, Egyptian control over Asia virtually ceased. But the Hittites had not yet consolidated their control of Syria and were concerned about a resurgent Assyria, constantly seeking to move west. Consequently, Egypt was able to recuperate under the Nineteenth-Dynasty pharaohs. Horemheb was succeeded by one of his generals, Rameses I, a descendant of the old Hyksos kings, who situated his capital at Avaris in the northeastern delta. His son Seti I set out to recoup Egypt's losses in Asia. He quickly gained control of Palestine and on his fourth campaign claims to have defeated a Hittite army under Muwattalis. Although this victory probably represents only a skirmish, full-scale war broke out under Seti's son Rameses II, who reigned sixty-seven years (1290-1224). In his fifth year Rameses II mounted a major attack on the Hittites, who ambushed him near Kadesh on the Orontes. Despite Rameses' personal valor and the timely arrival of reinforcements from the coast, the Egyptians were forced to retreat, and the Hittites penetrated Palestine as far as Damascus. Revolts against Egyptian rule flared as far south as Ashkelon, and Rameses took five years to restore order and regain control of northern Palestine. Although he occasionally raided Hittite territory, he never again seriously menaced Syria. In Rameses' twenty-first year, after Hattusilis III (1275-1250) took the Hittite throne, the two concluded a peace treaty. Fostered in part by exhaustion from the long strife, the treaty was also encouraged by the external problems each faced. The Hittites were continuously menaced by Assyria from the east and found it increasingly difficult to maintain themselves in Asia Minor against the pressure of the Indo-European peoples from the west. Egypt also faced continuous pressure from the Peoples of the Sea, Aegeo-Cretan tribes that had begun moving upon them from the west in the early years of Rameses II, a movement undoubtedly related to that faced by the Hittites in Asia Minor.

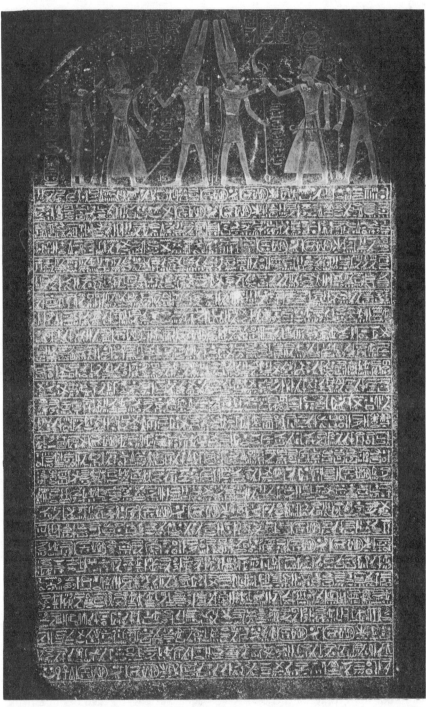

Israel stele of Merneptah (ca. 1220 B.C.), containing a hymn of victory which mentions Israel. (Egyptian Museum, Cairo)

In the main, though, Rameses II's concluding years were a time of peace and colossal building activity. He spent much of his time in the various palaces he built in the northeast delta, his favorite being Per-Rameses, "the House of Rameses," identified either with Tanis or Qantîr a few miles south (cf. Exod. 1:11).[2]

Peoples of the Sea. At the great battle of Kadesh in Rameses II's fifth year, both the Egyptians and Hittites used as mercenary troops some of the same Aegeo-Cretan "Peoples of the Sea," whom they had encountered in battles fought to defend their empires. These groups were but forerunners of a vast movement soon to inundate the coast of Asia Minor, Palestine, and Egypt, and to whom both the Hittites and Nineteenth-Dynasty Egypt were to succumb.

When Rameses II died, his thirteenth son Merneptah succeeded him. In his fifth year *ca.* 1220, Merneptah faced a horde of Peoples of the Sea who, together with Libyans, moved on Egypt from the west, along the coast of North Africa. In a fierce battle he defeated them and commemorated the event with a Hymn of Victory inscribed on a stele. This hymn, also celebrating an earlier campaign in Palestine, contains the first extrabiblical mention of Israel. It states: "Israel is laid waste, her seed is not." Merneptah died in 1211, and the Nineteenth Dynasty died out in internal chaos and disunity. Apparently even a Syrian usurper controlled Egypt for a time. Egyptian control of Palestine effectively had come to an end.

If Egypt struggled for its life, the Hittites met absolute disaster. They had concluded a treaty with Egypt in Rameses II's twenty-first year, *ca.* 1269, due in part to the pressure of Indo-European peoples to the west, undoubtedly related to the Peoples of the Sea. During the last decades of the thirteenth century these peoples poured across Asia Minor and shortly after 1200 erased the Hittites from the pages of history.[3] From Asia Minor they pushed by land and sea in wave after wave down the Palestinian coast to threaten once again Egypt's very existence.

Egypt's decline at the end of the Nineteenth Dynasty was reversed by Sethnakht and his son Rameses III (*ca.* 1183-1152), who inaugurated the Twentieth Dynasty. Early in his reign Rameses III regained control of Palestine, at least as far as Beth-shean (also called Beth-shan) in the Jezreel valley. But between his fifth and eleventh years, he faced a massive onslaught of Sea Peoples who came overland through Palestine; and he barely managed to keep Egypt from being overwhelmed. Exhausted by the struggle and racked by internal weakness

---

2. See C. deWit and K.A. Kitchen, "Raamses, Rameses," in J.D. Douglas–N. Hillyer, eds., *The Illustrated Bible Dictionary* (Wheaton: 1980) 3:1313f.; R. de Vaux, *Early History*, p. 325.

3. Except for occasional mention in the Bible of their cultural (if not racial) survivors in North Syria, they were lost to historical memory until excavations by the Deutsche Orient-Gesellschaft early in this century.

and dissension under the successors of Rameses III, Egypt's days of empire came
to an end.

Unable to take Egypt, elements of the Sea Peoples fell back upon Palestine
and occupied large areas of the coastal plain. Among them Egyptian sources
name the *Peleset*, unquestionably the Philistines.[4] Thus the nation that was to
mount a major threat to Israel's existence and trigger the rise of the Israelite
monarchy in the time of Saul and David arrived in Palestine at approximately
the same time as Israel.

Although the arrival of the Peoples of the Sea introduced new ethnic
groups into Canaan, it did not materially alter the culture or social structures.
Canaan continued to be organized in small city-states, the majority located on
the coastal plain and in the valley of Jezreel; the heavily-forested, mountainous
interior was only sparsely populated. The chief ethnic group was the Canaanites,
indigenous to the area since the third millennium.

Some notable features of this complex historical scene should be stressed.
First, Israel moved into a very advanced and cosmopolitan world when they left
Egypt. During the period of the Egyptian empire extensive and unprecedented
international contacts occurred in the whole of the ancient Near East, producing the cultural diffusion and cross-fertilization that J. H. Breasted termed the
"First Internationalism." In the Amarna letters Egyptians correspond with Babylonians, Assyrians, Mitannians, Hittites, Arzawans, Cypriots, and Canaanites,
primarily in an international Akkadian dialect that was the *lingua franca*. This
correspondence required a highly organized system of embassies in continued
and frequent contact through ambassadors, as well as scribal departments, with
scribes able to function in several languages, plus the means to educate them.[5]
The power politics of the day necessitated international alliances and an elab-

---

4. As indicated, the Sea Peoples were of Aegeo-Cretan origin. Tentative identification of their names with ethnic groups or places known elsewhere gives tantalizing
evidence of their migration and/or origin. Thus, Hittite and Egyptian sources for the
battle of Kadesh list *Luka*, who can be equated with the Lycians, a people in south-
central Asia Minor, and the *Sherden*, who perhaps later gave their name to Sardinia.
Merneptah and Rameses III mention the *Aqiwasha*, probably the Achaeans, known from
Homer and called the Ahhiyawa in Hittite sources; the *Turusha*, connected with the
Tyrsenians (or Etruscans) of Italy; and the *Tsikal*, who perhaps gave their name to Sicily.
This irruption of Aegean peoples very likely is related to events connected with the end
of the Mycenaean period in Greece, reflected in part in the Trojan war of Homer's *Iliad*.
See W.F. Albright, "Some Oriental Glosses on the Homeric Problem," *AJA* 54 (1950):
162-176. On the origin of the Philistines and the course of their occupation of Palestine,
see Albright, "Syria, the Philistines and Phoenicia," in *CAH* II/1 (1971): 24-33.

5. The Amarna letters contain one long letter completely in Hurrian (except for
the stylized opening lines), plus two shorter ones in a Hittite dialect, all in the international cuneiform script used for diplomatic correspondence. Several have marginal
notes in Egyptian hieroglyphics giving circumstances of the letter's arrival, one indicating
that it is a copy made for the archives (letter 27). At Ugarit, numerous copies of
vocabularies have been found, one in four languages: Akkadian, Sumerian, Ugaritic,
and Hurrian.

orate system of treaties to maintain them. For the first time the principle of law was extended beyond the boundaries of a nation or empire into the sphere of international relations. It was also a period of extensive identification of one nation's gods with similar deities in foreign pantheons. The Sumero-Akkadian gods were adopted into the pantheons of Hurrians, Hittites, Amorites, and Canaanites. The grain god Dagon originated in northwestern Mesopotamia among the Amorites, yet appears in the Bible as the principal god of the Philistines in southwestern Palestine.[6] Literary diffusion was extensive and widespread. Akkadian myths and epics were translated into Hurrian and Hittite and appear as school texts in the Amarna letters, used by Egyptian scribes to learn Akkadian. The Hurrians were apparently especially active in spreading Akkadian literature to Asia Minor and Syria-Palestine.[7] A Hurrian hymn to the goddess Nikkal has been found in Ugaritic; in the Amarna tablets from Tyre two Egyptian poems are translated into Akkadian; and the Canaanite myth of Astarte and the Sea is found in Egyptian hieroglyphics.[8] At Ugarit West Semitic scribes wrote religious texts in Hurrian for a Hurrian clientele. Thus, Israel entered a world in intimate contact that had produced a cross-fertilization and synthesis of culture hitherto unknown.

One quite remarkable development of this cultural situation is the appearance of alphabetic writing among the Canaanites of Syria-Palestine. Although writing developed shortly before 3000 in both Mesopotamia and Egypt, neither progressed beyond the cumbersome and complicated syllabic and ideographic cuneiform and hieroglyphic systems, with their hundreds of different signs. Although culturally dependent and less advanced, the Canaanites nevertheless developed an alphabet with less than thirty symbols, the economy of which made general literacy ultimately possible. The earliest alphabetic script thus far known is the "proto-Sinaitic," developed by West Semitic tribes impressed into service by Egyptian mining expeditions to Sinai. Other obviously closely-related scripts have been found in isolated discoveries in Palestine, e.g., Gezer, Lachish, Shechem, and Megiddo. The forms of the letters were obviously influenced by Egyptian hieroglyphics. These scripts date from *ca.* 1700 to 1200, with the largest and most important corpus, the Sinai inscriptions, dating to 1550-1450.[9]

---

6. In Amarna letter 23, Tushratta the Indo-European king of Hurrian Mitanni announces his intention to send Ishtar of Nineveh, an Assyrian deity famous for her healing powers, to Egypt to Amenophis III, who is apparently ill.

7. See E.A. Speiser, "The Hurrian Participation in the Civilization of Mesopotamia, Syria and Palestine," pp. 244-269 in J.J. Finkelstein and M. Greenberg, eds., *Oriental and Biblical Studies* (Philadelphia: 1967).

8. On the extent and transmission of this cultural diffusion, including widespread evidence of contact with the Aegean world as well, see C.H. Gordon, *Before the Bible* (New York: 1962), esp. pp. 22-46.

9. See Albright, *The Proto-Sinaitic Inscriptions and Their Decipherment* (Cambridge, Mass.: 1969).

The most remarkable texts of this period yet discovered are tablets from the fourteenth century from the city-state of Ugarit, modern Ras Shamra on the North Syrian coast opposite Cyprus. The Ugaritians were Northwest Semites, closely related to their Canaanite neighbors to the south. Their texts are also alphabetic, but written on clay in a cuneiform script. Although deeply influenced by the writing techniques of the dominant culture—Egypt for the proto-Sinaitic alphabet and Mesopotamia for Ugarit—both Ugaritians and Canaanites broke radical new ground in adapting them to an alphabetic principle.

The Ugaritic texts preserve a rich religious and epic literature (as well as epistolary and administrative texts) whose contents have many parallels with Old Testament culture and institutions and are of utmost importance for documenting the Canaanite religion and culture extant in Palestine when Israel entered the land. Indeed, Israel appeared at the right time and place to inherit the maximum cultural legacy the ancient world had yet attained.

Finally, the struggle for world empire in the third quarter of the second millennium ended in the death or exhaustion of all combatants. Only Assyria loomed large briefly in the late thirteenth century, but that nation also soon slipped into a period of weakness, prolonged late in the second millennium by incursions of the Aramean peoples who then flooded Syria and northwest Mesopotamia. Such an outcome was most propitious for the life and development of the people of God in the new land and statehood into which he was about to thrust them. Actually, from this point in time no nation was able to pursue world empire with permanent results until the rise of the Neo-Assyrian empire under Tiglath-pileser III, who came to the throne in 745. The struggle for power at the end of the Bronze Age produced a political power vacuum that lasted more than four hundred years. During this time Israel lived as the people of God free from the threat of any world power. Indeed, by the end of this period, Israel had so violated their covenant relationship to God that the biblical writers interpreted this new surge of world empires in the mid-first millennium as his judgment upon Israel.

Does the eye of faith see too much when it views Israel's emergence precisely at this time of maximum cultural synthesis and flowering and the beginning of a period of international political calm as God's providential guidance of the forces of world history for the sake of redemptive history? It surely would seem not.

EVIDENCE FOR THE EXODUS

Because placing the Exodus historically within the general period just outlined is exceedingly difficult, even a review of the problems is impossible here, and a general presentation of the more important facts and conclusions must suffice.[10]

---

10. For a thorough review of earlier views, replete with bibliography, see H.H. Rowley, *From Joseph to Joshua* (London: 1950). More general is J. Bright, *History*, pp. 118-130. Also helpful for the student are C. deWit, *The Date and Route of the Exodus*

First, the fact of the Exodus is incontrovertible. Although no direct historical evidence exists for either the oppression in Egypt or the escape,[11] the indirect evidence is overwhelming.[12] The Joseph story authentically reflects Egyptian life, customs, literature (especially in the northeast delta region), and even official titles as known from Egyptian records,[13] lending great historical credence to the sojourn in Egypt. It is now known that great numbers of Semitic peoples were employed as state slaves on building projects near Thebes in the Eighteenth Dynasty and in the northeast delta during the Nineteenth Dynasty.[14] Several Israelite names of the period, especially in Moses' family, are authentically Egyptian.[15] Even the escape of subject peoples from a major state is not without analogy in the ancient world.[16] Further, throughout the whole Old Testament period Israel looked back to the Exodus as the constitutive event that made them the people of God. Psychologically, it is most improbable that the story would have been invented. The only possible explanation of all the relevant facts is that God did indeed intervene to save his people.

DATE OF THE EXODUS

Even though the Exodus was certainly the central fact of Israel's history, no final solution can yet be offered to the complex chronological and geographical problems involved.[17] Exactly when and where it took place cannot be stated with certitude. However, the general period that seems to fit best most of the biblical and extrabiblical evidence is the first half of the thirteenth century. The main arguments are as follows:

(1) The Israel stele of Merneptah indicates that Merneptah encountered

---

(London: 1960) and K.A. Kitchen, *Ancient Orient and Old Testament* (Chicago: 1966). pp. 57-75. See also T. Brisco, "Exodus, Route of," *ISBE 2* (1982): 238-241 and J.M. Miller, "The Israelite Occupation of Canaan," pp. 213-284 in J.H. Hayes and Miller, eds., *Israelite and Judaean History*.

11. In the nature of the case, probably none will be found. The Israelites in Egypt were despised state slaves. Ancient rulers either did not record their defeats or else reported them as victories (e.g., Ramesses II's account of the battle of Kadesh), and the escape of a group of state slaves is unlikely to have been recorded in any form that would be preserved for posterity.

12. See, for example, the recent treatment of this evidence by Albright, *Yahweh and the Gods of Canaan*, pp. 35-52, 153-182.

13. See the excellent presentation by G.E. Wright, *Biblical Archaeology* (Philadelphia: 1962), pp. 54-58.

14. See Albright, *Yahweh and the Gods of Canaan*, pp. 89ff.; and R. De Vaux, *Early History* 1:325-27.

15. Albright, *Yahweh and the Gods of Canaan*, pp. 165ff.

16. See Kitchen, "Exodus," *IBD*, p. 489. For a striking parallel in modern times, see de Vaux, *Early History*, p. 374.

17. As Kitchen points out, numerous Near Eastern chronological problems are just as impossible to solve definitively in the present state of knowledge as is the date of the Exodus, despite evidence contemporaneous with the events in question. An example is the vexed problem of the date of Hammurabi; *Ancient Orient and Old Testament*, p. 75, n. 64.

Israel in Palestine in his fifth year, *ca.* 1220. The Exodus must have taken place earlier.[18]

(2) The Israelites were used as slaves to build the store cities of Pithom and Raamses, according to Exod. 1:11. Although some question still remains as to the exact location of these cities in the northeast delta,[19] the possible sites are all original foundations of Nineteenth-Dynasty pharaohs and primarily the result of Rameses II's building activities. The Exodus, then, must have taken place after his ascension to the throne, *ca.* 1300.[20]

(3) Evidence from the period of the Israelites' journey through the wilderness and the Conquest suggests the same period. They were forced to detour around Edom and Moab (Num. 20:14-21). Archaeological surveys have been interpreted as suggesting that these kingdoms did not exist prior to *ca.* 1300.[21] Excavations have established that a number of the cities taken by Joshua were destroyed in the latter part of the thirteenth century and occupied very shortly thereafter by people whose material culture was significantly simpler and poorer. The principal sites involved are Lachish, Bethel, Hazor, Tell Beit Mirsim, and Tell el-Ḥesi.[22] Although no proof exists that the enemy who destroyed these cities was Israel, the general pattern fits the biblical conquest quite well.

(4) Contemporary Egyptian documents provide historical parallels. Texts from the time of Merneptah and Rameses II document the use of Semites as slaves (using the Egyptian term for 'Apiru) in their building projects; another

---

18. How much prior is an open question. The stele gives no indication when Merneptah clashed with Israelite forces (conceivably in Sinai). It often is noted that on the stele "Israel" is written with the determinative for "people" rather than for "country," indicating that Israel was not yet sedentary. However, Egyptologists have observed that the stele is written carelessly, not always using determinatives with precision. Hence, this argument carries little weight in the absence of other evidence. It should further be noted that this view tacitly assumes that the group Merneptah met was the same group that had been in Egypt. Although it is a natural assumption, there is no evidence that such is the case.

19. See Kitchen, *Ancient Orient and Old Testament*, pp. 57ff. and de Vaux, *Early History*, p. 325.

20. A precise date is not possible, since there is an uncertainty of some fourteen years in the date of Ramesses' accession. See K. Kitchen, *The Bible in Its World*, p. 144 note 46.

21. N. Glueck, *The Other Side of the Jordan* (1940; repr. Cambridge, Mass.: 1970), pp. 114-125. More recent discoveries, however, call into question Glueck's conclusions. An exploration of new sites, together with a re-examination of a number that Glueck explored, undertaken in 1978, gives evidence that there was no occupational gap in the central Moab plateau in the Late Bronze (1550/1500-1200) or Iron I (1200-1000) periods. On this basis no argument for any specific Exodus date can be supported by the pottery evidence from the Moabite plateau. See J.R. Kautz, "Tracking the Ancient Moabites," *BA* 44 (1981): 27-35. For a review of other discoveries that suggest the same conclusion, together with reappraisals of Glueck's methodology and conclusions, see J.J. Bimson, *Redating the Exodus and Conquest*. JSOTS 5 (1978): 70-74.

22. Wright, *Biblical Archaeology*, pp. 80-83. Tell Beit Mirsim usually is identified with biblical Debir, but a much more suitable candidate for Debir is now Khirbet Rabud; see M. Kochavi, "Khirbet Rabud = Debir," *Tel Aviv* 1 (1974): 2-33. Tell el-Ḥesi is usually identified with biblical Eglon. On the difficult question of the destruction of Jericho and Ai, see Kitchen, *Ancient Orient and Old Testament*, pp. 62-64.

concerns permission for nomadic groups of Shasu Bedouin from Edom to cross the line of border fortresses to the pools at Pithom (Eg. *Pr-Itm*).[23]

(5) This date accords well with the view that the most likely setting for Joseph and the descent into Egypt is the Hyksos period. According to Gen. 15:13, the time spent in Egypt, viewed in prospect, would be 400 years,[24] or according to Exod. 12:40, in retrospect, 430 years. Thus, if the Exodus occurred in the first half of the thirteenth century, the descent into Egypt would have taken place during the first half of the seventeenth century—in the Hyksos period.[25]

The principal objection on biblical grounds is that this date does not fit the 480 years that 1 Kgs. 6:1 gives between the Exodus and the foundation of Solomon's temple *ca.* 970. This calculation would place the Exodus in the mid-fifteenth century. However, the Old Testament, as an ancient Near Eastern book, does not necessarily use numbers in the same way as modern chronology. Thus, the 480 years can be understood as an "aggregate" or "round number," probably based on the total of twelve generations of 40 years each.[26]

Hence, most scholars have concluded that the date of 1300-1250 suits the majority of evidence better than any other.[27] On this basis the Pharaoh of the oppression would be Seti I (1305-1290) and the Pharaoh of the Exodus

---

23. *ANET*, p. 259a. Especially interesting is information about the careful watch kept on passage through the border fortresses and particularly an account of the pursuit of two fleeing slaves who escaped through the line of fortresses into the desert north of Migdol. The latter mentions Succoth (Eg. Theku), Etam, and Migdol in the same order as the biblical account. *ANET*, p. 259; Y. Aharoni, *The Land of the Bible*, pp. 178f.; and de Vaux, *Early History*, p. 378.

24. Gen. 15:16 states that the Israelites would return to Canaan in the fourth *dōr*, usually translated "generation." Four generations equivalent to four hundred years is highly problematical. However, Heb. *dōr* means lit. "cycle of time," i.e., "age, period," rather than having the technical force of English "generation." Ugaritic and Assyrian evidence now shows that the word indicated a span of eighty years or more. Kitchen, *Ancient Orient and Old Testament*, p. 54, esp. note 99.

25. Wright, *Biblical Archaeology*, pp. 56-58.

26. Evidence exists in ancient literature that chroniclers did use such "aggregate" figures based on a total of selected figures; see Kitchen, *Ancient Orient and Old Testament*, p. 74. It often has been noted that the chronology of the period of Judges and Samuel involves periods of forty, eighty, and twenty years assigned to various leaders, oppressors, and deliverers of Israel. When this pattern in Judges is added to the forty-year reigns of Moses, Eli, Saul (so in Josephus and Acts), David, and Solomon, it is easy to see how an approximate calculation of the time span could have arisen on the basis of twelve generations of forty years. See D.N. Freedman, "The Chronology of Israel and the Ancient Near East," in *BANE*, pp. 271 and esp. 295 note 16. The three hundred years of Judg. 11:26 must be understood in the same way.

27. However, for discussions that present cogent arguments for a date in the fifteenth century, see Bimson, *Redating the Exodus and Conquest*; and W.H. Shea, "Exodus, Date of," *ISBE* 2 (1981): 230-38. Bimson's study is a thorough and well-documented treatment of all the lines of evidence used to establish the thirteenth-century date. His fifteenth-century date is largely based upon lowering the date for the end of Middle Bronze II to 1450/1400. The viability of this redating remains to be seen. However, his critique of the evidence on which the thirteenth-century date is based clearly reveals the tenuous nature of that conclusion.

Ramesses II (1290-1224). Nonetheless, present information cannot attest with certainty that the Exodus took place during this period.

ROUTE OF THE EXODUS

No more certain is the route of the Exodus or the location of Mt. Sinai. Here too one can deal only with probabilities, since direct evidence is lacking. With increased knowledge of the topography of the northeast delta, a few of the sites mentioned in Exod. 12:37; 13:17–14:4 and Num. 33:5-8 can be located with some certainty (see Map, p. 129). Raamses, the starting point, is almost certainly to be located at Tanis or Qanṭir.[28] Succoth, the next stopping point, is usually identified with Eg. *Theku*, modern Tell el-Maskhuṭah in the Wâdī Tumilat, the valley forming the main route to the east from the Nile area. This area is usually identified with Goshen, where the Israelites settled in Joseph's day. The next three sites, Etham, Pi-hahiroth, and Migdol, are quite uncertain, with numerous locations proposed.[29] The name usually translated "Red Sea" means literally "Sea of Reeds"[30] and doubtless refers to one of the reed-filled, sweet-water marshes between and around Lake Menzaleh and the Bitter lakes to the south, along the present Suez canal. Although Egyptian and biblical texts refer to such marshy bodies,[31] the location referred to in Exod. 13:18; 15:4, 22; etc. cannot be fixed definitely by current knowledge of the locations of Etham, Pi-hahiroth, and Migdol. The fourth site mentioned in connection with the crossing, Baal-zephon, generally is identified with Tell Defneh on the western shore of Lake Menzaleh about 5 mi. west of modern Qantara,[32] well within the area where the Sea of Reeds must be located. Thus, two plausible locations for the crossing of the Sea of Reeds may be established. One is in the south near the Bitter lakes, in which case the Israelites moved directly west or

---

28. The exact location is relatively unimportant for historical purposes; the general region establishes the starting point of the Exodus. Some scholars feel that the name Raamses (Ramesses) referred to a large area constructed by Ramesses II, comprising both Tanis and Qanṭir.

29. DeWit. *Date and Route*, pp. 13-20. See also de Vaux, *Early History*, pp. 378f.

30. The Hebrew word is *sûp*, "reeds," generally admitted to be a borrowing of Eg. *ṭwf(y)* "papyrus." It is so used in Exod. 2:3, 5, referring to the reeds in the Nile in which Moses was hidden as a baby. Elsewhere *yam sûp*, lit. "Sea of Reeds," also refers to the Gulf of Aqaba on the other side of the Sinai peninsula (e.g., 1 Kgs. 9:26), and to the Gulf of Suez, south of the region of the Exodus (e.g., Num. 33:10). The latter usage is an extension of the name of the reedy lakes lining the route of the Suez canal to the two northern arms of the Red Sea. Such a wider use of geographical terms can be seen in ancient times; Kitchen, "Red Sea," *IBD*, p. 1323.

31. An Egyptian text of the period of Rameses II speaks of "the Land of the Papyrus," that is, the papyrus marshes between Tanis-Qanṭir and the line of the Suez canal north of modern Ismailia. The same text refers to the "Waters of Horus" (Eg. Shihor), borrowed by Hebrew for the eastern boundary of Egypt; Josh. 13:3; 1 Chr. 13:5.

32. Albright, "Baal-Zephon," pp. 1-14 in W. Baumgartner et al., eds., *Festschrift für Alfred Bertholet* (Tübingen: 1950).

southwest from Succoth (Wâdī Tumilat), crossing a marshy lake, into the Sinai desert.[33] The other location is in the north, near Tell Defneh (Baal-zephon), in which case the Israelites doubled back from Succoth (14:1), crossing an arm of Lake Menzaleh, then south into Sinai.[34] However, it is not yet possible to establish the exact route.

It is very clear, though, that the Israelites did not take the normal route from Egypt to Canaan, somewhat anachronistically called "the way of the Philistines" (Exod. 13:17). This route began at Sile (modern Qantara) and paralleled the coast, reaching Canaan at Gaza (see Map). As this was the regular route of the Egyptian army, with forts and supply stations at requisite intervals, confrontation with Egyptian troops would have been certain (v. 17b). Rather, the Israelites went by the "Way of the Wilderness" (v. 18) and, after crossing the Sea of Reeds, entered the "Wilderness of Shur" (15:22; Num. 33:8), known from other references[35] to have been in the northwest Sinai peninsula, east of

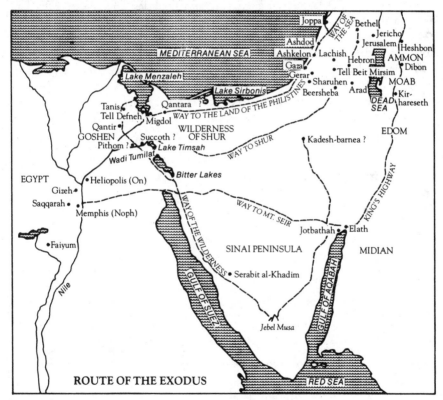

ROUTE OF THE EXODUS

33. Presented in detail in J. Finegan, *Let My People Go* (New York: 1963), pp. 77-89 and regarded as more probable by DeWit, *Date and Route*, pp. 13-20.
34. View adopted by Wright, *Biblical Archaeology*, pp. 60-62, and defended in detail in D.M. Beegle, *Moses, the Servant of Yahweh* (Grand Rapids: 1972), pp. 144-166.
35. E.g., 1 Sam. 15:7; 27:8.

the region between Lake Timsaḥ and Lake Menzaleh. From there they proceeded by various stations to Mt. Sinai.

Direct evidence for the location of Sinai and Israelite presence there may never be forthcoming. That presence was, historically speaking, ephemeral, and the Israelite tribes left behind no sedentary population to perpetuate their names for places they visited.[36] Further, Sinai itself has never had a sedentary population in historical times, so names have been attached to few sites with any permanence. Hence few names from the Mosaic period are likely to have survived in the Arabic nomenclature of the area, in contrast to the longevity of biblical names in sedentary regions.[37] However, the awesome granite mountains near the traditional site of Jebel Musa (Arab. "Mountain of Moses") and the Monastery of St. Catherine (see Map) still seem the most plausible site for Mt. Sinai (Horeb, in some passages), as strongly supported by several lines of evidence. The identification in Christian tradition reaches back at least to fourth-century A.D. monks from Egypt, and doubtless much earlier.[38] The Bible makes clear that Mt. Sinai was far south of Kadesh-barnea. Deut. 1:2 depicts the journey from Kadesh-barnea to Mt. Sinai as eleven days, and Elijah took "forty days and forty nights" (meaning a very long journey) to reach Sinai from Beersheba (1 Kgs. 19:8). The location thus appears to be in southern Sinai, a region whose stark, imposing beauty and solemn, awesome grandeur are most fitting for the moving events of Israel's Sinai experience.

---

36. Names of several Israelite campsites are drawn from geographical or other features, e.g., Marah (Exod. 15:23), "bitter," referring to the water found there; and Elim (v. 27), "trees," for the site had twelve springs and seventy palm trees. Other sites were named from events, e.g., Kibroth-hattaavah, "graves of lusting" (Num. 11:34).

37. This longevity has been demonstrated abundantly for sedentary areas since E. Robinson, *Biblical Researches in Palestine, Mount Sinai and Arabia Petraea* (Boston: 1841).

38. This has been suggested by surface examination of Tell el-Mekheret, in the oasis of Feiran, only a few miles from Jebel Musa on the direct road from the coast. The tell was occupied continuously from the Iron Age (*ca.* ninth-eighth centuries), through the Persian-Hellenistic and Roman-Byzantine periods, to the early Arab period. Further, geographical texts of the early Christian centuries show its name as Paran (source of Arab. Feiran) before Christian monks came to the area. The site, then, has been known since the biblical period. See Y. Aharoni, "Kadesh-Barnea and Mount Sinai," pp. 161-170 in B. Rothenberg, ed., *God's Wilderness* (London: 1961).

CHAPTER 10

EXODUS:
CONTENTS AND THEOLOGY

NAME AND CONTENTS

"EXODUS" in English Bibles is derived ultimately from Gk. *éxodus* "departure" (Exod. 19:1), the name given the book in the LXX. Although not wholly descriptive of the contents, it is an excellent name for the book, for one of its most important sections is the account of the "departure from Egypt" (1:1–15:21). In the Hebrew Bible the book is known from its first two words, *we'ēlleh šemôt* "these are the names" (often just *šemôt* "Names"), following ancient custom for naming a text.

The book centers in two most important events, the Israelite deliverance from slavery in Egypt through God's mighty act of salvation at the Sea of Reeds (1:1–18:26), and the establishment of his lordship through the covenant at Mt. Sinai (19:1–40:38). "Exodus" often is used in a broad sense for the whole complex of events from the deliverance to entry into the promised land (cf. 3:7-10). As such, it forms the high point of Old Testament redemptive history, as the means through which God constituted Israel as his vehicle for the redemption of all mankind.

The contents of the book can be outlined as follows:

Deliverance from Egypt and journey to Sinai (1:1–18:27)
 Oppression of Hebrews in Egypt (1:1-22)
 Birth and early life of Moses: his call and mission to Pharaoh (2:1–6:27)
 Plagues and Passover (6:28–13:16)
 Exodus from Egypt and deliverance at Sea of Reeds (13:17–15:21)
 Journey to Sinai (15:22–18:27)
Covenant at Sinai (19:1–24:18)
 Theophany on Sinai (19:1-25)
 Granting of covenant (20:1-21)
 Book of the Covenant (20:22–23:33)
 Ratification of covenant (24:1-18)

Instructions for tabernacle and cultus (25:1–31:18)
  Tabernacle and furnishings (25:1–27:21; 29:36–30:38)
  Priests and consecration (28:1–29:35)
  Craftsmen of tabernacle (31:1-11)
  Observance of Sabbath (31:12-18)
Breach and renewal of covenant (32:1–34:35)
  Golden calf (32:1-35)
  God's presence with Moses and people (33:1-23)
  Renewal of covenant (34:1-35)
Building of tabernacle (35:1–40:38)
  Freewill offering (35:1-29)
  Appointment of craftsmen (35:30–36:1)
  Building of tabernacle and furnishings (36:2–39:43)
  Completion and dedication of tabernacle (40:1-38)

ROLE OF MOSES

Moses dominates the Pentateuchal narratives from the second chapter of Exodus to the last chapter of Deuteronomy. Throughout the Old Testament he is portrayed as the founder of Israel's religion, promulgator of the law, organizer of the tribes in work and worship, and their charismatic leader through the deliverance, covenant at Sinai, and wilderness wanderings, until Israel was poised to enter the promised land from the Plains of Moab. To remove Moses from the traditions, regarding him as unhistorical or a later secondary addition,[1] renders inexplicable the religion and even the very existence of Israel.[2]

Name, Parentage, and Early Life. The book opens by recounting the great proliferation of Hebrew tribes in Egypt. So large had their numbers become that the king of Egypt regarded them as a considerable security threat. Such circumstances must have existed in Egypt after the Hyksos period, when Palestinian Semites in fact did seize power. To ensure control of his northeast frontier, Pharaoh reduced this faction to state slaves on the many building projects in the delta, notably Pithom and Raamses. When his stratagem to limit their number further failed (1:15-21), the king decreed that all males born to the Hebrews be drowned in the Nile.

In these circumstances Moses was born and hidden in a basket in the reeds along the Nile. A daughter of Pharaoh found the child, adopted him, and, through his sister Miriam, employed his own mother as his nurse. Although no details are given, Moses apparently grew up in the Egyptian court, receiving the education and training such a position would warrant (cf. Acts 7:22). This would have involved reading and writing, archery and other physical attain-

---

1. A not infrequent position in more extreme modern criticism. See the study of the treatment of Moses by M. Noth in J. Bright, *Early Israel*, pp. 51ff.
2. R. de Vaux, *Early History*, pp. 327-330; Bright, *History*, p. 124.

ments, and training in administration, for posts of confidence and responsibility were occupied by Egyptian and foreign princes—especially Semites—in New Kingdom Egypt.[3]

The daughter of Pharaoh named him Moses, "because I drew him out of the water" (2:10), a play on words between the Hebrew name Mōšeh and the verb māšâ "to draw out." Most scholars feel the name is actually Egyptian, as in names like Thutmosis or Ahmosis. If so, the explanation in 2:10 must be regarded as popular etymology, which is frequent in the Old Testament.[4]

The account of Moses' birth and early life in ch. 2 does not name his father or mother, noting only that both were from the tribe of Levi. Since the tradition probably would have preserved the names had they been known, it is more plausible that the four-member genealogy in 6:16-20 be understood as tribe (Levi), clan (Kohath), and family group (Amram by Jochebed) from which, an unknown number of generations later, came Moses and Aaron.[5]

Aside from the few brief facts recorded in 2:1-10, nothing is known about Moses' youth. He is portrayed next as a mature adult.

Moses in Midian. Having slain an Egyptian for beating a Hebrew, which reveals that Moses was conscious of his origin and race, he was forced to flee Egypt to the land of Midian.[6] There he settled with Jethro, priest of Midian, and married his daughter Zipporah, who bore him two sons.

Here the narrative flashes back to Egypt (2:23-25), noting that the king of Egypt had died during the "many days" Moses had been in Midian. It also notes that the people of Israel groaned under their cruel bondage and cried out to God, who heard them and remembered his covenant with Abraham, Isaac, and Jacob. This provides the setting and introduction to God's first step in delivering his people from Egyptian slavery—the call of Moses.

Call of Moses. While pasturing Jethro's sheep, Moses came to Horeb, "the mountain of God." There he saw the strange sight of a bush burning, yet not consumed (3:2). Turning aside to see what this might be, he was addressed by God, who introduced himself as "the God of your father, the God of Abraham,

---

3. See K.A. Kitchen, "Moses," *IBD*, pp. 1026-1030.

4. The question is difficult, however. In defense of the Egyptian origin, see J.G. Griffiths, "The Egyptian Derivation of the Name Moses," *JNES* 12 (1953): 225-231. For some cautions, see Kitchen, *IBD*, p. 1026.

5. Further evidence is the fact that four generations from Levi to Moses does not accord with the 400 years of Gen. 15:13 and the 430 years of Exod. 12:40f. for the period between the patriarchs and the Exodus, which other evidence suggests should be understood literally.

6. Midian proper was south of Edom and east of the Gulf of Aqaba, in the northern Hejaz of modern Saudi Arabia; but the nomadic Midianites ranged far and wide. In the Old Testament they are found in Moab (Gen. 30:35), Palestine (37:28), and especially raiding the Valley of Jezreel in the time of Gideon (Judg. 6:1-6). In the Exodus period they apparently had occupied western and southern Sinai (Num. 10:29-32; note also that this is where Moses saw the burning bush; Exod. 3:1ff.).

the God of Isaac, and the God of Jacob" (v. 6a), terminology associated with the traditions of his people. Moses knew immediately who was speaking to him and hid his face, "for he was afraid to look at God" (v. 6b). After describing the wretched state of his people in Egypt and affirming his intention to deliver them (vv. 7-9), God commissioned his messenger: "Come, I will send you to Pharaoh that you may bring forth my people, the sons of Israel, out of Egypt" (v. 10).

Suddenly, all was transformed: the shepherd was to become the deliverer. Indeed, so radical was the call that Moses raised a series of objections, to which God patiently responded (3:11–4:17). In this dialogue material of great theological import is set forth:

(1) Revelation of the divine name. Moses' first objection was elicited by the utter incongruity between his position in life and the enormity of his mission: "Who am I that I should go to Pharaoh . . . ?" God responded with the unconditional promise that he himself would be with Moses (3:11f.). Moses objected further that the people would respond to his commission with a question he could not answer:

> "If I go to the people of Israel and say to them, 'The God of your fathers has sent me to you,' and they ask me, 'What is his name?' what shall I say to them?" (v. 13)

God's response is stated three times in slightly different forms:

> "I Am who I Am. . . . Say this to the people of Israel, 'I Am has sent me to you. . . . Yahweh, the God of your fathers, the God of Abraham, the God of Isaac, and the God of Jacob, has sent me to you': this is my name forever, and thus I am to be remembered throughout all generations" (vv. 14f.)

Obviously of great theological importance, this passage has been discussed voluminously and with widely divergent interpretations, for the exact meaning is exceedingly difficult to elicit.

Did Moses posit that the Israelites, in asking for the name of God, were after factual information? Had they forgotten—or never really known—the name of their God? To grasp the force of Moses' question, it is necessary to understand that a name, in the Old Testament conception, is not merely a vocable to distinguish one person from another, but rather is bound up closely with the person's very existence,[7] representing and expressing his or her character and personality. To learn a person's name is to enter a relationship with his very being.[8] Thus, Moses actually is asking "What is God's relationship to

---

7. The force of "name" is but a special example of how the Israelites, as many ancient and modern peoples, attached a power to the word which now has been largely lost. In many ways their conception has a deeper and truer sense of reality. See the excellent study by J.L. McKenzie, "The Word of God in the Old Testament," pp. 37-58 in Myths and Realities (Milwaukee: 1963).

8. See esp. W. Eichrodt, Theology of the Old Testament, trans. J.A. Baker. OTL (Philadelphia: 1961) 1:206ff.

the people? He has been the 'God of the fathers'; who is he now?" In 23:20f.
God tells the Israelites that he will send his angel with them to Canaan and
admonishes them to reverence and heed him and offer no defiance, "for my
name is in him." The force of God's name can be seen especially in 33:18f.,
where Moses asks to see God's glory. He complies not only by permitting Moses
a mysterious, visible manifestation of himself (vv. 22f.), but also by promising
to proclaim his name before Moses (v. 19). This he then fulfills on top of the
mountain by proclaiming his name in a series of imposing affirmations that
stress his grace and mercy (34:5-7). Thus, God's name expresses his ineffable
and mysterious person, his glory.

God's response, usually translated "I am who I am," sounds like an evasive,
circular definition and hence a refusal of an answer.[9] But in 3:15 God does
reveal his name—Yahweh, which v. 14 explains. The whole context, and especially the import of Moses' question, strongly suggests that God is revealing
and not hiding himself. Throughout their history Israel looked back to the
events of this period when they learned who God was and what he was to be
to them.

The Hebrew phrase translated "I am who I am" reflects an idiom in which
something is defined in terms of itself, used when the speaker either does not
desire or does not have the means to be more explicit.[10] Hence it can express
something undetermined, but also totality or intensity.[11] Thus, "I will be gracious to whom I will be gracious, and will show mercy on whom I will show
mercy" (33:19) means "I am indeed he who is gracious and shows mercy."[12]
Taken with that force, "I am who I am" means "I am indeed he who is."[13]
Further, this existence is not a matter of being in the metaphysical sense—as

---

9. A number of interpreters contend that God here refuses to reveal the mystery
of his being: he is the Unnameable, the Ineffable, the Incomprehensible.

10. See further E. Schild, "On Exod. iii 14—'I am that I am,' " *VT* 4 (1954):
296-302.

11. See the excellent study by de Vaux, "The Revelation of the Divine Name
YHWH," pp. 48-75, esp. 67ff., in J.I. Durham and J.R. Porter, eds., *Proclamation and
Presence* (Richmond: 1970). Emphasis or intensity is expressed by repetition of the same
verb in the predicate (somewhat like the Hebrew cognate accusative).

12. This statement is immensely interesting here, since it immediately follows
God's promise to proclaim his name (v. 18). In fulfillment of the promise in 34:5-7,
when God does proclaim his name, the identical two verbs are used: "Yahweh, Yahweh,
a God merciful and gracious. . . ." In ch. 33 the revelation is connected with the fact
that God above all is merciful and gracious, reflected in the striking connection of his
name, revealed in 3:13-15, with the dramatic redemption from slavery in Egypt.

13. Recently a very forceful attempt has been made to understand both "I am who
I am" in v. 13 and "Yahweh" in v. 15 as derived from the causative rather than the
basic stem of the Hebrew verb. This would yield some such meaning as "I am he who
creates" or "I create what comes into being." Besides being somewhat hypothetical, this
interpretation does not commend itself simply because it requires emending the text to
make it conform to the hypothesis. Such a procedure in the interests of a theory is
arbitrary. See de Vaux, *Proclamation and Presence*, pp. 64f. For a full discussion of the
arguments for the interpretation as well as its weaknesses, see B.S. Childs, *The Book of
Exodus*, OTL (Philadelphia: 1974), pp. 62ff.

if a philosophical statement—but rather in the relative or efficacious sense: "I am he who is there (for you)—really and truly present, ready to help and to act." This interpretation is strongly supported by the expectations raised by the context. The people of Israel—and Moses, whose concern is thinly disguised—were in a hopeless situation and needed just such a word from God. By revealing his personal name, God indicates that he has opened to humankind his very being and given access to himself in fellowship and as savior.

Finally, a word must be said about the form of the name in v. 15, YHWH, the "tetragrammaton,"[14] and its relationship to the formula "I am who I am" in v. 14. The interpretation given in v. 14 takes the name to be the third person form of the verb *hāyâ* "to be," i.e., "he is."[15] But God, in speaking of himself, does not say "he is" but "I am." Others, speaking of God, must say "he is." Given the difficulty of simply translating such a name and the fact that pronunciation of the four consonants long had been lost by the end of the Old Testament period, most modern translations follow the KJV in translating LORD (usually in small capital letters to distinguish it from ordinary Heb. *'aḏōnay* "lord").

(2) Moses, the prophet. In the sequel to the revelation of the divine name, Moses continues to object to his call. In 4:10ff. he observes that he is not eloquent but slow of speech and tongue. To this God promises to be "with his mouth" and to teach him what to speak. Now, with all his objections answered by God's gracious promises of his presence and power, Moses must decide. He couches his refusal in the desperate plea that God send someone else (v. 13). Still, God will not bypass his stubborn messenger, but makes a concession. Aaron is commissioned as Moses' spokesman and Moses will play the role of God, giving Aaron the message to speak.[16] This paradigm of the prophetic role shows clearly that the task is primarily to bear a message, submerging one's own ideas, interests, and desires beneath those of the sender. This is also clear in

---

14. Something like "the four-lettered word," referring to the Hebrew consonants of the divine name, YHWH. Interpretation is complicated because the original pronunciation has not been preserved. Throughout its long history, until centuries after the New Testament period, Hebrew was written without vowels. When a system of vowels finally was invented to preserve traditional pronunciation of the sacred text, the name of God had become so holy that the Jews had long since ceased to pronounce it. Instead they read Heb. *'aḏōnay* "Lord" for YHWH, so eventually the vowels of *'aḏōnay* were written on the name YHWH. This is the source of the name "Jehovah." The pronunciation *Yahweh* comes from ancient transliteration into Greek and the grammatical requirements of the name's interpretation given in 3:13-15.

15. This interpretation sees the root of YHWH, *hāwâ*, as an old form of *hāyâ* "to be," occasioning much speculation and debate about whether the name existed before Moses. Some evidence now exists that YHWH may have been a name element among the Amorites from whom the Israelites apparently came, but no conclusive proof exists. Even if the name's prior use might some day be shown, the biblical teaching centers in the fact that, through the revelation to Moses and the deliverance at the Sea of Reeds, the name is filled with new meaning and significance. See de Vaux, "Revelation of the Divine Name," pp. 48-56.

16. Vv. 14-16; see also 7:1-2.

what follows. Having finally accepted his call (4:8), Moses is commissioned as messenger in characteristic prophetic fashion:

> And the Lord said to Moses in Midian, "Go back to Egypt. . . . And you shall say to Pharaoh, 'Thus says the Lord, Israel is my first-born son, and I say to you, "Let my son go that he may serve me. . . ." ' " (vv. 19-23)

and the commission is carried out:

> . . . Moses and Aaron went to Pharaoh and said, "Thus says the Lord, the God of Israel, 'Let my people go. . . .' " (5:1)

Here Moses' role is characterized in the "messenger formula" by which the prophetic word is authorized as the word of God, "Thus says the Lord." Although prophecy in Israel's history does not reach its fullest development until the period of the Monarchy, its form emerges full-blown in the call, commission, and task of Moses, prophet of God par excellence.[17]

PLAGUES AND THE PASSOVER

Pharaoh's response to God's demand to release the people is an unqualified "no":

> "Who is the Lord, that I should heed his voice and let Israel go? I do not know the Lord, and moreover, I will not let Israel go." (5:2)

A dramatic and classic confrontation between the power and authority of God and the stubborn will and hard heart of Pharaoh follows. God's power and authority is made evident through a series of ten catastrophes or "plagues" (9:14) that strike Egypt through the mediacy of Moses and Aaron. Through these plagues both Israel (6:7) and Pharaoh (7:5) learn who the Lord is, and Pharaoh ultimately allows Israel to leave (7:8–13:16).

Plagues. The first nine plagues are a continuous series (7:8–10:29), set apart from the tenth, the death of the firstborn. The nine are structured by a literary device that groups them into three sets of three plagues each. In the first plague in each set Moses is commanded to appear before Pharaoh at the river; in the second he is to "come before Pharaoh" at his palace; and in the third he is to make a gesture which brings the plague without warning to Pharaoh.

This pattern and other elements of literary structure[18] show that the accounts had a long history of oral and written transmission before reaching their current form. This has led many scholars to conclude that the narratives were

---

17. Deut. 18:15-20; Hos. 12:13. For the significance and role of the prophet as messenger, see C. Westermann, *Basic Forms of Prophetic Speech*, trans. H.C. White (Philadelphia: 1967), pp. 90-114.

18. De Vaux, *Early History*, pp. 361-65.

First Set	Second Set	Third Set	Structure
1. Water turns to blood	4. Land swarms with flies	7. Hail destroys crops	Moses appears before Pharaoh in morning at river
2. Frogs leave water, cover land	5. Cattle in field die of plague	8. Locusts devour all that is left	Moses "comes before" Pharaoh
3. Land filled with mosquitoes or gnats	6. Boils cover man and beast	9. Thick darkness covers land	Moses and Aaron do not appear before Pharaoh but use a symbolic gesture

not historical but rather "piously decorated accounts" whose actual value was "symbolic."[19] But recognizing that an account has long been transmitted by written or oral means does not necessarily prejudge its historical worth. This can be decided only by determining whether what is transmitted fits the background of the time and place of which it speaks and can be substantiated on independent grounds.

A recent study shows that the nine plagues fit rather precisely the natural phenomena of Egypt.[20] In this interpretation the plagues form a sequence of unusually severe natural events which exhibit a cause-and-effect relationship[21] in the very order of the scriptural text.[22] The plagues begin with an abnormally high inundation of the Nile from excessive rains. These extremely high waters would have washed down large quantities of characteristic bright red earth of the Abyssinian and Ethiopian plateau plus reddish-colored microorganisms called flagellates, turning the Nile blood red and foul, and creating conditions that would kill the fish (first plague). The decomposing fish would cause the frogs to desert the river banks (second plague) and infect them with the disease organism *Bacillus anthracis*, which in turn would cause the frogs' sudden death. The third and fourth plagues would be mosquitoes and the *Stomoxys calcitrans* fly, both of which would breed freely in the conditions created by the stagnant waters of the retreating Nile flood. The cattle disease (fifth plague) was anthrax, caused by the contaminated dead frogs; and the boils on men and cattle (sixth plague) would be skin anthrax, principally transmitted by the bite of the fly of the fourth plague. Hail and thunderstorms (seventh plague) in the time of year required by this sequence would destroy flax and barley but leave the wheat and

---

19. E.g., J.C. Rylaarsdam, "Introduction and Exegesis of Exodus," *IB* 1:839.
20. G. Hort, "The Plagues of Egypt," *ZAW* 69 (1957): 84-103; 70 (1958): 48-59. The editors note that this article, which differs so markedly from prevailing opinions, has been assured by those competent in the natural sciences to be geologically and microbiologically accurate.
21. Except the hail.
22. Described at length, without Hort's technical scientific material, in D.M. Beegle, *Moses, the Servant of Yahweh*, pp. 96-118.

Granite statue of Rameses II (1290-1224), pharaoh of the Exodus. (British Museum)

spelt for the locusts (eighth plague), whose immense numbers (10:6) would be favored by the same Abyssinian rains that had caused the initial flood. Finally, the thick darkness (ninth plague; v. 21) aptly describes an unusually strong ḥamsîn,[23] made far worse by the thick layer of fine red dust from the mud deposit of the inundation. In this natural interpretation the miraculous elements consist in the unusual severity of the events,[24] and their timing coincides with Moses' demands upon Pharaoh. God uses the created order for his own ends.

However, the tenth plague has no "natural" explanation.[25] This terrible catastrophe is described in a very complex section (12:1–13:16) that also narrates and gives regulations for the Passover meal, feast of Unleavened Bread (maṣṣôt), and redemption of the firstborn.

Passover. In the Passover meal (12:1-14) a year-old male animal from the flock (i.e., sheep or goat) was sacrificed, roasted, and eaten with the Israelites having "loins girded, . . . sandals on [their] feet, and . . . staff in . . . hand" (v. 11)—that is, ready for an immediate journey. Some blood of the sacrifice was placed on the lintel and two doorposts, marking the houses of the Israelites so God would pass over and spare their firstborn.

With the meat of the sacrifice, the Israelites were to eat unleavened bread and bitter herbs. When they left Egypt, they took this still unleavened dough (v. 34) and, upon reaching Succoth, baked cakes with it. This whole sequence is to be memorialized by the feast of Unleavened Bread, described in vv. 15-20, signifying the haste with which they left Egypt.

The original meaning of Heb. pesaḥ "passover" (Gk. pascha, hence Eng. "paschal") is unknown and much disputed. The verbal form (pāsaḥ) occurs only in vv. 13, 23, and 27. In vv. 13 and 27, the verb occurs immediately after the noun in a clearly explanatory construction meaning "to pass over, to spare."[26] When in vv. 21ff. Moses carries out God's instructions given him in vv. 1-14, he tells the Israelites to "kill the Passover lamb," without defining the term. Thus, many scholars believe that Moses was speaking of something already known, perhaps a spring festival customary to a shepherd people. Similarly, the feast of Unleavened Bread originally may have been a spring agricultural festival.[27] Evidence for the origin of these festivals prior to Moses and the Exodus

---

23. The desert "sandstorm" which begins to strike Egypt from the south in late February or early March and usually lasts two or three days.

24. As with the mosquitoes, flies, hail, and locusts under any interpretation.

25. The inundation of the Nile reaches the Delta region in late July or August. The tenth plague would have had to take place in March-April (Nisan) to provide the basis for the date of Passover.

26. Hence the aptness of the English translation "passover." The meaning of the verb is determined from context, with little likelihood that it is related to the homophonous verb pāsaḥ "to limp, to dance."

27. Thus, for example, in the description of the Passover in Lev. 23, the feast of Unleavened Bread is connected with the offering of the first sheaf of the spring barley harvest (vv. 10ff.).

is highly suggestive. However, they were reinterpreted radically as a result of the dramatic deliverance from Egypt. Whatever their original meaning, since that time they have commemorated God's free and gracious deliverance of his people.

As Israel's physical and religious circumstances have changed, so have the specific rites by which Passover has been celebrated. After the entry into Canaan, it was probably a home celebration, as in Egypt. Later, with the establishment of the temple, Passover became a pilgrim festival, with the slaughter of the lamb taking place in the temple (see Deut. 16). By New Testament times the communal meal was eaten in private. After the temple was destroyed in A.D. 70 and sacrifices ended, Passover again became a home festival. Yet despite changes in ritual, Passover has always been a communal, family celebration commemorating God's redemption of his people from slavery in Egypt.[28]

The Last Supper which Jesus celebrated with his disciples in the upper room certainly was patterned after a passover meal, if not the Passover itself.[29] Through this event the Passover was transformed in Christian belief into the Lord's Supper, again with strong emphasis on commemoration—of the person and death of Jesus the Messiah, through whom all that the Passover and old covenant anticipated has been brought to full fruition.[30]

DELIVERANCE AT THE SEA OF REEDS

Moses' role in the Exodus events was primarily as a prophet, a messenger. His message, "Thus says the Lord . . . 'Let my people go . . .' " (5:1), was his repeated and fundamental demand throughout his confrontation with Pharaoh during the plagues. Upon the death of the firstborn, Pharaoh finally acceded to this demand (12:29-32); and the Israelites, fortified and united by the solemn Passover meal, departed from Egypt (vv. 37-42). Although their exact route is not known (see pp. 128-130), they eventually arrived beside the "Sea of Reeds,"

---

28. The view which sees the original setting as a springtime festival of nomadic and "seminomadic" shepherds does have the most to commend it. In this view the sacrifice and festival was originally a rite to ensure safety and the fecundity of the flocks, especially at the point of embarking upon the annual journey to spring and summer pasturage. All elements of the Passover ritual fit this setting. For a clearer discussion, see de Vaux, Ancient Israel, trans. J. McHugh (New York: 1965) 2:488-493. Moses imaginatively reinterpreted this festival, providing the communal symbolic act which would unite the Israelites for their perilous journey. The meaning transferred to the old forms is not radically different but replete with meaningful analogy: the journey is not to pasture but to freedom; the dangers are not to the flocks but to themselves.

29. The question is much disputed. One of the best studies is J. Jeremias, The Eucharistic Words of Jesus, trans. A. Ehrhardt (Oxford: 1955). Whether or not it took place on the actual date of Passover is one of the difficult problems. See John 13:1 and J. Jocz, "Passover," Zondervan Pictorial Encyclopedia of the Bible (Grand Rapids: 1975) 4:608f. Cf. also W.S. LaSor, The Dead Sea Scrolls and the New Testament (Grand Rapids: 1972), pp. 201-5.

30. See I.H. Marshall, Last Supper and Lord's Supper (Grand Rapids: 1981).

which evidently impeded further progress toward Sinai. True to his character, Pharaoh had a change of heart and mustered his chariotry and troops in pursuit of the escaping Israelites. Trapped between the onrushing Egyptians and the sea, the Israelites then experienced the dramatic deliverance that was to become throughout the rest of the Old Testament the supreme example of God's saving acts (see pp. 55f.). At a signal from Moses, God sent a strong easterly wind all night that drove back the waters (14:21), and the Israelites, unencumbered by chariotry or plentiful supplies, crossed to the other side. The pursuing Egyptians, however, their chariot wheels mired in the soft ground, were engulfed by the waters of the returning flood.

> That day, Yahweh rescued Israel from the Egyptians, and Israel saw the Egyptians lying dead on the shore. Israel witnessed the great act that Yahweh had performed against the Egyptians, and the people venerated Yahweh; they put their faith in Yahweh and in Moses, his servant. (vv. 30f., JB)

A hymn of victory by Moses and the people follows (15:1-18), expressing in particularly beautiful poetry thanksgiving to God for his victory at the sea. This is the people's response of faith—the content of the belief attested in v. 31.[31] Remarkable parallels with Ugaritic literature in language and structure show that the poem is considerably earlier than the prose accounts that surround it.[32] On this basis, W.F. Albright and others have dated the poem as early as the thirteenth or twelfth century.[33] In the opening of the song, faith in the Lord is expressed in language rich in associations from both the recent and the distant past:

> Yahweh is my strength and my song,
> And he has become my salvation;
> This is my God, and I will praise him,
> The God of my father, and I will exalt him. (v. 2)

Yahweh, who so recently revealed himself to Moses and delivered his people from Egypt, is identified with the "God of the fathers," as he was known to the patriarchs, and the people affirm him as their God. The poem closes by looking ahead to the end of their journey, picturing the dismay of those in Canaan,

---

31. Note Childs, *Old Testament as Scripture*, p. 176: "The canonical effect of Ex. 15 in rehearsing the same event is to actualize the victory in the form of a liturgical celebration, concluding with the response, 'Yahweh will reign for ever and ever'. An event in past history has been extended into present time and freed for every successive generation to encounter."

32. Parallels in poetic structure are so close that some have suggested that actual verses of Canaanite poetry have been borrowed and adapted to suit the needs of Israelite religion. The evidence extends to such prosaic literary features as the use of verb tenses and archaic spelling.

33. W.F. Albright, *The Archaeology of Palestine*, pp. 232f.; F.M. Cross, Jr., and D.N. Freedman, "The Song of Miriam," *JNES* 14 (1955): 237-250; and Cross, *Canaanite Myth and Hebrew Epic* (Cambridge, Mass.: 1973), pp. 112-144.

and the ultimate presence of the Lord and his people in the hill country of Palestine (v. 17).

Throughout their history Israel looked back to this great deliverance as the constitutive event by which they became the people of God and the primary example of his redemptive purposes for them. The Psalms, particularly Ps. 78, especially dwell on the Exodus in praise of God for his mighty deeds. The prophets again and again extol Yahweh as he who brought Israel out of Egypt, led them through the wilderness, and gave them the law (cf. Isa. 43:16f.; Jer. 16:14; 31:32; Ezek. 20:6ff.; Hos. 2:15; 11:1; Amos 2:10; 3:1f.). The Exodus dominates the Old Testament perspective and becomes the first focus of divine redemption, which would be eclipsed only by that greater deliverance which God accomplished by the death of his Son on Calvary.

COVENANT AND LAW AT SINAI

After the deliverance at the sea, Israel traveled directly to Sinai (see pp. 128-130), a journey of three months (19:1). A few episodes on the way are related in 15:22–18:27, notably the provision of water at Marah (15:22-25) and at Rephidim, where Moses struck the rock (17:1-7), and of food—quails and manna (16:1-36).[34] At Rephidim they also fought the Amalekites (17:8-16).

At Sinai the people camped before the mountain, while Moses ascended. There God spoke with him, informing him that Israel would be God's own possession among all peoples "if you obey my voice and keep my covenant" (19:5). The instructions and events that followed revealed something momentous about to take place. In a three-day period of consecration the people were to wash their clothes and make themselves ready (vv. 9-15). Then they presented themselves at the foot of the mountain (v. 17), while God manifested himself in awe-inspiring greatness and majesty:

> Now at daybreak on the third day there were peals of thunder on the mountain and lightning flashes, a dense cloud, and a loud trumpet blast. . . . The mountain of Sinai was entirely wrapped in smoke, because Yahweh had descended on it in the form of fire. Like smoke from a furnace the smoke went up, and the whole mountain shook violently. (vv. 16-18, JB)

In the midst of this terrifying and awesome appearance,[35] God summoned Moses

---

34. The manna is presented as a miraculous provision, though a partial analogy is a sweet substance exuded by an insect which infests a species of tamarisk tree in southern Sinai. See F.S. Bodenheimer, "The Manna of Sinai," pp. 76-80 in G.E. Wright and Freedman, eds., *The Biblical Archaeologist Reader* 1 (repr. Grand Rapids: 1981).

35. The thunderstorm is often the scene of God's self-manifestation; see Pss. 18:7-14; 29; 1 Kgs. 19:11f. The cloud and fire are symbols of God's presence. See G.E. Mendenhall, "The Mask of Yahweh," pp. 32-66 in *The Tenth Generation* (Baltimore: 1973).

and delivered the Ten Commandments (20:1-17). After this the theophany was completed (vv. 18-21).

The meaning and role of the Ten Commandments have created great debate and have been understood in diverse ways. Their immense significance is made abundantly clear by the tenor of the whole presentation. On careful reading this passage is clearly the covenant which Israel is invited to accept in 19:5, obedience to which will constitute Israel as the people of God. Although this meaning is not explicit in the context of Exod. 19–20, reference to Moses' recounting of the event in Deut. 5 makes this abundantly clear:

> ". . . The Lord our God made a covenant with us, in Horeb. Not with our fathers did the Lord make this covenant, but with us, all of us who are alive here this day. . . . He said: 'I am the Lord your God, who brought you out of the land of Egypt. . . .' " (vv. 1-6)

As with God's covenant with Abraham in Gen. 15, a covenant is a means to establish a relationship (not naturally existing), which is sanctioned by an oath sworn in a ceremony of ratification. All the elements that make up a covenant are present at Sinai. In Exod. 19:3-8 Israel is summoned to a special relationship with God, described by three phrases: a special possession among all peoples, a kingdom of priests, a holy nation. Israel is to be God's own people, set apart from other nations for his own service just as priests were set apart from other men, and marked as such by a quality of life commensurate with the holiness of their covenant God.[36] Even though the specific contents of this covenant relationship are not yet revealed, Israel accepts with the solemn affirmation: "All that the Lord has spoken we will do" (v. 8). In 20:1-17 the covenant demands are set forth, and in 24:3-8 the covenant is ratified by a solemn ceremony. Here the oath is reaffirmed and given sanction by the sacrifice and the sprinkling of the blood, a symbolism whose implications are obvious.

This covenant relationship differs from the Abrahamic covenant only in that the party to the covenant binds himself to obligations by oath. This change, however, produces covenants that differ radically in both form and function. In the Abrahamic covenant God places himself under oath, bound by irrevocable promises to Abraham and his posterity. In the Sinai covenant Israel takes the oath, and the obligation is obedience to the covenant stipulations.

Recently the specific cultural background of the Sinai covenant has become clear. The covenant follows very closely the literary form and structure of the international treaty of the ancient Near East between an overlord (or suzerain) and his subject people (vassals).[37] Although the form was widely known and

---

36. Childs, *Exodus*, p. 367.
37. Initially set forth by Mendenhall, "Ancient Oriental and Biblical Law," *BA* 17 (1954): 25-46; and "Covenant Forms in Israelite Tradition," *idem* 59-76; both repr. in E.F. Campbell and Freedman, eds., *The Biblical Archaeologist Reader* 3 (Grand Rapids: 1981): 3-53. For numerous biblical and extrabiblical examples see J. Arthur Thompson, *The Ancient Near Eastern Treaties and the Old Testament* (London: 1964).

used during the second millennium, the largest number of examples of the suzerain-vassal treaty—and the most complete—are to be found in the fourteenth- and thirteenth-century Hittite texts from Boghazköy. Most of the elements of this form[38] may be found in the texts that deal with the Mosaic covenant, especially 20:1-17:

(1) Preamble (identifying the author and giving his titles): "I am Yahweh, your God" (v. 21). God needs no further titles, after the recent dramatic revelation of his name.

(2) Historical prologue (setting forth the previous relations between the parties and emphasizing the suzerain's benevolent deeds on behalf of the vassal; these acts are the grounds for the vassal's gratitude and future loyalty and obedience): "who brought you out of the land of Egypt, out of the house of slavery" (v. 2b). The historical survey here is succinct and minimal, but Israel's memory of God's dramatic deliverance is recent and fresh. In Josh. 24, the covenant renewal ceremony at Shechem, the historical prologue is long and detailed (vv. 2-13).

(3) Stipulations of the treaty, consisting of:
(a) the basic demand for allegiance and faithfulness: "You shall have no other gods before me" (20:3).
(b) specific stipulations (in treaty use, normalizing relationships within the empire): vv. 4-17.

(4) Provisions for:
(a) deposition of the text (treaties were kept in the temple): the tablets containing vv. 1-17 were placed in the ark of the covenant; 25:16; Deut. 10:1-5.
(b) periodic public reading: Deut. 31:10-13.

(5) Curses and blessings (invoked upon the vassal for breaking or keeping the covenant): Deut. 28:1-14 (blessings), 15-68 (curses).

Also, provision was made for a formal oath by which the vassal pledged obedience, and a religious ceremony, often with blood sacrifices, in which the treaty was ratified (cf. Exod. 24). The treaty was written in very personal terms, using an "I-Thou" dialogue pattern.

These close and detailed parallels show that the suzerain-vassal treaty form was adapted and expanded to serve the religious and theological needs of this special relationship. Thus the Ten Commandments very clearly were never intended to be a system of legal observances by obedience to which one could

---

38. The only one explicitly missing, and for obvious reasons, is the list of divine witnesses to and guarantors of the treaty. Yet Joshua used both the people as witnesses against themselves and a great stone which he set up in the sanctuary at Shechem; see Josh. 24:22-27.

earn God's acceptance. They are rather the stipulations of a covenant relationship rooted and anchored in grace. God has freely redeemed his people from slavery in Egypt and now binds them to him with his covenant. The prologue to the covenant looks back to this past deliverance and so forms a kerygma, a proclamation of good news. Redemption already has been accomplished.

But the covenant also proposes a dire and serious threat. It offers Israel not only blessing for obedience but curse for disobedience. Note the conditions posed in Exod. 19:5: "If you obey my voice and keep my covenant, you among all the peoples shall be my own possession." The covenant stipulations are not only the Lord's will for a redeemed people; they are also the source of his wrath and rejection should the people fail to keep them. Were Israel to break the covenant, they could in some sense cease to be the people of God. It was in the tension between these two affirmations that Israel lived under the Mosaic covenant, and this covenant alone makes their subsequent history understandable. Eventually their record of broken covenant promises became so virulent and long-standing that God invoked the curse of the covenant, sending the prophets with their call to repentance and their announcement of judgment.

The Ten Commandments, then, are not law in the modern sense, for they are not carefully defined and contain no penalties. They are rather "legal policy," a basic statement of that kind of behavior which the covenant community is willing to sustain by force.[39] When Israel accepted the covenant and these stipulations became normative, the need arose to implement and place them in a form more suitable to "law" in the normal sense. This development is found in the "Book of the Covenant" (20:23–23:33). Careful examination shows that most of the stipulations of 20:1-17 are repeated here as specific laws. Here Israel set down in concrete form those models of the shape of love that their life as the people of God demanded.[40]

THE TABERNACLE

Two long passages in Exodus describe the tabernacle.[41] In chs. 25–31 God reveals to Moses the plan, materials, and contents. Chs. 35–40, in which

---

39. This concept of the Decalogue as "legal policy" is set forth in detail in D.R. Hillers, *Covenant: The History of a Biblical Idea* (Baltimore: 1969), pp. 88ff.

40. These laws often are regarded as stemming from centuries later in Israel's life. Granted, they may have been supplemented and reshaped by Israel's subsequent experience; no system of laws can remain static as the life and circumstances of the people they regulate change. Nonetheless, there is every reason to believe that their original core goes back to Moses. The need, as indicated above, is manifest. Further, Moses is presented as administering justice and appointing judges when the task became too great (18:13-26). It is inconceivable that Moses did not begin the process of interpreting the covenant stipulations and organizing them into a form that could regulate conduct.

41. The Hebrew word most frequently translated "tabernacle" is *miškān*, which, it would appear, originally simply meant "a dwelling," specifically a tent. In Old Testament usage, however, it is almost totally restricted to the tent shrine that preceded the temple.

Moses carries out God's commands, repeat this account almost verbatim.[42]

The tabernacle was a portable shrine, consisting of a square latticework frame of acacia wood covered by two large linen curtains. One of the curtains formed the main hall, the Holy Place, while the second covered the Holy of Holies (i.e., the "Most Holy Place"), a smaller room at the back of the main hall and separated by a curtain. The Holy Place was 30 feet long by 15 feet wide by 15 feet high, while the Holy of Holies was 15 feet on each side. Inside the Holy of Holies was only the ark, a wooden chest containing the tablets on which were inscribed the Ten Commandments. In the Holy Place was the altar of incense, the lampstand, and a table with the "bread of the Presence." The tabernacle was placed in a court 150 feet by 75 feet, screened off from the rest of the camp by white curtains 15 feet high. In the court before the tabernacle stood the altar of burnt offering, and between it and the tabernacle stood the laver.

The long and detailed account of the tabernacle and its construction does not make easy or interesting reading. Further, the extravagant interpretations that earlier readers gave to the tabernacle and its furniture, arbitrarily considering them symbols and types of every kind of spiritual reality, has brought the subject into disrepute. Nevertheless, the tabernacle was of great importance to Israel, who had just accepted the Sinai covenant. In 25:8 God says: "Let them make me a sanctuary, that I may dwell in their midst." The tabernacle, then, was the localization of God's presence with his people, a visible symbol that he was their God.[43] Here Israel was to worship and atone for breaches of the covenant stipulations.[44] The tabernacle with its imagery and sacrificial system was the means by which the holy, transcendent, and infinite God could yet be present with his people—"tabernacling" or "tenting" among them. As the symbol of his presence, it looks forward to the time of fulfillment when God in the person of his Son truly would be present with his people, when "the Word became flesh and 'tabernacled' among us,[45] full of grace and truth" (John 1:14).

---

42. This literary device, which seems repetitive and unnecessary, is characteristic of that period. In the Keret epic from Ugarit, El reveals to King Keret in exhaustive detail how to conduct the military campaign to recapture his destined bride from her father's house. Later Keret carries out these commands, and the passage is repeated verbatim.

43. Scholars frequently have regarded the description of the tabernacle as unhistorical, a projection into the past of the later temple and its theology. Some features of the tradition indeed seem to have been embellished in light of later development. E.g., the silver required (38:25) would have weighed approximately 3.8 tons! However, many features in the tradition, together with extrabiblical examples, demonstrate that the core of the tradition goes back to the Mosaic period and institutions. See Cross, "The Priestly Tabernacle," in Wright and Freedman, eds., The Biblical Archaeologist Reader 1:201-228; Kitchen, "Some Egyptian Background to the Old Testament," Tyndale House Bulletin 5-6 (1960): 7-13.

44. On the significance of the tabernacle sacrifices, see pp. 153-57.

45. The JB notes that the literal translation reads "pitched his tent among us."

FOR FURTHER READING

Beegle, D.M. *Moses, The Servant of Yahweh*. Grand Rapids: 1972. (A good attempt at a "biography.")

Bimson, J.J. *Redating the Exodus and Conquest*. JSOTS 5. Sheffield: 1978. (A thorough review of the evidence for the date of the Exodus, positing a fifteenth-century date.)

Cassuto, U. *A Commentary on the Book of Exodus*. Trans. I. Abrahams. Jerusalem: 1967. (A stimulating treatment that eschews the standard literary critical views.)

Childs, B.S. *The Book of Exodus*. OTL. Philadelphia: 1974.

Finegan, J. *Let My People Go*. New York: 1963. (The story of the Exodus, attempting to place it historically and geographically.)

Stamm, J.J. and Andrew, M.E. *The Ten Commandments in Recent Research*. London: 1967. (Full discussion of recent interpretaion.)

Widengren, G. "What Do We Know About Moses? Pp. 21-47 in J.I. Durham and J.R. Porter, eds., *Proclamation and Presence*. Richmond: 1970. (Defends basic historicity from a critical evaluation of the literary sources.)

Zimmerli, W. *The Law and the Prophets*. Oxford: 1965. (Insightful treatment of the role of law in the Old Testament structure of faith and history.)

CHAPTER 11

LEVITICUS

Encamped in the shadow of Mount Sinai, the Israelites had experienced the great redemptive act of Yahweh—the deliverance from Egyptian bondage—that would remain central in their faith for all generations. They had seen and heard the thunders and lightnings on the holy mountain (Exod. 19:16-19), and Yahweh had given his commandments (20:1-17). He had declared that he was their God and they were his people. He was their suzerain who had bound them to him in treaty obligations.

But how was this relationship to be maintained? The Israelites could not dwell forever at Mt. Sinai, for that was not Yahweh's intention either in his promise to their fathers or in the deliverance from Egypt. They were to settle in a land where they could experience the benefits of being his people. Moreover, they were to become, in some way not yet spelled out, the source of blessing to all nations (Gen. 12:3), communicating their faith to other peoples. The wilderness of Sinai was the place for neither. Canaan was to be the land of the promise.

As the book of Numbers tells us, an entire generation of Israelites was to pass away before the people entered the land. During this period, they would learn through experience the results of both obeying and disobeying the word of the Lord. Prior to their entrance into Palestine, where they would be confronted by Canaanite cultic practices,[1] they were also to learn the proper ways to worship Yahweh. The details of this worship are given in Leviticus.

NAME AND CONTENTS

Name. Since ancient books actually were identified by their opening words (even as papal encyclicals are today), the title of the Hebrew book accordingly is *wayyiqrā'* "and he called" (Lev. 1:1). "Leviticus" comes from the Greek LXX

---

1. The primary meaning of "cult" (or cultus) is "worship" or "the rites and ceremonies of a religion."

through the Latin Vulgate. Basically it is an adjective, suggesting the complete title "the levitical (book)" or "the book pertaining to the Levites." The appropriateness of the name has been questioned, because the principal figure in Leviticus is Aaron, and the priesthood, which is described in the book, is limited to his sons. To them was committed the priestly service. Aaron, of course (like his brother Moses), was a Levite. However, a distinction was made between the "Aaronic priesthood"—descended from Levi (one of Jacob's twelve sons) through Aaron—and the "Levites," who could not claim Aaronic descent. Later a clear-cut distinction between "priest" and "Levite" developed.[2]

Perhaps too much has been made of the title "Leviticus." The predominant word is "priest," which is used more often than "Levite."[3] In the Sinai event, Yahweh had declared that the people of his covenant were "a kingdom of priests and a holy nation" (Exod. 19:6). Ideally the nation was a theocracy: every person was a priest, with Yahweh as king. However, such an ideal is less than practical, hence a representative principle was established. The firstborn son of each family should represent the family (13:2,13; 22:29). But Yahweh appointed the Levites to serve in place of the firstborn sons: "Behold, I have taken the Levites from among the people of Israel instead of every firstborn that opens the womb among the people of Israel" (Num. 3:12).

It seems, then, that to look upon Leviticus as "the handbook of the priests"—meaning officials of the cult—is to fall short of the biblical teaching; this book belongs to all the people.[4]

Contents. Leviticus is sometimes said to set forth the law, meaning the ritual laws of Israel. Such a statement usually is followed by a study of the contents as a simple collection of laws, with no attempt to understand the basic meaning of Heb. *tôrâ* (anglicized as "Torah"). In Hebrew usage, *tôrâ* means "instruction, discipline" (in the sense of disciplining as well as chastening). Thus the word is used of the instruction given by a father or mother (Prov. 1:8; 3:1). Principles derived from scientific observations can be called "laws." In some such sense "law" can designate the principles that govern the life of Yahweh's covenant people. In the Old Testament, "law" includes "statutes," "judgments,"

---

2. See R. Abba, "Priests and Levites," *IDB* 3:876-889, for a careful study. According to the classical Wellhausenian theory, the distinction between priests and Levites was postexilic, and the entire cult as described in Leviticus was a construction of postexilic Judaism. However, Abba shows that the Priestly Code was both preexilic and pre-Deuteronomic and thus of far greater historical value than previously thought. For further evaluation of Wellhausen's reconstruction, see D.A. Hubbard, "Priests and Levites," *IBD*, pp. 1266-1273.

3. The word *kôhēn* "priest" occurs 730 times; *lēwî* "Levite," 40 times; and the plural "Levites," 250 times. Often "Levites" is simply a tribal designation without official implication.

4. For an overview of the role of Israel as a "kingdom of priests," see A. Lacocque, *But As for Me* (Atlanta: 1979).

"commandments," and "precepts."[5] Therefore it is not erroneous to translate *tôrâ* as "law." Nonetheless, it is far more helpful to look upon Leviticus as a book of instructions for the priest-nation and their priestly representatives. These instructions concern cultic ritual and worship—the acts and attitudes which Yahweh's people are to maintain if they are to have unbroken fellowship with Yahweh.

The central theme of Leviticus might well be expressed by *qōḏeš* "holiness" and *qāḏôš* "holy" (see Lev. 19:2). Two questions are raised by this basic theme of holiness. First, how can sin be removed so people may become holy? Second, how can people maintain the holiness essential to fellowship with a holy God? Lev. 1–16 deals essentially with the first question; and the closing portion of the book, with the second.

Four-horned incense altar (ca. tenth century B.C.), from Megiddo, on which Israelites could offer "a pleasing odor to the Lord" (Lev. 2:2). (Israel Department of Antiquities)

5. For some idea of how the Israelites looked upon the "law of the Lord," see Ps. 119.

BIBLICAL CONCEPT OF HOLINESS

Basic Meaning. Originally *qāḏôš* meant simply "set apart," specifically for religious purposes. A piece of ground, a building, the furniture in the sanctuary, or even a horse could be "holy"—set apart for a religious or cultic usage. No moral quality was implied. There may have been a sense of the numinous, the sense of awe that the Israelite would have felt as he approached the tabernacle, or the high priest, as he entered the Holy of Holies. However, this feeling of the awesome power that holy things possess must not be confused with moral or ethical quality. Certain persons were "holy"—set apart for religious purposes—whether priests in the service of Yahweh or temple prostitutes of the Canaanite Baal.[6]

In the Figure, that which is inside the circle—set apart by the line—may be considered as "holy" or "sacred." That which is outside the circle is "profane," the biblical antonym of "holy." Note 10:10: "You shall distinguish between the holy and the profane and between the unclean and the clean" (lit.). That which is cultically "clean" is acceptable for the worship of Yahweh, and that which is "unclean" is not. Profanity, then, is the taking of a holy thing (such as the Lord's name) and using it in a profane, or common, way.

Profane (Holy) Profane

Derived (or Biblical) Meaning. The biblical concept of holiness is not limited to separation. Repeated use is made of the words "Yahweh is holy" or "I (i.e., Yahweh) am holy." This usage means that he is set apart, as already defined. He is spirit and mankind is physical. He is invisible and mankind is visible. More important, though, God is set apart from sin and sinful humanity. In the biblical tradition, God created Adam for fellowship with him, but sin broke that fellowship, and Adam and Eve were driven from the garden. Symbolically, God was in the sacred place and the human family was barred from it because of its sin. Yahweh's moral excellence, then, became part of the concept of his holiness; and his demand that the people of his covenant be holy was always bound up with the law. Holiness thus came to have the derived or biblical meaning of moral excellence.[7]

SACRIFICES AND OFFERINGS

Offerings. According to 7:37, five "offerings" were included in the law

---

6. It may come as a shock to learn that the *qᵉḏēšîm* "set-apart males" are cult-prostitutes (1 Kgs. 15:12) and *qᵉḏēšôṯ* "set-apart females" are harlots (Hos. 4:14; cf. Gen. 38:21f.).

7. Although seemingly wrong according to some philological methods, this is the only possible way to establish a correct biblical definition. A word must be understood in the way its users intend it to be used. In any discipline, whether medicine or mathematics, law or linguistics, certain words have specialized meanings for that field, a fact too often ignored by biblical scholars.

which Yahweh revealed to Moses on Mt. Sinai. One of these, always referred to in the plural as the "peace offerings," was divided into three kinds, hence there were seven offerings in all. Since all except the "cereal offering" involved the sacrificial killing of an animal, they are often referred to as "sacrifices." The Hebrew word for "offerings" in the passage means "presentation" or "the things which are brought near." (See Table.)[8]

The terminology, as translated from Hebrew, is not always uniform. The "whole burnt offering" or "burnt offering" sometimes is called a "holocaust," from a Greek word meaning "wholly burned." The "sin offering" is readily confused with the "guilt (or trespass) offering," for they are exactly the same except that the guilt offering requires restitution to the one harmed by the sin.[9] The "cereal offering" often is called the "meal offering," or in the KJV, the "meat offering."[10] Deut. 12:27 distinguishes between the burnt offering and the "sacrifice" (zebah), noting that the holocaust was entirely consumed by fire on the altar, whereas a portion of the "sacrifice" could be eaten by the priest, and in some cases by the offerer.

Role of the Person Making Offering. The actual presentation and immolation of the victim is described with precision (see Lev. 1:3-9). With a few exceptions (such as a sin offering for the whole congregation or the offering of small birds by a poor person), the ritual, up to the point of placing the sacrifice on the altar, is the same for all offerings.

The offerer was to present his offering personally at the altar or the door of the tent of meeting, "that he may be accepted before the Lord" (v. 3). The offering was to represent the offerer's own life—an animal he had raised or grain he had produced—and was to be of superior value (generally a male without blemish, or fine flour, or the best of firstfruits). The economic status of the offerer, however, was taken into consideration. Only later is there evidence that the offerer could purchase at the temple precincts an offering which had cost him no personal effort.[11]

The offerer then placed his hand on the head of the victim, probably indicating personal identification (1:4). Whether the offerer confessed his sin at the time of presenting the sacrifice is open to question. Since the ritual of the Day of Atonement clearly stipulates such a confession (16:20), it seems reasonable that this was part of every ritual of sacrifice. Moreover, specific sins are mentioned in connection with the sin and guilt offerings (5:1–6:7), and when the sinner recognized that he had sinned (4:14), or it was pointed out to him (v. 28), he was required to make a sacrifice. Thus, since he was making

---

8. Careful reading of the biblical passages along with study of the chart is recommended.

9. In 5:6 the terms are synonymous.

10. This term is confusing today, for "meat" in Elizabethan English meant "meal." No meat was included, although the cereal offering often was accompanied by a sacrifice of some kind.

11. Cf. Mark 11:15 and parallels; John 2:15f.

NAME OF OFFERING	PURPOSE	KIND OF OFFERING
'ôlâ Holocaust or burnt offering 1:3-17 6:8-13	To atone for unwitting sin in general	Male without blemish from herd or flock or two birds
ḥaṭṭā'ṯ Sin offering 4:1–5:13 6:24-30	To atone for specific unwitting sin	Priest: bull Whole congregation: young bull Ruler: male goat One of people: female goat or sheep Poor person: two birds; very poor: flour
'āšām Guilt or trespass offering 5:14–6:7 7:1-10	To atone for unwitting sin requiring restitution	Like sin offering (plus restitution)
minḥâ Cereal offering 2:1-16 6:14-23	To secure or retain good will	Fine flour or cakes or wafers or firstfruits with oil, frankincense, salt, but no leaven or honey Usually accompanied by animal sacrifice
šᵉlāmîm Peace offerings 3:1-17 7:11-21, 28-36	To render thanks to Yahweh . . .	Male or female from herd or flock without blemish
tôdâ Thank offering	For a blessing received	
neḏer Vow offering	Upon completion of a vow	
nᵉḏāḇâ Freewill offering	From a glad heart	

an offering for a specific sin, he apparently was making public confession of that sin.

Then came the terrible moment when the offerer had to slaughter his animal, skin it, and cut it in pieces. This bloody act was not in itself revolting; after all, most Israelite families raised and slaughtered their own animals for food. Yet anyone who has raised an animal can imagine the terrible feeling when it becomes necessary to put the animal to death, even if to end suffering. The levitical sacrifices were not designed to revulse but to impress upon the sacrificer a sense of identification with the victim (see 1:4). The offerer was

NATURE OF OFFERING	ACTIONS OF OFFERER	ACTIONS OF PRIEST
Completely burned	Brings offering Places hand on head Slays, skins, cuts in pieces	Accepts offering Throws blood against altar Places pieces on fire Washes entrails, legs
Fatty portions burned Remainder eaten	Brings offering (Elders do so for congregation)	Accepts offering Throws blood against altar Burns fat, etc., eats meat If own sin is included, burns portion outside camp
Like sin offering	Makes restitution first, Then same as sin offering	Like sin offering
Token (*'azkārâ*) burned	Brings offering Takes handful	Burns handful Priests and sons eat remainder
Fatty portions burned Remainder eaten	Brings offering Places hand on head Slays, skins, cuts in pieces Eats of remainder* (same day or next)	Accepts, Throws blood on altar Burns fatty portions Eats of remainder* (same day)

*Note the communion nature
of the thank offerings

sacrificing not only a choice animal which he had raised but a substitute for himself. The whole sequence of acts he performed could not help but impress him with the penalty invoked for sin: it cost a life.

Role of the Priest. The priest was obligated to keep the fire burning on the altar (1:7; 6:12f.). Presumably there was a ritual of accepting the sacrifice, perhaps partly preserved in the words, "it shall be accepted for him to make atonement for him" (1:4). When the offerer slew the animal, the priest caught the blood in a basin, threw part on the sides of the altar, and poured the rest around the base (v. 5). The ritual of the sin offering was somewhat more elaborate (cf. 4:4-7). The portion to be burned, after washing, was put on the altar. In the holocaust, the entire animal (except the hide) was to be burned; but in the other offerings, part of the sacrifice was the priest's portion and could be eaten by him. Again, however, a careful distinction was to be made. In the case of a sin offering, whether offered by the priest for his own sin or that of the whole congregation, the priest could not partake of it, for he was acting then as both priest and sinner. In that case, he carried his portion outside the camp and burned it. In the peace offerings, where the offerer's own sin was not part of the symbolism of the sacrifice, the offerer as well as the priest partook of a portion.

Every detail was significant. The responsibility of the priests to instruct the people, and the judgments upon them for failing to do so, play too large a part in the preaching of the prophets for us to overlook their import.

Significance of Blood. Throughout the law of the offerings the blood is emphasized. Reference to blood is particularly offensive to many, and the ritual of sacrifice has sometimes been called "butcher-shop religion." Nevertheless, both the fact and the symbolism in this insistence upon blood sacrifice must be understood. It lies also at the heart of the Christian faith, both in the sacrifice of Christ on the cross and in the symbolism of the Lord's Supper. The fact is simple: the shedding of blood means the death of the victim. The symbolic meaning lies in identifying the one making the sacrifice with the victim, for it symbolizes the death of the sinner. The penalty for sin is death, but the animal dies in place of the sinner. [12]

Day of Atonement. Of particular significance was the ritual of the Day of Atonement. Even though the temple and sacrificial system have disappeared, the Day of Atonement (Yom Kippur) remains the holiest day in the Jewish year.

"Atonement" and "to make atonement (for)" are difficult words to understand. The basic meaning of the Hebrew is "to cover over." English "atone" comes from the words "at one," and atonement is "at-one-ment" or reconciliation. Not all scholars agree that this is intended by the Hebrew, but it seems closer to the concept in Leviticus than "propitiation" (to please God). [13] The

---

12. In the New Testament, sacrifices of bulls and goats are viewed as only symbolic, "for it is impossible that the blood of bulls and goats should take away sin" (Heb. 10:4). On the other hand, the sacrifice of Christ is efficacious, offered once for all (v. 12).

13. In some works, the relationship of *kipper* with *kāpar* "to cover" is denied, and *kipper* is traced to a separate root "to propitiate." However, it is very difficult to support the idea of propitiation in Leviticus or the Old Testament as a whole. That concept is largely supported by comparative studies, since it is found frequently in non-Israelite religions. For a discussion of propitiation in the Bible, see L. Morris, "Propitiation", *NBD*, pp. 1287f.

emphasis here is not so much on pleasing God as on covering the sin, although the New Testament clearly uses propitiation as one facet of atonement (e.g., Rom. 3:25; 1 John 2:2). The blood atonement and the mercy seat in Leviticus help to prepare the way for this doctrine.

The high priest was the intermediary between the holy God and the sinful people. In the symbolism of the tabernacle (later, the temple), Yahweh was present between the cherubim in the Holy of Holies. On the Day of Atonement, Aaron the high priest put off his priestly robes, donned simple white garments, and performed the ritual. First, he made atonement for himself and his house (16:6), for he, too, was a sinner needing his sins covered. Then he offered a goat as sin offering for the people (v. 15). Both times he took blood and sprinkled it on the "mercy seat" in the Holy of Holies (vv. 13, 17). Because of the people's uncleanness, even the Holy Place was considered defiled and thus in need of atonement (v. 6).

Aaron then took a live goat, laid both hands upon its head, and confessed over it "all the iniquities of the people of Israel and all their transgressions, all their sins; and he . . . put them upon the head of the goat" and sent the goat into the wilderness (v. 21). It is specifically stated that "the goat shall bear all their iniquities upon him to a solitary land" (v. 22, certainly understood symbolically and not literally, as the prophets and the author of Hebrews clearly understood).

The goat (hence modern "scapegoat") is said to "go to Azazel" (v. 26, RSV). This expression has led to unending debate among both Jewish and Christian exegetes. Was Azazel the name of a place, or one of the deities of Sinai, or Satan? Was the goat "for Azazel" an offering to placate Satan or some demon? Each of these answers seems contrary to the basic spirit of the Day of Atonement, and is unsupported by anything else in the sacrificial rituals in the Bible. "Azazel" does not appear elsewhere. Despite the difficulties, the best explanation is to take "Azazel" as an unusual form derived from Heb. '$\bar{a}zal$ "to remove" and to translate the expression "for removal [of sin]."[14] This does full justice to the symbolism of the act, as the scapegoat carries the people's sins far away, where they will no longer stand between the people and the holy God.

LAWS OF HOLINESS

Holiness Code. Chs. 17–26 sometimes is called the Holiness Code. According to one form of the documentary theory (see p. 64), the Holiness Code (H) was one of the documents used in the formation of the Pentateuch (or Hexateuch), and was composed by a priestly author or school in the seventh or sixth century.[15]

---

14. The expression is simply *la'$\bar{a}$'zēl* "to/for Azazel/removal." "He who lets the goat go to Azazel" (v. 26, RSV) is really an interpretation, not a translation; the statement reads lit. "the one sending (or casting) the goat to/for Azazel (or destruction)."
15. See O. Eissfeldt, *Old Testament*, pp. 233-39.

It is hardly correct to call this a "code." Rather, it is a loose collection of principles representing the way of life of people called to be holy, and might better be called the Torah of Holiness. The principles are not set forth as points of law, but are details in which the people of Yahweh should seek to conform to the concept of holiness.

Included, for example, are a number of holy convocations (23:1-44), such as the Sabbath and Passover. The sabbatical year is to be observed every seventh year as a period of rest for the land (25:1-7), and the year of Jubilee, every fiftieth year as a time of redemption, when slaves are to be set free and property is to revert to the original family or clan (vv. 8-55). However, the Israelites did not observe these "sabbaths," and both Jeremiah (34:14-22) and Ezekiel (20:12-16) proclaimed that the Exile was God's punishment because of this.[16]

Law of Neighbor Love. When asked, "Which is the great commandment in the law?" Jesus replied with two commandments, the first from Deuteronomy ("You shall love the Lord your God with all your heart, and with all your soul, and with all your mind"; see p. 179), and the second from Leviticus ("You shall love your neighbor as yourself"; Matt. 22:36-40; cf. Lev. 19:18). The law of neighbor love in Leviticus comes at the end of a group of somewhat miscellaneous laws that express holiness (see v. 2) in such ways as revering mother and father, keeping sabbaths, avoiding idolatry, performing peace offerings, and leaving a portion of the harvest for the sojourner. The law of neighbor love follows admonitions against slander or "standing forth against the life" (making a capital charge?), or taking vengeance or bearing a grudge against one's neighbor. It is an excellent summary of one's relationship to those in the community of everyday life.

RELATIONSHIP OF LEVITICUS TO OTHER
PORTIONS OF THE BIBLE

Ezekiel. Leviticus and Ezekiel contain many points of similarity. Whether Ezekiel drew upon Leviticus or Leviticus was composed by priests dominated by Ezekiel's ideas is a matter of scholarly disagreement. If Leviticus contains, as a number of scholars now recognize, many early elements of Israelite cult, then one would expect Ezekiel, a priest (Ezek. 1:1) speaking to Jews in exile just before and after the destruction of the temple, to be unusually interested in reestablishing the levitical cultic regulations.

Hebrews. In several places, Hebrews quotes or cites Leviticus, mostly ch. 16 (the Day of Atonement passage).[17] Heb. 8–10 is interesting for two reasons:

---

16. It seems obvious that if both Jeremiah and Ezekiel speak of such long-term failure, the Sabbath could hardly be the invention of a postexilic priestly writer. On recent discussion of early material in the so-called Priestly Document, see R.E. Clements, "Pentateuchal Problems," pp. 118f. in G.W. Anderson, ed., *Tradition and Interpretation*.

17. Twenty-four such quotations or citations, according to data in the United Bible Societies' *Greek New Testament*, ed. K. Aland et al., 2nd ed. (Stuttgart: 1968), pp. 900f.

it gives a New Testament (and therefore canonical) concept of the significance of the levitical ritual, and provides insight into the community to whom Hebrews was written.

If Hebrews was written to Christian Jews faced with the fact that the temple had been (or was about to be) destroyed and the cultic system ended, the book would answer the problem of how to replace the sacrifices commanded by Moses.[18] The author shows that the animal sacrifices were merely "a shadow of the good things to come" (Heb. 10:1), with no power to take away sins. The sacrifice of Christ is the "true form of these realities," and therefore need never be repeated. The inference is that the ritual of the Mosaic law is no longer necessary; in fact, "what is becoming obsolete and growing old is ready to vanish away" (8:13).

Law and Grace. It sometimes is stated that salvation under the old covenant was by performing works of law, whereas under the new covenant people are saved by grace alone through the sacrifice of Christ. This is based largely on a somewhat distorted understanding of Paul's teachings in Galatians.

Careful study of the Torah as well as the rest of the Old Testament shows that man (in the generic sense) is never saved by his own efforts—but only by the grace of God. Man deserves condemnation and death for his sin; God is graciously willing to accept man on the basis of his faith and to provide the means by which he is redeemed. This is the revelation of redemption which the Bible proclaims. Paul so understood the basic covenant with Abraham, and declared that it was not annulled by the law given to Moses (Gal. 3:6-18).[19] The author of Hebrews, discussing the Old Testament cultic acts, stated it succinctly: "For it is impossible that the blood of bulls and goats should take away sin" (10:4).

Likewise, many Jews understood salvation to be by God's sovereign grace.

"Rabbi Jochanan said: 'Hence you may learn that man has no claim upon God; for Moses, the greatest of the prophets, came before God only with an appeal for grace.' " (*Deut. Rab. wa'ethanan* 2:1)

"It was not for their works that the Israelites were delivered from Egypt, or for their fathers' works, and not by their works that the Red Sea was cloven in sunder, but to make God a name. . . . So Moses told the Israelites, 'Not through your works were you redeemed, but so that

---

18. This is, of course, not the only explanation of the address of Hebrews. However, it seems quite unreasonable to suppose that the author was writing to a community that had no knowledge of the ritual laws and no reason to be concerned about performing those cultic acts.

19. This same passage plus the paragraphs that follow have been used to prove the contrary; and Gal. 3:23 is often cited to support the law/grace dichotomy. But salvation by works of the law is nowhere taught in the Old Testament. So the Old Testament was understood by Jesus and the apostles, including Paul—all of whom were Jews. See D.P. Fuller, *Gospel and Law: Contrast or Continuum* (Grand Rapids: 1980).

you might praise God, and declare His renown among the nations.' "
(*Midr. Ps.* 44:1)

Many Jewish prayers express dependence upon God for salvation:

"Sovereign of all worlds! Not in reliance upon our righteous deeds do
we lay our supplications before thee, but by reason of thine abundant
mercies. . . . Our Father, our King, though we be void of righteousness
and virtuous deeds, remember unto us the covenant with our fathers,
and our daily testimony to thy Eternal Unity."[20]

No magical concept of sacrifice is taught in the Old Testament. Man deserved to die for his sin, and in offering a sacrifice cast himself on the mercy
of Yahweh. The sacrifice was a substitute for himself, and the blood of the
sacrifice covered his sin. The Israelite knew, as the prophets pointed out, that
it was not the sacrifice that availed, but the covenant mercy of Yahweh (see
Mic. 6:6-8; Isa. 1:11-20; Hos. 6:6).

Types and Symbols. Because of the fanciful extremes of biblical interpreters,
who throughout the history of the Church[21] have sought by means of typology
to find the entire gospel in almost every verse of the Old Testament, typology
has been criticized and even ridiculed. Only recently has this trend been reversed. G. von Rad,[22] among others, has given the word "type" a degree of
"respectability."

The use of symbolism is well understood and thoroughly acceptable. Many
concepts can be represented better by symbols than abstract verbal description.
Symbols are all about us—the hand on the wristwatch, the calendar, the flag,
and the cross, to name a few.

Basically a symbol is a visible means of representing an abstract idea.[23] The
cross is a symbol of love, sacrifice, death, and salvation. The tabernacle in the
wilderness was a symbol of God's presence, his meeting place with his people.
Aaron was a man, but also high priest, and in that office symbolized holiness
(separation for God's service). The sacrifices which he offered on the Day of
Atonement were symbols: of his own sin, the nation's sin, and the sending
away of that sin into oblivion.

When a symbol is later replaced by the reality it symbolizes, it is called a

---

20. Rabbinic passages can be found in C.G. Montefiore and H. Loewe, *A Rabbinic
Anthology* (New York: 1974), ch. 3. Prayers are from *Siddur Avodat Israel*, but similar
ones can be found in any of the prayer books. The reference to "our daily testimony"
is to the Shema (Deut. 6:4f.), recited daily by religious Jews.

21. From Clement of Alexandria (*ca.* A.D. 150-215) and Origen (*ca.* 185-254) to
the present. In his commentary on Genesis even Luther indulged in fanciful typology.

22. Von Rad, *Old Testament Theology* 2:363-387.

23. The symbol may be expressed verbally, as when the written word "cross" calls
up a visual image. All language is, in a sense, symbolic; hence one can translate from
one language to another, using different symbols but conveying the same idea.

type,[24] and the reality can be called an antitype. The Old Testament tabernacle is an excellent example of a type. As a symbol, it represented visually the presence of the invisible Yahweh, clearly implied in the account of the coming of his glory upon the tabernacle (Exod. 40:34, 38). When "the word became flesh and tabernacled among us" (John 1:14), the symbol was replaced by a reality. Thus the tabernacle is a type of Christ.[25] Likewise, the levitical sacrifices are types, if the symbolic meaning is determined and the corresponding reality identified. In such manner the author of Hebrews saw the annual Day of Atonement sacrifice as a type of the once-for-all sacrifice of Christ (10:1, 11-14).

RELEVANCE OF LEVITICUS TODAY

In his commentary on Leviticus, N. Micklem asks, "Has such a book any place in the Christian Bible?" and answers in the affirmative.[26] However, not a few readers have found the book of no modern significance. Even Micah (6:6-8) and other prophets seem to question the validity of bloody sacrifices, and the author of Hebrews apparently set aside forever the levitical system (Heb. 8-10).

But if the love of God is relevant today, so is Leviticus.[27] Behind its stern requirements and strict regulations stands the loving heart of Yahweh who longs for the fellowship of his people. The same grace that snatched them from slavery in Egypt sought to maintain regular communion with them. God's holiness insisted that for fellowship to be enjoyed, sin must be dealt with, and on terms acceptable to him. Leviticus, thus, is much more than a compendium of sacrifices and feasts, for it spelled out the terms of that fellowship.

If the sacrifice of Christ is relevant, and also the discussion in Hebrews, then so is Leviticus. The sacrifice of Christ, as he himself described it prior to the event, and his apostles afterwards, can be understood only in the light of the Jewish sacrificial system. The epistle to the Hebrews underscores this.

However, Leviticus is relevant at a different level. In his revelation of redeeming love—that he loved the sinner but hated the sin—Yahweh used the symbols of Leviticus as preparation for his fuller revelation in Christ (cf. Heb. 1:1). The symbols or types have been replaced by a reality. Symbolic sacrifices are no longer necessary, for the real sacrifice of Christ has made them so. Yet, the ancient symbols do contain much that is profitable for instruction. In fact,

---

24. Gk. *týpos* "mark, impression, form, pattern, type" has significant usage in Acts 7:44; Rom. 5:14; and Heb. 8:5. Eng. "type" is derived from this word. As used in printing, the "type," however, may suggest the reality; and the impression ("antitype"), the image.

25. This in no way suggests that every detail of the tabernacle is a type of some corresponding detail in the person or ministry of Christ. See further W.S. LaSor, "Interpretation of Prophecy," *BDPT*, pp. 130-32.

26. "Introduction and Exegesis of Leviticus," *IB* 2:4.

27. See B.S. Childs, *Old Testament as Scripture*, p. 188.

one cannot fully understand the New Testament concepts of sin and salvation apart from the Old Testament, which prepares for the new revelation.

Occasionally the comment is made that the God and Father of Jesus Christ is not the Old Testament Yahweh. Jesus Christ himself strongly denies this, in both his words and his sacrifice. The God and Father of Jesus Christ is a holy God, offended by sin, who requires that blood be shed to remove sin. He has provided the substitute "lamb" in the person of his own Son, through whom has come "atonement" (Rom. 5:11, KJV; RSV "reconciliation"). Christ memorialized this for the entire present age ("until he comes") in the Lord's Supper, using Old Testament language in the words of institution (Matt. 26:26-28 par. Exod. 24:8; cf. also 1 Cor. 10:23-27). In faith sins are laid on the "Lamb of God," who, like the scapegoat of the Day of Atonement, "takes away" sins (see John 1:29). Without understanding the language and symbols of Leviticus, how can one fully understand the deepest meaning of the New Testament?

FOR FURTHER READING

Bigger, S.F. "The Family Laws of Leviticus 18 in their Setting." *JBL* 98 (1979): 187-203.

Cross, F.M., Jr. *Canaanite Myth and Hebrew Epic.* Cambridge, Mass.: 1973. (Essays on Israel's early priesthood, pp. 195-215; and the "Priestly Work," pp. 293-325.)

Davies, G.H. "Leviticus." *IDB* 3:117-122.

Gispen, W.H. "Leviticus, Book of." *NBD*, pp. 730-32.

LaSor, W.S. "Interpretation of Prophecy." *BDPT*, pp. 130-32. (Discussion of symbols and types.)

Noth, M. *Leviticus.* Trans. J.E. Anderson. OTL. Philadelphia: 1965. (Literary- and historical-critical.)

Snaith, N.H. *Leviticus and Numbers.* Rev. ed. Century Bible. London: 1967. (Text and notes.)

Wenham, G.J. *The Book of Leviticus.* NICOT. Grand Rapids: 1979.

CHAPTER 12

NUMBERS

THE Israelites had departed from Egypt on the fifteenth day of the first month (Num. 33:3; cf. Exod. 12:2, 5) and reached the wilderness of Sinai on the first day (new moon) of the third month (Exod. 19:1). On the third day, God revealed himself on the mountain (v. 16). The tabernacle was erected on the first day of the first month of the second year (40:17). The book of Numbers opens with a command from Yahweh to Moses dated the first day of the second month of the second year. On the twentieth day of that same month "the cloud was taken up from over the tabernacle of the testimony, and the people of Israel set out by stages from the wilderness of Sinai" (Num. 10:11f.). Deuteronomy opens with a reference to the first day of the eleventh month of the fortieth year, or about thirty-eight years, eight months, and ten days after departing from Sinai. In other words, Numbers covers a period of thirty-eight years and nine months, referred to as the period of wilderness wanderings.[1]

An obvious reason for the inclusion of this book is to fill the period from the Exodus and Sinai revelation to the preparations in Moab to enter the promised land. Upon further consideration, however, more than this is involved. The journey from Sinai to Kadesh-barnea by way of the Gulf of Aqaba takes only eleven days (Deut. 1:2), as demonstrated by Y. Aharoni.[2] The direct route would be but a few days less, and by way of Edom and Moab hardly more than a couple of weeks.[3] Numbers makes clear that the thirty-eight-year period was punishment for lack of faith, so none of the unbelieving generation would enter the land (cf. Deut. 1:35f.). Numbers, therefore, is not a mere bit of

---

1. No effort will be made to press these date formulas, for Numbers makes no theological significance of them other than a general reference to the "forty years" in the wilderness (cf. 14:33f.). However, it is highly unlikely that they were mere fictions of postexilic editors. It is not unreasonable to suppose that in addition to the written log of the stages of the journeyings (33:2) Moses also kept a record of the dates—at least those preserved in the account.

2. *The Holy Land.* Antiquity and Survival 2/2-3 (1957): 289f.

3. Comparison of Num. 33:38f. with Deut. 1:3 shows that the journey from Mt. Hor, where Aaron died, to Moab took six months.

history, but another recital of the acts of Yahweh. It is a complex story of unfaithfulness, rebellion, apostasy, and frustration, set against the background of God's faithfulness and forbearance.

Name. "Numbers" is a strange name for a book of this sort.[4] Its title in the Hebrew Bible, taken from words in the first verse, is "In the wilderness of [Sinai]." This title is quite fitting. The translators of the LXX gave it the name "Numbers" because of the lists of numbers recorded in the book, and that title was passed on through the Vulgate.

Outline. The book can be divided conveniently into three main portions, separated by accounts of the Israelite journeys. An assortment of material not closely related is added at the end.

At Sinai: Preparations for departure (1:1–10:10)
    First census (1:1-54)
    Tribal camps and leaders (2:1-34)
    Number and duties of the Levites (3:1–4:49)
    Miscellaneous laws (5:1-31)
    Nazirite vow (6:1-27)
    Dedicatory offerings (7:1–8:26)
    Supplementary Passover (9:1-14)
    Cloud to guide the people (9:15–10:10)
Journey from Sinai to Kadesh (10:11–12:16)
    Departure from Sinai (10:11-36)
    Incidents along the way (11:1–12:16)
At Kadesh in the wilderness of Paran (13:1–20:13)
    Spies' mission and report (13:1-33)
    People's decision and God's judgment (14:1-45)
    Miscellaneous laws (15:1-41)
    Korah's rebellion (16:1-50)
    Story of Aaron's rod (17:1-13)
    Priestly portions (18:1-32)
    Purification of the unclean (19:1-22)
    Closing events at Kadesh (20:1-13)
Journey from Kadesh to the Plains of Moab (20:14–22:1)
    Edom's opposition (20:14-21)
    Death of Aaron; victory over opponents (20:22–22:1)
On the Plains of Moab (22:2–32:42)
    Balaam and Balak (22:2–24:25)
    Apostasy at Peor and the plague (25:1-18)
    Second census (26:1-65)
    Daughters of Zelophehad, women's rights (27:1-11)
    Joshua appointed to succeed Moses (27:12-23)

---

4. Originally the book had no title. The earliest title occurs in the LXX.

Offerings at the feasts (28:1–30:16)
Vengeance on Midian (31:1-54)
Portions of the Transjordan tribes (32:1-42)
Miscellaneous matters (33:1–36:13)
Review of the journey from Egypt (33:1-56)
Boundaries of Israel in the land (34:1-29)
Cities of the Levites (35:1-34)
Daughters of Zelophehad and women's inheritance (36:1-13)

Critical Problem. At one time it was widely believed that Numbers, like the rest of the Pentateuch, was written entirely by Moses. With the rise of literary criticism, problems of this theory were pointed out. In its extreme form, the critical position rejected any historical validity of the book. Today, on the contrary, considerable support exists for the view that Numbers incorporates much historical material, although handed down in various forms and considerably worked over. Some of the elements of the problem are as follows:

(1) No mention is made of the book's author. Num. 33:2 indicates that "Moses wrote down their starting places, stage by stage, by command of the Lord," but this is the only mention of Moses' literary activity. Throughout the book, he is mentioned in the third person. It could be argued (and, indeed, has been) that Moses, like Caesar, could write of himself in the third person.[5] In comparing Numbers with Deuteronomy, it seems that while Moses was more likely the author of much of Deuteronomy, he probably did not write Numbers. Nevertheless, he is certainly the central figure of Numbers, and much of the material in the book comes from notes kept by Moses or one of his contemporaries, possibly Joshua.

(2) A considerable amount of early material is found in Numbers. At the same time, numerous problems exist in harmonizing the material, particularly certain laws, ordinances, and cultic practices. In some cases, scholars conclude that later practices are reflected.[6] Yet there is hardly a consensus. J. Arthur Thompson, for example, suggests:

> . . . although these institutions had a basic form already in the days of Moses, and although they preserved the spirit and the essential elements of the early forms, there were modifications at various times during the centuries of use, and . . . the form set out in Numbers represents the usage at the time of the final compilation of the source materials.[7]

The early material demonstrates intimate knowledge of the wilderness, the Israelite people, and their constant complainings and attitude toward Moses,

---

5. However, if Moses was in fact "very meek, more than all men that were on the face of the earth" (12:3), he could hardly have written such a statement.
6. Comparison of Num. 15:22-31 with Lev. 4:2-12 indicates some details of this problem. In general it is difficult to harmonize all the details of the offerings in Lev. 1–7 with sporadic references in Numbers.
7. "Numbers," *NBC*, p. 169.

Traditional site of Elim, an oasis where the Israelites encamped after crossing the Red Sea (Num. 33:9f.). (A.D. Baly)

as well as much descriptive material about Moses himself. Ancient rites, whose practice or significance seems later to have disappeared, are preserved in 5:11-22 and 19:1-22. Quotations from "The Book of the Wars of Yahweh" (21:14f., 17f., 27-30) also appear to be from an ancient source. In particular, several poetic passages (such as the utterances of Balaam in chs. 23–24), according to scholarly opinion, are in very ancient Hebrew, i.e., thirteenth or twelfth century B.C. Details of geography and historical allusions in these poems, notably 24:23f., may point to the time of the invasion of the Sea Peoples, *ca.* 1190.

Numbers in Numbers. According to 1:45f., "the whole number of the people of Israel, by their fathers' houses, from twenty years old and upward, every man able to go forth to war in Israel," totalled 603,550. This was at the first census, taken at Sinai on the "first day of the second month, in the second year after they had come out of the land of Egypt" (v. 1).[8] If the men of military age are estimated as between 20 and 25 percent of the population—based on records of other peoples—the total of all Israelites would have been 2.5 to 3 million persons. By any reckoning, the number can hardly be reduced below 2 million.

This number is extremely large, and the problems it raises are many and

---

8. A second census, taken on the Plains of Moab in the next generation, numbered 601,730.

CENSUS FIGURES IN NUMBERS 1 AND 26

Tribe	Cited	Figures	"A"[1]	"M"[2]	Cited	Figures	"A"[1]	"M"[2]
Reuben	1:20f.	46,500	46	500	26:5ff.	43,730	43	730
Simeon	1:22f.	59,300	59	300	26:12ff.	22,200	22	200
Gad	1:24f.	45,650	45	650	26:15ff.	40,500	40	500
Judah	1:26f.	74,600	74	600	26:19ff.	76,500	76	500
Issachar	1:28f.	54,400	54	400	26:23ff.	64,300	64	300
Zebulun	1:30f.	57,400	57	400	26:26f.	60,500	60	500
Ephraim	1:32f.	40,500	40	500	26:35ff.	32,500	32	500
Manasseh	1:34f.	32,200	32	200	26:28ff.	52,700	52	700
Benjamin	1:36f.	35,400	35	400	26:38ff.	45,600	45	600
Dan	1:38f.	62,700	62	700	26:42f.	64,400	64	400
Asher	1:40f.	41,500	41	500	26:44ff.	53,400	53	400
Naphtali	1:42f.	53,400	53	400	26:48ff.	45,400	45	400
Totals		603,550	598	5,550		601,730	596	5,730
Average		50,296	49.8	462.5		50,144	49.7	477.5
High		74,600	74	700		76,500	76	730
Low		32,200	32	200		22,200	22	200

Greatest increase: Manasseh (20,500)
Greatest decrease: Simeon (37,100)

[1]"A" = $^{e}l\bar{a}p\hat{i}m$ "thousands, clans"
[2]"M" = $m\bar{e}'\hat{o}\underline{t}$ "hundreds"

This table includes the censuses of Num. 1 and 26. The figures are given as commonly translated in the biblical texts: the following elements are broken down into the "thousands" (clans, chieftains) and "hundreds" (possibly the actual totals).

---

varied. If the Hebrews took with them "very many cattle, both flocks and herds" (Exod. 12:38), how could such a multitude have been kept in any kind of discipline during the departure from Egypt? How could the wilderness, with little pastureland and supplies of water, have supported them? And how could the original seventy Israelites who went down to Egypt have multiplied to more than two million in four or seven, or even ten, generations?[9]

There are four basic approaches to the problem of the numbers, and these may apply to other portions of the Old Testament as well as to the book of Numbers. These suggestions are:

(1) The numbers are to be taken literally. This interpretation is defended

---

9. Several scholars have attempted to demonstrate the mathematical possibility of this figure. E.g., T. Whitelaw shows that if fifty-one of Jacob's fifty-three grandsons had four male descendants each, the total in seven generations would amount to 835,584; "Numbers, Book of," ISBE (1939) 4:2166. Others have pointed out that the figures are unreasonable, particularly in view of the fact that out of the male population that included over 600,000 above the age of twenty, there were only 22,273 firstborn males over the age of one month (3:43)—which would require forty or forty-five males in every household. Little is gained from such discussions.

by several statements in Scripture.[10] The descendants of Israel "were fruitful and increased greatly . . . so that the land was filled with them" (Exod. 1:7). It was this population explosion that gave Pharaoh concern (vv. 9-12), and led to the order to kill all male babies born to the Hebrews (v. 22). As for the problems of the journey, the Israelites clearly were organized into smaller groups, which tribal leadership could handle. Food and water were miraculously provided as necessary; sometimes it is suggested that the wilderness was more fertile then than today, hence capable of supporting more people and flocks.

However, this approach does not deal with all of the problem, nor does it include all the biblical data. The peoples of Canaan were described as "seven nations greater and mightier than yourselves" (Deut. 7:1). Yahweh said: "It was not because you were more in number than any other people that the Lord set his love upon you and chose you, for you were the fewest of all peoples" (Deut. 7:7; cf. Exod. 23:29). If the data in Numbers are interpreted to mean that there were 2.5 million Hebrews, one is forced to conclude that they numbered as many as are found in the same area (Israel and the other parts of Cisjordan) at present—and this would have been less than the numbers of each of the other nations already in the land. Such a position is highly unlikely. Some figures from antiquity may be used for comparison. For example, the Assyrian king Shalmaneser III was opposed by a coalition of nations at the battle of Qarqar (853) including Hadadezer of Damascus, Irhuleni of Hamath, Ahab the Israelite, and eight other kingdoms. According to Shalmaneser's inscription, Ahab contributed 2000 chariots and 10,000 soldiers,[11] out of a total of about 3000 chariots and 70,000 fighting men—and this was at the height of the ten northern tribes. Since nothing less than the survival of his kingdom was at stake, presumably Ahab did not hold back a large part of his forces. When Sargon II

---

10. Some who take the numbers literally feel the problem probably is to be explained by supposing that at one time the numbers were written as numerals and not in words, as in the present Hebrew text. Hebrew letters have numerical value, so aleph is used for 1 and also for 1000, both equals 2 and also 2000, etc. However, there are no extant biblical texts in Hebrew where the numbers are so written. Any attempt to deal with the problem is purely hypothetical, even though the suggestion is valid.

11. Shalmaneser's figures are significant:

Hadadezer of Damascus	1200 chariots	1200 cavalry	20,000 men
Irḫuleni of Hamath	700	700	10,000
Ahab the Israelite	2000	—	10,000
From Que	—	—	500
From Musri	—	—	1,000
From Irqanata	10	—	10,000
Matinu-ba'lu of Arvad	—	—	200
From Usanata	—	—	200
Adunu-ba'lu of Shian	30	—	1?,000
From Gindibu in Arabia	—	1000 camel riders	—
Basa' ben Ruhubi of Ammon	—	—	?000

He speaks of "these twelve kings," although only eleven peoples are mentioned, and claims to have killed 14,000; *ARAB* 1 §611, *ANET*, p. 279.

captured Samaria, he reported that he "led away as booty 27,290 inhabitants of it" (presumably the city of Samaria) along with fifty chariots.[12] When Sennacherib invaded Judah (701), shutting up Hezekiah "like a bird in a cage," he besieged forty-six cities, and drove out 200,150 people, "young and old, male and female."[13] Every bit of available evidence, biblical and extrabiblical, seems to discourage interpreting the numbers in Numbers literally.

(2) The figures in Numbers are a "misplaced" census list from the time of the Monarchy.[14] This really does not deal with the basic problem, but simply shifts it to a later period. It does, however, remove such problems as the rapid multiplication of the Israelites, and the ability of the wilderness to sustain so great a number of men and animals.

(3) The word translated "thousands" also can be translated "tribes," or, with slightly different vocalization, "chieftains."[15] This attempt to solve the problem without doing violence to the biblical text was suggested by W.M.F. Petrie[16] and revised somewhat by G.E. Mendenhall in the light of archaeological discoveries.[17]

This theory is attractive, both because it can be carried over to deal with similar problems of great numbers during the Monarchy and divided kingdoms (e.g., 1 Sam. 6:19; 1 Kgs. 20:30; 2 Chr. 17), and because it requires minimum emendation of the Hebrew text.[18] However, it is not without problems. There seems to be no relation between the number of "tribes, clans" and the total in each group.[19] Furthermore, it is strange that a census dealing with numbers never greater than seven hundred would supply figures primarily in even hundreds.[20] Another possible problem is the relationship between the number of "thousands" and the fighting men in each—generally less than ten in each "thousand," which (using the ratio of 1:5) would indicate a total population of only about fifty persons in each "clan."

The most serious difficulty lies in numbering the firstborn males of Israel.

---

12. *ARAB* 2 §55; *ANET*, pp. 284f. For the problem of who actually captured Samaria, see p. 276, below.

13. *ARAB* 2 §240; *ANET*, p. 288.

14. W.F. Albright, *From the Stone Age to Christianity*, p. 291.

15. Heb. *'elep*, pl. *'elāpîm*, means either "one thousand" or a large group or family; cf. Mic. 5:2 (MT 5:1; "thousands," KJV; "clans," RSV). The same consonants could be pointed to read *'allûpîm* "chiefs, chieftains." The vowel points were not added until sometime between the sixth and ninth centuries A.D., but many scholars believe that the oral tradition on which this pointing was based was highly reliable.

16. *Egypt and Israel*, rev. ed. (London: 1911), pp. 42ff.

17. "The Census Lists of Numbers 1 and 26," *JBL* 77 (1958): 52-66; cf. B.S. Childs, *Old Testament as Scripture*, p. 200.

18. It would require rejecting the totals in Num. 1:46 and 26:51, among other details.

19. The 74 "thousands" of Judah would number only 600 fighting men, whereas the 62 of Dan would number 700, and the 41 of Asher, 500. Between the first and second census, the "thousands" of Simeon dropped from 59 to 22, but the "hundreds" only from 300 to 200.

20. One in the first census ends in fifty, and one in the second, in thirty.

According to Num. 3:43, the total was 22,273. The Levites, not required to supply fighting men, were to serve as surrogates for the firstborn (vv. 44f.). The Levites are numbered at 22,000. This can be meaningful only if 22,000 is a figure, not twenty-two "thousands."[21]

(4) The numbers are part of the epic style of narrative, intended to express the majesty and miracle of the deliverance from Egypt. R.K. Harrison, for example, feels that they are "not meant to be understood either strictly literally or as extant in a corrupt textual form."[22] Thompson is content to say: "The census lists represent an ancient tradition of tribal quotas of men available for war, so that the terms in question signify military units of some kind. . . . The exact numerical value of the terms is unknown."[23] To some students of the Bible, this is no solution, but rather an evasion of the problem. To others, it is an admission that, while the text is taken seriously, one does not presume to be able to answer all the problems with the limited knowledge available.[24]

THEOLOGY

Presence. In some way too marvelous for comprehension, the Lord made his presence with the Israelites visually known:

> On the day that the tabernacle was set up, the cloud covered the tabernacle, the tent of the testimony; and at evening it was over the tabernacle like the appearance of fire until morning. So it was contin-ually; the cloud covered it by day, and the appearance of fire by night. (9:15f.)

When the cloud was taken up, the people set out; and when it settled down, they encamped. As long as the cloud rested over the tabernacle, the people remained in camp (vv. 17-23).

Once, when Miriam and Aaron became exasperated with their brother Moses "because of the Cushite woman whom he had married" (12:1), the Lord called a meeting of the three at the "tent of meeting" (v. 4). "In a pillar of cloud," he appeared and uttered these solemn words:

---

21. The difference between the 22,273 firstborn males and the 22,000 Levites is accounted for by the levy of five shekels on each of the 273; cf. 3:46-48.

22. *Introduction*, pp. 631ff.

23. *NBC*, p. 169. It may be illuminating that the Qumran community, almost certainly comprising no more than 250 or 300 people at a time, uses the same termi-nology. The regulation concerning the annual census reads: The priests shall pass over first in order, according to their spirits, one after another; and the Levites shall pass over after them, and all the people shall pass over third in order, one after another, by thousands and hundreds and fifties and tens, so that every men of Israel may know his appointed position . . . (1QS 2:21).

24. See G.B. Gray, *Numbers*, ICC (New York: 1903), pp. 11-15; J. Garstang, *Joshua Judges* (New York: 1931), p. 120; R.E.D. Clark, "The Large Numbers of the Old Testament," *Journal of the Transactions of the Victoria Institute*, 87 (1955): 82ff.; J.W. Wenham, "Large Numbers in the Old Testament," *Tyndale Bulletin* 18 (1967): 19-53.

If there is a prophet among you, I the Lord make myself known to him
in a vision, I speak with him in a dream. Not so with my servant
Moses; he is entrusted with all my house. With him I speak mouth to
mouth, clearly, and not in dark speech; and he beholds the form of
the Lord. Why then were you not afraid to speak against my servant
Moses? (vv. 6-8)

In these and other ways, the Lord made his presence known. The stories of his
continual presence throughout the wilderness period must have been told and
retold for generations, for this theme recurs centuries later in the message of
the prophets.[25]

The Providence of Yahweh. If the wilderness period was a continual object-
lesson of the Lord's presence, it was also a constant demonstration of his provision for his people's needs. He provided "manna" for the people to eat; and
when they tired of this vegetarian diet, he sent quails (Exod. 16). This story
is elaborated in Num. 11, where the Lord's providential care is seen against the
background of the people's murmurings and complaints. The provision of quails
seems temporary; but the manna continued throughout the journey, ceasing
only when the Israelites entered Canaan (Josh. 5:12).[26] When Moses recounted
the wilderness experiences, he mentioned more than the marvelous provision
of food (Deut. 8:3): "Your clothing did not wear out upon you, and your foot
did not swell, these forty years" (v. 4). When the people lacked water and
complained to Moses, God told Moses and Aaron to assemble the congregation
and "tell the rock before their eyes to yield its water" (Num. 20:8). Moses was
irritated by the unreasonable complaints of the people and, in a moment of
anger, struck the rock twice (v. 20). For this he was told he would not enter
Canaan (v. 12). Throughout the Old Testament are many reminders of God's
providential care, often illustrated by reminiscences of the wilderness period of
Israel's history.

Patience. A cardinal point of Israelite theology is that the Lord is longsuffering. Numbers provides several incidents on which this belief was founded.
God was patient with Moses, both at the call in Sinai, when Moses tried to get
out of the task, and later in the wilderness. Moses himself usually was patient
with the people; his striking the rock at Meribah was quite out of character.

---

25. The theme of presence is developed in a way that embraces the message of the
Old Testament by S. Terrien, *The Elusive Presence: Toward a New Biblical Theology* (San
Francisco: 1978).
26. Many scholars believe the manna was the honeylike excretion of certain insects
on tamarisk branches that drops to the ground during the night. See F. Bodenheimer,
"Manna," *BA* 10 (1947): 1-6. This fails to explain why the manna ceased on Sabbaths;
why, regardless of the amount gathered, there was enough and only enough; and why
the phenomenon started when the Israelites entered Sinai and ceased when they left
Moab for Canaan.

Numbers is filled with accounts of the Israelites' grumblings and complainings. They complained about their misfortunes (11:1). They longed for the fish, cucumbers, melons, leeks, onions, and garlic of Egypt (v. 5), as if they had forgotten the terrible hardships of slavery. When the Lord sent them quails, they complained (v. 33, cf. Exod. 16). Miriam and Aaron complained about Moses' wife (12:1), and their anger spilled over so they were even jealous of Moses (v. 2). When the spies returned from Canaan with stories of giants and great walled cities, the people wanted to choose a captain and go back to Egypt (14:4). The Lord's patience wore thin at that point, and he declared that none of that generation would enter the land except Caleb and Joshua, the two spies who had encouraged the people to go in and possess the land. But even in that situation, God's great redemptive plan prevailed, and he extended his promise to include the children of those who refused to trust him. And in spite of the rebellions, he continued to provide food and water.

Intercession. In Leviticus, Yahweh's holiness was stressed, prompting the question: "How can a sinful people have fellowship with a holy God?" The biblical answer involves someone to intercede between them. As seen in Leviticus, the priesthood and sacrificial system provided one means of intercession. Numbers contains several examples of personal intercession.

One of the numerous Old Testament statements where God is portrayed in human terms[27] concerns Miriam's and Aaron's jealousy toward their brother Moses: "the anger of the Lord was kindled against them, and he departed." Miriam was stricken with leprosy, and Aaron cried to Moses: "Oh, my lord, do not punish us because we have done foolishly and have sinned." Moses then interceded: "Heal her, O God, I beseech thee." God did heal her, but only after a token punishment of seven days' banishment from the camp (12:9-15).

When the people rebelled at the spies' report and wanted to overthrow Moses and return to Egypt, God threatened to smite them with the pestilence and disinherit them (14:4-12). Moses argued that the Egyptians might hear of it and say: "Because the Lord was not able to bring this people into the land which he swore to give them, therefore he has slain them in the wilderness" (vv. 13-16). Arguing from his faith that the Lord is "slow to anger, and abounding in steadfast love, forgiving iniquity and transgression," Moses prayed that he would pardon the iniquity of the people. The Lord did, but refused to let that faithless generation enter Canaan (vv. 20-23). From such experiences, the Israelites developed a strong belief in the power of a righteous person to intercede on behalf of sinners. Like so many other points in their belief, this was based on the historic acts of Yahweh, not simply on a theological concept. Such intercession was not reserved to the priestly office, but was part of Moses' ministry as prophet (cf. Gen. 20:7; Amos 7:2-5).

---

27. The technical term is "anthropopathism" where God manifests human feelings. To describe him as if he had a human form is "anthropomorphism."

Yahweh and the Nations. The belief that the Lord was ruler of all nations is not fully expressed until the latter part of Isaiah; but, like other points in Old Testament theology, it was built on experience. The Lord had demonstrated in the Exodus that he was stronger than the gods of the Egyptians. When the people refused to accept the minority report of the twelve spies, they lost an opportunity to learn that Yahweh was stronger than the gods of Canaan. Probably the most graphic lesson, though, is found in the story of Balak and Balaam.

The Israelites had been forbidden to pass through Edom, so they had traveled around it (21:4). They had to pass through Amorite territory and requested permission to do so peaceably, but Sihon, king of the Amorites, refused. The Israelites defeated him and his people and took his land (vv. 21-25). Then they entered Moab, the last region to be traversed on their way to Canaan. Concerned, Balak, king of Moab, sought aid from Balaam, a Mesopotamian prophet renowned for his power to pronounce effective curses (22:6). The story includes an episode in which God persuades Balaam not to curse Israel. When Balak puts pressure on Balaam, God warns Balaam to say only what he tells him to say. Balaam saddles his ass and rides off with the princes of Moab. The angel of the Lord blocks the road, and when Balaam strikes his ass for refusing to go further, the ass speaks to him. The angel then prevails on Balaam to go with the Moabites, but instead of cursing Israel, to bless them. Balaam does so, three times. The story is delightfully told, and must have been a great favorite in the tents and around the campfires. But more than the story of a talking donkey, it contains a deep truth. The Lord of Israel is the one who controls people; even a Mesopotamian prophet, when confronted by Yahweh, can speak only what the Lord puts in his mouth.

There is a sequel to the story. Balaam—presumably the same person, for he is called "Balaam son of Beor" in both accounts (22:5; 31:8)—apparently joined himself to the Midianites and enticed Israelites to commit abominable sin against Yahweh by worshiping Baal of Peor (31:16; cf. 25:1-3). This likely involved ritual prostitution (25:6) and was the beginning of the harlotries—both spiritual and physical—that infested Israel[28] throughout the time of the prophets up to the Exile. The Lord commanded Moses to punish the Midianites; and in the brief war, Balaam was slain (31:8).

Star-and-Scepter Prophecy. After Balaam had blessed Israel a second time, the Spirit of God came upon him, and he uttered an oracle containing an often-quoted prophecy:

The oracle of Balaam the son of Beor,
    the oracle of the man whose eye is opened,
the oracle of him who hears the words of God,
    and knows the knowledge of the Most High,

---

28. See the discussion on Hosea, p. 343, below. See also Josh. 22:17.

who sees the vision of the Almighty,
    falling down, but having his eyes uncovered;
I see him, but not now;
    I behold him, but not nigh;
A star shall come forth out of Jacob,
    and a scepter shall rise out of Israel;
It shall crush the forehead of Moab,
    and break down all the sons of Sheth.
Edom shall be dispossessed,
    Seir also, his enemies, shall be dispossessed,
    while Israel does valiantly.
By Jacob shall dominion be exercised,
    and the survivors of cities be destroyed!
                                        24:15-19

The prophecy is remarkable for its reference to the dominion of Jacob, but most frequently quoted is that passage which speaks of the star and scepter. Many have taken it as a messianic prophecy. It was understood in some such sense at Qumran, where it is quoted in the Dead Sea scrolls.[29] In its context, the prophecy says nothing about a Messiah, and there is not even a vague suggestion of the beginning of the messianic age. "Star" and "scepter" are symbolic of rule,[30] so the prophecy speaks of a ruler that shall come forth from Israel to vanquish their nearby enemies. From such a small spark ultimately developed the burning fire of hope in a Messiah who would rule all nations with righteousness and peace.

FOR FURTHER READING

Albright, W.F. "The Oracles of Balaam." *JBL* 63 (1944): 207-233. (Text and notes; supports historicity.)

Elliott-Binns, L.E. *The Book of Numbers*. Westminster Commentaries. London: 1927. (Exegetical.)

Erdman, C.R. *The Book of Numbers*. Westwood, N.J.: 1952. (Expository.)

Fish, S. *The Book of Numbers*. Soncino Books of the Bible. London: 1950. (Text and translation with notes; oriented toward Jewish reader.)

Kennedy, A.R.S. *Leviticus and Numbers*. Rev. ed. Century Bible. New York: 1910.

Marsh, J. "Introduction and Exegesis of Numbers." *IB* 2:137-308.

Noth, M. *Numbers*. Trans. J.D. Martin. OTL. Philadelphia: 1968.

Wenham, G.J. *Numbers*. Downers Grove: 1981.

---

29. See W.S. LaSor, *The Dead Sea Scrolls and the New Testament*, p. 111.
30. See Gen. 37:9f.; 49:10; Ps. 45:6.

CHAPTER 13

DEUTERONOMY

$\mathbf{F}$OR thirty-eight years after they had refused to enter Canaan, the Israelites remained in the wilderness of Paran and at Kadesh-barnea,[1] until the old generation died off, and then they resumed their journey by a long detour around Edom. Now they were encamped in Moab, awaiting final instructions to go over and possess the land God had promised to their fathers. It was an awesome moment.

According to the book of Deuteronomy, Moses took this occasion to give three addresses to the people of Israel—farewell addresses, because he had been told that he could not enter the land with the people. The substance of the addresses is found in Deuteronomy. The first was delivered "beyond the Jordan, in the land of Moab" (1:5). The second—if the words of 4:44-49 are intended as a heading for the second portion and not as a summary of the first—was given "beyond the Jordan in the valley opposite Beth-peor, in the land of Sihon the king of the Amorites" (v. 46). The third was simply "in the land of Moab" (29:1). Quite possibly the same location is intended for all three messages.

OUTLINE AND CONTENTS

Outline. Most efforts to outline Deuteronomy begin with the three addresses. The book's hortatory or sermonic style has been noted by many scholars. But the three addresses would consist of four, twenty-four, and two chapters, respectively—a very disproportionate distribution. Moreover, the inclusion of a large number of laws in an order that has no clear-cut grouping or sequence raises problems of why they would be found in such an address. Even accepting

---

1. The list of names in Num. 33:19-35 must be fitted into the wilderness wanderings. It is not correct to think of the Israelites as remaining at Kadesh-barnea all that time. For a good comparative table of the places and references mentioned, see J.D. Davis and H.S. Gehman, eds., *Westminster Dictionary of the Bible* (Philadelphia: 1944), pp. 636-39.

G. von Rad's view that the "speaker is endeavouring to move from specifically legal formulations toward pastoral exhortation and encouragement,"[2] one wonders how the speaker could have held the attention of a large audience. Perhaps this difficulty is partly why M.G. Kline looks on Deuteronomy as a document rather than a speech—"the document prepared by Moses as a witness to the dynamic covenant which the Lord gave to Israel on the Plains of Moab."[3]

With some modifications, the outline of Deuteronomy, especially as presented by Kline, follows that of the suzerainty treaty as described by G.E. Mendenhall and others (see above, pp. 144-46).[4] The book does, however, far exceed in length any such treaty published to date. Nevertheless, whether Deuteronomy was prepared deliberately in the form of such a treaty or not, that structure is a good starting place. Thus the basic outline is as follows:

Introduction (1:1-5)
First Address: Acts of Yahweh (1:6–4:40)
   Historical Summary of Yahweh's Word (1:6–3:29)
   Israel's Obligations to Yahweh (4:1-40)
Appointing of Cities of Refuge (4:41-43)
Second Address: Law of Yahweh (4:44–26:19)
   Covenant Requirements (4:44–11:32)
      Introduction (4:44-49)
      Ten Commandments (5:1-21)
      Encounter with Yahweh (5:22-33)
      Great Commandment (6:1-25)
      Land of Promise and its Problems (7:1-26)
      Lessons from Yahweh's Acts and Israel's Response (8:1–11:25)
      Choice before Israel (11:26-32)
   Law (12:1–26:19)
      Concerning Worship (12:1–16:17)
      Concerning Officials (16:18–18:22)
      Concerning Criminals (19:1-32)
      Conduct of Holy War (20:1-20)
      Miscellaneous Laws (21:1–25:19)
      Liturgical Confessions (26:1-15)
      Concluding Exhortations (26:16-19)
Ceremony to be Instituted at Shechem (27:1–28:68)
Third Address: Covenant with Yahweh (29:1–30:20)
   Purpose of Yahweh's Revelation (29:1-29)

---

2. *Deuteronomy*, trans. D. Barton. OTL (Philadelphia: 1966), pp. 19f.
3. *Treaty of the Great King* (Grand Rapids: 1963), p. 48.
4. BA 17 (1954), repr., pp. 25-43 in E.F. Campbell, Jr., and D.N. Freedman, eds., *The Biblical Archaeologist Reader* 3; *Law and Covenant in Israel and the Ancient Near East* (Pittsburgh: 1955); "Covenant," *IDB* 1:714-723, esp. 716. D.J. Wiseman, *The Vassal-Treaties of Esarhaddon*. Iraq 20 (1958): 23ff.; J. Muilenburg, "The Form and Structure of the Covenantal Formulations," *VT* 9 (1959): 347-365; M. Tsevat, "The Neo-Assyrian and Neo-Babylonian Vassal Oaths and the Prophet Ezekiel," *JBL* 78 (1959): 199-204.

Nearness of Yahweh's Word (30:1-14)
Choice Set before Israel (30:15-20)
Moses' Closing Words; His Song (31:1–32:47)
Moses' Death (32:48–34:12)

Whether originally presented orally as three addresses or written as a farewell document, the book sets forth the theme of God's covenant with Israel. It may be summarized thus:

> And now, Israel, what does the Lord your God require of you, but to fear the Lord your God, to walk in all his ways, to love him, to serve the Lord your God with all your heart and with all your soul, and to keep the commandments and statutes of the Lord, which I command you this day for your good? (10:12f.; see vv. 12-22)

COMPOSITION

The book of Deuteronomy often is called the keystone of the entire documentary hypothesis of the Pentateuch. The date of its composition has been set forth as one of the "assured results" of higher criticism. However, in recent years the theory as originally presented has almost completely deteriorated among modern students of Deuteronomy. Therefore a survey of the critical views of the book's composition is in order.

Classical Documentary Hypothesis. In the Graf-Wellhausen theory of the composition of the Pentateuch, the four documentary sources were J, E, D, and P. The D document was the major portion of Deuteronomy. In the eighteenth year of king Josiah of Judah (621 B.C.), workmen repairing the house of the Lord found "the book of the law." When it was read to the king, he tore his clothing, recognizing that his people had been disobeying the words of this book; and a religious revival was begun (2 Kgs. 22–23). As early as Jerome (fourth century A.D.), it was believed that the book found was Deuteronomy. In 1805, W.M.L. de Wette used critical scholarship to show that Deuteronomy came from a source not found in the first four books of the Pentateuch and therefore was dated in the seventh century, later than J and E. Wellhausen, toward the end of the nineteenth century, was convinced that Josiah's reforms were sparked by contemporary religious leaders who, in order to advance these reforms, composed "the book of the Law" and buried it in the temple. Subsequently, it was "discovered," and, since it purported to date from the time of Moses, gave great support to the reforms.[5] Some scholars were convinced that "the book of the law" consisted of Deut. 12–26; others, that it was chs. 5–26.

---

5. The term "pious fraud" was used on occasion with reference to this book. See J. Wellhausen, *Prolegomena to the History of Israel*, pp. 25-28.

Hammurabi stele (ca. 1700 B.C.) containing 282 laws, which suggest interesting comparisons in form and detail with the laws of the Pentateuch (e.g., Deut. 19:21). (Louvre)

Deuteronomic Historian. The date of "the book of the Law," according to the majority of scholars, was determined clearly by the theory that it was composed just prior to discovery in 621. In the twentieth century, however, scholars became disenchanted with this date. Some pushed the date of Deuteronomy back to the time of Manasseh or Hezekiah, or earlier than Amos, or even as early as Samuel. Others put the work in the time of Haggai and Zechariah, or even later.[6] Meanwhile, scholars were noticing that Deuteronomy has more in common with 1–2 Kings than with the first four books of the Pentateuch.

As a result of these varied conclusions, the term "Deuteronomist" became more common, and scholars began speaking of the "Tetrateuch" (Genesis–Numbers) and "Deuteronomic history" (Deuteronomy, Joshua, Judges, Samuel, and Kings).[7] Scholars who had followed the Wellhausenian theory had insisted that the major purpose of the D document was to establish Jerusalem's claim as the sole sanctuary, even though the city is mentioned nowhere in Deuteronomy. Von Rad noted that this theory was at odds with the command to erect an altar on Mt. Ebal (Deut. 27:4-8).[8] A.C. Welch and others pointed out that Deuteronomy has some points in common with Hosea and concluded that, rather than a product of the southern kingdom, it was a northern composition.[9] It is addressed to Israel as a whole, rather than Judah, Zion, and the Davidic line.[10] The main purpose of the book, as T. Oestreicher succinctly stated, was not *Kulteinheit* (unity of worship, i.e., at the central sanctuary) but *Kultreinheit* (purity of worship).[11] Some scholars concluded that Deuteronomy was the result, not the cause, of the Josianic reforms.[12] Obviously the same data were leading scholars in quite opposite directions.

Present Status. No scholarly consensus exists at present. Form-critical studies have led more and more scholars to recognize quite early elements in Deuteronomy. The possibility that the book is structured like the second-millennium suzerainty treaties (see above), rather than those of the mid-first millennium, would point to an earlier date. The hortatory style convinces some modern

---

6. For a quick summary, with references, see G.T. Manley, *The Book of the Law* (Grand Rapids: 1957), pp. 18-22. For a fuller discussion, see C.R. North, "Pentateuchal Criticism," pp. 48-83 in OTMS, or H.F. Hahn, *The Old Testament in Modern Research*, pp. 1-43.

7. According to M. Noth, there never was a "Hexateuch" (Genesis–Joshua); *Überlieferungsgeschichtliche Studien* 1, 3rd ed. (Tübingen: 1967): 180-82.

8. *Studies in Deuteronomy*, trans. D.M.G. Stalker (London: 1953), p. 68.

9. A.C. Welch, *The Code of Deuteronomy* (London: 1924).

10. See von Rad, *Deuteronomy*, p. 26.

11. *Das deuteronomische Grundgesetz*. Beiträge zur Förderung christlicher Theologie 27/4 (1923).

12. G.E. Wright, "Introduction and Exegesis of Deuteronomy," *IB* 2:321, mentions especially R.H. Kennett, G. Hölscher, F. Horst, and J. Pedersen, with references.

scholars that the book rests on a tradition going back to Moses himself.[13] Others put the tradition in the early Monarchy.

If one removes apparently late glosses and possibly some material in the final chapters, nothing remains in Deuteronomy that could not have come from the time of Moses. It is certainly more likely that Deuteronomy greatly influenced the prophets than that they produced it. None of the major points of contemporary tension in the prophets, such as the "high places," Baal worship, or specific types of idolatry, is found in Deuteronomy. Moses, not the prophets after him, established the great principles of Israelite religion; the prophets developed those principles and applied them to the spiritual and moral problems of their day. The results of two centuries of critical scholarship, at this moment, seem to indicate that if Deuteronomy is not the actual words of Moses, at least it is a tradition that accurately represents him and his application of the covenantal laws and statutes of Yahweh to the needs of the Israelites about to enter Canaan.[14]

THEOLOGY

Deuteronomy is a treasure chest of theological concepts that have influenced the religious thought and life of Israelites, Jews, and Christians. If the basic ideas came from Moses, as has been argued above, expanded and adapted by the Spirit's nurture, and influenced the early prophets who were responsible for the "Deuteronomic history"—the "Former Prophets"—as well as the later ("Latter") prophets, then there is excellent reason to seek to understand the theological ideas of Deuteronomy, because of both their antiquity and their dominance in Old Testament thought.

Creed. Deut. 6:4f. is the "Creed" of Israel, or, to use the opening word which has become its Jewish name, the "Shema":

Hear, O Israel: The Lord our God, the Lord is one; and you shall love the Lord your God with all your heart, and with all your soul, and with all your might. (Literal translation)

These words were to be upon the hearts of the Israelites, who were to teach them diligently to their children. The words were to be bound "as a sign" on

---

13. Wright, *ibid.*, p. 326; cf. S.R. Driver, *Deuteronomy*. ICC (New York: 1895), p. lxi. For a summary of recent discussion on the background of Deuteronomy, see R.E. Clements, "Pentateuchal Problems," pp. 117f. in G.W. Anderson, ed., *Tradition and Interpretation*.

14. B.S. Childs, *Old Testament as Scripture*, p. 212, stresses the homiletical style which belongs to the present shape of the book as an essential part of the explanation of the law: "The new interpretation seeks to actualize the traditions of the past for the new generation in such a way as to evoke a response of the will in a fresh commitment to the covenant."

the hand and "as frontlets" between the eyes. They were to be written on the doorposts of the house and on the gates. These instructions, immediately following the Shema, have become part of the Jews' daily religious rituals. Jesus took the words of v. 5 as the first and greatest commandment (Matt. 22:37).

The creed sets forth the unity and uniqueness of Yahweh the God of Israel, specifically in the relationship established between him and his people. The word used for "one" is the numeral—literally, "The Lord our God, the Lord, one." If this passage specifically taught monotheism, another Hebrew word could have been used, hence, "The Lord our God is the only God."[15] At the same time, Deut. 6:4f. does exclude any concept of polytheism in Israel's God, for he is not many but one. Above all, there is an exclusiveness about Yahweh which demands total love from his people. If the creed does not set forth monotheism as a philosophical idea, it certainly sets forth the Lord as the only God the Israelite could love and serve, for to love him with all the heart and soul and might leaves no place for devotion to another god. The name "monolatry" (worship of one god) is sometimes given to the early Israelite view, since it does not explicitly deny the existence of other gods. However, both monotheism and monolatry are philosophical concepts, and the Israelites do not appear to have been philosophers. They did not speculate about God. They knew him from their experiences with him. He had delivered them from Egypt and demanded their complete devotion. Their faith was the result of experience and not the conclusion of logic.

God Who Acts. The concept of Yahweh as one who enters into activities with selected human beings is not presented for the first time in Deuteronomy. It was an essential part of the creation story, the flood narrative, and certainly the Abrahamic covenant; and it was illustrated in a mighty way when Yahweh overthrew first the determination of Pharaoh not to release the Israelites, and then the effort of his army to recapture the escaped slaves.

However, in Deuteronomy, the historical acts of Yahweh become a basic part of the book's viewpoint, particularly as these acts relate to the claims Yahweh makes on the Israelites both at that moment and after they entered the land of promise. Moses reminds them "what Yahweh did at Baal-peor" (4:3), which is to instruct future behavior in the promised land (v. 5). "What great nation is there that has a god so near to it as Yahweh our God is to us, whenever we call upon him?" asks Moses (v. 7). The events which engendered such faith are to be made known "to your children and your children's children" (v. 9).

The doctrine that God is invisible and the commandment against making images in any form to represent God are both drawn from the Horeb experience (vv. 15f.). "And beware lest you lift up your eyes to heaven, and when you see the sun and the moon and the stars, all the host of heaven, you be drawn away

---

15. Because the word translated "one" appears to be a predicative adjective and not an attributive adjective, the translation "one Lord" is rejected here.

to worship them and serve them, things which the Lord your God has allotted to all the peoples under the whole heaven," Moses goes on to say. "But the Lord has taken you, and brought you forth out of the iron furnace, out of Egypt, to be a people of his own possession . . ." (vv. 19f.). The sun, moon, and stars belong to everyone—by God's decree—but the deliverance from Egypt was his action on behalf of Israel alone, designed to make them his own people.

If Israel forgets these experiences and their implications, Yahweh will certainly punish his people, driving them out of the land and scattering them among the nations. On the other hand, if Israel returns to Yahweh and obeys his voice, he is merciful and will not forget the covenant he swore to their fathers (vv. 25-31).

> For ask now of the days that are past, which were before you, since the day that God created man upon the earth, and ask from one end of heaven to the other, whether such a great thing as this has ever happened or was ever heard of. Did any people ever hear the voice of a god speaking out of the midst of the fire as you have heard, and still live? Or has any god ever attempted to go and take a nation for himself from the midst of another nation, by trials, by signs, by wonders, and by war, by a mighty hand and an outstretched arm, and by great terrors, according to all that the Lord your God did for you in Egypt before your eyes? To you it was shown, that you might know that the Lord is God; there is no other besides him. (vv. 32-35)

In Moses' final address, he declares: "you have seen all that the Lord did before your eyes in the land of Egypt . . . but to this day the Lord has not given you a mind to understand or eyes to see or ears to hear" (29:2-4). Again the fact that Yahweh had led them through the wilderness and provided for their needs is mentioned. Then Moses remarks that this was so "he may establish you this day as his people and that he may be your God as he promised you and as he swore to your fathers, to Abraham, to Isaac, and to Jacob" (vv. 12f.).

Election of Israel. The concept that Yahweh has chosen Israel to be his possession is called "election." The basis of the doctrine is found in the call of Abraham (Gen. 12:1-3; 15:1-6), where God's promise is directed to the "seed" or descendants of Abraham. This idea is thrust into the forefront of God's call to Moses (Exod. 3:6). It is found in the revelation of the law at Sinai (cf. 20:2, 12) and in the sacrificial system set forth in Leviticus (cf. Lev. 18:1-5, 24-30). The reference to the promise is found in the account of sending the spies into Canaan (Num. 13:2) and in their minority report (14:8). But most of all, it is the pervasive idea in Deuteronomy.

The word most often used to set forth the doctrine of election in the Old Testament is the verb "to choose." It occurs quite frequently in Deuteronomy.[16]

---

16. Heb. *bāḥar* occurs 30 times in Deuteronomy, 20 each in Isaiah and 1–2 Samuel, and 15 in 1–2 Kings.

But the idea of election—that God had chosen Israel to be his people—is expressed in many other ways and is often implied when no explicit word is used (cf. 4:32-35). It should be remembered that God's choice of Israel was effected by his creating it as a new people. Divine election is not an arbitrary act, as though God picked an already existing nation while snubbing others. His new work of redemption called for a new people, hence his call to Abraham and the formation of a new nation from Abraham's family and the subsequent events of its history.

"For you are a people holy to the Lord your God," says Moses; "the Lord your God has chosen you to be a people for his own possession, out of all the peoples that are on the face of the earth" (7:6). This choice was made not because of the numerical superiority of Israel (v. 7), but "because the Lord loves you, and is keeping the oath which he swore to your fathers . . ." (v. 8). Because of this election, Israel was to destroy the nations in the land of Canaan, "seven nations greater and mightier than yourselves" (vv. 1f.). Israel was to make no covenant with them and to show no mercy to them. There was to be no intermarriage between Israelites and the peoples of the land, for this could only turn the Israelites from Yahweh to serve other gods (vv. 3f.). Above all, they were to destroy all the religious symbols of the peoples of Canaan (v. 5). These may seem to be harsh obligations. If Yahweh is equally the God of all nations, and, therefore, all men are equally his children, then these teachings seem to raise objections. But they must be put in their proper context, against the background of election. Yahweh has chosen Israel, and he is the God of Israel. He makes no commitment to other nations, except as it involved his covenant with Israel. This basic idea of election lies behind the exclusivist portions of the New Testament, such as the difference set between the followers of Christ and the "world" (cf. John 1:12; 8:42; 15:18f.; 1 John 2:15).

But there is another side to this concept of election. God's choice of Abraham and his descendants had a purpose: "by you all the families of the earth will be blessed" (Gen. 12:3, RSV mg.). God's jealousy for Israel does not stem from his indifference to other peoples; rather, it arises from his concern that Israel transmit the truth to other peoples. If Israel is not careful to guard the truth which Yahweh revealed in words and acts, the truth will never reach the rest of the world. Accordingly, Deuteronomy stresses that the Israelites are to do all that the Lord commanded, once they enter Canaan. This is the reason behind the law of the "single sanctuary" (Deut. 12:1-14). The injunction was that Israel not worship at any of "the places where the nations whom you shall dispossess served their gods" (v. 2). "But you shall seek the place which the Lord your God will choose . . ." (v. 5). That place, wherever it might be— Ebal, Shechem, and finally Jerusalem—was to be the exclusive place of worship for those whom Yahweh had chosen to be his people. Only thus could the faith remain uncontaminated by Canaanite religion, and only thus could there be a clear witness to the nations.

The purpose of election—witness to the nations that were to be blessed because of Israel's election—is not at all stressed in Deuteronomy. Moses' central point was to place before the Israelites the dangers of contaminating their faith, of losing the truth revealed to them, when they entered into the land.[17]

Covenant Relationship. The relationship that resulted from God's election of Israel is spoken of as a "covenant relationship." The word "covenant" occurs many times in the Old Testament.[18] Although sometimes described as a "contract" or "agreement," the biblical covenant is not exactly the same. A contract has a *quid pro quo* ("something for something"): "for value received I agree to pay. . . ." If either party fails to keep his side, the other is freed from obligation. Even the suzerainty treaty is not exactly the same as the biblical covenant, although it seems a closer parallel. Here, the ruler has conquered the vassal people, and therefore they have certain obligations to him. In turn, he promises to provide certain benefits. The biblical covenant, on the other hand, originates neither in a *quid pro quo*, nor in conquest. It begins with love: "because the Lord loves you . . ." (7:8). Therefore, even though the people fail to keep their part of the obligation—they certainly did in the wilderness period—God will not break his covenant (4:31).

For the prophets, the covenant relationship is prominent; indeed, it becomes the cornerstone of the hope they construct. There were three basic elements to that hope: formation of the people God had chosen to be his, their inheritance of the land he had sworn to give the patriarchs and their descendants, and establishment of the throne he had promised David and his posterity. Each of these promises was incorporated in a covenant, whether that which God had sworn to Abraham and reiterated to Isaac, Jacob, Joseph, and Moses, or that sworn to David (2 Sam. 7). Because the Lord is a God who keeps his promises, the prophets knew that ultimately he must redeem his people, restore them to the land, and establish the king on the throne. The elements of this hope are present already in Deuteronomy; and in setting forth his convictions, Moses is truly the archetypal prophet (cf. 9:26-29; 17:14-20; 18:15-18).

One must not suppose, however, that no obligations were incumbent upon Israel in this relationship. In fact, the law given at Sinai, which Moses reiterates with sermonic applications, is composed of the obligations resulting from the covenant relationship. Here it is essential to understand the fine distinction between a contract and a covenant. If the relationship between Israel and Yahweh had been that implied in a modern contract, Yahweh's commitment would have been contingent upon Israel's keeping its obligations. In the covenant relationship, Yahweh keeps his part (the promises) because of his love

---

17. On the concept of election, see H.H. Rowley, *The Biblical Doctrine of Election*, 2nd ed. (Naperville: 1965), p. 210.

18. The Hebrew word *bᵉrîṭ* occurs 285 times throughout the Old Testament, including 26 in Deuteronomy, 24 in Genesis, 23 each in Joshua and 1–2 Kings, 20 in Psalms, 19 in Jeremiah, and 17 in Ezekiel.

and because he is God. He may punish Israel for disobedience, and may even punish whole generations for stubborn disbelief. But his covenant remains in force—simply because of his nature.

Israel, on the other hand, is obligated to keep the covenantal requirements—not to put Yahweh in debt to Israel, but because Israel is his people and so should behave accordingly. Moses appeals to the foundational principle laid down in Leviticus—"You shall be holy; for I the Lord your God am holy" (Lev. 19:2)—as he repeats the law:

All the commandment which I command you this day you shall be careful to do, that you may live and multiply, and go in and possess the land which the Lord swore to give to your fathers. And you shall remember all the way which the Lord your God has led you these forty years in the wilderness. . . . Know then in your heart that, as a man disciplines his son, the Lord your God disciplines you. So you shall keep the commandments of the Lord your God, by walking in his ways and by fearing him. . . . (Deut. 8:1-6)

Concept of Sin. The basis for the biblical doctrine of sin is set forth in the story of the Fall (Gen. 3) and illustrated in the subsequent chapters, culminating in the Flood (Gen. 4–9). In Numbers, the sin of Israel was illustrated in several events of murmuring and rebellion. In Deuteronomy, it is seen against the background of the covenant relationship.

The redemptive act by which the Lord brought the Israelites out of Egypt is mentioned in connection with the commandments (Deut. 6:20-25). The obligation of the Israelites to keep and do his ordinances stemmed from the fact that they were chosen to be his possession (7:6). Thus, when they entered the land, they were to remember these facts and keep his commandments (8:1-10). However, they were in danger of forgetting this relationship and turning to other gods (vv. 11-18), for which they would "surely perish" (v. 19). Loving God and keeping his commandments are set side by side (11:1, 13), and blessing in the land is to follow from such obedience (vv. 8-12). Implicitly, disobedience would bring the withholding of blessing.

The worst sin, therefore, is turning to other gods. Many detailed laws and statutes are set forth in Deuteronomy, but rarely is a penalty for infraction mentioned. Rather, blessing is promised for keeping the laws:

Because you hearken to these ordinances, and keep and do them, the Lord your God will keep with you the covenant and the steadfast love which he swore to your fathers to keep; he will love you, bless you, and multiply you; he will also bless the fruit of your body and the fruit of your ground, . . . the increase of your cattle and the young of your flock, in the land which he swore to your fathers to give you. (7:12f.)

But when apostasy or idolatry is mentioned, a threat of punishment is attached:

Beware lest there be among you a man or a woman or family or tribe, whose heart turns away this day from the Lord our God to go and serve the gods of these nations. . . . The Lord would not pardon him but rather the anger of the Lord and his jealousy would smoke against that man and the curses written in this book would settle upon him and the Lord would blot out his name from under heaven. (29:18-20)

So serious is the sin of idolatry that the Israelite was commanded to kill a brother, son or daughter, wife, or friend who sought to lead him to serve other gods: "You shall not yield to him or listen to him, nor shall your eye pity him, nor shall you spare him, nor shall you conceal him; but you shall kill him; . . . You shall stone him to death with stones, because he sought to draw you away from the Lord your God, who brought you out of the land of Egypt . . ." (13:6-10). If the inhabitants of a city were to try to lead Israelites away from Yahweh, that city and everything in it were to be destroyed (13:15f.).

Despite the humanitarian nature of many of the laws set forth in Deut. 15–26, the penalties for idolatry were terribly severe. The only answer that can be derived from Deuteronomy, or any other portion of the Bible, is the nature of the covenant relationship. As a general rule, the Bible does not enjoin the people of God to slaughter unbelievers. The only such policy is in connection with the Israelite possession of Canaan. As shown in Joshua and Judges, the covenantal nature and purpose of the land of promise underlies the requirements for Israel to remove the Canaanites. The ancients knew little of the tolerance that modern, pluralistic societies have developed. The typical Middle Eastern nation—like tribal peoples today—had a uniform culture and religious belief adhered to by all who lived within their region. Uniqueness was best preserved by intolerance of other cultures. As set forth in Samuel and Kings and presented in the background of the messages of the prophets, failure to obey Yahweh's command to destroy the Canaanites led to gross idolatry on the part of the Israelites and ultimately to the destruction of the kingdom and exile from that land.

Like the marriage covenant, the relationship between Yahweh and his people is a covenant of mutual love and trust. Like adultery, apostasy breaks the relationship by despising the love on which it is based, violating the trust, and treating the person as unworthy of exclusive and all-consuming commitment. The covenant relationship is impossible under such conditions, as argued at length in the prophets. The person who turns from God to serve other gods is warned of grave results. He who attempts to lead someone else into idolatry is the worse sinner; he is condemned to death.

The concept of progressive revelation (see above, p. 11) applies here. One type of law was necessary at the time the Israelite nation was getting established in Canaan. Gross idolatry at that point could have destroyed completely the means of conveying God's redemptive revelation to future generations. Gross idolatry several centuries later brought the nation to defeat and destruction, and only by God's grace was a remnant spared. In the light of revelation through Jesus Christ and the Apostles a gentler law applies.

God in History. The concept that God has actually entered into history is a unique biblical doctrine, one not found in the same way in the literature of any other religion. It is taught consistently throughout the Bible. In Deuteronomy, however, it is set forth in a unique way which greatly influences the later writings and gives rise to the idea of "Deuteronomic history."

To cite chapter and verse is largely superfluous, for the entire book is a recital of God's acts on behalf of his people. It is an account of how God led Israel out of Egypt, gave them the law at Sinai, patiently endured their stubborn displays of unbelief in the wilderness, and brought them to the verge of the Jordan. This sequence of events is perhaps summarized best in chs. 6–12, several portions of which are quoted above.

Ch. 5 contains the second account of the Ten Commandments (or Decalogue; the first is in Exod. 20:1-17). Their implications are set forth in the chapters that follow. The story moves back and forth between the obligations of the future, when Israel will have entered the land of Canaan, and the experiences of the past, when Israel saw the mighty acts of Yahweh and heard his words. This interplay of past and future gives rise to a "prophetic" view of history, in which the past not only provides lessons for the future but even becomes the source of movements that influence the future. When God acted in the past—in the time of Abraham, for example—he not only said or did something which can be a lesson for today or give hope for tomorrow, but he also revealed part of his ongoing activity, by which he will fulfill his redemptive purpose. So Moses, the prophets, and the New Testament writers understood the history of God's activity.

The biblical view is neither that of Kismet, the fatalism of Islam, nor that of Karma, the deterministic cause-and-effect of Hinduism and Buddhism. The human actors always behave as if free in their choices and therefore responsible for them. Yahweh often is portrayed as if angered or frustrated by human activities, but in the end, his purpose prevails. He brought Israel out of Egypt despite the power and wisdom of Pharaoh. He brought Israel through the wilderness despite the unbelief of the majority. He gave them victory over the kings and nations who sought to bar their way. He turned the curses of Balaam into blessings. And despite their utter disbelief that they could enter the land of Canaan, he had them on the shore of the Jordan and was giving instructions for the time when they would enter the land.

This same concept of history—sometimes called *Heilsgeschichte*, the history of salvation—can be seen in the prophets. In the Former Prophets it is applied primarily to the contemporary situation; in the Latter Prophets, to the future as well. It pervades the works of the Psalmist. It sustains the people of God in the Exile and afterwards, days that would otherwise be hopeless. It is even intertwined with the events set forth in Esther—where the name of God does not even appear. To God's people, history becomes "his story."

INFLUENCE OF DEUTERONOMY

How can the influence of a book be measured? One yardstick is the number of books written about it or that quote it. Another indication would be some great achievement that can be traced directly to motivation which the book supplied. Of course, one could never record precisely the individual decisions influenced by reading the book or the number who received hope from it.

Some Bible students see the influence of Deuteronomy on Samuel and Elijah, on Hosea and Jeremiah, and on Jesus. Judging from the number of quotations or citations of Deuteronomy in the New Testament, it ranks as one of the most influential.[19] Based on the number of manuscripts of the individual Old Testament books found among the Dead Sea scrolls, Deuteronomy was one of the five most influential works at Qumran.[20] Jesus thrice found strength in Deuteronomy to turn back Satan's tempting (Matt. 4:1-11; cf. Deut. 8:3; 6:13, 16). When asked which commandment was greatest, he quoted Deut. 6:5 in reply.

But this is only the peak of the iceberg. How many times was Deuteronomy quoted in the home of Joseph and Mary, that Jesus came to know it so well? In how many Jewish homes, where the Shema (6:4f.) is recited several times a day, has the book brought faith and inspiration? How many Christians have found help and strength in its pages? Every indication points to the conclusion that Deuteronomy is one of the most significant books in the Old Testament. In any generation it deserves careful study.

FOR FURTHER READING

Carmichael, C.M. *The Laws of Deuteronomy*. Ithaca, N.Y.: 1974. (Examines literary and historical problems.)

Clements, R.E. *God's Chosen People*. London: 1968. (Theological interpretation of Deuteronomy.)

————. *Prophecy and Covenant*. London: 1965.

Craigie, P.C. *The Book of Deuteronomy*. NICOT. Grand Rapids: 1976. (Espouses conservative position regarding date and unity.)

Daane, J. *The Freedom of God*. Grand Rapids: 1973. (Contrasts biblical view of election with that of Reformed scholastic theology.)

McCarthy, D.J. *The Old Testament Covenant*. Oxford: 1972. (Expansion of CBQ 27 [1965]: 217-240.)

————. *Treaty and Covenant*. Analecta Biblica 21 (1965). (Form-critical study of ancient Near Eastern documents and the Old Testament; esp. 109-140.)

---

19. Based on the United Bible Societies' *Greek New Testament*, Deuteronomy is quoted or cited 195 times in the New Testament, exceeded only by references to Psalms, Isaiah, Genesis, and Exodus, in that order.

20. Thus far, 27 are of Psalms, 24 of Deuteronomy, 18 of Isaiah, and 15 each of Genesis and Exodus.

Nicholson, E.W. *Deuteronomy and Tradition*. Philadelphia: 1967. (Literary and historical problems.)

Phillips, A. *Deuteronomy*. Cambridge Bible Commentary. Cambridge: 1973. (Commentary on NEB.)

Robertson, E. *The Old Testament Problem*. Manchester: 1950. (Examines classic Wellhausenian theory.)

Rowley, H.H. *The Faith of Israel*. London: 1956. (Includes essay on Israelite equation of the good life with obedience to the will of God.)

Weinfeld, M. *Deuteronomy and the Deuteronomic School*. Oxford: 1972. (Studies sermonic composition, relationship to wisdom, and the law as rationalistic ideology.)

Zimmerli, W. *The Law and the Prophets*. Trans. R.E. Clements. Oxford: 1965. (Esp. pp. 31-45 on Law and Covenant.)

CHAPTER 14

THE FORMER PROPHETS

As indicated in the discussion of the canon (Ch. 3), the second main division of the Hebrew Bible is known as the "Prophets," and is subdivided into "Former Prophets" and "Latter Prophets." The Former Prophets consist of four books: Joshua, Judges, Samuel (later divided into 1–2 Samuel), and Kings (later divided into 1–2 Kings).

PROBLEMS OF CLASSIFICATION

"Prophets" or "History"? In the English Bible, these six books (counting Samuel and Kings as four books) are included in the "historical" division along with 1–2 Chronicles, Ezra, Nehemiah, and Esther. Why did the Jews who arranged the Hebrew canon call these books "prophets"? And why are they now considered as "history"?[1] At this point it is sufficient to note that to the ancient Hebrew mind, at least, the Former Prophets had more the nature of "prophecy" than of "history."[2]

As noted in the discussion of Genesis (pp. 107-9, above), the question of what constitutes "history" is very complicated, and scholars have come to various conclusions. Behind any history lie the "brute facts"—what actually happened. An attempt to record every fact would be impossible, yet to record only the principal or most important events immediately interposes, between the events and the reader, the person making the record.

Some would not consider such a record as history. Rather, it is a "chronicle" or "journal." It makes no attempt to relate the events, to study their effects on

---

1. Luther probably was responsible for the order of the Protestant canon. For an extended study of this problem, see H.E. Ryle, *The Canon of the Old Testament*, 2nd ed. (New York: 1895), pp. 221-249.
2. Quite probably the Hebrews focused both on the office of prophet and on the book's oracular nature. Only a western way of thinking attempts to judge the work deficient as history prior to understanding the *oracular* nature of the work.

one another,[3] or to relate the events of one chronicle to those of another chronicle from another region or period. The books of Kings contain many references to "the chronicles of the kings of Israel" or "of Judah" and similar titles.[4] These were probably journals or daybooks in which principal events were recorded and which were used as source materials in the composition of 1–2 Kings. The "annals" of a number of Assyrian kings likewise represent a kind of chronicle. History could be defined as the product of a process of selection from such chronicles and of editorial arrangement to tell a story, whether a history of painting or of the rise and fall of the German Third Reich.

The individual books that comprise the Former Prophets are not really a history—at least not one satisfactory to the modern historian. Joshua tells the story of the settlement of Israel in Canaan; but as history, the account is not all of the same detailed character. The crossing of the Jordan, the religious rites at Gilgal, the capture of Jericho and of Ai are all given with considerable detail. But the conquest of southern Canaan is told very succinctly, and that of the north even more briefly. In some cases, the peoples involved or cities taken are not indicated. Judges is even more tantalizing—a series of stories apparently from various parts of the country and various times. An attempt to build a continuous account of the new nation's development reveals that the purpose of Judges was not to give that kind of history, but to lay out the pattern of God's dealings with his people in judgment and grace. The books of Samuel seem more satisfactory as history, for they do give a good picture of the establishment of the Monarchy and of the first kings. 1–2 Kings is a rather full chronological account, complicated somewhat because the histories of the northern and southern kingdoms are interwoven; but even here kings are evaluated by their religious practices rather than their political significance. Throughout the Former Prophets, the religious viewpoint dominates. This, then, is not history as modern historians might write it. Rather, to oversimplify considerably, it is history from a prophetic point of view: (1) picturing God's control of history by deed and word; (2) featuring acts of prophets like Samuel, Nathan, Elijah, and Elisha; (3) demonstrating the great prophetic themes of divine rescue in the Exodus, gift of the land, covenant obligations in the exclusive worship of Yahweh and justice in the community, blessing and punishment as Yahweh's reward for obedience or rebellion.

Historical Significance. To make such a statement, however, is not to denigrate the historical value of the biblical books. All historical writing is selective, and all is written for some purpose. There is a great difference between the

---

3. Even this question is often rejected by historians of the modern "scientific" school influenced by the philosophy of D. Hume, wherein events are viewed as having no real relationship to one another.

4. The person responsible for such works was originally called *mazkîr* (lit. "one who causes to remember"). Later the office of *mazkîr* seems to have developed into more than simply the chronicler.

strongly biased annals of the Assyrian kings and the histories of Herodotus and Josephus[5]—even if the historical worth of many statements in Herodotus or Josephus may be questioned. The historian has a purpose in the selection of materials.[6] He does not invent or falsify (although it may seem so to those with differing purposes), but selects in light of that purpose. The Former Prophets contain historical data chosen from the prophetic viewpoint.

It usually will be conceded today that the Old Testament contains more historical material than any other single book prior to Herodotus, the "father of history."[7] Archaeological discoveries repeatedly have demonstrated its high degree of historical accuracy.[8] Nonetheless, the historical element in the Former Prophets—or throughout the Old Testament—is incidental to (and integral with) the religious message. The Former Prophets are primarily prophecies (in the basic Hebrew sense of speaking the word which God has given). In these books, the purpose of God is set forth; the message of God, perceived through his acts and words, is proclaimed.[9]

"Former" and "Latter Prophets." A temporal difference can be demonstrated between the "Former" and the "Latter Prophets." The "Former" belong mostly to the period of settlement in Canaan and the early Monarchy, even though they continue the story to the Exile. The "Latter Prophets" belong to the closing centuries of the two kingdoms. But it would be entirely incorrect to think of this temporal distinction as the only difference. A more fundamental difference may be found in the nature of the books.

The Former Prophets are more "historical," approaching a continuous narrative of the events in Israel's history. From Joshua through 2 Kings, can be reconstructed—in outline form, at least, and in some cases with considerable detail—the sequence of Israel's history from the entrance into Canaan until the Exile, roughly 1250-586 B.C. Precisely for this reason these books are called

---

5. See the annals of Assur-nasir-pal (*ARAB* 1 §§437-483) or Shalmaneser III (*ANET*, pp. 276-281). See also the account of the campaigns of Thutmose III (*ANET*, pp. 234-241). Several editions of Herodotus and Josephus are available.

6. For instance, exactly the same historical data are available to the writer of "black history" as to any other historian. Because of their justifiable view that previous historians tended to omit data that did not (in their opinion) concern nonblacks the writers of "black history" have selected data that are important to blacks. Future historians, seeking to present a more "balanced" picture, will doubtless select data of concern to both blacks and nonblacks.

7. Herodotus dates to the fifth century B.C.; *History of the Persian Wars*, trans. A.D. Godley. Loeb Classical Library (London: 1921-24).

8. See W. F. Albright, *History, Archaeology, and Christian Humanism* (New York: 1964); E. Yamauchi, *The Stones and the Scriptures* (Philadelphia: 1972); J. Finegan, *Light from the Ancient Past*, 2nd ed. (Princeton: 1959); W. Keller, *The Bible as History*, trans. W. Neil (New York: 1956); J. Arthur Thompson, *The Bible and Archaeology*, 3rd ed. (Grand Rapids: 1982); W.S. LaSor, "Archeology," *ISBE* (1979) 1:243f.

9. For all this, these writings form the best historical writings in antiquity. By every measure, they give the most complete account with exceptional accuracy and with sensitivity to the social, political, religious, and other concerns of the time.

"historical" in the English canon. In contrast, only a vague outline of history can be reconstructed from the Latter Prophets. Historical persons and events are mentioned, but no sequence of events can be found. Even with the outline of history available from the Former Prophets, there is great difficulty arranging chronologically the details found in the Latter Prophets.

On the other hand, the Latter Prophets are more "prophetical," containing more of the preaching message of the prophets[10]—an element almost entirely absent from the Former Prophets. The book of Joshua, for example, reports about the man Joshua, including some of what he said and did; but Joshua, unlike a prophet such as Amos, gives no oracle of Yahweh. Many of Nathan's words are recorded in connection with the story of David, but Nathan's words cannot be classified as prophecy in the same sense as Jeremiah's. Probably the most extensive prophetic writing in the Former Prophets is the "Elijah cycle" (1 Kgs. 16–2 Kgs. 1). Yet even these chapters and the "Elisha cycle" (2 Kgs. 2–9) which follows form nothing approaching a "prophecy of Elijah (or Elisha)" similar to that of Micah or Zephaniah.

Therefore, though the Former Prophets are principally prophetic—in the sense that they set forth the acts of Yahweh and the interpretation thereof—they are at the same time historical. They do indeed give a continuous history of Israel, but always through the eyes of a prophet. It is history interpreted by the Spirit of God through his spokesmen.

PROBLEMS OF DATE AND COMPOSITION

Source Theory. In a previous generation, the documentary hypothesis, the theory that there were four sources (J, E, D, P) in the Pentateuch, was applied also to the Former Prophets (see above, p. 64). It was common to include Joshua with the preceding books and to speak of a "Hexateuch." More recently, scholars are inclined to separate Deuteronomy from the first four books (the "Tetrateuch") and include it with the Former Prophets to form the "Deuteronomic history." The reasons for such attempts are essentially the same as with the Pentateuch, namely, alternate forms of the divine name, differences in style, "doublets" or "triplets" in which the same or remarkably similar details occur or where different causes or reasons for the same event are found,[11] reference to later situations or place names in an account of an earlier period, and the citing of sources ("the book of Jashar," "the book of the chronicles of the kings of Judah"). Detailed analyses of these critical theories can be found in any standard introduction to the Old Testament.

---

10. Most of the books of the great prophets (the Latter Prophets) are collections of the prophets' oracles or messages.

11. One of the most notable is David's first introduction to Saul (1) as a musician who could bring therapy to the king (1 Sam. 16:14-22), or (2) in the contest with Goliath (17:12-54, particularly vv. 55-58).

Literary Forms in Kings. A number of literary forms (*Gattungen*) occur in the books of Kings. Any theory of composition of these books must take them into account.

Sources can be identified behind the recorded accounts. For example, the "Solomon cycle," the series of stories about Solomon, from his proclamation as king until his death, is told in 1 Kgs. 1:1–11:40. Following these stories is the statement, "Now the rest of the acts of Solomon, and all that he did, and his wisdom, are they not written in the book of the acts of Solomon?" (11:41). Similarly, after the account of Solomon's son Rehoboam, reference is made to "the Book of the Chronicles of the Kings of Judah" (14:29). Again, following the brief account of Baasha king of Israel, the source is mentioned: "the Book of the Chronicles of the Kings of Israel" (16:5).[12] Many such references occur in the books of Kings. These chronicles were court records, the journals or daybooks in which the king's scribe entered the events of the day.

Also included are prophetic stories, or stories about prophets. Most extensive are the "Elijah cycle" (1 Kgs. 17:1–19:21; 22:41–2 Kgs. 1:18) and the "Elisha cycle" (2:1–10:36), but these stories seem to be interwoven with other accounts. Among the shorter stories about prophets is the account of Ahijah the Shilonite and Jeroboam (1 Kgs. 11:29-39). 2 Chr. 13:22 refers to a prophetic story: "The rest of the acts of Abijah, his ways, and his sayings, are written in the story (*bᵉmidrāš*) of the prophet Iddo."

Prophetic oracles often are interwoven with the story about the prophet. Ahijah's oracle to Jeroboam (1 Kgs. 11:31-39) occupies most of the story. Shorter oracles are contained in the long story of Elijah, such as the oracle to Ahab (21:21-24).

Similar to the prophetic oracle is the divine revelation to the prophet, such as the words of Yahweh to Elijah in 19:15-18. Note that the revelations generally are recounted in the third person: "And the Lord said to him" (v. 15).

Prophetic evaluations are particularly noticeable in the accounts of the kings of Israel and Judah. In introducing the reign of Jehoash (Joash), the writer says: "And Jehoash did what was right in the eyes of the Lord all his days, because Jehoiada the priest instructed him" (2 Kgs. 12:2). On the other hand, the account of Jehoahaz of Israel comments: "He did what was evil in the sight of the Lord, and followed the sins of Jeroboam the son of Nebat . . ." (13:2). According to these evaluations, there were good and bad kings in Judah; the prophets did not simply follow a political party line.

Of course it is possible to construct a theory of inspiration that explains the various types of literature as the result of direct revelation. However, as seen with regard to revelation and inspiration (Ch. 2, above), such a position

---

12. These are not to be confused with the biblical books of Chronicles. 1–2 Chronicles had not yet been written, and "the rest of the acts (*dibrê*)" of such named kings are not found in them. As further evidence, the same references occur in Chronicles; cf. 2 Chr. 20:34.

is not biblically derived, and never has been the historical position of the Church. Therefore the details should be considered as *indicia* of the process by which God brought the Scriptures into existence. There must have been a storehouse of prophetic tradition, possibly compiled and preserved by the prophetic institution known as "the sons of the prophets." Judging from passages in Chronicles,[13] the prophets or their followers kept accounts such as "the midrash of the prophet Iddo" (2 Chr. 13:22) and the "acts (*dibrê*) of Shemaiah the prophet and of Iddo the seer" (12:15). These were not oral accounts, for each statement includes the word "written," as do the summarizing statements in Kings. Subsequent to the latest recorded event, an author or editor apparently wove together the various accounts to form the basic structure of Kings.[14]

Deuteronomic History. The relating of historical events into a purposeful sequence as the acts of Yahweh is apparently a concept unique to the Bible. Certain events are attributed to the actions of deities in other ancient Near Eastern literature, but nowhere else is the idea consistently carried through a historical period, nor are all events related to only one deity.

The origin of this concept is debatable. Recent scholarship attributes it to a seventh-century "Deuteronomic historian." Perhaps the most sustained illustration of the concept is in Judges, where it is clearly set forth that sin brings punishment in the form of oppression by a foreign nation, while repentance causes Yahweh to raise up a deliverer (see Ch. 16). But the same understanding of history is found in evaluations of the kings of Judah and Israel throughout 1–2 Kings.

Such a concept, carried through with a consistency far exceeding that of any other nation, and so completely different from that found in any other ancient literature, must be indigenous to Israel. It requires at least a superior religious insight—the kind that ultimately comes from divine revelation to a mind capable of comprehending the revelation. The essential question is simply: Is it more reasonable to assume that the originator of this concept of history was an unknown figure in the days of Josiah, when the kingdom was rapidly drawing to a close, or Moses? Or was it a combination of both?

The answer is not simple. The best time to develop a philosophy of history is at the end of a period, rather than the beginning. Only after looking back over the great deeds of God can it be said: "God meant it for good." At earlier times one may question his goodness or wisdom. The time of Jeremiah and Josiah would be a fitting period to develop a philosophy of history. Yet, it is remarkable that relatively unimportant prophets, such as Gad, Iddo, or even Obadiah and Habakkuk, are known by name, their memory cherished by the people of God, while the great genius who saw God at work in all that was happening remains completely unknown.

---

13. Although quite late (4th cent.), Chronicles certainly contains earlier material.
14. See W.S. LaSor, "1 and 2 Kings," *NBC*, p. 320.

Moses is consistently presented as having remarkable experiences of God which none other had ever known. If certain statements in Deuteronomy are taken at face value, the bulk of that work presents a philosophy of history, an explanation of the great works of Yahweh. According to many scholars, this is "the book of the law" discovered by Hilkiah in the temple in the days of Josiah (2 Kgs. 22:8-13). But this seems too simplistic. It stresses the final stage of composition, and seems to ignore the roots found in earlier periods, and the process by which Israel's history came under the interpretation of divine judgment and grace. If the outline of the suzerain vassal treaty is indeed seen in the law of Moses at Sinai, then the concept of blessings and curses is present already. It underlies the events as preserved in Judges. The stories of Saul and David, in the early Monarchy, depict divine blessing and rejection. The cultic literature, much of which stems from the Monarchy, is filled both with testimony of the blessings of Yahweh and with the sense of divine displeasure and chastisement for failure to obey his law. This view of judgment and grace is largely applied to individuals at first, but certainly by the time of Amos the concept is applied to the nation. Then the Deuteronomic concept of history seems to have been forgotten for a time, only to be "discovered" with a new sense of the divine imperative in the days of Josiah. The final form of the recital of the acts of Yahweh certainly must have come from the deuteronomic editor or editors at the end of the kingdom, but the deuteronomic concept of history seems to have originated much earlier. Indeed, it is most reasonable to assume that as the people of Yahweh applied the germinal Mosaic truth to the events of the ensuing centuries, the Deuteronomic concept of history came into its fully developed form.[15]

FOR FURTHER READING

Miller, J.M. *The Old Testament and the Historian.* Guides to Biblical Scholarship. Philadelphia: 1976.

Porter, J.R. "Old Testament Historiography." Pp. 125-162 in G.W. Anderson, ed. *Tradition and Interpretation.* (Pp. 132-152 on the Deuteronomic historical work.)

---

15. "In sum, the book has not been redacted primarily to offer an explanation of the past, but to function as scripture for the new generation of Israel who are instructed from the past for the sake of the future"; B.S. Childs, *Old Testament as Scripture*, p. 238. See Childs, *ibid.*, for a discussion of the suggested purposes of the final editors of the Deuteronomic history. The viewpoint taken in this survey is close to that held by H.W. Wolff as summarized by Childs: "the book's rehearsing of the history of the destruction of the nation has the pattern of divine judgment and forgiveness built into it in such a way as to offer to the nation under judgment a renewed promise of forgiveness."

CHAPTER 15

JOSHUA

THE book of Joshua takes up where Deuteronomy left off. The Israelites were encamped in the Plains of Moab, awaiting the Lord's command to go over and possess Canaan. Moses, who had led them thus far, was not to enter the land (Deut. 3:23-27; 32:48-52). God had instructed Moses to turn over the leadership to Joshua (3:28, and again just before the death of Moses, 31:23). Shortly after he had done so, Moses died (34:5).

> And Joshua the son of Nun was full of the spirit of wisdom, for Moses had laid his hands upon him; so the people obeyed him, and did as the Lord had commanded Moses. (v. 9)

The book of Joshua resumes the story at this point:

> After the death of Moses the servant of the Lord, the Lord said to Joshua the son of Nun, Moses' minister, "Moses my servant is dead; now therefore arise, go over this Jordan, you and all this people, into the land which I am giving to them, to the people of Israel. . . . No man shall be able to stand before you all the days of your life; as I was with Moses, so I will be with you; I will not fail you or forsake you. (1:1-5)

OUTLINE AND CONTENTS

The story is told in two main parts, each approximately half of the book: a rapid survey of the conquest of the land; and a description of how the land was divided among the twelve tribes.

Outline

Commission of Joshua (1:1-9)
Entry into the land (1:10–5:12)
   Preparations to cross the Jordan (1:10-18)
   Spies in Jericho (2:1-24)
   Crossing the Jordan (3:1–4:18)
   Camp at Gilgal (4:19–5:12)

Conquest of the land (5:13–12:24)
    Commander of the army of the Lord (5:13-15)
    Fall of Jericho (6:1-27)
    Campaign against Ai (7:1–8:29)
    Altar built on Ebal (8:30-35)
    Treaty with the Gibeonites (9:1-27)
    Campaign in the South (10:1-43)
    Campaign in the North (11:1-23)
    Summary of the Conquest (12:1-24)
Division of the land (13:1–22:34)
    Allotment of the Transjordan tribes (13:1-33)
    Portion of Caleb (14:1-15)
    Portion of Judah (15:1-63)
    Portion of Joseph (16:1–17:18)
    Portion of the remaining tribes (18:1–19:51)
    Cities of refuge (20:1-9)
    Levitical cities (21:1-42)
    Conclusion and departure of Transjordan tribes (21:43–22:9)
    Altar by the Jordan (22:9-34)
Joshua's last days (23:1–24:33)
    Joshua's first address (23:1-16)
    Joshua's second address and the covenant at Shechem (24:1-28)
    Burials of Joshua, Joseph's bones, and Eleazar (vv. 29-33)

Contents. Joshua began immediately to prepare for crossing the Jordan. One of the first obstacles would be the ancient and well-fortified city of Jericho, a few miles from the river. Joshua sent two spies to reconnoiter the land and city, and they were remarkably protected by the innkeeper, the harlot Rahab (2:1-24). The crossing of the Jordan, which was in flood,[1] was made possible by the damming-up of the waters a dozen miles or so north, so Israel might pass over on dry ground. Then, according to the well-known account, Jericho was taken by the intervention of Yahweh. The Israelite army marched around the city for seven days, with seven priests blowing rams' horns. Though one might get the impression that the conquest of Canaan would be easy, such is usually not so for God's people.

The campaign to take the area at the ancient ruins of Ai (the Hebrew word means "the ruins") resulted in a setback. When Joshua sought the reason from the Lord, he received the answer: "Israel has sinned; they[2] have transgressed my covenant . . ." (7:11)—by secretly keeping spoils of battle, which should have been "devoted"[3] to Yahweh. Apparently the guilty party was de-

---

1. According to 3:15 "the Jordan overflows all its banks throughout the time of harvest," that is, springtime, when the Jordan waters flowed over the narrow bed of the river into the Zor. See p. 49.

2. Israel sometimes is referred to in the singular ("he" or "she") and sometimes the plural ("they"). In this sentence both occur.

3. This meant to destroy utterly a person, possessions, or a city. See pp. 207-9.

Excavations at Jericho, a city "devoted to the Lord for destruction" (Josh. 6:17). (Jericho Excavation Fund, photo K.M. Kenyon)

termined by casting lots, which the people of the Old Testament believed were guided by Yahweh. By the process of elimination, the tribe of Judah, the clan of the Zerahites, the family of Zabdi, and finally Achan were chosen. Achan confessed his sin in taking a beautiful mantle, a quantity of silver, and a gold bar. He and his entire household, his sons, daughters, large and small cattle, and his tent, as well as the booty, were destroyed by stoning and fire. Then Ai was conquered by ambush (7:16–9:17) (p. 203).

The next problem developed when Joshua and his forces were planning to move to the top of the central mountain range, probably to begin the campaign in the south of the land. Some of the Gibeonites met them, dressed as though they had just come on a long journey. They persuaded Joshua to enter a covenant (or treaty) with them (9:13). Without seeking the Lord's direction, Joshua agreed, only to learn that they were inhabitants of the cities he had to capture to unify the land. Because of his treaty, sworn by solemn oath, Joshua did not kill them or "devote" their cities, thus permitting the first of the Canaanite enclaves (small cities and villages occupied by non-Israelites, in the midst of Israelite territory). Later, this coalition of Gibeonite cities astride the main north-south route would become a factor in disunifying the land and the subsequent division into northern and southern kingdoms.

Five Amorite kings of the city-states south and southwest of Gibeon received news of the conquest of Ai, and hastened to confront Joshua and the Israelites. Once again Yahweh gave the Israelites victory, and the enemy fled past Beth-horon toward the maritime plain to the west. Yahweh sent a storm with large hailstones and then stayed the sun (10:6-14) on this "long day of Joshua" (pp. 209-210).

The conquest of the south, including the Negeb and Shephelah (10:1-43), is told very briefly, without detailed accounts of the battles (vv. 28-43). This is followed by a similarly brief account of the conquest in the north, including a battle by the waters of Merom (11:7) and the conquest of Hazor (v. 10).

The style changes notably in the second half of the book, with somewhat tedious accounts of the division of the land among the tribes. Perhaps most interesting is the story of the altar which the Transjordanian tribes erected by the Jordan as they returned to their lands. The purpose of the altar was misunderstood by the Cisjordan tribes (those in Canaan), and only a prompt explanation that it was a witness of unity rather than a sign of division prevented a serious breach between the tribes on opposite sides of the river (22:21-29).

How Total Was the Victory? A casual reading of Joshua, with no attempt to consider some of the incidental statements or the data in the book of Judges, may suggest that the Israelite victory over the Canaanites was quick and complete. Several statements could easily foster such a conclusion: "Joshua defeated the whole land" (10:40); "Joshua took all that land" (11:16); "they put to the sword all who were in it, utterly destroying them; there was none left that breathed" (v. 11); "there was not a city that made peace with the people of

Israel, except the Hivites, the inhabitants of Gibeon, they took all in battle" (v. 19).

However, the book itself notes that there remained "yet very much land to be possessed," and spells out the details (13:1-7).[4] Included was the Philistine territory, and some land north of Palestine. But much of it remained unconquered, particularly in the Canaanite enclaves, with Canaanite altars and high places that proved later to snare the Israelites into sin.

THE MAN JOSHUA

The leading character in the book is Joshua[5] bin Nun, an Israelite of the tribe of Joseph (the "half-tribe" of Ephraim) who was born in Egypt and was a young man at the time of the Exodus (Exod. 33:11). He was named "Hoshea" ("salvation"; cf. Num. 13:8), but Moses called him "Jehoshua" or "Joshua" ("Yahweh is salvation"; v. 16).[6] Joshua was chosen by Moses to be his "minister"—probably his personal attendant—and was present on the mountain when Moses received the law (Exod. 24:13ff.). He was also guardian of the tent of meeting when Moses met with Yahweh (33:11).

Joshua was given charge of a detachment of Israelites called upon to repel an Amalekite attack at Rephidim in the Sinai wilderness (17:9). Later, he was one of the twelve sent to spy out Canaan (Num. 13:8) and, with Caleb, submitted the minority report urging the people to go in and take the land. As a result, he and Caleb were permitted to enter Canaan (14:30). Finally, he was commissioned by Yahweh to become leader when Moses died (Deut. 31:14f., 23). His strategy in setting up a base at Gilgal, which effectively cut the land in two and enabled him to take first the south and then the north, has been recognized by military experts as excellent. But the biblical point would be missed by attributing the Conquest simply to superior military genius. Yahweh fought the battles (cf. Josh. 5:14f.) and gave the Israelites victory. Joshua was his servant.

But Joshua was a servant who had experienced the deliverance from Egypt, the giving of the law at Sinai, the terrible frustrations and sufferings of the wilderness, and the tremendous faith of Moses. It is entirely inconsistent with the whole thread of the story to suppose, as did scholars of a previous generation,

---

4. According to a number of scholars, a distinct contradiction appears in the accounts of the Conquest. But J. Bright says: "No essential contradiction therefore exists between the various conquest narratives. Chapters 1–12 schematize the story under three phases; they do not declare that nothing remained to be done"; IB 2:547. See also W.F. Albright, "The Israelite Conquest of Canaan in the Light of Archaeology," BASOR 74 (1939): 11-23; and G.E. Wright, "The Literary and Historical Problem of Joshua 10 and Judges 1," JNES 5 (1946): 105-114.

5. The title of the book probably stems from this fact and does not imply that he wrote it. The book gives no such indication, and very few scholars today accept that ancient Jewish tradition.

6. The Greek form is Iēsous "Jesus" (see Acts 7:45, KJV).

that various strands of stories involving the gradual migration of Hebrews in Canaan over perhaps two or three centuries were woven into the story, and that only then was Joshua attached as its hero.

COMPOSITION AND AUTHENTICITY

In the nineteenth century, most scholars were convinced that the same sources that had been discovered for the Pentateuch could be traced in Joshua (see p. 193, above). Chs. 1–12 were composed almost entirely by JE and D, and chs. 13–24 were almost entirely the work of P. According to this theory, the first twelve chapters include a number of etiological tales, stories made up in earlier times to explain certain facts or answer questions such as "Where did the Israelites come from?" or "Why are the Gibeonites menial servants (hewers of wood and drawers of water)?" (9:17).

As previously mentioned (p. 178 note 7), M. Noth came to reject the earlier view and insisted, after critical study, that Deuteronomy had more in common with Joshua, Judges, 1–2 Samuel, and 1–2 Kings than with the J, E, and P elements of the books which preceded it. To the earlier material compiled by the Deuteronomic historian in chs. 1–12 were added later such materials as lists of towns and border descriptions—whose dates are disputed. J. Bright is inclined to place these additions in the time of the Monarchy, the tenth century B.C.[7] Shortly afterward a Deuteronomic addition (chs. 13–21) was appended,[8] and other additions were made later.[9]

Authenticity. Some material in Joshua seems to have an eyewitness quality, particularly chs. 5–7. In addition, quite a few details in later chapters suggest that those accounts were either contemporary with Joshua or not much later.[10] However, glosses, such as the phrase "to this day," clearly suggest a time later (but not much later) than the event itself. Therefore, it would seem that the work consists of material (oral or written) from the time of Joshua, on which are imposed some reworking and some clearly later material.[11] Unless the Deu-

---

7. *IB* 2:545.

8. Bright notes "No doubt by the same hand"; *IB* 2:545.

9. E.M. Good says: ". . . it seems justifiable to doubt that the Pentateuchal documents continue into Joshua. . . . In its present form Joshua is thoroughly Deuteronomic"; "Joshua, Book of," *IDB* 2:990.

10. For example: (1) the chief Phoenician city was Sidon (13:4ff.; 19:28), but later, Tyre; (2) Rahab was still alive (6:25); (3) the sanctuary was not yet permanently located (9:27); (4) the Gibeonites were still menial servants in the sanctuary (v. 27; cf. 2 Sam. 21:1-6); (5) the Jebusites still occupied Jerusalem (15:8; cf. 2 Sam. 5:6ff.); (6) the Canaanites were still in Gezer (16:10; cf. 1 Kgs. 9:16); and (7) old place names are used and must be interpreted (15:9ff.).

11. Later material includes: (1) Joshua's death (24:29-32); (2) relocation of Dan (19:40; cf. Judg. 18:27ff.); (3) reference to the "hill country of Judah" and "of Israel" (11:21), which seems to presuppose the division of the kingdom after Solomon's death; (4) passages which summarize the life of Joshua (4:14) or later Israelite history (10:14); (5) reference to the book of Jashar (10:13; cf. 2 Sam. 1:18); (6) reference to Jair (13:30; see Judg. 10:3-5); and (7) expansion of the territory of Caleb (15:13-19; see Judg. 1:8-15).

teronomic historian is dated quite early—in the Monarchy or earlier—the "Deuteronomist theory" does not account for these features.

In addition to a considerable body of material in Joshua which must go back to the events referred to, significant archaeological evidence must be considered. A number of important Canaanite cities were destroyed in the thirteenth century, suggesting an invasion of the land. Excavations at such widely separated places as Beitin (Bethel), and Tell el-Duweir (Lachish), Tell el-Ḥeṣi (Eglon?), Tell Beit Mirsim (Anshan?), and Tell el-Qedah (Hazor) indicate that this invasion was widespread, leaving its effects in the south, center, and north. The extent of the damage, which left thick layers of ash and, in some cases, almost complete destruction, indicates that the warfare was severe. As a result, a number of modern scholars have expressed confidence in the historicity of the pertinent portions of Joshua.

In view of this evidence, the book's authenticity would appear much more firmly established than the theories of the Wellhausenian school (that the Hexateuch is the product of eighth- and seventh-century sources and a post-exilic editor) or Noth (that the Deuteronomic history is the product of the seventh-century historian using earlier sources, reworked by a postexilic editor) would admit. Such American scholars as W.F. Albright, G.E. Wright, and Bright concur.[12]

Many problems remain to be solved (to paraphrase 13:1). J. Garstang's conclusions after his 1929-1936 excavations,[13] that Jericho gave evidence of conquests as described in Joshua and indeed in the fifteenth and early fourteenth centuries, have been severely challenged by the excavations of K.M. Kenyon.[14] In fact, she found no evidence that Jericho was occupied, much less destroyed, at the time of Joshua's invasion. Excavations at et-Tell (Ai) by J. Marquet-Krause indicate that the city was destroyed ca. 2200 and never rebuilt.[15] In addition, literary and textual problems both in Joshua itself and in its relationship to other Old Testament writings remain to be solved.

Perhaps the most important problem arises from numerous indications that certain Hebrew peoples (it is uncertain whether they were "Israelites" or specific Israelite tribes) entered Canaan at periods both before and after the invasion by Joshua.[16] Indeed, the question has been asked whether there was an actual

---

12. Albright, "Archaeology and the Date of the Hebrew Conquest of Palestine," BASOR 58 (1935): 10-18; BASOR 74 (1939): 11-23; Archaeology of Palestine, pp. 229f.; Wright, "Epic of Conquest," BA 3 (1940): 25-40; JNES 5 (1946): 105-114; Bright, IB 2:546f.

13. "The Walls of Jericho," Palestine Exploration Fund Quarterly Statement (1931): 192-94.

14. Digging up Jericho (New York: 1957).

15. Les fouilles de 'Ay (et-Tell) 1933-1935, 2 vols., Bibliothèque Archéologique et Historique 40 (1949); Albright's note in BASOR 118 (1950): 31 corrects Marquet-Krause's date of 2000. For four suggested explanations arising from the account of the conquest of Ai, see H.J. Blair, "Joshua," in NBC, p. 240.

16. See H.H. Rowley, From Joseph to Joshua, pp. 1-56.

invasion of Canaan, led by Joshua, in the days immediately following Moses.
According to some scholars,[17] nothing took place that could be called a "conquest of Canaan." Some Hebrew peoples, probably to be identified in part with
the "Ḫabiru" of the Amarna letters (see p. 206), entered Canaan over a
period that stretched from Abraham to the Monarchy.[18] The variant forms of
this view allow little material of historical value in Joshua.[19] Other scholars
conclude that there were two invasions of Canaan, and possibly even two
emigrations from Egypt, although this is unlikely. The first invasion would have
been in the Amarna age (fifteenth century), and the Hebrews again would be
identified with the Ḫabiru of the Amarna letters. This exodus would be
connected with Moses. The second invasion of Canaan would have been led
by Joshua in the thirteenth century, when Israelite tribes were already in the
land.[20]

Archaeological evidence does not seem to support a fifteenth-century invasion, nor does the picture of the Ḫabiru obtained from the many references
in ancient Near Eastern literature agree with the biblical picture of the Israelite
invaders. Further, the entire range of biblical material, from Moses to Malachi,
knows of only one exodus from Egypt, in which all twelve tribes participated,
and only one entrance into Canaan. This is the picture presented in Joshua,
and archaeological evidence seems to support it.

An alternate explanation of the settlement period is found in G.E. Mendenhall's theory that Israel's historical existence in Canaan found its roots in
a rebellion of nomads who were already in or near the land and overthrew the
oppressive power of the urban, Canaanite overlords.[21] This theory has been
expanded from a sociological viewpoint and coupled with a Marxist interpretation of class struggle in a massive study by N.K. Gottwald.[22] While there is
no way in which such theories can dislodge the role of the historic Exodus and
Conquest, they can serve as a reminder that the formation of Israel's tribes and
their settlement in Canaan may have had complexities which have not yet
been fully grasped.

HISTORICAL SCENE

For any book of the Bible, but especially one like Joshua, which gives an
account of the entrance of the Israelites into the land that they would inhabit
for the next several centuries, a knowledge of the historical background is

---

17. See M. Noth, *History of Israel*, pp. 68-84.
18. See Rowley, *From Joseph to Joshua*, pp. 109-163.
19. See Bright, *Early Israel in Recent History Writing*, pp. 39f.
20. For an excellent survey of the theory of two invasions of Canaan, see Rowley,
From Joseph to Joshua.
21. G.E. Mendenhall, *The Tenth Generation: the Origins of the Biblical Tradition* (Baltimore: 1973).
22. N.K. Gottwald, *The Tribes of Yahweh: A Sociology of the Religion of Liberated Israel,
1250–1050 B.C.E.* (Maryknoll, N.Y.: 1979).

certainly important. But Joshua contains an initial problem: the date of the entrance into Canaan.

Date of Joshua's Invasion. As seen in Ch. 9, the biblical data, if interpreted rightly, lead to two different dates for the Exodus. On the one hand, according to 1 Kgs. 6:1, it was in the 480th year after the people of Israel came out of Egypt that Solomon commenced building the temple. Since this is dated in the fourth year of his reign (probably 967), the date of the Exodus would be 1446. On the other hand, the Hebrew slaves built the store cities Pithom and Raamses (Exod. 1:11); and since the name Raamses (or Ramses, or Rameses) has not been found prior to Rameses I, and building operations in the eastern delta were not carried out to any extent before Seti I (1305-1290) and Rameses II (*ca.* 1290-1224), the Exodus would be *ca.* 1290.[23]

The account of Moses' dealings with Pharaoh (Exod. 7–12) strongly implies that Pharaoh's residence was not far from the Hebrews, in other words, in the Delta region. In the fifteenth century, the Pharaohs were located at Thebes in Upper Egypt, about five hundred miles south. This, plus archaeological evidence of the Canaanite cities destroyed in the thirteenth century, as well as evidence of the time of the Edomite and Moabite occupation of the Transjordan regions,[24] and other factors,[25] favors the thirteenth-century date. The invasion of Canaan, then, would have taken place *ca.* 1250.

International Scene. The powerful Eighteenth Dynasty had ended in Egypt. Located at Thebes, it nevertheless had controlled Palestine and Syria and waged campaigns to the Euphrates. However, it had been weakened by the revolt of Amenophis IV (Akhenaten; 1369-1352) against the Amon priesthood, and his relocation of the capital at Akhetaten (el-Amarna),[26] and the dynasty never

---

23. This analysis is greatly simplified. Actually there are more biblical data—the number of generations between certain persons, and figures about years or generations between persons or events—some of which support the earlier date, some the later. See *NBC*, pp. 232f.

24. See N. Glueck, *The Other Side of the Jordan*, pp. 153-160.

25. E.g., in the fifteenth century, according to the Amarna letters, Palestine was under Egyptian hegemony and there scarcely could have been any sizeable invasion without Egyptian intervention. But admittedly, the Amarna letters could be interpreted to support a fifteenth-century invasion. Also favoring the thirteenth century, Israel is first mentioned in the stela of Merneptah (*ca.* 1224-1211), but this evidence also is ambivalent.

26. Popularly known as "Tell el-Amarna" (although there is no tell). Approximately 348 letters formed part of the diplomatic correspondence of Amenophis III and Amenophis IV (Akhenaten) with vassal kings in Palestine and Syria and others:

    13 with Kadasman-enlil and Burnaburias of Babylon
     2 from Assur-uballit of Assyria
    13 with Tusratta of Mitanni
     8 with king of Alasia (Cyprus?)
     1 with the Hittite Suppiluliuma
     1 from Zita, probably brother of Suppiluliuma

See E.F. Campbell, Jr., "The Amarna Letters and the Amarna Period," *BA* 23 (1960): 2-22; repr. in *The Biblical Archaeologist Reader* 3:54-75.

fully recovered. The end was brought about by a military take-over in the late fourteenth century. At the beginning of the Nineteenth Dynasty Seti I began building a capital at Avaris (Tanis) or at Qanṭir 30 km. south in the eastern Delta, and Rameses II continued the work on a grand scale. Egyptian control of Palestine had begun to fade in the Amarna period as the Amarna letters clearly show. Rameses II attempted to hold back the Hittites who were pushing down into Syria, but after a nearly tragic campaign he signed a treaty with Hattusilis III (ca. 1275-1250),[27] confirmed by a marriage alliance between Hattusilis' daughter and Ramesses, and the Orontes river became the limit of Egypt's influence.[28] Both the Hittite and Egyptian empires were weakened by the long struggle. The Hittite capital was destroyed, and the Hittite empire fell to the Sea Peoples ca. 1200. Egyptian power in Palestine was never again great, and the Nineteenth Dynasty fell ca. 1197. The Assyrian empire did not arise until ca. 1100; hence Palestine was in the center of a "power vacuum"—a highly favorable time for a young nation.

Amarna Letters and the Ḥabiru. The discovery at el-Amarna in 1887 of the diplomatic correspondence of Amenhotep III and Amenhotep IV and their allies and vassals in the nearer parts of Asia[29] fills in a number of details concerning Palestine ca. 1400-1350.

A number of the letters were written by kings of city-states in Palestine and Syria, frantically appealing for help against invaders plundering the lands of the Egyptian king and warning that, unless aid was sent quickly, his lands would be lost. Scholars favoring a date of 1446 for the Exodus and 1400 for Joshua's invasion of Canaan have suggested that the Amarna correspondence may actually reflect conditions resulting from this invasion. It sometimes has been claimed that the name Joshua occurs in these letters.[30]

Quite often the Amarna letters mention a people or class denoted by the Sumerian word SA.GAZ and Akkadian ḫa-bi-ru, both taken as the same peo-

---

27. The Hittite campaign was led by Muwatallis (ca. 1306-1282) and the battle is dated in Ramesses' fifth year, ca. 1286. Ramesses apparently withdrew, and the struggle continued for about a decade. Hattusilis, brother of Muwatallis, had seized the throne from Muwatallis' son. Copies of the treaty have been found in Egypt and the Hittite capital, Boghazköy. The latter part of the reign of Ramesses II was a time of peace and much building activity in Egypt.

28. S.H. Langdon, "Letter of Ramesses II to a King of Mirā," *Journal of Egyptian Archaeology* 6 (1919): 179ff.; J. H. Breasted, *The Battle of Kadesh* (Chicago: 1903); *ANET*, p. 319.

29. J.A. Knudtzon, *Die El-Amarna-Tafeln*, 2 vols. Vorderasiatische Bibliothek (Leipzig: 1907-1915); S.A.B. Mercer, *The Tell el-Amarna Tablets*, 2 vols. (Toronto; 1939). Selections in *ANET*, pp. 482-490, include correspondence with the Hittites, Mitanni, Assyria, city-states in Palestine and Phoenicia, and Babylon.

30. Yašuya occurs only once, in tablet EA 256:18; Mercer, *The Tell el-Amarna Tablets*, 2:664. In the same tablet, Ayab (Job) and Benenima (Benjamin?) also occur, but there is no basis to suppose that these are the biblical figures. Tablet EA 256 refers to a revolt, but hardly conquest by a foreign power.

ple.[31] Since '*pr* occurs in both Egyptian and Ugaritic, and since the Akkadian can be read *ḫa-pi-ru*, the word is Anglicized as both "Ḫabiru" and "Ḫapiru." The earliest mention of the SA.GAZ or Ḫabiru occurs in a text from the Third Dynasty of Ur (*ca.* 2050); if the '*pr* and Ḫabiru are the same—which is not at all firmly established—references to the Ḫabiru can be found in Assyrian, Babylonian, Ugaritic, Egyptian, and Hittite texts for the next seven or eight hundred years.

Identification of the Ḫabiru with the Hebrews is tempting, and a number of scholars have adopted it. However, it is impossible to interpret most references to the Ḫabiru as also indicating the Hebrews. Moreover, the Ḫabiru are described as warriors, mercenaries, marauders, and caravaneers all over the ancient Near East—which does not fit the biblical picture of the Hebrews. If the Exodus was in 1446, then at the same time the Hebrews were in the wilderness of Sinai, Amenhotep II (1438-1412) was reporting the capture of 89,600 prisoners, among them 3,000 'Apiru,[32] from his campaign in Syria and Palestine. If it was in 1290, then the Hebrews were still slaves in Egypt at the time of Amenhotep. Neither case permits an easy identification.

The problem of the Ḫabiru cannot be solved here.[33] The important point is that identification of the Ḫabiru with the Hebrews is not easy.[34]

Ḥerem, or Killing in the Name of Yahweh. When the Israelites captured Jericho, they burned the city, including all inhabitants except Rahab and her family (Josh. 6:24f.). They did the same at Ai (8:24-29) and elsewhere. The word for this total destruction is *ḥerem* "devotion," and the verb is translated "utterly destroyed" (RSV; cf. 6:17 "devoted to the Lord for destruction").

If the biblical presentation of this subject were couched in language implying that such "devotion" was practiced because the Israelites thought the Lord wanted it (although he nowhere asked them to do it), the idea would still be somewhat offensive. But it is stated several times that Joshua acted "as the Lord God of Israel commanded" or "as Moses the servant of the Lord had commanded" (10:40; 11:12).

The suggestion that God could command anyone to kill another, or that he should command the complete extermination of every living being in a city, is so offensive that some have proposed that the God (or "Jehovah") of the Old

---

31. Oriental Institute, *The Assyrian Dictionary* (Chicago: 1956) 6:84f., cites usage and variant spellings.

32. *ANET*, p. 247.

33. Assyriologists who met in a world congress at Paris in 1953 to discuss the problem in depth came to varying conclusions. See M. Greenberg, *The Ḫab/piru.* American Oriental Series 39 (New Haven: 1955); J. Bottéro, *Le Problème des Ḫabiru à la 4ième rencontre assyriologique internationale.* Cahiers de la Société asiatique 12 (1954).

34. For further reading, see G.L. Archer, Jr., *A Survey of Old Testament Introduction* (Chicago: 1964), pp. 253-59; Albright, *Yahweh and the Gods of Canaan*, pp. 73-91; A. Haldar, "Habiru, Hapiru," *IDB* 2:506; T.O. Lambdin, "Tell el-Amarna," *IDB* 4:529-533.

Testament is not the same as the Father of Jesus Christ. This, of course, runs counter to the teachings of Christ and the apostles, who clearly identify their God with the God of Abraham and Isaac and Jacob, and the God who revealed himself to Moses and the prophets.

A partial answer to this problem is the fact that this kind of religious "devotion" was part of the religious culture of the day. It was common practice for many ancient Near Eastern peoples to devote persons and possessions and captives to their gods. That such action was customary does not, of course, make it right, but it does help explain why the Israelites did not think it wrong. God's revelation, as mentioned, is progressive. He takes his people where they are, and leads them step by step until at last they will be where he is. At this point, the Israelites were not ready for such teachings as the Sermon on the Mount ("love your enemies"). If they had been, God would have given them such revelations.

But this is not the only answer. The biblical position regarding the Canaanites is not simply "Exterminate them!" There is a reason behind the command, which is best understood against the background of Canaanite culture and religion. In Yahweh's eyes, the Canaanites were exceedingly great sinners, who not only committed abominations but also sought to entice Israel to join them in these "religious" acts. The discovery of Ugaritic documents at Ras Shamra in Syria has opened up detailed information about Canaanite religious practices. Religious prostitution, child sacrifice, and other features of this religion led Albright in one lecture to describe it as perhaps the most depraved religion known to man.[35]

Yahweh, the Israelites were reminded many times, is a holy God. He cannot tolerate such abominable practices, especially in the name of serving a deity. The Canaanites must be punished. Further, the purity of Israelite religion must be preserved, and certainly the sensual attractions of Canaanite religion would prove (as at Baal-peor) a serious threat to the stern Yahwistic ethic. A surgeon does not hesitate to remove an arm or a leg, or even a vital organ, when life is at stake. The spiritual life of Israel—and ultimately of the world Yahweh wanted to bless through Israel—was at stake, so Yahweh ordered surgery.

Admittedly, this is only a human interpretation and an attempt to justify the difficult biblical position. In addition, though, there is the verdict of history. The Israelites, sickened by slaughter or seduced by sensual religious rites, ceased exterminating Canaanites. Canaanite religious practices gradually pervaded Is-

---

35. In *Yahweh and the Gods of Canaan*, p. 152, he is more cautious: "We are as yet in no position to say that the North-western Semites were more 'depraved' (from a Yahwist point of view) than the Egyptians, Mesopotamians and Hittites, but it is certainly true that human sacrifice lasted much longer among the Canaanites and their congeners than in either Egypt or Mesopotamia. The same situation seems to hold for sexual abuses in the service of religion, for both Egypt and—on the whole—Mesopotamia seem to have raised the standards in this area at a much earlier date than was true in Canaan."

raelite religion, as will be seen in the prophets, and brought upon Israel terrible punishments from Yahweh—foreign oppression, invasion, destruction of Israelite cities, and, at last, the destruction of Jerusalem and exile.

To repeat, Yahweh did not order the Israelites to exterminate all gentiles—only the Canaanites. This policy was not to become permanent, but was for the immediate situation, when the Israelites were occupying the land God had promised their fathers. Later, the moral and ethical teachings of prophets such as Amos, Micah, and Isaiah would be presented to Israel as the word of Yahweh, and still later Jesus Christ would claim that he came to fulfill the law and prophets. The devotion of the Canaanites must be seen against all these factors.

Did Joshua Make the Sun Stand Still? Josh. 10:12f. reads:

Then spoke Joshua to the Lord in the day when the Lord gave the Amorites over to the men of Israel; and he said in the sight of Israel,
  "Sun, stand thou still at Gibeon,
  and thou Moon in the valley of Aijalon."
And the sun stood still, and the moon stayed, until the nation took vengeance on their enemies. Is this not written in the Book of Jashar? The sun stayed in the midst of heaven, and did not hasten to go down for about a whole day.

At face value, this seems to indicate that the sun and moon stopped their movement across the sky for approximately an entire day. Support for such a miracle has been reported in folklore throughout the world in legends of a day when the sun did not set. The question, though, is whether the occurrence of such a day is what the biblical passage actually implies.

It is important to keep in mind that belief in the possibility of miracles, on the one hand, and interpretation of a passage of Scripture that may or may not refer to a miracle, on the other, are entirely different matters. No doubt is raised at this point regarding God's ability to perform miracles. The question is whether this passage actually teaches that the sun stood still.

The passage in question is poetry, or at least contains a few lines of poetry. In poetry, literal meanings often are replaced by figures of speech. Moreover, the translation quoted above is not precise. Words are added to make the language pleasing. Literally, it reads:

Sun on Gibeon be still,
  And moon in the valley of Aijalon!
And the sun was still, and the moon stood. . . .

The verb translated "be still," as in English, can mean either "remain motionless" or "be quiet." Therefore it is an open question whether Joshua was asking the sun to "stand still" or "be still" (not give forth its terrible heat). The words that follow in v. 13 ("the sun stood in the middle of heaven, and did not hasten to go [or, set] for about a complete day") seem to support the meaning "stand still."[36]

Secondly, reference is made to "the Book of Jashar." Just what this was, who wrote it, and even how much of the passage in Joshua is taken from it, are unresolved questions. If this reference is to the words that follow, then support for the interpretation "stand still" must be attributed to the book of Jashar.

Perhaps most important is application of the principle that the Bible draws a moral relationship between the nature of the miracle and the purpose for which it was performed. God thus does not just arbitrarily "work a miracle"; he always has a purpose, whether to deliver his people, sustain them with food and water, heal them from the bites of serpents, or deliver them from their enemies. As a general rule, a relationship also exists between the "size" of the miracle and its purpose. A miracle of cosmic proportion would be necessary to slow the rotation of the earth for twenty-four hours. Was such a tremendous effort required to give Joshua the victory?

Not all scholars come to the same answers. Some dismiss the entire story as imported from a pagan source. Those who do believe that a miracle occurred understand it in different ways. Some believe that Joshua was asking for relief from the sun's heat; others, that the rays of the sun and the moon were bent by an alteration of the refracting power of the atmosphere, so the sun and moon appeared to stand still. Whatever happened—and something must have occurred—the faith of the Israelites was greatly strengthened thereby.

THEOLOGICAL INSIGHTS IN JOSHUA

The Promise-Keeping God. Centuries before, Yahweh had entered into a covenant with Abraham to give the land of Canaan to his descendants. This promise had been repeated to Isaac and Jacob, renewed to Moses, repeated to the Israelites in the wilderness, and again when Joshua was commissioned to lead them across the Jordan. Yahweh fought for Israel and gave them victory. When at last Joshua began to describe the boundaries of the tribal possessions, it was the fulfillment—in part—of Yahweh's promise. A considerable amount of land remained unconquered, but Yahweh promised to drive out the inhabitants before the people of Israel (13:2-6a). As for the land already taken, he said: "Allot the land to Israel for an inheritance."

The concept of promise and fulfillment plays a large part in the story of Israel's faith. The story of how Yahweh delivered the Israelites from Egyptian

---

36. While the exact location of Joshua and his forces is impossible to determine, the verse indicates that the sun was in the east, and the moon in the west. This would suggest a time just before or after sunrise when the moon was waning. Joshua had made an all-night march (v. 9), and may have been asking not for more sunlight but more darkness. Blair (*NBC*, p. 244) adopts this interpretation and suggests that the verb "to go" may here mean "to rise," although this is contrary to its common use with reference to the sun; it usually refers to the setting of the sun.

slavery, sustained them in the wilderness, and gave them Canaan is remembered many times as the prophets seek to call the people back to their God.

The Covenantal Idea. The concept of the relationship between Yahweh and Israel as a covenant has been presented in preceding chapters. In Joshua the concept is seen largely in the conquest of the land: "Thus the Lord gave to Israel all the land which he swore to give to their fathers" (21:43); "Not one of all the good promises which the Lord had made to the house of Israel had failed; all came to pass" (v. 45).[37]

Throughout the Old Testament, the land is a fundamental element in the covenant. The Israelites were to obey the words of Yahweh that their days might be long in the land, and that there might be prosperity in the land. When idolatry and apostasy became serious problems, the prophets declared that unless they repented, the people would be driven out of the land. Then the word was given through the prophets that because of his promise, Yahweh would cause a remnant to return, that he might reestablish them in the land. During the Exile, this promise of restoration was the basis for hope.

Likewise, the *herem* (p. 207) must be placed within the covenant relationship. Yahweh acted on behalf of Israel and against Israel's enemies because of his covenant with the fathers. In fact, this makes the idea of total destruction an understandable item in biblical religion, for the covenant's ultimate purpose is to provide for all the nations of the earth the knowledge of Yahweh and the covenant blessings. Anything or any person that would prevent the working out of this redemptive purpose must be removed. Although this may seem a harsh verdict, the alternative is the hatred and hostility that prevail among people who have not come to know the redemptive work of God.

The Achievement of Rest. One of the insights of Joshua has been expressed more often in hymns than in the balance of the Scripture, namely that in reaching Canaan the people gained rest from the hardships of the wilderness and the rigors of conquest (e.g., 1:13; 11:23). Israel was to live as God's own nation, a witness to the other nations, once they were established in Canaan. Israel's failure arose from too little application of religious truth to the problems of everyday life. The prophets of the eighth century speak out strongly on that matter.

Nevertheless, there is a rest for the people of God. This basic truth develops into a rich doctrine of future hope and blessing (e.g., 2 Sam. 7:1), with heaven ultimately a place of rest from the rigors of the earthly pilgrimage. The author of Hebrews can speak of a "rest of the people of God" and draw his imagery from the wilderness experience and the land of Canaan (Heb. 3:7–4:10).

---

37. A stimulating summary of the role of the land in Israel's faith is found in W. Brueggemann, *The Land* (Philadelphia: 1977).

FOR FURTHER READING

Driver, S.R. *Introduction to the Literature of the Old Testament*. (Pp. 116-159; argues for Hexateuch.)

Freedman, D.N. "Hexateuch." *IDB* 2:597f. (Useful bibliography.)

Gevirtz, S. "Jerusalem and Shechem: A Religio-literary Aspect of City Destruction." *VT* 13 (1963): 52-62. (Salting of devastated city intended to purify site for consecration.)

Jensen, I.L. *Joshua: Rest-Land Won*. Chicago: 1966.

Kaufmann, Y. *The Biblical Account of the Conquest of Palestine*. Trans. M.B. Dagut. Jerusalem: 1953. (Former Prophets not a "Deuteronomistic historical work.")

Lapp, P.W. "The Conquest of Palestine in the Light of Archaeology." *CTM* 38 (1967): 283-300. (Examines relationship of inscriptional, biblical, and archaeological evidence.)

McCarthy, D.J. "The Theology of Leadership in Joshua 1-9." *Bibl* 52 (1971): 165-175.

Miller, J.M., and Tucker, G.M. *The Book of Joshua*. Cambridge Bible Commentary. New York: 1974. (Literary, historical, theological study.)

Nielsen, E. *Shechem: A Traditio-historical Investigation*. 2nd ed. Copenhagen: 1959. (Examines city's role in formation of amphictyony.)

Soggin, J.A. *Joshua: A Commentary*. Trans. R.A. Wilson. OTL. Philadelphia: 1972. (Supports hypothesis of a "Deuteronomistic" school.)

Weippert, M. *The Settlement of the Israelite Tribes in Palestine*. Trans. J.D. Martin. SBT 21. Naperville: 1971. (Critical survey of "classical" hypotheses.)

Woudstra, M.H. *The Book of Joshua*. NICOT. Grand Rapids: 1981. (Stresses proleptic and programmatic nature of Hebrew narrative.)

Yeivin, S. *The Israelite Conquest of Canaan*. Istanbul: 1971. (Successive waves of incoming Israelites.)

CHAPTER 16

JUDGES

AT the end of Joshua, the tribes of Israel were in the land Yahweh had promised to the patriarchs. They had subdued some of the enemies, but not all. Ultimately they would become a nation with a king, but not for two hundred years or more. The interval, when the tribes were learning to live together and to meet the problems of living with Canaanite cities in their midst and hostile nations on their borders, is known as "the period of the Judges." The story is told in the book of Judges.

After an introductory portion (Judg. 1) which gives a sketchy summary of the conquest of Canaan and notes the portions not conquered,[1] the story is resumed where it ended in Joshua:

> When Joshua dismissed the people, the people of Israel went each to his inheritance to take possession of the land. And the people served the Lord all the days of Joshua, and all the days of the elders who outlived Joshua, who had seen all the great work which the Lord had done for Israel. . . . And all that generation also were gathered to their fathers; and there arose another generation after them, who did not know the Lord or the work which he had done for Israel. And the people of Israel . . . forsook the Lord, the God of their fathers . . .; they went after other gods, from among the gods of the people who were round about them. . . . (2:6, 12)

A central problem is immediately clear—the Israelites' forsaking of Yahweh and turning to the gods of the Canaanites.

CENTRAL CONCEPT

Whether the common definition of what is called "Deuteronomic history" is accepted is unimportant. What is important at this point is the fact that a

---

1. For the problems arising from the seeming differences in Joshua and Judges, see G.E. Wright, *JNES* 5 (1946): 105-114; H.H. Rowley, *From Joseph to Joshua*, pp. 100-104; Y. Kaufmann, *The Biblical Account of the Conquest of Palestine*.

definite concept of history was developing in the Old Testament. According to this concept, the things that happened to Israel were all interrelated and specifically related to the acts of Yahweh. This understanding of history unfolds rather clearly in the book of Judges.

Yahweh Tests Israel. The words from 2:6-12 provide the background for the book. A few other details remain, such as why Canaanite enclaves were left, the part the surrounding nations played in Yahweh's dealings with Israel, and the concept of the "Judge" who appears from time to time.

The reason Canaanites were left in the land is given in a few words. Yahweh had brought his people from Egypt to fulfill the covenant he had made with them. Part of this covenant is expressed by the "angel of the Lord" at Bochim: "You shall make no covenant with the inhabitants of this land; you shall break down their altars" (2:2); but Israel had disobeyed the Lord. A careful reading of Joshua would give the impression that the Israelites had "devoted" every city and destroyed every pagan altar. The story of the Conquest stresses that side. But here it is seen that many cities were not conquered, and many altars were left standing. So the angel of the Lord continues: "I will not drive them out before you" (v. 3), and later: "Now these are the nations which the Lord left, to test Israel by them . . ." (3:1). In other words, the disobedience of the Israelites would become the means whereby God would bring them to a deeper understanding of the election purpose and a deeper understanding of his relationship to Israel. The testing will demonstrate clearly the twofold truth that Yahweh is faithful to the covenant even though his people are not, and that when they call upon him he will save them.

What Is a "Judge"? The book gets its name from the eleven or twelve persons in its pages who "judged" Israel. Having read the account of the giving of the law on Sinai, and associated the law of Yahweh with the Israelite people, one might easily conclude that the Judges were officials appointed to try the people for violating that law. The term "Judge" is apt to be misleading, for these persons, except on rare occasions, are not at all like the modern concept of the judge. Normally they did not hold court, nor was their main task to hear complaints or make legal decisions. The elders or family heads usually did so in the social sphere, while priests were the final interpreters of religious law. The "Judges" here were leaders or deliverers.[2]

---

2. Heb. *šōpēṭ*, usually translated "judge," is related to Phoenician (Punic) and Ugaritic words that help clarify its meaning. The Romans referred to the civil rulers of Carthage as *sufes* or *sufetes*, which Z.S. Harris takes as Phoen. *špṭ*; *A Grammar of the Phoenician Language*. American Oriental Series (New Haven: 1936), p. 153. Livy compares them to the Roman consuls; *History* xxx.7.5. The Ugaritic story of Anat has this couplet:

> *mlkn. aliyn b'l*
> *ṭpṭn. win d'lnh*
> Our king is Aliyan Ba'al,
> Our judge, there is none who is above him (51.iv.43f.)

Ch. 3 furnishes a useful paradigm for understanding succeeding accounts of the Judges. Here Israel dwells among the other peoples of the land, intermarries, and serves the pagan gods (vv. 5f.). This intermingling is evil in Yahweh's eyes, and his anger is kindled against them. He brings against them Cushan-rishathaim, king of Mesopotamia, who oppresses them (or they serve him) for eight years (vv. 7f.). Then the Israelites cry to Yahweh, who raises up for them a "deliverer," Othniel, brother of Caleb. "The Spirit of the Lord came upon him and he judged Israel; he went out to war, and the Lord gave Cushan-rishathaim king of Mesopotamia into his hand" (vv. 9f.). Then the land "had rest" (v. 11). The pattern established here and followed in the stories of other Judges is this:

> The people "do evil" by serving other gods.
> Yahweh sends a nation to oppress them.
> The people cry to Yahweh.
> He raises up a deliverer.
> The oppressor is defeated.
> The people have rest.

Not all parts are mentioned each time, but in general the pattern is the same (cf. vv. 12-30; 4:1-24; 5:31b).

The "Judge," then, was a charismatic leader, raised up by Yahweh, on whom his Spirit came to empower the "Judge" to deal with a certain situation. He was not a king and did not establish a dynasty or ruling family. The Judge was the person—man or woman (for Deborah, too, was one)—selected by Yahweh to drive out the oppressor and give the land rest.

OUTLINE

Brief reign of Abimelech (8:33–9:57)
    Jotham's fable (9:7-15)
Israel in the period of the Judges; close of the period (10:1–12:15)
    Tola and Jair, minor Judges (10:1-5)
    Jephthah's period as leader (10:6—12:7)
    Ibzan, Elon, Abdon, minor Judges (12:8-15)
Philistine oppression and the exploits of Samson (13:1–16:31)
    Annunciation and birth of Samson (13:1-25)
    Samson and the woman of Timnah (14:1–15:20)
    Samson and the harlot of Gaza (16:1-3)
    Samson and Delilah (vv. 4-31)
Other events of the period (17:1—21:25)
    Micah and his priest (17:1-13)
    Migration of the tribe of Dan (18:1-31)
    Outrageous act at Gibeah (19:1-30)
    War between Benjamin and Israel (20:1-48)
    Reconciliation of the tribes (21:1-25)

HISTORICAL BACKGROUND

As noted regarding Joshua, a political vacuum had resulted from the long struggle between the Egyptians and the Hittites. A few other details can be added
for the period of the Judges.

Migration of Peoples. In the latter part of the second millennium, population
movements in southeastern Europe and southwestern Asia seriously disturbed
the distribution of peoples that had prevailed for centuries. The Minoan and
Mycenean culture of Crete and the Peloponnesus was brought to an end. Invaders in Asia Minor destroyed the Hittite capital and pushed the Hittites
eastward into Syria.

Contributing to the fall of the Hittite empire as well as of Syrian kingdoms
like Ugarit were the Sea Peoples, who left their homes on the coasts of Greece,
Asia Minor, and the Aegean islands (particularly Crete, biblical Caphtor), and
inundated the Mediterranean coast by a series of invasions. Although Rameses
III was able to repel their raid on the Egyptian coast during the eighth year of
his reign (*ca.* 1188), they met no similar resistance in Canaan. The Philistines
from Caphtor (cf. Amos 9:7) settled on the southern end of the maritime plain
in Palestine, joining others already there. The non-Semitic invaders rapidly
established five strongholds: Gaza, Ashkelon, Ashdod, Gath, and Ekron—
names found many times in Judges and Samuel. This league of cities, often
called "the Philistine pentapolis," represented a united threat with which the

loosely-knit Israelite tribes were unable to cope. The "Samson cycle," tales about the Judge Samson (13:1–16:31), deals with the Philistines.[3]

The migrations in southeastern Europe and the eastern Mediterranean involved mainly Indo-European peoples, though from time to time there were migrations of Semites from the Arabian desert. Available evidence suggests an invasion of the Transjordanian region in the thirteenth century, resulting in the establishment of Edom, Moab, and Ammon. The Israelites, in journeying from Kadesh-barnea to Moab under Moses, had problems with the Edomites and Moabites; and in the period of the Judges they were oppressed by the Moabites and Ammonites. It is not clear where to fit the Midianites. They were in the area earlier and appear to have been tolerated by the Moabites, for Midianite clans lived in Moab—indeed, the Moabite king solicited their cooperation against the Israelites (Num. 22:4); later the camel-borne Midianites were involved in a protracted series of raids on Israel (Judg. 6:1-6). The Midianites were likely a nomadic people from the region east of the Gulf of Aqaba, who were not limited to a specific territory, but roamed, as do Bedouin today.

Introduction of the Iron Age. The Iron Age in the Middle East generally is dated beginning *ca.* 1200. In this period widespread application of the newly-discovered means of refining iron ore and manufacturing iron implements and artifacts brought an end to the preceding Bronze Age (when tools and metal artifacts were made of bronze, a mixture of copper and tin). The Hebrew word for iron (*barzel*) apparently is borrowed from Hittite; iron metallurgy seems to have been introduced first in the district of Kizzuwatna, in the eastern Hittite empire. Probably as early as 1400 (prior to the Hittite conquest of the Mitanni *ca.* 1370), Mitannian kings sent presents of iron objects to Egyptian pharaohs. The early references to iron in the Old Testament include the iron bedstead (or sarcophagus) of Og, king of Bashan (Deut. 3:11, if properly interpreted), the chariots of the Canaanites (Josh. 17:16) and of Sisera (Judg. 4:3), and the Philistine monopoly of iron metallurgy (1 Sam. 13:19-22). However, the monopoly enjoyed by the Hittites and later the Philistines soon was broken, and iron was a common commodity in the Middle East by the twelfth century.[4]

Canaan and Its Peoples. Largely a land of mountains and valleys (see pp. 44f.), Palestine was better suited to house a large number of small city-states than an

---

3. See O. Eissfeldt, *Philister und Phönizier* (Leipzig: 1936); G.U. Bonfante, "Who Were the Philistines?" *AJA* 50 (1946): 251-262; C.H. Gordon, "The Role of the Philistines," *Antiquity* 30 (1956): 22-26; J.C. Greenfield, "Philistines," *IDB* 3:791-95. On the power void caused by their invasions, see S. Moscati, *The Face of the Ancient Orient* (Chicago: 1960), p. 204.

4. The reduction of iron ore and the use of nonmeteoric iron implements now is known to have been considerably earlier than the 1200 B.C. date for the beginning of the Iron Age. See N.K. Gottwald, *The Tribes of Yahweh*, pp. 656-58 and notes 335, 584-86.

integrated people, for it engendered isolation rather than communication. Among the nations left in the land to test the Israelites were "the Canaanites, the Hittites, the Amorites, the Perizzites, the Hivites, and the Jebusites" (3:5). What is known about these peoples?

"Canaanite" is an imprecise term, used sometimes in the larger sense of all who lived in Canaan, and sometimes in reference to a particular people (compare Josh. 7:9 and 11:3). When finally the Israelites became dominant in Palestine, the center of Canaanite population shifted to what is now Lebanon, and the term "Phoenician" came to be applied to them.[5] K.M. Kenyon suggests that an amalgamation of Amorite nomads with the previously existing culture in the region around Byblos resulted in the people known as Canaanites; they migrated to Palestine ca. 2300.[6] References to Canaanites and their religious practices appear throughout most of the Old Testament.

The "Amorites" are also difficult to define. Babylonian sources refer to a people with the same name who came from the land of Amurru, whose capital was at Mari on the Euphrates. They invaded southern Mesopotamia very early in the second millennium and founded an Amorite dynasty at Isin and Larsa. Hammurabi conquered Mari, and soon thereafter the Hittites brought an end to the Amorite dynasty. Amorites also occupied city-states in Syria, as known from the Amarna letters; and Amorites were in both Palestine and Transjordan (Judg. 10:8; 11:19ff.).[7]

Still fewer data exist for the other peoples. The Jebusites were the inhabitants of Jerusalem (1:21). The Perizzites are mentioned many times, but nothing is known about them. Possibly the name meant those who did not live in walled cities, but there is no proof. The Hivites settled at Mt. Lebanon (3:3), Mt. Hermon (Josh. 11:3), along the route from Sidon to Beersheba (2 Sam. 24:7), and in the Gibeonite cities (Josh. 9:7; 11:19). Many times, confusion of the Hivites with the Horites occurs within accounts or between the Hebrew and Greek texts; sometimes these terms are also confused with "Hittites." The three words are quite similar in Hebrew writing.

The Hittites are mentioned in the Old Testament as early as patriarchal times, but no record exists of Hittite movements into Syria until about the twelfth century. However, the term "Hittite" needs definition, for the original Hittites (Ḫatti or Proto-Hittites) and the later "Hittites" who invaded the land of the Hatti (ca. 2000) were not the same people. Furthermore, the Hyksos penetration of Egypt (ca. 1700) was accomplished by a mixture of peoples, some

---

5. B. Maisler (Mazar), "Canaan and the Canaanites," *BASOR* 102 (1946); J. Gray, *The Canaanites* (New York: 1964); D. Harden, *The Phoenicians* (New York: 1962); S. Moscati, *Ancient Semitic Civilizations* (New York: 1957), pp. 99-123.

6. *Amorites and Canaanites* (New York: 1966), p. 76. Recent discoveries at Tell Mardikh (Ebla) may cause revision of theories about the early Canaanites.

7. According to Kenyon, the biblical evidence suggests that the Amorites lived in the hill country (central mountain range), while the Canaanites lived in the coastal plain, Valley of Esdraelon, and Jordan valley; *Amorites and Canaanites*, p. 3.

of whom were Indo-Europeans (as were the Hittites). When the Hyksos were expelled from Egypt (*ca.* 1370), it is not unlikely that some settled in Palestine. Some of the peoples mentioned in the biblical account as inhabitants of Canaan may have been there as a result of this Indo-European movement through the land.

Centrifugal Situation in Israel. Putting together these various elements helps to clarify the picture of Israel in Judges. The geography, continuing struggles with the other inhabitants, and internal tensions between strong personalities all tended to pull the tribes apart. Some scholars have applied the Greek concept of "amphictyony" to Israel, meaning that there was a very loose association of twelve tribes unified only by the single sanctuary located at Shiloh. Use of the term is questionable, for the ark and its palladium (tent-shrine) at Shiloh play little if any part in Judges. The unifying factor in Judges, therefore, is the concept that Yahweh, who made a covenant with his people, repeatedly was willing to act on their behalf by raising up deliverers.

Chronology of Judges. The book of Judges contains numerous references to periods of time. For example, after the deliverance from Cushan-rishathaim, king of Mesopotamia (3:10), the land had "rest" for 40 years (v. 11). Then the people sinned again and were delivered into the hand of Eglon, king of Moab, for 18 years (v. 14). The Israelites cried to the Lord, who delivered them by sending Ehud, and the land had rest for 80 years (v. 30). Added together, the time references in Judges total 410 years. Adding to this the years for the invasion of the land and the years between the end of Samson's judgeship and the beginning of Solomon's temple yields a figure that seems close to the dates obtained on the basis of 1 Kgs. 6:1—*ca.* 1440 for Exodus and *ca.* 1400 for the entrance into Canaan.[8]

As noted, there are serious obstacles to accepting these dates (p. 205). If the entrance into Canaan took place *ca.* 1250, what is to be done with the figures in Judges? Two different approaches have been attempted. In one, the figures are taken as "round numbers," since 40, 80, and 20 occur several times. Interspersed with them, however, are others—18, 8, 7, 3, 6—and it would be questionable exegesis to ignore these. Morever, even "round" numbers must mean something; 410 hardly can be reduced to about 200 and the numbers still be taken seriously.

A second approach is to look upon the various periods of oppression and the corresponding judgeships as local and overlapping. The nations that oppressed Israel were situated on various sides or in various parts of Canaan. Jabin "king of Canaan" ruled Hazor in the north; the conflict was in the Plain of Esdraelon (4:2, 4) and only a few northern tribes were involved (vv. 6, 10). The Midianite attacks came from the east (6:3), and, although their raiding extended to Gaza (v. 4), the conflict took place in the valley of Jezreel (Esdraelon) and involved northern tribes (vv. 34f.). The Ammonite oppression was in Gilead in Transjordan; it then extended into central Palestine (10:8f.), but Jephthah was from Gilead (11:1), and the conflict was in Transjordan (vv.

---

8. J. Garstang has given a remarkably close parallel between the history of Egypt in Palestine and the details of Judges based on this system of chronology; *Joshua Judges*, pp. 51-66, esp. 65. However, he has handled the biblical figures rather loosely, for if taken as found, the Exodus has to occur at least one hundred years earlier, between 1554 and 1544. In that case, his correlation between Israelite and Egyptian history breaks down.

29-33). The oppression of the Philistines, when Samson was Judge, was localized in the southwest. Thus no compelling reason exists to reject the view that the Judges were raised up to meet more or less regional situations; if so, the period of "rest" in one region could have overlapped the "oppression" in another.[9]

AUTHORSHIP AND COMPOSITION

Author. Nowhere does the book give any indication of the author. According to Jewish tradition, it was written by Samuel, but few scholars are willing to accept this. As with Joshua, there are both early and late elements in Judges.[10] Scholars agree that the Song of Deborah is among the earliest portions of the Old Testament.[11]

Composition. The development of theories of the book's composition has largely paralleled that of Joshua (see pp. 202-4). It seems reasonable to assume that a period in which the stories were told by word of mouth (twelfth to tenth centuries) was followed by a period when some or most were put in written form (tenth and ninth centuries). To this were added editorial comments (e.g., "in those days there was no king") and possibly additional stories not always in the same form or location in the Greek version (e.g., the story of Shamgar). Editing may have continued through the eighth and seventh centuries. Judges, along with Samuel and Kings, probably was put in final form about the sixth century.[12]

Careful study of Judges points up different styles, such as the Gideon story compared to the Samson cycle. This would support the theory that the stories were composed by different authors and transmitted in different forms; the final "author" or "editor" made no great effort to conform them to a uniform style.

---

9. Objection has been made that in each case the Judge is said to have judged "Israel," and nothing indicates that only a portion is intended; see A.S. Geden, "Judges, Book of," *ISBE* (1939) 3:1774. On the other hand, the Judges usually are identified with a local region, and in several instances only a few tribes are involved in the "deliverance."

10. Early elements: Song of Deborah (ch. 5); Jebusites in Jerusalem (1:21); Sidon still the chief city of the Phoenicians (3:3); Canaanites still in Gezer (1:29). Late elements: destruction of Shiloh had occurred (18:31); "in those days there was no king in Israel" (17:6; 18:1), implying a date in the Monarchy; "until the captivity of the land" (v. 30), suggesting a date after Assyrian invasions had begun, unless הארץ "the land" was a corruption of הארון "the ark"—a very simple confusion; see J.E. Steinmueller, *Companion to Scripture Studies* 1:79; E.J. Young, *An Introduction to the Old Testament* (Grand Rapids: 1958), p. 180.

11. See W.F. Albright, "The Earliest Forms of Hebrew Verse," *JPOS* 2 (1922): 69-96.

12. J.M. Myers ("Introduction and Exegesis of Judges," *IB* 2:678f.) and C.F. Kraft ("Judges, Book of," *IDB* 2:1019f.) seek to reconstruct the history of composition, putting the final stage after the Exile.

RELIGIOUS SIGNIFICANCE

In a sense, the religious lessons of Judges are taught mainly by negation and contrast. "In those days there was no king in Israel; every man did what was right in his own eyes" (21:25)—but this was often wrong in God's eyes, just as it is even to the modern reader.

Deuteronomic History. The work of the "Deuteronomic historian" is often identified in the book of Judges and reduced to the following pattern: sin brings punishment, but repentance brings deliverance and peace. The basic assumption of this pattern, which the longer stories in Judges seem to follow, is that Yahweh is sovereign. He uses non-Israelite peoples in Palestine and surrounding areas to punish the Israelites for their idolatry and its concomitant practices. He raises up deliverers when his people turn to him, and endues them with the power of his Spirit, so they can defeat the enemy and give the land peace once more. The lessons are positive, but begin from the negative position of unbelief and idolatry.

Deceit and Treachery. A number of the stories contain elements that may be taken as offensive. Ehud takes tribute to Eglon king of Moab, then sends the bearers away, saying: "I have a secret message for you, O king." Since Ehud is left-handed, he could hide his sword under his garment on his right thigh, where it would not be detected. He seizes it suddenly, attacks the king, and escapes (3:15-25).

Mt. Tabor, where the armies of Deborah and Barak assembled to combat Sisera (Judg. 4). (W.S. LaSor)

When Sisera is fleeing Deborah and Barak, Jael gives him refuge in her tent; she gives him milk and covers him with a rug. After asking her to stand watch, he takes a nap. Jael thereupon takes a tent peg and mallet and drives the peg through his skull (4:17-21).

Only when the biblical characters are viewed as being "on our side" can such incidents be overlooked. Nothing is to be gained by attempting to defend such offensive behavior. The heroes and heroines of the stories in Judges were following principles which may have been sometimes acceptable in that day, but are not acceptable now. As God himself recognized, these people were doing what they thought was right. But they had much to learn, and through his prophets and apostles God would continue to teach his people.

Jephthah and His Daughter. When Jephthah is called upon to deliver Gilead from the Ammonites, he makes a vow to Yahweh: "If thou wilt give the Ammonites into my hand, then whoever comes forth from the doors of my house to meet me, when I return victorious from the Ammonites, shall be the Lord's, and I will offer him up for a burnt offering" (11:30f.). When he returns his daughter, his only child, comes out to meet him. He fulfills his vow (vv. 34-39).

So objectionable is this story that many scholars have interpreted it to mean that Jephthah's daughter was bound to a vow of perpetual virginity.[13] The Israelites never practiced human sacrifice; hence Jephthah never would have intended such sacrifice in his vow and certainly would not have performed it in fulfillment. However, the text is clear. He "did with her according to his vow" (v. 39).

Although he may be judged by modern standards, Jephthah was not brought up under those standards. He was a Gileadite, and the non-Israelites in that region in that day followed Chemosh, whose worship included the sacrifice of children as burnt offerings (2 Kgs. 3:27). According to the concept of progressive revelation, God takes his people where they are and leads them to a more complete knowledge of his person and will. Jephthah was a product of his own day. It is difficult to understand how he could be a worshiper of Yahweh—even more, a deliverer raised up by Yahweh—and still practice what is later described as an "abominable act." Yahweh had not asked him to make such a vow, or any vow at all, according to the biblical account. It was an impulsive act on Jephthah's part, made with good intention. When the Israelites learned that Yahweh does not require such actions, they learned to view Jephthah's vow and its fulfillment accordingly. The significant fact is that even though they came to regard child sacrifice as an abomination in Yahweh's eyes, they did not remove this story from their sacred Scriptures. Lessons can be learned even from well-intentioned mistakes.

---

13. See C.F. Keil and F. Delitzsch, *Commentary on the Old Testament* 2, trans. J.D. Martin (repr. Grand Rapids: 1973), pp. 388-395.

Samson's Exploits. The story of Samson has been told and retold, both in expurgated form and in lurid detail. What is to be made of a man who cavorted with Philistine women and finally let the woman who had betrayed him three times know the secret of his strength (ch. 16)? Can the story be dismissed as a "solar myth," as some have done, or Samson's deeds compared with the twelve labors of Hercules?[14]

The story of Samson's birth is somewhat similar to that of Samuel (1 Sam. 1). It comes as the result of the prayer and faith of his parents. At birth he is dedicated as a Nazirite (cf. Num. 6), specifically bound to the instruction that "no razor shall come upon his head" (Judg. 13:5; 16:17). Yahweh blesses the child, and the Spirit is in him (13:24f.). After that, the story becomes somewhat bizarre. Samson demands that his father arrange a marriage with a Philistine girl. ("His father and mother did not know that it was from the Lord; for he was seeking an occasion against the Philistines" [14:4].) Before the ceremony is over, the wedding gives way to the first of his personal campaigns against the Philistines (vv. 10-20). Following several other exploits, the story of Samson and Delilah presents the tragic end of Samson. By Delilah's deceit and collusion with the Philistine "lords"[15] and by Samson's folly or stupidity, the secret of his great strength is discovered, and his hair is cut while he sleeps. His strength gone, the Philistines are able to bind him, put out his eyes, and imprison him. But they unwisely let his hair grow, and, in a final burst of strength accompanied by a cry to Yahweh, Samson collapses a Philistine temple by pulling away the pillars that support the roof, killing a large number of Philistines (16:18-31).

The story of Samson certainly illustrates no New Testament ethic! But Samson, too, is a child of his day. Moreover, he was selfish and showed little or no control of his passions. C. F. Kraft describes him as "a negative religious hero—an example of what God's charismatic individual should not be."[16] But aspects of Samson's life and ministry should be viewed as positive examples as well. For instance, Samson trusts in Yahweh and is put in such situations precisely for the purpose of punishing the Philistines. In Hebrews Samson is named as one of the great heroes of faith (11:32ff.).

Central Truth. The lesson from each of the Judges is, above all, that those who are dedicated to Yahweh can be used by Yahweh. Elements in their lives may not be in keeping with the Lord's will. Their methods may not stand up as exemplary. But these matters can be resolved by later revelation of what Yahweh is like and what he desires of his people. Again and again God's servants fall short in their private and public thoughts and acts. Something to censure

---

14. See C.F. Burney, *The Book of Judges*, 2nd ed. (repr. New York: 1970), pp. 391-409; G.F. Moore, *Judges*. ICC (New York: 1910), pp. 364f.

15. The word used is peculiar to the Philistines and has been compared to the Greek "tyrant," a name used for rulers in the region from which the Philistines are thought to have originated.

16. "Samson," *IDB* 4:200.

can be found in almost everyone mentioned in Heb. 11, or, for that matter, in the Old Testament—and certainly in Judges. Nonetheless, because of their dedication, Yahweh could use them to deliver Israel from its oppressors and to keep the tribal federation alive until Israel was ready for the next stage in his great redemptive purpose.

THEOLOGICAL CONTRIBUTIONS

God Is the Savior. Though the Judges are called "Savior," obviously in the mind of the author God is the Savior. (Cf. the view presented in Isaiah, pp. 383f.). He hears the cry of his people, and on each occasion raises up a Judge whom he endows with his Spirit.

View of History. Part of the message of Judges is its concept of history. The book includes a series of reminders of the constant loyalty of God in the face of the Canaanite testings, which basically form an internal problem of God's people. At the same time, the temptation to put false trust in foreign alliances, which often called for a compromise with foreign gods, is brought into clearer light.

Monarchy. Is the book of Judges a low-key apology for the Davidic monarchy? Does the statement "there was no king in Israel in those days" suggest a time when there was a king and an implicit effort to contrast the days under the Monarchy with those prior to it? Perhaps this prepares for understanding the Monarchy in its unique role whereby the central shrine is perpetuated and Yahweh's covenant with his people repeatedly emphasized. The messianic concept of the king is stated in the words "He shall judge the people with equity" (Ps. 72:2; Isa. 11:4).

FOR FURTHER READING

Albright, W.F. "The Song of Deborah in the Light of Archaeology." *BASOR* 62 (1936): 26-31.
Alt, A. "The Settlement of the Israelites in Palestine." In *Essays on Old Testament History and Religion.* Trans. R.A. Wilson. Oxford: 1966, pp. 135-169; Garden City: 1968, pp. 175-221.
Blenkinsopp, J. "Structure and Style in Judges 13–16." *JBL* 82 (1963): 67-76.
Boling, R.G. *Judges.* Anchor Bible 6A. Garden City: 1975. (Form critical; applies recent archaeological finds.)
Crenshaw, J.L. *Samson: A Secret Betrayed, A Vow Ignored.* Atlanta: 1978. (Applies "aesthetic criticism" to Samson "saga.")
Glueck, N. *Explorations in Eastern Palestine III.* AASOR 18-19 (1937-38): 241-251.
————. *The Other Side of the Jordan.* 1940; repr. Cambridge, Mass.: 1970. (Esp. pp. 167-172, boundaries of Moab.)

Grohman, E.D. "Moab." *IDB* 3:412-15. (Rise of Iron Age civilization.)

Lind, M.C. *Yahweh Is a Warrior*. Scottdale, Pa.: 1980. (Esp. Ch. 4, "The Conquest as Yahweh's War.")

McKenzie, J.L. *The World of the Judges*. Englewood Cliffs, N.J.: 1966. (Thorough study, emphasizing cultural, religious, and historical background.)

Martin, J.D. *The Book of Judges*. Cambridge Bible Commentary. New York: 1975.

Mayes, A.D.H. *Israel in the Period of the Judges*. SBT. Naperville: 1974. (Argues against amphictyony hypothesis, favoring community whose members acknowledge Yahweh as God and whose unity was founded at Kadesh.)

Noth, M. "The Background of Judges 17–18." Pp. 68-85 in B.W. Anderson and W. Harrelson, eds., *Israel's Prophetic Heritage*. New York: 1962. (Sees book as pro-monarchical.)

———. *Das System der zwölf Stämme Israels*. Stuttgart: 1930. (Classic reconstruction of premonarchical history of Israel, stressing twelve-tribe amphictyony.)

Robertson, E. "The Period of the Judges: A Mystery Period in the History of Israel." *BJRL* 30 (1946): 91-114.

Rogers, M.G. "Book of Judges." *IDBS*, pp. 509-514.

Simpson, C.A. *The Composition of the Book of Judges*. Oxford: 1957. (Three separate and distinct traditions.)

Smend, R. *Yahweh War and Tribal Confederation*. Trans. M.G. Rogers. Nashville: 1970. (Esp. pp. 43-75, "Major and Minor Judges.")

Snaith, N.H. "The Historical Books." Pp. 90-95 in *OTMS*.

Wharton, J.A. "The Secret of Yahweh: Story and Affirmation in Judges 13–16." *Interp* 27 (1973): 48-66.

CHAPTER 17

BIRTH OF THE MONARCHY
1 Sam. 1–31

INTRODUCTION

THE period of Israel's history described in 1–2 Samuel and 1 Kgs. 1–11 displays a number of sweeping changes in political, social, and religious life. Beginning amid the chaos and degradation of that era under the Judges when there was no king in Israel, the period ends with Solomon's splendid empire. Israel begins as a twelve-tribe confederacy unified by certain ethnic ties but even more strongly by a common faith in Yahweh. At the end of the period Israel is the strongest nation in western Asia. In 1 Samuel, people make pilgrimages to the simple shrine of Eli at Shiloh; by 1 Kgs. 11 they have an elaborately constructed royal temple whose building and maintenance have sorely taxed their resources and good will.

The story of these startling changes is largely the story of four people—Samuel, Saul, David, and Solomon. But before exploring this fascinating story, the documents in which it is preserved must be considered.

Originally one book, 1–2 Samuel probably were divided early in the Christian era; perhaps the division was first made in the LXX, which treats Samuel and Kings as parts of a unified work called the book of Kingdoms.[1] The tragic death of Saul marks the division between 1–2 Samuel, but the artificiality of the division is clearly indicated in that David's response is recorded in 2 Sam. 1. The division between 2 Samuel and 1 Kings also is artificial, since the story of Solomon's rise to power and David's last days in 1 Kgs. 1–2 is linked in style and contents to 2 Sam. 9–24. As seen in the Pentateuch, size seems to have prompted the divisions between some of the books.

Jewish tradition names Samuel as author of these books,[2] but they more likely bear his name because of his dominant role in the first twenty-five chap-

---

1. 1–2 Samuel, 1–2 Kings are called 1–2–3–4 Kingdoms. Jerome, in the Vulgate, followed the same pattern but called the books 1–2–3–4 Kings.
2. Talmud B.Bat. 14b. But 1 Sam. 25:1; 28:3 go beyond Samuel's death.

ters. He may have been responsible for some of the material in 1 Samuel, especially the early history of David, as 1 Chr. 29:29f. suggests:

> Now the acts of King David, from first to last, are written in the Chronicles of Samuel the seer, and in the Chronicles of Nathan the prophet, and in the Chronicles of Gad the seer, with accounts of all his rule and his might and of the circumstances that came upon him and upon Israel, and upon all the kingdoms of the countries.

This passage is instructive in its reminder that the ancient editors of the historical books had several sources at their disposal.[3]

Many attempts have been made to trace the influence of the Yahwist and the Elohist in 1–2 Samuel,[4] but the difficulties inherent in the documentary hypothesis are even more impressive here. Thus recent studies of Samuel have tended to stress the background and origin of various sections of the book rather than look for parallel strands dovetailed by an editor.[5] C. Kuhl, for instance, holds that the stories have been combined into "individual cycles with a special literary aim." These cycles deal with the rise of Saul and David, the story of the ark, the prophecy of Nathan,[6] a report of the Ammonite war, and especially the history of the succession to David.[7] Somewhat similarly, A. Weiser stresses four "independent fundamental literary units": the story of the ark (1 Sam. 4–6; 2 Sam. 6); the rise of Saul (1 Sam. 9:1–10:16, 11, 13f.); the rise of David (1 Sam 16:14–2 Sam. 5); and David's reign (2 Sam. 9–20; 1 Kgs. 1–2).[8]

1–2 Samuel refer to sources, although so cryptically as to be of little help. 1 Sam. 10:25 depicts the kingmaker Samuel recording the rights and duties of kingship in a book, while 2 Sam. 1:18 cites the book of Jashar, familiar from Josh. 10. When these stories were combined is a moot question, and the editor's identity is just as vexing. In contrast with Judges and especially Kings, the editorial framework is scarcely discernible, with a maximum of straightforward

---

3. The Chronicles of Samuel, Nathan, and Gad have not been identified, but sections from them and other sources possibly are included in Samuel, Kings, and Chronicles.

4. K.F.R. Budde, *Die Bücher Richter und Samuel, ihre Quellen und ihr Aufbau* (Giessen: 1890), was apparently the first to apply the documentary approach systematically to Samuel.

5. E.g., J. Mauchline, *I & II Samuel*. New Century Bible (Greenwood, S.C.: 1971), pp. 16-30.

6. Was this (2 Sam. 7) part of the Chronicles of Nathan the prophet (1 Chr. 29:29)? Could the story of Nathan's encounter with David after the Uriah-Bathsheba incident (2 Sam. 12) be derived from these Chronicles?

7. C. Kuhl, *The Old Testament, Its Origins and Composition*, trans. C.T.M. Herriott (Richmond: 1961), p. 134. See also O. Kaiser, *Introduction to the Old Testament*, trans. J. Sturdy (Minneapolis: 1975), p. 160: ". . . the way opened up by L. Rost (*Überlieferung von der Thronnachfolge Davids*, Beiträge zur Wissenschaft vom Alten [und Neuen] Testament III [1926]) of looking for older, originally independent single works, is winning the day."

8. *The Old Testament: Its Formation and Development*, trans. D.M. Barton (New York: 1961), p. 162.

narration and a minimum of interpreting, advising, or exhorting.[9] Because the final author rarely intruded his own observations, the stories frequently have a remarkable firsthand freshness and the unblurred perspective of an eyewitness. Apart from minor alterations, the books seem to date close to the end of David's reign.[10] As with Judges and Kings, the compiler and editor likely was strongly influenced by a prophetic view of history and selected and shaped his material so as to highlight Samuel and Nathan's roles in dealing with Saul and David. In so doing he showed that the kings of Israel were obligated to be sensitive to the prophets, who interpreted the covenant for the nation.[11]

SAMUEL—PRIEST, PROPHET, JUDGE (1 SAM. 1–7)

Perhaps the greatest Old Testament figure since Moses, Samuel played a pivotal role in the crucial transition from confederacy to monarchy. He was the last of the Judges and the guiding light in the establishment of the kingship. A true charismatic leader, he embodied the great offices of his time. Nothing that happened among the tribes was beyond his concern. Acting in a variety of capacities, he served the tribes faithfully in a crucial period of biblical history, when the external pressures brought upon Israel by the Philistines called for far-reaching social and political changes. To his credit, Samuel was able to shape Israel's future while still clinging to and insisting on their ancient ideals.

Samuel's Childhood (1:1–3:21). (1) Pious Hannah (1:1–2:11). Judges gives a picture of almost unrelieved darkness. Apart from sporadic revivals in times of invasion and oppression, the scene was gloomy. Yet, Israel's covenant ideals were not completely neglected; the book of Ruth and the story of Samson's

---

9. The framework of Judges and Kings usually is credited to a late seventh-early sixth-century "Deuteronomist" editor who gave these books their final form under the influence of the newly discovered "book of the law" (2 Kgs. 22:8ff.), Deuteronomy. Such a theory frequently, but not always, dates Deuteronomy in the seventh century. But Y. Kaufmann has shown that many of the chief emphases of Deuteronomy, including the pattern of judgment for sin and reward for righteousness, are detectable as early as the Judges; *The Biblical Account of the Conquest of Palestine*, pp. 5-7. He finds no Deuteronomistic influence in Samuel. This verdict receives some support, though for different reasons, in E. Sellin–G. Fohrer, *Introduction to the Old Testament*, trans. D.E. Green (Nashville: 1968), pp. 194f.

10. The Hebrew text of Samuel apparently has suffered much and is among the poorest preserved of Old Testament writings. The monumental studies of S.R. Driver (*Notes on the Topography and Text of the Books of Samuel*, 2nd ed. [Oxford: 1918]), along with the inquiries of P.A.H. deBoer (*Research into the Text of 1 Samuel I-XVI* [Amsterdam: 1938]; "1 Samuel XVII," *Oudtestamentische Studien* 1 [1942]: 79-103; "Research into the Text of 1 Samuel XVIII-XXXI," 6 [1949]: 1-100), have helped clarify the text, while the Qumran scrolls include a Hebrew fragment of Samuel akin to the Hebrew prototype of the Septuagint. See F.M. Cross, Jr., "A Report on the Biblical Fragments of Cave Four in Wâdi Qumran," *BASOR* 141 (1956): 9-13.

11. For a review of contemporary attitudes toward the composition of Samuel, see N.H. Snaith, pp. 97-102 in *OTMS*, and O. Eissfeldt, *Old Testament*, pp. 268-281, where Eissfeldt's own three-document theory (J, E, L) is expounded. (L is a lay source not influenced by priestly considerations.) Also J.R. Porter, "Old Testament Historiography," pp. 132-152 in G.W. Anderson, ed., *Tradition and Interpretation*.

parents (Judg. 13) show that piety and family loyalty were not altogether absent. The story of Hannah gives an even clearer look at the brighter side of this bleak time.

Among the annual pilgrims to the central shrine at Shiloh, in central Palestine about midway between Shechem and Bethel, were Elkanah of Ephraim and his wives, Hannah and Peninnah. Though Judges clearly indicates the existence of other shrines, some private, there seems to be ample evidence of a central sanctuary at Shiloh from the time of settlement until its destruction by the Philistines in Samuel's day. This shrine may have been a more permanent and less portable form of the wilderness tent, which was designed for use by the tribes while on the march. The feast which drew Elkanah and his wives is not identified. Most likely it was the autumn harvest festival, the feast of Booths (or Tabernacles; Lev. 23:33-36; Deut. 16:13-15).[12] The feasts during this period do not seem to have been elaborate affairs. In fact an atmosphere of simplicity hangs over the whole story: no bustling temple complex was this, but a modest shrine managed by a priest, Eli, and his two sons, Hophni and Phinehas. Hannah had ready access to the chief priest, and he took a personal interest in her circumstances.

Wellhausen and his followers interpreted this simplicity as indicating that the elaborate structure of the tabernacle and its staff in Exodus, Leviticus, and Numbers was a much later development and actually represented the postexilic religious patterns.[13] Another possibility is that this simplicity was part of the general degradation of a period when there was almost no central authority to enforce the laws. In such times the pious of the land did their best to preserve the spirit if not the letter of the law.

The story focuses on Hannah's distress at not being able to obey the "imperative of fruitfulness," compounded by the scornful chidings of her rival. Her plight resembles Sarah's (Gen. 16:1ff.; 21:9ff.) but was even more vexing; Peninnah had full stature while Hagar was a slavewife. As was customary for Israelites in desperate need, she made a strong vow to the Lord (1 Sam. 1:11). She may have considered the offering her husband had sacrificed as a votive offering, a type of peace offering (cf. Lev. 7:11ff.). If so, Elkanah's sacrifice was a festive occasion, accompanied by eating and drinking (v. 9).[14] Hannah's pledge seems to indicate that she would consecrate her son as a Nazirite, al-

---

12. Deut. 16:16 enjoins attendance at the central sanctuary three times a year: the feasts of Unleavened Bread, Weeks, and Booths. This law, however, like much Pentateuchal legislation, may represent an ideal not systematically carried out. Practical considerations may have limited the pilgrimages to one per year.

13. E.g., J. Wellhausen, *Prolegomena to the History of Ancient Israel*, pp. 130, 135f.; R.H. Pfeiffer, *Religion in the Old Testament*, ed. C.C. Forman (New York: 1961), pp. 78f.

14. J. Bright suggests that such occasions also may have involved a recital of God's gracious deeds and a renewal of allegiance to him; *History*, p. 171. Deut. 31:9-13 provides for such ceremonies during the feast of Booths at least every seven years. Thus, Hannah's despair may have been deepened by memory of God's past blessings, which seem to have passed her by. Psalms of complaint customarily rehearse God's past redemptive acts so as to make the prayer for rescue more poignant (Ps. 22:4f.; 44:1-3).

though she mentions only the most obvious prohibition—"no razor shall touch his head."[15]

This vow is particularly appropriate for Samuel who stood firmly for Israel's ancient standards, which were being sorely tested by compromise and indifference. To be a Nazirite meant to stand for the ancient way, favoring the semi-nomadic simplicity of earlier generations over the sophisticated influence of Canaan.[16] Amos (2:11f.) may have had Samuel in mind when he mentioned Nazirites as messengers from God whom the people had failed to heed.

Hannah's silent praying marked her off from the other worshipers and caught Eli's eye (1 Sam. 1:12ff.). The Israelites, like most Orientals, prayed aloud regardless of the circumstances ("I cry aloud to the Lord"; Ps. 3:4; "Hear my voice, O God"; 64:1). Israelite worship must have been quite exuberant, but Hannah was in no such mood. Eli's rebuke for what he interpreted to be drunkenness may indicate both the rarity of silent prayer and the drunken excesses of these ceremonies. The Canaanites regularly turned ritual into orgy, and the Israelites were prone to do the same, as prophets like Hosea (e.g., 4:11, 17f.) indicate.

When Hannah's prayer was answered by the birth of Samuel,[17] she refrained from further pilgrimages to Shiloh until she had weaned him, probably at age three.[18] Then she brought him to Eli and dedicated him to the service of the Lord with what was probably a thank offering (Lev. 7:11ff.).

The power and beauty of Hannah's prayer (1 Sam. 2:1-10) often has evoked comment. The prayer shows that devout Israelites did not necessarily compose their own prayers but used established patterns, which they may have altered to suit their needs. Hannah's prayer is based on a song of thanksgiving for success in battle (cf. "the bows of the mighty," v. 4; destruction of adversaries, v. 10). So great was her victory over Peninnah and others who derided her for her barrenness that she expressed her jubilation in the strongest terms, not hesitating to lord it over those who had made fun of her.[19]

---

15. Num. 6:1-21 describes these vows—abstinence from wine, strong drink, use of a razor, and contact with a corpse. Note also Samson in Judg. 13:4ff.

16. Regarding those Nazirites called Rechabites (descendants of Jonadab ben Rechab; 2 Kgs. 10:15-17), Bright observes: "[abstinence from wine and refusal to live settled lives] was rather a symbolic renunciation of the agrarian life and all that it entailed. It moved from the feeling that God was to be found in the ancient, pure ways of the desert, and that Israel had departed from her destiny the moment she came into contact with the contaminating culture of Canaan"; *The Kingdom of God* (Nashville: 1953), pp. 55f.

17. Samuel probably means "El is his name," "name of El," or "name of God." Hannah's explanation (1:20) is a popular etymology. Perhaps she connected Samuel (*šᵉmûʾēl*) with the phrase "asked of God" (*šāʾûl mēʾēl*) because of the similar sound.

18. R. Patai (*Sex and Family in the Bible and the Middle East* [Garden City: 1959], pp. 192-95) cites other biblical passages to show that sucklings or children just weaned could walk, talk, and comprehend (see Isa. 11:8; 28:9; Ps. 8:2). 2 Macc. 7:27 mentions a three-year suckling period. This custom still prevails in parts of Jordan, where a case is known of a child being nursed until his tenth year.

19. V. 10 is problematic because of the final words: "He will give strength to his king, and exalt the power of his anointed." Many have considered the whole prayer an addition from the Monarchy.

(2) Eli's wicked sons (2:12-36). Symbolic of the toll Canaanite corruption had taken on Israel's values were Phinehas and Hophni, the sons of Eli. They flagrantly disregarded the laws limiting the priests' share of the sacrifice (vv. 13-17), going so far as to demand pieces of meat before the sacrificer offered it.[20] Furthermore, they engaged in fornication with the women attendants at the shrine. Whether or not this was sacred prostitution, such conduct was repulsive to some Israelites, at least, who brought the shocking report to Eli (vv. 22-25).

The doom of these wicked sons was announced to the old priest by a nameless prophet called "a man of God" (vv. 27ff.), perhaps a member of one of the bands of itinerant prophets active during this period (e.g., 10:5ff.). Only the gist of his message is given.

This section is connected with the preceding by the mention of Hannah's annual visits, her loving ministries to Samuel, and continued fruitfulness in bearing children (vv. 18-21). It anticipates the following section by noting Samuel's faithfulness before the Lord (vv. 18, 21, 26),[21] in marked contrast to the deplorable conduct of the sons of Eli.

(3) Samuel's call (3:1-21). The prophetic influence discernible in various parts of 1–2 Samuel stands out clearly in this chapter, especially in the emphasis on the word of the Lord (vv. 1, 7, 19-21). Samuel was dedicated to priestly service by his mother, in accordance with Israel's ancient custom of consecrating the firstborn to the Lord in commemoration of the preservation of the firstborn during the final plague in Egypt (Exod. 13:2, 15). Perhaps because of the impracticality of this practice, the Mosaic legislation substituted the tribe of Levi for the firstborn of all the tribes (cf. Num. 3:11ff.). Hannah, however, felt her obligation to God so keenly that she conformed to the tradition literally.[22]

This chapter announces the expansion of Samuel's ministry from mere priestly apprenticeship to full prophetic office. The story of the voice which Samuel mistook for Eli's shows that Samuel had a direct call from God to be a prophet.[23] This experience, which ushered in a new era of prophetic activity, must be compared with Moses' burning bush or the visions of Isaiah, Jeremiah,

---

20. That the editor took pains to explain the customary method of determining the priestly portions suggests that he was sufficiently removed from the time of Samuel to sense the need for explanation. Cf. Ruth 4:7.

21. Luke's description of the growth of the boy Jesus (2:25) reflects 1 Sam. 2:26, just as his version of the Magnificat, Mary's song of triumph (1:46-55), closely resembles Hannah's song.

22. The precise relationship between Samuel and the tribe of Levi is hard to determine. 1:1 suggests that Elkanah, Samuel's father, is an Ephraimite, while 1 Chr. 6:28 lists Samuel among the descendants of Levi. Samuel's family may have been Levites dwelling in Ephraim, or Samuel may have been an adopted member of the tribe because of his priestly activities.

23. H.H. Rowley has stressed the importance of this sense of vocation: ". . . It is clearly held that what made him a genuine prophet was not parental dedication, but the fact that when he was still a child the word of God came to him by divine initiative"; *The Servant of the Lord*, pp. 112ff.

and Ezekiel. Samuel had heard the voice of God. He was never the same afterward, and Israel knew it (v. 20).

The Philistines and the Ark (4:1–7:17). (1) Capture of the ark (4:1–7:2). Much of the Philistine strength lay in their possession of iron weapons, for which the bronze armament of the Israelites was no match. While the conflict between the two peoples was spasmodic for a century or more, by the time of Samuel (*ca.* 1050 B.C.) the invaders had mustered sufficient strength to indulge their lust for conquest. Though probably not numerous themselves, they brought substantial numbers of Canaanites under their sway and organized them into disciplined, well-equipped fighting units. For these Canaanites the Philistine invasion had not meant the loss of liberty. Rather, it marked a transfer of allegiance from the Egyptian pharaohs of the Eighteenth through Twentieth Dynasties.

When the Philistines finally attacked Israel, they were not to be denied. After losing the initial skirmish and four thousand troops (4:1-4), the Israelites called for the spiritual support of the ark of the covenant. But the ark served more to spark the Philistines to fever pitch than to bolster the sagging hopes of Israel. Israel lost thirty thousand men, Phinehas and Hophni (whose death the man of God had predicted), and the ark (vv. 5-11). The news was too much for the aged Eli, who collapsed and died when he heard it (vv. 12-18). Phinehas' widow wrote the epitaph for Israel's dying hopes after this stunning defeat when she named her son Ichabod—"No glory";[24] for the glory of God departed when the ark, the symbol of his presence in Israel, fell into Philistine hands (vv. 19-22).

The Philistines, however, got more than they had bargained for. When their idol Dagon collapsed in the presence of the ark, their cities refused to let the ark within their gates (5:1-10).[25] An epidemic, apparently bubonic plague, followed. The chastened Philistines prepared a guilt offering of five golden tumors and five golden mice and dispatched the ark to Beth-shemesh in Israelite territory (5:11–6:21). Probably the mice and the tumors, suggestive of the plague, are to be connected with sympathetic magic, in which one makes a representation of the curse he wants to avoid or the blessing he wants to attain.

(2) Judgeship of Samuel (7:3-17). Though no record exists in Samuel,

---

24. Kuhl claims that the "writer of this part" misunderstood the name, which probably meant "man of glory" (Heb. *'iš kābôd*); *The Old Testament, Its Origins and Composition*, p. 121 note 34. Kuhl cites no evidence for this suggestion, which does not fit the context.

25. Some have interpreted Dagon as a fish god (Heb. *dāg* "fish"), but he was more likely a grain god (Heb. *dāgān* "grain"). His name is found also in Ugaritic, Phoenician, and Babylonian texts. Whichever explanation is correct, the Philistines clearly adopted a Semitic name for their chief god. Philistine proper names were often of Semitic derivation. This and other linguistic data would indicate a cultural interchange between the Philistines and the Canaanites. See Gordon, *The World of the Old Testament*, pp. 121f.

Shiloh most probably was destroyed in a Philistine raid and its shrine demolished. Memory of such an event persisted until the time of Jeremiah, who uses it to warn against false trust in the security afforded by the Jerusalem temple (7:12; 26:6; cf. Ps. 78:60). That the ark, after seven months among the Philistines (1 Sam. 6:1), remained for twenty years (7:2) at Kiriath-jearim (where it had been brought from Beth-shemesh) would be added testimony that the shrine at Shiloh had been leveled.[26]

It was after these crushing defeats from the Philistines that Samuel came into his own as a Judge. Like his noble predecessors, Deborah, Barak, Gideon, and Shamgar, he rallied the people to repentance (vv. 3-9). When the Lord routed the Philistines at Mizpah, apparently by sending a thunderstorm to confuse their troops, the Israelites recovered confidence in him and were able not only to hold the Philistines at bay but also to recapture much of their lost territory. This passage (vv. 3-17), which reads like an episode in Judges, is the last glimpse of the old order. Clamor for a king was growing.

SAMUEL AND SAUL—TIME OF TRANSITION (8:1–15:35)

The pressure of constant Philistine opposition called for a new tactic from Israel. Neither the aging Samuel nor his irresponsible sons could provide the consistency and quality of leadership the times demanded. The threat posed by the highly-organized, closely-knit Philistine communities could be answered only in kind. Israel needed a king.

Quest for a King (8:1–12:25). (1) Monarchy versus theocracy. The request of Israel's elders for a king was greeted with mixed emotions. Some passages seem to oppose the idea (8:1-22; 10:17-19; 12:1-25), others favor it (9:1–10:16; 10:20–11:15). One explanation is a documentary theory in which two documents reflecting contrasting attitudes toward kingship have been combined by an editor who made no attempt to smooth out the apparent contradictions. Typical of this approach is the analysis of A.R.S. Kennedy,[27] who holds that the source favorable to the monarchy, which he labels M, is the older source and included most of 1 Sam. 13–2 Sam. 6. The source which opposes the monarchy he identifies as Deuteronomic (D) and associates with the framework of Judges, in that it depicts Samuel as Judge of all Israel.

A slightly different approach is suggested by J. Bright. Though recognizing two or three parallel narratives, he sees in them not "a reflection of subsequent

---

26. No evidence exists that Samuel had anything to do with the ark at Kiriath-jearim. His activity as Judge took him throughout the land (1 Sam. 7:15f.), but Ramah, where he built an altar, seems to have been the center of his religious activity.

27. *Samuel*, rev. ed. Century Bible (New York: 1905). Kennedy's view probably is more widely received now than when first formulated. See Snaith, *OTMS*, p. 101; G.W. Anderson, *A Critical Introduction to the Old Testament*, 2nd ed. (Naperville, Ill.: 1960), pp. 74ff.

bitter experience with the monarchy," but an accurate picture of the mixture of feelings which must have been present from the beginning. Samuel shared this ambivalence.[28]

However, the contrast between the two attitudes toward kingship may be somewhat overdrawn. C.R. North, while attributing the supposedly hostile passages to Deuteronomists, contends that

> it is going beyond the evidence to argue that the author of 1 Samuel 7:2–8:22, 10:17–24:12, was inveterately hostile to the monarchy as such. . . . Theocracy was his ideal; but even so Yahweh would need a vicegerent, either a judge or a king, through whom He could act.[29]

Monarchy was necessary for Israel's survival, but, like every turning point in their history, carried great risk. How could Israel have a king like their neighbors (8:5) without the loss of freedom inherent in such centralization (vv. 10-18)? The old order was obviously passé, but what would the new order bring? These and other questions undoubtedly troubled Samuel and other advocates of Israel's covenant tradition (see Deut. 17:14-20).

In view of the absolutist tendencies of ancient oriental monarchies, one can see how their patterns threatened both Israel's tradition of personal freedom and their conviction that Yahweh was the true king. As shall be seen more clearly in the Psalms, Israel's tradition of sacral kingship (as opposed to secular kingship) did not elevate the king to divine status, as that of their neighbors frequently did.[30] Rather, it viewed him as God's representative charged with the responsibilities of enforcing (and embodying) the covenant. Far from a dictator, he was, ideally at least, a servant of his people.

1–2 Samuel reflect accurately both the necessity of kingship and the dangerous implications of such a move. God's use of the kingship as part of the preparation for the King of Kings is witness to the validity of monarchy in Israel. That the vast majority of Israel's kings failed to fulfill their ordained role is testimony to kingship's intrinsic dangers. The truly successful pattern of government for Israel was a delicate balance—not theocracy *or* monarchy but theocracy *through* monarchy. God must always be the true ruler if Israel was to be his people. Nonetheless, he could exercise his rule through a human king. Amidst this tension, Saul proceeded to the throne.

(2) Long live the king! Saul's ascent was accomplished in stages, according to 1 Sam. 9–13. Saul was anointed by Samuel (in response to God's command [9:16]) after the two had met while Saul was tracking his father's stray asses. Later, at Mizpah he was singled out by lot from the clan of Matrites of the tribe

---

28. *History*, p. 188. See Mauchline, *I & II Samuel*, pp. 20-24.
29. *The Old Testament Interpretation of History* (London: 1946), p. 98.
30. Isa. 14:4ff. and Ezek. 28:1ff. accurately reflect the attitude of true Israelites toward the sacral kingship of their neighbors. See further H. Cazelles, "The History of Israel in the Pre-Exilic Period," in G.W. Anderson, ed., *Tradition and Interpretation*, pp. 293-95.

of Benjamin (10:21). The political expedience of choosing a Benjaminite frequently has been noted. As Saul himself suggested, Benjamin's political insig-
nificance ("least of the tribes of Israel"; 9:21) minimized the threat for the other
tribes in choosing a king from one tribe to rule over all the others. Saul's
modesty also showed at Mizpah when he hid behind the baggage as Samuel
attempted to introduce him (10:20-24). A striking figure, Saul gained a good
deal of popular support despite the opposition of some rabble-rousers (vv. 25-27).

An Ammonite invasion put Saul's charismatic gifts to the test (11:1-15).
Though privately anointed king and publicly hailed as such, he was still farming
in Gibeah when he learned of the Ammonite raid on Jabesh-gilead. The tribes
were mustered and the Ammonite forces ravaged or routed. Saul seems still to
have regarded Samuel as coregent or fellow judge (cf. v. 7). Saul's success
quelled any opposition to his regency; and once again, at Gilgal, Samuel proclaimed him king. These stories of Saul's rise to power need not be viewed as
separate and independent accounts,[31] but perhaps as stages in the transition
from judgeship to monarchy. Indeed, their variety speaks for their authenticity.
The times required several public proclamations and the display of charismatic
gifts before Saul could be accepted uniformly by the tribes.

The hero's acclaim given Saul seemed to sharpen Samuel's awareness of
the monarchy's potential menace to Israel's life and faith. Perhaps he, like Saul
himself (11:13), resented the new king's being given the credit due to God for
the victory. He seized the occasion to defend the integrity of his ministry as
Judge, to recount the mighty acts of God in the Exodus and the theocratic
confederacy, and to admonish the people concerning the implications of the
quest for a king (12:1-18). Part of Samuel's speech may well summarize his
attitude and that of his prophetic successors toward the kingship: ". . . if both
you and the king who reigns over you will follow the Lord your God, it will be
well; but if you will not hearken to the voice of the Lord, but rebel against the
commandment of the Lord, then the hand of the Lord will be against you and
your king" (vv. 14f.).

(3) Is Saul among the prophets? 1–2 Samuel afford interesting glimpses of
prophetic activity in the centuries before the golden age of prophecy, the eighth
century. In this early period the moral and ethical ministry of the prophets,
though not altogether absent, as Samuel's speeches indicate, was not always
prominent. Their messages sometimes concerned religious protocol, as in the
indictment of Eli's sons for failure to honor God in the sacrifices. At other
times they were like diviners with access to special knowledge, often very practical, like the location of Saul's lost asses (9:6ff.). Such information generally
required payment or a gift.

Ecstatic behavior—dancing or chanting to music, uttering oracles in a
trancelike state (note Balaam in Num. 24:4)—seems to have been characteristic
of at least some prophets of this period. The band of prophets, bearing harp,

---

31. As by Weiser, The Old Testament, p. 163.

tambourine, flute, and lyre, among whom Saul prophesied was typical (10:3ff.).[32] Their connection with the high places, established centers of worship, should not be overlooked. Samuel probably was not alone in performing both priestly and prophetic functions.

In considering the nature of prophecy during this period 9:9 is curious: ". . . for he who is now called a prophet was formerly called a seer." The simplest explanation seems to be that in Israel's early days, there were two offices, seer and prophet, which later were merged under the title "prophet." The distinction between the terms was not hard and fast. 2 Kgs. 17:13 would suggest that they were separate offices, while the prophet Amos is also called a seer (Amos 7:12). Possibly the seer's chief function originally was looking into the future to give guidance concerning it, whereas the term prophet, while including a predictive element, may have embraced a wider meaning.[33]

Saul's Military Exploits (13:1–14:52). The Philistines put constant pressure on the young monarchy. By monopolizing the metal industry (13:19-22) and taking advantage of their superior chariotry (v. 15) where the terrain permitted, they were able to maintain a distinct military advantage over the Israelites. To the time of Saul the tribes had no standing army but in times of emergency were dependent on volunteers. When Saul or his son Jonathan defeated a Philistine garrison (e.g., at Geba; 13:3), raids of reprisal were sure to follow (cf. vv. 17f.). In a lightning attack, the crafty and courageous Jonathan and his armor bearer inflicted such losses on the Philistines that Israel's courage was kindled (14:1-15). By clearing them out of the hill country of Ephraim, Saul gained freedom of movement and respite from the relentless Philistine pressure, enabling him to wage war against other neighbors like Moab, Ammon, Edom, and Amalek (see vv. 47f.).[34]

Though Saul did little to change the old political order and made almost no attempt at centralization, he did sense the necessity of a trained military leadership. Since so much of the fighting remained in the hands of volunteers from the tribes, a corps of highly skilled recruits was essential for Saul's daring raids (v. 52).

Saul's Fatal Choice (15:1-35). If Saul's rise to power was gradual, so was his descent. The daring and brashness which made him mighty in battle made him

---

32. This is not the only instance of Saul's ecstatic activity. An even more startling description of ecstatic behavior is found in 1 Sam. 19:24: "And he too stripped off his clothes, and he too prophesied before Samuel, and lay naked all that day and all that night."

33. See H.H. Rowley, *The Servant of the Lord*, pp. 99ff., for a discussion of 9:9. The verse is an explanatory gloss on the term "seer," inserted into the narrative by an editor whose readers apparently were more familiar with the office of prophet.

34. See Bright, *History*, pp. 188-191, for an excellent summation of Saul's military feats and the structure of his government.

dangerously unpredictable in dealing with his people, particularly with conservative religious leaders like Samuel. His explosive disposition caused trouble more than once with both people and prophet. His rash vows, although fulfilling the need of the hour, can scarcely have endeared him to his countrymen (11:7; 14:24). Jonathan's protest (vv. 29f.) may have reflected a widespread attitude.

However, Saul's flagrant disobedience of Samuel caused his final rejection. Two episodes are recounted. First, Saul waited seven days at Gilgal for Samuel to arrive and supervise the pre-battle sacrifice which prepared the Israelites for further combat with the outraged Philistines (13:8ff.). The impatient Saul presumptuously usurped Samuel's priestly rights by sacrificing the animals himself. Saul's insensitivity to the limitations of his office suggested to Samuel that his first experiment in monarchy was doomed to fail.

When the king ignored the command to put to the sword all the Amalekites, their livestock, and their goods, Samuel's suspicion was confirmed. Like Achan (Josh. 7:1ff.), Saul had not taken the holy war seriously. This was no mere foray to restock depleted supplies or capture troops for slave labor. It was to be vengeance in the name of God (1 Sam. 15:1-3). The casualness with which Saul treated the divine directive was viewed by Samuel as symptomatic of a rebellious spirit. The stern prophet remained resolute despite Saul's pleadings (vv. 24-31). The lesson had to be made clear, regardless of the cost; for king and commoner alike, obedience was better than sacrifice (v. 22).

Saul and David—Struggle for Power (16:1–31:13). The search for a new king had to begin. In spite of Saul's abject failure, the question of returning to the confederacy was never considered. The factors which called the monarchy into being still existed. The call was not for a change of government but for a new king. In response to God's command Samuel went to Bethlehem to find him.

The account of the selection of David (16:6-13)[35] suggests a familiar biblical pattern: elder brothers bypassed in favor of younger—Isaac over Ishmael, Jacob over Esau, Joseph over the other ten. Rather than accidental, this pattern highlights these events as turning points in God's redemptive program. He is breaking into the ordinary practices of the time and culture and is doing a new thing. These choices are based not on the laws of authority or inheritance but on God's sovereign will and power. Consequently the mighty accomplishments of these men are not their own. God is their source.

David, Court Favorite (16:1–20:42). The anointing of David was followed by the departure of charismatic power from Saul (16:14). Instead of the Spirit

---

35. Many have connected this name with *dawidum*, apparently "leader" or "chieftain" in the Akkadian letters found at Mari. Recent interpretation, however, understands the word in the Mari texts to mean "defeat" and renders the connection with David most improbable. See H. Tadmor, "Historical Implications of the Current Rendering of Akkadian *daku*," *JNES* 17 (1958): 129-141.

of the Lord, an evil spirit had come upon him. That this spirit is said to be from the Lord suggests that its coming is part of God's judgment on Saul and that the Israelites viewed all reality as under God's control. Saul apparently began to experience spells of acute depression which could be relieved only by music. It is this curious circumstance that caused Saul's and David's paths to cross (vv. 18-23). Saul's servant gives as good a description of the future king's varied talents as the narrative contains: ". . . skilful in playing, a man of valor, a man of war, prudent in speech, and a man of good presence; and the Lord is with him" (v. 18).

The story of the slaying of Goliath (17:1–18:5) originally may have been a separate account incorporated by an editor during the compilation of the books of Samuel. It introduces David again (v. 12), although he is already well-known from the preceding chapter. Perhaps this story had been circulated separately as one of David's mighty acts and then found its place in the text without much alteration.[36]

Goliath's challenge to the Israelites (vv. 4-16) is an instance of representative warfare, a custom attested in antiquity. The battle was to be decided by a contest between a representative of each side. Perhaps the principle of corporate personality, in which the power of a tribe or family could be summed up in one member, helped foster this practice.

David's victory over Goliath elevated him to a position of responsibility in Saul's army and endeared him to Saul's son, Jonathan (18:1-5). When David's popular appeal began to exceed Saul's, the king became jealous and suspicious and tried to kill him (vv. 6-11). Though David still had access to the court, his acceptance by Saul faded as the king's behavior became more and more turbulent.

Saul's offers of his daughters, Merab (vv. 17-19) and Michal (vv. 20-29), to David were doubled-edged. Ostensibly, they would have supported David's claim to the throne. The monarchy, particularly in Judah, had a strong matriarchal tinge: queen mothers were always to be reckoned with. To be married to the king's daughter would have given David considerable leverage. However,

---

36. The Goliath story is found in at least three separate accounts. While 1 Sam. 17 (see also 19:5; 21:9; 22:10, 13) credits the slaying to David, 2 Sam. 21:19 mentions an Elhanan as conqueror of Goliath. 1 Chr. 20:5 states that it was Lahmi, brother of Goliath, whom Elhanan slew. One thing is certain: the text of 1–2 Samuel contains numerous difficulties and frequently must be amended, especially with the aid of the LXX. E.J. Young has suggested two possible reconstructions in this case, both naming Elhanan as slayer of Goliath's brother; Introduction, p. 182. Another possibility is to view Elhanan as another name for David. Ancient kings frequently assumed throne names, as do modern monarchs and popes. Elhanan would be the given name and David the regnal or throne name. See A.M. Honeyman, "The Evidence for Regnal Names Among the Hebrews," JBL 67 (1948): 23-25; J.N. Schofield, "Some Archaeological Sites and the Old Testament," Expository Times 66 (1954-55): 250-52. The troublesome name of Elhanan's father, Jaareoregim (2 Sam. 21:19) may actually be a garbled version of "Jesse"; 'or^{e}gim obviously has been miscopied from the end of the verse, where it is translated "weavers."

when Saul asked for the foreskins of one hundred Philistines as marriage price, his strategy was betrayed: he really hoped that David would be killed.[37] The plan miscarried when David and his band slew twice the required number without hurt to David.

More than once, only Jonathan stood between David and death (19:1ff.; 20:1ff.; 20:30). The two had formed a pact of friendship, solemnized by a covenant ritual. As Abraham had given animals to Abimelech (Gen. 21:27ff.) in pledge of his faith, so Jonathan gave David his robe and armor. This was undoubtedly a covenant of parity[38] binding them as equals, although the circumstances thrust the heavier burden on Jonathan. The sincerity and solemnity of this relationship is shown by its being stated, renewed, or reaffirmed four times in 1 Samuel: 18:3; 20:16, 42; 23:18.[39] Jonathan's sober vow—"the Lord so do to Jonathan, and more also" (20:13)[40]—is a stern reminder that death was the judgment upon one who broke such a covenant. Considering the Israelites' strong family loyalties, Jonathan's concern for David seems all the more remarkable.

David, the Hunted Refugee (21:1–27:12). Even Jonathan's intervention could not protect David permanently. With exile or death his only alternatives, David fled (21:10). Later, others of his clan, doubtless fearing retaliation, joined him in exile. With his motley band of about four hundred fellow fugitives (22:2), David frequently hid by day and traveled by night to escape Saul. The Philistine borders, southern hill country of Judah, the Negeb, Edom, and Moab were laced with the tracks of his bandit raiders. At times he attacked the Philistines (23:1ff.); at other times his dread of Saul forced him to sojourn among them (at Gath; 27:1ff.).

David's tactics with Saul were defensive, not aggressive. Twice he could have taken the king's life handily (24:4ff.; 26:6ff.) but refused. His attitude toward Saul remained one of respect and reverence; even when he craftily cut off a piece of Saul's skirt, he regretted the insult against his ruler (24:5f.).

Saul, by contrast, was relentless in stalking David. Despite the constant Philistine threat, Saul compulsively pursued David and his outlaw band to the neglect of other responsibilities and the detriment of the nation. Saul's unbalanced state became increasingly apparent. His ruthless butchery of Ahimelech,

---

37. Though severed heads or hands were customary evidences of the number of battle victims, foreskins were requested because the Philistines did not practice circumcision; Gordon, *The World of the Old Testament*, p. 161 note 20. Similarly, Egyptians often cut off the male genitals of the uncircumcised Libyans they had slain.

38. This term often is used in contrast to the covenant of suzerainty which a great king imposes on lesser rulers, usually after he has done them some great favor.

39. See Young, *Introduction*, p. 181, for a concise summary of the steps in this covenant relationship.

40. Note David's vow to avenge the insult of Nabal (25:22): "God so do to David and more also. . . ." Such a statement undoubtedly was accompanied by a suggestive gesture such as feigning to slit one's throat.

who had given aid and comfort to David (21:1ff.), and of a priestly company of more than eighty together with their families (22:11ff.) showed the depths of his dementedness. This latest of a series of outrages against the priests' authority contrasts with the attitude of David, who from the outset enlisted their support and was sensitive to their religious leadership. Indeed, Ahimelech's son Abiathar escaped Saul's bloody coup and joined David's exiled company (22:20ff.).

David's willingness to consult the Lord is evidence of his concern for the priestly ministry. That the narrative records this immediately after the arrival of Abiathar suggests that it was through Abiathar that David determined God's will for his journeys and battles (23:1ff.). The ephod (a priestly garment to which a pouch was attached) which the fleeing priest clutched probably contained lots or other forms of oracles for divining (see 23:6). In contrast with David's ready access to Yahweh's will, Saul tried desperately but unsuccessfully to discern it by dreams, Urim (sacred lot?),[41] and prophetic activity (28:6).

Not surprisingly, Samuel's death draws scant notice (25:1), for the aged kingmaker had been upstaged for some time by David and Saul. More prominent is David's encounter with the ill-tempered Nabal and his gracious wife Abigail (25:2ff.). Nabal's failure to receive David and his men with the courtesies demanded by custom would have cost him dearly had his wife not intervened. David's rough-and-ready life as a fugitive is amply documented in this episode. He took food where he could find it and was willing to spill the blood of him who refused it. He wooed the widowed Abigail and married Ahinoam as well. Those were days of dash and daring. And David was equal to them.

Decline of Saul (28:1–31:13). It was a desperate Saul who faced a Philistine onslaught from the North and could find no word from God for guidance. He zealously had banned all wizards and mediums (28:3), yet in his panic he found himself consulting one (28:8ff.). The scene, fittingly shrouded in mystery, shows Saul at the end of his tether begging for advice from one he had disobeyed consistently in life. In this brief glimpse, Samuel is shown to be as dauntless in the afterlife as in the days of his flesh, bringing from the underworld only a more trenchant version of what he had announced at Gilgal (15:17ff.): Saul's disobedience had cost him the crown.

If the scene at Endor was fraught with mystery, that at Gilboa was charged with tragedy (31:1ff.). Giving no quarter, the Philistines forced the battle against Saul and his sons. The younger men fell first, and the wounded Saul pleaded for the coup de grâce. When his armor bearer refused, Saul fell on his own sword. The Philistines, customarily looting the battle dead, severed his head and took his armor as trophies of their triumph over one who had dogged

---

41. The lots may have been flat disks with "yes" and "no" sides. When both agreed the answer was clear. When they disagreed, further guidance was sought.

Tell el-Ḥuṣn, where the Philistines displayed the corpses of Saul and his sons (1 Sam. 31:10-12). (W.S. LaSor)

them for a decade or more. The Philistines rejoiced at Saul's death and Israel's vulnerability. But they had yet to reckon with David.

FOR FURTHER READING

Ackroyd, P.R. *The First Book of Samuel*. Cambridge Bible Commentary. New York: 1971.
————. *The Second Book of Samuel*. Cambridge Bible Commentary. New York: 1977.
Albright, W.F. "Reconstructing Samuel's Role in History." Pp. 42-65 in *Archaeology, Historical Analogy, and Early Biblical Tradition*. Baton Rouge: 1966.
Campbell, A.F. *The Ark Narrative*. SBL Dissertation. Missoula: 1975. (Form-critical, traditio-historical study of 1 Sam. 4–6; 2 Sam. 6.)
Gordon, R.P. "David's Rise and Saul's Demise: Narrative Analogy in 1 Samuel 24–26." *Tyndale Bulletin* 31 (1980): 37–64.
Hertzberg, H.W. *I and II Samuel*. Trans. J.S. Bowden. OTL. Philadelphia: 1964.
Hoffner, H.A., Jr., "A Hittite Analogue to the David and Goliath Contest of Champions?" CBQ 30 (1968): 220-25.
McCarter, P.K., Jr. *I Samuel*. Anchor Bible. Garden City: 1980. (Comprehensive.)
Miller, P.D., and Roberts, J.J.M. *The Hand of the Lord*. Baltimore: 1977. (Literary and historical reassessment of ark narrative, including comparative and structural studies.)
Ou-Testamentiese Werkgemeenskap in Suid-Afrika. *Studies on the Books of Samuel*. Pretoria: 1960. (Papers on historical, cultural, and textual background.)

Payne, D.F. *Kingdoms of the Lord: A History of the Hebrew Kingdoms from Saul to the Fall of Jerusalem*. Grand Rapids: 1981. (An excellent account of the history of this period and its impact on Israel's faith.)

Petersen, D.L. *The Role of Israel's Prophets*. JSOTS 17. Sheffield: 1981. (Analysis of meaning and function of various prophetic titles: Seer, Man of God, etc.)

Segal, M.H. "The Composition of the Books of Samuel." *JQR* 55 (1964): 318-339; 56 (1965): 32-50, 137-157. (Sees later compilation including stories of the ark, Saul, Samuel, first and second stories of David.)

Tsevat, M. "Studies in the Book of Samuel." *HUCA* 32 (1961): 191-216; 33 (1962): 107-118; 34 (1963): 71-82; 36 (1965): 49-58.

Vannoy, J.R. *Covenant Renewal at Gilgal*. Cherry Hill, N.J.: 1977. (Study of 1 Sam. 11:14–12:25.)

CHAPTER 18

ISRAEL'S GOLDEN AGE—
DAVID AND SOLOMON
(2 Sam. 1–1 Kgs. 11)

INTRODUCTION

THE eighty years or so outlined in this section saw an almost total transformation in Israel's political and economic life. David and his son forged Judah and Israel into a military entity able to dominate their neighbors, and into a mercantile enterprise bringing unprecedented wealth and fame. The loose-knit tribes were welded together by a strong monarchy that was the model for almost four centuries. It was indeed Israel's golden era.

DAVID'S POWERFUL REIGN (2 Sam. 1:1–8:18)

These chapters continue the story of David's rise to power begun in 1 Sam. 16. The death of Saul left Israel leaderless and subject to Philistine domination. But with firm and measured steps David marched to the throne of Judah and all Israel, more than filling the vacuum. If Saul's obsession to destroy David left him vulnerable to Philistine invasions, David's dedication to protecting and enlarging Israel's borders drove him to subdue the Philistines and bring all of Israel's immediate neighbors under his sway.

King Over Judah at Hebron (1:1–4:12). (1) How Are the Mighty Fallen (1:1-27)! David's respite from Saul's persecution and his return from exile among the Philistines were clouded by his remorse at the slaughter on Mt. Gilboa. His grief over the loss of Saul, for whom he seems to have had great regard, and especially of Jonathan probably was compounded by his concern for the cause of Israel, now in need of stout convoy. The fate of the Amalekite opportunist who sought David's favor by reporting the king's death and claiming a hand in it proves the depth of David's emotions.

Further proof is his moving lament uttered in reflection upon Israel's (and his) great loss (vv. 19-27). Using dramatic contrast (in which past glories of the heroes are recited to sharpen feeling for their present humiliation) and the short, sobbing lines of the funeral dirge, David invokes all Israel, including the mountains of Gilboa which witnessed the tragic scene, to lament the king and his son.[1]

(2) Struggle for the Throne (2:1–4:12). David's triumphal return from his sojourn in Ziklag resulted in his acclamation as king of Judah in Hebron (2:1-4). This ancient town, rich with memories of Abraham's day, was his capital for seven and a half years (5:5). Meanwhile, Saul's family still was to be contended with. At the instigation of Abner, Saul's crafty general, Ishbosheth (more correctly, Eshbaal),[2] Saul's son, had been made king of the other tribes, including those fragments of the nation dwelling in Transjordan. Nothing indicates that Ishbosheth's government gained extensive popular support. That its capital was in Transjordan greatly curtailed its influence among the tribes, who apparently looked increasingly to David as leader.

After about two years of skirmishes between the two contestants for the throne (2:10; 3:1), Ishbosheth angered Abner by accusing him of intimacy with Saul's concubine (vv. 6-11). If true, this probably would suggest that Abner was himself ambitious for the crown. Sexual union with one of Saul's partners would have been interpreted as one credential for kingship. This break with the king forced Abner to make overtures to David (vv. 12-16), who responded by demanding that Saul's daughter Michal be restored to him as wife. The political reason behind this request (granted by Ishbosheth) is apparent: a son by Michal would help consolidate under David those factions loyal to Saul.[3]

The turncoat Abner spearheaded David's drive to unite the nation by traveling through the land to confer with the elders of the tribes (vv. 17-19). Apparently jealousy and desire for revenge goaded David's general, Joab, to slay his rival who, overtly at least, had become his ally. Abner's death both grieved David (note his brief lament, vv. 33f.) and dismayed Ishbosheth, who shortly afterwards was assassinated by two cutthroats who previously had served Saul (4:2f.). This did not please David, and he summarily slew the murderers who had sought to impress him by their deed.

King Over All Israel at Jerusalem (5:1–8:18). The rival gone, David was hailed at Hebron as king of all Israel (5:1-5). The house of Judah, which at this time included Simeonites, Calebites, Othnielites, Jerahmeelites, and Kenites (1 Sam. 27:10; 30:29), was united with the northern tribes ("Israel"[4]).

---

1. For fuller discussion of the Qinah (dirge) form and its use of dramatic contrast, particularly with the exclamation "how!" (see vv. 19, 25), see Ch. 47 on Lamentations.

2. Eshbaal ("Man of Baal" or, more probably, "Baal exists") is used in 1 Chr. 8:33; 9:39. Scribal resentment toward Baal has in 2 Samuel resulted in the change of *ba'al* to *bōšet* "shame."

3. See J.D. Levenson and B. Halpern, "The Political Import of David's Marriages," *JBL* 99 (1981): 507-518.

4. Only the context can tell whether the entire people or the northern tribes are meant.

Site of David's capital city at Jerusalem, south of the present Old City. (W.S. LaSor)

That the latter never wholeheartedly accepted Judean kingship is proved by the readiness with which the kingdom split at the time of David's grandson, Rehoboam.

(1) Capture of Jerusalem (5:6-16). The Canaanite stronghold of Jerusalem had remained outside Israel's control during their two-and-a-half-century occupation of the land. An ancient city (cf. Gen. 14:18),[5] Jerusalem was ideally situated to be David's capital. Lying between the two halves of his kingdom in territory to which no tribe could lay claim, it was sufficiently neutral to serve as a unifying factor. The details of David's conquest are obscure, but his men may have crept through a water shaft (5:8).[6] David's enmity for the Jebusites and the psychology he used in whipping his men to battle pitch are shown in his references to the enemy soldiers as the lame and blind apparently recalling Jebusite mockery of him. Such taunts were a common tactic in ancient warfare.

David set out immediately to fortify and beautify his capital. Though no match for Solomon's lavish splendor, his building projects brought a tone of luxury which Saul's best days had not known. The size of David's family alone (see 3:2-5; 5:13-16) suggests an extensive court. Israel's pattern of life was changing, and David was spearheading the change. Jerusalem was his own city, taken with his private troops instead of a tribal army. It was the spoil of his victory, and he treated it accordingly. Firmly entrenched in his fortress capital,

---

5. The identity of Salem and Jerusalem seems to be confirmed by Ps. 76:2.
6. See W.S. LaSor, "Jerusalem," *ISBE* 2 (1982): 1006.

he set out to do what Saul had failed to do: to rid the land of the Philistines. Dauntless as ever and well-versed in Philistine tactics, David was able both to win decisive victories and to control and confine the enemy to their own borders (5:17-25)[7] for the first time in 150 years.

(2) Religious Reforms (6:1–7:29). One of Saul's basic mistakes had been his insensitivity to Israel's religious institutions, particularly the central shrine and priesthood. But David grasped the importance of his people's spiritual heritage and sought to perpetuate and promote it. Israel could not have been truly united unless their political head was also their religious leader. By bringing the ark, long neglected by Saul, to Jerusalem and establishing it in a tent home, David made his city the religious as well as political capital, a master stroke which greatly enhanced his people's loyalty to him. His active participation (apparently too active for his decorous wife Michal; 6:20) in the ceremonies of dedication marked him off as one who revered Israel's God and fostered their faith, a reputation he well deserved and never lost.

Saul's rise to power had produced misgivings in the prophet Samuel, but David's had Nathan's full support (7:1-3). At divine command the prophet announced to David the special relationship the king and his seed were to enjoy with God. In terms reminiscent of the Abrahamic covenant, Nathan promised him "a great name"—a lofty and well-earned reputation; stability for his people in the land; an everlasting dynasty; and an intimate relationship between God and David's successors. While David was forbidden to build a permanent temple, he was assured that his son would do so. The importance of this covenant can scarcely be exaggerated.[8] Prophetic expectation of a Davidic king to reign in future glory over Israel (Isa. 9:6ff.; 11:1ff.) hinges on this covenant, as does prophetic censure of the non-Davidic kings of the northern kingdom. New Testament faith traces Christ's right to rule to his descent from David (Matt. 1:1; Luke 1:32).

To administer the numerous details of public worship, David appointed as priests Zadok and Ahimelech (8:17). Ahimelech's father Abiathar apparently was still active as well (15:24), perhaps as a "priest emeritus" maintaining some influence even though his son had succeeded him. The families of both priests seem to have had roots that go back to the sanctuary at Shiloh and beyond that to Aaron, founder of the priestly line.[9] But not all priests were descendants

---

7. The accounts of wars with the Philistines in 21:15-22 may be summaries of battles early in David's reign rather than at the end, as their place in the narrative might be taken to indicate.

8. For a detailed discussion of its uniqueness and possible relationships with the Abrahamic covenant of Gen. 15, see R.E. Clements, *Abraham and David* (Naperville: 1967), pp. 47-60.

9. The genealogies, however (1 Chr. 6:4-8; 24:1-3), are not without problems. Many attempts have been made to disassociate the line of Zadok from that of Aaron. Though the precise connection may not be clear (the genealogies may skip generations or include names adopted but not born into the line), the reasons usually given for disassociating the two lines are not compelling.

of Aaron, for David's own sons were numbered among them (8:18). While the description of official religion is sketchy in 2 Samuel, the Chronicler spares no effort to give a full account (1 Chr. 23:1–29:30). His record is testimony to the strategic role of David in shaping the transition from the simplicity of the shrine at Shiloh to the elaborate cultic functions characterizing the reigns of Solomon and his successors.

(3) Unparalleled Military Success (8:1-18). Ch. 8 is a concise summary of David's military activities, with details sometimes given in succeeding passages (e.g., his conflict with the Ammonites and their Syrian allies, ch. 10). When the dust of the various battles had settled, the Philistines as well as the Edomites, Moabites, Ammonites, and the great city-states of Syria like Damascus, Zobah, and even Hamath were either in David's control or subject to him.

Two decades before, the Israelites had been trying to avoid strangulation by the Philistines. But the Philistine pentapolis had been broken, and David had greatly enlarged the areas of Israel's influence. Now indeed the most powerful kingdom in Western Asia, Israel's borders stretched from the desert to the Mediterranean, and from the Gulf of Aqabah to the outskirts of Hamath on the Orontes.

(4) Political Centralization. David's religious reforms, military outreach, and political and social reorganization called for sweeping changes in administrative structure. How elaborate this structure became is hard to calculate. Two lists of David's chief officials are given (8:15-18; 20:23-26). They include a commander-in-chief of the Israelite troops (Joab); leader of the Philistine mercenaries (Cherethites and Pelethites);[10] the two priests mentioned above; two officers responsible for official records, documents of state, and administrative details; and for part of the time at least, a superintendent of the corvée, who apparently managed the foreign labor force. These officials had no independent authority, but were closely supervised by the king, a complete leader whose judgment was final in every area, military, religious, or political.[11]

Strong prophetic opposition to David's census in ch. 24 probably stems from objections to its purpose. This was no mere counting of the people, but an attempt to determine the strength of the various tribes in order to levy taxes and recruit troops.[12] Although Israel was more secure from outward intervention under David, the citizens had less personal freedom. This adjustment from tribal confederacy to centralized monarchy was hard, and subsequent history reveals that the Israelites never did quite succeed.

---

10. C.H. Gordon observes: "Foreign mercenaries have no [family or local loyalties] and tend to be well disciplined, loyal to their commander and interested in his personal welfare, for on him depends their professional welfare"; *The World of the Old Testament*, p. 170.

11. J. Bright (*History*, pp. 205f.) points out that David's administration is patterned, in part at least, on Egyptian models.

12. In spite of what seems to be a move toward internal taxation, David's chief sources of revenue were undoubtedly the spoils of war and the tribute of conquered or fearful nations around him.

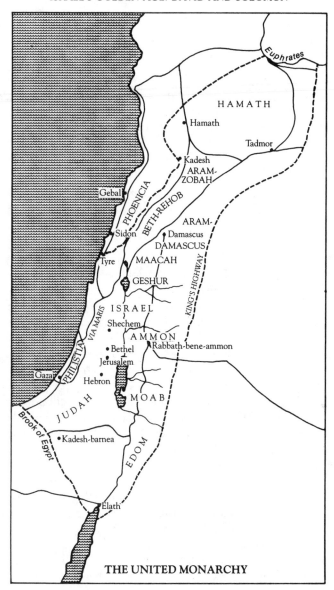

THE UNITED MONARCHY

DAVID'S AMBITIOUS SONS (2 Sam. 9:1–1 Kgs. 2:46)

The transition from charismatic to dynastic leadership was not resolved by David's ascent to the throne. Saul's son Eshbaal had made a thwarted attempt at succession, and later the Benjaminite Sheba would seek to rally Israel against David (20:1-22). But, tragically, not all competition for the throne came from without. David, who handled international and national affairs so readily, had trouble in his own household, for at least three sons desired the throne. Theirs is a tragic human story of glory and shame, intrigue and counterintrigue, love and blood, shining success and wretched failure.

These chapters are generally considered the finest piece of history writing in antiquity—the Court History of David (2 Sam. 9–20; 1 Kgs. 1–2):

> Its author has equal command of the art of the dramatic construction of a tale and of the realistic characterization of the persons whom he presents true to life and unadorned. He keeps himself in the background, and yet quite a number of indications (. . . 11:27; 12:24; 17:14) reveal the fact that he regards even the ultimate relationships in history to be between earthly events and divine dispensation.[13]

The detailed knowledge of court life and language point to a member of the court as author—perhaps Ahimaaz, Solomon's son-in-law, or Abiathar, priest to David.

David's Strengths and Foibles (2 Sam. 9:1–12:31). The picture of David's kindness to the house of Saul and his profound regard for Jonathan, sketched throughout the narrative, is enhanced by his mercy to Jonathan's son Mephibosheth (9:1-13).[14] The pointed mention of the lameness highlights the king's condescension, for such infirmities often were considered divine judgments (see John 9:1f.). David's kindly treatment of a member of the rival's household is all the more remarkable in view of the frequent oriental custom of doing away with the male line of the opposing royal family. David kept his pledge to Jonathan and spared his line (see 1 Sam. 20:14-17). His loyalty to that covenant was tested again when revenge had to be taken for Saul's outrage against the Gibeonites (2 Sam. 21:1-6). Apparently, Mephibosheth responded to David's kindness and remained loyal to the end, although his guardian and servant, Ziba, turned traitor during Absalom's revolt and tried to undermine David's confidence in Mephibosheth (16:1-4).

An episode during the Ammonite war (11:1-27) shows another side of David. Invading armies, especially the Assyrians, usually timed their campaigns between the latter rains in March and the grain harvest in May and June. Roads were dry enough to be passable, and the soldiers could sustain themselves on their enemies' ripening crops. But while his armies were on the march, David remained in the capital, and his illicit encounter with the lovely Bathsheba then occurred. By his desperate plot to get rid of her husband Uriah, David added murder to adultery. Nathan's parable, a subtle yet forceful rebuke of David, is convincing evidence of the great prophets' crucial role in Israel's life

---

13. A. Weiser, *Introduction to the Old Testament*, p. 165. For a thorough study of the literary style and intent, see R.N. Whybray, *The Succession Narrative*. SBT (Naperville: 1968). A survey of recent discussions on this section is found in J.R. Porter, "Old Testament Historiography," pp. 151f. in G.W. Anderson, ed., *Tradition and Interpretation.*

14. His name, like Ishbosheth's, stems from scribes who altered its original form Meribbaal (1 Chr. 8:34; 9:40) to show their contempt for the Canaanite fertility god Baal. The Israelites referred sometimes to their covenant Lord as Baal ("master"). Hosea, however, rejected this title for Yahweh because of its pagan connotations (Hos. 2:16f.).

(12:1-15). The king, whose chief obligation was to enforce the terms of the covenant and insure justice at every level of society, had himself grossly violated the covenant. David crumbled before the righteous indictment of the stern prophet. God's mercy was his only hope; and although his sin had such dire effects as the death of Bathsheba's baby (12:15-19) and the loosening of the moral fibers of David's sons (e.g., Amnon; 13:1-39), that mercy spared him.[15] The remarkable honesty of the Old Testament is apparent here, for no attempt is made to hide or excuse the great king's glaring moral lapses.

Absalom's Lust for Power (13:1–18:33). A strong ruler is sure to make enemies, and David was no exception. His wars had taken toll on the morale of the troops levied from Israel, forced to bear arms for long periods along with David's private army of mercenaries. Within the court itself scheming and conniving undoubtedly increased—particularly among David's wives—as the question of David's successor was raised.

Open conflict for the crown was triggered when Amnon, David's oldest son (3:2), took unfair advantage of his half-sister, Tamar, then cruelly rejected her, even though he could have asked her hand in marriage (13:1-19). Absalom, undoubtedly with mixed motives, set out to avenge his sister's honor and also to remove a rival for the kingship. Seething bitterly over his father's failure to punish Amnon, Absalom waited two years, had Amnon slain, and fled to the Aramean state of Geshur, his mother's home (vv. 20-39).

Joab, David's general, also was a powerful political figure. Although his cunning attempt to effect reconciliation between David and Absalom was discovered by the king, he succeeded in getting the king to allow Absalom's return to Jerusalem, where for two years the young man had no access to his father's court (14:1-33). Absalom's personal grace and beauty were coupled with an irresponsible opportunism. This dangerous combination showed itself when he stirred discontent among litigants in the gate by saying he would judge in their favor were he in charge of Israel's affairs. This and other ploys made him a serious threat to David's security (15:1-6). Surreptitious threat became open rebellion when Absalom had himself proclaimed king at Hebron (vv. 7-12).

As support for Absalom's coup grew stronger, David gathered his band of steadfastly loyal Philistine mercenaries and fled Jerusalem. The picture of the beaten king trudging barefoot up the Mount of Olives, head covered in mourning, cheeks wet with tears, is as touching as any in the Old Testament. Particularly grievous to David was the report that his wise counselor and friend, Ahithophel, had abandoned him for Absalom (14:30f.; 16:15-23). One of the few bright spots was the loyalty of Hushai, whom David commissioned to stay in Jerusalem to spy on Absalom's activities (15:32-37; 16:16-19).[16] Ch. 17

---

15. Jewish tradition appropriately connects the prayer for forgiveness in Ps. 51 and the thanksgiving for forgiveness in Ps. 32 with this episode.

16. One of Absalom's activities was to associate publicly with David's concubines (16:20-22), an act that would help Absalom tighten his grip on the crown.

records Hushai's success in thwarting the advice of Ahithophel, who recommended immediate pursuit of David.[17] So crushed was Ahithophel that he took his own life.

After consolidating his forces in Transjordan, David, probably joined by groups of loyal citizens, sent three armies to battle Absalom, whom they smashed decisively. Absalom himself was killed, in defiance of his father's orders, by the realistic Joab, who knew that peace was impossible while Absalom lived (17:24–18:33).

David's Last Days (2 Sam. 18:1–1 Kgs. 2:46). The exiled king, barely recovered from his grief over Absalom, had not yet returned to Jerusalem when Sheba, a Benjaminite, rallied Israel against her ruler. Keenly aware of the enmity the supporters of the house of Saul carried against him, David lost no time in sending Amasa to crush the revolt. The final victory, however, was credited to Joab, who treacherously killed Amasa and took control of his troops (20:1-26). That Joab was not put in charge of the chase at the outset probably reflects David's strong disapproval of his slaying of Absalom (18:14f.).

Despite the obvious instability of the land and the people's apprehension concerning the future, David took no definite steps to appoint his successor until the close of his life. Adonijah, his oldest surviving son (3:4), made a strong bid for the throne by enlisting the support of Abiathar and Joab, David's priest and general. When the report reached Jerusalem that Adonijah had actually held a coronation feast at En-rogel, Nathan the prophet and Bathsheba, mother of Solomon, pressured the king to name Solomon. Responding affirmatively to his favorite wife, David sealed Solomon's appointment with an oath and gave concrete evidence by turning over to him his private army of Philistine mercenaries. With Zadok as priest, Nathan as prophet, and Benaiah, son of Jehoiada, as general, Solomon was crowned at Gihon, while Adonijah's festivities turned to mourning (1 Kgs. 1:1-53).

But Adonijah, who, fearful of his life, had taken sanctuary at the altar, made one more desperate attempt to unseat Solomon: he asked for David's consort, Abishag, as wife after his father's death. Solomon, sensing the political implications of his brother's request (cannily made through the influential Bathsheba), executed Adonijah.[18] After banishing Abiathar to Anathoth (cf. Jer. 1:1) and slaying Joab in fulfillment of David's dying request for vengeance upon the murderer of Absalom and Amasa, Solomon reigned without rival upon the

---

17. Hushai and Ahithophel seem to be early examples of the wise men or counselors who played major roles in determining policy in Israel (see Jer. 18:18) and who later were instrumental in shaping the biblical wisdom literature. Hushai's simile (2 Sam. 17:18) is a familiar wisdom technique. For background on these wise men, see W. McKane, *Prophets and Wise Men.* SBT 44 (Naperville: 1965), pp. 13-62.

18. The influential women in David's court (e.g., Michal and Bathsheba) seem to have set the pattern for other queen mothers of Judah. Note that the author of Kings records without fail the name of each king's mother (e.g., 15:2, 10).

throne of Judah and Israel (1 Kgs. 2:1-46). Dynastic rule had been established. For almost four centuries the kings in Jerusalem would be sons of David.

David, despite his moral lapses, high-handed policies, and failure to order his own household, gave Israel some of their finest moments. All future kings were measured by their likeness to him.

SOLOMON IN ALL HIS GLORY (3:1–11:43)

Solomon's stony path to the throne was followed by an era of unparalleled prosperity and glory. His forty-year reign (ca. 971-931) saw Israel rise to splendid heights in peaceful pursuits, just as his father's forty-year rule had witnessed unprecedented military success. Originally named Jedidiah ("beloved of the Lord") by Nathan (2 Sam. 12:24f.), Solomon (probably his regnal name) stands in the background in the biblical account until the last days of David. When others like Amnon, Absalom, and Adonijah had been set aside, Solomon stepped to the throne and enhanced its power and prestige.

Authorship and Composition of Kings. Solomon's story dominates the first eleven chapters of Kings. The admirable Court History of David ends at 1 Kgs. 2:46. 1 Kgs. 3–2 Kgs. 25 is the work of a gifted and inspired compiler who gave the books their uniform theological outlook and highly stylized presentation of Israel's history. He probably lived at the close of Judah's history (ca. 590).[19] The emphasis on Elijah, Elisha, and other prophets, together with the editor's general prophetic outlook, has led many to attribute 1–2 Kings to Jeremiah. Indeed, the author did view Israel's history from a perspective akin to Jeremiah's and wrote under many of the same influences. Here, as in 1–2 Samuel, the mere chronicling of events has given way to a subjective approach. Rather than a court apologist whose aim was to celebrate the exploits of the king—as was common among ancient peoples (the Hittites are probably an exception)—the historian evaluates and frequently criticizes the rulers, comparing each with David, the great royal prototype.

The compiler of Kings has given some clues as to his sources. Probably most of the material concerning Solomon in 1 Kgs. 3–11 was drawn from the book of the Acts of Solomon (11:4), while many of the other stories were found in the book of the Chronicles of the Kings of Israel and its counterpart for Judah. The LXX suggests that 8:12f. (LXX 8:53) was taken from the book of Jashar (cf. Josh. 10:13; 2 Sam. 1:18). The deeds of Elijah and Elisha may have been transmitted orally among the schools of the prophets.

All of these materials have been skillfully formed into a synchronized historical narrative. Chronicles of the two kingdoms, originally separate, have

---

19. Jehoiachin's release from prison (ca. 560) described in 2 Kgs. 25:27-30 sets the earliest possible date for completion of the book. However, most of it probably was compiled and edited two or three decades earlier.

been painstakingly combined and interwoven with the editor's own prophetic comments.[20] The result is that

> the Book is a history written with a religious and a practical aim.
> . . . The remarkable note is that when all was lost, someone found the history of that tragic period worth recording as a lesson of God's discipline of His people.[21]

Solomon—the Master Sage. As Israel's first dynastic ruler, Solomon took office with no obvious charismatic powers. In a vision he had at Gibeon, however, God offered him his choice of gifts (1 Kgs. 3:5-14). Realizing the magnitude of his responsibilities, Solomon requested a wise and discerning mind. He took full advantage of his international contacts, wealth, and respite from war, and dedicated himself to literary pursuits. His collections of wise sayings earned for him a reputation beyond that of his Egyptian, Arabian, Canaanite, and Edomite contemporaries (4:29-34) and made him the great patron of Israel's wisdom literature. The precise role of Solomon in Old Testament literature will be discussed in connection with Proverbs, Ecclesiastes, and Song of Solomon.

Solomon not only attained heroic status in Israel but also captured the imagination of many peoples in widespread areas. No figure of antiquity (with the possible exception of Alexander the Great) is so widely celebrated in folk literature among Jews, Arabs, and Ethiopians.

Solomon—Merchant and Statesman. David had bequeathed to his son a substantial empire. Solomon's task was to control it and strengthen the centralized government which his father had founded and which was essential to maintaining the empire. Disregarding to some extent the traditional tribal boundaries, Solomon set up administrative districts, each responsible for providing support to the court one month during the year (4:7-19), a formidable task (vv. 22f.).

Another unpopular policy was Solomon's drafting of laborers from the tribes. Though the 30,000 Israelites engaged in public projects (5:13-18) were not technically slave laborers as were the Canaanite workers (9:15-22), they relished their freedom too much to submit uncomplainingly. The assassination of Adoniram, superintendent of the labor crews (4:6; 5:14; 12:18), indicates the strong feelings toward Solomon's rigid policies.

The most lasting and influential legacy of Solomon's era was the temple at Jerusalem. Only during this period did Israel have the combination of wealth,

---

20. Materials from official records of the northern kingdom probably were brought south by refugees after the fall of Samaria in 722. See further B.S. Childs, *Old Testament as Scripture*, pp. 287-89.

21. J.A. Montgomery and H.S. Gehman, *The Book of Kings*. ICC (Edinburgh: 1951), pp. 44f.

centralized government, and relief from enemy attack necessary to complete a project of this scale. The resources of Solomon's kingdom and the ties of friend-ship with Phoenicia (5:1) were fully exploited to provide a worthy dwelling for God. Foreign artisans were indispensable both because the pastoral life of the Israelites did not stimulate craftsmanship and because their prohibition against making any replica of the deity (Exod. 20:4) tended to curtail artistic activity.

Archaeological discoveries in Canaan together with the fairly detailed bib-lical descriptions (1 Kgs. 5–8) permit reasonable reconstruction of the temple and its furnishings. However, nothing of the temple itself remains, and no tenth-century Phoenician temple has yet been discovered. The ninth-century shrine of Tainat in Syria contains the same tripartite division—porch, nave (holy place), and inner sanctuary (holy of holies).[22]

Solomon's foreign policy was based mainly on friendly alliances, sometimes sealed by marriage, and maintenance of a formidable army. Among his wives was Pharaoh's daughter, for whom he built a special wing on his palace (3:1; 7:8). This profitable alliance is testimony both to Solomon's prestige and Egypt's weakness, for, although Egyptian kings frequently wed foreign princesses, they rarely married their daughters to non-Egyptians. For a dowry Pharaoh (probably one of the last of the feeble Twenty-first Dynasty) gave Solomon the border city of Gezer (9:16).

Solomon's alliance with Hiram of Tyre also was profitable (5:1-12). The Phoenicians, just entering the heyday of their colonial expansion, supplied architectural skill and many materials, especially Lebanese timber, for the tem-ple and palaces. They built and manned his ships and provided a market for Israel's wheat and olive oil. This tie proved especially lucrative when Hiram extended to Solomon a substantial loan (9:11).

Solomon was the first Israelite to use chariotry effectively. Quartered in a ring of fortified border cities (vv. 15-19), his militia included 4,000 stalls for horses,[23] 1,400 chariots, and 12,000 horsemen (4:26). Recent excavations at Hazor, Eglon, and Gezer have yielded Solomonic remains, while the Megiddo stables, previously attributed to him, more recently have been credited to Ahab.[24]

Trading was Solomon's forte. Grasping the significance of controlling the land bridge between Asia and Egypt, he governed the chief north–south caravan routes. Merchant ships carried his cargoes from ports like Ezion-geber to harbors in Asia and Africa. The famed visit of the queen of Sheba (10:1-13) may have

---

22. For a brief but helpful description of the temple, see A. Parrot, *The Temple of Jerusalem*, trans. B.E. Hooke (London: 1957). See also J. Gutmann, ed., *The Temple of Solomon* (Tallahassee: 1976).

23. 40,000 is apparently a scribal error; cf. 2 Chr. 9:25.

24. Y. Yadin, "New Light on Solomon's Megiddo," *BA* 23 (1960): 62-68. Whether the large buildings were actually stables is now open to question. See J.B. Pritchard, "The Megiddo Stables: A Reassessment," pp. 268-276 in J.A. Sanders, ed., *Near Eastern Archaeology in the Twentieth Century*; Yadin, "The Megiddo Stables," pp. 249-252 in F.M. Cross, Jr., W.E. Lemke, and P.D. Miller, Jr., eds., *Magnalia Dei: The Mighty Acts of God*. Festschrift G.E. Wright (Garden City: 1976).

had a commercial purpose. Her people, the Sabeans in southwest Arabia, were apparently in danger of economic suppression by Solomon's tight hold on their caravan routes. Though the queen's journey was successful, she probably had to share her profits with Solomon. He was also middleman between the Hittites and Arameans in the north and the Egyptians, who sold chariots to these northerners. The king held a similar monopoly on the horse-trading enterprises of Cilicia, biblical Kue (10:28f.). Unfortunately Solomon's commercial enterprises, though bringing fabulous wealth to Jerusalem, did not benefit all classes in Israel. The commoner, in fact, may have been less comfortable under Solomon than under David and Saul. The tendency toward centralization of wealth which angered the great prophets of the eighth century began in Solomon's golden reign.[25]

Restiveness among Israel's neighbors revealed that Solomon was losing his grip on the empire. Hadad led a revolt in Edom, and, more formidably, Rezon seized Damascus, which greatly jeopardized Solomon's hold on the Aramean city-states (11:14-25). The author of Kings interpreted these events as tokens of divine judgment for Solomon's serious religious compromises. He does not chide Solomon for his sensuality or amoral living but for disobedience to Israel's monotheistic ideal. Embracing the religions of his wives, Solomon forsook his Israelite heritage and shirked his kingly responsibilities as guardian of the faith. Judgment had to come, if not in Solomon's lifetime (he was spared for David's sake), then afterward. And come it did.

FOR FURTHER READING

Albright, W.F. "The Administrative Divisions of Israel and Judah." *JPOS* 5 (1925): 17-54.

Alt, A. "The Formation of the Israelite State." In *Essays on Old Testament History and Religion*. (Esp. pp. 171-237 [1966]; 223-309 [1968] on David and Solomon.)

Bright, J. "The Organization and Administration of the Israelite Empire." Pp. 193-208 in F.M. Cross, Jr., W.E. Lemke, and P.D. Miller, Jr., eds., *Magnalia Dei*. (Role of David's personality, development of central administration.)

Carlson, R.A. *David, the Chosen King*. Trans. E.J. Sharpe and S. Rudman. Stockholm: 1964. (Traditio-historical approach to 2 Samuel.)

Cross, F.M., Jr. "The Ideologies of Kingship in the Era of the Empire: Conditional Covenant and Eternal Decree." Pp. 219-273 in *Canaanite Myth and Hebrew Epic*.

Davey, C.J. "Temples of the Levant and the Buildings of Solomon." *Tyndale Bulletin* 31 (1980): 107-146.

---

25. For an assessment of the way in which Solomon's power contributed to the deterioration of Israel's ideals, see W. Brueggemann, *The Prophetic Imagination* (Philadelphia: 1978), pp. 28-43. An analysis of the role of Israel's kings in the administration of justice is found in K.W. Whitelam, *The Just King: Monarchical Judicial Authority in Ancient Israel*. JSOTS 12 (Sheffield: 1979).

Gray, J. *I and II Kings*. 2nd ed. OTL. Philadelphia: 1970. (Extensive bibliography.)

Gunn, D.M. *The Story of King David: Genre and Interpretation*. JSOTS 6. Sheffield: 1978.

Malamat, A. "Aspects of the Foreign Policies of David and Solomon." *JNES* 22 (1963): 1-17. (Examines kingdom of Hadad-ezer, Hamath, David's and Solomon's foreign marriages.)

Mendenhall, G.E. "The Monarchy." *Interp* 29 (1975): 155-170. (Israel followed model of Syro-Hittite state, introducing a paganization with fateful social and political consequences.)

Porten, B. "The Structure and Theme of the Solomon Narrative (1 Kings 3–11)." *HUCA* 38 (1967): 93-128. (Argues for structures, unified account.)

Robinson, J. *1 Kings*. Cambridge Bible Commentary. New York: 1972.

_____. *2 Kings*. Cambridge Bible Commentary. New York: 1976.

Snaith, N.H. *Notes on the Hebrew Text of 1 Kings XVII–XIX and XXI–XXII*. London: 1954. (Grammatical notes for beginning Hebrew students.)

Thornton, T.C.G. "Solomonic Apologetic in Samuel and Kings." *Church Quarterly Review* 169 (1968): 159-166. (Much of 2 Samuel and 1 Kgs. 1–2 composed in latter part of Solomon's reign to justify his accession and actions.)

Tsevat, M. "Ishbosheth and Congeners, the Names and Their Study." *HUCA* 46 (1975): 71-87.

Wifall, W.R. *The Court History of Israel*. St. Louis: 1975. (Commentary on Kings for general reader.)

Yeivin, S. "Social, Religious, and Cultural Trends in Jerusalem under the Davidic Dynasty." *VT* 3 (1953): 149-166.

CHAPTER 19

DIVIDED MONARCHY
(1 Kgs. 12:1–2 Kgs. 18:12)

REHOBOAM AND JEROBOAM—THE KINGDOM RENT
ASUNDER (1 Kgs. 12:1–14:31)

SOLOMON'S death brought Rehoboam to the throne. With this transition surfaced all the latent feelings of oppression and abuse which the Israelites had suppressed under the iron rule of David and Solomon. Fostering this resentment was an able young Ephraimite named Jeroboam, son of Nebat, whom Solomon had made superintendent of the work crews of the northern tribes (11:28) during the building of certain fortifications in Jerusalem. A man of humble birth (his mother was a widow), Jeroboam had apparently chafed under Solomon's stern policies. When the prophet Ahijah, resentful of the idolatrous practices corrupting the court, prophesied that Jeroboam would lead the ten northern tribes to independence,[1] Jeroboam's rebellion evidently became known, and he fled to Egypt to escape Solomon's wrath (vv. 26-40).

Rehoboam's Drastic Policy (12:1-24). The showdown with Jeroboam took place at Shechem, where Rehoboam presented himself as king to the northern tribes. This ancient city had seen important convocations, but none so dramatic or crucial as that described in ch. 12. There the people of Israel, tired of Solomon's high-handed policies, sought redress of grievances and assurance of future leniency from his son. The brash Rehoboam overestimated his hold on the northern clans and underestimated the intensity of their resentment. He discounted the counsel of the elders (in itself a serious breach of his people's traditions) and yielded to his callow and ambitious associates. Then Jeroboam, who had hurried back from Egypt at the news of Solomon's death, led the

---

1. The "one tribe" left of the house of David was Benjamin (11:32, 36). Judah was not mentioned because it was assumed that they would remain loyal to their own king. Actually, Benjamin, the border area between north and south, was a bone of contention throughout the Divided Monarchy.

Israelites in declaring independence. That made official the separation between north and south, a separation which had, in fact, been true even during David's day. Their battle cry probably had been decades in the making:

> What portion have we in David?
> We have no inheritance in the son of Jesse.
> To your tents, O Israel!
> Look now to your own house, David. (v. 16)

Rehoboam's attempts to enforce his demands were doomed when his taskmaster Adoram was assassinated and prophetic intervention kept his troops from marching north. Only Judah remained completely loyal (v. 20). Benjamin's loyalties were mixed, but their proximity to Jerusalem required that Rehoboam maintain a tight grip (cf. vv. 21-24). But God used Rehoboam's shortsightedness and obstinacy to bring long overdue judgment on Judah. Solomon's idolatrous and oppressive practices needed judging, and Jeroboam's insurrection became the means that God used.

Jeroboam's Rival Shrines (12:25–14:20). Jeroboam astutely sensed that, if the north-south breach was to become permanent, it must be total. If David had used the royal shrine at Jerusalem to bind the nation together, Jeroboam set up rival shrines to keep the two halves apart, forbidding the regular pilgrimages to Jerusalem. Instead, he capitalized on the rich traditions of Dan and Bethel and set up shrines there. Disregarding the well-established pattern, he appointed priests and attendants who did not stem from Levi. Worse still, he equipped these "high places" with golden calves, reminiscent of Israel's revelry at Sinai (Exod. 32:1ff.). Archaeology suggests that these calves probably were only pedestals on which the invisible Yahweh was believed to be mounted, just as the ark of the covenant is sometimes described as his throne or footstool (cf. Ps. 132:6-8).[2] Though this was the calves' official significance, the people of the land undoubtedly identified them with the images of the Canaanite fertility cult and began to merge the worship of Yahweh and Baal. This syncretism accounts for the prophetic rebuke of Jeroboam and his shrines (e.g., from the man of God, 13:1-32; from Ahijah, 14:14-16). Even changing the date for the main feast, Jeroboam sought to divorce his cult completely from the religion of Judah. The prophetic editors of Kings, outraged at his innovations, constantly remind their readers that it was he who led Israel into open and flagrant sin (e.g., 16:26; 22:52).[3]

---

2. W.F. Albright, *From the Stone Age to Christianity*, pp. 299-301.
3. The stories in Kings were given their final setting by the prophetic schools in Judah, which operated after the northern kingdom had fallen and thus had the advantage of hindsight. See B.S. Childs, *Old Testament as Scripture*, p. 290. Jeroboam himself may have been a devout worshiper of Yahweh, but his zeal for his own shrines, priesthood, and patterns of worship proved ultimately destructive to Israel's historic faith. For his failure to hedge against compromise he was condemned.

Whereas most of the events during Jeroboam's reign are concisely sum-marized in Scripture, one episode is narrated at length—the tragic story of the man of God. Having fulfilled God's will by proclaiming doom to the usurper Jeroboam and his altars, he disobeyed the terms of his mission and paid with his life (13:1-34). Probably this story was handed along in oral form and treas-ured by the prophets of Judah, not only because it promised that a son of David would destroy Jeroboam's shrine and slay his priests (v. 2),[4] but also because it stressed complete obedience. It gives a quaint picture of prophetic activity in this period and helps prepare for the stories of Elijah and Elisha.

There is a touch of irony in Jeroboam's desperate appeal to the prophet Ahijah at Shiloh (14:1-20). When his son Abijah fell ill, he sent to the old prophet who had first predicted his rise to power. Though Ahijah had once supported Jeroboam, who had come to him in disguise, the prophet's words were fraught with doom. The corruption of Canaan was taking its toll on Israel's religious life; and though the old seer's eyes were dim, he could read the hand-writing on the wall.[5] Jeroboam's kingdom, formed to bring judgment on Judah, was also to fall victim to God's judgment.

Struggles Within and Without (14:21–15:34). Judah was scarcely more righ-teous than Israel. The religious apostasy of Solomon's day became more blatant under Rehoboam, as the mention of Asherim and male cult prostitutes (vv. 23f.) indicates. Jeroboam's disruption of the kingdom was not the end of the judgment upon Judah. The powerful Libyan-Egyptian, Sheshonk (biblical Shi-shak), who had toppled the weak Twenty-first Dynasty, invaded Judah (*ca.* 926 B.C.) and exacted heavy tribute (vv. 25-28). When the brief biblical record is supplemented by Sheshonk's inscriptions in the temple at Karnak, something of the sweep of his campaign is made clear. More than 150 places are named as victims of his assaults. From Esdraelon in the north to Edom in the south, Palestine was ravaged by the Egyptian troops. This campaign would have been even more devastating had not instability in Egypt prevented Sheshonk's taking full advantage of his conquests.[6]

Since both Israel and Judah were stunned by the Egyptian raiders, neither

---

4. The mention of Josiah (v. 2) is considered by many scholars as "prophecy after the event." It may be, of course, a rare biblical example of specific prediction, or possibly the name refers not to Josiah specifically but to a descendant of David, given the symbolic name "he whom Yahweh supports"; see C.F. Keil and F. Delitzsch, *Commentary on the Old Testament*, in *loc.* Also, it may be that while the original prophecy of victory (cf. Amos 7:11-13) contained no name, the editors, seeing Josiah's reforms as fulfillment of the prophecy, added his name to highlight the connection.

5. The Asherim denounced in v. 15 took their name from the Canaanite goddess Asherah, consort of El or Baal. Customarily they were sacred trees or posts planted or erected at sacred shrines. Evidently worship of the golden calves opened the door for other acts of idolatry. See K.G. Jung, "Asherah," *ISBE* 1 (1979): 317f.

6. Earlier he had shown disdain for Judah by harboring the fugitive Jeroboam (11:40).

was in a position to deal telling blows to the other, and they remained stale-mated throughout the reigns of Jeroboam and Rehoboam. Little is known of Jeroboam's political system. Presumably he perpetuated many of Solomon's ad-ministrative policies, yet trying to maintain the goodwill which had thrust him into office. His building projects at Shechem, Penuel (on the Jabbok in Trans-jordan), and Tirzah probably required substantial work crews, and his need to keep troops prepared for attack by Egypt or Judah (14:30) certainly demanded a well-organized standing army. Meanwhile Rehoboam struggled to keep the house of David intact, despite storms without and strife within. Jerusalem's glory was badly tarnished by Sheshonk's attack, and the statement that Reho-boam replaced Solomon's gold shields, plundered by the Pharaoh, with shields of bronze is symbolic. Judah's golden age was gone (vv. 26f.).

Following a brief but eventful reign by Abijam (15:1-8; called Abijah in 2 Chr. 13:1), during which strife between the two kingdoms continued and the borders of Judah were extended (see 2 Chr. 13:1-22), Asa began his lengthy rule (*ca.* 911-870). The introductory formula is typical in Kings for the rulers of Judah: (1) the king's accession to the throne is synchronized with the rule of the northern king; (2) length of his rule is stated; (3) his mother's name is given;[7] (4) his reign is evaluated, usually in terms of conformity to or departure from David's standard of piety and devotion (vv. 9-11).[8] Asa is one of the few kings of Judah to receive a favorable evaluation.

Asa was deeply embroiled in power politics. The Chronicler recounts an episode which the authors of Kings omit: Asa's decisive victory over the Ethi-opian vassal of Egypt who had sought to repeat and extend Sheshonk's con-quests. The Judean king so smashed the invading hosts that impotent Egypt was unable to venture into Palestine for a century and a half (2 Chr. 14:9-15). In the north, Baasha, of Issachar, had wrested the throne from Jeroboam's son Nadab and built fortifications at Ramah, thus partially blockading Asa's capital. Asa established an unhappy pattern for later kings when he appealed for help to Ben-hadad of Damascus, and backed his appeal with monetary gifts from the

---

7. The same queen mother, Maacah, is named for both Abijam (15:2) and Asa (v. 10). While Asa and Abijam may have been brothers and "son" in v. 8 a scribal error, more likely the queen mother was such a powerful figure that she continued to wield influence in the court under her grandson Asa (probably just a lad at the outset of his rule) and thus overshadowed his mother. Terms of relationship in the Bible should not always be taken literally, for they often are used for wider relationships (cf. Matt. 1:1).

8. Accession of a northern king usually is synchronized with that of his southern counterpart; the length of his reign is stated; usually his mother is not mentioned; and the evaluation is always negative, normally including the verdict, "He did what was evil in the sight of the Lord, and walked in the way of Jeroboam and in his sin which he made Israel to sin." Vv. 33f. show the typical introductory formula. The formula which closes the rule of a king usually is sterotyped as well. Note v. 31: "Now the rest of the acts of Nadab, and all that he did, are they not written in the Book of the Chronicles of the Kings of Israel?" (This is not the biblical book but the official court records from which the editors of Kings drew.)

temple and palace treasuries. The Syrian king's aid forced Baasha to retire from
Ramah, and the threat to Jerusalem was removed when Asa dismantled Baasha's
fortifications (1 Kgs. 15:16-33).[9]

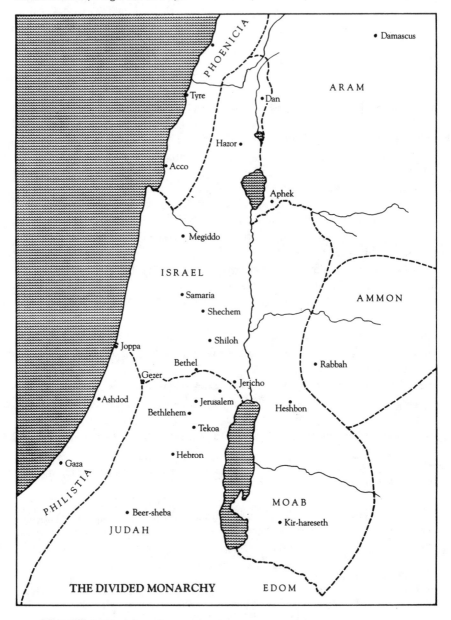

THE DIVIDED MONARCHY

9. A fine summary of the turbulent relations between Damascus, Israel, and Judah
is found in M.F. Unger, *Israel and the Arameans of Damascus* (Grand Rapids: 1957).

HOUSE OF OMRI—BUILDING THE NORTHERN CAPITAL
(16:1-34)

The northern kingdom never achieved dynastic stability. Jeroboam had no dynastic claim to the throne, and his son reigned only two years before Baasha seized the crown and stamped out the royal family (15:27-30). But Baasha's household was no more fortunate. His son Elah and his entire family were wiped out by Zimri, who, with Omri, was commander of a portion of the royal troops (16:8-14). Zimri's reign lasted but seven days. Omri was hailed as king and laid siege to Zimri's capital at Tirzah. Zimri's death (suicide?) divided the loyalty of the people between Omri and Tibni, but Omri's forces prevailed.

This political instability was reflected in the search of Jeroboam and his successors for a suitable capital. It is testimony to the political skill and military insight of Omri that he selected Samaria—an admirable site near Shechem—and legally purchased it, so that, like David's Jerusalem, it was his city. As a measure of the aptness of his choice and the degree of his skill as architect and builder, Samaria remained the capital for a century and a half, falling only after a prolonged Assyrian siege.

Samaria's strategic location has been described concisely by K.M. Kenyon: "Samaria lies athwart the main north-south route, watchful of any advance up from Judah and in easy contact with Phoenicia. . . . It was equally important

Remains of a large, columned building at Megiddo, formerly identified as Solomon's stables but now dated to the reign of the Omride dynasty and probably built by Ahab. (Oriental Institute, University of Chicago)

for him [Omri] to have easy communication to the west, where lay the richest lands of his kingdom. On all counts, Samaria was a much better focus than Tell el Far'ah [Tirzah]."[10] Excavations have laid bare Omri's lavish building enterprises, which were continued by his son Ahab. The luxury Amos denounced a century later began under Omri.[11] Omri's shrewdest political move was probably his alliance with Phoenician Tyre, then in its heyday of colonization. With this alliance, he could find a ready market for Israel's agricultural products and also maintain sufficient military strength to keep the Arameans of Damascus from invading his territory in Transjordan, which stretched south and included Moab. Undoubtedly the crowning achievement of this negotiation was the marriage of his son Ahab to Jezebel, daughter of the king of Tyre (16:41). This unholy union assured Israel's political strength and religious degradation. The spiritual mettle of the tribes was put to its severest test. But God had not left his people without a witness to the true faith; Elijah the prophet was more than equal to the occasion.

ELIJAH—ISRAEL AT THE CROSSROADS (17:1-22:53)

Ahab's reign is recounted in detail in Kings, not so much because of his political importance (the equally important Omri is dismissed with six verses) but because of his conflict with Elijah, who symbolized the opposition of the true Israelites to the innovations of the king and his Phoenician queen.

Ahab's Political Prowess. Ahab made the most of the opportunities bequeathed him by Omri. He lavishly expanded and fortified the royal quarter on the hill of Samaria. Realizing the folly of the constant strife with Judah under Jeroboam and Rehoboam and their successors, both Omri and Ahab pursued peace. In Jehoshaphat (*ca.* 873-848) of Judah, Ahab found a ready ally (cf. 22:1-4).

Cooperation between the kingdoms was essential not only because of the Arameans, who constantly slashed at the Israelite borders, especially the outposts in Transjordan, but also because of the rapid rise of Assyria. Under Ashurnasirpal II (*ca.* 883-859), the Assyrians marched to the Mediterranean, bringing some of the lesser Syrian city-states under their sway.

The threat of enemy invasion often forges strange partnerships, such as Ahab's alliance with Ben-hadad of Damascus. The two kings already had fought three rounds; the Syrian won the first (20:1-6) but Ahab soundly whipped Benhadad in the second (vv. 19-21), and in the third took him captive (vv. 26f.). But in an important episode, which the biblical authors did not record, the two joined with Irhuleni of Hamath and other western rulers to meet the coastward

---

10. *Archaeology in the Holy Land* (New York: 1960), p. 262.
11. See Kenyon, *ibid.*, pp. 260-69, and esp. A. Parrot, *Samaria, the Capital of the Kingdom of Israel* (London: 1958), for the archaeological findings.

thrust of the Assyrian Shalmaneser III (*ca.* 859-824), carrying on his father's ruthless territorial expansion. The outcome of the clash at Qarqar on the Orontes is not quite certain. Shalmaneser III, in Assyrian fashion, claimed a brilliant victory; but he failed to return to follow up his successes for several years, suggesting that he was licking his wounds. According to the Kurkh stele of Shalmaneser, Ben-hadad (called in the text Adad-'idri, i.e., Hadadezer) furnished 1,200 chariots and 20,000 men, while "Ahab the Israelite" contributed 2,000 chariots and 10,000 men.[12] Ahab's charioteers seem to have been especially skilled in maneuvering in hilly terrain. After the Syrians had been routed by Ahab's men in the second battle mentioned above (vv. 19-21), they cried out for an opportunity to fight the Israelites on the plains, where they felt the Syrian gods would be more effective (vv. 23-25)!

The alliance with the Arameans lasted only as long as the Assyrian threat was imminent. Galled that Ramoth-gilead in northern Transjordan was in Aramean hands, Jehoshaphat and Ahab joined battle against an unnamed king of Aram, probably Ben-hadad I (22:1-4). The professional prophets unanimously concurred that the excursion would be successful. Zedekiah, son of Chenaanah, even constructed and wore horns of iron, to symbolize the military might with which the Israelites would drive back the Syrians (v. 11). The display of prophetic symbolism (by which the prophets acted out their message, giving it a concrete existence thought to guarantee its fulfillment) proved mere wishful thinking because it lacked the authority of the Lord. As shall be seen, true prophets sometimes used prophetic symbolism, but in response to the initiative of God, not as a means of controlling his activity.

Only Micaiah, who often had goaded Ahab with gloomy prophecies (v. 8), saw the real outcome—the defeat of Israel and loss of her leader.[13] Like Elijah on Carmel, Micaiah proved that the minority may be right, even when represented by a solitary individual, providing he has listened to the word of God. Micaiah must take his place alongside Moses, Samuel, Nathan, Elijah, Amos, and John the Baptist as one who declared God's truth to royalty, heedless of the cost.

A random shot by a Syrian archer proved Micaiah right and the glib optimists wrong (vv. 34-40). Ahab was dead, but Jehoshaphat was spared, presumably because he was loyal to Yahweh and carried on Asa's reform. The

---

12. J. Bright, *History*, p. 240 note 34, now rejects his earlier position (2nd ed. [1972], p. 236 note 36) which followed Albright ("A Votive Stele Erected by Ben-Hadad I of Damascus to the God Melcarth," *BASOR* 87 [1942]: 28) in suggesting that Hadadezer was the king's personal name, while Ben-hadad was his regnal name. D.J. Wiseman (*DOTT*, p. 48) names Hadadezer as a possible successor of Ben-hadad. M. Black follows Wiseman (*DOTT*, p. 240), listing the major objections to Albright's view, while acknowledging that the Melqart stele lends support to the identification of Ben-hadad and Hadadezer.

13. Micaiah's first answer was affirmative (v. 15), but Ahab must have detected uncertainty or sarcasm, for he demanded a truthful answer (v. 16). See S.J. DeVries, *Prophet Against Prophet* (Grand Rapids: 1978).

author's evaluation is positive, but notes two weak links in Jehoshaphat's spiritual armor: failure to destroy the shrines outside Jerusalem and peaceful relations with Israel's wicked king (vv. 41-46).

Despite Ahab's military prowess and genius for making profitable alliances, his final defeat was not his only major setback. In the Moabite stone (ca. 830), Mesha, the king of Moab (2 Kgs. 3:4), boasts a smashing victory ending forty years of oppression by Omri and his son. "Israel," he exults, "perished utterly forever."[14] Ahab's preoccupation with Assyria and Aram undoubtedly contributed to his neglect of Israel's holdings in southern Transjordan and paved the way for the crushing defeat of Ahab's son Jehoram and his ally Jehoshaphat at the hands of the vengeful Mesha (vv. 4-27).[15]

Jezebel's Flagrant Opposition to Israel's Faith. By himself Ahab would have been a menace to Israel's covenant tradition. Plainly an opportunist, he seems to have had few convictions or scruples. But he was not by himself. Jezebel was by his side, using her prestige and influence as insidiously and maliciously as possible. Like Solomon's foreign wives, she continued her pagan worship, maintaining it on a lavish scale. When the prophets of Yahweh opposed her heathen ways, she set out viciously to destroy them, ruthlessly and thoroughly. The foresight of Obadiah, steward of Ahab and devout worshiper of Yahweh, saved a hundred of them, but many must have perished (1 Kgs. 18:3f.).

Having bent every effort to suppress true prophetic activity, Jezebel imported to her court hundreds of false prophets dedicated to Baal and Asherah (v. 19). Such zeal in so strategic a position posed an incalculable threat to Israel's historic faith. The corruption of Canaanite religion had long been seeping in from the Israelites' Canaanite neighbors, but under Jezebel it was pumped from the palace with extraordinary pressure.

Submitting to the worship of Baal was not unpleasant or distasteful for most Israelites. The idols of the Canaanite fertility god offered a tangible element to which they could tie their worship, while the festive occasions afforded opportunity to give full vent to their passions for wine and immorality. Indeed, riotous drinking and sexual incontinence were a religious duty of Baalism. Baal was lord of the vine. Intimate relations with the cultic prostitutes (both male and female) were believed to encourage Baal to enjoy intercourse with his consort, thus insuring fertility for the whole land. Furthermore, Baal had become for the Canaanites a universal god, although worshiped in local forms as well. Jezebel's god was Baal Melqart (or simply Melqart; also spelled Milqart), the form of Baal worshiped in her home city Tyre, but she had no trouble

---

14. See E. Ullendorff's translation and discussion, *DOTT*, pp. 195-98.

15. Mesha, like the Israelites, credited his defeats and victories to the anger or approval of his god. Chemosh, to whom he apparently offered human sacrifice, is mentioned frequently in the Old Testament (Num. 21:29; 1 Kgs. 11:7; 2 Kgs. 23:13; Jer. 48:46). The presence in Israel of shrines to Chemosh was viewed as religious compromise.

transferring his authority to Israel. Ugaritic texts seem to imply that Baal's title Melqart (lit. "king of the city") branded him lord of the underworld and his authority was not limited to any one geographical area.[16]

Small wonder that the prophets, with Elijah as spokesman, firmly opposed Jezebel's religious program. She was clutching at the vitals of their faith. One reason for the spate of miracles by Elijah and Elisha was to demonstrate that Yahweh, not Baal, controlled nature; note, for instance, the terrible drought predicted by Elijah (17:1-7).[17] But Ahab's understanding was dulled, and the frenzied Jezebel was consumed with hatred of Yahweh's prophets. The lessons did not get across.

Nowhere is Jezebel's flagrant contempt for Israel's ancient ideals seen more clearly than in her vile plot to seize Naboth's vineyard (21:1-26). As shown in the book of Ruth, real estate was not readily salable among the Israelites. Land was passed through successive generations as part of the family inheritance. It could be sold only in dire emergencies and then preferably to a kinsman. Thus, Naboth was appalled at Ahab's presumptuous offer to buy or trade the vineyard.

While Ahab pouted, Jezebel plotted, with utter disdain of the customs and practices of the tribes. Schooled in a more dictatorial approach to kingship in Tyre, she could not understand Ahab's distress when Naboth balked at his request. She wanted the land beside the country palace in Jezreel, and as queen would not be denied. Hiring thugs as false witnesses, she had Naboth condemned to death by the elders on trumped-up charges.

Elijah, incensed at Jezebel's inhumanity, confronted Ahab at Jezreel and pronounced doom upon him, his despised wife, and his entire household. The king's subsequent show of contrition, however, postponed this judgment from his day to his son's (vv. 27-29).

Both Elijah and Elisha are depicted in Kings as ministering to the unfortunate classes (notably the widows). As true prophets, they were to embody the covenant faith and demonstrate it in their relationships with others. Never was this more needful than this crisis hour when "Israel was full of people who, like Jezebel, had no conception of covenant law or, like Ahab, little concern for it."[18]

A noteworthy contrast may be drawn between David's response to Nathan (2 Sam. 12:13) and the attitudes of Ahab and Jezebel to Elijah. Even a good king was not above base conduct, but David acknowledged his sin when it was pointed out. Ahab and his queen, however, were too calloused to the covenant

---

16. Ben-hadad of Syria dedicated a monument "for his Lord Melqart," showing that he was worshiped beyond Israel and Tyre. Ahab and Ben-hadad may have had more in common than their fear of Assyria. For text and comments on the Melqart stele, see Black, DOTT, pp. 239-241.

17. The drought may have spanned a complete year and part of a year on either side. This would accord with the statement in 18:1, "in the third year." Menander of Ephesus mentions a year-long drought in Phoenicia. Cf. Josephus Ant. viii.13.2.

18. Bright, History, p. 245.

obligations and too far removed from the pattern of Israel's kingship. If earlier kings had bent before the chastening rod of the prophetic word, this royal pair sought to break the rod and destroy the prophet who wielded it.

Elijah's Contest on Mt. Carmel (18:1-46). Elijah's name ("Yahweh is my God") summarized his message. He sensed better than anyone since Moses the exclusive nature of Yahweh's claim upon Israel. Yahweh alone was God and would brook no rivals or partners. Elijah put Israel's problem squarely and concisely when he asked the people (v. 21): "How long will you go limping with two different opinions? If the Lord is God, follow him; but if Baal, then follow him." Some issues must be settled in absolutes, and the choice of a God to serve is one of them.

With a courage born of confidence in his convictions, Elijah challenged the prophets of Baal (sponsored by Jezebel) and their followers to a contest to determine who should be worshiped in Israel—Baal or Yahweh. The site was Mt. Carmel, long considered sacred and capped by shrines to Baal and Yahweh (Yahweh's had apparently been desecrated; v. 30). Handicapping himself by giving the prophets of Baal the choice of a sacrificial animal, allowing them to call first on their god to ignite their sacrifice, and drenching his own sacrifice and wood before invoking Yahweh's fire from heaven, Elijah dramatically proved the superiority of his God.[19]

The contrast between the conduct of the prophets is interesting. Apparently the trademark of a pagan prophet was ecstatic behavior, not the content of the message. Baal's prophets are classic examples of the use of frenzied activity to coerce God's response. They first limped around the altar, then gashed themselves with knives while raising their voices in prayer to Baal. Throughout the day their desperate raving continued in vain. Elijah, by contrast, calmly yet fervently voiced his petition, and the fire fell.[20]

Though, from the Judeo-Christian perspective, one may not condone Elijah's zeal in slaughtering the false prophets, the harsh act can be understood. Judgment had to come upon these frauds, and the prophet apparently considered himself the instrument. Although his ardor seems excessive, the menace had been great. The pagan zeal of Jezebel and her followers had not left the prophets of Yahweh unscathed. This was Elijah's day, and he made the most of it.

---

19. H.H. Rowley rejects the view that the pouring out of water was rainmaking magic: "At the moment it was not rain that was wanted, but fire, and all that Elijah was doing was loading the dice against himself even more, to demonstrate his confidence and to make his triumph the more spectacular"; "Elijah on Mount Carmel," *BJRL* 43 (1960): 210.

20. See Rowley, *ibid.*, for a discussion of various theories explaining this miracle by natural means, such as use of an inflammable liquid instead of water, and a mirror to ignite it with the sun's rays. However, as Rowley points out, Baal's prophets would have been watching Elijah's every move. Any trick would have tumbled Yahweh's cause to shameful defeat. The explanation must be, as the narrator states, that God sent the fire.

Few men in Scripture stand taller than the lonely Tishbite (17:1) on Mt. Carmel. His strategic role at a crucial time has been well summarized by Rowley:

> Often in the history of the world great issues have depended on lone individuals, without whom events would have taken a wholly different turn. Yet few crises have been more significant for history than that in which Elijah figured, and in the story of the Transfiguration he rightly stands beside Moses. Without Moses the religion of Yahweh as it figured in the Old Testament would never have been born. Without Elijah it would have died.[21]

A word of praise is due for the artful simplicity with which this story is told. It is not spoiled with excessive detail, uncalled-for commentary, or melodramatic sentimentalizing. The narrator uses irony and humor, and conveys a sense of the dramatic, giving Elijah his richly-deserved place as protagonist, while never forgetting that it was not Elijah so much as Elijah's God who won the day.[22]

EXPLOITS OF ELISHA (2 Kgs. 1:1–8:29)

By the beginning of 2 Kings, Ahab was dead; but Elijah was not, and his opposition to Canaanite religion was as strong as ever. When the injured Ahaziah, Ahab's son and successor, sought to consult the priests or prophets of Baal-zebub, god of Ekron, in the land of the Philistines, Elijah resorted to drastic measures to stop him (1:2-16). Many ancients believed that to predict the future was to control it; for a powerful man, like a prophet, to utter the will of a god was to determine the will of that god. Ahaziah's mission to Baal-zebub was a tacit admission that Baal, not Yahweh, was lord of Israel and shaper of their future.

Apparently the memory of the contest on Carmel had begun to pale. Jezebel was still alive, so there could be no letup in the prophets' vigorous opposition to the inroads of paganism. In fulfillment of Elijah's prophecy, Ahaziah failed to recover from his injury. His brief reign (ca. 853-852) gave way to that of his brother Jehoram (or Joram), which lasted until about 841.

Elijah and Elisha. What Elijah had been to Ahab, Elisha was to Jehoram. Elisha apparently had accompanied Elijah as one of his "sons," a follower or apprentice. When Elijah was dramatically yet mysteriously taken from him, Elisha cried out: "My father, my father! the chariots of Israel and its horsemen!" (2:12). Elisha's last illness evoked the same tragic lament from Israel's king Joash some years later (13:14). Israel's strength lay in godly leaders, not mighty armies; her prophets were her true defense.

---

21. *Ibid.*, p. 219.

22. The honesty of his treatment of Elijah is seen also in the picture of Elijah in despair at Mt. Horeb. Perhaps James had in mind this gloomy episode: "Elijah was a man of like nature with ourselves . . ." (5:17).

Realizing that he was heir to Elijah's ministry, Elisha begged also to be heir to his power (2:9). The request for a double share of Elijah's spirit should not be understood as meaning twice what Elijah had—a presumptuous request—but rather two portions of it as an inheritance, i.e., the lot of the firstborn son who was entitled to a double share of the estate (cf. Deut. 21:17).[23]

Elisha and Jehoram (ca. 852-841). To deal with Jehoram, Elisha needed all the power possible. Despite token reforms like tearing down Ahab's pillar to Baal, Jehoram made little effort to undo his parents' damage (3:1-4). Religiously and ethically his reign was marked by the same cavalier attitudes toward the covenant faith. The story of the prophet's widow who begged Elisha to rescue her from the creditor who threatened to enslave her two sons reflects the same neglect of social justice, if not the same violence, as the story of Naboth's vineyard (4:1-7). Still, the Elisha stories contain more evidence of the seven thousand that had not bowed to Baal than does 1 Kings. Despite the young delinquents who mocked the bald-headed prophet (2:23f.),[24] there was the devout and generous Shunammite (4:8-37). Despite the temptation to consult pagan oracles (1:2, 6, 16), there were active bands of prophets loyal to Yahweh who responded to the leadership of Elisha (2:15-18; 3:4-8; 6:1-7).[25] The infiltration of foreign religions was a hazard to Israel's faith, but Israel itself was not without missionary outreach, as shown by the Israelite maid who pointed her master, Naaman, commander of the Syrian army, to the prophet of the true and living God (5:1-27).

Politically, two episodes marked the reign of Jehoram. First, Mesha, king of Moab, whose land had been dominated by Omri and Ahab and who was forced to pay heavy tribute in sheep and wool, revolted against Israel (3:4-8). After initial setbacks against Jehoram and his ally, Jehoshaphat of Judah,[26] Mesha was driven to drastic measures. He took his eldest son, who was to succeed him, and offered him to Chemosh as a burnt offering upon the wall. This appalling sight apparently caused Israel's troops to panic. The exact meaning of the words "And there came a great wrath upon Israel" is hard to discern (v. 27). Perhaps God used their confusion at this bizarre sight to put them to

---

23. C.H. Gordon suggests that the Hebrew idiom indicates a fraction; *The World of the Old Testament*, p. 200. The request, then, would be for two-thirds of Elijah's spirit.

24. Gordon, *loc. cit.*, notes that even recently in Arab Palestine some villages had reputations for generous hospitality, while others were known for disrespectful and even harmful treatment of strangers. Perhaps the taunting of Elisha was the latest of a number of incidents which revealed that the lads of Bethel really were lawless young hoodlums. Such disregard for ancient ideals of hospitality and respect for age is no shock in a society where the elders also were casual toward the standards of the past.

25. Elisha may have been more ecstatic in his prophetic activity and, therefore, more at home with the prophetic guilds than Elijah (see 3:15; see also 1 Sam. 10:5-12).

26. The strong ties between Israel and Judah, forged by Omri, remained binding for several generations. Intermarriage between the ruling houses was a contributing factor (e.g., Jehoshaphat's son, Jehoram of Judah, was married to a daughter of Ahab; 8:18).

rout so the Moabites could defeat them. Or perhaps some of the superstitious soldiers of Israel (not all had the insights of Elijah or Elisha!) feared the wrath of Chemosh in a land where he, not Yahweh, was thought to rule.[27]

The second noteworthy event was the series of skirmishes between Israel and Syria. In 5:2 and 6:8 there are hints that raiding Israel may have been a regular Syrian practice. Elisha doubtless viewed the wars of Israel as holy wars and was consulted frequently before battle by the king (e.g., 3:13-19; 6:9ff.). If he was an aid to the king of Israel, Elisha was a goad in the side of the king of Syria, who took drastic but vain action to rid himself of the prophet who knew the king's battle strategy almost before he himself did (6:8-14).

Elisha and the Syrians. One striking story from this period concerns a Syrian siege of Samaria which almost starved the city. The king of Israel blamed Elisha for the disaster (6:31), perhaps because the prophet had recommended clemency for captured Syrian raiders (vv. 20-23); or possibly because Elisha had predicted the defeat in an unrecorded prophecy. Calmly weathering the king's fury, Elisha prophesied the end of the famine on the morrow (7:1f.). The word was fulfilled when the Syrians, terrified by strange noises they took to be an attacking army, fled, leaving their equipment and rations.

This was not the only time that Elisha had a finger in Syrian affairs. On a journey to Damascus he learned that the aged Ben-hadad, ruler of Damascus and head of the league of Aramean city-states for about forty years, was ailing (8:7-9). Desperate to discover his fate, Ben-hadad sent gifts to the man of God by his trusted steward Hazael. Elisha's response is puzzling: "Go, say to him, 'You shall certainly recover'; but the Lord has shown me that he shall certainly die" (v. 10). The apparent answer to Ben-hadad was that the illness would not be fatal. Elisha, however, knew that Hazael would plot against the king, and this was to be the cause of Ben-hadad's death.[28] The firm gaze which the prophet fixed on Hazael was prompted by his knowledge of both the pending assassination and the suffering that subsequently would befall Israel (v. 12). When Hazael smothered Ben-hadad with a wet bedsheet, the throne of Damascus was his.[29]

---

27. Mesha boasts of this and subsequent victories in the Moabite stone. He dated his revolt against Israel at the midpoint of the reign of Omri's son. While no record of Moabite revolt against Ahab survives, the slackening of hold upon Moab may have begun during his reign and been completed during that of Jehoram, Ahab's son. Another means of correlating the inscription with the biblical account is to interpret "son" as "grandson," i.e., Jehoram.

28. Hebrew scribes, sensing the contradictory nature of Elisha's statement, changed "to him" (*lô*) in the first statement to "not" (*lō'*) so both statements would agree in announcing that Ben-hadad would not recover but would die. The RSV rendering, however, seems to represent the original idea.

29. An Assyrian inscription of Shalmaneser IV confirms the biblical account: "Adadidri [Ben-hadad] forsook his land [i.e., died an unnatural death]. Hazael, son of a nobody, seized the throne." See Unger, *Israel and the Arameans of Damascus*, p. 75; M. Burrows, *What Mean These Stones?* (Baltimore: 1941), p. 281.

Jehoram of Israel and Ahaziah (*ca*. 841) of Judah, his kinsman, took advantage of the chaos stemming from the change of administration in Damascus to recapture Ramoth-gilead from the Syrians (vv. 25-29). Although Jehoram was wounded and Ahaziah either contracted or aggravated an illness so that both withdrew from the front and returned home, the venture was successful.

While Jehoram of Israel was confronted with the Syrians throughout his reign, Jehoram of Judah (*ca*. 853-841), Ahaziah's father, had troubles of his own (vv. 20-24). Edom followed Moab (3:4-8) and revolted against their masters. This show of independence is proof of the weakness of the southern kingdom, no longer able to hold their southern neighbor in check.[30]

With amazing courage and vitality, Elisha ministered throughout the land to commoner and aristocrat, Israelite and foreigner. More than once he drew the fire of his own king and that of Syria. Yet when either wanted word of the future, he called upon Elisha. Clad in Elijah's rude mantle of haircloth (1:8; 2:13), he soothed a widow's anxiety, helped a servant recover an axe head (6:5-7), baffled Ben-hadad, and infuriated Jehoram. Moreover, he initiated the plan which toppled the wicked and compromising house of Omri, fulfilling Elijah's prophecies of the utter ruin that Ahab's callousness and Jezebel's corruption would bring on themselves and their family.

JEHU AND HIS HOUSE—TROUBLE IN ISRAEL (9:1–14:29)

The man selected by Elisha to bring vengeance on the house of Omri was Jehu, a hard-driving, swashbuckling officer in Jehoram's army, quartered at Ramoth-gilead to guard against a Syrian counterattack (9:1-37). In the ancient charismatic manner, Jehu was anointed by Elisha's representative and acclaimed king by the Israelite soldiers. With this mandate Jehu set out on a bloodstained purge that included a host of victims: Jehoram of Israel (9:24), his ally Ahaziah of Judah (vv. 27f.), Jezebel (vv. 30-37), the male descendants and associates of Ahab (10:1-11), forty-two members of Ahaziah's clan (vv. 13f.), and all the worshipers of Baal in Samaria (vv. 18-27).

Not only did Jehu carry his revenge on Ahab's household to vicious extremes, but he showed little talent for stable rule after the revolution. His coup substantially changed Israel's foreign policy: the murder of Ahaziah resulted in a tragic breach in the alliance with Judah which had been maintained since Omri.

Jehu's savagery prepared the way for the low point in relations between Israel and Judah during the reign of Jehu's grandson Jehoash (*ca*. 798-782). Judah's king Amaziah (*ca*. 796-767), flushed with success against Edom (14:7), sent a brash challenge to Jehoash of Israel. The northern king's reply is typical of the sage expressions in which the ancient kings and wise men took pride:

---

30. The loss of Edom probably carried with it the loss of access to the copper mines and harbor facilities at Ezion-geber on the Gulf of Aqaba.

"A thistle on Lebanon sent to a cedar on Lebanon, saying, 'Give your daughter to my son for a wife'; and a wild beast of Lebanon passed by and trampled down the thistle" (v. 9).[31] When Amaziah persisted, Jehoash crushed his forces at Beth-shemesh. Pursuing Judah's routed army, Israel stormed Jerusalem, smashed a portion of her wall, and looted the temple and royal treasury (vv. 11-14).[32]

Jehu's massacre of Ahab's family and widow probably severed also the friendly ties between Israel and Phoenicia, forged by Omri's diplomacy and strengthened by Ahab's marriage to Jezebel. Hence to the west and south, where Omri's dynasty had found friends, the house of Jehu faced enemies.

To the north and east the situation was even more perilous. Hazael of Syria, as courageous as he was impetuous, raided and ravaged Israel, chipping away particularly at her holdings in Transjordan (10:32f.). Shalmaneser III records on his famous Black Obelisk that he took tribute from Jehu of the house of Omri (ca. 841).[33] Whereas Ahab had joined with Damascus against Shalmaneser at Qarqar (ca. 853), Jehu decided to pay tribute to Assyria instead. He refused to join forces with Hazael against Assyria, thus engendering a hatred which blazed throughout the Syrian's life. Jehu's death only encouraged the Syrians to take greater liberties, and the reign of Jehu's son Jehoahaz saw Israel brought to the brink of disaster. The cryptic note in 13:7 shows the impotence which Hazael's attacks had produced: "For there was not left to Jehoahaz an army of more than fifty horsemen and ten chariots. . . ." (A half-century earlier Ahab had fielded two thousand chariots at Qarqar!) Looking back on those dark days, the authors of Kings had no other explanation for Israel's survival than the covenant loyalty of God who had pledged his faithfulness to the patriarchs (vv. 22f.).[34]

Athaliah and Joash (ca. 841-835; ca. 835-796). Events in Judah during this period were only slightly less turbulent than those in the northern kingdom. Ahaziah's death at the hand of Jehu enabled his ambitious mother Athaliah to seize control of the throne and use her power to further the worship of Baal

---

31. See Jotham's fable, which also involves a conversation among plants (Judg. 9:7-15). The interchange between Ahab and Ben-hadad also illustrates the use of witty or proverbial expressions between enemy rulers: "Ben-hadad . . . said, 'The gods do so to me, and more also, if the dust of Samaria shall suffice for handfuls for all the people who follow me.' And the king of Israel answered . . . 'Let not him that girds on his armor boast himself as he that puts it off'" (1 Kgs. 20:10f.).

32. 2 Chr. 25:5-13 supplies the motive for the conflict. The Judean king had hired Israelite mercenaries to aid in his conquest of Edom, but in obedience to a prophet he sent them north without allowing them to take part in his southern campaign. The embittered Israelites raided Judean cities, thus provoking Amaziah to challenge Israel.

33. "House of Omri" became standard Assyrian nomenclature for Samaria for a century or more after Omri's death, eloquent testimony to the prestige he enjoyed and brought to his nation.

34. Israel's fortunes took a slight turn for the better under Jehoahaz' son Jehoash, who defeated Hazael's son Ben-hadad II three times, as Elisha had prophesied just before his death (vv. 14-25).

Melqart. Her plot to destroy all competitors was foiled when the boy Joash (also spelled Jehoash) was saved and taken into protective custody by the priest Jehoiada (11:1-4), who later forced enthronement of the lad as king. The chief accomplishment of Joash was the refurbishing of the temple, probably both neglected and desecrated under the influence of Athaliah (12:1-21). Joash's attempts to assert himself over the priests who had reared him and served as regents in his youth could not have endeared him to them. Perhaps the palace conspiracy which took his life resulted from his high-handed policies in regard to the temple project. His compromising attitude toward Hazael of Damascus, to whom he paid tribute during the Syrians' campaign to Philistine Gath, may have made him unpopular with the more warlike elements of his people.

Jeroboam II (ca. 793-753). During the reign of Amaziah of Judah, Joash's son, Israel's fortunes took a decided turn for the better when the skillful administrator and soldier Jeroboam II began his lengthy and affluent reign. Aided by several decades of weakness in Syria and Assyria, Jeroboam pushed Israel's borders north as far as the entrance to Hamath in northern Syria and south as far as the Dead Sea, undoubtedly including substantial areas in Transjordan, perhaps as far south as Ammon and Moab. This expansion had been prophesied by Jonah ben Amittai (14:23-29). Prophetic evaluation of Jeroboam's rule is mixed: he was viewed as a savior of Israel who lifted the nation from the edge of ruin (vv. 26f.); yet Amos saw, in Israel's empty ritual and the social oppression of the poor by the rich, grounds for full-scale judgment. It seems that Jeroboam gave Israel respite from judgment at the outset of his reign only to ripen them for judgment after its close.

LAST DAYS OF ISRAEL (15:1–18:12)

From the battle of Qarqar (*ca.* 853) to the fall of Samaria (*ca.* 721), the threat of Assyrian attack was never far from the minds of the Israelites. Responses to this threat differed: Ahab joined with Ben-hadad I to thwart Shalmaneser's westward advance; Jehu chose rather to pay tribute to the Assyrians and left Hazael in the lurch. But the threat was always there, even though its immediate pressure was not always felt; sometimes there was sufficient respite to allow Israel and Syria or Judah to go at each other. If there was some relief under Jeroboam II (*ca.* 793-753) while Assyria waged war elsewhere, the threat returned even more menacingly under Tiglath-pileser III (*ca.* 745-727) and his successors. Menahem (*ca.* 752-742), Pekah (*ca.* 742-732),[35] and Hoshea (*ca.* 732-722), the three most important Israelite kings of this final period, had to reckon seriously with Assyrian invaders, whether in paying tribute or being ravaged (15:19f., 29; 17:3-6).

---

35. See Ch. 21 for a discussion of Pekah's dates and the problems raised by them.

Coupled with this almost constant external pressure was serious internal instability. The houses of Jeroboam I, Baasha, and Omri were leveled by rebellion. Similarly, Jehu's house collapsed, as Hosea predicted (1:4), when Zechariah (ca. 753-752), son of Jeroboam II, was slain by Shallum (2 Kgs. 15:8-12). Shallum in turn was assassinated by the ruthless Menahem (vv. 13-16) after only a month on the throne (ca. 752). Menahem ruled about a decade and seems to have died a natural death, the only one of the last half dozen kings of Israel to do so.[36] Pekahiah (ca. 742), Menahem's son, was slain by his officer, Pekah, who occupied the throne until ca. 732 when Hoshea (ca. 732-722) conspired against him and gained the crown. It was to this relentless pattern of intrigue and counterintrigue that the prophet Hosea, an eyewitness, referred:

> All of them are hot as an oven,
>   and they devour their rulers,
> All their kings have fallen;
>   and none of them calls upon me. (7:7)

Jeroboam had forcibly grabbed the throne of Israel from Rehoboam and thus had set a pattern for his successors throughout two centuries.

Uzziah, Jotham, Ahaz (ca. 790-715). Meanwhile the kings of Judah generally followed a program of appeasement of Assyria. After the death of the pagan queen mother Athaliah (ca. 835), Davidic kings ruled in Jerusalem in unbroken succession, despite occasional mishaps like the palace coup against Joash (12:20). The dynastic stability of the southern kingdom is a great point of contrast between Judah and Israel. A contributing factor was the practice of establishing coregencies, i.e., a father's placing a son on the throne to see that he was duly recognized as heir apparent well before the old king's death. This prevented such difficulties as experienced at the death of David (1 Kgs. 1). However, after the long, prosperous reign of Uzziah (also called Azariah),[37] Judah was forced to struggle for survival against an alliance between Pekah of Israel and Rezin of Damascus (ca. 750-732), whose primary aim was opposition to Assyria (15:37). Uzziah's son Jotham (ca. 750-731) refused to join this coalition and incurred their wrath. His son Ahaz (ca. 735-715) was threatened even more seriously when they laid siege to Jerusalem (16:5). Though the invasion failed, apparently it forced Ahaz to neglect Judah's holdings in Edom. The Edomites thrust off Ahaz' yoke and took over his port and industries at Elath (Ezion-geber) on the Gulf of Aqabah. At this juncture, when Ahaz was harassed from north and south,[38] Isaiah brought hope and comfort in his famous Immanuel prophecy

---

36. The clause "And . . . slept with his fathers" (e.g., 15:22) seems to indicate a natural death. The only apparent exception in Kings (1 Kgs. 22:40) is Ahab, who died in battle (vv. 34-37).

37. Counting coregencies at both ends, Uzziah's reign (15:1-7) stretched some fifty-two years (ca. 790-739), although leprosy curtailed his public activities much of this time. Only Manasseh (ca. 695-642) ruled longer.

38. The Chronicler indicates that the Philistines joined in by pressuring Judah's western frontiers (2 Chr. 28:18).

(Isa. 7:1-17). Tiglath-pileser's invasions of Syria and Israel brought relief to Judah, although at a high price: Ahaz depleted the treasuries and partially stripped the temple to raise tribute with which to curry the Assyrian's favor (2 Kgs. 16:5-9, 17-20).

The tactics of Jotham and Ahaz deferred an Assyrian attack on Judah for a few decades, but Israel's prospects were dim. Their resources were depleted by decades of fighting Syria and Assyria or paying tribute to avoid battle, their morale broken by want of purposeful leadership, their covenant faith weakened by pagan incursion and perversion of the worship of Yahweh. Consequently, they barely survived the slashing thrusts of Tiglath-pileser, who pared away huge portions of Israel, leaving intact only the core around Samaria.

Hoshea (ca. 732-721). When Hoshea seized the throne (*ca.* 732), he had no choice but to yield to Tiglath-pileser's demands for tribute. Sometime after Shalmaneser V (*ca.* 727-722) succeeded Tiglath-pileser, Hoshea defied his Assyrian lord and courted Egypt's support against him (17:4). But Egypt was too weak to help. Shalmaneser swept into Israel and stormed Samaria. The fortress capital held out for a couple of years, during which time Shalmaneser died. His successor Sargon II (*ca.* 722-705) finished the task with a vengeance (*ca.* 721).

Israel's proud kingdom was fallen, no more to rise (vv. 1-6; Amos 5:2). Here the authors pause to survey the rubble of this once lofty realm and meditate on its demise. In true prophetic fashion they view the Assyrians as mere instruments of a God who had to judge Israel's unbridled license and unrelieved spiritual depravity. Their contempt for the covenant, say the authors, fired God's fury, leaving no alternative but judgment, a judgment compounded by deportation of much of the surviving Israelite remnant and importation of pagan hordes, who contributed to the delinquency of the land by introducing alien religions. Such a mixture of populations was standard Assyrian practice, intended to curb revolt by thinning the warm blood of patriotism. The ethnic and religious syncretism of the Samaritans (17:41) plus their opposition to the restoration in Judah (recorded by Ezra and Nehemiah) helps explain hostile attitudes toward them in the New Testament times (e.g., John 4).

FOR FURTHER READING

Aberbach, M., and Smolar, L. "Jeroboam's Rise to Power." *JBL* 88 (1969): 69-72. (Text-critical study.)
Ap-Thomas, D.R. "Elijah on Mount Carmel." *PEQ* 92 (1960): 146-155.
Cross, F.M., Jr. "The Stele Dedicated to Melcarth by Ben-hadad of Damascus." *BASOR* 205 (1972): 36-42. (New reading of inscription, with implications for ninth-century Aram.)
Malamat, M. "Origins of Statecraft in the Israelite Monarchy." *BA* 28 (1965): 34-65.

Repr. pp. 163-198 in E.F. Campbell and D.N. Freedman, eds., *The Biblical Archaeologist Reader* 3.

Miller, J.M. "The Fall of the House of Ahab." *VT* 17 (1967): 307-324. (Shows importance of charismatic-dynastic controversy.)

Parker, S.B. "Jezebel's Reception of Jehu." *Maarav* 1 (1978-79): 67-78. (Reexamination of Jezebel's motives in 2 Kgs. 9:30-37.)

Parzen, H. "The Prophets and the Omri Dynasty." *HTR* 33 (1940): 69-96. (Discusses sources of antagonism.)

Tadmor, H. "Assyria and the West: The Ninth Century and Its Aftermath." Pp. 36-48 in H. Goedicke and J.J.M. Roberts, eds., *Unity and Diversity*. Baltimore: 1975.

Whitley, C.F. "The Deuteronomic Presentation of the House of Omri." *VT* 2 (1952): 137-152. (Historical accuracy sacrificed in presentation of theocratic view.)

CHAPTER 20

JUDAH ALONE
(2 Kgs. 18–25)

HEZEKIAH'S REFORMS (2 Kgs. 18:1–20:21)

Rebellion Against Assyria. The lessons of Israel's collapse were not lost on Hezekiah, who was coregent of Judah with Ahaz from *ca.* 729 B.C. and ruled alone from *ca.* 716 to 687. Spurred on by the prophet Isaiah, Hezekiah sought two commendable goals: to break Assyria's dominance in the west and to purify Judah's covenant faith by wiping out the altars and shrines to Canaanite and Assyrian deities. The two tasks were related. In the ancient Near East, vassal states normally were required to observe their masters' religious practices along with their own.

Assyria's troubles with their northern neighbors, particularly Armenia (Urartu), kept Sargon busy at home for nearly a decade (720-711). Meanwhile, Egypt was in no mood to foment revolt because of Nubian invasions led by Piankhi, who ultimately dominated the Nile valley and established the Twenty-fifth Dynasty of Nubian rulers (715-663). Hezekiah took advantage of the respite from Assyrian invasion to slacken his ties with Nineveh and await the right moment for revolt. The statement, "he rebelled against the King of Assyria and would not serve him" (18:7), probably summarizes Hezekiah's actions beginning in 711, when he may have joined Philistine Ashdod and the kingdoms of Edom and Moab in revolting against Sargon. Though the Nubians in Egypt may have promised help, their hold on the throne was still too shaky. Sargon readily slapped down the rebellion and set up an Assyrian governor in Ashdod.

Hezekiah's rebellion came into the open when Sargon died in 705, leaving his son Sennacherib to mount the throne. Ancient kings knew that a garment rips most readily at the seams; hence transitions between rulers frequently were occasions for revolt on the outposts of the empire.

Intrigue with Egypt. Hezekiah was not alone in his will to revolt. This worried Isaiah, who knew that revolt was too simple a solution for Judah's problems. Revolt would mean losing in two ways: Judah would suffer the ravages of Assyrian invasion, and their covenant faith would again be compromised by the influence of Egypt and their other pagan allies. Isaiah's warning took the form of a dire woe, a threat of judgment in which God's wrath would cause Judah's plan to tumble in on their own heads:

"Woe to the rebellious children," says the Lord,
    "who carry out a plan, but not mine;
and who make a league, but not of my spirit,
    that they may add sin to sin;
who set out to go down to Egypt,
    without asking for my counsel,
to take refuge in the protection of Pharaoh,
    and to seek shelter in the shadow of Egypt!
Therefore shall the protection of
    Pharaoh turn to your shame,
and the shelter in the shadow of
    Egypt to your humiliation." (Isa. 30:1-3)

All foreign military alliances were anathema to the prophets, but especially those with Egypt, which were viewed as rejections of the Exodus. Israel's Lord had proved himself master of Pharaoh and his host in the plagues and at the Red Sea. To trust Egypt for help could only mean that Judah had turned their backs on the grandest event of their past and had lost confidence in the covenant God.

Overtures from Babylon. It is against this backdrop that one should understand the emissary sent to Jerusalem by the Babylonian ruler Merodach-baladan (20:12-19).[1] Though the ostensible reason was Hezekiah's illness, there is little doubt about the true agenda. The Babylonians, long vassals of Assyria, wanted to see whether Hezekiah's will and resources would make him a stout ally against Sennacherib. When Hezekiah showed them the royal wealth, supplies, and military equipment, Isaiah seized the opportunity for a dire prediction. Any treaty with the Babylonians would be like a snare that catches the fowler instead of the bird. And Hezekiah's own offspring would be the first to feel the captors' noose. All such alliances were uneasy at best, but this one would prove damaging beyond repair. A century later Isaiah's words came true when Babylonian armies three times marched west against Judah and their neighbors, leaving Jerusalem's walls and temple in ruins and bringing to a bitter end the reign of Hezekiah's sons (ch. 25).

Isaiah's advice against foreign covenants and armed rebellion could not counter Hezekiah's willfulness, supported by a strong cadre of political advisers.[2]

---

1. Bab. *Marduk-apal-iddina.* Banished from Babylon by Sargon, he had recovered his throne in 709. His long-standing quarrel with Assyria had honed to a fine edge his desire to revolt.

2. The statesmen of Judah who counseled such action are often called the pro-Egyptian party. Whether technically a party is uncertain. Certainly numbers of them lobbied hard for their view.

Hezekiah busied himself fortifying Jerusalem for the inevitable siege. The authors of Kings singled out especially his steps to assure an adequate supply of water: ". . . he made the pool and the conduit and brought water into the city . . ." (20:20). More than 1700 feet long, the tunnel that carried water from the Virgin's Fountain (also called the spring of Gihon; 1 Kgs. 1:33) in the Valley of Kidron, outside the city walls, to the pool of Siloam, inside the walls, was a remarkable feat of engineering.[3] Isaiah, however, read these preparations as arrogant self-reliance, where trust in God was needed. He even pointed out that Hezekiah gave no credit to other architects and workmen who had worked on the reservoir system earlier (Isa. 22:8-11).

Invasion by Sennacherib. Hezekiah's defiance did not escape the attention of Sennacherib, who consolidated around him the resources of his homeland

Sennacherib's attack on Lachish (701 B.C.), depicted on relief from his palace at Nineveh. (British Museum)

3. In 1880 a Hebrew inscription was discovered that describes the tunnel's completion, when crews digging from each end met in the middle. For the text of the Siloam inscription, see N.H. Snaith, in *DOTT*, pp. 209-211. Hezekiah's water project was also mentioned in 2 Chr. 32:30 and Ecclus. 48:17. See W.S. LaSor, "Jerusalem," *ISBE* 2 (1982): 1011.

and marched against his enemies. By 703 he had defeated Merodach-baladan and set an Assyrian prince over Babylon. Then he marched west, crushing the coastal rebellion of Tyre, Acco, Joppa, and Ashkelon. Near Ekron, he defeated an Egyptian army that had marched north to support the rebels.

Then he turned to Judah and confirmed Isaiah's worst fears. The account in Kings is brief: "In the fourteenth year of King Hezekiah [701] Sennacherib king of Assyria came up against all the fortified cities of Judah and took them" (2 Kgs. 18:13). The actual mayhem is more clearly seen in Sennacherib's own descriptions, which tally the capture of 46 fortified cities, 200,150 captives, plus innumerable horses, mules, donkeys, camels, large and small cattle. In vivid detail the Assyrian king described his tactics: piling earthen ramps against the city walls, assailing the gates with battering rams, and tunneling under the stones and brick fortifications.

Sennacherib's account of the siege is noteworthy: "He himself [Hezekiah, the Jew] I shut up like a caged bird within Jerusalem, his royal city. I put watch-posts strictly around it and turned back to his disaster any who went out of its city gate."[4] Sennacherib's silence about the fall of Jerusalem is explained by the narrative in Kings which describes the annihilation of the Assyrian army by the angel of the Lord. The means used is not mentioned. Bubonic plague is a likely explanation.[5]

The death of Sennacherib at the hands of his sons (2 Kgs. 19:36f.) occurred some twenty years later (681). The chronology used here does not accept the theory of J. Bright and others that the account in chs. 18–19 and Isa. 36–37 telescopes two Assyrian invasions under Sennacherib—one in 701, the other some years later.[6]

The historical background of Sennacherib's invasion is as fully documented as any event in Israel's history. In addition to the Siloam inscription are several references from Sennacherib himself. The Taylor prism contains the fullest account, detailing the tribute that Hezekiah was forced to pay: thirty talents of gold, three hundred talents of silver, plus other valuable objects and numerous slaves (18:14-16). The Bull inscription and the Nineveh Slab inscription both contain summary references to Hezekiah's submission.[7]

The events at Lachish (Tell ed-Duweir) outlined in 18:17-37 also have left

---

4. D.J. Wiseman in *DOTT*, p. 67.

5. Herodotus ii.141 reports that an invasion of field mice devoured the quivers, bows, and shield straps so the Assyrians were unable to fight effectively or defend themselves.

6. Bright, *History*, pp. 298-309. F.F. Bruce (*Israel and the Nations* [Grand Rapids: 1969], p. 72) implies and Wiseman ("Sennacherib," *IBD*, pp. 1414-15) clearly states that the biblical records and Assyrian texts are best understood as describing one invasion. The mention of the Egyptian Tirhakah as king (2 Kgs. 19:9; Isa. 37:9) has raised the possibility of two invasions, for his reign seems not to have begun until 690. K.A. Kitchen (*IBD*, p. 1571) suggests that Tirhakah was an army commander then, but was called king because he later assumed the throne. Evidence cited by Bright and questioned by Kitchen would indicate that he was too young to have led the Egyptian troops in 701.

7. For full translations, see Wiseman, in *DOTT*, pp. 64-69.

archaeological testimony. A relief on the palace wall at Nineveh shows Sennacherib seated on his portable throne outside Lachish receiving the homage of the defeated inhabitants of that part of Judah.[8] After the fall of Lachish, apparently Sennacherib's headquarters before the assault on Jerusalem, the Assyrian king sent three high officials with a large number of soldiers to persuade Hezekiah and his counselors to surrender the city.[9] The Assyrian delegation did its best to intimidate the leaders of Jerusalem by denouncing their Egyptian allies, questioning whether Yahweh would come to their aid, maligning Hezekiah's leadership, and pointing out the failure of the local gods to save Hamath and Samaria. Such cajoling and sarcasm were apparently standard ploys of ancient diplomacy.

Strengthened by Isaiah's comfort (19:6f.), Hezekiah rejected the call to surrender. Sennacherib reminded him by letter of the chain of victories with which he had enslaved Syria and Palestine. Once more Isaiah encouraged the king by denouncing, in the Lord's name, the arrogance of the Assyrians and specifically promising the relief of Jerusalem: "He shall not come into this city or shoot an arrow there, or come before it with a shield or cast up a siege mound against it" (v. 32).

The deliverance predicted by Isaiah and implemented by the angel of the Lord caused problems for later prophets like Jeremiah. The relief that came to Hezekiah was interpreted as evidence that Zion, with its Davidic palace and Solomonic temple, was inviolable. The covenant God would never destroy his own city and house. Thus God's act of rescue became grounds for complacency and compromise. And the authors of Kings, who had narrated the story of miraculous preservation, had the sad task of ending with the tragic narrative of Jerusalem's collapse (ch. 25).[10]

MANASSEH'S REBELLION (21:1-26)

Few kingdoms in history have seen reversals of policy as drastic as that of Manasseh when he succeeded Hezekiah, with whom he apparently had been

---

8. *ANEP*, pp. 371-74.

9. The Tartan (*tartannu* "second") was apparently the highest military officer of Assyria; the Rabsaris (lit. "chief of the eunuchs"), a high administrative official in the palace bureaucracy; and the Rabshakeh, probably not the chief cupbearer as once thought, but chief of the nobles (lit. "high ones" from *šaqu* "to be high"). As spokesman for the emissary, the Rabshakeh seems to be the ranking diplomatic official. That such senior officials were sent shows how seriously Sennacherib viewed the mission. For a thoughtful meditation on the Rabshakeh, see J. Ellul, *The Politics of God and the Politics of Man*, trans. G.W. Bromiley (Grand Rapids: 1972), pp. 143-161.

10. God's miraculous care was evidenced also in Hezekiah's recovery from seemingly terminal illness. The sign given by Isaiah—the shadow that moved back ten steps on the sundial—is as puzzling astronomically as Joshua's sun that stood still. No obvious correlation with an eclipse seems possible given the date of the healing, which took place at least fifteen years before Hezekiah's death in 687 and probably before Merodachbaladan was permanently expelled from Babylon in 703. Franz Delitzsch's theory of a miracle in the form of an optical illusion may be as good as any; Keil-Delitzsch, *Commentary* at 2 Kgs. 20:11.

coregent for about ten years. Ironically, Judah's most flagrantly apostate king reigned the longest of any of the sons of David—fifty-five years (696-642).

Compromise with Assyria. Manasseh was as bent to collaborate with Assyria as Hezekiah was to resist such a move. Political submission was accompanied by a startling reversion to pagan practices.[11] High places, altars, and images were erected, including an image of the Canaanite Asherah in Solomon's temple. The Assyrian astrological cult was celebrated, and all manner of magic and soothsaying was practiced. Once, probably in some national emergency, Manasseh sacrificed his own son. Any opposition—such as that of the prophets—was brutally crushed. Two summary statements show the horror with which the authors of Kings viewed his reign: ". . . Manasseh seduced them to do more evil than the nations had done whom the Lord destroyed before the people of Israel" (21:9); "Moreover Manasseh shed very much innocent blood, till he had filled Jerusalem from one end to another . . ." (v. 16).[12]

Conflict with the Prophets. Manasseh's path brought him to a head-on collision with the prophets, whose theme was judgment: "and I will wipe Jerusalem as one wipes a dish, wiping it and turning it upside down" (v. 13). No more could a promise be forthcoming, as came through Isaiah in the days of Sennacherib, that Jerusalem and her splendid temple would be spared. Though the prophet Zephaniah is dated to Josiah's reign, his account of Jerusalem's evil—capitulation to foreign cults and compromise with foreign fashions—aptly describes Manasseh's vicious legacy (see Zeph. 1:1-9).

The reign of Amon, Manasseh's son, was short and ill-fated (642-640). Like his father, Amon was faulted specifically for his idolatry. His assassination by political underlings ("servants," 2 Kgs. 21:23) was probably the result of growing antipathy toward the basically pro-Assyrian policies of Manasseh and Amon. The assassins in turn were slain by "the people of the land," apparently some landed gentry who feared the implications of full-scale revolt against Assyria.[13]

The trend had been set. The narrative in Kings moves relentlessly toward its disastrous denouement. Even Josiah's splendid attempts to revive the covenant faith could not measurably alter the plot.

---

11. Prisms of Esarhaddon and Ashurbanipal mention Manasseh as paying tribute to Assyria; *ANET*, pp. 291, 294.

12. 2 Kings is silent about Manasseh's captivity in Babylon and his subsequent repentance (2 Chr. 33:10-17). Whatever reformation may have resulted was both superficial and short-lived. The major purpose of Kings was to show that divine judgment on Manasseh's wicked rule was inevitable. Any mention of modest reform would have been a digression. See Bruce, *Israel and the Nations*, p. 75, for the circumstances (probably some involvement with Egypt in plotting against Assyria) leading to Manasseh's captivity.

13. See Bright, *History*, p. 316.

JOSIAH'S REVIVAL (22:1–23:30)[14]

In some ways Josiah's reign (639-609) paralleled Hezekiah's, beginning when Assyria was preoccupied with military and political pressures close to home. This time, however, Assyria would not recover. By the time of Josiah's tragic death, the dire prophecies of Nahum about Nineveh's demise were about to be fulfilled.

Josiah's desire to reform the faith and rearrange the politics of Judah was aided by two closely contemporary events (626): the death of Ashurbanipal, Assyria's last great ruler; and the successful revolt of Nabopolassar of Babylon, who assumed the throne of what had been a vassal state.[15]

Book of the Law. Even more important to Josiah's reign than these political changes was the discovery of the book of the law in 621 (22:3-20).[16] Josiah had already taken renewed interest in the temple. The law book was found during its refurbishing, which Josiah had sponsored. The law gave him the impetus and direction needed to undo much of Manasseh's damage (23:4-20). In an all-out effort, he purged the temple of pagan vessels, deposed idolatrous priests throughout the land, abolished sacred prostitution, and defiled the sites of pagan shrines so no worshiper would dare approach them. All his royal resources were put to the task, supported undoubtedly by prophets like Zephaniah and Jeremiah as well as many who had joined their king in entering into solemn covenant with the God of their fathers (23:1-3).

Yet Josiah's spiritual revival was not enough, even though it included celebration of the Passover with more enthusiasm and thoroughness than at any time in centuries. The authors of Kings, intent on showing the terrible toll of sin on Israel's welfare, saluted the reforms but cited their inadequacy to stay the Lord's wrath against Judah "because of all the provocations with which Manasseh had provoked him" (vv. 26f.).

Battle with Neco. Josiah's death (23:28-30) adds to the tragedy that echoes throughout the last chapters of 2 Kings. The need for judgment was so great that even the good king was not spared. The circumstances that led to Josiah's death show how confused international affairs had become at the close of the

---

14. Since the historical and political events from Josiah to the fall of Judah under Zedekiah are essential to understanding Jeremiah, they will be treated more thoroughly there.

15. The role of the Scythians (a West Siberian people who settled in the Black Sea–Caspian area *ca.* 2000 and later invaded northern Persia and Urartu) is not well understood. Some scholars following Herodotus i.104-106 (e.g., Bruce, *Israel and the Nations*, p. 77) believe that a Scythian invasion hastened Assyria's undoing. Others (e.g., Bright, *History*, p. 315) leave the question open.

16. Since Jerome (*Commentary on Ezekiel*, 1:1), this scroll customarily has been identified with Deuteronomy, esp. chs. 12–26. For the various theories of the date of Deuteronomy see above (p. 177).

seventh century. Assyria was on its last legs, harried especially by Nabopolassar and his allies, the Medes, who had moved west from the steppes of northwest Persia to put pressure on the Tigris valley. Egyptian policy now took a new turn. After centuries of contesting Assyrian domination of the Mediterranean coast, Egypt, led by Pharaoh Neco, sought to support Assyria against the co-alition of Babylonians and Medes. Apparently the Egyptians preferred to reckon with a sickly Assyria than a virile Babylonia.

Josiah seemed to view Neco's invasion as a threat to the growing political sovereignty he wanted to exercise in the region north of Judah's borders from which the tribes of Israel had been deported (vv. 19f.). Boldly, Josiah marched to Megiddo to cut off Neco's army in its rush to the Euphrates, where it would contest the armies of Babylon under Nebuchadnezzar, who was then military commander. Josiah was slain in battle. The arrival of the chariot bearing his body was surely one of the most shocking sights Jerusalem had ever witnessed. The words of the prophetess Huldah were fulfilled, but not as expected (22:20). Josiah had not lived to see judgment fall on Jerusalem, but his own death was certainly a harbinger of it. Few episodes would prove more puzzling to the faith of God's people—and more maturing. God seemed to reserve the right to deviate from his own patterns: the wicked Manasseh lived to a ripe age; the righteous Josiah was cut off in his prime.

JERUSALEM'S FALL (23:31–25:30).

With Josiah's death at Megiddo, the fall of Jerusalem was inevitable, even though it took more than twenty years. Josiah's successors ruled only on terms set by their Egyptian or Babylonian superiors.

Egypt's Dominance. Jehoahaz, Josiah's oldest son, ruled only three months (23:30-33). Neco, though he apparently had failed to aid Assyria, considered Syria and Palestine his territory. His victory over Josiah made Judah a tributary. Summoning Jehoahaz to his camp at Riblah in northern Syria, Neco removed him from power and exacted massive tribute.

Eliakim, another son of Josiah, was appointed puppet ruler (608-597) by Neco, who gave him the regnal name Jehoiakim (24:34f.) and forced him to tax his countrymen almost unbearably to pay the tribute.

Babylon's Conquests. Egyptian dominance lasted only a few years (609-605). When Nebuchadnezzar defeated Neco at Carchemish in 605, the Babylonians reigned unrivaled as masters of the Middle East. Jehoiakim (*ca.* 603) was forced to pledge allegiance to Nebuchadnezzar (24:1). When a battle between Egypt and Babylon on the Egyptian frontier proved a stalemate (601), Jehoiakim was given heart to rebel despite the stern warnings of Jeremiah. Not until 598 could Nebuchadnezzar march west again, but when he did Jehoiakim was done in, possibly by those who hoped for clemency from their foreign masters (vv. 2-7).

Judah's defeat was made more painful because their neighbors—Syria, Moab, and Ammon—aided Nebuchadnezzar in the siege. The authors of Kings have no doubt that behind the political turmoil was the hand of God, judging Judah for Manasseh's crimes (vv. 3f.).

Jehoiachin, Jehoiakim's son and a lad of eighteen, was placed on the throne (vv. 6-9). His three-month reign ended when Nebuchadnezzar himself marched on Jerusalem and took the young king with his family and courtiers hostage to Babylon (597). In an attempt to nip in the bud any further revolt, the Babylonians also deported Judah's finest leaders and craftsmen. Judah was left with neither will nor ability to rebel for another decade (vv. 10-16).

Zedekiah's Rebellions. Mattaniah, Josiah's youngest son and Jehoiachin's uncle, was appointed ruler by Nebuchadnezzar, who named him Zedekiah (597-586). As if plagued with a death wish, Judah made rebellion against Babylon the dominant drive of Zedekiah's reign. Two circumstances made the king's lot insufferable: many nobles envisioned measurable profit from economic and political independence; and some countrymen pledged primary loyalty to Jehoiachin, still alive in Babylon. A stronger person might have ruled peacefully and sensibly, as Jeremiah constantly urged, but not Zedekiah.

Though Judah did not join an abortive revolution threatening to spread west in 593, the suicidal urge prevailed a few years later. Jeremiah's opposition to rebellion and Zedekiah's uncertainty were crushed under the juggernaut of chauvinistic ambition and misguided confidence. Egypt's role was unclear, though Pharaohs Psammetichus (593-588) and Hophra (588-569) undoubtedly were involved. Other help seemed limited to token support from Tyre and Ammon.

Judah's arrogance left Nebuchadnezzar no choice. Early in 588 his armies surrounded Jerusalem, while Judah's foolish nobles waited in vain for the angel of the Lord to help as in Hezekiah's day. Over two years of siege left the capital weakened and unnerved by hunger and fatigue. Zedekiah's desperate bolt for freedom was intercepted, and he reaped the full wrath of Nebuchadnezzar. Blinded, bound, bereft of his sons, who were murdered while he yet had sight, he was carted to Babylon, the tattered remnant of David's ancient glory (25:1-7).

The authors of Kings spared no details in describing Jerusalem's suffering (given poetic expression in Lamentations)—sacking and burning, spoiling and looting. The thorough savagery of ancient conquerors is documented in vv. 8-21. But more, the authors saw an explicit commentary on the righteousness of God who inflicted judgment on a people that played false with him. One line could label the next half century: "So Judah was taken into exile out of its land" (24:20).

Even the puppet governor, Gedaliah, could not long survive such chaotic days. The last smoldering sparks of rebellion flared briefly when Ishmael, a member of the royal family, assassinated Gedaliah, probably out of spite for the

Babylonian conquerors. The assassins had no choice but to flee to Egypt (25:22-26). Tragically, they forced Jeremiah to go with them.

Jehoiachin's Release. 1–2 Kings end on a more hopeful note: at Nebuchadnezzar's death, when Evil-merodach mounted the throne of Babylon (562), Jehoiachin, still alive after thirty-seven years in captivity, was freed and accorded royal treatment (vv. 27-30). This passage is a reminder that the final touches were not put on 2 Kings until well into the Exile, when the full implications of the events recorded were perceived.

Moreover, Jehoiachin's release had its own theological message. The necessary judgment, so long promised by the prophets and so ruthlessly executed by the Babylonians, had done its work. Jehoiachin, whose captivity was the first chapter of the Exile, lived to see the last chapter begin. The same God who sent the dove to signal the end of the Flood prompted the sacred writers to depict Jehoiachin, free from fetters and dining at the king's table. The storm was past; a better day was at hand. That story, however, belongs not to Kings but to Ezra and Nehemiah.

FOR FURTHER READING

Albright, W.F. "King Joachin in Exile." *BA* 5 (1942): 49-55. Repr. pp. 106-112 in G.E. Wright and D.N. Freedman, eds., *The Biblical Archaeologist Reader* 1. (Based on Babylonian ration tablets discovered by E.F. Weidner.)

Malamat, A. "Josiah's Bid for Armageddon." *Journal of the Ancient Near Eastern Society* 5 (1973): 267-279. (Assumes that Megiddo was in Egyptian hands in 609.)

————. "The Last Kings of Judah and the Fall of Jerusalem." *IEJ* 18 (1968): 137-156. (Chronological study.)

Rowley, H.H. "The Prophet Jeremiah and the Book of Deuteronomy." Pp. 157-174 in *Studies in Old Testament Prophecy*. Edinburgh: 1950. (Summary of discussion to 1950 plus bibliography.)

Torczyner, N.H. et al. *The Lachish Letters*. New York: 1938.

Wiseman, D.J. *Chronicles of the Chaldean Kings (626-556 B.C.)*. London: 1956. (Translation of Neo-Babylonian texts plus commentary.)

CHAPTER **21**

THE CHRONOLOGICAL
PUZZLE

T HE Old Testament contains not only hundreds of names of persons and places (see p. 40 above), but also many chronological data. In the books dealing with the earlier periods, these usually are expressed only in years,[1] and they cannot be attached to any extrabiblical data. But in Kings and Chronicles and several prophets (e.g., Jeremiah, Ezekiel, Daniel, Haggai, Zechariah, Ezra, and Nehemiah) there is a spate of chronological material. Some of these dates can be converted to the present system of calendration quite readily. But others offer various seemingly insoluble problems. Before discussing these, some idea of the ancient systems of counting time and building calendars will be helpful.

THE YEAR AND ITS DIVISIONS

Accounts that Methuselah lived 987 years (Gen. 5:25) or that Abraham was 100 years old when Isaac was born (21:5) usually prompt an inquiry into whether the ancients counted time the same as moderns do. Basically, the answer is affirmative. Components of time in antiquity were derived from observation of natural phenomena just as, ultimately, are modern time divisions.

Day. In the Semitic world the day began at sunset. This was refined to coincide with the appearance of the first star; later, when the day was divided into hours, it began at 6 p.m. (the hour does not yet appear in the Old Testament).[2] Since a "day" which begins in the evening and extends into the following period of daylight actually encompasses parts of two "days" in the

---

1. E.g., Gen. 5:3, 5f., etc. An exception is the flood account where even the month and day are given; cf. 7:11; 8:13.
2. The Sumerians marked a "double hour"; it is relatively easy to divide the sky into halves and thirds, and mark approximately when the sun is one- or two-thirds of the way to "noon" or has declined by similar amounts. Sundials were in use by the eighth century B.C., and the Greeks and Romans used the hour as a unit. Where "hour" occurs in the Old Testament, it simply means "time, occasion"; cf. Dan. 3:6.

modern sense, it is customary for scholars who desire accuracy to use a double date, e.g., "6/7 June," i.e., the day that begins the evening of the sixth and ends at sundown on the seventh.[3]

Month. As the day was determined by the sun's apparent movement, so the month was determined by the moon. Earliest records show that it began with the new moon (the first appearance of the thin crescent in the western sky at sunset). The moon's cycle is 29.5 days, hence months were alternately 29 and 30 days.[4]

Obviously the lunar month only occasionally coincides with the modern calendar month. The equivalent is customarily represented by a compound, e.g., "Nisan = March/April." But this is not always precise. For example, in 1970 Nisan began on 6 April, and Nisan was April/May. In a year requiring an intercalary month (see below), the normal equivalents as a rule will not hold.

Year. The concept of year, as far back as records exist, was associated with the change in seasons, occasioned in turn by the solar cycle of 365.25 days. But months derived from the lunar cycle and years derived from the solar cycle cannot be synchronized exactly. Suppose that in the year x, the new moon of Nisan coincided with the spring equinox so both solar and lunar cycles began

Astronomical calendar from tomb of Rameses VII (1149-1142 B.C.) at Thebes. (Egyptian Museum, Cairo)

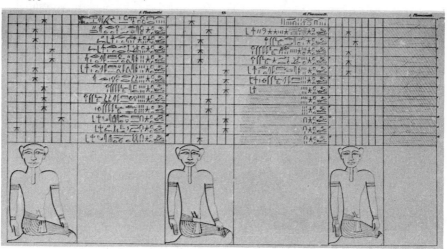

3. R. de Vaux cites evidence that the Hebrews originally had a morning-morning day; see *Ancient Israel*, p. 181. This theory has not found general acceptance.

4. The earliest Semitic words for "month" were derived from the word for "moon" (cf. English "month," essentially "moonth"). Later, the common Hebrew ḥōdeš "new-ness" replaced the earlier word.

at the same time. Twelve months later (i.e., $12 \times 29.5 = 354$ days), the first of Nisan would be about eleven days before the spring equinox. The year of twelve lunar months is a lunar year; that of approximately 365 days is a solar year.

The lunar year is satisfactory for nomads, who move their flocks with the seasons and need not know when to plow and plant. But the farmers of Palestine needed a calendar related to the solar year. Likewise in Egypt, where the annual flooding of the Nile was essential to agricultural production, a solar year was necessary. In Mesopotamia, approximate correlation of the lunar and solar years was achieved by intercalation. In Egypt, a calendar of twelve months of thirty days each (hence, not a lunar calendar), plus five extra days each year, yielded an approximate solar calendar.[5]

Intercalation. The Hebrews, like the Babylonians from whom they derived their calendar, added an intercalary month when needed to bring the lunar year into phase with the solar year. Such intercalation is necessary seven times in nineteen years, and was decreed by the priest or king, either to bring the month Nisan into phase with the spring equinox or to bring Tishri into phase with the fall equinox.[6]

Civil Year and Sacred Year. In addition to these confusing practices, the Hebrews had two ways of marking the new year. According to Exod. 12:2, Yahweh told Moses that Nisan was to be the first month.[7] But the Jewish New Year, Rosh Hashanah ("the head of the year"), is in the fall, in Tishri. This shows that there was a civil year, which began with Tishri (around the autumnal equinox), and a religious year, which began with Nisan (in the spring). Different kings and nations alternated between the two.[8]

Calendar. Using names derived from Babylonian, the Hebrew year was as follows:

---

5. The Egyptians anchored their calendration to the heliacal rising of the star Sothis or Sirius (the Dog Star), but failed to adjust for leap year, and as a result, their calendar fell short one day in four years, or one year in 1,460 (the "Sothic cycle"). Nevertheless, they did keep careful records of the amount the calendar year diverged from the rising of Sothis.

6. The time of intercalation appears to have been somewhat arbitrary at first. Later, a system was developed ("Metonic cycle," adopted *ca.* 432) in which intercalary months were added to the third, sixth, eighth, eleventh, fourteenth, seventeenth, and nineteenth years. The Babylonians had no uniform time for intercalation, for the intercalary month was sometimes added between Elulu and Tišritu (in the fall) and sometimes between Addaru and Nisanu (in the spring). The Hebrews finally decided to add the month after Adar, even though their year began in the fall.

7. Nisan is not mentioned, for then the month was called Abib (13:4). Later the Babylonian name was adopted.

8. De Vaux argues that the autumnal year was original, since the first month was called *Tišritu* "beginning"; *Ancient Israel*, p. 191. But he apparently overlooked that the next month was *Waraḥ-šamnu* "eighth month."

Hebrew	Babylonian	Approximate Equivalent	Sacred Year and Name	Order in Civil Year
Nisan	Nisanu	Mar./Apr.	1st	7th
Iyyar	Ayaru	Apr./May	2nd	8th
Sivan	Siwanu (Simanu)	May/Jun.	3rd	9th
Tammuz	Du'uzu	Jun./Jul.	4th	10th
Ab	Abu	Jul./Aug.	5th	11th
Elul	Elulu/Ululu	Aug./Sep.	6th	12th
Tishri	Tišritu	Sep./Oct.	7th	1st
(Mar)ḥesvan	(W)araḫ-šamnu	Oct./Nov.	8th	2nd
Kislev	Kisliwu (Kislimu)	Nov./Dec.	9th	3rd
Ṭebet	Ṭebitu	Dec./Jan.	10th	4th
Sheḇaṭ	Šabaṭu	Jan./Feb.	11th	5th
Adar	Addaru	Feb./Mar.	12th	6th
(Veadar)		(Intercalary month)		

Regardless of when the year began, "first month" refers to Nisan, "second month" to Iyyar, etc. Thus in Jer. 36:22, where a Tishri-Tishri year is used, the "ninth month" was in the winter—Kislev (November/December), not Sivan (May/June).[9]

Accession Years and Nonaccession Years. Years of the modern calendar are designated by numbers attached to a known event, so A.D. 1973 means 1973 years "in the year of the Lord," counting from the presumed year of the birth of Jesus. But before years were reckoned in eras, events might be dated according to the year of a king's reign, as in the formula "in the second year of Darius" (Hag. 1:1).

Kings, however, were not considerate enough to die at the end of a year so the new king could start his reign on New Year's day. What should be done, then, with the portion of a year that was left? Suppose that King Z died on 19 August, and his son succeeded him on 20 August, but the New Year began in Tishri (hypothetically here, 20 September). Sometimes the new king would call the period from 20 August to 19 September the "first year" of his reign. But if the "first year" were taken to begin 20 September, the new king might call the part of the year from his accession to the next New Year the "accession year," with the "first year" starting the next New Year's day. The two methods of counting are called the accession-year system and the nonaccession-year

---

9. A similar phenomenon is evident in modern calendar names. Originally September meant "seventh month" (from Lat. *septem* "seven"); October "eighth month" (from *octo*); November "ninth month" (from *novem*); and December "tenth month" (from *decem*). When the year was changed, these names were retained.

system. Obviously, the total number of years of a succession of kings using one system differs from that calculated by the other system. To give the modern equivalent for the formula "In the second year of Darius the king, in the sixth month, on the first day of the month," one must first know whether Darius used the accession-year or nonaccession-year method. The sixth month would be Elul, regardless of whether he used the Tishri-Tishri or the Nisan-Nisan year (see above), and the first day would be the day of the new moon—which, if the year can be determined, can be calculated by astronomical tables.

THE CHRONOLOGICAL PUZZLE IN KINGS AND CHRONICLES

Basis of the Puzzle. 1–2 Kings and 1–2 Chronicles abound in chronological details. Their authors have left a rich legacy of information concerning the length of reign of every king of Judah and Israel, the relationship of the reigns of the rulers of both kingdoms to each other (called "synchronisms"), and the age of the kings of Judah at their accession. Furthermore, important events sometimes are synchronized with the year of the king's rule. Especially important are chronological references to events also recorded in secular history—e.g., the invasion of Shishak (1 Kgs. 14:25), Sennacherib's assault on Jerusalem (2 Kgs. 18:13). On occasion the biblical writers even synchronized an event with a year in the reign of a foreign king; e.g., Jer. 25:1 identifies the fourth year of Jehoiakim with the first of Nebuchadnezzar, while 32:1 connects the tenth year of Zedekiah with Nebuchadnezzar's eighteenth.

Thus, a lavish supply of material exists from which to construct a chronology and thereby measurably advance detailed knowledge of Hebrew history.[10] The trouble is that much of the information appears at first glance self-contradictory. For instance, 2 Kgs. 1:17 records that Joram, son of Ahab, began to reign in the second year of Jehoram, son of Jehoshaphat of Judah, while 3:1 puts it in the eighteenth year of Jehoshaphat. Similarly, some puzzling results are achieved in totaling the years of the reigns. A checkpoint ought to be the time from the division of the kingdom under Rehoboam and Jeroboam I (1 Kgs. 12), who began to rule about the same time, to the deaths of Joram of Israel and Ahaziah of Judah, victims of Jehu's purge (2 Kgs. 9:24, 27). But when the figures for each kingdom are totaled, the span is ninety-eight years and seven days for Israel and ninety-five years for Judah. The figures for the next period are even more puzzling. Jehu of Israel and Athaliah of Judah rose to power at the same time, so the totals of the years from their accession to the fall of Samaria (placed in the ninth year of Hoshea and the sixth of Hezekiah; 18:10) should agree. But for Israel the total is 143 years, seven months; for Judah, 166

---

10. For an excellent summary of approaches to the chronological problems and the canonical function of this material, see B.S. Childs, *Old Testament as Scripture*, pp. 294-300.

years. The situation is complicated by Assyrian chronological information which allows about 120 years for the same events.[11]

Even more vexing are attempts to harmonize the lengths of reign of the various kings with synchronisms of their rules and those of their counterparts in the other kingdoms. For instance, Jeroboam II ruled Israel for forty-one years (14:23). Simple subtraction would suggest that he died and was succeeded by his son Zechariah in the fourteenth year of Azariah (Uzziah), who had ascended the throne of Judah in Jeroboam's twenty-seventh year (15:1). The text, however, marks Azariah's thirty-eighth year as the time of Zechariah's accession (v. 8). This leaves twenty-four years unaccounted for.

These examples suggest the scope of the problem. Until recently attempts to make sense of the numbers as they stand in the text have encountered almost insurmountable difficulties. What appears to be a major breakthrough has been presented in E.R. Thiele's important book, *The Mysterious Numbers of the Hebrew Kings*.[12] The strength of Thiele's solutions to these vexing puzzles is that they make possible the interpretation of the biblical data without recourse to emendation or drastic adjustments. Since the problems vary for different historical periods, each period will be surveyed independently, with Thiele's suggested solutions briefly presented.

From the Division of the Kingdom to the Accession of Pekah (ca. 931-740). The accession-year system of reckoning, discussed above, was generally used in Assyria, Babylonia, and Persia during the biblical period. An initial problem is to determine which method each kingdom of Israel used.

A related question is the month in which regnal years began. The importance of this is increased by the fact that the Hebrews sometimes reckoned Nisan (March/April) as the first month of the year and sometimes Tishri (September/October). When did they begin their regnal years? Did both kingdoms use the same month, and was each kingdom consistent? How would a scribe refer to dates of a kingdom which used another method? Would he merely reproduce the alien system or would he transpose it into familiar terms? These are some of the questions which relate to the knotty problem of biblical chronology.

Again, one must consider the possibility of coregencies, where one king begins to rule before another dies. This overlap would mean that actual reigns were not so long as the individual years of rule added together might indicate. Another factor is the possibility of interregnal periods when no king was on the throne.

By carefully checking the various possible answers to the above questions

---

11. Jehu, at the outset of his reign, paid tribute to Shalmaneser III *ca*. 841. Samaria fell to Sargon II *ca*. 721.

12. Rev. ed. (Grand Rapids: 1965). The authors are deeply indebted to Thiele's work for the material in this section.

to see which approaches best satisfied all the numerical data in Kings and Chronicles, Thiele came to some strikingly convincing conclusions. First, during the first sixty years or so after the schism under Jeroboam I and Rehoboam, royal scribes in Judah used the accession-year system, and those in Israel, the nonaccession-year. Furthermore, whenever data are given about a king of Judah, the accession-year method is used both for his figures and the synchronism with Israel's king. Similarly, for a northern king the nonaccession-year scheme is followed not only for his reign but for his contemporary in the south.[13] Again, Thiele demonstrates that Judah's regnal year ran from Tishri to Tishri throughout the Monarchy and beyond (see Neh. 1:1 and 2:1). Israel, however, perhaps to be different from Judah and perhaps in imitation of Egypt and Assyria, followed a Nisan-Nisan regnal calendar.[14]

Adding to these observations the possibility of coregencies, particularly in Judah, and the fact that neither kingdom shows evidence of interregnal periods, the chief clues are at hand for resolving the numbers of the Hebrew kings. The great strength of Thiele's approach, and the most cogent argument for its validity, is that it provides a means of understanding the data without conjecture and correction.

During the fifty-two-year period from the beginning of the reign of Jehoram to the end of that of Joash (ca. 848-796), all evidence points to a switch in Judah's reckoning from accession-year to nonaccession-year. The reason is clear: this was the period of close alliance between the kings of Judah and the Omrides who followed Ahab. Thiele suggests that the pagan queen mother Athaliah brought this innovation. Apparently she encouraged the royal scribes to make the change retroactive to include the reign of Jehoram.[15]

Political pressures evidently forced both Israel and Judah to an accession-year system at the beginning of the eighth century. The growth of Assyrian influence is the probable explanation for this change, which begins with Jehoash in Israel (ca. 798) and Amaziah in Judah (ca. 796). Both kingdoms used the accession-year scheme until the close of their histories.

How can dates in antiquity be established with any assurance of accuracy? Archaeological findings such as pottery or other ancient ruins can give only relative chronology. That is, time sequences in various stages of civilization may be noted and correlated with similar stages at other sites; but one cannot by archaeology alone put an absolute date on any finding. Recently the method of dating objects made from organic matter by testing the amount of radioactive carbon 14 has been refined. But even this can tell only the order of antiquity within a margin of about ten percent. By what method can one say that the

---

13. Thiele more than once notes the care taken by the official scribes and later editors and copyists: ". . . the individuals who first recorded these data must have been dealing with contemporary chronological materials of the greatest accuracy and the highest historical value. . . ."; *ibid.*, p. 26.

14. *Ibid.*, pp. 27-32.

15. *Ibid.*, pp. 68-72.

battle of Qarqar was fought in 853 or that Nebuchadnezzar destroyed Jerusalem in 586?

Actually, Israel's enemies, especially the Assyrians, have given the most help in placing the relative chronology of the Bible against an absolute chronology in ancient history. Not only did the Assyrians follow a solar year corresponding to the modern year, but they established an office of eponym (Assyrian *limmu*) to which they appointed annually a high official, governor, or king. By keeping lists of these eponyms, they provided a system of reference to every year from 891 to 648. Furthermore, one text mentions an eclipse which astronomers fix at 15 June 763. When compared with Assyrian king lists, the eponym lists provide the means of establishing the Assyrian royal chronology. The importance of the Assyrian texts for biblical chronology can scarcely be exaggerated because they concentrate on the most significant period for biblical chronology—the Divided Monarchy.

Of special interest for the late and post-Assyrian periods is the Canon of Ptolemy (*ca*. A.D. 70-161), which both corroborates and augments the Assyrian lists. Ptolemy traces the rulers of Babylon from 747 B.C. onward, the Persian kings, Alexander and his successors in Egypt, and the Roman kings to his own day. His knowledge of astronomy as well as geography and history makes his work all the more valuable, with more than eighty observations on solar, lunar, or planetary positions. His mention of the accession of Sargon II of Assyria to the throne of Babylon in 722/21 provides an important cross check with the Assyrian eponym lists.

Fixed points in biblical chronology can be determined on the basis of synchronisms between Assyrian and Israelite history. The reign of Shalmaneser III, who fought Ahab at Qarqar in 853 and took tribute from Jehu in 841, provides an excellent opportunity to correlate Israel's history with the absolute Assyrian chronology. The campaigns of Tiglath-pileser III, Shalmaneser V, Sargon II, and Sennacherib afford further cross-references.

Accession of Pekah to Death of Ahaz (Ca. 740-715). This brief period is one of the most frustrating chronologically. The accuracy of Kings here has often been questioned.[16] While 2 Kgs. 15:30 says that Hoshea of Israel came to power in the twentieth year of Jotham, v. 33 notes that Jotham reigned just sixteen years! Even more startling are the problems involving Pekah of Israel. Hebrew chronology suggests that his reign began in 740, while Assyrian records of Tiglath-pileser suggest that it closed in 732. However, v. 27, which gives the

---

16. The chronological data of the kings of Judah in 1–2 Kings, as W.S. LaSor points out (*NBC*, p. 323) are extremely detailed, giving the father's age when the son (the succeeding king) was born, the son's age when he began to reign, the years that he reigned, his age at death, and other facts. From these data, LaSor has constructed a tightly-woven chronology of the kings of Judah which is remarkably self-consistent. No variation can be introduced into these figures without affecting all related figures—which would require a highly improbable amount of textual alteration.

synchronism for Pekah's succession, also states that he reigned twenty years! The difficulties become more disturbing in the reigns of Ahaz and Hezekiah. Comparison of 15:27, 30; 16:1f.; 18:1 leads to the impossible conclusion that Ahaz was twenty-six when his twenty-five-year-old son, Hezekiah, began to reign! As Thiele points out, the synchronism of 18:1, which brings Hezekiah to the throne in Hoshea's third year, cannot be correct.[17]

According to the evidence mustered by Thiele, Pekah was the culprit. Apparently he reckoned his reign as beginning in 752, even though this was actually the year of Menahem's accession. A possible explanation is that Pekah was a co-conspirator with Menahem against Shallum. In 740 when Pekah, in turn, disposed of Pekahiah, Menahem's son, he apparently decided to take credit for the twelve years of the combined reigns of Menahem and Pekahiah. When Pekah's accession is reckoned from 752, the entire chronology of the period begins to take shape.[18]

The puzzling synchronisms which place Hoshea's accession in the twelfth year of Ahaz (i.e., 719) and seek to correlate Hoshea's reign with Hezekiah's, thereby telescoping the careers of Hezekiah and his father Ahaz, are found in 2 Kgs. 17:1; 18:1, 9f. Thiele's explanation seems credible: long after the events a scribe or editor, who failed to understand Pekah's "twenty" years, assumed that Pekah had died in 720 and incorrectly synchronized Hoshea's accession in 720, which he knew to be the twelfth year of Ahaz. This was done despite the correct synchronization of Hoshea's reign in 15:30 ("the twentieth year of Jotham"). Knowing that Hezekiah came to the throne in the sixteenth year of Ahaz, the scribe or editor incorrectly synchronized events in Hezekiah's reign with Hoshea's and vice versa. In other words, the synchronisms of 17:1; 18:1, 9f. are to be disregarded, since Hoshea had been carried into captivity by the Assyrians several years before Hezekiah was crowned. By misunderstanding the twelve-year coregency of Jotham (his father, Uzziah, had contracted leprosy) and Pekah's crediting himself with the twelve years of Menahem and Pekahiah, the reviser inaccurately correlated the reigns of Jotham and Ahaz so they overlapped by about twelve years.[19]

Thiele's painstakingly thorough researches have provided the key to one of the great riddles of Old Testament history. Not only does he demonstrate the accuracy of the Scripture, but he shows how beautifully it harmonizes with the highly reliable Assyrian chronological records. Furthermore, in identifying the four faulty synchronisms he has isolated a source of some major difficulties. W.A. Irwin's evaluation is a fitting conclusion to this brief summary:

---

17. *Mysterious Numbers*, pp. 119-123.

18. *Ibid.*, pp. 123-131. It is exceedingly important that Pekah's twenty-year reign give way to Hoshea's in 732 if the events concerning the fall of Samaria are to be fitted accurately into Assyrian accounts.

19. *Ibid.*, pp. 131-39. An additional slip of one year in connection with Pekah's accession means that during this period the dates for Israel are off by thirteen years and for Judah, by twelve.

He [Thiele] has taken passages commonly regarded as patent disclosures of carelessness, if not of ignorance, on the part of the Hebrew historians, and has shown them to be astonishingly reliable. . . . And it is a matter of first-rate importance to learn now that the Books of Kings are reliable in precisely that feature which formerly excited only derision.[20]

FOR FURTHER READING

Campbell, E.F. "The Ancient Near East: Chronological Bibliography and Charts." Pp. 281-293 in BANE.

DeVries, S.J. Yesterday, Today and Tomorrow. Grand Rapids: 1975. (Critical study of Israelite concept of time.)

Ehrick, R.W., ed. Chronologies in Old World Archaeology. Chicago: 1965. (Esp. pp. 395-461.)

Finegan, J. Handbook of Biblical Chronology. Princeton: 1964. (Good introduction to problems involved.)

Neugebauer, O. The Exact Sciences in Antiquity. 2nd ed. New York: 1969. (Esp. pp. 71-96, Egyptian mathematics and astronomy; pp. 97-144, Babylonian astronomy.)

Parker, R.A., and Dubberstein, W.H. Babylonian Chronology, 626 B.C.–A.D. 75. Providence, R.I.: 1971. (Data relating to chronological problems, tables for translating Babylonian calendar to Julian.)

Thiele, E.R. "Coregencies and Overlapping Reigns Among the Hebrew Kings." JBL 93 (1974): 174-200.

Wifall, W.R. "The Chronology of the Divided Monarchy of Israel." ZAW 80 (1968): 319-337.

---

20. Ibid., pp. xxii–xxiii.

CHAPTER 22

PROPHETS AND PROPHECY

In the Old Testament the term "prophet" is used relatively often, and certain types of writings are called "prophecy." In popular usage, a "prophet" is someone who can foretell the future, and "prophecy" means predictions of things to come. Although containing elements of truth, these popular definitions are by no means proper for the biblical terms. Before studying the prophets,[1] therefore, it is important to gain an understanding of the biblical meaning of these concepts.[2]

NAMES USED FOR THE PROPHET

Prophet. The most common term for the person and office is "prophet," which has come into English from Greek. Gk. *prophētēs* means, basically, "one who speaks for a god and interprets his will to man."[3] It is composed of two elements, the second of which means "to speak." The first can mean both "for, forth" and "beforehand,"[4] so the word can mean either "to speak for, proclaim," or "to speak beforehand, foretell." Many writers claim that a prophet is a "forthteller" rather than a "foreteller," but both meanings are implicit and both usages found.

The Hebrew term, which the Greek attempts to translate, is *nābî.* The derivation and basic meaning have long been debated, partially on the basis of the formation and meaning of the Greek word, rather than the Hebrew. It now

---

1. The Former Prophets have been discussed above in Chs. 14–20. However, as indicated in Ch. 14, the Former and Latter Prophets differ significantly, so that the Former Prophets today commonly are not considered as "prophets," and some of the peculiar methods of interpretation often (and incorrectly) applied to the Latter Prophets usually are not applied to them.

2. For a helpful summary of recent study, see W. McKane, "Prophecy and the Prophetic Literature," pp. 163-188 in G.W. Anderson, ed., *Tradition and Interpretation.*

3. H.G. Liddell and R. Scott, *A Greek-English Lexicon*, ed. H.S. Jones, 9th ed. (New York: 1940) 2:1540a.

4. *TDNT* 6 (1968): 783f.

seems well established that the root *nb'* means "to call" and that its morphology supports the meaning, "one called."[5] The prophet, then, was one called by God, and as seen in the Old Testament, called to speak for God. Thus the Greek term accurately describes the prophet even if it does not precisely translate the Hebrew.

Biblical usage is best illustrated in God's message to Moses, where Moses is likened to "God" and Aaron is described as his "mouth" (Exod. 4:15f.), and where Moses is described as "God to Pharaoh" and Aaron is his "prophet" (7:1f.). The prophet is pictured here as God's mouth.

"Seer" and Other Terms. The prophet also was called a "seer," meaning "one who sees in a vision." Two different Hebrew words are so translated and, it would seem, are completely interchangeable. One passage (1 Sam. 9:9) indicates that the term "seer" was earlier and came to be replaced by "prophet," but if there was ever any clear-cut difference, it had become indistinct by Old Testament times.[6]

Other terms for the prophets include "man of God," "watchman," "messenger of Yahweh," and "man of the Spirit." These terms are actually descriptions of the prophet's activities, although at times they seem to have become titles. They add significant aspects to an understanding of the prophet.

CHARACTERISTICS OF THE PROPHET

Ecstasy. According to one widely-held view, the major characteristic of the prophet is ecstatic behavior. This theory was stated by G. Hölscher,[7] but is probably best known from the description by T.H. Robinson:

> We can now call before our minds a picture of the prophet's activity in public. He might be mingling with the crowd, sometimes on ordinary days, sometimes on special occasions. Suddenly something would happen to him. His eye would become fixed, strange convulsions would seize upon his limbs, the form of his speech would change. Men would recognize that the Spirit had fallen upon him. The fit would pass, and he would tell to those who stood around the things which he had seen and had heard.[8]

In a few instances in the Old Testament a person was seized by sudden ecstasy. When King Saul was grasped by the Spirit, the people asked: "Is Saul among the prophets?" (1 Sam. 10:11). But there are many more examples of

---

5. For the derivation see Akk. *nabû* "to call"; cf. Hammurabi i.17. For the morphology or word formation, see W.S. LaSor, *Handbook of Biblical Hebrew* (Grand Rapids: 1979) 2 §24.2441. See also W.F. Albright, *From the Stone Age to Christianity*, pp. 231f.

6. See H.H. Rowley, *The Servant of the Lord*, pp. 105-8.

7. *Die Profeten* (Leipzig: 1914).

8. *Prophecy and the Prophets in Ancient Israel* (London: 1923), p. 50.

prophets who exhibit normal behavior. W.R. Smith, prior to publication of Hölscher's work, said that God "speaks to His prophets, not in magical processes or through the visions of poor phrenetics, but by a clear intelligible word addressed to the intellect and the heart. The characteristic of the true prophet is that he retains his consciousness and self-control under revelation."[9] This aptly summarizes the biblical portrayal of the prophet.

"*Call.*" The biblical prophet was certain not only that God had spoken to him, but also that he was called to speak God's message.[10] In some instances, the call is described in considerable detail, and each account has distinctive elements not found in the others. Thus the call was an individual event, not a stereotyped formula used by prophets to validate their activity. Isaiah seems to have accepted his call willingly, while Jeremiah was reluctant and contended with Yahweh. Amos seems to have had a single call, while Ezekiel cites the day, month, and year of several occasions when the Lord called him and gave him a message.[11] Any purely humanistic explanation that would interpret the experience of a call as merely a convergence of events or a subjective psychological experience is not consonant with the biblical data. On the other hand, God did use historical situations and personal feelings in communicating with the prophets.

Character. Peter, referring to prophecy, said: "Moved by the Holy Spirit holy men of God spoke."[12] While biblical statements about the holiness of the prophets are rare, it is generally accepted that God would only use holy people as his prophets. One might argue that God saw fit to use those whose moral behavior was not always above reproach in other offices, such as Moses the lawgiver, Aaron the high priest, or David the king. But it is difficult to think that Nathan would have had any effective word of reproach for David if he himself had been a man of unbridled passions. Still, it is closer to the biblical data to stress the prophet's wholehearted dedication to Yahweh rather than his or her moral excellence.

CLASSIFICATION OF THE PROPHETS

Before Samuel. Samuel sometimes is called "the last of the judges and the first of the prophets" (see Acts 3:24; 13:20). However, the term prophet is used also of a number of persons prior to Samuel. About all that can be deduced

---

9. *The Old Testament in the Jewish Church*, 2nd ed. (London: 1908), quoted by Rowley, *The Servant of the Lord*, p. 100.
10. Note accounts of the call in Isa. 6:1-13; Jer. 1:4-10; Ezek. 1:1-3; Hos. 1:2-9; 8:1-5; Amos 3:1-8; 7:12-15.
11. See J. Lindblom, *Prophecy in Ancient Israel* (Philadelphia: 1962), pp. 182-197.
12. 2 Pet. 1:21 (RSV mg.). However, evidence for "holy men" or simply "men" seems about evenly divided.

from the material may be summarized as follows: (1) the concept of revelation from God to a chosen servant (the basic element of prophecy) was familiar prior to Samuel; (2) since Moses is taken as the prototype of the prophet (see Deut. 18:18), his prophetic ministry should be taken into account in defining the prophetic task; (3) the idea that prophecy had diminished and then resumed with Samuel is implicit in Eli's reaction to Samuel's call (1 Sam. 3:7-9). The implications are quite significant, for studies of prophecy can no longer begin with the prophetic writings of the Old Testament, or even the prophetic sayings of Samuel, Nathan, Elijah, and Elisha. They certainly must include the prophetic ministry of Moses, and, probably, the prophetic elements in the patriarchs.

PROPHETS

Prior to Samuel
    Enoch (Jude 14)
    "Holy prophets from the beginning" (Luke 1:70; Acts 3:21)
    Abraham (Gen. 20:7; cf. Ps. 105:14f.)
    Moses (Num. 12:1-8; Deut. 34:10; Hos. 12:13)
    Miriam (prophetess; Exod. 15:20)
    Eldad, Medad, and the Seventy (Num. 11:24-29)
    Deborah (prophetess; Judg. 4:4)
    "Man of God" (13:6ff.)
    Prophetic vision rare in the days of Eli (1 Sam. 3:1)

Monarchy [ca. 1075-931]
    Samuel (1 Sam. 3:1) [time of Saul and David]
    Gad (2 Sam. 22:5) [Saul and David]
    Nathan (12:1) [David]
    Ahijah (1 Kgs. 12:22) [Rehoboam and Jeroboam I]
    Saul, David, Solomon; experiences with prophetic characteristics
    Asaph, Heman, and Jeduthun (Ethan) (1 Chr. 25:1)
    Iddo (seer; 2 Chr. 9:29) [Solomon, Rehoboam, and Ahijah]

From division of the Monarchy to the Assyrian period [931-ca. 800]
    Shemaiah (1 Kgs. 12:22) [Rehoboam]
    Ahijah, Iddo (see above)
    Hanani (seer; 2 Chr. 16:7) [Asa]
    Jehu son of Hanani (1 Kgs. 16:1) [Asa and Jehoshaphat]
    Elijah (17:1) [Ahab and Ahaziah of Israel]
    Elisha (19:16) [Ahab–Jehoash of Israel (860-ca. 795)]
    Micaiah ben Imlah (22:4) [Ahab]
    Jehaziel and Eliezer (2 Chr. 20:14, 37) [Jehoshaphat of Judah]
    Zechariah (24:19) [Joash]
    Unnamed prophet (1 Kgs. 20:13) [Ahab]
    Unnamed prophet (2 Kgs. 9:4) who anointed Jehu
    "Sons of the prophets" (1 Kgs. 19:10)
    "False" prophets (ch. 13; etc.)

Eighth-century [ca. 800-ca. 675]
    Obadiah
    Joel [reign of Joash (?)]
    Jonah [Jeroboam II (?)]

Amos [Uzziah of Judah and Jeroboam II]
Hosea [before fall of Jehu's dynasty]
Micah [Jotham, Ahaz, and Hezekiah]
Isaiah [Uzziah, Jotham, Ahaz, and Hezekiah]
("Deutero-Zechariah" [prior to 722 (?)])
Oded (2 Chr. 28:9)

Seventh-century [*ca.* 675-597]
Nahum [between 663 and 612]
Habakkuk [perhaps shortly after 605]
Zephaniah [Josiah]
Jeremiah [626-586]

Sixth-century [*ca.* 597-538]
Ezekiel [592-572 (or 570)]
(Daniel [605-538, or considerably later])
Isaiah 40-66 [*ca.* 550-538 (possibly later)?]

Postexilic (*ca.* 538-*ca.* 450)
Haggai [520]
Zechariah 1–9 [520 and 518]
Malachi [between *ca.* 486 and 450]

(Note: problems of dating, authorship of portions of Isaiah and Zechariah, and similar matters that would too greatly complicate this table are discussed under the individual prophets.)

Tenth and Ninth Centuries. With the call of Samuel, a new period of prophetism begins in the biblical account. Since it coincides with the inauguration of the Monarchy one may conclude that the prophet was specifically intended to serve as the voice of God to the king. In support of this, the end of the prophetic activity of the Old Testament is approximately contemporary with the end of the Israelite kingdom. From the material preserved in the Scriptures, a specific prophet cannot be associated with every king; but there are several unnamed prophets and a "school of the prophets," so it seems reasonable that God had "mouths" to speak to all the kings of Israel and Judah. This appears to be supported by the reaction of the kings to prophetic activity. It seems that they rather expected some prophet to bring messages from Yahweh, and no evidence exists that they were surprised by such activity.[13]

The prophets of the Monarchy and early Divided Monarchy are sometimes called the "oral" or "nonwriting" prophets. This means that the Bible has no books which are solely the products of individual prophets of this period, such as a "prophecy according to Elijah." In contrast, the prophets of the later period of the Divided Monarchy are called "literary" or "writing" prophets. But these terms are unfortunate, for they fail to elucidate the facts as derived from the

---

13. The various relationships between the prophets and the political and religious establishments of their day have been explored thoroughly by R.R. Wilson, *Prophecy and Society in Ancient Israel* (Philadelphia: 1980).

Scriptures. On the one hand, one book (or two) bears the name of Samuel. (Whether he wrote it or not is beside the point.) On the other hand, one should not assume that the "writing" prophets set out to write books of prophecy. The evidence in the book that bears Jeremiah's name indicates that he was for the most part an "oral" prophet, and that the writing down of his prophecies was largely the work of Baruch (Jer. 36:4, 32). It is clear from their contents that most of the prophetic books were first spoken messages, written down later, perhaps by the prophet himself, perhaps by his disciples.[14]

Eighth and Seventh Centuries. Prophecy changed markedly in the eighth century. In general, the prophets of the tenth and ninth centuries were "advisors to the kings." They may have had prophetic messages for the people, but most evidence indicates that they counseled the kings, either encouraging them to walk in the way of Yahweh or, more often, rebuking them for failing to do so. In the eighth century, the prophets turned their attention more to the people, the nation,[15] or in some cases foreign nations.[16]

Along with this change of the object of address came the introduction of written prophecies. True, earlier prophetic speeches survive, such as Samuel's words to Saul and David, Nathan's rebuke of David, and the words of Elijah to Ahab or Jezebel. But with the eighth-century prophets came longer messages and collections that constitute books bearing the prophets' names. At the same time, the "sons of the prophets" were less prominent, perhaps having developed into a state-supported institution. There was also considerable criticism of "false" prophets.

It does not seem unreasonable, therefore, to say that a crisis had come upon Israel and Judah. Within the century, indeed within the lifetime of the eighth-century prophets and in some cases during their prophetic ministry, the northern kingdom would be brought to an end. God's judgment was about to be visited upon the kingdom of Israel. The kings and the leaders had gone so far into sin that there was no hope of salvation. The prophets, therefore, sounded clear warnings, seeking to move the people to repentance. Inscripturation of the prophecies seems to be a way to get the message to a wider audience, as well as to a future generation.

What had happened to Israel in the eighth century was used as an illustration to Judah, whose end would come at the end of the seventh and begin-

---

14. It is helpful to remember that the greatest of all prophets, Jesus Christ, did not write his prophecies; they were written down by others and preserved in the Gospels.

15. Amos, sent by Yahweh to proclaim a message to Samaria (Israel), was the first prophet to confront the nation.

16. It seems highly unlikely that prophetic messages addressed to Edom, Tyre, Egypt, etc., were actually intended to be delivered to and read by the rulers of those nations, or, if so, that they would have had any effect. More likely, they were intended for Israel, the people of God, in the contemporary generation, and even more, in future generations. God's word does not return empty; it accomplishes what he wills it to do.

ning of the sixth century. The seventh-century prophets therefore shared a more urgent sense of judgment and issued a strengthened plea for repentance. At the same time, the element of hope for the remnant was sounded ever more clearly.

Exile and Postexilic Period. With the end of the southern kingdom and the destruction of Jerusalem, the old way had come to an end. Many of the people were in captivity, needing hope and encouragement to begin again. They had to be reminded that Yahweh's covenant was still in force, and that he would complete his redemptive purpose in the world. Accordingly, these elements abounded in the prophets of the sixth and fifth centuries.

At the same time, Israel's basic beliefs had to be enlarged so Yahweh could be seen as God of all nations, not of Israel alone. The revelation of his purpose, including its dual nature as originally expressed in the covenant with Abraham, had to be made clear. Israel was to continue distinct from the nations (or gentiles). Nevertheless, Yahweh's purpose was to bring the nations to worship him and learn his laws from Israel. As this became clearer, more references were made to the "latter days" or "those days." The study of events leading up to and following the "end" of the age (eschatology) assumed greater prominence.

Specifically, postexilic prophets encouraged rebuilding the temple, reestablishing the kingdom and throne of David, and resuming the cultus that helped preserve Israel's separate identity. But it is suggested also that even this would not be the ultimate achievement of God's redemptive purpose. Troubles, persecution, and even another destruction of Jerusalem lay beyond the immediate future. The temple was nothing like the previous temple in its glory, and the nation was only a tolerated and almost insignificant bit of a large empire. These were not the "latter days" that had been foretold. Accordingly, stress was placed on still-future blessings. Apocalyptic elements were introduced claiming that God himself would intervene to destroy Israel's enemies and set up his king on Zion. There would be a time of judgment that would be a refining fire for Israel. Then would come an age of righteousness and peace. Having sounded that note, the prophets became silent.

PROPHECY

In general, there are two simplistic approaches to prophecy, one stressing the predictive element, the other emphasizing the message as applied to the contemporary situation. In biblical prophecy, both elements are present.

God's Message to the Present Situation. By simply picking verses from the prophets and pasting them together to give "prophecies that prove the Bible" or "Jesus Christ in prophecy," one creates the impression that prophecy is "history written in advance." However, when one studies the prophets, this glamorous concept suddenly disappears. It is necessary to plow through chapters that have nothing to do with the future in order to find a single verse, or even part of a verse, that is "prophecy."

A careful study of the prophet and his (or her) message reveals that he is deeply involved in the life and death of his own nation. He speaks about the king and his idolatrous practices, prophets who say what they are paid to say, priests who fail to instruct the people in Yahweh's law, merchants who use false balances, judges who favor the rich and give no justice to the poor, greedy women who drive their husbands to evil practices so they can bask in luxury. All this is prophecy in the biblical sense. It is God's message to his people and the king who rules them in his place. It is a message of judgment because God's people are constantly in need of correction. At the same time, it is a message of hope, for Yahweh has not broken his covenant and will complete his redemptive purpose.

God's Message Concerning the Future. God is never concerned with the present simply for the sake of that moment. Ever since creation, he has been working out his purpose for humankind, and he never forgets where he is going and what he is doing. The prophets are let in on that purpose (Amos 3:7). Prophecy is therefore not simply God's message to the present situation, but is intended primarily to show how that situation fits into his plan, how he will use it to judge and refine or comfort and encourage his people. Prophecy is God's message to the present in the light of his ongoing redemptive purpose.

On exceptional occasions, he gives rather precise details about what he is going to do. Yet even in this instruction, usually called "predictive prophecy," the predictive element almost always is firmly attached to the present situation. The prophet speaks about what has meaning for his listeners. He does not suddenly forget them and utter an irrelevant "prophecy of things to come." Rather, he takes them from that moment into the sweep of divine redemptive activity and centers on a truth that will become a beacon to God's people.

Since God's redeeming purpose culminates in Jesus Christ, all prophecy somehow must point to Christ. In that sense he "fulfills" prophecy, or, rather, prophecy is fulfilled in him. While this may not be what is commonly understood by "fulfillment of prophecy," it is the definition properly derived from the biblical evidence.

Prophecy is a window that God has opened for his people by his servants the prophets. Through it one can see more of God's purpose in his redemptive work than would be possible otherwise. It gives a better understanding of what he has done for and with and through his people in the past, and a clearer comprehension of his purpose in the present. And, while it may never satisfy insatiable demands for specific details of the future, it nevertheless gives a clear view of where God is taking humanity and what obligations therefore are laid upon his people.

FOR FURTHER READING

Albrektson, B. *History and the Gods*. Lund: 1967. (Historical events as divine manifestations in the ancient Near East and Israel.)

Beecher, W.J. *The Prophets and the Promise*. Repr. Grand Rapids: 1963.

Crenshaw, J.L. *Prophetic Conflict*. BZAW 124 (1971). (Effect on Israelite religion.)

Davies, E.W. *Prophecy and Ethics: Isaiah and the Ethical Traditions of Israel*. JSOTS 16.
Sheffield: 1981. (Analysis of the traditions that influenced the prophetic message.)

Fohrer, G. "Remarks on Modern Interpretation of the Prophets." *JBL* 80 (1960): 309-319.
(Critique of form-critical approach.)

Freeman, H.E. *An Introduction to the Old Testament Prophets*. Chicago: 1968. (Conservative introduction to each book.)

Interpretation 32/1 (January 1978). (Review articles suggesting revision of standard views:
R.R. Wilson, "Early Israelite Prophecy," pp. 3-16; H.W.Wolff, "Prophecy from the
Eighth through the Fifth Century," pp. 17-30; G.M. Tucker, "Prophetic Speech,"
pp. 31-45; B.S. Childs, "The Canonical Shape of the Prophetic Literature,"
pp. 46-55; J. Limberg, "The Prophets in Recent Study: 1967-1977," pp. 56-68.)

Johnson, A.R. *The Cultic Prophet in Ancient Israel*. 2nd ed. Cardiff: 1962.

Lambert, W.G. "Destiny and Divine Intervention in Babylon and Israel." OTS 17
(1972): 65-72.

Orlinsky, H.M. "The Seer in Ancient Israel." *Oriens Antiquus* 4 (1965): 153-174.

Petersen, D.L. *The Roles of Israel's Prophets*.

Rabe, V.W. "The Origins of Prophecy." *BASOR* 221 (1976): 125-28. (Summary and
critique of current theories.)

Rowley, H.H., ed. *Studies in Old Testament Prophecy*.

Synave, P. and Benoit, P. *Prophecy and Inspiration*. Trans. A.R. Dulles and T.L. Sheridan.
New York: 1961. (Roman Catholic scholars' views; stimulating.)

Wilson, R.R. "Prophecy and Ecstasy: A Reexamination." *JBL* 98 (1979): 321-337.

Winward, S.F. *A Guide to the Prophets*. Richmond: 1968. (Emphasis on teachings.)

CHAPTER 23

HEBREW POETRY

THE Old Testament contains a great deal of poetry. Some versions indicate it by the arrangement of the lines (RSV, JB). An understanding of the basic principles of Hebrew poetry is essential to interpret some of these passages. Poetry in any tongue is highly compressed language, generally using word images to convey larger meanings, emotive figures rather than rationalizations.[1] Therefore one must recognize that the message to some extent is controlled by the form. Also, frequent suggestions that a passage be emended or deleted "for the sake of the meter"[2] require an awareness of the value and limitations of such treatment of the text. Occasionally, the poetic structure will help restore a broken text, or understand a difficult one.[3] Thus, one should at least know what Hebrew poetry is and how to recognize it.

CHARACTERISTICS

Parallelism of Members. The distinctive characteristic of Hebrew poetry (and other Semitic poetry from the same period) is formal parallelism of thought.[4] Sometimes this is obscured in translation, for to retain the beauty of poetry

---

1. Consider these images: "Ephraim is joined to idols" (Hos. 4:17); "Ephraim is a cake not turned" (7:8); "Ephraim is like a dove, silly and without sense" (v. 11); "Ephraim was a trained heifer that loved to thresh" (10:11); "It was I who taught Ephraim to walk" (11:3); "Ephraim herds the wind" (12:1).

2. See the proposed emendation in *Biblia Hebraica* of Joel 1:4 and discussion, p. 310 below.

3. E.g., Amos 6:12 reads: "Do horses run upon rocks? / Does one plow with oxen?" Clearly, the second strophe should be as incredible as the first, hence it is sometimes emended to read: "Does one plow *there* with oxen?" or "Does one plow *the sea* with oxen?"

4. The classical work on the subject is R. Lowth, *De sacra poesi Hebraeorum* (London: 1753). See also E. Sievers, *Metrische Studien*, 7 vols. (Leipzig: 1901-1919); G.B. Gray, *The Forms of Hebrew Poetry*, rev. ed. (New York: 1970); T.H. Robinson, *The Poetry of the Old Testament* (1947; repr. New York: 1976). Although anticipated by Ibn Ezra (A.D. 1093-1168) and others, Lowth's work was foundational.

words often are rearranged. To make the basic structure obvious, this study will use baldly literal translation, hyphenating words to show that the Hebrew uses a single word, and otherwise attempting to reproduce the original form as closely as possible.[5]

(1) Synonymous parallelism, the simplest form, consists of two lines (stichs) which say approximately the same thing.[6] For various reasons, principally stylistic, the simplest form is not often used, but has a number of variations. For example:

Wine (is)	a-mocker	a	b	
Strong-drink	a-brawler	a'	b'	(Prov. 20:1)

This statement consists of two stichs, each having two words. The first word in the first stich (wine) is paralleled by the first word in the second (strong drink). Likewise the second words are parallel. The first line is a b, and the second is a' b' (read "a prime, b prime").

When a stich has three or more units, often one is omitted in the parallel stich, and another element is lengthened to compensate. C.H. Gordon calls this a "ballast variant," while N.K. Gottwald terms it "compensation." This is sometimes called "incomplete parallelism":

And-I-will-turn	your-feasts	to-mourning,	a	b	c
	and-all-your-songs	to-lamentation.		B'	c'

(Amos 8:10)

The verb, although not repeated, is understood with the second stich. The second unit in the second stich is somewhat longer than its parallel, hence is marked B' ("heavy-b' prime"):

Binding	to-a-vine	his-foal,	a	b	c
	and-to-a-choice-vine	the-son-of-his-ass,		B'	C'
He-washed	in-wine	his-garment,	d	e	f
	and-in-the-blood-of-grapes	his-clothes.		E'	f'

(Gen. 49:11)

"Emblematic parallelism"[7] describes synonymous parallelism where one stich is to be taken literally but the parallel is figurative. Note the following:

---

5. Hebrew poetry may open a window into the Hebrew mind. Whereas westerners build logical arguments with many different points, hoping to use supplemental statements to convince, the Hebrews attempted to say the same thing in complementary or contrasting ways. "Doublets" and other scriptural phenomena, sometimes thought to result from the conflation of different sources, actually may have been the Hebrew way of presentation, by synonymous or complementary or contrasting accounts from the same creative mind.

6. Also called "identical parallelism." Various scholars use various terms; see N.K. Gottwald, "Hebrew Poetry," *IDB* 3:831. Because of the clarity of his system, it is used here. *Stichos* often is used for "stich," and *stichoi* for "stichs."

7. The term and the illustration are from F.F. Bruce, "The Poetry of the Old Testament," *NBC*, p. 45.

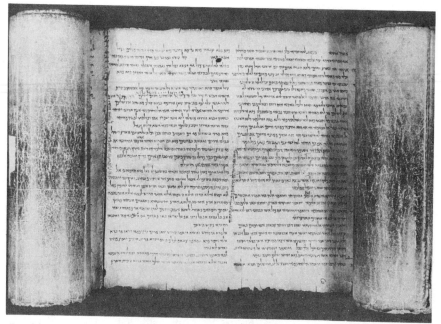

Dead Sea Isaiah scroll (1QIsaᵃ), containing the Song of Hezekiah (Isa. 38:10-20) and the beginning of the Book of Consolation. (J.C. Trever)

| As-a-father | pities | his-children, | *a* | *b* | *c* |
| So-Yahweh | pities | those-who-fear-him. | *a'* | *b'* | *c'* |

(Ps. 103:13)

Not all scholars deem it necessary to make this distinction between the literal and figurative lines.

(2) Antithetic parallelism, in which the second stich expresses the same idea but in a negative or contrasting manner, while rare in the prophets, is quite common in Proverbs and Psalms:

| A-son wise | gladdens | a-father | $(a+b)$ | *c* | *d* |
| And-a-son foolish | grieves | his-mother. | $-(a+b)$ | $-c$ | *d'* |

(Prov. 10:1)

In this example, the first unit is a noun and adjective $(a+b)$, while the parallel stich has its opposite (indicated by $-$). Likewise, the verbs are opposites. In such a contrasting form, the conjunction "and" is better translated "but." "Father" and "mother" could be rendered as "parents." A likely prose—but prosaic—equivalent would be "A wise son makes his parents happy, but a foolish son gives them grief."

The following illustration from Isaiah begins with antithetic parallelism, but the entire verse is somewhat more complex, with the author's message developing from a basic principle to a practical application:

Cease	the-evil	$-a$	$-b$
Learn	the-good.	a	b
Seek	justice;	c	d
Set-straight	oppression.	c'	$-d$
Vindicate	the-fatherless;	e	f
Litigate-for	a-widow.	e'	f'

(1:16b–17)

(3) In synthetic parallelism, which is not well named, the second stich advances the thought of the first, rather than repeating it:

And-I-will-send	fire	on-the-wall-of Gaza,	a	b	c
	and-it-shall-devour	her-palaces.		d	e

(Amos 1:7)

The verb "shall-devour" is not truly parallel to "fire," but is rather the effect of the fire. "The-wall-of-Gaza" and "her-palaces" are complementary statements, implying the entire city. The rest of the passage illustrates synonymous parallelism:

And-I-will-cut-off	inhabitant	from-Ashdod,	a	b	c
	and-holder-of scepter	from-Ashkelon,		B'	c'
And-I-will-turn my-hand		against-Ekron,	D	c''	
And-they-shall-perish		the-remnant-of-the-Philistines,	e	C'''	

said Lord Yahweh. (v. 8)

"And-they-shall-perish" is the result of "and-I-will-cut-off," showing "synthetic" parallelism. The Philistine cities (Gaza, Ashkelon, Ekron) are parallel with "the-remnant-of-the-Philistines." The entire passage, then, has three distichs (verses of two stichs each), forming one message, directed against the Philistines. The words, "said Lord Yahweh," form a "prose cliché," and such lines should always be set outside the structural pattern (clearly demonstrated by Ugaritic poetry; see below). Thus there is no reason to delete such statements.

(4) The chain figure ("sorites") is an example of synthetic parallelism:

The leaving-of	the-palmerworm	ate	the-locust,	$a+b$	c	d
And-the-leaving-of	the-locust	ate	the-hairy-locust	$a+d$	c	e
And-the-leaving-of	the-hairy-locust	ate	the-wingless-locust.	$a+e$	c	f

(Joel 1:4)

Biblia Hebraica (Kittel) suggests dropping the second stich, but this would spoil the effect of the chain, designed to portray judgment that comes in steps and is total.

(5) External and internal parallelism are Gottwald's terms to describe the correspondence between distichs (external) as a supplement to correspondence within a distich (internal):

		internal		*external*
Hear-ye	the-word-of-Yahweh	*a*	*b*	A
Rulers-of	Sodom;	*c*	*d*	B
Give-ear-to	the-Torah-of-our-God,	*a'*	*b'*	A'
People-of	Gomorrah.	*c'*	*d'*	B'

(Isa. 1:10)

Clearly, the units of the first stich parallel those of the third, as those of the second do those of the fourth. The capital letters in this illustration represent the stichs, "A" consisting of *a b*, etc. The passage could just as well be analyzed as two distichs, each consisting of verb, object, and vocative: *a b c : a' b' c'*. In the following example, such reduction is not possible:

Knows	the-ox	his-owner,		*a*	*b*	*c*
	and-the-ass	the-crib-of	his-lord:		*b'*	*C'*
Israel	negative	knows,		*d*	−A	
My-people	negative	understand.		*d'*	−A'	

(Isa. 1:3)

The first distich is clearly synonymous parallelism, as is the second, as the schematization *a b c : b' C'* and *d −A : d' −A'* indicates. But the first distich is in antithetic parallelism with the second, hence −A and −A' are ballast variants that are the negative of "knows" in the first stich.

(6) The variety of Hebrew poetry is almost endless, and new patterns can be found throughout the Old Testament. Little can be gained from trying to identify and analyze every type, but there is value in attempting to analyze a sufficient number to get the feeling of Hebrew poetry and see the essential message in the verse:

And-a-controversy	to-Yahweh	against-Judah	*a*	*b*	*c*	
And-visitation		upon-Jacob	*a'*		*c'*	*d*
		according-to-his-ways;				
According-to-his-deeds	I-will-bring-back to-him		*d'*	*b'*	*c'*	

(Hos. 12:2 [MT 3])

Since Hebrew has no verb "to have," "A-controversy to-Yahweh" means "Yahweh has a controversy," and therefore is parallel with "a-visitation." "Jacob" parallels "Judah." "According to his ways" is clearly parallel with "according to his deeds."

"I-will-return (=bring back) to-him" is the result of Yahweh's having a controversy with Judah. The verse therefore seems to be a tristich (a verse of three
stichs). Note the chiasm in the third stich (see below), *d'* being placed first.

(7) Quite often, the order of the units in a stich will be reversed in the
parallel. If connected with lines, the parallel members form an X, Gk. *chi*, hence
this structure is called "chiasm."

Thou-shalt-break-them	with-a-rod-of iron;			*A*	*B*
Like-a-vessel-of a-potter	Thou-shalt-crush-them.			*B'*	*A'*

(Ps. 2:9)

In-the-wilderness	prepare	the-way-of	Yahweh,		*a*	*b*	*c*	*d*
Make-straight	in-the-desert	a-highway	for-our-God.		*b'*	*a'*	*c'*	*d'*

(Isa. 40:3)

In both illustrations, the chiasm (crossing) of the elements is obvious. In the
second example, it is apparent in the form presented, but it would have been less
obvious if arranged as a tetrastich:

a	*b*
c	*d*
b'	*a'*
c'	*d'*

Chiasm is a very common element of Hebrew poetry, both internally and exter-
nally, but is not always readily apparent. In Ps. 2:9, above, it is external, for if set
down as a tetrastich, it would look like this:

a+b	A
c d	B
e f	B'
a'+b	A'

Even so, this is not obvious, for "with a rod of iron" and "like a potter's vessel" are
not exact parallels. The basic thought of the verse is: "Thou shalt break and crush
them like a potter smashing a pot with an iron rod."

Rhyme, Rhythm, and Meter. Scholars of Hebrew poetry long have struggled
with problems of meter and rhythm. It is generally agreed that rhyme is very rare
in biblical poetry, and seems to be coincidental when it does occur. But the
majority of scholars in the past have argued strongly for the presence of meter and
rhythm. Possibly this was because knowledge of ancient prosody came largely
from the classical Greek and Latin poets.[8]

---

8. Greek and Latin poetry can be "scanned," identifying the rhythm of short and
long syllables (Wĕ sing thȳ prāise, Ŏ Lōrd oŭr Gōd), then giving names to the beat
pattern of the measures ("feet") of each line. Terms such as "iambic pentameter" (five
measures, each an iamb or short-long [˘ ¯] rhythm) and "dactylic hexameter" (six measures, each a dactyl [¯ ˘ ˘]), etc., were used. Such terms sometimes have been applied
to Hebrew poetry, but many scholars today recognize that this cannot be done without
forcing the pattern or seriously altering the text.

(1) Earlier studies therefore attempted to identify the meter of Hebrew verses, and terms such as "2 + 2" or "3 + 2 meter," indicating that a distich had two heavy beats in each stich, or three beats followed by two, are common. If a line could not be fit into the hypothetical meter, it often was emended, and *Biblia Hebraica* (Kittel) bristles with the emendational note "m cs" (*metri causa*, "for the sake of the meter").[9] But these theories were developed before the discovery of Ugaritic poetry.

(2) Since 1929, many tablets have been discovered at Ras Shamra (ancient Ugarit) in Syria. Some contain religious texts, including quantities of poetry quite similar to that in the Old Testament. The tablets have not been touched since they were buried by the destruction of the library of Ugarit in the fourteenth century B.C., hence there is no possibility of subsequent editorial or scribal alteration, so here are the brute facts on which to build a theory of Semitic poetry. The Ugaritic evidence does not support regular patterns of either rhythm or meter.[10] The following examples, again translated with bald literalness, will give some idea of how remarkably like Old Testament poetry are the Ugaritic materials:[11]

| And-depart, | O-king, | from-my-house, | *a* | *b* | *c* |
| Be-distant, | O-Keret, | from-my-court. | *a'* | *b'* | *c'* |

(Krt. 131f.)

| Departed | Kothar | from-his-tents | *a* | *b* | *c* |
| Hayum | departed | from-his-tabernacles. | *b'* | *a* | *c'* |

(2 Aqht V.31)

Lo, thine-enemies,	O-Baal,		*a*	*b*	*c*
Lo, thine-enemies		thou-shalt-smite;	*a*	*b*	*d*
Lo, thou-shalt-vanquish		thy-foes.	*a*	*d'*	*b'*

(68:9; cf. Ps. 92:9 [MT 8])

| I-shall-give | her-field | for-a-vineyard, | *a* | *b* | *c* |
| | the-field-of her-love | for-an-orchard. | | *B'* | *c'* |

(77:22)

| They-shout, | Athirat | and-her-sons, | *a* | *b* | *c* |
| | The-goddess | and-the-band-of her-kin. | | *b'* | *C'* |

(Anat V.44)

| She-washes | her-hands, | the-virgin-Anat, | *a* | *b* | *c* |
| | her-fingers, | the-sister-in-law-of nations, | | *b'* | *C'* |

---

9. The latest revised edition of this work, *Biblia Hebraica Stuttgartensia*, ed. K. Elliger and W. Rudolph (Stuttgart: 1967-1977), is much more reserved in this regard.

10. See the evidence presented by W.S. LaSor, "An Approach to Hebrew Poetry through the Masoretic Accents," pp. 327-353 in A.I. Katsh and L. Nemoy, eds., *Essays on the Occasion of the Seventieth Anniversary of the Dropsie University* (Philadelphia: 1979); "Samples of Early Semitic Poetry," pp. 99-121 in G. Rendsburg et al., eds., *The Bible World*. Festschrift C.H. Gordon (New York: 1980).

11. Many more illustrations could be given. For extended portions, see C.H. Gordon, *Ugaritic Literature* (Ventnor, N.J.: 1947).

| She-washes | her-hands | in-the-blood-of | soldiers, | *a b d* |
| | her-fingers | in-the-gore-of | troops. | *b' d'* |

(Anat II.32)

"Prose clichés" similar to "thus said Yahweh" may be found in every column, always outside the parallelism.

(3) In view of Ugaritic studies it is no longer possible to assume a fully developed rhythmic pattern in Hebrew poetry, such as iambic (˘ ¯) or anapestic (˘ ˘ ¯) measures. Wholesale emendation "for the sake of the meter" is no longer acceptable. The total disregard of joined words in construct, as found throughout *Biblia Hebraica* (Kittel), in order to fit a predetermined scheme of meter is unacceptable. However, the recognition of a pattern of stress accents, which develops naturally from the words and word groups in the stichs, is certainly beyond question. This pattern, however, need be no more regular than the patterns found in Ugaritic poetry.

Word-Pairs and Other Devices. H. L. Ginsberg pointed out that the poets of Syria and Palestine had a regular "stock-in-trade" of fixed pairs of synonyms that recur repeatedly, and as a rule in the same order.[12] Cassuto lists twenty-six such pairs, including:

> *r'š* "head"—*qdqd* "pate"
> *'rṣ* "earth"—*'pr* "dust"
> *yd* "hand"—*ymn* "right hand"
> *'yb* "enemy"—*ṣr* "foe"
> *'lp* "thousand"—*rbb* "ten thousand"[13]

These and others are used similarly in Hebrew poetry. S. Gevirtz has given numerous examples,[14] of which here are just a few, using both Ugaritic and biblical citations:

> May Ḥoron break thy head (*r'š*)
> Athtart-šem-Ba'al thy pate! (*qdqd*)   (127:56-57)

> Yea, God shall smite the head (*r'š*) of his enemies,
> The hairy pate (*qdqd*) of one walking in his guilt.   (Ps. 68:22 [MT 21])[15]

> We have planted thy foes in the earth (*'rṣ*)
> In the dust (*'pr*) those who rise against thy brother.   (76 II 24-25)

> And their land (*'rṣ*) shall be soaked with blood,
> And their dust (*'pr*) shall be made rich with fat.   (Isa. 34:7b)[16]

---

12. "The Rebellion and Death of Ba'lu," *Orientalia* 5 (1936): 172.
13. M.D. Cassuto, *ha-Elah 'Anat* [U. Cassuto, *The Goddess Anath*] (Jerusalem: 1953), pp. 24-28 [Hebrew].
14. *Patterns in the Early Poetry of Israel* (Chicago: 1963), pp. 7-10 and passim.
15. See also Gen. 49:26; Deut. 33:16; Ps. 7:17 (MT 16).
16. See also v. 9.

[Let her place] a cup in my hand (*yd*),
  A goblet in my right hand (*ymn*). (1 Aqht 215-16)

Your hand (*yd*) will find out all your enemies,
  Your right hand (*ymn*) will find out those who hate you. (Ps. 21:8 [MT
                                                   9])[17]

What enemy ('*yb*) has risen against Ba'al,
  Or foe (*ṣr*) against the Rider of the clouds? (Ant. IV 48)

I would soon subdue their enemies ('*yb*)
  And turn my hand against their foes (*ṣr*). (Ps. 81:14 [MT 15])[18]

He casts silver by thousands ('*lp*),
  Gold he casts by ten-thousands (*rbb*). (51 I 28-29)

There shall fall at thy side a thousand ('*lp*)
  And ten thousand (*rbb*) at thy right hand. (Ps. 91:7)[19]

There are many such pairs, and probably some not yet recognized. The following are noteworthy: hear // give ear; Jacob // Israel; silver // gold; gold // fine gold; voice // speech; gift // present; man // son of man (or their plurals); wine // strong drink (or beer, *skr*); serve // bow down; fashion // create // make; people // nation; reside // dwell; count // number. One should be on the alert for other pairs. Note that such pairs are often used in prose passages for emphasis.

Another noteworthy phenomenon is the use of "graded numbers" or the "*x, x* + 1" pattern:

Once has God spoken
  Twice have I heard this. (Ps. 62:12 [MT 11])

For three transgressions of Damascus,
  Yes, for four I will not reverse it. (Amos 1:3)

Six things does Yahweh hate,
  Yea, seven are an abomination to him. (Prov. 6:16)

We shall raise against him seven shepherds,
  And eight leaders of man. (Mic. 5:4)

The same patterns often are found in Ugaritic. In addition to the $x, x + 1$ pattern, there is the $10x + x$, $10(x + 1) + (x + 1)$ (such as sixty-six // seventy-seven; seventy-seven // eighty-eight), and the $10x$, $10(x + 1)$ (such as eighty // ninety). These patterns, while common in Ugaritic, are not found in the Hebrew Bible.

---

17. See also Ps. 26:10.
18. See Ps. 89:42 (MT 43).
19. See also Deut. 32:30; Mic. 6:7; Dan. 7:10 (Aramaic).

EXEGETICAL VALUES OF THE STUDY OF POETRY

As noted, the pieces of the parallelisms in a passage are parts of the message. One must take the total passage and study the contributions of the parts to the total message.

Analyzing the Passage. The first step is to analyze the passage into its components, as illustrated above. Whether this is by schematic arrangements, such as "*a b c : a' b' c'*," is secondary. But the ability to recognize the elements is essential. For example, Amos 1:8 clearly deals with the Philistines. Therefore the component parts must help illuminate the message to the Philistines. Likewise, Prov. 10:1 deals with the effects of a child's behavior on the parents.

Analysis, but Not Fragmentation. The total message must be kept in view. To conclude, for example, that a wise son brings joy to his father, while a foolish son grieves his mother, suggesting that the mother has no joy in a wise son or the father no grief over a foolish son, is to miss the entire point. Likewise, to conclude that the Lord will cut off the inhabitants of Ashdod but not the other Philistine cities, or take away the king from Ashkelon but not from the other cities, is to misunderstand the nature of Hebrew poetry. Quite often, the component parts compose an important lesson. Isa. 1:16b-17 quoted above gives a fairly comprehensive picture of "doing good," particularly toward those with no one to look out for them, such as the orphan (the fatherless) and widow.

Recognizing Poetic Figures of Speech. Poetry in any language is to be distinguished from prose. Expressions such as "the trees clap their hands" or "the little hills skip like lambs" are to be understood as poetry, not botanical or geological descriptions. But the Bible, it is said, is "literally true." So it is, and as such it must be handled as the commonly accepted norms of literature require. When Isaiah addresses the "rulers of Sodom" and the "people of Gomorrah" (1:10; see above), one must look not only at his surface meaning, for Sodom and Gomorrah had disappeared long ago. Isaiah was comparing the people of Israel with the greatest sinners the land had ever seen. When Amos refers to "the pastures of the shepherds" and "the head of the Carmel" (1:2), he probably is using merism, whereby the extremes of mountain and valley stand for the entire land. Many figures of speech are used in the Bible, particularly in poetic passages. One must learn to recognize and interpret them as the author intended.

Alliteration, Assonance, Paronomasia, Onomatopoeia. In all literature, authors may use stylistic devices to catch attention or impress their message on the hearer or reader. In poetry, the use of devices which play on the sounds of language is particularly marked. With alliteration, words or syllables begin with the same or similar sounds. Assonance uses the same or similar sounds (usually vowels) within words. Paronomasia (pun) plays on words with the same or similar sounds but different meanings. Onomatopoeia is the use of words that sound similar to or suggest the concept they describe. Unfortunately, these devices can rarely be carried over in translation. For example, when God asks Amos: "What do you see?" and Amos answers: "A basket of summer fruit" (8:1f.), the Hebrew word that means "summer fruit" sounds almost like that for "end." This similarity of words prepares Amos for God's statement, "The end has come upon my people Israel." But the pun is lost in the translation.[20]

Striving to Retain the Beauty of Expression. Although not everyone is a poet or even appreciates poetry, the beauty of poetic expression is generally recognized. When dealing with the word of God, it is particularly important to attempt to preserve every appealing feature, including the poetry. Since much of the teaching of Jesus is in poetic form as are also snatches of hymns (Phil. 2:6-11), fragments of creeds (1 Tim. 3:16), and bursts of song (Rev. 4:11; 5:9f.), sensitivity to poetry in the Old Testament will enhance one's ability to understand the New. Scholars struggle for hours with a single verse, striving to find words and phrasing that convey the meaning with the same beauty as the original. Perhaps the main quality that made the KJV so well beloved was its beauty of language. When dealing with poetic passages, one should work in the original languages, or at least study several recent English translations, testing each for beauty as well as accuracy. God is the author of beauty. Striving to demonstrate the beauty of his word honors and glorifies him.

SUMMARY

In attempting to speak about God, two methods can be used: negation and analogy. Since God is infinite (without limitations) it is impossible to define (place limits about) him. One can say only what he is not. He is "infinite" (not finite), "immaterial" (not matter), "eternal" (not subject to space-time categories), "unchangeable" (not changing), and so on. This method is derived from Western rationalism, shaped largely by Greek philosophical methods. The other approach is to compare God to something known within the space-time system. Here one enters the imagery and symbolism of the biblical world. While found throughout the Bible, nowhere is it more prominent than in the poetry. The Unseen can be known by comparison or analogy with what one has seen. Ultimately God is known most fully as seen in the incarnate image, his Son. In many ways, the biblical approach is superior to the philosophical,[21] for people learn far more, and better, through the senses than through speculation. The poetry of the Bible has universal appeal. Its structure and imagery are not

---

20. For other illustrations, see Gottwald, *IDB* 3:835.
21. This not to deny the value which certainly exists in the philosophical approach.

lost in translation. It speaks to "every nation and kindred and people and tongue."

Likewise, there is no more adequate way to express faith in God and devotion to him than through song. Much of the Old Testament poetry started at just this point. Rather than purporting to be a source of theological doctrines, it was simply the expression of the faith of the singer, whether an individual or a community. It maintained its appeal through centuries because the believing community could join in the song, which expressed their faith and devotion. Even so, it remains not only a way of knowing God, but even more, a way of praising him who alone is worthy to be praised.

FOR FURTHER READING

Albright, W.F. "Verse and Prose in Early Israelite Tradition." Pp. 1-52 in *Yahweh and the Gods of Canaan*.

Cross, F.M., Jr., and Freedman, D.N. *Studies in Ancient Yahwistic Poetry*. SBL Dissertation 21. Missoula: 1975. (Orthographic and linguistic analysis of Exod. 15; Gen. 49; Deut. 33; 2 Sam. 22 = Ps. 18.)

Culley, R.C. "Metrical Analysis of Classical Hebrew Poetry." Pp. 12-28 in J.W. Wevers and D.B. Redford, eds., *Essays on the Ancient Semitic World*. Toronto: 1970. (Descriptive approach.)

Dahood, M. "Hebrew Poetry." *IDBS*, pp. 669-672. (Summary of literary techniques detected through comparison with Ugaritic poetry.)

Freedman, D.N. "Pottery, Poetry, and Prophecy: An Essay on Biblical Poetry." *JBL* 96 (1977): 5-26. (Character and function of Hebrew poetry in light of recent study.)

_____. "Prolegomenon." Pp. vii-lvi in G.B. Gray, *The Forms of Hebrew Poetry*. Repr. New York: 1972.

Kugel, J.L. *The Idea of Biblical Poetry: Parallelism and its History*. New Haven: 1981. (A new approach to the meaning of parallelism.)

Muilenburg, J. "A Study in Hebrew Rhetoric: Repetition and Style." *VTS* 1 (1953): 97-111.

O'Connor, M.P. *Hebrew Verse Structure*. Winona Lake: 1980. (Reassessment based on comparative poetic study, linguistics, and literary criticism.)

Robertson, D.A. *Linguistic Evidence in Dating Early Hebrew Poetry*. SBL Dissertation 3. Missoula: 1972. (Comparison of early and "standard" poetry of the eighth century and later.)

Robinson, T.H. "Hebrew Poetic Form: The English Tradition." *VTS* 1 (1953): 128-149.

CHAPTER 24

AMOS

"COME to Bethel and sin!" said Amos, with sharp irony. "Go back home, you seer!" said Amaziah, priest of Bethel. "Prophesy there, never again prophesy at Bethel, for it is the king's sanctuary" (see Amos 4:4; 7:12f.). This confrontation between the prophet of Yahweh and the priest of a rival shrine introduces well the study of the prophets, for those who proclaimed Yahweh's words were in continual conflict with the rulers, priests, and others who would not accept these utterances.

AMOS AND HIS PREACHING

Prophet. When Amaziah warned Amos to return to Judah to "earn your bread there, do your prophesying there" (7:12, JB), he was implying that Amos was a professional prophet. To his words of contempt, Amos replied: "I (was) no prophet; I (was) no son of a prophet; but I (was) a herdsman[1] and a piercer of sycamore figs, and the Lord took me from (following) after the flock, and the Lord said to me, 'Go, prophesy to my people Israel' " (7:14f.).

Amos was a shepherd of Tekoa (1:1), a village on the edge of the wilderness of Judah about six miles (10 km.) south of Bethlehem, in the southern kingdom of Judah. In addition to herding sheep, he pierced (or pinched) sycamore figs, a fruit that must be punctured or slit shortly before ripening to be edible.[2] Since figs are not found in Tekoa, Amos must have supplemented a meager income with seasonal work in western Judah, where such trees were found (see 1 Kgs. 10:27).

His statement, "I not a prophet" (lit.), has elicited continuing debate. In

---

1. Heb. *nōqēḏ*, sometimes translated "rancher," may suggest that Amos was a wealthy owner of many small cattle, not a simple shepherd (*rō'ēh*). But then why would he have to supplement his earnings by piercing sycamore figs?
2. See H.N. and A.L. Moldenke, *Plants of the Bible* (Waltham, Mass.: 1952), pp. 106-8; J.C. Trever, "Sycamore," *IDB* 4:470-71. See also 1 Chr. 27:28.

such a verbless clause the verb tense must be supplied from context, and in this case it would seem to be the present tense: "I *am* not a prophet." Following this interpretation, scholars have argued that Amos disclaimed any connection with prophetic office and in fact was repudiating it as an instrument of Yahweh's revelation. Other scholars feel this is contradicted by what follows: "Go, prophesy to my people Israel."[3] How could Amos say, "I am not a prophet," and immediately following say that God had commanded him to be just that? Thus these scholars suggest that the clause be past tense: "I *was* no prophet."

Likewise the next clause would read: "I (was) no son of a prophet." The "sons of the prophets" were members of the prophetic guild in training to be professional prophets. In the days of Elijah and Elisha they apparently were highly regarded (see 2 Kgs. 2:3, 15f.); but there were also professional prophets and their young trainees who prostituted their services, saying what the rulers wanted (see 1 Kgs. 22:6-23). Without judging the prophetic office, Amos simply said that he had not been a prophet, but one day the Lord called him to prophesy to the northern kingdom.[4]

Nothing further is known about Amos. Presumably he went back to Tekoa, after delivering the Lord's words, and edited his messages. Subsequently he wrote them substantially as they are today. There is no basis to assume that disciples followed him about and later recorded his words. The Lord had raised up the first prophet, or one of the first, to leave a written legacy.

Times. Without doubt Amos' words were delivered in the days of Jeroboam ben Joash (Jeroboam II), who ruled Israel 793-753,[5] for the clash between Amos and Amaziah (7:10-17) is an integral part of the message. To excise this passage would leave the book virtually meaningless. Since v. 10 therefore is to be accepted as authentic, there can be no basic objection to the claim that 1:1 also is accurate. Now, since the reigns of Uzziah of Judah and Jeroboam II of Israel overlapped for the period 767-753[6] (removing the portions of each reign that were coregencies with the previous kings), Amos' prophecy can be placed within that period, possibly *ca.* 760.

Amos indicates that the revelation was given "two years before the earthquake" (1:1). That must have been a very severe seismic phenomenon, for it

---

3. *Hinnābē'* (niphal), lit. "make yourself a prophet" or "act the part of a prophet."

4. See H.H. Rowley, "The Nature of Old Testament Prophecy," *The Servant of the Lord*, p. 120, for a discussion of the problem and valuable bibliography. For a fuller study, see his article, "Was Amos a Nabi?" p. 191 in J.W. Fück, ed., *Festschrift Otto Eissfeldt* (Halle: 1947).

5. See 2 Kgs. 14:23-29. Jeroboam was apparently coregent from 793-782, for the fifteenth year of Amaziah would be 782, and the forty-one years of Jeroboam's reign must be dated so as to end in 753; see W.S. LaSor, "1 and 2 Kings," *NBC*, p. 358.

6. For Amaziah of Judah, see 2 Kgs. 14:1-22; for Azariah (Uzziah), 15:1-7. Azariah must have been coregent 790-767. For detailed chronology, see LaSor, *NBC*, p. 323; see also p. 358 on 14:17-22.

was remembered well over two centuries later as "the earthquake in the days of Uzziah" (Zech. 14:5). However, it does not help us date the prophecy any more precisely. On the other hand, it does indicate that whereas the revelation from Yahweh was given two years before the earthquake, it actually must have been written down after it.

The Assyrian king Adad-nirari III (811-784), in a series of campaigns against the Aramean city-states (805-802), had broken the power of Damascus and removed for a time the Syrian threat to Israel. The succeeding kings of Assyria were checked by the advances of Urartu, and the Aramean (Syrian) city-states of Hamath and Damascus battled each other for supremacy. As a result, Uzziah of Judah and Jeroboam II of Israel could extend their boundaries almost to those of David and Solomon (see Map).[7] Jeroboam's northern border was at the entrance of Hamath, and for a while he ruled both Hamath and Damascus (2 Kgs. 14:25).

Such successes inspired national pride and the feeling that Yahweh favored Israel. The development of international trade made the merchants rich. Wealth brought injustice and greed; the poor were neglected, then persecuted. Religion became formalistic. The rich dominated everything and everyone from prophets and priests to judges and the poor who sought justice.

Message. This is precisely the picture painted in the message of Amos. Two classes had developed, rich and poor (Amos 5:10f., 15; 6:4f.). The poor were oppressed (2:6f.; 5:11; 6:3-6) and even sold into slavery (2:6, 8). The rich had summer and winter palaces of ivory (3:15), with couches and damask pillows (v. 12) and vineyards and precious oils for anointing (5:11; 6:4-6). The women, fat and pampered "cows of Bashan," drove their husbands to injustice so they might have drinks (4:1). Justice was bought at the shrines of Bethel, Gilgal, and other places, but Yahweh was not there (5:4f.), and, indeed, could not truly be worshiped there. He despised their ritual (vv. 21-24).

The Israelites were serving another god who could not help them (8:14). Their religion needed reform (3:14; 7:9; 9:1-4). Yahweh abhorred the "pride of Jacob" (6:1-8) and planned to end it (6:9-14).

HIS PROPHECY

Its Nature. Obviously, Amos did not sit down in Tekoa of Judah and write a prophecy against Israel. The confrontation with Amaziah at Bethel and the message Amaziah sent to Jeroboam indicate clearly that Amos had gone to the northern kingdom and preached with such power and persistence that Amaziah could write, "the land is not able to bear all his words" (7:10). Thus, Amos

---

7. According to 2 Kgs. 14:25, this had been foretold by the prophet Jonah ben Amittai; cf. Jonah 1:1.

Ivory comb from Megiddo, representative of the wealth and luxury assailed by Amos (3:15; 6:4). (Oriental Institute, University of Chicago)

must have given his prophetic messages orally, probably at Samaria and other places as well as Bethel. Basically his message could be summarized in these words:

> Jeroboam shall die by the sword,
> and Israel must go into exile away from his land. (7:11)

But this prophecy, as preserved today, is well structured. Scholars generally agree that it hardly could have been delivered orally in this form. Some think they can see smaller units that were probably the original messages, while others think certain key words ("locusts," "plumb-line," "basket of summer fruit," etc.) were symbols Amos used in his brief messages, and the expanded form was written later. It is unlikely and of no great importance that such problems shall ever be solved. Like the preaching of Jesus, that of Amos probably was given in both shorter and longer forms on many occasions, until at last it stirred enough reaction that the official religious leaders had to take note. The written form can only be a summary or a number of samples of the original spoken words, yet it is a summary of great form, precision, and beauty.

Contents. The written prophecy can be divided into three parts: lion's roar (1:1–3:8); Yahweh's indictment of Israel (3:9–6:14); and Yahweh's judgment (7:1–9:15).

The first part consists of eight indictments of six surrounding nations plus Judah and Israel, along with the punishment Yahweh threatened. Each begins with the formula, "For three transgressions of . . . , and for four, I will not revoke the punishment" (1:3, 6, 9, etc.).[8] This is the "x, x + 1 pattern," found elsewhere in the Old Testament and other ancient Near Eastern literature; here it probably indicates that the nations had sinned "enough and more than enough" to warrant God's judgment. The list includes nations bordering Israel and Judah, three of which (Edom, Ammon, and Moab) were related to Israel by blood. The indictments against the six nations were based on crimes against humanity, but Judah was indicted "because they have rejected the law of the Lord, and have not kept his statutes" (2:4). Israel was cited because of specifically forbidden sins of human behavior involving their neighbors and therefore their relationship to Yahweh (vv. 6-12).

As noted in Hebrew poetry (p. 316, above), the elements of parallel stichs often must be combined to get the full meaning. The same is true when interpreting larger parallel portions. In this case Judah and Israel are parts that make up the greater Israel or Yahweh's people. The second elements, then, may be taken as supplementary, and the sin of Judah and Israel interpreted as rejecting Yahweh's law, further specified as selling the righteous for silver, the needy for a pair of shoes, and including the other crimes listed. It would be misleading and incorrect interpretation to conclude that the sins of Judah were religious, while those of Israel were social. The religion of Yahweh is expressed in both its vertical and horizontal components, relating the Israelite to both God and neighbor.

Ethical Monotheism. In a former generation it was a common belief that Amos introduced ethical monotheism—the concept that there was only one God, who demanded ethical behavior.[9] Many scholars now reject the idea that the prophets were introducing a new religion, holding rather that they based their words on the covenant tradition.[10] Amos certainly did, referring often to

---

8. See Ps. 62:11 (MT 12): "Once God has spoken; twice have I heard this"; Prov. 30:15: "Three things are never satisfied; four never say 'Enough' "; see Ugaritic "with thee thy seven lads, thine eight swine" (67:5, 8f.); "Behold, a day and a second day the fire eats into the house, the flame into the palace" (51:6, 24-26). The numbers are usually incidental, indicating repreated incidents or numerous persons or things. Often the "x + 1" item is elaborated upon and considered most significant; see Prov. 6:16-19.

9. See J. Wellhausen, *Prolegomena to the History of Ancient Israel*, p. 474, and more recently, see C.F. Whitley, *The Prophetic Achievement* (Leiden: 1963), pp. 93ff. The theory that Amos introduced ethical monotheism was tied to J (eighth century) as the earliest source of the "Hexateuch" (p. 64, above). The two theories were used in a basically circular argument.

10. See R.E. Clements, *Prophecy and Covenant*, pp. 14-17; H.H. Rowley, *The Faith of Israel*, p. 71.

an earlier tradition,[11] and frequently using the covenant name "Yahweh."[12] Kaufmann is clearly close to the truth in noting that the prophet's demands for social justice are mostly a restatement of the ancient covenant laws, not simply applied to individuals, but understood as deciding even national destiny.[13] The idea that Yahweh is God of all nations, after all, only extends the Abrahamic covenant to all the families of the earth (Gen. 12:3; 18:18; 22:18), and the concept that Yahweh will punish other nations basically only extends the Exodus tradition that Yahweh punished Egypt and its gods.

The charge that the "social gospel" is "another gospel" (see Gal. 1:8) and is contrary to the true gospel of salvation by the grace of God is to be rejected. True, erroneous emphases have been placed on the biblical doctrine of social justice, both in the pre-Reformation period and in recent decades, and the stress on social responsibility (or "good works") has sometimes become a legalistic system opposed to the biblical doctrine of salvation. But human interpretations should not distort the clear teachings of Scripture. Amos was not the first to stress social justice—nor the last. Human responsibility to one's fellow is part of biblical religion from the story of Cain and Abel to the closing chapters of Revelation, and nowhere is emphasized more than in Jesus' teachings and Paul's epistles.[14]

Judgment and Hope. A former generation also held, as some still do, that the eighth-century prophets were "prophets of doom and gloom," and that elements of hope must be excised as later insertions. This view is generally rejected today, but scholars still question whether Amos 9:11-15 is part of the original work. The principal objection is that it is inconsistent with the rest of the book, where Amos consistently pronounces judgment. It therefore is held to be inconceivable that he would change his stance at the very end of his prophecy.[15]

However, at least two questions must be answered. First, is Amos otherwise

---

11. For example, the law of Yahweh (2:4), prophets and Nazirites (v. 11), sacrifices, tithes (4:4), leaven (v. 5), offerings (5:22), songs, harps (v. 23), new moon and sabbath (8:5), Sheol (9:2), destruction of the Amorite (2:9), the Exodus (v. 10; 3:1), pestilence as in Egypt (4:10), Sodom and Gomorrah (v. 11), day of Yahweh (5:18), David (6:5), Joseph (v. 6), and the temple (8:3). To remove any of these because they belong to a "later" tradition is circular reasoning; see R.H. Pfeiffer, *Introduction*, pp. 582f.

12. "Yahweh" is named fifty-two times; "the Lord Yahweh," nineteen; and "Yahweh God of Hosts," six.

13. *The Religion of Israel*, ed. and trans. M. Greenberg (Chicago: 1960), p. 365; see also J. Lindblom, *Prophecy in Ancient Israel*, pp. 311f.

14. A handy summary of prophetic teaching on social justice is found in J. Limburg, *The Prophets and the Powerless* (Atlanta: 1977).

15. Note, for instance, Eissfeldt's acceptance of the view of Wellhausen; *Old Testament*, p. 401, citing *Die Kleinen Propheten*, 4th ed. (Berlin: 1963), p. 96. But cf. Clements, *Prophecy and Covenant*, pp. 49 note 1, 111f. For an assessment of this matter in terms of the canonical function of ch. 9, see B.S. Childs, *Old Testament as Scripture*, pp. 405-8.

utterly devoid of hope? On two occasions, when given visions of judgment, Amos interceded for "Jacob" (7:2, 5). If Yahweh would listen to such intercession—and he did; see vv. 3, 6—was it too much to believe that Yahweh would restore the nation after he had punished it? The second question is more fundamental, for it begins not with the prophet but with covenant theology. Since Amos was building on God's revelation in light of the covenantal relationship, is it not axiomatic that ultimate restoration is necessary to fulfill Yahweh's purpose? Admittedly, not all Israelites would perceive this truth, but would not Yahweh's prophets? How could Yahweh fulfill his covenants with Abraham and David if total and final destruction of Israel were to be the end of the matter?

A further objection to the authenticity of 9:11-15 is based on the reference to the "booth of David that is fallen" (v. 11). This, it appears, requires a date subsequent to the fall of Jerusalem. However, this position relies on English translation rather than the Hebrew text. The passage says "the booth of David (which is) falling," a participial form. It also could be translated "the falling booth of David." The house of David, presumably the "booth," already had begun to fall when the kingdom was divided following the death of Solomon (931), and the northern kingdom viewed the Davidic dynasty as ended. In the apostasy of the northern kingdom, and certainly since Ahab and Jezebel (874-853), the kingdom of Israel was "falling." This was so in the loss of land to the Assyrians and the payment of tribute to Assyria by Jehu. And beyond doubt, the punishment revealed by Yahweh to Amos foretold the fall of Samaria as well as Judah. Therefore, there seems no valid argument against the use by Amos himself of the language of 9:11.[16]

Did Amos Oppose the Cult? Several statements in Amos seem to belittle Israel's cultic practices (see 4:4f.; 5:21-24, and esp. v. 25), so some writers have suggested that he opposed the cult. In fact, scholars often posit a fundamental rivalry between the prophets and priests, or hold that the cultic ideas in the Old Testament developed when the priests triumphed over the prophets after the Exile.[17] This problem again is in no way limited to Amos.

However, Amos utters no statement against the principle of sacrifice or against the sanctuary. His criticism is directed against specific sins in the northern kingdom. The people of this sinful nation had violated the sanctity of the house of their God (2:8), and Yahweh's servants, both Nazirites and prophets, had been forced into disobedient acts (v. 12). Punishment of the altars of Bethel is pronounced because of Israel's transgression (3:14). The religious ritual of 4:4f. is juxtaposed with the greed and inhumanity of the people, stressing the emptiness of their religion. Certainly the vigorous statements in Amos are reactions against meaningless ritual:

---

16. See also G. von Rad, *Old Testament Theology* 2:138.
17. See Rowley, *Worship in Ancient Israel*, pp. 144-175. See also H. Graf Reventlow, *Das Amt des Propheten bei Amos*. Forschungen zur Religion und Literatur des Alten und Neuen Testaments 80 (1962).

I hate, I despise your feasts,
    and I take no delight in your solemn assemblies.
Even though you offer me your burnt offerings and cereal offerings,
    I will not accept them,
and the peace offerings of your fatted beasts
    I will not look upon.
Take away from me the noise of your songs;
    to the melody of your harps I will not listen.
But let justice roll down like waters,
    and righteousness like an ever-flowing stream. (5:21-24)

THEOLOGICAL INSIGHTS

Yahweh the Supreme God. Amos is not a professional theologian and offers no doctrinal treatises. Rather, his messages from God reveal something of God's actions and attitudes. Thus it is easy to overlook his great insights about God and, as did scholars of the early twentieth century, reduce Amos to a haranguer on social justice. In fact, Amos' cry for justice arose from the very nature of God.

Yahweh judges all nations. This is implicit in the opening cycle of indictments against the surrounding nations (chs. 1–2). He is everywhere (9:2) and in all natural phenomena (9:5f.). He made the Pleiades and Orion (5:8). He forms the mountains and creates the wind (4:13). Yahweh not only brought up Israel from Egypt, but also the Philistines from Caphtor and the Syrians from Kir (9:7). This God, who rules heaven and earth, is the God with whom all nations must deal.

Yahweh is a God of moral perfection, and he requires moral behavior of all people. He gives a general revelation to all (see p. 54, above), and all will be held accountable for their actions. Amos speaks of Damascus as threshing Gilead (1:3)—literally driving threshing sleds with pieces of iron or flint imbedded in their underside over the wounded and dying bodies of the conquered. Gaza sold a people into slavery to Edom (v. 6), as did Tyre. These acts of inhumanity are sins against the God who made all people. He likewise sits in judgment upon Israel for similar sins of inhumanity.

Yahweh the God of Israel. Israel, however, is not just another nation among nations. Rather, Israel stands in a special relationship. "You only have I known of all the families of the earth," says Yahweh (see 3:2). The essence of the Old Testament covenantal religion is that Yahweh chose Israel to be his people.

This is shown by constant use of the covenant name Yahweh (see p. 134, above), first intimately associated with Israel in the Exodus account. But the name does not merely identify God with Israel; more importantly it bespeaks the redemptive purpose, for Yahweh is the one who delivers his people from bondage (see 2:10), destroys their enemies (see v. 9), and raises up their sons for prophets (see v. 11). He is the revealing God (3:7f.).

The special relationship between Yahweh and Israel is brought out also in the judgments pronounced. Because of that relationship God finds Israel guilty. "You only have I known of all the families of the earth; therefore I will punish you for all your iniquities" (v. 2). Yahweh tried famine, rain, blight, mildew, and pestilence to turn Israel back to him, but to no avail (4:6-11).[18] He must now proceed to punishment (v. 12). One of the most noteworthy judicial acts is his sending famine—not of bread, but of hearing the words of Yahweh (8:11). He is not only the revealing God but the God who withholds revelation, especially when his prophetic word is not heeded.

Election Responsibility. The close relationship between the covenant name of the Lord and the judgment upon the people for their sins—whether religious or cultic or social—underscores a great Old Testament truth, that election by Yahweh carries the responsibility to live according to his revealed will. This was stressed when the law was revealed at Sinai (see Ch. 9, above), and reiterated often in Numbers, Deuteronomy, and Joshua. It is the basic theme underlying many of the prophetic utterances.

In Amos, the people's sins are related to the law of Yahweh. This is not readily apparent, for Amos does not cite chapter and verse nor quote exact words. Nonetheless, the elements of the law are present, including care of the poor and needy, administration of justice, use of just weights in commerce, and, above all, the obligation to worship Yahweh alone. Even more significantly, Amos repeatedly cites past historical situations and associates them with the name Yahweh.[19]

But there is another side to the responsibility of election. Since Yahweh has chosen Israel, he has a special responsibility to them. While sinful Israel cannot count on any special leniency because of election (see 9:7f.), but rather will be held to an even higher standard of moral responsibility than the other nations, nevertheless Yahweh will not completely destroy the house of Jacob. Only the sinners of his people will die (vv. 8-10). This is not elaborated upon, and a complete doctrine must not be built on just a few verses. Leviticus distinguishes between inadvertent sins (sins of ignorance) and high-handed sins (sins of presumptuousness). For the covenant people the former could be forgiven; the latter could not. Since Amos already has stressed that Yahweh repeatedly tried to cause his people to return to him, certainly implying the possibility of forgiveness, the "sinners" he now speaks about must be those who

---

18. "Turn, return, turn back, repent," etc., all translate one Hebrew verb (*šûḇ*), used many times in the prophets. Unfortunately, the English translations obscure this. The KJV, for example, translates *šûḇ* 123 different ways!

19. A common expression in Amos is *nᵉʾûm yhwh*, variously translated in English: "says the Lord" (RSV), "it is Yahweh who speaks" (JB), "declares the Lord" (NASB). It occurs many times in nearly all the prophets. Yahweh, the covenant name of the God of Israel, appears to be used almost exclusively when the covenant relationship lies behind a situation or statement.

EIGHTH-CENTURY PROPHETS AND THEIR WORLD

	Prophet	Judah	Israel	Syria	Assyria	Egypt
800	Isaiah (?) Micah Amos Hosea Jonah (?)		Jehoash 798-782		Adad-nirari III 810-783	
790		Amaziah 796-767	Jeroboam II *793-753			
780		Azariah (Uziah) *790-740			Shalmaneser IV 782-772	
770					Ashur-dan III 771-754	
760						Sheshonk IV 763-727
750		Jotham *751-732	Zechariah 753 (6 mos.) Shallum 752 (1 mo.) Menahem 752-742	Rezin 750-732	Ashur-nirari V 753-744 Tiglath-pileser 747-727	
740			Pekahiah 741-740 Pekah ¶752-732			
730		Ahaz *735-716	Hoshea 731-722 Fall of Samaria 722	Fall of Damascus 732	Shalmaneser V 727-722	Osorkon IV 727-716
720		Hezekiah *728-687			Sargon II 722-705	
710						Shabako 715-702
700		Manasseh *696-642			Sennacherib 705-681	Shabataka 702-690 Tirhaqa 690-664
690						

*Coregency   ¶Rival claim to throne

sin presumptuously. They presume that because they are Israelites, Yahweh will accept any kind of behavior.

But Amos ends on a happier note. He foresees clearly that Yahweh's covenant has not been destroyed. The "tottering hut of David" (v. 11, JB) will be repaired, raised up, rebuilt "as in the days of old." But the covenant goes beyond that. Yahweh does not just simply patch the nation like a cosmic junk dealer. He promises, through Amos, something far more glorious in prosperity, stability, and security.

"Behold, the days are coming," says the Lord,
  "when the plowman shall overtake the reaper
  and the treader of grapes him who sows the seed;
the mountains shall drip sweet wine,
  and all the hills shall flow with it.
I will restore the fortunes of my people Israel,
  and they shall rebuild the ruined cities and inhabit them;
they shall plant vineyards and drink their wine,
  and they shall make gardens and eat their fruit.
I will plant them upon their land,
  and they shall never again be plucked up
  out of the land which I have given them,"
    says the Lord your God. (vv. 13-15)

FOR FURTHER READING

Barton, J. Amos' Oracles Against the Nations. SOTS Monograph. Sheffield: 1980.

Brueggemann, W. "Amos IV 4-13 and Israel's Covenant Worship." VT 15 (1965): 1-15. (Shows prophetic dependence on older traditions.)

Coote, R.B. Amos Among the Prophets: Composition and Theology. Philadelphia: 1981. (Attempts to trace in the composition of the book three distinct stages from Amos' day to the Exile.)

Craghan, J.F. "The Prophet Amos in Recent Literature." Biblical Theology Bulletin 2 (1972): 242-261.

Cripps, R.S. A Critical and Exegetical Commentary on the Book of Amos. London: 1929. (A standard work.)

Gold, V.R. "Tekoa." IDB 4:527-29.

Hammershaimb, E. The Book of Amos. Trans. J. Sturdy. Oxford: 1970. (Exegetical.)

Hoffmann, Y. "Did Amos Regard Himself as a nābî?" VT 27 (1977): 209-212. (Natural lack of perspective prevented Amos' realizing his position as pioneer of a new prophetic movement.)

Honeycutt, R.L. Amos and His Message. Nashville: 1963. (Expository commentary.)

Kapelrud, A.S. Central Ideas in Amos. Repr. Oslo: 1961.

Mays, J.L. Amos. OTL. Philadelphia: 1969. (A thorough yet readable study.)

Rector, L.J. "Israel's Rejected Worship: An Exegesis of Amos 5." Restoration Quarterly 21 (1978): 161-175.

Robertson, J., and Armerding, C. "Amos." ISBE 1 (1979): 114-17.

Smith, G.A. *The Book of the Twelve Prophets.* Expositor's Bible 4. Rev. ed. Grand Rapids: 1956. Pp. 456-549. (Excellent.)

Watts, J.D.W. *Vision and Prophecy in Amos.* Grand Rapids: 1958. (Includes form analysis of the visions.)

Wolff, H.W. *Amos the Prophet: The Man and His Background.* Trans. F. McCurley. Ed. J. Reumann. Philadelphia: 1973.

————. *Joel and Amos.* Trans. W. Janzen, S.D. McBride, Jr., and C.A. Muenchow. Hermeneia. Philadelphia: 1977. (The most analytic and powerful commentary available; strong emphases on form criticism and clan wisdom in Amos' background.)

CHAPTER 25

HOSEA

A decade or so after Amos came north to denounce Jeroboam's court, the Lord called Hosea, a son of the northern kingdom, to the prophetic ministry. His message, proclaimed over many years, demonstrates God's grace and judgment.

The book of Hosea was chosen to head the collection of Minor Prophets (written on one scroll and called "the Book of the Twelve") not only because he was among the earliest (Amos actually preceded him by a few years) but because his is the longest of the preexilic writers (Zechariah's postexilic book is slightly longer).

INTRODUCTION

Prophet. Nothing is known of Hosea's life or upbringing, except that he was the son of Beeri (1:1). Anything else about his personal circumstances, except his tragic marriage, must be reconstructed from the style, tone, and contents of his message.

The compassionate tone of his work seems to stem from several sources. He seems, first, a tenderhearted person, and the frequent comparisons with Jeremiah in the Old Testament and John in the New are not out of place. Overwhelmed by God's boundless and changeless love (see 11:8f.), he reached out in concern for his countrymen. Furthermore, in contrast to Amos, he preached to his own people; and though at times he was unsparing in his indictments, he was never detached from them, never cold or heartless toward them. Without doubt the dominant influence which gave Hosea's message its ring of compassion was his own suffering and disappointment. He, like Jeremiah, had been asked by God to walk a path of grief and anguish known to only a few, and he could not be the same again. He had felt something of God's own heartbreak and was stamped with an imprint of divine compassion.

Nothing is known of his station before his call. Some number him among the priests because of his intimate knowledge of religious affairs in the northern kingdom and his grave concern for the corruption of the priesthood (e.g.,

4:5-9). Others link him with the official prophets because he quotes a frequent jibe: "The prophet is a fool, the man of the spirit is mad" (9:7). But neither conclusion can be maintained with certainty.

This much can be said: his outstanding knowledge of both the political tensions of his own day and the great events of Israel's past mark him as an unusual prophet. Like Isaiah he was extremely sensitive to political currents and analyzed their implications shrewdly. Also, his outstanding literary gifts, particularly his figures of speech, are additional evidence that he was probably from the upper classes.[1]

Date. The introductory verse (1:1) places Hosea's ministry in the reigns of Uzziah, Jotham, Ahaz, and Hezekiah of Judah and Jeroboam II of Israel. Its minimum length was about forty years, since Jeroboam II died *ca.* 753 and Hezekiah ascended the throne *ca.* 715 and was coregent from *ca.* 728. The book itself gives little evidence that Hosea continued to preach after the fall of Samaria in 721.

When the prophet's first son was born, Jehu's dynasty still reigned, for the Lord specifies that Jehu's house was still to be avenged (1:4). But it is not certain whether the ruler then was Jeroboam II or his ill-fated son, Zechariah, assassinated by Shallum *ca.* 752. If his ministry began at the close of Jeroboam's reign, the bulk of it took place during the hectic days of Menahem (*ca.* 752-742), Pekah (*ca.* 740-732) and Hoshea (*ca.* 732-722). These were desperate times when Assyrian armies thrust westward repeatedly and the Israelites sought vainly, whether by war or appeasement, to preserve their security and integrity as a nation.

Hosea's ministry coincided closely with the reign of Tiglath-pileser III (*ca.* 745-727), who brought unprecedented vigor and vision to the throne of Assyria. Both biblical history (2 Kgs. 15:19) and Assyrian records report that Menahem paid heavy tribute to Tiglath-pileser (called here Pul, after the Babylonian form of his name). Hoping to use Assyrian support to bolster his tottering throne, which had been seized from Shallum who had reigned only a month, Menahem raised the tribute by taxing wealthy Israelites. Hosea makes veiled references to this courting of Assyrian favor:

Israel is swallowed up;
> already they are among the nations as a useless vessel.
For they have gone up to Assyria. . . .
> Ephraim has hired lovers.
Though they hire allies among the nations,
> I will soon gather them up. (8:8-10)

Ephraim herds the wind,
> and pursues the east wind all day long;
they multiply falsehood and violence;
> they make a bargain with Assyria,
> and oil is carried to Egypt. (12:1)

---

1. See A. Weiser, *Old Testament*, p. 233.

Threatened without by Assyria, Israel was unsettled within by political intrigue. A basic instability, an inability to maintain a ruling dynasty over long periods, is most clear during this period. Hosea sensed the situation perceptively:

> For like an oven their hearts burn with intrigue;
>   all night their anger smolders;
>   in the morning it blazes like a flaming fire.
> All of them are hot as an oven,
>   and they devour their rulers.
> All their kings have fallen;
>   and none of them calls upon me. (7:6f.)

> They made kings, but not through me.
> They set up princes, but without my knowledge. (8:4)

The references to Egypt probably relate to the second half of King Hoshea's reign, when, after an initial period of playing vassal to Assyria, he sought Egyptian support for his opposition to Shalmaneser V, who succeeded Tiglath-pileser in 727.[2] Hosea aptly characterized the rapid and capricious vacillations in foreign policy:

> Ephraim is like a dove,
>   silly and without sense,
>   calling to Egypt, going to Assyria.[3] (9:3)

In short, Hosea's ministry spanned the troubled third quarter of the eighth century (ca. 750-725). His lot was to watch Israel's last illness when all attempted cures came to naught. Neither a quelling of internal revolt nor aid from allies like Egypt could stay Israel's demise. Judgment had to come. Whether Hosea lived to see the end is not known. But the prophetic word from God and his own understanding of the times convinced him of its certainty, a certainty which he faithfully proclaimed but cannot have rejoiced in.

HOSEA'S MARRIAGE (1:2-3:5)

Few Old Testament passages have prompted more discussion than the opening chapters of Hosea. God's demand on Hosea is unique:

---

2. See J. Bright, *History*, p. 275.
3. It is uncertain whether Hosea directly mentions the Syro-Ephraimitic coalition between Pekah of Israel and Rezin of Damascus. Isaiah described the threat this alliance presented to Ahaz of Judah (see Isa. 7) and its downfall at the hands of Tiglath-pileser. Possibly the battle call of Hos. 5:8 refers to conflict between Israel and Judah in the border towns of Benjamin:

> Blow the horn in Gibeah,
>   the trumpet in Ramah.
> Sound the alarm at Beth-aven [a derogatory name for Bethel,
>   meaning "house of nothing" instead of "house of God"];
>   Tremble, O Benjamin!

Go, take to yourself a wife of harlotry and have children of harlotry,
for the land commits great harlotry by forsaking the Lord. (1:2)

The details are few and the whole account so condensed that much is left to
the interpreter's imagination. But the questions about the story's meaning are

Canaanite fertility goddess such as those for whom Israel "played the harlot" (Hos. 2:5); Ras Shamra. (Louvre)

not merely academic. It is the foundation of Hosea's ministry. A clear understanding of the marriage is essential to a clear grasp of his message.[4]

Problems of Interpretation. Are the narratives of chs. 1 and 3 the prophet's
actual experience (history) or a story he composed to convey a spiritual truth
(allegory)? They will be treated here as history for several reasons. First, the
book itself does not suggest that it be taken other than at face value. Second,
certain details do not fit an allegorical pattern: no suitable meaning for Gomer's
name has been found; no purpose is apparent in references to the weaning of
Not-pitied (1:8) or in the order of the children's births. Furthermore, use of
such an allegory would have strange effects on the reputation of the prophet
and his family. If he were married, his wife's reputation would suffer; if not, his
own status in the community would be questioned. Finally, the traditional
reason for considering the story as allegory is to avoid the stigma on the morality
of God and the prophet which the command to marry a harlot apparently
involves. But does what is morally doubtful as history become any less questionable when viewed as allegory?

A second main question is the relationship between chs. 1 and 3. The
approach here is that the two chapters are not two parallel accounts of the
same incident—Hosea's taking of Gomer as wife.[5] Rather, ch. 3 is the sequel
to ch. 1. Not only does this seem more natural, but certain details tend to
support it. Ch. 3 says nothing of the children, so prominent in ch. 1. Again,
ch. 3 strongly suggests that the woman is barred for some time from any contact
with a man, including her husband, as a disciplinary measure, just as Israel is
to be chastened by exile (3:3f.). But ch. 1 implies that Gomer conceived her
first child shortly after marriage (1:3). Furthermore, ch. 3 seems quite clearly
to symbolize Israel's return to God, her first husband, as prophesied in 2:7:

> She shall pursue her lovers,
>   but not overtake them;
> and she shall seek them,
>   but shall not find them.
> Then she shall say "I will go and return to my first husband,
>   for it was better with me then than now."

Several scholars have held that the woman in ch. 3 is not Gomer but a
second wife. Although the wording of v. 1—"love a woman who is beloved of

---

4. The treatment here is based on the masterful presentation of the problems by
H. H. Rowley, "The Marriage of Hosea," *BJRL* 39 (1956-57): 200-233. For a contrasting
view, see B. S. Childs, *Old Testament as Scripture*, pp. 377-380.

5. Those who take these chapters as parallel accounts would call attention to the
difference in literary form. Ch. 1 is prose narrative written in the third person and
frequently is thought to have been composed by disciples of the prophet. Ch. 3 is prose
narrative in the first person—a kind of memoir, usually thought to have come from the
prophet himself.

a paramour"—is strange, it seems highly unlikely the prophet would marry two women if his marriages are to symbolize God's relationship with one nation, Israel. Since the whole purpose of the story is to illustrate this relationship, would not the taking of a second wife confuse rather than clarify the message that God is to restore Israel to himself, as made clear in 2:14-23?

> Therefore, behold, I will allure her,
> and bring her into the wilderness,
> and speak tenderly to her.
> . . . . . .
> And there she shall answer as in the days of her youth,
> as at the time when she came out of the land of Egypt. (vv. 14f.)

Another problem of interpretation is the kind of a woman Gomer was. In other words, what is the meaning of God's command (1:2): "Go, take to yourself a wife of harlotry"? Some view this harlotry as religious fornication, i.e., idolatry. Gomer, then, would not be an immoral woman but a member of an idolatrous people. This would fit every member of the northern kingdom, dedicated to calf worship, including the prophet himself. The desire to protect Gomer's reputation stems, in part, from the moral problem in God's command and Hosea's response. Many have held that Gomer was not wicked when Hosea married her but turned to evil later. The command in v. 2 would represent not God's actual call but Hosea's interpretation in retrospect. Hosea realized that the call came when he took his wife, who proved as unfaithful to him as Israel had to God. If Gomer was evil when they married, her husband knew nothing about it. Even if this approach is acceptable for ch. 1, what about ch. 3? Here Hosea knows full well what kind of woman he is taking. To an Israelite, reconciliation with an adulteress would be scarcely less repugnant than marrying one in the first place, since stoning was the customary prescription for adultery (Lev. 20:10; Deut. 22:22; John 8:5).

Another interpretation is that Gomer, like many Israelite virgins, had participated in a Canaanite ritual of sexual initiation with a stranger prior to her marriage. The purpose was to assure fertility of the marriage. Though this theory has the strong support of H. W. Wolff,[6] it is by no means widely accepted, chiefly because of insufficient Old Testament evidence for this practice.[7]

Many recent scholars have considered Gomer a cult prostitute, but this is by no means certain. She is called an adulteress in 3:1, but the technical form for religious harlot ($q^e\underline{d}\bar{e}\check{s}\hat{a}$) nowhere is used of her. Further, it is unlikely that marriage to such a person would have been any less distasteful to Hosea, who scathingly denounced cult prostitution, than marriage to an ordinary harlot. So little is known about the role and status of cult prostitutes in Israel that it is hazardous to conjecture how Hosea's marriage to one would have been viewed.

---

6. *Hosea*, trans. G. Stansell. Hermeneia (Philadelphia: 1974), pp. 14f.
7. See W. Rudolph, "Präparierte Jungfrauen?" ZAW 75 (1963): 65-73; also J.L. Mays, *Hosea*. OTL (Philadelphia: 1969), p. 26.

Character and Meaning of the Marriage. Quite clearly Hosea connected his prophetic call with his marriage to Gomer, but the relation between the two is puzzling. Was he called before the marriage, or did his call grow out of his experience with Gomer? If 1:2 is taken at face value, as seems best, his call came immediately before he married. His prophetic naming of his first son Jezreel is strong evidence that he was already a prophet at his marriage. No doubt, however, his tragic experiences with Gomer had a profound influence, refining his character and enriching his ministry. In a sense, his call was continuous, beginning when he took Gomer and growing and deepening throughout his years of suffering.

(1) Gomer and her children. Drastic situations sometimes call for drastic measures. This was the situation in Israel in Hosea's day. The combination of corruption and luxury throughout Jeroboam's lengthy reign had brought the nation to spiritual and moral bankruptcy. Baal worship, introduced officially by Ahab's queen Jezebel, was still rampant despite Jehu's drastic measures to wipe it out. In turning to the Baals Israel had played false with their first love, Yahweh. In order to illustrate memorably this spiritual adultery God commands Hosea to marry a woman whose reputation was evil. Many have sought to defend both Hosea and Gomer on the grounds that their relationship must have been pure at first, just as Israel's relationship with God was pure in the Exodus experiences:

> I remember the devotion of your youth,
>   your love as a bride,
> how you followed me in the wilderness,
>   in a land not sown.
>
> Israel was holy to the Lord
>   the first fruits of his harvest. (Jer. 2:2f.)

However, Hosea's marriage was not meant to recapitulate God's dealings with Israel but to thrust into sharp relief Israel's present degeneracy. How could this be done more effectively and dramatically than by a marriage between a prophet and a wicked woman?[8] Whether Gomer's prostitution was commercial or religious is unknown. The text suggests that she was not a typical Israelite woman.

The three children symbolize aspects in God's dealing with his people. The first-born, Jezreel, seems quite clearly to have been Hosea's son: "She conceived and bore him a son" (1:3). His divinely appointed name was a prophecy of judgment upon the house of Jehu, whose vicious purges began with the murder of Joram and Jezebel at Jezreel (2 Kgs. 9:16-37). The threat ("I will break the bow of Israel in the valley of Jezreel," v. 5) seems to have been fulfilled in the

---

8. The prophets did not always enjoy obeying God's commands. Walking "naked and barefoot for three years as a sign and a portent against Egypt and Ethiopia" was certainly not a task that Isaiah relished (Isa. 20:2f.).

murder of Jeroboam's son Zechariah, the last of Jehu's dynasty (15:8-12).[9] Jezreel's name is aptly chosen because it not only speaks of judgment for Jehu's act at Jezreel but can also suggest restoration (Hos. 2:22f.), since it means "God will sow."

The second child is a daughter, Not-pitied (*Lo-ruhamah*), who symbolizes a reversal in God's attitude toward Israel. His mercy has been spurned and trust in his deliverance replaced by confidence in arms and alliances. God has little choice but to withdraw his mercy and let Israel understand through judgment the full significance of their faithlessness (1:6f.). The third child, a son, is called Not-my-people (*Lo-'ammî*) to symbolize the broken covenant. God does not reject Israel; rather, they had rejected him and refused to be his people (vv. 8f.).

The relationship between Hosea and these two children is not clear. The text does not state specifically that Gomer bore them to him as it does in Jezreel's case. Furthermore, the tone of ch. 2 suggests that they are children of Gomer's adultery:

> Plead with your mother, plead—
>   for she is not my wife,
>   and I am not her husband—
> that she put away her harlotry from her face
>   and her adultery from between her breasts.
>   . . . . . .
> Upon her children also I will have no pity,
>   because they are children of harlotry. (2:2, 4)

This interpretation, if correct, is another graphic illustration of Israel's corruption.

Ch. 2 is an extended commentary on 1:2. Beginning with references to Gomer and her children, it then deals with the infidelity of the Israelites, who worship the Baals without realizing that it was Yahweh, not Baal, who had blessed them abundantly (2:8). As the chapter proceeds the focus shifts from Gomer's wandering ways to those of Israel.

(2) God's forgiveness and Hosea's. Following the threat of judgment (vv. 9-13), which comes because Israel had forgotten Yahweh, the tone in ch. 2 changes abruptly: Israel will not return to God so he will fetch his people back himself (vv. 14-23). The very names of Baal are to be erased from their memory and a new marriage is to take place: "And I will betroth you to me for ever; I will betroth you to me in righteousness and in justice, in steadfast love, and in mercy, I will betroth you to me in faithfulness; and you shall know the Lord" (vv. 19f.). Israel, previously scattered in judgment, will be sown in the land (note above the meaning of the name Jezreel), pity will be poured out on Not-pitied, and Not-my-people will again be God's people. God's grace will reverse the judgment and bring restoration (vv. 21-23).

---

9. The RSV (v. 10) follows the LXX in placing this murder at Ibleam near Jezreel (cf. 9:27).

Then God commands Hosea to follow his example and restore Gomer as his wife (3:1-5). The order is important. God pledges forgiveness to Israel, and Hosea follows suit. The sequence of chs. 2 and 3 is theologically profound. Forgiving does not come naturally; those who have felt God's forgiveness learn to forgive (cf. Eph. 4:32).

Hosea bought Gomer for the price of a slave, apparently the equivalent of thirty pieces of silver, and took her back. The degrading state into which she had fallen is itself emblematic of the wages which sin pays. Rebellion against God issues in slavery to something else. God's forgiveness does not mean that he treats sin lightly. His love for Israel involved exile as well as exodus, and Hosea disciplines Gomer to demonstrate both the seriousness of her sin and God's chastening of Israel in captivity (3:3f.). But discipline is not the last word: "Afterward the children of Israel shall return (or repent) and seek the Lord their God, and David their king; and they shall come in fear to the Lord and to his goodness in the latter days" (v. 5).

A remarkable story, this. A prophet is called to bear a cross, to experience both the suffering heart and the redeeming love of God. With unflinching obedience Hosea drank a bitter cup. His home was his Gethsemane. And in bending to a will not his own, he not only left a most poignant illustration of divine love but helped prepare the way for One who most fully embodied this love.[10]

HOSEA'S MESSAGE (4:1–14:9)

Chs. 4–14 summarize Hosea's preaching ministry. In contrast with the carefully shaped structure of Amos, they reveal no discernible order. Oracles of various subjects are placed side by side without apparent connection. Movement or progression throughout the book is almost undetectable. This does not mean that Hosea is not a gifted poet. Indeed, his are among the most moving poems of the Bible. He has a gift of expression, particularly with figures of speech, that few Old Testament poets match. How better, for instance, could the weakening effects of Israel's foreign alliances be described?

Ephraim mixes himself with the peoples:
   Ephraim is a cake not turned.[11]
Aliens devour his strength,
   and he knows it not;
gray hairs are sprinkled upon him,
   and he knows it not. (7:8f.)

---

10. See Rowley, "Marriage of Hosea," p. 233: "Like Another, he learned obedience by the things that he suffered, and because he was not broken by an experience that has broken so many others, but triumphed over it and in triumphing perhaps won back his wife, he received through the vehicle of his very pain an enduring message for Israel and for the world."

11. Burnt on one side and underdone on the other.

Hosea's metaphors frequently are rural:

> Ephraim was a trained heifer
>> that loved to thresh,
>> and I spared her fair neck;
> but I will put Ephraim to the yoke,
>> Judah must plow,
>> Jacob must harrow for himself.
> Sow for yourselves righteousness,
>> reap the fruit of steadfast love;
>> break up your fallow ground,
> for it is time to seek the Lord,
>> that he may come and rain salvation upon you. (10:11f.)

The lyric quality of Hosea's poetry is typified by his combination of strength and sensitivity in this love song, whose closest parallels are in the Song of Solomon:

> I will heal their faithlessness;
>> I will love them freely,
>> for my anger has turned from them.
>
> I will be as dew to Israel;
>> he shall blossom as the lily,
>> he shall strike root as the poplar;
>
> his shoots shall spread out;
>> his beauty shall be like the olive,
>> and his fragrance like Lebanon.
>
> They shall return and dwell beneath my shadow,
>> they shall flourish as a garden;
> they shall blossom as the vine,
>> their fragrance shall be like the wine of Lebanon. (14:4-7)

The themes explored in chs. 4–14 are too numerous for detailed comment. A brief look at Hosea's more important emphases will illustrate the mood and tone of his messages and his poetic power.

Knowledge of God. Repeatedly Hosea traces Israel's spiritual and moral problems to their lack of knowledge of God:

> Hear the word of the Lord, O people of Israel;
>> for the Lord has a controversy with the inhabitants of the land.[12]
> There is no faithfulness or kindness,[13]
>> and no knowledge of God in the land;

---

12. Note the formal tone of this indictment, using literary forms which probably originated in the legal sphere; see Mic. 6:1-16. On the literary forms used in Hosea, see W. Brueggemann, *Tradition for Crisis* (Richmond: 1969), pp. 55-90.

13. Heb. *ḥesed*, a favorite word of Hosea, blends the ideas of loyalty and love. Used of God, it means "covenant love" or "steadfast love"; for persons, as here, "kindness" or "charity" is implied.

there is swearing, lying, killing, stealing, and committing adultery;
   they break all bounds and murder follows murder. (4:1f.)

My people are destroyed for lack of knowledge;
   because you have rejected knowledge,
   I reject you from being a priest to me.
And since you have forgotten the law of your God,
   I also will forget your children. (v. 6)

The relationship between knowing God and obeying the law is obvious here. Knowledge of God is not merely knowing about God; it is being properly related to him in love and obedience. Israel did not need more information about God but to respond fully to what was known. Even more important than obedience is fellowship. "In the Old Testament knowledge is living in a close relationship with something or somebody, such a relationship as to cause what may be called communion."[14]

Obedience to the law, for Hosea and the prophets, is not a sterile legalism but a vital, vibrant fellowship. In response to what God had done in the Exodus and after, they pledged loyalty to his will as revealed in the law. In refusing to respond, Israel broke fellowship with God as Gomer had with Hosea.[15] Sin shattered the communion, and only repentance could restore it:

Their deeds do not permit them
   to return to their God.
For the spirit of harlotry is within them,
   and they know not the Lord. (5:4)

Empty ritual cannot substitute for cordial communion:

For I desire steadfast love and not sacrifice,
   the knowledge of God, rather than burnt offerings. (6:6)

Against the present apostasy, Hosea sees a brighter day, when God in grace will again take Israel to wife. The consummation will be renewed communion:

I will betroth you to me in faithfulness;
   and you shall know the Lord. (2:20)

Lack of the knowledge of God is the root of all other sin. In depicting Israel's relationship with God, Hosea prepares for Jeremiah (e.g., Jer. 4:22) and the New Testament. His teachings provide rich meaning for certain statements

---

14. T.C. Vriezen, An Outline of Old Testament Theology, 2nd ed. (Newton Centre, Mass: 1970), p. 154. The relationship between knowledge and communion is illustrated in the use of "to know" (yāda') for sexual intercourse (e.g., Gen. 4:1).

15. Citing H.B. Huffmon, "The Treaty Background of Hebrew Yada'," BASOR 181 (1966): 31-37; and with S.B. Parker, "A Further Note on the Treaty Background of Hebrew Yada'," BASOR 184 (1966): 36-38, Brueggemann concludes: "It is now beyond dispute that 'know' means to acknowledge covenant loyalty and the accompanying demands"; The Land, p. 105 note 21. Lack of this knowledge is the root of all other sin.

of Christ: "All things have been delivered to me by my Father; and no one knows the Son except the Father, and no one knows the Father except the Son and anyone to whom the Son chooses to reveal him" (Matt. 11:27). And especially, "And this is eternal life, that they know thee the only true God, and Jesus Christ whom thou has sent" (John 17:3).[16]

Folly of Ingratitude. Perhaps more than any other prophet, Hosea recalls Israel's past as he speaks to their present.[17] Beginning with the Exodus, he traces God's care for his people and their rebellion against him. History, according to Hosea, is the story of God's graciousness and Israel's ingratitude.

> Like grapes in the wilderness,
>   I found Israel.
> Like the first fruit on the fig trees,
>   in its first season,
>   I saw your fathers.
> But they came to Baal-peor (cf. Num. 25:1-3),
>   and consecrated themselves to Baal,
>   and became detestable like the thing they loved. (9:10; see 12:13f.)

Israel's present conduct scarcely matches God's blessing upon them. Having spurned his grace in both past and present, they are ripe for judgment.

> I am the Lord your God
>   from the land of Egypt;
> You know no God but me,
>   and besides me there is no savior.
> It was I who knew you in the wilderness,
>   in the land of drought;
> but when they had fed to the full,
>   they were filled, and their heart was lifted up;
>   therefore they forgot me.
> So I will be to them like a bear robbed of her cubs.
>   I will tear open their breast,
> And there I will devour them like a lion,
>   as a wild beast would rend them.[18] (13:4-8)

Israel's failure to thank God properly is definitely linked to their idolatry. They credit the Baals for what God had done (2:8). Indeed, the more abundantly he blessed Israel, the more they pursued false gods:

---

16. See also 1 John 2:3-6 where love and obedience define knowing God.

17. His book abounds with references to Israel's antiquity: Jacob's exploits (12:3ff.); idolatry at Baal-peor (9:10; cf. Num. 25); terrible debauchery at Gibeah (9:9; 10:9; see Judg. 19:24-26); destruction of the cities of the plain (11:8; cf. Gen. 19:23-25); Achan's sin at Achor (2:15; cf. Josh. 7:24-26).

18. This is a powerful example of Hosea's literary ability. Combining tenderness with strength, Hosea gently rehearses God's care for Israel, then immediately lashes out with savage threats of judgment.

Israel is a luxuriant vine
   that yields its fruit.
The more his fruit increased
   the more altars he built;
as his country improved
   he improved his pillars. (10:1)

This sketch by Hosea is not unlike Paul's picture of pagan practices in Rom. 1:21: "for although they knew God they did not honor him as God or give thanks to him. . . ." Ingratitude toward God results either in idolatry or self-adulation. To fail to credit him means to attribute blessings incorrectly to some other source—or even to oneself. To do either denies God's sovereignty and grace.

Futility of Mere Religion. The prophets did not oppose Israel's formal religion (cult) in itself. When this religious structure served its true purpose in celebrating the mighty acts of God and reminding the people of their present obligation and future expectations, the prophets could give full support.[19]

But in Hosea's day the cult failed miserably to fulfill its purpose. The people were intensely religious. Feasts were kept judiciously (10:1), sacrifices and offerings burnt continually (5:6; 6:6), altars built in abundance (10:1). This outward show, however, masked an inward corruption of the worst kind.

The priests were a special target of Hosea's ire. They were as corrupt as the people they should have been helping (4:9). Having neglected their duty to teach the law, they, in a sense, were chiefly responsible for Israel's defection (4:4-9; 5:1f.). Their sacrifices and libations were meaningless because the terms of the covenant—righteousness and justice—were being ignored.

Pagan practices were observed side by side with divinely established forms of worship. Israel's faith, grounded in the redemptive experiences of the Exodus, had degenerated virtually to another fertility cult in which the Baals were thanked for the spring crops (2:11f.) and immorality was celebrated as a religious obligation (4:12-14). The people did not seek Yahweh's word, but were content to discern the future by magic (v. 12). Canaanite ritualistic orgies were performed by the Israelites, who wailed and gashed themselves (like the prophets of Baal contesting with Elijah's God on Mt. Carmel) to gain answers to their prayers (7:14; cf. 1 Kgs. 18:28). The drunken revelries (4:11) and criminal outbursts (v. 2; 6:7-9; 7:1) make the picture of religious failure bleak indeed.

Perhaps Hosea's simplest summary of Israel's sinful state is "Men kiss calves!" (13:2), illustrating graphically the abysmal depths to which God's covenant people descended by pouring out their love to metal images. In the name of God these people were denying and denouncing all that name stood for.

---

19. A helpful resume of the attitudes of Amos and Hosea to the cult is R. Vuilleumier, *La tradition cultuelle d'Israël dans la prophétie d'Amos et d'Osée.* Cahiers Théologiques 45 (1960).

God's Changeless Compassion. The dreary picture of decadence is neither Hosea's last nor best word. God's love for Israel is greater than their sin. Few Old Testament passages are more moving or profound than Hosea's description of God's compassion for Israel in 11:1-9. Hosea first pictures God complaining of Israel's failure to be a grateful son:

> When Israel was a child, I loved him,
>   and out of Egypt I called my son.
> The more I called them
>   the more they went from me;
> They kept sacrificing to the Baals,
>   and burning incense to idols.
> Yet it was I who taught Ephraim to walk,
>   I took him up in my arms;
>   but they did not know that I healed them.
> I led them with cords of compassion,
>   with the bands of love. . . . (11:1-4)

No rebellion can quench such love. The passage then shows how God's compassion triumphs over Ephraim's inconstancy:

> How can I give you up, O Ephraim!
>   How can I hand you over, O Israel!
>   . . . . . .
> My heart recoils within me,
>   my compassion grows warm and tender.
>
> I will not execute my fierce anger,
>   I will not again destroy Ephraim;
> for I am God and not man,
>   the Holy One in your midst,
>   and I will not come to destroy.[20]

"I am God and not man"—this is the secret of God's righteousness and love. He cannot stoop to the level of sin or corruption, and so cannot be fickle or inconstant. Free from human weaknesses and limitations, God's love abides despite rebellion and hostility. Of all the prophets, Hosea knew what it was to love, be sinned against, and go on loving; he was the best equipped to bring this message of "the quite irrational power of love as the ultimate basis of the covenant relationship."[21]

Hosea took a certain risk in couching the relationship between Yahweh and his people in terms of love. The Canaanite nature cult put great stress on

---

20. "To destroy" is based on a textual emendation. The text of Hosea apparently has suffered more than any other Old Testament book in editing and copying through the centuries. The classic textual study is H.S. Nyberg, *Studien zum Hoseabuche.* UUÅ (1935); see also Wolff, *Hosea.*

21. W. Eichrodt, *Theology* 1:251.

the erotic nature of the divine-human relationship and the role of physical love in maintaining the order of the universe. Hosea fended against the danger of misunderstanding by his studied insistence that God's love revealed itself first and best not in sexual terms, in the cycles of the seasons or spring fertility, but in the redemptive acts of the Exodus. Hosea was able to convey the warmth and vitality of God's love in his intimate communion with his people without contributing to this basic misunderstanding. He did this, in part, by depicting God as the father who cares for and educates his son (11:1-4) as well as the husband who draws back his wayward wife. More than passion is involved; there is the deliberate activity of God's will throughout Israel's history, itself a continuity of divine instruction and discipline. [22]

Hosea strikes a fine balance between love and law as the ground of Israel's relationship to Yahweh. For him the covenant religion can never be reduced to purely legal terms but involves a personal fellowship between God and Israel. Rather than opposing or criticizing the law, Hosea says much in its support (e.g., 4:6ff.; 8:12f.). He shows that behind and beneath the law lies love. Israel's response to God can never be merely formal obedience because God's overture came first not by law but by love. For Amos sin was the breaking of the covenant; but for Gomer's husband sin was the spurning of God's love.

This love, in Hosea, is never reduced to mere sentiment. His view of the holiness of God guards against this. In fact, few prophets sound the note of God's sharp anger as strongly. What seem almost contradictory emphases stand side by side—"I will love them no more" (9:15) and "I will love them freely" (14:4). Wrath and love, or "the wrath of love,"[23] are expressed clearly in God's willingness to woo his wicked wife Israel and yet punish the nation's wickedness. He loves and judges them simultaneously. Hosea makes no attempt to reconcile this seeming paradox, presenting it as part of the personality of God. At times he sees God virtually wrestling within himself, vexed by his people's rebellion, yet relentlessly drawn to them in love (11:8f.). [24]

Here Hosea doubtless reflects some of the struggle within his own breast as he ponders his relationship with Gomer. Revelation comes in many and strange ways, none more mysterious than that of God's intense feeling toward his people through a prophet's conflicting emotions toward a faithless yet beloved wife. This is enacted prophecy[25] at its highest Old Testament level. In a certain sense in the life of Hosea the word became flesh.

---

22. Ibid., 1:251f.
23. Ibid., 1:252.
24. J.M. Ward, *Hosea: A Theological Commentary* (New York: 1966), pp. 191-206, captures the power and poignancy of that struggle.
25. Sometimes called prophetic symbolism; the prophet demonstrates or acts out his message, and God uses the demonstration to fulfill the message. See also Childs, *Old Testament as Scripture*, pp. 381f.

FOR FURTHER READING

Andersen, F.I., and Freedman, D.N. *Hosea.* Anchor Bible. Garden City, N.Y.: 1980.
(A monumental and devout work that will influence future study of Hosea.)

Farr, G. "The Concept of Grace in the Book of Hosea." *ZAW* 70 (1958): 98-107.
(Comparison with Amos.)

McKenzie, J.L. "Knowledge of God in Hosea." *JBL* 74 (1955): 22-27. (Equates with the practice of traditional Hebrew morality.)

Morgan, G.C. *Hosea: The Heart and Holiness of God.* Repr. London: 1964. (Twelve sermons.)

Östborn, G. *Yahwe and Baal: Studies in the Book of Hosea and Related Documents.* Lund: 1956.

Snaith, N.H. *Mercy and Sacrifice: A Study of the Book of Hosea.* London: 1953.

CHAPTER 26

JONAH

IN all but one of the prophetic books, the major characteristic is the message of Yahweh to the prophet, and through the prophet to Israel.[1] The prophecy of Jonah is unique in that it is an account of what happened to a prophet and not a report of his message. Since this book was placed in the canon among the prophets, one may conclude that the story of what happened to Jonah *is* the message. And the story involves much more than the account of being swallowed by a fish.

STORY OF JONAH

Divine Command and Its Consequences. Jonah ben Amittai (Jonah 1:1) was a prophet who foretold the expansion of Israel in the days of Jeroboam II (2 Kgs. 14:25). There seems to be no good reason to assume that the story of Jonah concerns another prophet with the same name.[2] The book of Jonah tells nothing of his prophetic activity in Israel. It simply begins with the word of Yahweh: "Arise, go to Nineveh, that great city, and cry against it; for their wickedness has come up before me" (Jonah 1:2). But instead of going east toward Assyria, Jonah took a ship at Joppa that was bound for Tarshish—in the opposite direction,[3] "away from the presence of the Lord" (v. 3).

Yahweh stirred up a mighty storm, and the small ship was in danger of

---

1. Sometimes the message is addressed to a foreign nation, but it is hardly likely that it was delivered to, or even directly intended for, any other than Yahweh's people Israel.

2. To state that the story is told about a ninth-century prophet neither affirms nor denies its historicity (see below), nor does it establish a ninth-century date for its writing.

3. The location of Tarshish has been much debated and is still not certain. Whether in Spain (Tartessus; see Herodotus *History* iv.152), Sardinia, or elsewhere, it must have been on (or possibly beyond) the Mediterranean. See C.H. Gordon, "Tarshish," *IDB* 4:517f.; Josephus (*Ant.* ix.10.2 § 208) identified it with Tarsus in Cilicia.

breaking up. The pagan[4] sailors began to pray to their gods and to lighten the
ship by casting things overboard. The captain awakened Jonah, sleeping in the
inner part of the ship, and urged him to pray to his God. The sailors cast lots
to determine the blame for the angry seas, and the lot fell to Jonah. He confessed that he was trying to get away from Yahweh (v. 10) and urged them to
throw him into the sea (v. 12), but they were not willing. They attempted to
row back to land but could not, "for the sea grew more and more tempestuous
against them" (v. 13). Finally, they did throw Jonah overboard, "and the sea
ceased its raging" (v. 15).

Yahweh "appointed a great fish to swallow up Jonah; and Jonah was in the
belly of the fish three days and three nights" (v. 17). Then Yahweh spoke to
the fish, "and it vomited out Jonah upon the dry land" (2:10).[5]

Second Command and Results. Yahweh gave Jonah a second chance, again
commissioning him to go to Nineveh; this time Jonah went. The only words
of his prophetic message recorded are these: "Yet forty days, and Nineveh shall
be overthrown!" (3:4). But his preaching must have been with great conviction,
for "the people of Nineveh believed God; they proclaimed a fast, and put on
sackcloth, from the greatest of them to the least of them" (v. 5). News reached
"the king of Nineveh," who decreed a national fast, prayer to God, and turning
from evil (vv. 7f.). Yahweh saw how the people "turned from their evil way"
(v. 10), and he repented of what he said he would do to the city.

Jonah was greatly displeased and, indeed, angry. "Is this not what I said
when I was yet in my country?" he said to Yahweh. "This is why I made haste
to flee to Tarshish; for I knew that thou art a gracious God and merciful, slow
to anger, and abounding in steadfast love, and repentest of evil" (4:2). Then
Jonah set up a little hut outside the city, to see "what would become of the
city" (4:5). Yahweh appointed a plant, probably the castor oil plant (v. 6, RSV
mg.), which grew rapidly and sheltered Jonah from the blistering sun (v. 6).
But the next day, God appointed a worm which attacked the plant, and then
an east wind[6] that not only dried up the vegetation, but even affected Jonah,
so he begged God to let him die.

Conclusion of the Story. Jonah, who desperately tried to avoid going to
Nineveh to preach, and was angry because the Ninevites had repented of their

---

4. No doubt they were pagan (see 1:5). Probably many were Phoenicians, since at
that period most shipping on the Mediterranean was the province of Phoenician (or
Punic) merchants. When Solomon built his fleet at Ezion-geber on the Gulf of Aqaba,
Hiram of Tyre (1 Kgs. 9:12) staffed it with his servants, "men of ships, knowers of the
sea" (v. 27, lit.). The Hebrews faced life with their back to the sea: "east" was *miqqedem*
("before, in front") and "west" was *mě'āḥôr* ("from behind, in back"); see Isa. 9:11.
5. The traditional location, the "Gate of Jonah" near Iskanderun (Alexandretta)
in Turkey, has little to commend it. Josephus (*Ant.* ix.10.2 § 213) located this on the
Black (Euxine) Sea, which is certainly wrong. It is generally assumed that Jonah was
returned to land not far from where he started.
6. The hamsîn or sirocco; see p. 50, above.

Skin-covered boat used to transport materials on the Tigrus and Euphrates; relief from Sennacherib's palace at Nineveh (704-681 B.C.). (British Museum)

evil when he did preach to them, was deeply affected by the death of the plant—a plant for which he had done nothing. To this Yahweh said: "And should I not pity Nineveh, that great city, in which there are more than a hundred and twenty thousand persons who do not know their right hand from their left, and also much cattle?" (v. 11).

INTERPRETATION OF THE STORY

Former generations of biblical scholars in general understood the story of Jonah in a literal or historical sense. Modern scholars, for a variety of reasons, have been inclined to treat the story not as history but as myth, allegory, or parable.

The didactic quality of a story does not necessarily depend on its historicity. For example, the parables of Jesus have their intended teaching-value whether the events happened or not.[7] Whether or not the details of the parable of the

---

7. This does not mean "whether Jesus spoke them or not." The authority of these teachings depends on the historicity of Jesus and the Incarnation.

Good Samaritan (Luke 10:30-35) are historically accurate, or the event itself historical, the parable in any event makes its point. Likewise, the story of Jonah could have been told simply to get across a lesson. Other details must be examined in order to determine whether or not it was intended as a historical account.

Historical Interpretation. The surface indications of the story lead naturally to the historical interpretation. Jonah ben Amittai actually lived in the days of Jeroboam II (2 Kgs. 14:25). The story is introduced just as are prophecies in other books: "Now the word of the Lord came to Jonah . . ." (Jonah 1:1). The presentation is not in the form of a dream or a vision, but in a situation requiring Jonah to get up and go to Nineveh. The details of buying a ticket, boarding the ship, and the destination of the ship, as well as its port at the moment, appear to be historical data. The account of the storm, the sailors' reactions, their pagan practices, and even their eventual cries to Yahweh and sacrifices to him are told as historical details. There are a few difficulties to be considered later, but on the whole, this sounds like a historical account.

The introduction of the "great fish" (commonly called a "whale") suggests that this is no ordinary story, but another factor must be taken into consideration. Jesus used the story of Jonah in the belly of the fish for three days and nights as a "sign" of his own burial and (by implication) resurrection (Matt. 12:39f.).[8] It has been argued strenuously by those who hold to the historical interpretation of Jonah, that Jesus placed this story on the same historical level as his own resurrection. The alternate point also has been made, that if the Jonah story is not true, then the resurrection of Jesus cannot be defended—but this is false logic, for Jesus was using a simile built only on the positive and not concerned with the negative possibility.

Again, in connection with Jonah's visit to Nineveh, the words of Jesus must be considered: "The men of Nineveh will arise at the judgment with this generation and condemn it; for they repented at the preaching of Jonah, and behold, something greater than Jonah is here" (Matt. 12:41). In the same context, Jesus mentioned the visit of the queen of Sheba to Solomon, suggesting that the preaching of Jonah in Nineveh was on the same historical footing (Matt. 12:41f.; cf. Luke 11:29-32).

Those who reject the historical interpretation find several bases for challenging this position. First and foremost is the story of the "whale." A number of books bluntly state that a whale cannot swallow a man, although more recent works admit that there is a species of whale with a gullet large enough to accommodate a man. In any event, Jonah could not have survived for three days in the belly of the fish, because of both lack of oxygen and the action of the gastric fluids. Various replies have been written to such objections, including

---

8. Since he was to be in the heart of the earth for three days and nights, it is implied that Jesus would not be in the earth after that period.

accounts of persons who survived being swallowed by fish.[9] In fact, the arguments over 1:17 and 2:10 often have pushed the study of the message of Jonah into limbo.[10]

The objection sometimes is raised, that if Jonah had been swallowed, as written, and lived, he hardly would have composed a psalm while in the fish's belly (see 2:1-9). Such reasoning is unworthy. Those who raise the objection refuse to allow the author what they themselves attribute to him, artistic creativity. Surely Jonah prayed when he found himself in the belly of the fish! Accepted at face value, the story must have been written at a later time. Could not Jonah, writing later, have worked his prayer into poetic form?[11]

More cogent is the argument concerning Nineveh. According to 3:3, Nineveh was an exceedingly great city, about sixty miles in diameter, or perhaps in circumference.[12] The location of Nineveh is known, and the walls have been partially excavated, and it is not nearly that large. Some expositors therefore have interpreted the passage as referring to "Greater Nineveh," including surrounding cities.[13] G.A. Smith—well known as a careful critical scholar of Bible geography—was content to accept the sixty miles as referring to the circumference of the "district" of "greater Nineveh." But no available evidence indicates that such a "district" was ever a geographical or political entity.

The explicit verb used, "Now Nineveh was[14] an exceedingly great city," implies that the city no longer existed. If Jonah lived in the days of Jeroboam II (793-753), it is highly unlikely that he was still living to tell this story after the fall of Nineveh (612). But again, this may be a scribal addition or simply the idiom of the storyteller.

Much more serious is the argument that the details of Nineveh's repentance have no historical verisimilitude. In what language did Jonah preach? Had he miraculously learned Assyrian, or did the people miraculously understand Hebrew, or was this a miracle of glossolalia? What of the king's decree that even the herds and flocks should not feed or drink water? How could this be enforced on dumb brutes, and what would be its religious significance? Why dress the

---

9. See, among others, R.K. Harrison, *Introduction*, pp. 907f., and G.A. Archer, *Survey*, p. 302 note 8.

10. See G.A. Smith: "And this is the tragedy of the Book of Jonah, that a Book which is made the means of one of the most sublime revelations of truth in the Old Testament should be known to most only for its connection with a whale"; *The Book of the Twelve Prophets*. Expositor's Bible (1956) 4:679.

11. The Old Testament contains much evidence that poetic form was the more common form of prayer. There is little doubt that the Lord's Prayer is also in poetic form.

12. "Three days' journey in breadth" seems to refer to the distance across the city. A day's journey can be calculated at twenty or thirty miles.

13. Sometimes Gen. 10:12 is quoted: "that is the great city." Nineveh in that passage is joined with Rehoboth-Ir, Calah, and Resen. Smith takes Kuyunjik, Nimrud, Khorsabad, and Balawat as the four corners of the district; cf. *The Book of the Twelve* 4:531 note 3.

14. Jonah 3:3, *hāy^etā*. In such a clause, the verb "to be" is usually omitted unless necessary to give the tense.

animals in sackcloth? Furthermore, what evidence is there that Nineveh ever underwent such religious conversion? And when was the king of Assyria ever called "king of Nineveh" (3:6)? For such reasons, the historical nature of the account is strongly challenged. Those who defend the historicity of Jonah have sought to answer such objections point by point.[15] For the moment, judgment must be reserved.

Mythological, Allegorical, and Parabolic Interpretations. Grouping these interpretations is not to suggest that they are the same, but rather that they view the general intent of the book as something other than historical.

(1) Myth. Myth seeks to present truth about human experience or natural origins (usually involving the gods) in a form that purports to be historical. In ancient myths, the struggle of humanity against nature, or even of nature itself with its seasons of seedtime and harvest, may be portrayed as contests with a god or between gods. In ancient Canaan, Yamm (the Sea) was one of these gods, and a sea monster (here a great fish, but elsewhere Leviathan or Lothan) was a hostile force. The name "Nineveh" also has been compared with the word for "fish" (cuneiform *Ninā*). However, while elements in the story might be associated with mythic language, there is no clearly recognizable mythic plot.

(2) Allegory. In allegory, a story told to convey a message, each detail contributes to the whole. Thus in Jesus' parable of the wheat and weeds (Matt. 13:37-43), the sower, seed, field, wheat, weeds, enemy, harvest, and reapers all have symbolic meaning.[16] Likewise here, the name Jonah means "dove," a symbol of Israel (Hos. 11:11; Ps. 74:19). Other details are less obvious. Israel was disobedient and did not preach the truth to the gentile nations, symbolized by the attempt to sail to Tarshish; therefore Yahweh punished Israel with exile, symbolized by the swallowing up of Jonah. In the postexilic period, Israel only reluctantly witnessed to the gentiles, and never really understood the heart of Yahweh for the "Ninevites." The theory is ingenious, but hardly convincing. When compared with literary examples that are clearly allegories, the story of Jonah falls far short, since it contains no key to its own interpretation.

(3) Parable. The parable is a short story which symbolizes a moral or spiritual truth.[17] Unlike the allegory (with which it is often equated), it does not have meaning attached to every part. Thus Jonah, taken as a parable, sets forth the unwillingness of "Jonah" (whether a person, the people of Israel, or any other group hearing the story) to make the message of God known to "Nineveh," and Jonah's inability to understand the heart of Yahweh. Election

---

15. For a strong presentation of the traditional view, see Archer, *Survey*, pp. 295-303.

16. Jesus' parables are clearly parables and not allegories. However, this (and a few others) include allegorical details, hence its use here.

17. A parable may convey other categories of truth, but the definition here fits the biblical parable.

by Yahweh has become an end rather than a means, and the divine purpose, stated by Yahweh to Abram, "that in you all the nations of the world shall be blessed" (Gen. 12:3, RSV mg.), has been almost completely forgotten. The basic similarity of the allegorical and parabolic interpretations is obvious. The parabolic interpretation is not forced to find a meaning for each detail and therefore is preferable.

Which Interpretation is Correct? No simple solution exists. Adoption of the historical interpretation requires recognition that fully satisfactory answers to the questions raised are not available. Selection of parabolic or religious-fiction interpretation necessitates coming to grips with Jesus' use of Jonah in the Gospels.[18] Those who subscribe to the authority of the Lord's words cannot lightly dispose of them.

The motivation for one's choice of interpretation is of great significance. If one decides on the parabolic or symbolic interpretation simply because the miraculous element is offensive, then the decision is based on an a priori conclusion contrary to the biblical position. Yet it is entirely possible to decide on grounds of literary form that the book is intended as a parable or drama.

A firm principle in biblical study is that even in a clearly historical passage, the religious message is more important than the historical details.[19] The Bible is not simply a book to satisfy curiosity about peoples and events in the ancient Near East. It is inspired by God's Spirit, with doctrinal, spiritual, and moral intent.[20] As part of the biblical canon, Jonah must be studied with primary attention on the religious message. At this point the historical and parabolic interpretations come together, for either approach yields the same lesson: Yahweh is concerned about pagan peoples and commands his servants to proclaim his message to the nations.

RELIGIOUS CONTRIBUTIONS OF JONAH

Concept of God. The God of Jonah was, of course, Yahweh, the Lord, God of Israel. Apparently Jonah was among those who believed that Yahweh was limited to the land where his people dwelt, for he sought to get "away from the presence of the Lord" (1:3) by fleeing to Tarshish. Still, he believed that Yahweh

---

18. It has been suggested that since the Markan and Lukan parallels to Matt. 12:38-41 do not refer to the whale (Mark 8:12; Luke 11:29), Matt. 12:40 may be a Matthean interpolation. This appears to be an argument *in extremis*, but in any event the reference to Nineveh is found in the Lukan parallel (11:30), and what seems to be dominical support for the historicity of Jonah and his mission to Nineveh remains.

19. B.S. Childs bypasses as a theological issue the impasse regarding the historicity of the story by determining its canonical function as a "parable-like story," an analogy; *Old Testament as Scripture*, p. 426.

20. Paul described inspired Scripture as "profitable for teaching, for reproof, for correction, and for training in righteousness" (2 Tim. 3:16). In the context, there can be no doubt that he meant only religious or spiritual teaching.

was "the God of heaven, who made the sea and the dry land" (v. 9). He recognized a connection between his disobedience and the violent storm, and believed that if he were cast overboard the storm would cease (v. 12). He believed that Yahweh heard and answered prayer (2:2, 6) and so he turned to him in time of distress (v. 7). Jonah also knew that Yahweh was "a gracious God and merciful, slow to anger, and abounding in steadfast love" (4:2) and believed that Yahweh would display this grace even to the Ninevites if they repented (3:10; 4:2a).

The concept of God found in Jonah is to some scholars too advanced for the preexilic period, and they therefore date Jonah as postexilic, usually around the fourth century. But this fails to consider some elements of the story. By the fourth century, Assyria and Nineveh were long gone (Nineveh fell in 612), and no Israelite would have had the sharp animosity displayed by Jonah, for there were nearer and stronger enemies. Moreover, it is highly unlikely that a post-exilic Jew still would have harbored the notion that he could flee from the presence of Yahweh. Certainly a great lesson of the Exile was that Yahweh was not limited to Palestine. There is nothing in Jonah, except possibly one item, that cannot be found in the preexilic scriptures.[21]

Universality of Yahweh and His Redemptive Purpose. The one concept in Jonah not generally found in the preexilic prophets is that Yahweh would command his prophet to preach to a gentile nation and that Yahweh would spare that nation if it would repent. The preexilic prophets were so concerned with the Israelites' idolatry that they tended to isolate and insulate them. Elijah (1 Kgs. 17–19) and Elisha (2 Kgs. 8) visited foreign lands and performed certain ministries in them, and others prophesied concerning the surrounding nations, but none was sent to preach repentance except Jonah. Since this is not consistent with the biblical accounts of the preexilic prophets, some scholars conclude that Jonah must be a postexilic writing.

But this reasoning is not fully convincing. The mediatorial role of Israel is basic to the covenant concept, as has been seen repeatedly. True, the role had not been fulfilled, nor had it been stressed, but nevertheless the idea was already present. Even to Jonah the commission did not come as a new idea, but rather as one whose consequences he was unwilling to accept. Yahweh had to break through Jonah's antigentilism—which was not easy! But this is precisely what the Old Testament is all about. At various times and in various ways God made known his redemptive purpose to chosen individuals. That his elect people were to be a light to the gentiles was a truth he had revealed to Abram, Isaiah, Jonah, and others, yet it still had not broken through in Jesus' day (see Matt. 21:43). God's commission to Jonah is no more characteristic of fourth-century Jewish theology than it is of ninth- or eighth-century Israelite

---

21. Unless, of course, such ideas are excised from the preexilic prophets wherever found—but that is based on a priori grounds that amount to circular argument.

practices. The truth that Yahweh is God of all nations and desires all people to know him and his redemptive purpose was not arrived at by human reason. It was a revelation of God to his prophets, and it came to Jonah in a most unusual way.

FOR FURTHER READING

Aalders, G.C. *The Problem of the Book of Jonah.* London: 1948.

Burrows, M. "The Literary Category of the Book of Jonah." Pp. 80-107 in H.T. Frank and W.L. Reed, eds., *Translating and Understanding the Old Testament.* Nashville: 1970. (Treats book as satire; summary of recent scholarship.)

Childs, B.S. "Jonah: A Study in Old Testament Hermeneutics." *SJT* 11 (1958): 53-61.

Fretheim, T.E. "Jonah and Theodicy." *ZAW* 90 (1978): 227-237. (Jonah examines new aspect of theodicy: are God's *compassionate* actions just?)

Johnson, A.R. "Jonah ii, 3-10: A Study in Cultic Phantasy." Pp. 82-102 in H.H. Rowley, ed., *Studies in Old Testament Prophecy.* (Examines parallels of thought and language in Jonah and Psalms.)

Landes, G.M. "The Kerygma of the Book of Jonah." *Interp* 21 (1967): 3-31. (Contextual interpretation of psalm [Jon. 2:2-9].)

Wolff, H.W. *Jonah: Church in Revolt.* St. Louis: 1978. (Translation and exposition.)

CHAPTER 27

MICAH

ALTHOUGH Isaiah was to overshadow him in fighting the religious and social corruption of his countrymen, Micah proved a stout ally in prophesying the twin themes of doom and hope.[1] In contrast to Isaiah's massive, bold treatment of the tensions of the times, this younger contemporary offered a delicate and precise description. In a sense, the brevity of his work is compensated for by its intensity. Indeed, few passages from the prophets can match the fiery fury of his denunciations of Jerusalem's leaders in chs. 2 and 3.

INTRODUCTION

The Prophet. Most of what is known about Micah's life and background must be inferred from the contents and tone of his writings, for he offers almost no direct information about himself. His name is an abbreviation of Mîkayāhū "who is like Yahweh?" (note the Hebrew text of Jer. 26:18). Moresheth, his hometown, is probably Moresheth-gath (see Mic. 1:14), a Judean village about twenty-five miles southwest of Jerusalem near Philistine Gath. Several lines of evidence mark him as a country man, perhaps a peasant farmer. He attacks the crime and corruption of Jerusalem and Samaria as one not really at home in either capital (vv. 1, 5-9; 3:1-4, 12), and takes great pains to show how the impending judgment is to affect the villages and towns of his home region, southern Judah (1:10-16). His protests against oppression and exploitation of the poor and underprivileged mark the conviction and vehemence of one who identifies with their lot.

Isaiah and Micah are an interesting combination: a nobleman, confidant

---

1. The affinities of Micah to Isaiah may reflect more than a common date and place of ministry. The collecting and editing of Micah's prophecies may have been performed by the same group of disciples (the "Isaiah School") responsible for the final composition of Isaiah's words. B.S. Childs sees this process, in which Micah's words are edited in a framework theologically kin to Isaiah, as a step in the development of a canon of prophetic literature; *Old Testament as Scripture,* pp. 434-36, 438.

of kings and statesmen; and a peasant farmer or landowner, whose occasional visits to the capital had confirmed reports heard in his own town. While the two differ in background and breeding, their courage and conviction is the same. Both staunchly uphold the covenant, dedicatedly defending Israel's historic faith.

Like Amos (Amos 7:14f.) Micah does not seem to have been a professional prophet. In fact he criticizes unsparingly the prophets who "divine for money" (Mic. 3:11) or tailor their message according to how they are treated (v. 5), pointedly contrasting himself with them. His credential is the Spirit of the Lord, which gives him courage and strength to speak out forcefully and clearly (v. 8). This strong sense of call is vindicated in virtually every line. Fervently yet concisely he speaks to the issues of his day in terms of Israel's covenant

Spring Gihon, at the eastern end of the water tunnel constructed by Hezekiah, during whose reign Micah prophesied. (G. Nalbandian)

obligations. Behind the covenant, steadfast in spite of Israel's failure to maintain that bond, is the God of the covenant who yet will lead his people to future glory.

Date. The book's title (1:1) places Micah in the reigns of Jotham, Ahaz, and Hezekiah (*ca.* 735-700 B.C.). General consensus places at least vv. 2-9 before the destruction of Samaria in 721. The appeal of Jeremiah's supporters to the prophecy of Micah confirms the latter's connection with Hezekiah:

> And certain of the elders of the land arose and spoke to all the assembled people, saying, "Micah of Moresheth prophesied in the days of Hezekiah king of Judah. . . ." (Jer. 26:17f.)

Exact dates for other parts of the prophecy are difficult to determine. Some hold that the judgment on Judah depicted in 1:10-16 refers to Sennacherib's invasion in 701, but A. Bentzen, among others, dates it before 711, claiming that Gath was not yet under Assyrian domination.[2] The reference to human sacrifice (6:7) often is taken to reflect Manasseh's terrifying reign when the rite was common practice, but 2 Kgs. 16:3 attributes it to Ahaz as well.

In short, there is no reason to question and much evidence to support the tradition that Micah, like Isaiah, prophesied just before and after the fall of the northern kingdom. The threat of doom hanging over Jerusalem (see 3:12) and the references to Assyria as the prime national enemy (5:5f. [MT 4f.]) suggest the period between the fall of Samaria in 721 and the miraculous rout in 701 of Sennacherib's army, which had laid siege to Jerusalem. The affinities in theme and emphasis to Isaiah, especially in the peace oracle in 4:1-4 (see Isa. 2:2-4), support this conclusion.

Unity. While chs. 1–3 have been accepted almost universally as genuine oracles of Micah,[3] considerable question has arisen over dating the speeches in chs. 4–7. The reference to Babylon, for instance, has been interpreted as indicating a later origin of the oracles in 4:6-8, 9-13. However, Hezekiah's alliance with Merodach-baladan (2 Kgs. 20:12-19) indicates that the ancient city was prominent in Micah's day, even though its heyday was not to come for nearly a century.

During the past century or so biblical scholars have tended to limit the great prophets' role to preaching doom. Consequently, the notes of hope which frequently accompany those passages of judgment were commonly considered to be later, usually postexilic, additions not the work of the original prophets. For Micah, it has been fashionable to relegate the passages regarding Judah's future hope (e.g., 2:12f.; 4:1-4; esp. 7:8-20) to an exilic or postexilic editor.[4]

---

2. *Introduction* 2:147.

3. Many scholars have viewed 2:12f. as out of place in the midst of otherwise unrelieved gloom; however, see L.C. Allen, *The Books of Joel, Obadiah, Jonah, and Micah*. NICOT (Grand Rapids: 1976), p. 242, for a persuasive argument for Mican authorship of those verses.

4. E.g., C. Kuhl, by no means the most radical critic, claims that in the last four chapters "have been inserted a number of prophecies of salvation from exilic and post-

Happily, in recent years emphasis has turned to the element of future deliverance. A. Kapelrud summarizes the dual aspect of the prophetic oracles— doom and hope:

> The stress may have been laid on doom and imminent destruction; but there is good reason to believe that though such oracles predominated they were not the last word of the prophets. They may have been reticent in their promises for the future, because the situation usually gave them more occasion to underline the gloomy side of their message.[5]

Though allowing for an editorial process, Kapelrud objects, with good reason, to the idea that the editors composed and inserted new passages in the writings of the prophet.

After analyzing various eschatological passages which some have denied to Micah, Kapelrud concludes: "We cannot a priori say that chs. iv-v and vii have such contents that they must necessarily be considered as additions to the words of the prophet."[6]

It is indeed hazardous to approach these writings with set ideas. As Christ said: "The Spirit [or wind] blows where it wills" (John 3:8). The prophets were creative thinkers, inspired by the Spirit of the Lord and under control of the word which they received—a word of both judgment and grace.[7]

MESSAGE

Structure. The double note of judgment and grace gives the book its basic structure, which reflects a thematic rather than chronological order of the oracles. When they were uttered historically is not so important to the arrangement as what they say.

Some divide the book into two parts, each with an oracle of doom followed by a message of hope:

Part One
Messages of doom (1:2–3:12)
(brief glimmer of hope in 2:12f.)
Messages of hope (chs. 4–5)

---

exilic times" and that "the end of the book dates from the exilic or early post-exilic period"; *The Old Testament: Its Origins and Composition*, p. 214. See also A. Weiser, who is a bit more restrained in his judgment of the book's unity: ". . . no convincing proof can indeed be adduced either for or against the authenticity of the oracles in chapters 4–7. On the other hand the prophetic liturgy in 7:8-20 must evidently be taken out of Micah's time" and assigned to the postexilic period; *Old Testament*, pp. 254f.

5. "Eschatology in the Book of Micah," *VT* 11 (1961): 394.
6. *Ibid.*, p. 405. In contrast to Kapelrud's caution, J.L. Mays takes an extreme position: "Micah's sayings are found only in the first three chapters"; *Micah.* OTL (Philadelphia: 1976), p. 13.
7. Note the soundly cautious conclusion of G.W. Anderson: "When we consider the variety of denunciation and promise found in the teaching of other prophets, such as Micah's contemporaries, Hosea and Isaiah, it is unrealistic to claim that a prophet could not predict severe punishment . . . and also, at some other stage in his ministry, promise restoration"; *A Critical Introduction to the Old Testament*, p. 156. For a thorough discussion see K. Jeppesen, "New Aspects of Micah Research," *JSOT* 8 (1978): 3-32.

Part Two
  Messages of doom (6:1–7:7)
  Messages of hope (7:8-20)[8]

A somewhat more satisfactory, though more complicated, analysis is the three-part division proposed by L.C. Allen:[9]

Part One (1:2–2:13)	
Long doom	(1:2–2:11)
Short hope[10]	(2:12f.)
Part Two (chs. 3–5)	
Long doom	(ch. 3)
Short hope	(4:1-5)
. . . .	
Hope for remnant in distress	(vv. 6-8)
Long distress; short hope	(vv. 9f.)
Short distress; long hope	(vv. 11-13)
Short distress; longer hope	(5:1-6 [MT 4:14–5:5])
Hope for remnant in distress	(vv. 7-9 [MT 6-8])
. . . .	
Long doom	(vv. 10-14 [MT 9-13])
Short hope	(v. 15 [MT 14])
Part Three (chs. 6–7)	
Long doom	(6:1–7:7)
Short hope	(7:8-20)

This arrangement does not seem accidental but was probably a deliberate attempt by Micah or his disciples to underscore the twofold nature of his prophecy, the concept of the remnant to be rescued, and the central hope of messianic deliverance (5:1-6 [MT 4:14–5:5]).

First Messages of Doom (1:2–2:11). Following a solemn introductory announcement of judgment in which all people are summoned before the bar of justice (1:2-4), both capitals are indicted as sources of the pollution having contaminated the nation. The judgment on Samaria is spelled out in detail

---

8. See Mays, *Micah*, pp. 4-12, 23-33. Childs rightly criticizes Mays for arguing that the basic message of Part One (chs. 1–5) is Yahweh's lordship over the nations, while Part Two (chs. 6–7) deals with his lordship over Israel. Though the nations surely are included in Micah's hope (4:1-4), the bulk of the oracles, esp. in chs. 1–3, is directed to Israel; *Old Testament as Scripture*, p. 432. J.A. Soggin finds a similar structure but describes it as four parts: "chs. 1–3, threats; chs. 4–5, promises; ch. 6:1–7:6, further threats; ch. 7:7-20, new promises"; *Introduction*, p. 271.

9. *Micah*, p. 260; he acknowledges his debt to E. Nielsen, *Oral Tradition*. SBT 11 (Chicago: 1954); B. Renaud, *Structure et attaches littéraires de Michée IV-V* (Paris: 1964); and J.T. Willis, "The Structure of the Book of Micah," *Svensk Exegetisk Årsbok* 34 (1969): 5-42.

10. "Long" and "short" refer to the length of the passage dealing with doom, distress, or hope.

(vv. 5-9). Then, in concise, almost telegraphic, phrases, Judah's doom is described in its impact on the towns and villages of the hill country and lowlands (vv. 10-16). Scarcely any prophetic passage can match this sustained series of wordplays, which English translations cannot possibly transmit, and the cryptic allusions to the various towns make interpretation difficult. Perhaps rather than try to determine historic situations one should try to capture the mood of desperate weeping, shameful mourning, and shroudlike despair to fall upon the whole land when judgment strikes.[11] The capitals may be the source and center of evil, but its impact has crept to the furthest reaches of the land.

Next Micah, employing a woe oracle, furiously attacks the sins which made the judgment necessary. Like Amos (e.g., 4:1; 5:10-12) he was incensed at the high-handed and heartless oppression of the underprivileged poor by the rich upper class (2:1-5, 8f.). And like Isaiah (e.g., 30:10f.; cf. Amos 2:12), Micah denounced Israel's calloused resistance to the prophetic word, especially when it foreboded doom (2:6-11).

First Hint of Hope (2:12f.). This oracle of salvation is a chink of light in the book's first three chapters. It is placed here not because Micah preached doom and hope simultaneously—which could only have confused his audience—but because those who preserved and edited his utterances wanted to stress that judgment was never the Lord's last word for the covenant people.

The probable context for this promise of divine deliverance is God's victory over Sennacherib and his Assyrian army in 701. Note the similarity between these verses and Isaiah's prediction of the rescue of a remnant (2 Kgs. 19:30-34; cf. Isa. 37:31-34). Both Micah and Isaiah foresaw a time when a beleaguered group of survivors would take refuge in Jerusalem and be held virtual captives there by a foreign invader, finally to be released by the power of Yahweh, their king, to return to their cities and towns—perhaps those so savagely assaulted in 1:10-16.

Second Message of Doom (ch. 3). To Micah Judah's leadership had collapsed completely. Far from defending the covenant, they had become cannibal-like in exploiting the wretched peasant class, neglected by all but a few prophets (3:1-4). With a hostility akin to contempt, Micah, as God's true messenger (v. 8), singles out particularly the false prophets (vv. 5-7, 11). These professionals had lost all sense of true mission, offering messages both empty and false. When the stipend was to their liking, they spoke optimistically; when it was not, they prophesied harsh things. Rather than the word from God, reward from their hearers determined what they said. Lacking both courage and insight, they vainly trusted in the security of God's presence in the temple, unaware that this covenant symbol would itself be leveled by God (v. 12).

---

11. Two possible occasions, both Assyrian invasions, have been suggested for this picture of judgment on southwest Judah: the campaigns of Sargon II against the Philistines (720 or 714-711) and the ravaging sieges of Sennacherib (701).

Second Message of Hope (4:1–5:15 [MT 14]). From the bleak present of religious and social degeneracy, the prophet looks to a brighter future in which the covenant ideal would be fully realized. Ch. 4 gives Micah's picture of the messianic kingdom; ch. 5, his portrait of the messianic king. The contrast between the prophet's day and the latter days (4:1) is apparent in almost every line.

(1) Messianic kingdom (ch. 4). The centrality of the temple (v. 1), the universal rule of God (v. 2), unparalleled peace (v. 3), unbroken prosperity and security (v. 4), and unerring devotion to God (v. 5) are some of the chief characteristics of Israel's brilliant future. Vv. 1-3 seem to have been a song familiar to both Isaiah and Micah, who probably borrowed it from a common source, most likely the temple services (see Pss. 46, 48, 76). V. 4 is Micah's addition, perhaps based on concern for his rural countrymen whose land was being savagely snatched away:

> but they shall sit every man under his vine and under his fig tree,
>   and none shall make them afraid.

His compassion for the hapless members of his society is revealed again in his picture of the prominent role of the outcast and lame in the new era (vv. 6f.).

The great day to come involved not only a return to the covenant faith but a revival of the political splendor of David's time (4:8). After a period of exile (vv. 9f.), Judah would be regathered to a place of prominence over other nations. Once again would come holy war, and Israel would be an instrument of judgment on the other nations (vv. 11-13; cf. Ps. 2).

(2) Messianic king (5:1-15 [MT 4:14–5:14]). Following Isaiah's lead Micah looks forward to the rule of a true son of David who will embody the ideal features of his ancient ancestor. The birthplace in Bethlehem is mentioned (v. 2 [MT 1]) to stress the simple and humble origin of both David and his future successor, who will be a true shepherd of the people (v. 4 [MT 3]). The marvel of this familiar prophecy is not so much that Micah mentions Bethlehem, but rather that the sovereign Lord saw to it that the Christ was born there despite the fact that his family home was in Nazareth (Luke 2:1-20).

Israel's future victory is said to be over Assyria (5:5f. [MT 4f.]), which had been the dominant enemy for a century and a half. Characteristically, the prophets do not predict time elements (exceptions are Jeremiah's seventy years of exile and Daniel's seventy weeks), seeing the what of the future but not always the when. Assyria, then, stands for any nation that opposes God's people. Judah ultimately will gain supremacy not because of their might but because of their God (vv. 7-15 [MT 6-14]).

Third Message of Doom (6:1–7:7). This section, like some other judgment speeches, begins with the word "hear" (see 1:2; 3:1, 9; 6:9; Amos 3:1; 4:1; 5:1). The scene is a courtroom or, more accurately, the city gate, where most litigation took place. The mountains are called as witnesses to the controversy between the Lord and his people.[12] Then, in true prophetic fashion, God's mighty and gracious deeds in the Exodus are rehearsed as evidence for his faithfulness to his people (6:3-5). God assumes a triple role in the lawsuit as plaintiff, prosecutor, and judge. In response, the nation, personified as an individual, asks how it may atone for its disobedience:

> Will the Lord be pleased with thousands of rams,
>   with ten thousands of rivers of oil?
> Shall I give my first-born for my transgression,
>   the fruit of my body for the sin of my soul? (v. 7)

But God wanted more than even the most costly ritual obedience. The prophetic answer is a classic expression of the ethical and spiritual aspects of true covenant faith: upright conduct; compassion, especially to the weak and poor; devout obedience to and fellowship with God (v. 8).

In the next oracle, a judgment speech (vv. 9-16), God's indictment becomes more specific. Violence, deception, crooked business practices, and other unrighteous and unjust deeds will bring desolation and frustration upon the land.[13] The reference to Omri and Ahab may indicate that this oracle was uttered before the fall of Israel in 721 or that the same kinds of corruption which destroyed the northern kingdom had spread to Judah (v. 16).

The picture of treachery and oppression concludes in 7:1-7, actually a psalm of individual complaint. Distressed, almost undone, by the degradation of his countrymen, and vexed by the total collapse of personal and social values (vv. 5f.), Micah affirms his confidence in the redeeming God who alone is ultimately dependable (v. 7).[14]

Third Word of Hope (7:8-20). Prominent here is not the return or repentance of the people but the intervention of God. It is he who brings light and executes judgment (vv. 8f.), puts to shame the enemy who had mocked Israel in their weakness (vv. 10, 16f.), and returns to shepherd his people as in days of old (vv. 14f.). Micah closes with a reminder not of Israel's uniqueness but of God's. He is the hero of redemption's story—the pardoning, compassionate, faithful God:

---

12. Hittite legal documents, especially treaty-forms of covenants, begin with summoning the gods as witnesses. Rejecting this polytheism, Old Testament court scenes call on elements of creation; e.g.:

> Hear, O heavens, and give ear, O earth;
> for the Lord has spoken (Isa. 1:2).

13. Note the "therefore" (v. 13) which regularly introduces announcements of intense judgment (1:14; 2:3, 5; 3:12; cf. Amos 3:11; 4:12; 5:16).

14. B. Reicke suggests that the "I" in vv. 1-10 is a representative of the nation, perhaps a royal representative, who leads the people in a liturgical ritual used in the autumn festival which included the Day of Atonement; "Liturgical Traditions in Mic. 7," *HTR* 60 (1967): 349-367.

Who is a God like thee, pardoning iniquity
and passing over transgression
for the remnant of his inheritance?
. . . . . .
Thou wilt show faithfulness to Jacob
and steadfast love to Abraham,
as thou hast sworn to our fathers
from the days of old. (vv. 18, 20)

The literary form of vv. 8-20 seems to continue the liturgical pattern of vv. 1-7:

vv. 8-10—confession of confidence in Yahweh's rescue (pronounced by a representative of the people)

vv. 11-13—promise of restoration (salvation speech) for Israel and judgment on the nations (probably by a prophet in the temple)

v. 14—prayer for God's blessing (by the people)

v. 15—promise of divine deliverance as a new Exodus (probably by a prophet)

vv. 16f.—elaboration of that promise (salvation speech): dismay of the nations and their subsequent fear of Yahweh

vv. 18-20—hymn of praise to Yahweh for his unique forgiveness and unbroken faithfulness (by the congregation)

This liturgical pattern points to the influence of Israel's worship on the prophetic writings. The prophets denounced the laxity of public worship (e.g., Amos 5:21-24) only because they believed so deeply in it as a necessary expression of covenant commitment. But even more, the pattern of confession, prayer, hymn, and prophetic response in ch. 7 may indicate that the prophets' words influenced the form and content of Israel's worship and thus contributed to its renewal. If so, Micah's lines well may have been repeated as part of the temple liturgy long after his passing—a witness that the final purpose of all God's words to his people is not information but celebration of his grace and goodness, in worship and obedience.[15]

FOR FURTHER READING

Smith, L.P. "The Book of Micah." *Interp* 6 (1952): 210-227. (Good concise survey.)

Snaith, N.H. *Amos, Hosea and Micah.* London: 1956. Pp. 83-111. (Exegetical and expository commentary.)

Wolff, H.W. *Micah the Prophet.* Trans. R.D. Gehrke. Philadelphia: 1981. (Exposition and modern applications.)

van der Woude, A.S. "Micah in Dispute with the Pseudo-prophets." *VT* 19 (1969): 244-260.

---

15. On the importance of liturgical influence for Micah's role in the canon, see Childs, *Old Testament as Scripture*, pp. 437, 439.

CHAPTER 28

ISAIAH: BACKGROUND

ISAIAH is one of the largest books in the canon—along with Psalms and Jeremiah—and a very important book. As a measure of its importance, the remains of no less than fifteen manuscripts of Isaiah have been identified among the Dead Sea scrolls, making it second only to Deuteronomy in this regard. Moreover, Isaiah greatly influenced John the Baptist, Jesus, and certainly the New Testament writers, whose works include 411 quotations from Isaiah.[1] Analysis of the number of books about Isaiah or the size of articles devoted to the book in Bible dictionaries or encyclopedias will underscore its importance. Having admitted that since (as he contends) only chs. 1–39 can be attributed to Isaiah "his status may seem less than it was," C.R. North remarks that "he must have been far and away the greatest man of his time."[2] Certainly the measure of the man has been determined largely by the measure of his work, which has been called, among many superlatives, the greatest book in the Old Testament.

The Prophet. Before discussing the prophet and his work, it is necessary to define the basis for the statements to be made. One serious weakness of some modern scholarship has been to cite the almost universally recognized greatness of Isaiah—which is derived from the entire book—while denying that much of the book, including the magnificent chapters in the second part, comes from the same prophet. The view taken here, to be defended below, sees only one Isaiah, who was responsible for, although not necessarily the final author or editor of, the entire work. Only a tremendous figure could have produced a work with such immense influences, and the only known figure of such stature in the history of the prophets is Isaiah.

Isaiah ben Amoz (to be distinguished from the prophet Amos) was a Ju-

---

1. As a means of comparison, these quotations account for 9¾ columns in the United Bible Societies' *Greek New Testament*, compared to 9½ columns for quotations from Psalms and 5¾ each for Genesis and Exodus.
2. "Isaiah," *IDB* 2:733.

dean, probably a Jerusalemite, whose ministry extended from the year of Uz-ziah's death (740 B.C.; cf. 6:1) through the reigns of Jotham, Ahaz, and Hezekiah (certainly to 701), and according to tradition, which finds some support in the prophecy itself, into the reign of Manasseh (696-642). Tradition also records that Isaiah was a cousin of Uzziah or a nephew of Amaziah (Talmud *Meg*. 10b), born in or near Jerusalem. Modern scholars call this "simply a guess,"[3] but Isaiah's ready access to king (7:3) and priest (8:2) lend support to the tradition. He was married to a prophetess and had two sons (7:3; 8:3); according to Jewish tradition, the second son was born of a second marriage to a "virgin" (see 7:14; RSV "young woman"). Another tradition reports that Isaiah was martyred in Manasseh's day by being sawed in two (Assumption of Isaiah, possibly the basis for Heb. 11:37). Thus Isaiah's ministry extended over a period of at least forty years (740-701), and possibly more, since Hezekiah's death did not occur until 687 and it is doubtful that the coregent Manasseh would have dared to martyr Isaiah while Hezekiah was still alive.

The prophet clearly felt a sense of mission resulting from his divine call (6:8-10). Despite a previous sense of unworthiness, prompted by the vision, and his description as "a man of unclean lips" (v. 5), he believed that Yahweh had cleansed him in preparation for his work (v. 7). His mission was difficult, and he stood in awe before the nature and extent of it (vv. 11-13). The names he gave his sons—Shear-jashub "a remnant will return" and particularly that of the younger, Maher-shalal-hash-baz "speed spoil, hasten prey"[4]—are indic-ative of his mission. A very close relationship exists, as will be seen, between these names and the message given to Isaiah in his call (vv. 11-13).

According to 2 Chr. 26:22, Isaiah ben Amoz had written the "acts" of Uzziah, implying that he was the scribe or keeper of the official chronicle of that king. The prophecy implies that Isaiah moved easily in official circles and was close to the kings (see 7:3; 8:2; 36:1–38:8, 21f. par. 2 Kgs. 18:3–20:19). Such a position would satisfactorily explain Isaiah's knowledge of world affairs.[5]

The Times. The chapters on Amos, Hosea, and Micah already have shown something of the national and international situation. For at least part of his ministry Isaiah was contemporary with these prophets. Although his call came in the year that Uzziah died, one may assume from 2 Chr. 26:22 that he had been active in the court for at least a few years prior to that date. If the record of Sennacherib's death (Isa. 37:38) is accepted as coming from Isaiah's pen, this would mean that his court life and prophetic ministry extended from *ca.* 745 to *ca.* 680. But even cutting this down to "the last four and a half decades

---

3. O. Eissfeldt, *Old Testament*, p. 305.
4. The verbs are imperatives and not imperfects, as RSV mg. "The spoil speeds, the prey hastes."
5. See W. S. LaSor, *Great Personalities of the Old Testament* (Westwood, N.J.: 1959), pp. 136-143; North, *IDB* 2:733.

of the eighth century" as does O. Eissfeldt, one would have to agree that they "were filled with the most momentous events, more so than almost any other period of Israelite history."[6]

Tiglath-pileser came to the Assyrian throne in 745, and by 740 had conquered all of northern Syria. In 738 he subjugated the Aramean city-state of Hamath and forced other small kingdoms to pay tribute to escape the same fate. Included in this group were Israel under Menahem (2 Kgs. 15:19f.), and one Azriyau of Ya'udi, taken by some to be Azariah (Uzziah) of Judah.[7] In 734 Tiglath-pileser led an expedition to the Philistine territory and set up a base of operations at the River of Egypt (Wâdī el-'Arîsh). A number of small states allied against him in the so-called Syro-Ephraimite war (733). Israel participated in this war, but Ahaz of Judah refused; hence the coalition turned against him, planning to overthrow the Davidic dynasty and put someone on the throne who would join the alliance (2 Kgs. 15:37; 16:5; Isa. 7:1). Rejecting Isaiah's advice, Ahaz turned to Assyria for help (2 Kgs. 16:7-9). Tiglath-pileser invaded the upper Jordan region, took Gilead and Galilee, and carried off many of the Israelites to Assyria, in line with his policy of displacing peoples (15:29). Assyria was now almost at the borders of Judah.

About this time Pekah of Israel was overthrown, and his successor Hoshea paid tribute to Tiglath-pileser after the Assyrian king had devastated Damascus terribly (732). Tiglath-pileser died in 727, and soon thereafter Hoshea refused to pay tribute to the successor Shalmaneser. Egypt seems to have been implicated in this action (2 Kgs. 17:4). Assyria moved against Israel and seized the king and his land, but was unable to take Samaria the capital. After a three-year siege Samaria fell (721), either to Shalmaneser or his successor Sargon II (who claimed the victory), and the rest of the Israelites were carried into captivity. The land was resettled by captives from other lands, including Babylonians (v. 24), which may explain the intimate knowledge that Isaiah and other prophets had of Babylon. With the fall of the northern kingdom, Assyria extended to the northern boundary of Judah, a fact reflected in the sense of crisis and imminent doom found in Isaiah.

In 720 some of the city-states in Syria and Palestine rebelled but were suppressed. Gaza tried to revolt with the help of Sib'u of Egypt. In the battle that ensued, Assyrian forces drove the Egyptians back into their own land, leaving Judah practically an island. In 716 Ahaz died, and Hezekiah (who had acted as coregent for twelve years) succeeded him. In 714 the Twenty-fifth (Ethiopian) Dynasty came into power in Egypt (possibly reflected in Isa. 18:1-6). In 713-711 an anti-Assyrian uprising occurred at Ashdod, in which Edom, Moab, and Judah participated. Sargon of Assyria sent his Turtan ("second") to

---

6. Eissfeldt, *Old Testament*, p. 305.
7. Others understand this to refer to the city-state of Ya'ud (Sam'al) in the Karasu valley of northern Syria. It is most difficult to see how it could have been Judah, as M. Noth admits; *History*, p. 257 note 3.

Deportees from Ekron with Assyrian escort, depicted on seventh-century relief from Nineveh. (Louvre; photo W.S. LaSor)

Ashdod (ch. 20), and Ashdod and Gath became an Assyrian province. Judah was losing territory.

Sargon died in 705, setting off an immediate rash of revolts against Assyria, including Hezekiah's effort (2 Kgs. 18:4), which was doubtless encouraged by Egypt (cf. Isa. 30:1-5; 31:1-3). Merodach-baladan led a revolt in Babylon, and most likely sent envoys to Hezekiah to lay the groundwork for a two-pronged revolt or attack (2 Kgs. 20:12-19; Isa. 39:1-4). Sennacherib of Assyria was busy stamping out revolt and could not focus on Judah until 701. On that campaign he crushed Sidon, and caused Ashdod, Ammon, Moab, and Edom to pay tribute. He also subjugated Ashkelon and Ekron and was victorious over Egyptian forces under Tirhakah at Eltekeh.[8] Lachish was besieged, Hezekiah was

---

8. Whether this was in 701 or 687 has been much debated; see L.L. Honor, *Sennacherib's Invasion of Palestine* (New York: 1926); J. Bright, *History*, pp. 298-309.

"shut up like a bird in a cage"[9] and forced to pay tribute to Sennacherib (2 Kgs. 18:13-16). More of his land was taken and given to Philistine kings. According to some scholars, only Jerusalem was left of the southern kingdom; if so, much of the land appears to have been regained later.

The history of the times is so interwoven with Isaiah's prophecy that the prophecy cannot be understood without a knowledge of the events. Hence Eissfeldt says that Isaiah's message "remains unintelligible without an exact knowledge of contemporary history."[10]

The Prophecy. Not until the rise of modern criticism was any indication given that the book of Isaiah existed in two or more parts. The LXX (third century) gives no evidence of "First" and "Second" Isaiah, although it does divide other books (e.g., Samuel, Kings, Chronicles). The complete Isaiah manuscript found among the Dead Sea scrolls (1QIsa^a) makes not the slightest break at the end of ch. 39; rather, 40:1 is the very last line of the thirty-second column, with no indentation or any unusual space at the end of the preceding line.[11] In the Jewish count of canonical books, Isaiah was always counted as one book. Therefore, the book will be studied here as a single work.

On the basis of content, the book breaks into two great parts, which can be further subdivided. Some find a "historical interlude" between the two parts.

Part One: Judgment (chs. 1–35)
　Judah's sins (chs. 1–12)
　　Arraignment (ch. 1)
　　Jerusalem: Yahweh's and Israel's contrasted (chs. 2–4)
　　Song of the Vineyard (ch. 5)
　　Isaiah's vision and commission (ch. 6)
　　Immanuel: the sign to Ahaz (chs. 7–8)
　　Prince of Peace (9:1-7 [MT 8:23–9:6])
　　Yahweh's anger; Assyria his rod (9:8 [MT 9:7]–10:34)
　　Future hope: the Branch (ch. 11)
　　Song of thanksgiving (ch. 12)
　"Burdens" of judgment (chs. 13–23)
　　Burden concerning Babylon (13:1–14:27)
　　Burdens concerning Philistia, Moab, Damascus, Cush, Egypt,
　　　the wilderness of the west, and Tyre (14:28–23:18)
　Yahweh's purpose in judgment (chs. 24–27)
　　Judgment on the nations (ch. 24)
　　Salvation of Yahweh's people (ch. 25)
　　Song of trust (ch. 26)
　　Deliverance of Israel (ch. 27)

---

9. *ARAB* 2:240; *ANET*, p. 288.
10. *Old Testament*, p. 305; cf. Noth, *History*, pp. 257-269.
11. However, a space of three lines at the bottom of col. 27 does separate ch. 33 from 34.

Warning against humanistic efforts to save (chs. 28–35)
    Ephraim a warning to Jerusalem (ch. 28)
    Hypocrisy of Zion (ch. 29)
    Reliance on Egypt of no avail (chs. 30–32)
    Salvation from Yahweh (ch. 33)
    Yahweh's day of vengeance (ch. 34)
    Zion's blessed future (ch. 35)
Historical interlude (chs. 36–39)
    Sennacherib's invasion and failure (36:1–37:20)
    Isaiah's message (37:21-38)
    Hezekiah's illness (ch. 38)
    Envoys from the king of Babylon (ch. 39)
Part Two: Comfort (chs. 40–66)
  Deliverance (chs. 40–48)
    Comfort from Yahweh (chs. 40–41)
    Yahweh's servant (ch. 42)
    Yahweh the divine redeemer (ch. 43)
    Idols no gods (ch. 44)
    Cyrus, Yahweh's anointed, but Yahweh supreme (ch. 45)
    Judgment on Babylon (chs. 46–47)
    Israel's lack of faith rebuked (ch. 48)
  Expiation (chs. 49–59)
    Yahweh's servant a light to the nations (ch. 49)
    Opposition to Yahweh's servant (ch. 50)
    Yahweh's comfort of Zion (51:1–52:12)
    Yahweh's servant a redeemer of the people (52:13–53:12)
    Heritage of Yahweh's servants (ch. 54)
    Mercy freely offered (ch. 55)
    Righteousness and wickedness contrasted (chs. 56–58)
    Confession of the nation's transgressions (ch. 59)
  Glory (chs. 60–66)
    Future glory of Zion (ch. 60)
    Good tidings to the afflicted (ch. 61)
    Vindication of Zion (ch. 62)
    Yahweh's wrath on the nations (ch. 63)
    Prayer for mercy (ch. 64)
    Rebellious punished (ch. 65)
    New heavens and new earth (65:17–66:24)

Note how the closing verses (66:15-24) are reminiscent of the opening verses (1:1-26).

Basing his analysis of a two-part division (bifid) which may have been indicated by the three-line break in the Dead Sea 1QIsa^a, R.K. Harrison finds a slightly different breakdown in which he sees an "overlapping." The first half ends with the hope of restoration of the Davidic regime (chs. 32–33), and the second half (34–66) opens with a renewal of the note of judgment (34–35).[12]

PROBLEM OF AUTHORSHIP

The traditional view that Isaiah wrote the entire book is held today by exceedingly few scholars. The more conservative critics today accept two books (1–39 and 40–66); the moderate position finds three books (1–39, which includes several later additions; 40–55; 56–66); and the extreme positions find five or more authors.[13] The influence of the critical process on Roman Catholic scholars, historically more conservative critically than Protestant scholars, illustrates the point. The Pontifical Biblical Commission in 1908 asked:

> Should the philological argument drawn from language and style to impugn identity of authorship throughout the Book of Isaias be deemed of such force as to compel a man of sound judgement with competent knowledge of Hebrew and of the art of criticism to recognize several authors in the same book? Answer: in the negative.[14]

The Catholic Commentary on Holy Scripture (1953) reads: "It is undoubted however that the book as a whole owes its present form not to Isaias but to a post-exilic redactor, to whom also introductory indications, when not autobiographical or narrated in the first person, usually belong."[15] Finally, the Jesuit scholar J.L. McKenzie, in his Dictionary of the Bible (1965), which contains the official imprimatur, can state: "Most of the book of Isaiah does not come from the prophet Isaiah. . . . The book is a compendium of many types of prophecy from diverse periods."[16]

Arguments for Plural Authorship. Four major arguments have been given for dividing the prophecy of Isaiah among two or more authors: the historical perspective, the mention of Cyrus (in reality, an extension or specification of the first), the style, and the theological viewpoint.

S.R. Driver presents three independent lines of argument in considerable detail:[17] (1) The internal evidence of the prophecy itself points to the period of Babylonian captivity. Jerusalem is ruined and deserted (44:26; 58:12; 61:4; 63:18; 64:10). The prophet is addressing exiles in Babylonia (40:21, 26, 28; 43:10; 48:8; 50:10f.; 51:6, 12f.; 58:3ff.). (2) The literary style of 40–66 is very

---

12. *Introduction*, p. 764.
13. For the history of critical study of Isaiah, see G.L. Archer, *Survey*, pp. 318-339; CCHS §§421f.; B.S. Childs, *Old Testament as Scripture*, pp. 316-338; Eissfeldt, *Old Testament*, pp. 303-346; North, *IDB* 2:737-743; E.J. Young, *Introduction*, pp. 199-207.
14. *Acta Apostolicae Sedis* 41 (1908): 613f.
15. §421a.
16. P. 397.
17. *Introduction*, pp. 236-243.

different from that of 1–39, for which Driver gives considerable evidence.[18] He also discusses points that cannot be specifically illustrated, such as the terse, compact style of Isaiah contrasted with the lengthy development of an idea in Second Isaiah and the grave, restrained rhetoric of Isaiah contrasted with the warm and impassioned rhetoric of Second Isaiah. (3) The theological ideas of 40–66 differ remarkably from those which in 1–39 appear to be distinctive of Isaiah. The author of the second part "moves in a different region of thought from Isaiah; he apprehends and emphasizes different aspects of Divine truth."[19]

Eissfeldt, without lengthy elaboration, likewise lists three arguments:[20] the mention of Cyrus, designated as "my Shepherd" (44:28) and "his anointed" (45:1); Babylon (not Assyria) threatened with downfall (47:1; 48:14); and the peculiarities of linguistic usage and of thought.

Arguments for a Third Isaiah (Trito-Isaiah) are summarized by A. Weiser:[21] (1) "The nation is living in Palestine; Jerusalem is built up again." (2) "The subject-matter . . . is no longer the great longing for deliverance and for the return home, but miserable conditions, details and quarrels in the life of the community" (56:9ff.; 57:3ff.; 65:1ff.; 66:3ff.). (3) "The expectations of salvation bear a marked worldly and materialistic colouring." (4) "The conception of God is not as lofty as that of Deutero-Isaiah and his strong trustful optimism will be sought in vain." Weiser notes that in chs. 60–62 "sayings of Deutero-Isaiah are frequently employed and quoted, their original meaning being distorted." He views this as a "deep gulf" between Deutero- and Trito-Isaiah.[22]

Many recent works give no reasons for holding to two or three Isaiahs. The authors state as accepted fact that chs. 1–39 were written by "Isaiah of Jerusalem" and 40–66 (or 40–55) by "an unknown prophet of the Exile."

Discussion of Arguments for Multiple Authorship. Even with the view of inspiration stated in Ch. 2, it is no more difficult to accept the concept of "an unknown prophet of the Exile" than that of an unknown author of the epistle to the Hebrews. One could concede that the religious values of "Second" or "Third" Isaiah are just as great, assuming their divine inspiration, regardless of one's views of authorship. A person's position concerning Isaianic authorship should not be made a test of orthodoxy. Nevertheless, it is as much a violation of critical principles to say without further explanation that "Isa. 40–66 was written by an unknown prophet of the Exile" as it is to say "Isaiah wrote the entire book." One must therefore examine the evidence.

(1) Is Eissfeldt's argument from the reference to Cyrus an antisupernaturalistic a priori? (It is not necessarily so!) If so, it must be rejected at once.

---

18. *Ibid.*, pp. 238-240.
19. *Ibid.*, p. 243.
20. *Old Testament*, p. 304.
21. *Old Testament*, p. 206.
22. See also T. Henshaw, *The Latter Prophets* (London: 1958), p. 255.

Antisupernaturalism is basically antitheism, which has no place in biblical religion, for the Bible is theistic from beginning to end. The argument based on Cyrus, however, often is advanced by thoroughgoing theists, who point out that it is contrary to the nature of prophecy, as illustrated everywhere else in the prophetic literature of the Bible, to announce the names of individuals in advance. (One exception is the specific mention of Josiah in 1 Kgs. 13:1f., more than three centuries before he came on the scene.) Some scholars who hold to single authorship of Isaiah believe that the name "Cyrus" in 44:28 and 45:1 is an addition to the text.[23] But consider the startling statement made by von Rad in another context: "In fact, Deutero-Isaiah puts in bold relief the question of who is the controller of world-history, and the answer he gives almost takes one's breath away—the Lord of history is he who can allow the future to be told in advance."[24] On the other hand, O.T. Allis holds that Cyrus is the subject of the entire context (from ch. 41 on), and that the name cannot be excised without destroying the literary structure of the passage.[25] Josephus (Ant. ii.1.1-2 §§1-7) writes that Cyrus was so impressed with finding his name in a book "140 years before the temple was destroyed" that he gave the Jews leave to go back to their own land and rebuild the temple. However, most scholars today find no valid basis in Josephus for either the position that Isaiah wrote the prophecy of Cyrus or that this was the reason for Cyrus' action.

Therefore, this argument may be dismissed, first, because its refutation is not necessary for a single-author position, and second, because the two-author view of von Rad (and others) does not depend on it.

(2) All scholars admit that any argument based on style is precarious. An author's style may vary according to his purpose, audience, mood, age, and other factors. In fact, scholars often admit that the "unknown author" of chs. 40–66 deliberately sought to imitate the style of Isaiah of Jerusalem. The remarks of J.L. McKenzie are apropos: "Relationships in vocabulary and in thought make us conclude that Second Isaiah not only knew the oracles of Isaiah of Jerusalem, but also that he thought of himself as the continuator of Isaiah of Jerusalem."[26] McKenzie's admission concerning style and vocabulary is not to be taken as special pleading by a defender of single authorship, for he holds to at least a two-author view.

Likewise, style is not a decisive factor in Trito-Isaiah. Henshaw notes that "the style for the most part is inferior,"[27] but later comments: "The style of these chapters closely resembles that of Deutero-Isaiah, but it is not uniform

---

23. See Harrison, Introduction, p. 794.

24. Old Testament Theology 2:242, with a footnote to 41:25ff.; 48:14.

25. The Unity of Isaiah (Philadelphia: 1950), pp. 51-61.

26. Second Isaiah. Anchor Bible 20 (Garden City: 1968), p. xxi. McKenzie also reports an in-depth study of style by J. Reinken using modern statistical methods: "This study simply does not support the thesis of different authorship nor does it support the thesis of unity of authorship. This is to say that the vocabulary alone is not decisive. Nor is the style alone any more decisive"; p. xvi.

27. The Latter Prophets, p. 256.

throughout, that of some passages being much inferior to that of others."[28] In fact, on the basis of style alone scholars find no agreement in their results, whether for Isaiah or any other part of the Old Testament.

(3) The argument based on the geographical and historical situation cannot be disposed of in quite as summary a fashion. One cannot dispute that the viewpoint of ch. 40–66, in general, does not anticipate the Exile, but rather stands within the Exile. An accepted principle of the grammatico-historical hermeneutic holds that prophecy always arises from the historical situation and speaks to people of that situation (Ch. 22). For prophecy to be given exclusively in advance of a situation is a violation of this principle—i.e., while it may refer to a future time, it must do so from within the present situation, for otherwise it would have no relevance to people of its own day.

Although this principle is acceptable in general, it must not be taken to exclude predictive prophecy. Predictive prophecy, as a rule, shows its own historical setting. E.g., in the Olivet discourse (Mark 13; Matt. 24–25), Jesus clearly is sitting on the Mount of Olives with his disciples not long before the Crucifixion, talking about the future. But in Isa. 40–66 there is nowhere any indication that Isaiah of Jerusalem is in the Jerusalem of his own time talking to contemporaries about a future exile. Rather, numerous indications show that the author is living within the Exile, talking to people who are living under exilic conditions.[29]

However, the argument is not quite so simple. If it were, all scholars might be among the disciples of B. Duhm[30] and his approach to Deutero-Isaiah. For even chs. 1–39 contain segments (chs. 13, 24–27, 32–35, and according to some scholars much more) which do not have the eighth-century viewpoint of Isaiah. Therefore, most scholars deny their Isaianic authorship. Chs. 56–66 contain so many references that do not have a Babylonian *Sitz im Leben* (setting) that many scholars insist that these were delivered in Jerusalem—after the Exile, of course.[31] But the details of the Jerusalem or Palestinian passages in chs. 56–66 are frequently not at all in harmony with the postexilic period. The idolatry, high places, and similar sins (see 57:3-13) are characteristic of the period before the Exile, but not after. Scholars of Old Testament history and religion long have pointed out that the Exile cured Israel of idolatry. The kinds of sin mentioned in 59:1-8 sound much more like those in Amos, Micah, and the original Isaiah, than like those in Haggai, Zechariah, Malachi, or Ezra-

---

28. *Ibid.*, p. 265.

29. See Driver, *Introduction*, p. 237.

30. *Das Buch Jesaja*, 4th ed. HKAT (Göttingen: 1922).

31. C.C. Torrey, who held the strange view that there never was a Babylonian exile, pointed out that if the few references to Babylon and Cyrus could be eliminated as later glosses, almost all of chs. 40–66 could be assigned to a Palestinian situation; *The Second Isaiah: A New Interpretation* (New York: 1928), pp. vii-viii. The word "Babylon" occurs 13 times in Isaiah: once each in chs. 21, 43, 47; twice each in chs. 13, 14, 48; and 4 times in ch. 39.

Nehemiah. The serious student of this problem should read the postexilic prophets and then Isa. 56–66 and make careful comparisons. Chs. 40–55 have points
in common with both the earlier and the later chapters of Isaiah. In fact,
scholars are so completely confused by the data that they have tended to frag-
mentize Isaiah into numerous sources, possibly as many as ten, stretching over
a period from 740 to the second century B.C. As to geography, numerous minor
details are given about Jerusalem, but no details about Babylonia. (Compare
this with Ezekiel or Daniel, which include details about Babylonia.) If "Deutero-
Isaiah" ("Isaiah of Babylon") wrote from Babylon, he managed to hide the fact
very well.

Looking at the problem from another angle, would the viewpoint of the
book of Isaiah have been so far removed from the experience of the eighth-
century Judeans? In 722 the people of the northern kingdom had been taken
into captivity and deportees from Babylon relocated in Israel. Many of the
northerners had fled south, doubtless with tales to tell, so talk about exile would
be quite relevant. Would references to Babylonia have been meaningful? The
visit of envoys of Merodach-baladan, the Babylonian revolutionary, in the days
of Hezekiah (ca. 701; see 2 Kgs. 20:12; Isa. 39:1) must have raised the possibility of alliance with Babylon in an attempt to overthrow Assyria. Isaiah opposed that position. With divine revelation (or even without it) he might
indeed have foreseen that the future would bring divine retribution upon Judah
at the hands of Babylon—a message certainly not irrelevant to his day.

Moreover, Isaiah indicates clearly that his message is intended not for his
own day alone, but for a future time. Just after the account of Ahaz' refusal to
heed Isaiah's advice (ch. 7), and just before the promise of the coming Davidic
ruler (9:2-7 [MT 1-6], accepted as Isaianic by many critics), Isaiah speaks of
binding up the testimony and sealing the teaching among his disciples (8:16).
The passage is not without linguistic difficulties,[32] but the intent is clear: Isaiah,
whether by command from Yahweh or by personal decision, is looking to a
distant time when his message will be more completely relevant.[33]

A reasonable possibility is that Isaiah's messages were collected and pre-

---

32. The verbs ṣôr and h^aṭōm are imperative forms as pointed—but who is speaking?
If Yahweh, then "my disciples" seems out of place, and "your disciples" (Isaiah's) would
make better sense. If Isaiah, then to whom is he giving the command? If to his disciples,
then "my disciples" is again difficult, and "yourselves" would seem preferable. Scholars,
therefore, are inclined to emend the pointing and read the words as infinitives, thus
"I have bound up, etc." or "I will bind up, etc.," indicating a conclusion to which Isaiah
has come.

33. The verb ṣārar "to bind up" means to shut in, confine, hold together, and ḥtm
"to seal" means to authenticate with a seal, to protect, to seal up; see Dan. 12:4. The
intent is not to keep anyone from seeing or knowing the contents—in fact, the contents
of Isaiah's prophecy (and also Daniel's) were known to every generation. The idea of
safeguarding and authenticating the message for a future time, both in Isaiah and in
Daniel, is clear from the contexts.

served by his disciples[34] and later edited and put into written form. This would
be sufficient to account for the introduction of a later viewpoint. What Isaiah
said with immediate relevance, as well as with reference to the future, was put
into language that was more meaningful at the time of writing. Isaiah's immediate disciples (born, perhaps, no later than 700) could hardly have lived
until the capture of Jerusalem (597), much less the return from exile (537 or
later). Therefore, it is the better part of wisdom to keep an open mind on the
subject.

(4) The theological ideas in Isaiah and the argument that those in Deutero-
Isaiah are much advanced beyond those of Proto-Isaiah will be discussed in the
following chapter. Here, note only that in some respects this is a circular
argument. Some scholars seek to determine what the level of theological thought
must have been in the eighth century. Then they proceed to excise from the
texts of Amos, Micah, Hosea, Isaiah, or the Deuteronomic history what does
not fit that a priori. Then, on the basis of the emended texts, they offer proof
for the original thesis. Such logic fails to carry conviction.

There can be no question concerning the development of ideas in the book
of Isaiah. A notable difference can be seen between chs. 1–39 and 40–66, as
even a perusal of the outline (pp. 369f. above) will show. Furthermore, it is
exceedingly difficult, even impossible, to reconstruct the process whereby original utterances of the prophet and the final inscripturated form are connected.
Taking the book at face value, one must assume that various prophesies were
remembered, possibly written down, and preserved beginning ca. 740 and continuing through the Exile and return, until the canonical shape of the book
was achieved. No scholar should attempt this reconstruction without an overwhelming sense of humility.

Therefore, although there must be some degree of flexibility in considering
various suggestions, no reason suffices to reject the view that Isaiah was the
dominant personality responsible for the entire prophecy that bears his name.
The presence of later interpolations and explanatory glosses is not only a possibility but a demonstrable fact. The theory of the activity of Isaiah's disciples
is not unreasonable; quite the opposite, it is suggested, if not required, by the
text itself. The Gospels are essentially the teachings of Jesus Christ, although
he did not write a word of them. The gospel of Mark is very likely the preaching
of Peter or the catechetical instruction that accompanied Peter's preaching,
even though the literary form and structure are almost certainly Mark's. The

---

34. "Disciples" and "school" must not be viewed as some kind of formal systema-
tization. It is highly likely that a great and influential religious leader could gather a
cadre of followers, some of whom would continue his work and ideas after his death. A
possible comparison would be the "disciples" and "schools" of great critical and theological scholars in Germany in the past few centuries. Some hint of such a school may
be found in Talmud B. Bat. 15a: "Hezekiah and his company wrote Isaiah, Proverbs,
the Song of Songs, and Ecclesiastes"—which, in the light of other Talmudic tradition,
seems to imply the gathering, editing, and publishing of sayings; cf. Prov. 25:1.

Torah is essentially Mosaic, although how much of it actually was written down by Moses is not at all clear. Here, then, are three different types of transmission of the teachings of religious leaders, and doubtless others can be found within the Scriptures. Any similar process is acceptable when one says "Isaiah was responsible for the entire prophecy."

What is strongly rejected is any view that leaves only a microscopic Isaiah of Jerusalem and a gigantic anonymous figure of the Exile. Such a view raises more problems than it solves.

Authority. More significant than the discussion of authorship is the question of authority. What does the prophecy of Isaiah say to the believing community? Without debate, the critical division of Isaiah resulted in the loss of much of the message:

> First of all, critical scholarship has atomized the book of Isaiah into a myriad of fragments, sources, and redactions which were written by different authors at a variety of historical moments. To speak of the message of the book as a whole has been seriously called into question, and even such relatively conservative scholars as W. Eichrodt have been forced to isolate a small number of 'genuine' or 'central' passages from which to interpret the rest of the book. Again, critical exegesis now rests upon a very hypothetical and tentative basis of historical reconstructions. Since it is no longer possible to determine precisely the historical background of large sections of Isaiah, hypotheses increase along with the disagreement among the experts. Finally, the more the book of Isaiah has come into historical focus and has been anchored to its original setting, the more difficult it has become to move from the ancient world into a contemporary religious appropriation of the message.[35]

The question that must be asked first is not, "What value has this work for the church today?" but rather, "What value did this work have to the believing community that caused it to be preserved, revered, and considered as sacred Scripture?" For if it had not been regarded so, the prophecy—or rather, according to the critical view, the snips and patches that became the prophecy—would have disappeared long ago. The solution proffered by Childs, namely the canonical process, while of great merit, is not completely satisfactory. According to his view, First Isaiah underwent "theological redaction . . . to assure that its message was interpreted in the light of Second Isaiah."[36] But why was First Isaiah preserved for 150 years or more? Childs notes: "In the light of the present shape of the book of Isaiah the question must be seriously raised if the material of Second Isaiah in fact ever circulated in Israel apart from its being

---

35. Childs, *Old Testament as Scripture*, p. 324.
36. *Ibid.*, p. 333.

connected to an earlier form of First Isaiah."[37] His answer, which delays production of the canonical Isaiah for two centuries or more, does not speak to
the prior question concerning First Isaiah. The element of hope of future redemption must have been ignited in Isaiah's disciples, and it must have burned
so fiercely that the destruction of the temple, exile of the nation, and disap-
pointments of the return, all combined, could not quench it. Second Isaiah—
and Third, and as many other "Isaiahs" as critical scholars may identify—never
circulated without First Isaiah. The hypothetical book contains no heading, no
date formula, no statement "The vision of 'Second Isaiah' which he saw in the
days of Zerubbabel" such as is found in every other prophetic work. As far as
can be ascertained, only one prophecy of Isaiah existed, however scholars finally
may succeed in getting from Isaiah of Jerusalem to the canonical book that
bears his name.

The authority of the book, then, is the message of the entire book. It
combines judgment and deliverance, despair and hope. Childs' landmark work
makes this truth undeniable. Therefore to study the prophecy of Isaiah, in the
light of the analysis above, is not to claim that Isaiah plotted his work in outline
and then wrote it. It is entirely likely that he wrote little, if any, of it, except
for the portions of chs. 36–39 that are also found in 2 Kgs. 18–20. Rather, the
entire process may be attributed to the action of God's Spirit, as the ultimate
Author, both on the prophet Isaiah and on his "disciples," whoever they were
and whenever and however they put the work in its canonical form. Since the
people of God were more in need of this message earlier than later, a similar
date is favored for the work.

This leads to the hermeneutical principle that is a guide in deriving the
message of Isaiah that will be authoritative today. One must seek, as always,
to know the situation to which "the prophet" spoke. But in this case, the *Sitz
im Leben* extends from preexilic Israel facing the awful judgment of the Lord
whom they had rejected, to the exiles who needed to know that their warfare
had been accomplished and who were very much in need of comfort. This is
one reason for the greatness of the prophecy of Isaiah: it stands astride two
worlds, speaking to the sinners who face an angry God (1:21-26) and also to
the remnant who are to receive salvation from that same God (40:1f.), now
revealed as Father and Redeemer (63:16). For this reason, Isaiah's prophecy
speaks with authority to every man and woman of every age. Like Israel, all
have sinned repeatedly, in thought, word, and deed. Like Israel all need salvation. The book of Isaiah proclaims that salvation is provided by the God who
is in full control of this world and who can reveal to his prophets what is to
take place in the future.

---

37. *Ibid.*, p. 329.

CHAPTER 29

ISAIAH: MESSAGE

PROPHETIC VISION

WHETHER the divine call (Isa. 6:8-10) marked the beginning of Isaiah's prophetic ministry or came later is a debatable point. Since it does not open the book, some would argue that it happened later; others see it as an editor's insert (but why would an editor not place it at the beginning?). In any event, chs. 1–5 appear to be a brief overview of the entire message and therefore serve well as an introduction to the book. Included are the indictment of the people for their stupid and stubborn sin (1:1-26) and the promise of redemption for those who repent (vv. 27-31); a vision of the glory of the latter days (2:1-4) and of the judgment on the proud, haughty, and idolaters (vv. 6-19); another alternation, this time in reverse order, of the judgment (3:1–4:1) and glory to come (4:2-6); and the beautiful "song of the vineyard" (ch. 5). At least two visions are indicated (1:1; 2:1), and possibly several discrete messages have been combined to form this introduction.

Vision. The vision of Yahweh himself (ch. 6) is dated "in the year that King Uzziah died" (740 B.C.). Some commentators suggest here a cause-and-effect relationship: before that event, Isaiah saw only the glories and splendor of the royal court; but when Uzziah died, God was able to break through to Isaiah with a vision of the heavenly court. The vision contains a revelation of the thrice-holy (i.e., incomparably holy) One (vv. 1-3), seated on a throne "high and lifted up," whose train fills the temple. The seraphim[1] serve to guard the throne, worship the Lord, and minister to Isaiah in his sinful need (v. 7). Isaiah also has a vision of himself: a sinner dwelling in the midst of sinners (v. 6), in need of mercy because his eyes had "seen the King, the Lord of Hosts" (v. 5). At this point Isaiah receives the revelation of his appointed ministry (vv. 8-13).

---

1. See R.K. Harrison, "Seraphim," *IBD*, p. 1417.

Wadi or dry brook at Elah, which, with heavy rainfall, might become a "river in the desert" (Isa. 43:19f.; cf. 30:25; 32:2). (W.S. LaSor)

Mission. Isaiah's mission is complex. It appears, at first glance, to be a message of the rejection of Israel. Yahweh seems to be telling Isaiah that he is to make it impossible for the people to see and hear and repent (6:10).[2] Some commentators have suggested the Pharaoh-Moses confrontation as a parallel: Pharaoh first hardens his own heart, and then Yahweh seals the process (see Exod. 7:3, 14). However, a redeeming feature is found in the words "the holy seed is its stump" (Isa. 6:13). This concept of the future hope springing forth from the stump is found again (see 11:1), and becomes part of the language of the messianic promise in several prophets. A number of scholars have rejected this portion of ch. 6 as non-Isaianic, much as they have removed all elements of hope or redemption from the eighth-century prophets; but, as seen above (p. 376), this requires extensive tampering with most of the texts from the

---

2. This portion of the vision is quoted 5 times in the New Testament: Matt. 13:14f.; Mark 4:12; Luke 8:10; John 12:39-41; Acts 28:26f.

eighth century or earlier. Moreover, it removes the only element that had redeeming significance, and, if true, would have left Israel with no hope.[3]

DOCTRINE OF GOD

In some respects Isaiah is the theologian of the Old Testament. In this book appear not only the elements for a well-defined doctrine of God, but—particularly in the latter portion—expressions of faith that are in essence formulations of doctrine (see 11:1-5; 48:12f.; 63:15-17). This very fact (as seen in Ch. 28) has been used to argue for the late date of such passages. The theology allegedly is too well developed for the eighth century. But great theological statements come, humanly speaking, from great individual minds able to comprehend many data and compress them into a form useful to the believing community. From another angle, the elements of theology come from an appreciation and assimilation of the acts of God.[4] Israel's history was the result of many acts of God, and formulating the theological significance of those acts was the work of Moses and the prophets. Indeed, as supported by the prophetic books in their present form, all of the elements for Isaiah's theology are found by the eighth century.

The Holy One of Israel. It is appropriate that Isaiah, whose temple vision was a revelation of the thrice-holy Yahweh, should stress the holiness of God. His characteristic expression, "the Holy One of Israel," is found twenty-five times in the book (twelve in chs. 1–39, eleven in chs. 40–55, and twice in chs. 56–66).[5] In all the rest of the Old Testament, it occurs only six times, once in a quotation attributed to Isaiah (2 Kgs. 19:22), twice in the closing chapters of Jeremiah (50:29; 51:5), and three times in Psalms (71:22; 78:41; 89:18 [MT 19]). In no case can it be demonstrated that the expression was used either before Isaiah's time or long after Jeremiah's time.

Idea of the Holy. The root *qdš* carries the idea of "separate, set apart." N.H. Snaith contends that it means "set apart to" rather than "set apart from," and

---

3. Some idea of the extent of emendation required can be seen in that the following portions of chs. 1–12, all presenting some form of redemptive hope, would have to be excised: 1:16-20, 27-31; 2:2-5; 4:2-6; 6:13b, c; 8:16-18; 9:1-7 (MT 8:23–9:6); 10:12–12:6. Needless to say, the artistic structure obvious in the work as it stands is completely destroyed. Furthermore, not a single line of these excisions need be deleted on any critical basis other than the view that the eighth-century prophets were prophets of doom unrelieved by hope of redemption. Happily, many scholars now reject this position.

4. Isaiah's temple vision, as it now stands, reflects the community's later understanding of its significance.

5. The expression occurs in the following passages: 1:4; 5:19, 24; 10:20; 12:6; 17:7; 29:19; 30:11f., 15; 31:1; 37:23; 41:14, 16, 20; 43:3, 14; 45:11; 47:4; 48:17; 49:7; 54:5; 55:5; 60:9, 14. Note "the Holy One of Jacob" (29:23); "God the Holy One" (5:16); "your holy One" (43:15); "his holy One" (10:17; 49:7); "whose name is Holy" (57:15). In 40:25 "Holy One" (Heb. *qādôš*) stands alone; also Hab. 3:3; Job 6:10; the plural form is used of God in Hos. 11:12 (MT 12:1); Prov. 9:10; 30:3.

concerns the suprahuman world.[6] Thus, when Moses received his call in Sinai at the burning bush, he was told "the place on which you are standing is holy ground" (Exod. 3:5), ground set apart to Yahweh.

Although no moral or ethical quality is implied in the earliest uses of the word "holy," certainly by the Mosaic period a moral or ethical connotation was intended. At Sinai Yahweh said to Moses: "You (Israel) shall be to me a kingdom of priests and a holy nation" (Exod. 19:6); this relationship required fidelity to Yahweh their God and obedience to his moral code as specified in the covenant. Holiness to Israel, then, implied a separateness to Yahweh that was characterized by the way the members of the congregation believed and acted.

Isaiah, however, is the one who actually pointed up the moral nature of holiness, citing "unclean" (Heb. ṭāmē') rather than "profane" as the characteristic of sinfulness, and stressing its moral or behavioral more than its ritual significance. In the Wilderness and the post-Mosaic periods, holiness was bound up with the cult of Yahweh,[7] one purpose of which was to inculcate the Torah. The elaborate details of the sacrificial system were designed to impress upon the Israelites that disobedience to the revealed law alienated them from Yahweh and required atonement or reconciliation. But cult had become an empty form. "Unclean" came to be used more with reference to ceremonial or ritual uncleanness than to immoral behavior or disobedience of the precepts of Torah.[8] The prophets sought to reestablish the relationship between worship and obedience.[9] In the temple vision, Isaiah realized that the reason for Yahweh's separateness (or holiness) was not a cultic deficiency on the prophet's part, but Yahweh's moral perfection over against Isaiah's own uncleanness (6:5). Yahweh confirmed the accuracy of Isaiah's perception by sending a seraph to cleanse his lips with a burning coal from the altar, saying: "Your guilt is taken away, and your sin forgiven" (v. 7). This is not to be understood as anticultic, for the entire episode takes place in the temple, the center of the cult.

The sin of the people to whom Isaiah was sent—supposedly a holy nation— was not unsatisfactory cult but refusal to hear the word of Yahweh (6:9f.), as brought out in the opening indictment of Israel (1:2-6, 10-17). The elements of worship without obedience were meaningless (vv. 11-15). What Yahweh wanted from his people was proper behavior (vv. 16f.). The once-faithful city had lost the moral nature of holiness and had become a harlot (zônâ, 1:21; Isaiah avoids use of qāḏēš or qᵉḏēšâ), a condition demonstrated by the loss of justice and righteousness (vv. 22f.; see below).[10]

---

6. *The Distinctive Ideas of the Old Testament* (London: 1944), pp. 30f.

7. See H.H. Rowley, *Worship in Ancient Israel*, pp. 37-70.

8. See BDB, pp. 379f., for a detailed study of the word ṭāmē'.

9. Greatly misunderstanding this effort, some scholars have insisted that the prophets were anticultic and antipriesthood. A much-needed corrective was supplied by R.E. Clements, *Prophecy and Covenant*, esp. chs. 4-5.

10. For further reading, see Snaith, *Distinctive Ideas*, pp. 21-50; J. Muilenburg, "Holiness," *IDB* 2:616-625; W. Eichrodt, *Theology* 1:270-282.

J. Muilenburg[11] points out that Second Isaiah stresses the relationship of the Holy One to his redemptive activity (41:14; 43:3, 14; 47:4; 48:17; 49:7; 54:5). Even with the view of authorship presented in this study, the observation is still valid. For if the punishment of the nation was because of uncleanness, which is a violation of Yahweh's holiness, then restoration of the nation must require some kind of cleansing, which is involved in salvation and redemption. To present the indictment of uncleanness without the remedy of divine salvation would be of little help, and to speak of salvation or redemption without making clear the reason for such divine activity would—as in much present-day preaching—verge on nonsense. Isaiah's own experience, namely the realization of his own sin and the receiving of God's gracious salvation, became the basis of his message to Israel:

> Come now, let us reason together, says the Lord: though your sins are like scarlet, they shall be as white as snow; though they are red like crimson, they shall become like wool. (1:18)

Yahweh as Savior. Isaiah's name (Heb. $y^e\check{s}a'y\bar{a}h\hat{u}$) means "Yahweh will save" or possibly "Yahweh is salvation," which may partly explain the prophet's great interest in salvation.[12] In chs. 1–39, Yahweh is "the God of your salvation" (17:10), which has special reference to deliverance from Assyria (see 11:11-16; 12:1). Salvation is personal ("my salvation," 12:2; "the Lord will save me," 38:20), but it also refers to the city (37:35) and the people who cry to the Lord (19:20). Salvation is mentioned in connection with "stability of your times," and is joined with "wisdom," "knowledge," and "the fear of the Lord" (33:6). It is deliverance in the time of trouble (v. 2), but also has reference to "that day" for which the people of God have waited (25:9), which in context appears to be a future time of blessing.

In chs. 40–55 salvation is also deliverance from foes and oppressors (45:17;

---

11. *IDB* 2:621.
12. The noun $y^e\check{s}\hat{u}'\hat{a}$ "salvation" occurs about 77 times in the Old Testament: 18 times in Isaiah (7 in chs. 1–39, 6 in chs. 40–55, and 5 in chs. 56–66), often in the Psalms, and only twice in the other prophets. The noun $y\bar{e}\check{s}a'$ "salvation" occurs 36 times: 5 times in Isaiah (1 in chs. 1–39, 2 each in chs. 40–55 and 56–66), 20 times in the Psalms, and only 4 times in the other prophets. The noun $t^e\check{s}\hat{u}'\hat{a}$ "deliverance, salvation" occurs 34 times: twice in Isaiah (45:17; 46:13), 13 times in Psalms, once in Jeremiah, and nowhere else in the prophets. The verb $y\bar{a}\check{s}a'$ "save" (in the hiphil and niphal stems) occurs 206 times: 27 times in Isaiah (8 in chs. 1–39, 12 in chs. 40–55, and 7 in chs. 56–66), 56 in Psalms, 11 in Jeremiah, as well as all other prophets. The hiphil participle occurs 33 times, usually translated "savior." This form is found 9 times in Isaiah (1 in chs. 1–39, 6 in chs. 40–55, 2 in chs. 56–66); with the meaning "savior" it occurs only 3 times in the other prophets. Taking all the forms from the root $y\check{s}'$ together, of some 342 occurrences in the Old Testament, 122 are found in Psalms, and about 50 in Isaiah (15 each in chs. 1–39 and 56–66, 20 in chs. 40–55). Word counts were made from a Hebrew concordance; the figures vary slightly in other sources. The H-participle figures are also counted in the forms under the verb, hence are duplicated there; however, they are counted only once in the totals.

49:25). The idea of ransom is connected with salvation, for Yahweh gave Egypt, Ethiopia, and Seba in exchange for Israel's salvation (43:3). Yahweh is the only Savior (vv. 11f.). Idols were unable to save (46:7), as were sorcerers and astrologers (47:13). In Second Isaiah, the idea of righteousness is connected with salvation (45:8, 21). Moreover, righteousness is to be extended to the ends of the earth (v. 22; 49:6), and, as a result of the rule of Yahweh, is to be forever (51:5f.).

In chs. 56–66 salvation is contingent on doing justice and righteousness (56:1) and is parallel to "deliverance." The parallel to righteousness is found also in 59:17 and 61:10, and to justice in 59:11. Righteousness, salvation, vengeance, and fury are all combined as the garments of the Lord when he comes in judgment (v. 17), and salvation is parallel to reward and recompense (62:11). Salvation is triumph over the foe and hence victory (59:16; 60:16; sometimes used to translate forms of *yš'*, since a result of salvation is victory). The mysterious One who comes from Edom in crimsoned garments becomes the Savior by being afflicted with the people's affliction, and redeems them in love and pity (63:1f., 8f.).

Since Isaiah's idea of salvation is connected with the concepts of redemption, deliverance, righteousness, and justice, it is necessary to take up these ideas also to get a complete picture of what the prophet meant by the words "save," "savior," [13] and "salvation."

Yahweh as Redeemer. The verb *gā'al* "redeem" and its participle *gô'ēl* "redeemer" also are brought into prominence in Isaiah. The Hebrew root in its various forms occurs some 122 times in the Old Testament, of which about 26 occurrences are in Isaiah (1 in chs. 1–39, 18 in chs. 40–55, and 7 in chs. 56–66). Otherwise the bulk of its occurrences will be found in Leviticus (21 times in chs. 25 and 27), Ruth (19 times in chs. 3–4), and Numbers (6 times). Two other words are used to convey the idea of "redemption," namely *pāḏâ* "ransom" and forms of *kipper* "covering, atonement, propitiation," but their use in Isaiah is insignificant.

The basic idea of *g'l* is to recover property (including persons) no longer held by the original owner. In Lev. 25:47-49 the "near kinsman" (*gô'ēl*) could redeem a person who had had to sell himself into slavery. In Ruth, the "near kinsman" had the privilege and responsibility of marrying Ruth and raising up progeny in the name of the dead relative, to protect the inheritance of the deceased. [14] The *gô'ēl* kinsman-redeemer figure is presented in Isaiah without

---

13. Of the name Savior, Snaith says: "this appellation is by no means confined to Second-Isaiah, for it is the theme of many Psalms and of most of the prophets. The name Saviour is, however, so frequent in Second-Isaiah as to be a marked feature of his vocabulary"; *Distinctive Ideas*, p. 86. The word counts simply will not support this statement. "Salvation" may be the "theme" of most of the prophets, but the word is a hallmark of Isaiah.

14. See W.S. LaSor, *Daily Life in Bible Times* (Cincinnati: 1966), pp. 45-47.

detailed application of the various shades of meaning, but the basic idea is retained: "For thus says the Lord: 'You were sold for nothing, and you shall be redeemed without money' " (52:3). In an extended passage about the redemption of Israel (ch. 43, esp. vv. 1, 14), Yahweh says: "I give Egypt as your ransom, Ethiopia and Seba in exchange for you" (v. 3).

Chs. 1–39 do not contribute to the study of the word—which is not strange, for without captivity there is no need for redemption. However, the very unusual word g^e'*ûlîm* "redeemed (ones)" occurs in 35:9; 51:10; 62:12; 63:4 (i.e., all three "Isaiahs"), and elsewhere only in Ps. 107:2.

Chs. 40–55 offer the most productive study of the root. "Your Redeemer is the Holy One of Israel," says Yahweh (41:14; cf. 43:14; 47:4; 48:17; 54:5). Clearly Isaiah uses the word primarily with reference to redemption from captivity (43:14, cf. 47:4 and its context; 52:3-9). However, the contexts also show that this redemptive activity is not an end in itself, but part of a process moving on toward something greater. This Redeemer will make his people victorious, and they shall rejoice in Yahweh (41:14-16). His redemption reveals the truth that he is the first and the last; beside him there is no god (44:6f.; cf. vv. 24-28). It is connected with his judicial acts (47:3ff.), yet is at the same time instructive to his people (48:17) and a revelation to the kings of the earth (49:7). Yahweh's redemptive activity results in his glorification (44:23).

Chs. 56–66 add the crowning touch:

In all their affliction he was afflicted,[15]
    and the angel of his presence saved them;
In his love and in his pity he redeemed them;
    he lifted them up and carried them all the days of old. (63:9)

Therefore they say, and all the redeemed with them:

Thou, O Lord, art our Father,
    our Redeemer from of old is thy name. (v. 16)

To this add the words of Isa. 35:

No lion shall be there,
    nor shall any ravenous beast come up on it;
they shall not be found there,
    but the redeemed shall walk there.
And the ransomed of the Lord shall return,
    and come to Zion with singing;
    everlasting joy shall be upon their heads;
they shall obtain joy and gladness,
    and sorrow and sighing shall flee away. (35:9f.)[16]

---

15. Following Qere; Kethib reads "he did not afflict." Some MSS read with Q; LXX and Syriac follow K.

16. See further R.C. Dentan, "Redeem, Redeemer, Redemption," *IDB* 4:21f.

Yahweh as Father. The concept of God as "father" seems to have been avoided in the Old Testament during the period when Israel was in contact with nature religions such as Baal worship. Israel indeed was called God's "son" (Hos. 11:1), but God was not referred to as "father" until the danger of contaminating the word with some kind of sexual connotation no longer existed. Yahweh is Creator and refers to his creatures as his "children" (Isa. 45:11). But only toward the end of Isaiah can be found such statements as: "For thou art our Father. . . . Thou, O Lord, art our Father, our Redeemer from of old is thy name" (63:16); "Yet, O Lord, thou art our Father" (64:8 [MT 7]).[17]

Yahweh as Supreme and Only Ruler. One of Isaiah's greatest theological contributions is his absolute monotheism. Yahweh's glory is the whole earth (6:3), therefore the other gods are nothing (2:8, 18, 20f.): "They were no gods, but the work of men's hands, wood and stone" (37:19).

Some scholars have insisted that this concept is too advanced for the eighth century (but see Amos 1-2, 9) and therefore must be excluded from the authentic Isaianic passages. But someone had to originate the idea so clearly taught in Isaiah. According to one view the Israelites finally realized that gods made with hands are no gods when Babylon was about to be taken by the advancing Persian forces, and the Babylonians were scurrying about trying to save their gods (see Ps. 115:3-8; 135:15-18). That the experiences of the Exile made deep theological impressions on the Jews cannot be doubted, but were these experiences sufficient to make them monotheists? Many other peoples lived in exile, even at the same time the Israelites did; yet only the worshipers of Yahweh became monotheists. Was it not because some of Yahweh's prophets had already sown the seed which germinated in exile? The Lord's method was always to tell his people through the prophets what he was going to do and why, to carry out that activity, and to explain to his people what he had done and why. He is not only "the God who acts"; he reveals to his servants the prophets the reasons for these acts.

When the great superpowers developed, beginning with the Assyrian period, and first Israel and then Judah were swallowed up by pagan nations, the people of Yahweh faced the frightening question of whether Yahweh was weaker than the gods of Assyria or Babylonia. The practice of the nations was to carry off the gods from the temples of the peoples they conquered, symbolizing the supposedly greater strength of their own gods. But Isaiah looked at the situation and proclaimed that Assyria was only a rod in Yahweh's hand (10:5) to punish Israel, and he soon would punish Assyria for their arrogance and pride (vv. 12f.). Even though deep darkness was to come upon the land, light would come to dispel that darkness because of the "zeal" of Yahweh (cf. 8:21–9:2, 7 [MT 9:1, 6]).[18]

---

17. See J. Daane, "Father," *ISBE* 2 (1982): 284-86.
18. For the meaning of *qin'â* "zeal, jealousy," see BDB, p. 888; G.A. Smith, *The Book of Isaiah.* Expositor's Bible, rev. ed. (1927; repr. Grand Rapids: 1956) 3:649; A. Stumpff, "*zēlos*," *TDNT* 2:878-880.

In the second part of Isaiah, however, is found the most sustained presentation of the universality and power of God. Disregarding the critical invention
of Servant Songs as irruptions into the text, and reading chs. 40–49 from
beginning to end, one cannot help but feel the cogency of the presentation.
Yahweh is not only the protector and sustainer of his people Israel, but the
controller of all nations (40:11, 13-17). The One who gives power to the faint
is the Creator of the ends of the earth (vv. 28f.). Yahweh stirred up one leader
from the east (41:2) and one from the north (v. 25)—and "declared it from
the beginning, that we might know" (v. 26; cf. 44:6-8). Yahweh, who created
heavens and earth (42:5), called his servant Israel in righteousness, intending
them to be a light to the nations (v. 6; cf. 41:8)—but his servant was blind
and deaf (42:19). Even in the chastisement that must come (43:2) Yahweh is
with his people as Redeemer and will deliver them (vv. 6f.). He will break
down the bars of Babylon (v. 14), make a way in the wilderness and rivers in
the desert (v. 19), and blot out the transgressions of his chosen people (v. 25;
cf. 44:1). Yahweh is the first and the last; besides him there is no god.

Yahweh forms light and creates darkness; he makes weal and creates woe
(45:7). The Maker of Israel (v. 21), Creator of the earth, and the One who
stretched out the heavens (v. 24) is also Maker of Cyrus, his "shepherd" (v. 28),
who shall build his city and set his exiles free (45:13). Bel and Nebo, who must
be carried on beasts and cattle and cannot share the burden, themselves must
go into captivity, but Yahweh, who has borne and will continue to carry Israel,
is the only God (46:1-9). He is the One who declares the end from the beginning, because he is the One who brings it to pass. What he purposes he will
do (46:10f.). Babylon will be reduced to shame (ch. 47), but Yahweh will defer
his anger on the house of Jacob for his name's sake (48:1-11).

The same doctrine of God is found in chs. 56–66 with the added promise:
"For behold, I create new heavens and a new earth; and the former things shall
not be remembered or come into mind" (65:17). "For as the new heavens and
the new earth which I will make shall remain before me, . . . so shall your
descendants and your name remain" (66:22).

Spirit of Yahweh. Isaiah has more to say about the Spirit than any other Old
Testament writer. In spite of the difficulties inherent in determining a doctrine
of the Spirit,[19] a strong and clear teaching is evident in all parts of Isaiah. The
key passage is 11:2, in a context that promises the advent of "a shoot from the
stump of Jesse" (v. 1). Some critics view this passage as a later addition, but
others find no compelling reason to deny it to First Isaiah. The "Spirit of

---

19. The basic difficulty lies in the Hebrew word *rûaḥ*, which may mean "wind" as
well as "spirit." In addition is the problem of interpretation, for a passage may refer to
the "Spirit (of Yahweh)" or to the "spirit (of man)." Furthermore, "spirit" may be a
quality or an attribute, even when used of God. For example, is "a spirit of justice" in
28:6 a human attribute or a gift of the divine Spirit (see 30:1)? In 37:7 is Yahweh going
to put some evil or perverse spirit in the king of Assyria, or is it the Spirit of Yahweh
who will give the king the false rumor?

Yahweh" will rest upon this "shoot," and is described further as "the spirit of
wisdom and understanding, the spirit of counsel and might, the spirit of knowledge and the fear of the Lord."[20] E.J. Kissane points out that the description
"comprises intellectual, practical and spiritual gifts."[21] Christians who find fulfillment of the messianic promise in Jesus may connect this passage to the time
of the baptism (Matt. 3:16 and par.). To the degree that "the Church is an
extension of the Incarnation" ("the body of Christ") the description of the
Spirit in Isa. 11:2 may be compared with the "gifts" or "fruit" of the Spirit in
the New Testament (see 1 Cor. 12:4-11; Gal. 5:22f.).

In the day of desolation the people of Yahweh will wait "until the Spirit
is poured upon us from on high" (32:15), bringing justice and righteousness;
the result will be peace, quietness, and trust forever (vv. 16-18). In 34:16 the
Spirit is mentioned in parallel with "the mouth of the Lord," but since the
stichs are in the nature of action—result ("synthetic parallelism"), it is not clear
whether the two should be equated. A possible interpretation would be that
Yahweh commanded and his Spirit carried out the action.

Is the prophet speaking of "Spirit" or "wind" in 40:7 ("The grass withers,
the flower fades, when *rûaḥ yhwh* blows upon it")? The reference to "the word
of our God" (v. 8) favors "Spirit." In v. 13 the divine Spirit seems clearly
intended, but to insist that this is the "third person" of a triune being goes
beyond the teaching of the passage. In 42:1 Yahweh says he has put his *rûaḥ*
upon his servant, that he might bring forth justice to the nations; interpretation
of this passage is further complicated by making it a messianic promise.[22] In
44:3 "I will pour my Spirit (spirit?) upon your descendants" is parallel with
"and my blessing on your offspring." "And now the Lord God has sent me and
his Spirit" in 48:16 presents difficulty because the speaker is not clear; if it is
an introductory statement to what follows, then one may infer that the Spirit
has inspired the prophet to proclaim that message.

In 59:19 is the prophet speaking of the "wind" (so RSV) or the "spirit"
(NEB)? To judge from v. 21 (which may be questionable to do, since the
passage seems to end after v. 19), the Spirit is again related to the "words which
I have put in your mouth." On the other hand, the prophet clearly is speaking
of the Spirit of Yahweh in 61:1 (lit., "the Spirit of the Lord Yahweh is upon
me, because Yahweh has anointed me, to proclaim good news to the poor he
has sent me, to bind up the brokenhearted . . ."). Jesus used this passage in
the synagogue at Nazareth, and said that it was fulfilled "this day," "in your

---

20. Occasionally writers connect this verse with the seven spirits mentioned in
Rev. 1:4. Even casual exegesis of Isa. 11:2 will make it clear that only one Spirit is
intended; the other phrases are attributes of that Spirit.

21. *The Book of Isaiah*, rev. ed. (Dublin: 1960) 1:135.

22. While this interpretation could be a *sensus plenior* ("fuller sense"), it can hardly
be derived from the passage in its context. See LaSor, "Interpretation of Prophecy,"
BDPT, pp. 128-135; "The *Sensus Plenior* and Biblical Interpretation," pp. 260-277 in
W.W. Gasque and LaSor, eds., *Scripture, Tradition, and Interpretation*. Festschrift E.F.
Harrison (Grand Rapids: 1978).

hearing" (Luke 4:18-21).[23] The term "Holy Spirit" is used twice in Isa. 63:10f., and "the Spirit of Yahweh" in v. 14.

Obviously Isaiah contains nothing like the fullness of the New Testament doctrine of the Spirit, but this should not be expected. Scripture was revealed "at various times and in various ways" (*polymerōs kai polytrōpos*, Heb. 1:1), and the revelation was not complete until its completion in the Son. Nonetheless, Isaiah represents a marked advance in the revelation concerning the Spirit over what had been given previously even if Joel is accepted as antedating Isaiah.

MAN'S RELATIONSHIP TO GOD

To consider the entire range of theological anthropology in Isaiah would be a large task, and much of it would duplicate what has already been discussed from Genesis on. Rather, attention will be given to Isaiah's specific contributions, particularly as contained in the concepts of righteousness and justice.

Righteousness. Heb. *ṣedeq* and *ṣᵉdāqâ* "righteousness" occur 273 times in the Old Testament, of which 58 are in Isaiah. In all the other prophets combined, the words occur about 12 times. The bulk of the occurrences is in Psalms.

Snaith takes the original meaning to have been "straightness," hence "that which is, or ought to be, firmly established, successful and enduring in human affairs."[24] Perhaps a simpler definition of the basic meaning is conformity with accepted standards.[25] Conformity with a divinely revealed law is a later and biblical definition. This can be illustrated by the story of Judah and Tamar (Gen. 38). According to custom, Judah was out of step for having failed to provide for the widow of his dead son; Tamar, who had taken steps to provide by playing the harlot and thereby tricking Judah into fulfilling his responsibility, actually was "more righteous" (v. 26).[26]

In the prophets, however, particularly Isaiah, "righteousness" means conformity to God's way, especially as set forth in God's Torah. Usually this involves ethical behavior, but, as Snaith points out,[27] it is not mere ethics. According to Eichrodt, "God's *ṣᵉdāqā* or *ṣedeq* is his keeping of the law in

---

23. It is important to recognize that Isa. 61:1 stands on its own feet, apart from any New Testament claim that it has been fulfilled. The passage, without any such interpretation, had to make sense to those who first heard or read it, and to all who read it prior to its "fulfillment." This is not to deny fulfillment of Scripture, but to insist on putting it in its proper order.

24. *Distinctive Ideas*, pp. 72f.

25. See E.R. Achtemeier, "Righteousness in the OT," *IDB* 4:80.

26. "Every relationship brings with it certain claims upon conduct, and the satisfaction of these claims, which issue from the relationship and in which alone the relationship can persist, is described by our term *ṣdq*"; H. Cremer, *Biblisch-theologisches Wörterbuch*, 7th ed. (Gotha: 1893), p. 233, quoted in G. von Rad, *Old Testament Theology* 1:371; see von Rad's treatment, pp. 370-383.

27. *Distinctive Ideas*, pp. 68-78.

accordance with the terms of the covenant."[28] He warns against any concept of distributive justice, such as is familiar from Roman law, and points to Isaiah's "picture of the conduct of the Prince of Peace, who establishes his kingdom with judgment and righteousness (Isa. 9:7), and puts an end to all violence and oppression, so that his people are united in the harmony of a purpose in keeping with the nature of their God (Isa. 11:3-5, 9)."[29] This righteousness is not the result of human effort, but rather is the gift of God, for only such righteousness "can lead to that conduct which is truly in keeping with the covenant."[30] Accordingly, "righteousness" and "mercy" often are found in parallelism in the Psalms. As a result of this stress on God's mercy, the term "righteousness" comes to be used of human benevolence, for if people act in God's way, they shall be merciful. This is the sense in which New Testament *dikaiosýnē* sometimes means "deeds of righteousness, religious duties."[31]

Isaiah reports that in Jerusalem righteousness had been replaced by murderers (1:21) and bloodshed (5:7), but when God's redemptive work was finished, it would be called the city of righteousness (1:26). Righteousness rained down from heaven and brought forth righteousness on earth (45:8). Righteousness and justice frequently are mentioned in poetic parallel (e.g., 1:27; 16:5; 28:17). It is sometimes seen as judicial (cf. 10:22), and is learned from God's judgments (26:9f.). Righteousness is an attribute of the messianic figure that is to arise from the stump of Jesse and it governs his acts (11:3-5). One result of righteousness is peace (32:17; cf. 48:18). The redeemed Israelite rejoices and exults in Yahweh for having covered him with the robe of righteousness (61:10). The idea of deeds of righteousness is often implicit and sometimes explicit (cf. 56:1; 64:5 [MT 4]).

English translations present a problem in studying the concept of "righteousness." The RSV often translates Heb. *ṣeḏeq* and *ṣᵉḏāqâ* as "deliverance," sometimes "victory," and occasionally "vindication." The result of Yahweh's righteousness with reference to his covenant people is deliverance or victory and therefore vindication (see 41:2, 10; 51:1, 5, 7; 54:17), Therefore, righteousness in Isaiah may be defined as a quality of Yahweh; the actions in accordance with that quality, particularly with reference to his covenant people; and results of those righteous acts not only on his people but on the entire earth (see Ps. 71:15f., 24).[32]

Justice. Heb. *mišpāṭ* "judgment" occurs some 420 times in the Old Testament and is translated 29 different ways in the KJV (239 times as "judgment"). It is

---

28. *Theology* 1:240.
29. *Ibid.*, 1:245.
30. *Ibid.*, 1:247. Heb. *ṣiḏqaṯ yhwh* is used of the saving acts of Yahweh, often in the Psalms; cf. BDB, p. 842, 6.a.
31. See Matt. 6:1f.; W. Bauer, *A Greek-English Lexicon of the New Testament*, trans. and rev. W.F. Arndt and F.W. Danker (Chicago: 1979), p. 196; G. Schrenk, "*dikaiosýnē*," *TDNT* 2:192-210.
32. For further reading, see Snaith, *Distinctive Ideas*, pp. 51-78, 87-93; Eichrodt, *Theology* 1:244-47; Schrenk, *TDNT* 2:182-210; Achtemeier, *IDB* 4:80-85.

used throughout the Old Testament, but principally in Psalms (65 times), Isaiah (40), Deuteronomy, Ezekiel (37 each), and Jeremiah (31). In about 18 of the passages in which the word occurs in Isaiah, it is either parallel with or in close proximity to the word ṣeḏeq or ṣeḏāqâ "righteous(ness)."

The root meaning seems to have suggested something like "judge," and therefore developed into such meanings as "to judge, govern," "justice, decision," "manner, custom, the way of living under the judgments that have been made," "vindication or condemnation, the judgment issued," "to enter into judgment" (43:26), and the like. Because of this range of meanings, the only practical way to study this word is to observe its usage in many contexts.

Snaith says: "Neither this word, nor its early companion *torah* (later 'The Law') can ever wholly be separated from God. For us, 'justice' means either the demands of some moral law, or, more often, the king's justice. To the Hebrew it meant the demands of God's law, and God's justice."[33] L. Morris says: "Judgment, as the Hebrews came to understand it, is first and foremost an activity of God. Yahweh is 'a God of judgment' (Is. xxx. 18), or even 'the God of judgment' (Mal. ii. 17). Judgment is His own activity, for no-one 'taught him in the path of judgment' (Is. xl. 14)."[34] Human judgment ideally considered, therefore, is judgment in conformity with God's judgment. Accordingly, Snaith says: "But no judge, whether priest or prophet, could give any other judgements than those which are regarded as being the veritable word of God. It is necessary therefore to think of 'doing mishpat' (Micah vi. 8) as meaning 'doing God's will as it has been made clear in past experience' "[35]—or, perhaps preferably, as has been made clear in past revelation.[36]

Isaiah sees the breakdown of Israel to be due, at least in part, to the collapse of judgment. "How the faithful city has become a harlot! She that was full of *mišpāṭ*! Ṣeḏeq lodged in her, and now murderers" (1:21; cf. 5:7). He also sees redemption to be accomplished by judgment, but whether this means the action of Yahweh or of the people is perhaps not clear; v. 27b seems to suggest that it is by the action of the people: "Zion shall be redeemed by *mišpāṭ*, and her penitents by *ṣeḏāqâ*." The judicial act of Yahweh certainly is not absent, for the day of holiness comes "when Yahweh shall have washed away the filth of the daughters of Zion and cleansed the bloodstains of Jerusalem from its midst by a spirit of judgment and by a spirit of burning" (4:4). Yahweh enters into judgment with the elders and princes of his people (3:14). Yahweh is a God of judgment (or justice), exalted in justice (5:16; 30:18). "Those who decree iniquitous decrees" refuse to grant justice to the needy (10:2). But the child who is to be born will uphold his kingdom with justice and righteousness (9:7 [MT 6]; cf. 16:5). The Lord Yahweh says that he is laying a cornerstone in Zion

---

33. *Distinctive Ideas*, p. 74.

34. *The Biblical Doctrine of Judgment* (Grand Rapids: 1960), pp. 7f.

35. *Distinctive Ideas*, p. 76.

36. While the Old Testament is concerned with the rights of all people, it expresses particular concern for the rights of those who cannot normally obtain justice, i.e., the widows and fatherless, the poor and the resident alien.

and "will make justice the line and righteousness the plummet" (28:17). The servant of Yahweh receives the Lord's spirit in order to bring forth justice to the nations, and "he will not fail or be discouraged till he has established justice in the earth" (42:1-4). The Lord says: "I . . . love justice, I hate robbery and wrong" (61:8), and tells his people: "Keep justice, and do righteousness, for soon my salvation will come, and my deliverance (ṣᵉḏāqâ) will be revealed" (56:1).

Clearly mišpāṭ is a complex idea to Isaiah, involving Yahweh, his nature, acts, and requirements of all his creatures, but especially of his covenant people. He manifests good judgment, and in that judgment brings justice. He longs for the same in his people. In his judgment he will establish mišpāṭ in the earth through his servant.[37]

Servant of the Lord. One of the most significant contributions of Isaiah is the figure of "the servant of Yahweh." Much has been written on the subject, from many points of view, with a vast measure of disagreement and misunderstanding.

In the first edition of his commentary on Isaiah,[38] B. Duhm separated certain passages, namely 42:1-4; 49:1-6; 50:4-9; and 52:13–53:12, from the rest of chs. 40–55, and designated them as the "Servant Songs," or songs of 'eḇeḏ yhwh. Since that time, it has been almost an axiom to consider these passages as independent poems. J. A. Soggin says: "They are marked out not only by a special theme, independent from that of the rest of the work, but also by the fact that they have evidently been interpolated in their present context, from which they can be removed without any resultant damage or interruption."[39] Scholars are not in complete agreement over the extent of the poems, and some scholars count five Servant Songs, and some even six or seven.[40] According to some, the poems existed before "Second Isaiah" and were used by him; others say they were written later and inserted into "Deutero-Isaiah" by a redactor. A very few scholars reject the independent existence of the Servant Songs.[41]

---

37. For further study, see Morris, *The Biblical Doctrine of Judgment*, pp. 7-25; Snaith, *Distinctive Ideas*, pp. 74-77; Eichrodt, *Theology* 1:374-381.

38. *Das Buch Jesaja*. HKAT (Göttingen: 1892).

39. *Introduction*, p. 313.

40. For specifics, see the very detailed note in H. H. Rowley, *The Servant of the Lord*, p. 6 note 1.

41. After having accepted the theory of the Servant Songs for about forty years, W.S. LaSor, on the basis of continuing study of the text, came to a different conclusion: "a careful reading of the entire section, extending from chapter 41 (not 42) through chapter 53, will show that it is *all* about the Servant of the Lord"; *Israel: A Biblical View* (Grand Rapids: 1976), p. 16. P.-E. Bonnard, independently, came to much the same conclusion. Calling those who isolate the poems "victims of prejudice," he says: "Isaiah 40–55 constitutes rather a symphony on the Servant Israel"; *Le Second Isaie: son disciple et leurs éditeurs*. Études Bibliques (Paris: 1972), p. 7; see his discussion, pp. 37-56, and table, pp. 39f.

Attempts to identify the Servant of Yahweh have been equally confused and confusing. Is the Servant Israel, the prophet himself, Cyrus, or someone else? Christians, on the basis of Acts 8:35, contend that the Servant is Jesus, but neither that reference nor Isa. 53 requires such a conclusion on the basis of pure exegesis. That Jesus used the term "servant" with reference to himself is clear, and that the early Church called him "servant of God" (*pais theóu*) is also clear. By seeking a fuller or deeper meaning in the Servant passages in Isaiah, it is possible to find "fulfillment" in Jesus. But first of all, the Isaianic text must be considered exegetically. What did the prophet mean, and how did the early hearers or readers understand the statements?

At the outset, Israel is the servant (41:8f.). The purpose of a servant is to do the will of the master, and Israel was chosen to do Yahweh's will, to "bring forth justice to the nations" (42:1), to be "a light to the nations" (v. 6). But Israel was a blind, deaf servant (v. 19) and therefore had to be punished (v. 24). Some interpreters detect two persons in dialogue in this portion: Israel the nation and a righteous individual or remnant in Israel. All admit that interpretation is difficult. Some believe that Cyrus of Persia is Yahweh's servant (and some even claim that this entire portion of Isaiah is about him). This is based on the passages in 44:28, where Cyrus is called "my shepherd," and 45:1, where he is called "his (Yahweh's) anointed (or messiah)." There is no doubt that Cyrus is called upon to serve Yahweh, and that the portion seems to extend at least to v. 13 ("he shall build my city and set my exiles free"). However, careful reading will indicate that Israel is still the servant (44:1f.; cf. v. 21). But most important, the text clearly states that the calling of Cyrus was "for the sake of my servant Jacob, and Israel my chosen" (45:4). Only by detaching the Servant Songs from the context can such a conclusion be avoided.

In 48:1 the house of Jacob is still being addressed, but in 49:1-6 it becomes clearer that two persons are in view: Jacob and "my servant, Israel" (v. 3) who was "formed from the womb" to be Yahweh's servant, "to bring Jacob back to him, and that Israel might be gathered to him" (v. 5). This seems to be the prophet himself, whose task—and a very difficult one—is to "raise up the tribes of Jacob" (v. 6). Ch. 50 describes some of the sufferings and persecutions that this servant had to undergo (see vv. 5-7). Ch. 51 reads at times like the preaching of the prophet, yet at others it seems that God himself is speaking to the people. (The attempt of Bible editors to put some passages in quotation marks may help to point out this characteristic, but the lack of agreement about where quotations begin and end permits no great confidence in the results.)

In the great passage in 52:13–53:12, however, the prophet now joins himself with the people in looking at another servant: "All we like sheep have gone astray, . . . and the Lord has laid on him the iniquity of us all" (53:8). Careful study of the personal pronouns—"we, our, us" on the one hand, and "he, his, him" on the other—requires the interpretation that the servant is neither the blind and deaf nation Israel, nor the righteous remnant or prophet called "Israel," but the true Israel, the obedient servant.[42] A servant is one who serves his master, and the more faithful that service, the more the servant approaches the ideal.

The Servant of the Lord can be represented by a triangle or cone. The bottom represents the entire nation, thus the servant of chs. 41–48. The middle portion represents the more faithful servant, whether interpreted as the righteous remnant or the prophet himself (or even someone else). The apex represents the servant who perfectly serves his Lord, having "borne our griefs and carried our sorrows" (53:4). He is the one who made himself an offering for sin (v. 10) and made many to be accounted righteous (v. 11). He is the true Israel, who fulfills to the utmost the will of Yahweh and the purpose which Yahweh had in mind when he first chose Israel. "Accordingly, the fuller meaning of the servant passages has to do with the perfect Servant, and the Christian rightly identifies this Servant with the one who came in the form of a servant and who was obedient even unto death (cf. Phil. 2:7-8)."[43]

A servant may well become so disobedient, rebellious, and hostile to his lord's will that he must be banished. On the other hand, a servant also may be obedient and become a perfect servant. In ch. 14 the satanic servant (the one who became an adversary to the Lord) is portrayed as fallen from heaven, cast away, nevermore to be named (vv. 4-21). In ch. 53 the obedient servant is portrayed as the sin bearer, who will have his portion with the great (v. 12). Yahweh uses a satanic servant as a "rod" by which to lead his rebellious people into captivity. He uses his "shepherd," Cyrus, to bring his people back to their land—but that is not the end of sin. Yahweh uses the suffering servant to bring his ransomed people into the kingdom of righteousness and justice, the eternal realm of peace.

In the final chapters of the book, the prophet's notion of servanthood reflects the opening portion of Isaiah's prophecy:

> I was ready to be sought by those who did not ask for me;
>   I was ready to be found by those who did not seek me.
> I said, "Here am I, here am I,"
>   to a nation that did not call on my name.
> I spread out my hands all the day
>   to a rebellious people . . . (65:1f.)

But the fulfillment of God's eternal purpose also is reflected:

> "For behold, I create new heavens and a new earth;
>   and the former things shall not be remembered or come into mind.
> But be glad and rejoice for ever in that which I create;

---

42. See D.J.A. Clines, *I, He, We, and They: A Literary Approach to Isaiah 53.* JSOTS 1 (Sheffield: 1976).

43. LaSor, *BDPT*, p. 135.

for behold, I create Jerusalem a rejoicing,
and her people a joy.
I will rejoice in Jerusalem,
and be glad in my people;
no more shall be heard in it the sound of weeping
and the cry of distress.

. . . . . .

The wolf and the lamb shall feed together,
the lion shall eat straw like the ox;
and dust shall be the serpent's food.
They shall not hurt or destroy
in all my holy mountain,
says the Lord." (65:17-25)

FOR FURTHER READING

Childs, B.S. Isaiah and the Assyrian Crisis. SBT, 2nd ser. 3 (London: 1967).

Clements, R.E. Isaiah 1–39. NCBC. Grand Rapids: 1981. (See chs. 36–39 as early link between 1–35 and 40–55.)

Holladay, W.L. Isaiah: Scroll of a Prophetic Heritage. Grand Rapids: 1978. (Study guide for lay people; canonical book represents "a whole array of voices.")

Kaufmann, Y. The Babylonian Captivity and Deutero-Isaiah. Trans. C.W. Efroymson. New York: 1970. (Challenges view that Israel only first accepted monotheism in post-exilic period.)

Kissane, E.J. The Book of Isaiah. 2 vols. Rev. ed. Dublin: 1960. (Fine study by Roman Catholic author.)

Knight, G.A.F. Deutero-Isaiah: A Theological Commentary on Isaiah 40–55. Nashville: 1965.

Kruse, C.G. "The Servant Songs: Interpretive Trends Since C.R. North." Studia Biblica et Theologica 8 (1978): 3-27.

Millar, W.R. Isaiah 24–27 and the Origin of Apocalyptic. HSM 11. Missoula: 1976.

Muilenburg, J. "Introduction to Isaiah 40–66." IB 5:381-414.

Neubauer, A., and Driver, S.R., eds. The Fifty-third Chapter of Isaiah According to the Jewish Interpreters. 2 vols. 1876-77; repr. New York: 1969. (Texts and translations.)

North, C.R. The Suffering Servant in Deutero-Isaiah. 2nd ed. London: 1956. (Thorough treatment with exhaustive bibliography.)

Power, E. "Isaias." CCHS §§ 419a–451s. (Thorough bibliography; interesting development of prophet's message.)

Skinner, J. The Book of the Prophet Isaiah. 2 vols. Cambridge Bible. Cambridge: 1897-98. (A classic.)

Smart, J.D. History and Theology of Second Isaiah. Philadelphia: 1965.

Ward, J.M. Amos and Isaiah. Nashville: 1969. (Pp. 143-279; sees literary and theological affinity between "First Isaiah" and Amos.)

Westermann, C. Isaia 40–66. Trans. D.M.G. Stalker. OTL. Philadelphia: 1967.

Whybray, R.N. Isaiah 40–66. NCBC. Grand Rapids: 1981.

Young, E.J. The Book of Isaiah. 3 vols. Grand Rapids: 1965-1972. (Conservative, careful exegesis, dogmatically controlled.)

CHAPTER 30

MESSIANIC
PROPHECY

THE word "Messiah" does not occur in the Old Testament. How then can one speak of "messianic prophecy"?

Because the Christian is principally concerned with Christ, he or she has a special interest in looking for prophecies of Christ in the Old Testament. In fact, this quest seems to be the only interest some Christians have in the Old Testament. In Isaiah in particular, and to a lesser extent in Micah, this survey already has encountered prophecies that are usually associated with Jesus Christ, and more will be found in other prophets; therefore it seems appropriate to discuss at this point the subject of messianic prophecy.

MESSIANIC PROPHECY AND PROPHECY IN GENERAL

Like biblical prophecy in general (see Ch. 22), messianic prophecy is not "history written in advance." Yet it does somehow relate to the coming Messiah.

The Word "Messiah." The English word derives from Heb. *māšîaḥ* (sometimes written *mashiach*), a common adjective meaning "anointed." It was translated into Greek as *christós* "anointed," from which come "Christ" and "christen." The words "Messiah" and "Christ" have the same basic meaning,[1] and in referring to Jesus as "the Christ," the New Testament writers identified him with the Jewish Messiah.

But to begin with Christ is to work backwards. Rather, one first should ask what the people of Israel thought of when they heard the Hebrew word. Used as an adjective meaning "anointed," it occurs a number of times, often as "the anointed priest," and several times with reference to kings. Sometimes it is used as a substantive, "anointed one," applied even to the Persian king Cyrus (Isa.

---

1. As the terms develop in usage, "Christ" takes on additional meanings, and the word in Christian usage is much broader than the Jewish "Messiah."

45:1). But nowhere in the Old Testament does the word occur with the technical meaning of "Messiah."[2]

In the intertestamental period, after the close of the Old Testament canon but prior to the time of Jesus, the word came to be used as a technical term, usually with the article, "the Anointed" (Pss. Sol. 17:36; 18:8; cf. 1 Enoch 48:10; 52:4). By the time of Jesus the word was in common use as a title.[3] When the rulers sent priests and Levites to interrogate John the Baptist, he replied: "I am not the Messiah" (John 1:20). His reply was understood perfectly, for they asked next: "Are you Elijah?" (according to Jewish teaching, Elijah was to come just prior to the advent of the Messiah; see Mal. 4:5 [MT 3:24]). Likewise, when Jesus asked the apostles: "Who do men say that I am?" Peter replied: "The Christ . . ." (Matt. 16:15f.). The early Church adopted this title for Jesus (see Acts 2:36), and subsequently "Jesus the Christ (Messiah)," simplified to "Jesus Christ," became a proper name.

Messianic Prophecy without Messiah? It already has been asked how there can be messianic prophecy in the Old Testament if the word "Messiah" does not occur. To answer that question one must first understand that prophecy is a message from God (see Ch. 22) which relates the present situation to his ongoing redemptive activity. This activity culminates in Jesus Christ. Therefore, any prophecy that ties the present with the ultimate purpose of God may be called "messianic." But although the term "messianic prophecy" is used in a broad sense, it is better to narrow the definition and give it precision by formulating several distinctives.

(1) Soteriological prophecy. Many prophetic passages express the general idea that God is working to save his people, and that the time is coming when this purpose will be achieved. Such a hope can be found in the story of the Fall, where God tells the serpent that the seed of the woman will crush the serpent's head—i.e., that the adversary of God's creative work will be defeated in the long run (see Gen. 3:15). Although often called "messianic prophecy," this passage might better be placed in the category of soteriological prophecies, prophecies which proclaim God's ultimate victory over everything opposed to his saving purpose.

(2) Eschatological prophecy. Quite a number of prophecies, especially in books later than the fall of Samaria, relate to the days to come or the end of the age. As early as Amos[4] occur statements such as the following:

---

2. Some scholars read "Messiah" in Dan. 9:25f., but there it lacks the article and is translated better "an anointed one, a prince" (RSV), "an anointed prince."

3. For a fuller discussion, see W.S. LaSor, "The Messianic Idea in Qumran," pp. 344-351 in M. Ben-Horin, B.D. Weinryb, and S. Zeitlin, eds., *Studies and Essays in Honor of Abraham A. Neuman* (Leiden: 1962); "The Messiah: An Evangelical Christian View," pp. 76-95 in M. Tanenbaum, M.R. Wilson, and A.J. Rodin, eds., *Evangelicals and Jews in Conversation on Scripture, Theology, and History* (Grand Rapids: 1973).

4. For the authenticity of these verses, see p. 324. See also G. von Rad, *Old Testament Theology* 2:138; R.E. Clements, *Prophecy and Covenant*, pp. 111f.

"In that day I will raise up
  the booth of David that is fallen
and repair its breaches,
  and raise up its ruins,
  and rebuild it as in the days of old." (Amos 9:11)

"Behold, the days are coming," says the LORD,
  "when the plowman shall overtake the reaper
  and the treader of grapes him who sows the seed. . . .
I will restore the fortunes of my people Israel,
  and they shall rebuild the ruined cities and inhabit them. . . ."
(vv. 13f.)

These passages are taken here as referring to the "messianic age" (see below).
Still, they mention no messianic person; God himself is central. Since such
passages concern the end time, they might be classified as eschatological
prophecy.

(3) Apocalyptic prophecy. In a few prophecies, particularly exilic and postexilic, divine intervention brings about the final victory over the enemies of
God's people. Sometimes this is connected with the "day of Yahweh," an expression already in use prior to the time of Amos (see Amos 5:18). The day of
Yahweh, or day of the Lord, is a day of judgment (Isa. 2:12-22), wrath (Zeph.
1:7-18), and salvation or victory (3:8-20). When Gog of the land of Magog
comes against Israel "in the latter years," it is God himself, using earthquake,
pestilence, torrential rains, and every kind of terror, who defeats Gog and saves
his people and their land (Ezek. 38:1-39:29). This irruption or breaking-in of
God into the normal or historical chain of events is sometimes called "apocalyptic," and such prophecies are best classified as apocalyptic.

(4) Messianic prophecy. Only when the Messiah is clearly in view, or when
the messianic reign is described, should prophecy be called messianic. Otherwise
great confusion arises.[5] But if the term "Messiah" does not occur in the Old
Testament, how can one learn about the person or kingdom of the Messiah?

MESSIANIC PERSON AND OFFICE

Son of David. According to Jewish usage of the intertestamental and New
Testament periods (ca. 300 B.C.–A.D. 300), "Messiah" meant specifically the
Son of David who was to appear as the messianic king. The New Testament
uses it precisely in this sense. Thus Jesus asked the Pharisees: "What do you
think of the Messiah? Whose son is he?" and they replied, "The son of David"
(Matt. 22:42). When Jesus rode into Jerusalem in a manner suggesting the

---

5. For a strong protest against this confusion of terms and a fine contribution to
the clarification, see J. Coppens, "Les origines du messianisme: Le dernier essai: de
synthèse historique," pp. 35-38 in L'Attente du Messie. Recherches bibliques (Bruges:
1954).

fulfillment of Zechariah's prophecy (Matt. 21:5; cf. Zech. 9:9), the crowds shouted: "Hosanna to the Son of David!" (Matt. 21:9). When the apostles were concerned with establishing Jesus' messianic claims, they centered on Old Testament passages that mentioned David (Acts 1:16; 2:25), and argued that it was actually the Messiah who was intended (see 2:29-31, 34-36, substituting "Messiah" for "Christ").[6]

Davidic Dynasty. When David was planning to build a temple (or "house") for Yahweh, the prophet Nathan was sent, first to veto that plan, and then to promise that "the Lord will make for you a house" (2 Sam 7:11). The following words are from the "Davidic covenant":

> "I will raise up your offspring after you, who shall come forth from your body. . . . I will establish the throne of his kingdom for ever. . . . And your house and your kingdom shall be made sure for ever before me; your throne shall be established for ever." (vv. 12-16)

On the basis of this covenant the terms "house of David," "throne of David," and "son of David" assume a large role in Old Testament prophecy.

In reviewing Samuel and Kings (see above, Chs. 17–20) it was noted that the Davidic dynasty continued until the fall of the southern kingdom. The postexilic prophets and the hagiographa (Ezra and Nehemiah) demonstrate that the Davidic line was established once more in the person of Zerubbabel. In the New Testament genealogies of Jesus, Jesus was of the line of David (on the place of David in the beliefs of the early Church, see above). This centrality of the Davidic dynasty became the essential element of the messianic hope, and is expressed in a variety of ways.

Isaiah proclaimed a hope concerning the "latter time" (Isa. 9:1), when a child would be born and would take upon himself the government, "to establish it, and to uphold it with justice and with righteousness from this time forth and for evermore." This government was to be "upon the throne of David" (vv. 6f.). Isaiah also mentioned "a shoot out of the stump of Jesse, and a branch . . . out of his roots" (11:1), referring to David as the son of Jesse and the fact that even though cut down, the Davidic line would spring up again from the same roots.

Jeremiah refers to the covenant with David (Jer. 33:17, 20f.), citing "a righteous branch" and "a shoot of righteousness to grow up unto David" (Jer. 23:5f.; 33:14-16). He even announces that "they shall serve . . . David their king, whom I will raise up for them" (30:9).

Ezekiel says: "I will set up over them one shepherd, my servant David,"

---

6. Although "Messiah" and "Christ" were practically interchangeable terms at first (see p. 396), New Testament uses frequently are taken as referring exclusively to Jesus. The apostles were arguing that Jesus was the Messiah and that the Messiah was David's son.

Tomb of King David, from whose line would spring forth "a righteous Branch" (Jer. 33:15). (G. Nalbandian)

who shall be prince among them (34:23f.). Similar statements are found in other prophets.

Royal Psalms. Apart from any specific theory of enthronement rituals (see below, Ch. 40),[7] it should be pointed out that a number of Psalms on the surface appear to be addressed to the king, but they contain expressions that seem to indicate some being who is greater than the individual occupying the throne at that moment.

Ps. 2, for example, refers to the king on Zion (the portion of Jerusalem where the palace was located), but it addresses him as Yahweh's "son" (v. 7) and promises that God will give him the nations for a heritage and the ends of

---

7. For a balanced study, see J.L. McKenzie, "Royal Messianism," *CBQ* 19 (1957): 25-52. See also D.J.A. Clines, "The Psalms and the King," *Theological Students Fellowship Bulletin* 11 (1975): 1-8.

the earth for a possession (v. 8). This affirmation seems to look forward to a time when the king would rule not only over Israel but even over the gentiles.

Ps. 45 is addressed "to the king" (v. 1 [MT 2]), and describes the glory of his kingship. But it goes on to say: "Your throne, O God, endures for ever and ever" (v. 6 [MT 7]),[8] and concludes: "I will cause your name to be celebrated in all generations; therefore the peoples will praise you for ever and ever" (v. 17 [MT 18]). Certainly this looks beyond the reign of the incumbent king!

Ps. 110 opens: "Yahweh says to my lord: 'Sit at my right hand, till I make your enemies your footstool' " (v. 1). Other expressions are used that elsewhere are connected with the end of the age, such as "the day of his wrath" (v. 5) and "execute judgment among the nations" (v. 6).

These few examples show that the king who sat on the throne of David was a symbol of something greater in space and time than himself and his reign, and could even be a symbol of Yahweh. Psalms that express faith in God's promise to establish an eternal kingdom, and that also refer to the king or throne in Jerusalem, can properly be called messianic Psalms. They are closely related to messianic prophecy.

Messianic Kingdom:. Attention to details expressed in the messianic prophecies shows that the prophets envisioned more than simply the continuity of the Davidic dynasty. The very expression "son of David" should suggest a broader or deeper idea; while individual kings are called "son of Jeroboam," "son of Nebat," or "son of Ahaz," the prophetic passages concerning continuity of the dynasty always cite the "son of David." Thus the original covenant with David is called to mind, and with it the original ideal king and kingdom.

As seen above, the kingdom to be established in the latter days is to be "for ever and ever." It includes the nations (or gentiles) and extends to the ends of the earth. But it is more than an extension in space and time of the kingdom of Judah. It differs in its very essence, being founded on righteousness and peace. The Spirit of the Lord rests upon the messianic king, who judges with righteousness and equity (Isa. 11:2-4). Even changes in the natural order are part of the prophetic picture of the messianic kingdom:

> The wolf shall dwell with the lamb,
>   and the leopard shall lie down with the kid,
> and the calf and the lion and the fatling together,
>   and a little child shall lead them.
>
> . . . . . .
>
> They shall not hurt or destroy in all my holy mountain;
> for the earth shall be full of the knowledge of the Lord
>   as the waters cover the sea. (vv. 6-9)

---

8. The Hebrew also could be translated "Your throne is God," but not "your divine throne," as in the RSV.

Though the focus of this chapter has been on the *kingly* aspects of Messianism, the subject as featured in the New Testament is considerably broader. Jesus is pictured there not only as the fulfillment of the royal ideal as Son of David but of many other Old Testament themes as well: as wise man he is greater than Solomon (Matt. 12:42); as Son of Man he fulfills Daniel's vision (Dan. 7:14ff.); as prophet and lawgiver he is a second Moses (Matt. 5–7); as priest he outranks Aaron (Heb. 5–7); as Servant of Yahweh he gives his life a ransom for many (Mark 10:44). Strands, including the royal one, that were originally separate in the Old Testament, Jesus braided together himself, as part of his consciousness of being God's Anointed and Chosen.

FOR FURTHER READING

Bentzen, A. *King and Messiah*. London: 1954. (Expounds Scandinavian viewpoint.)

Klausner, J. *The Messianic Idea in Israel*. Trans. W.F. Stinespring. New York: 1955. (From time of Moses to third century A.D.)

Landman, L. *Messianism in the Talmudic Era*. New York: 1979. (Essays on origins, natural and supernatural aspects of Jewish and Christian messianic phenomena.)

Motyer, J.A. "Messiah." *IBD*, pp. 987-994.

Mowinckel, S. *He That Cometh*. Trans. G.W. Anderson. Nashville: 1956. (Includes discussion of "Son of Man.")

O'Doherty, E. "The Organic Development of Messianic Revelation." *CBQ* 19 (1957): 16-24.

Ringgren, H. *The Messiah in the Old Testament*. SBT 18. London: 1956. (Supports traditional interpretation, using historical exegesis.)

Rivkin, E. "The Meaning of Messiah in Jewish Thought." *USQR* 26 (1971): 383-406. (Spontaneous answer to problems of Judaism in Greco-Roman world.)

Scholem, G. *The Messianic Idea in Judaism*. Trans. M.A. Meyer and H. Halkin. New York: 1971. (Essays stressing complex relationship of Jewish mysticism and messianism.)

Teeple, H.M. *The Mosaic Eschatological Prophet*. JBL Monograph. Philadelphia: 1957. (Examines views of return of Moses or a prophet like him in the eschatological age.)

CHAPTER 31

JEREMIAH

CHALLENGING times both demand and produce people capable of meeting the challenge. Jeremiah's day, the most momentous period in Judah's lengthy history, had as its chief interpreter a prophet without peer in his grasp of the prophetic message and his ability to express it. Through four turbulent decades, Jeremiah declared the word of God to king and commoner alike at great personal cost. He demonstrated not only what a prophet should say but what he should be. His book recounts both his life and message and provides the paradigm for all true prophecy.[1]

INTRODUCTION

The Prophet. The biographical and autobiographical sections of his book make Jeremiah better known than any other writing prophet. Born in the village of Anathoth north of Jerusalem (1:1; 11:21, 23; 29:27; 32:7-9), he was the son of Hilkiah, a priest. Whether, as frequently suggested, Hilkiah's family had been deprived of the right to practice their profession by Josiah's sweeping reforms, which abolished shrines outside of Jerusalem, is not certain. It does seem likely that the family was descended from Abiathar, the priest banished to Anathoth by Solomon for his part in Adonijah's play for the throne (1 Kgs. 2:26). What Jeremiah's home was like is not known; but H.L. Ellison's suggestion is worth noting: "The way in which Jeremiah was steeped in the prophecies of his predecessors, especially Hosea, suggests that his home may have been one of those where the light of the persecuted prophetic tradition was kept alive in a dark age."[2] This heritage does not mean that Jeremiah's family

---

1. See A. Bentzen: ". . . a book on prophecy will always be, to a great extent, a book on Jeremiah"; *Introduction* 2:116.
2. *Men Spake from God*, 2nd ed. (Grand Rapids: 1958), p. 79; see J. Skinner, *Prophecy and Religion: Studies in the Life of Jeremiah* (Cambridge: 1922), p. 19, where the family line is traced back to Eli and the shrine at Shiloh:

always understood and accepted his message. To the contrary, the men of Anathoth, including his brothers and his father's household, attacked him vigorously, probably because he supported Josiah's reforms (see 11:21; 12:6).

Josiah and Jeremiah seem to have been about the same age. The prophet calls himself a youth when the word of God first came to him in the thirteenth year of Josiah's reign, ca. 627 B.C. (1:2).[3] Thus, he probably was born shortly after 650. Although his prophetic call came well before Josiah's reforms were given impetus by the finding of the book of the law (2 Kgs. 22:8ff.), most of the written prophecies concern events after Josiah's tragic death in 609. Jeremiah's ministry spans more than forty years (until after 586, when Jerusalem fell to Nebuchadnezzar) and embraces the reigns of Josiah's four successors, the last kings of Judah.

His Call. Jeremiah was marked for misunderstanding from the beginning. His call established him as a true prophet and set the tone of his ministry:

> Then the Lord put forth his hand and touched my mouth;
> and the Lord said to me,
> "Behold, I have put my words in your mouth.
> See, I have set you this day over nations and over kingdoms,
> to pluck up and to break down,
> to destroy and to overthrow,
> to build and to plant!" (1:9f.)

Like Moses, Jeremiah felt inadequate for the task, especially since his youth would hamper his delivering this word of gloom to a hostile audience. Such preaching cannot have been popular, and the guarantee implicit in the vision of the almond rod, that God would see that his word was carried out, was essential before Jeremiah could accept his burdensome responsibilities (see 20:7-18). Hosea suffered shame and reproach because of a wicked wife; Jeremiah was deprived completely of marriage and fatherhood to symbolize the barrenness of a land under judgment (16:1-13). Such celibacy was rare among the Jews and undoubtedly reinforced questions about his normalcy.

In addition to these inner conflicts, Jeremiah was harassed by repeated threats from without. Indeed, "conflict is the keynote of Jeremiah's public career."[4] The men of his own town and household set themselves against him (11:21-23; 12:6). Later, a coalition of priests and prophets charged him with blasphemy for predicting destruction of the temple (26:1-6). His militant stand

---

. . . There was no family in Israel whose fortunes had been so closely bound up with the national religion as that into which Jeremiah was born. And nowhere would the best traditions and the purest ethos of the religion of Yahweh be likely to find a surer repository than in a household whose forbears had for so many generations guarded the most sacred symbol of its imageless worship, the Ark of God.

3. J.P. Hyatt's proposal (IB 5, p. 779) to read "twenty-third" instead of "thirteenth" and begin Jeremiah's ministry in 616 has not been accepted widely.

4. H.T. Kuist, Jeremiah, Lamentations. Layman's Bible Commentary (Richmond: 1960), p. 8.

was vindicated when it was recalled that Micah had made a similar prediction in the days of Hezekiah and went unscathed. Yet the people were so riled that only the protection of Ahikam, a Jewish noble, saved the prophet's life (26:24). Beaten and put in stocks by Pashhur the priest (20:1-6), and left to die in a mire-filled cistern by the princes of Judah (38:6-13), Jeremiah had more than one brush with death. Worst of all was the fury of Jehoiakim, enraged by the indictments of his people's sins and the announcements of his country's doom (36:1-7). Both Jeremiah and his faithful scribe Baruch escaped the royal wrath only by divine protection (v. 26).

Adding to Jeremiah's woes were the misunderstanding and opposition of the false prophets, professionals more attuned to the people's whims than to the word of God. Rather than support and reinforce Jeremiah's message, they contradicted it, preaching peace and security instead of judgment. So embroiled were they in the sins of their countrymen that they could not cry against them:

"But in the prophets of Jerusalem
   I have seen a horrible thing:
they commit adultery and walk in lies;
   they strengthen the hands of evildoers,
so that no one turns from his wickedness." (23:14)

They claimed to know the word of the Lord, but their claim was empty:

"I did not send the prophets,
   yet they ran;
I did not speak to them,
   yet they prophesied.
But if they had stood in my council,
   then they would have proclaimed my words to my people,
and they would have turned them from their evil,
   and from the evil of their doings." (vv. 21f.)

The contrast between true and false prophet is most clear in Jeremiah's conflict with Hananiah (28:1-17). As a prophet over the nations as well as Judah (1:10), Jeremiah had proclaimed that the surrounding kingdoms—Edom, Moab, Ammon, Tyre, Sidon—should bow to Nebuchadnezzar's suzerainty, disregarding any prophet or diviner who advised otherwise. To dramatize this submission Jeremiah secured a wooden yoke around his neck with thongs. Claiming divine inspiration Hananiah announced that the exile in Babylon would be short-lived and that the captives, including Jehoiachin the deported king, would return within two years (28:2-5). He then broke Jeremiah's wooden yoke (vv. 10f.). It takes little imagination to feel how such opposition vexed the prophet's righteous soul.

His Character. The abundant autobiographical and biographical material in the book gives important insights into the prophet's character. Five chief characteristics can be seen:[5]

---

5. H. Cunliffe-Jones, *The Book of Jeremiah*. Torch Bible Commentary (Naperville: 1960), pp. 32ff.

Late Bronze Age cistern at Jerusalem (cf. Jer. 38:6). (Israel Department of Antiquities)

(1) Jeremiah possessed a deep-seated personal honesty, especially in his relationship with God. Unlike the false prophets, he gave no glib answers, but wrestled with God to be certain of understanding his word in each situation. This frankness could approach insubordination or even blasphemy:

> "I sat alone, because thy hand was upon me,
> for thou hadst filled me with indignation.

Why is my pain unceasing,
   my wound incurable,
   refusing to be healed?
Wilt thou be to me like a deceitful brook,
   like waters that fail?" (15:17f.)

And again:

"O Lord, thou hast deceived me,
   and I was deceived;
thou art stronger than I,
   and thou hast prevailed.
I have become a laughingstock all the day;
   every one mocks me." (20:7)

Jeremiah readily admitted that his ministry was distasteful at times. He felt trapped. He could not escape God's call, and the word burned within him. Yet when he did preach, God made a fool of him by delaying fulfillment of the prophecy (see 20:8-10). But Jeremiah trusted God so much that his directness was an asset. Like Habakkuk he wanted to believe, and cried out for help in his unbelief. In his personal fellowship with God he found strength to go on despite questions and fears, for God himself gave assurance:

"If you return, I will restore you,
   and you shall stand before me.
If you utter what is precious, and not what is worthless,
   you shall be as my mouth.
They shall turn to you,
   but you shall not turn to them.
And I will make you to this people
   a fortified wall of bronze;
they will fight against you,
   but they shall not prevail over you.
for I am with you,
   to save you and deliver you,"
     says the Lord. (15:19f.)

(2) Jeremiah was courageous in carrying out his convictions. As seen above from the partial catalog of Jeremiah's suffering at the hands of his enemies, none of the threats from family, royalty, or priesthood caused him to diminish his message. He knew what he had to do, and he did it . . . not always happily, but always faithfully and courageously.

(3) Jeremiah also demonstrated a passionate hatred of morally or spiritually unsound conduct. His fiery blasts against idolatry (e.g., chs. 2–5), social injustice (e.g., 5:26-29), and false prophecy (e.g., vv. 30f.) are examples of his righteous indignation. So relentless was his call for judgment that his prayers for the vindication of his message at times became pleas for vengeance on his enemies:

"Remember how I stood before thee
  to speak good for them,
  to turn away thy wrath from them.
Therefore deliver up their children to famine;
  give them over to the power of the sword,
let their wives become childless and widowed.
  May their men meet death by pestilence,
  their youths be slain by the sword in battle." (18:20f.)

If he expressed himself too strongly at times, it was not so much a sign of weakness as of greatness. Jeremiah took sin seriously because he took God's righteousness seriously. It remained for a later Sufferer to show how to hate transgression, and yet make intercession for the transgressors.

(4) Jeremiah combined a sensitivity to his people's sufferings and a gracious humanity. His role as a prophet of doom often clashed with his love for his people and land.[6] To see impenitence and indifference to imminent judgment put a sword through his soul:

"Let my eyes run down with tears night and day,
  and let them not cease,
for the virgin daughter of my people is smitten with a great wound,
  with a very grievous blow." (14:17)

Though serious, as his lot demanded, Jeremiah was not morbid. He found a certain joy in his intimate communion with God and his fellowship with fervent and loyal friends like Baruch. That Zephaniah the priest seemed responsive to his message (29:29); that Ahikam, a prince of Judah, protected him (26:24); that the Ethiopian steward dared save him from the miry cistern (38:7-13); and that Zedekiah was secretly receptive combine to suggest that Jeremiah was capable of warm friendships despite his prophetic austerity.

(5) A final and outstanding characteristic was Jeremiah's hope for the future, a hope grounded not in glib optimism but in the sovereignty and loyalty of God. As relentless was his proclamation of doom, so was his heralding of hope for the land after it had been purified by judgment. In the face of disaster, he displayed his confidence by purchasing property at Anathoth, thus testifying to his expectation that God would allow his people to resettle their land (32:1-44).

Composition of the Book.[7] Although the details are far from complete, more is known about the compilation of Jeremiah than any other prophetic book.

---

6. Cunliffe-Jones, *ibid.*, p. 34, lists several passages which reflect Jeremiah's intimate knowledge of and concern for his land: e.g., 1:11; 2:23, 31; 4:7, 11; 5:6; 6:29; 7:11, 18, 34; 8:7; 12:5; 14:6; 17:8, 11; 18:3f.; 22:6. See also E.F.F. Bishop, *Prophets of Palestine: The Local Background to the Preparation of the Way* (London: 1962), pp. 115ff.

7. For a description of the complex structure and the various types of literature found in Jeremiah, see J. Bright, "The Book of Jeremiah: Its Structure, Its Problems, and Their Significance for the Interpreter," *Interp* 9 (1955): 259-278.

Part of the prophet's message was written down in the fourth year of Jehoiakim (*ca.* 605). Apparently, written prophecy was the exception, since God specifically commanded Jeremiah to write down all that he had spoken to him since the days of Josiah (36:1-3). Baruch's first scroll was written in response to this command and seemingly summarized the first twenty years of Jeremiah's ministry. It probably contained much of what is recorded in chs. 1–25, centering in the dire fate awaiting Judah and Jerusalem for their deep moral and spiritual corruption.

After Jehoiakim brazenly burned the first scroll, Jeremiah dictated a second, even longer scroll (36:32), which probably corresponded even more closely to chs. 1–25. That substantial portions of the first half of the book are in the first person suggests that they had been either dictated by Jeremiah himself or preserved as originally preached. The second half of the book uses the third person and contains much more prose in proportion to poetry.

The usual theory, which has considerable merit, is that, whereas the first part of the book contains oracles (both prose and poetry), personal prayers (confessions), and some autobiographical sketches (the call, 1:4-19; the symbolic burying of the waistcloth, 13:1-11), the second half is largely an account of episodes in Jeremiah's life during the reigns of Jehoiakim and Zedekiah and after the fall of Jerusalem. Those narratives usually are credited to Baruch, who as a close friend and associate recorded these events and appended them to the early collection written at Jeremiah's behest. Virtually all of chs. 26–52 is prose (even the recorded speeches), in contrast with the preponderance of poetic oracles in chs. 1–25. Chief exceptions are chs. 30–31, which form part of the Book of Consolation (chs. 30–33), and the oracles against the nations in chs. 46–51.

Biblical scholars have questioned the Jeremianic authorship of some sections of the book. The text itself seems to indicate that ch. 52, which closely resembles 2 Kgs. 24:18–25:30, is not to be ascribed to Jeremiah, since the last line of 51:64 says: "Thus far the words of Jeremiah." This chapter must have been added to the edition of Jeremiah and Baruch to show by its graphic account of the fall of Jerusalem how Jeremiah's prophecies had been fulfilled literally.

The sabbath passage in 17:19-27 has frequently been denied to Jeremiah,[8] usually because its emphasis on rigid enforcement of the sabbath laws seems out of harmony with Jeremiah's stress on inward obedience rather than ritual observance. But Jeremiah may well have viewed sabbath observation not as a means of grace but as a sign of repentance. Probably the sabbath commandment had been seriously neglected during Manasseh's lawless reign. Reestablishing its authority and resisting the temptation to commercialize the day (see Amos 8:5) might well be excellent evidence of a change of heart.[9]

---

8. E.g., Cunliffe-Jones, *The Book of Jeremiah*, pp. 136f.
9. See Ellison's defense of authenticity, "The Prophecy of Jeremiah," *Evangelical Quarterly* 34 (1962): 24f.

Other passages sometimes denied to Jeremiah are ch. 10 (whose thought and tone recall parts of Isa. 40–55) and some of the oracles against foreign nations in chs. 46–51.[10] However, interpreters still debate these questions at length. What seems clear is that a prophet who ministers over a lengthy period of time amid changing circumstances and who is so thoroughly steeped in the messages of his fellow prophets should be allowed considerable variety in what he says and how he says it, without any narrow limitations as to tone or message.

Another critical question concerns the so-called deuteronomic editor, who is said to have reworked the book after Baruch gave it its basic shape. He is said to be responsible for prose passages which stress obedience to the law (7:1–8:3; 11:1-17; 17:19-27).[11] While such editing may well have taken place, it is just as likely that Baruch himself gave these speeches their final form. Perhaps if more were known about the development of Hebrew prose style, the so-called deuteronomic style might be seen as a normal prose style of the seventh and sixth centuries.

The history of the composition of Jeremiah is further clouded by the book's form in the LXX, where it is considerably shorter than the Hebrew[12] and preserves the oracles in somewhat different order. Chs. 46–51, the indictment of the nations, is inserted between 25:13 and 15, omitting v. 14. A likely explanation is the editors' desire to shape the book according to the patterns of Isa. 1–39 and Ezekiel: oracles of doom against Judah, oracles of doom against the nations, and oracles of hope for Judah.[13] This stylized arrangement argues against priority of the LXX structure. The vast differences may show that the final book was published in more than one form.

CONTENTS

A basic difficulty in analyzing the contents of Jeremiah's prophecy is their lack of consistent chronological order. Oracles and episodes from various periods of the prophet's lengthy career appear side by side. Thus the reader must be alert to changes in the historical situation involved. Some oracles are undated in the text, and can be attributed to a particular period in Jeremiah's life only with great hesitancy. Yet since Jeremiah is so much the interpreter of his times and so vitally linked to their epoch-making events, it seems best to attempt to organize his writings chronologically and expound them in connection with the reigns of Judah's last tragic kings.

---

10. Some have questioned also the oracles of consolation in chs. 30–31.

11. Bentzen summarizes recent approaches to the composition of Jeremiah, including that of S. Mowinckel, the backbone of contemporary analyses; *Introduction* 2:119. Mowinckel has given a digest of his own views in *Prophecy and Tradition* (Oslo: 1946), pp. 61-65.

12. Bentzen says that one-eighth of the MT is missing in the LXX; *Introduction* 2:118. G.W. Anderson estimates the difference as 2700 words; *A Critical Introduction to the Old Testament*, p. 124.

13. (1) 1:1–25:13; (2) 46:1–51:64 plus 25:15-38; (3) 26:1–35:19. The remainder of the book describes Jeremiah's sufferings (chs. 36–45).

Josiah's Reign. As noted, Jeremiah's call is dated in the thirteenth year of Josiah (1:2). Although the only other clear reference to Josiah's reign is in 3:6, it seems virtually certain that at least chs. 1–6 stem from this period. The oracles in this section concern the two major themes found in the description of the call: the destruction upon Judah from the north because of their idolatry (1:13-19) and the assurance that God was watching over his word to bring it about (vv. 11f.).

In describing the sins of idolatry which were about to plunge Judah into judgment, Jeremiah mustered all his considerable poetic skills to make his indictment the more pressing and convicting. Judah's faithlessness was shocking for several reasons. First, they had spurned God's many overtures of love and grace and reversed their past practices of devotion:

> "I remember the devotion of your youth,
>   your love as a bride,
> how you followed me in the wilderness,
>   in a land not sown.
> Israel was holy to the Lord,
>   the first fruits of his harvest.
> All who ate of it became guilty;[14]
>   evil came upon them."
>   says the Lord. (2:2f.)

Furthermore, Judah's forsaking of their Lord for other gods is unparalleled even among their pagan neighbors:

> "Has a nation changed its gods,
>   even though they are no gods?
> But my people have changed their glory
>   for that which does not profit.
>   . . . . . .
> for my people have committed two evils:
>   they have forsaken me,
> the fountain of living waters,
>   and hewed out cisterns for themselves,
> broken cisterns,
>   that can hold no water." (vv. 11, 13)

This was done in spite of the clear example of Israel, who had been made desolate for similar sins:

> "She saw that for all the adulteries of that faithless one, Israel, I had sent her away with a decree of divorce; yet her false sister Judah did not fear, but she too went and played the harlot." (3:8).[15]

---

14. I.e., Israel's enemies who attacked them.

15. Such passages which treat Judah's idolatry as spiritual harlotry show most clearly the influence of Hosea's message.

The corruption and deep-seated rebellion bring in their wake judgment from without. Zion, the great city of God, was to be ravaged by invaders from the north. Chs. 4–6 are a collection of brief oracles which herald this doom and offer some reasons for it. The religious leaders—prophets and priests—are singled out in ch. 5 as chief contributors to Judah's delinquency:

"An appalling and horrible thing
    has happened in the land:
the prophets prophesy falsely
    and the priests rule at their direction;
my people love to have it so,
    but what will you do when the end comes?" (5:30f.)

The identity of the northern enemy is debatable. Traditionally, the Scythians, also mentioned above (Ch. 32) in relationship to Zephaniah's prophecies, were thought most likely. But Herodotus' description[16] of their exploits in Syria, Palestine, and Egypt has received little confirmation from other sources. Contemporary scholars, therefore, tend to find in Jeremiah either general references to foreign enemies, who usually invaded Judah from the north, or specific references to Babylonia, who just started toward prominence under Nabopolassar during Jeremiah's early ministry. Whatever its identity, the enemy is terrible:

"They lay hold on bow and spear,
    they are cruel and have no mercy,
    the sound of them is like the roaring sea;
they ride upon horses,
    set in array as a man for battle,
    against you, O daughter of Zion!" (6:23)

Curiously, Jeremiah tells little of Josiah's reform. Certainly he supported it, particularly the earlier phases, and his preaching (e.g., ch. 3) set the pace for it. But just as certainly, he cannot have been satisfied with the results, for the reform dealt too much with externals and left the heart of the people untouched. No surface reform could erase the ingrained wickedness fostered by decades of rebellion. Jeremiah searched vainly among poor and rich alike to find a righteous person (5:1-5), but the verdict was always the same:

"But this people has a stubborn and rebellious heart;
    they have turned aside and gone away." (v. 23)

Reformation without was a shoddy substitute for repentance within.

Just as puzzling is Jeremiah's virtual silence about the king's tragic death at Megiddo in 609. The Chronicler notes that the prophet felt it keenly: "All Judah and Jerusalem mourned for Josiah. Jeremiah also uttered a lament for Josiah . . ." (2 Chr. 35:24f.). But the prophet himself makes only passing

---

16. *History* i.103-6.

reference in 22:10. No doubt he was stunned, especially since it came at the hands of the Egyptians, frequent targets of Jeremiah's ire (e.g., 2:16-18). Perhaps his silence indicates both feelings too deep for words and the conviction that what is past is past: the present was the pressing problem.

Jehoahaz. Josiah's son and successor received only brief mention in Jeremiah, and that only after his three-month reign was brought to an abrupt end by deportation to Egypt (2 Kgs. 23:31-35). Apparently Pharaoh Neco, bent on aiding the beleaguered Assyrians and halting the resurgence of Babylonian power, felt that Jehoahaz (also known as Shallum) was not a loyal vassal. Rather than risk revolt in Judah and the disruption of supply and communication lines, Neco placed Eliakim, another son of Josiah, on the throne and sent Jehoahaz to Egypt to die. In a brief oracle (22:10-12), Jeremiah exhorts the survivors not to weep for the dead Josiah but for the exiled king, "for he shall return no more to see his native land."

Jehoiakim. As soon as Eliakim—whose coronation name was Jehoiakim—mounted the throne, Jeremiah joined battle with him on three fronts. Encouraged by the dramatic defeat of Sennacherib in the reign of Hezekiah, Jehoiakim urged his people to trust in the temple and its sacrifices as a defense against foreign invasion. Complacency became part of public policy, however corrupt the domestic life and however threatening the foreign scene. But the temple would suffer the fate inflicted by the Philistines on the shrine at Shiloh (1 Sam. 4–6). The chant of false security ("This is the temple of the Lord, the temple of the Lord, the temple of the Lord"; Jer. 7:4) was to give way to the laments of captivity, unless king and people mended their ways (7:1–8:7; 26:1-24).

Jeremiah also attacked Jehoiakim for flagrantly violating the terms of the Book of the Covenant, which his father had rediscovered. Oppression of aliens, widows, and orphans, bloodshed, idolatry, stealing, adultery, and even child sacrifice were among the sins specifically forbidden yet blatantly practiced (7:5-10, 30f.). In a few short years, Jehoiakim had succeeded in undoing his father's reforms.

This violent oppression was accompanied by luxury altogether unfitting for a servant king of Judah:

> "Woe to him who builds his house by unrighteousness,
> and his upper rooms by injustice . . .
> who says, 'I will build myself a great house . . .
> paneling it with cedar, and painting it with vermilion.
> Do you think you are a king
> because you compete in cedar?
> Did not your father eat and drink and do justice and righteousness?
> Then it was well with him." (22:13-15)

He, to whom royal splendor meant so much, must bear ignominy and shame as judgment. As usual in prophetic judgment speeches, the punishment fit the crime:

"Therefore, thus says the Lord concerning Jehoiakim . . .
With the burial of an ass he shall be buried,
    dragged and cast forth beyond the gates of Jerusalem." (vv. 18f.)

Jeremiah also assaulted Jehoiakim's foreign policies. Neco's victory at Megiddo had left Egypt in a position to dominate Judah and her neighbors. In direct defiance of God, Jehoiakim joined a coalition led by Egypt in an attempt to resist the growing power of Nebuchadnezzar's Babylon. Naively these peoples counted on their circumcision to charm them to victory over the uncircumcised Babylonians. But the penitent heart, not the removed foreskin, was the key to victory according to Jeremiah:

"Behold the days are coming, says the Lord, when I will punish all those who are circumcised but yet uncircumcised—Egypt, Judah, Edom, the sons of Ammon, Moab, and all who dwell in the desert that cut the corners of their hair;[17] for all these nations are uncircumcised, and all the house of Israel is uncircumcised in heart." (9:25f.)

From this period of conflict with Jehoiakim come Jeremiah's confessions, poignant complaints lifting to God deep questions about the rightness of the Deity's ways. God had called him to denounce sin and proclaim judgment. Yet sin persisted, and judgment was postponed. Beyond his persecution by the vicious king, Jeremiah's sharpest anguish was caused by God's silence (see 11:18-20; 12:1-6; 15:15-18; 18:19-23; 20:7-18).[18]

Jeremiah's plea for judgment was answered by the marching troops of Nebuchadnezzar. In 605 the Babylonians routed Neco's army at Carchemish (see 46:2-24), bringing a marked shift in the balance of power. The death of his father Nabopolassar kept Nebuchadnezzar from exerting authority over Canaan and Judah for several months. But invasion was inevitable, and for two decades, Babylon's long shadow dimmed the light of Judah's independence:

Thus says the Lord:
"Behold a people is coming from the north country,
    a great nation is stirring from the farthest parts of the earth.
They lay hold on bow and spear,
    they are cruel and have no mercy. . . ." (6:22f.; cf. 5:15-17)

By destroying the scroll containing these indictments and threats (ch. 36), Jehoiakim did more than show disdain for the prophet; he sought to break the

---

17. A pagan custom outlawed in Lev. 19:27.
18. Many of these passages resemble psalms of individual complaint in which the sufferer describes his pain and pleads for God's help. The almost suicidal despair of 20:14-18 has its closest parallel in Job's dark soliloquy (Job 3:1-26).

power of the prophecy. Its power, however, lay not in carbon scrawls on Baruch's parchment but in the word of the eternal Lord that could not be broken.

At this pivotal point in history, Jeremiah summarized the message he had preached for twenty-five years and reminded his countrymen of their failure to repent. For seventy years they would serve the king of Babylon, as God banished from them "the voice of mirth and the voice of gladness, the voice of the bridegroom and the voice of the bride, the grinding of the millstones and the light of the lamp" (25:1-38, esp. vv. 10f.).

To this period can be attributed several of Jeremiah's oracles against the nations (chs. 46–49). The victory at Carchemish made Babylon the major power, whose ruthless policies would but hurt the smaller nations. Jeremiah's speeches to Judah's neighbors in Egypt, Moab, Ammon, Edom, and Damascus reinforce his statements about Yahweh's sovereignty, remind Judah of the awesome power of their oppressor, and renew the hope that all their enemies would ultimately fall.

In 601, Jehoiakim tried to free himself from Babylonian suzerainty. Encouraged by Nebuchadnezzar's failure to conquer Egypt, Judah made a play for independence. This was a misstep that proved painful at the beginning and fatal at the end. Nebuchadnezzar's first response was to send against Judah bands

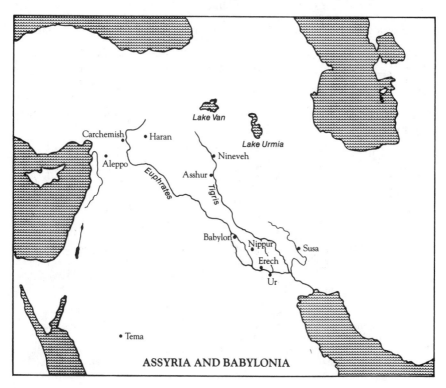

ASSYRIA AND BABYLONIA

of Chaldeans, Syrians, Moabites, and Ammonites (2 Kgs. 24:2), perhaps the "shepherds" over whom Jeremiah lamented:

> "Many shepherds have destroyed my vineyard,
>   they have trampled down my portion,
> they have made my pleasant portion a desolate wilderness." (12:10)

Three years later Nebuchadnezzar himself invaded Judah and laid siege to Jerusalem. About this time, the apostate Jehoiakim died,[19] still a young man, as Jeremiah had foretold (22:18f.; 36:30).

Jehoiachin. Jehoiachin's brief (three months) reign is recorded in 2 Kgs. 24:8-17: the invasion of Jerusalem, the capture of the king and his family, the looting of the temple, the exile of Judah's best warriors and artisans. Jeremiah preserves the pathos of the events. In Nebuchadnezzar's ravaging of the land, Jeremiah sees the Lord's own hand:

> "I have winnowed them with a winnowing fork
>   in the gates of the land;
> I have bereaved them, I have destroyed my people;
>   they did not turn from their ways." (15:7)

The stern threat of exile brings loud lament:

> "For a sound of wailing is heard from Zion:
>   'How we are ruined!
>   We are utterly shamed,
> because we have left the land,
>   because they have cast down our dwellings.' " (9:19; cf. 10:17f.)

Worst of all, the deportation of Jehoiachin (also called Coniah and Jeconiah) spells the end of the Davidic dynasty:

> "As I live, says the Lord, though Coniah the son of Jehoiakim, king of Judah, were the signet ring on my right hand, yet I would tear you off and give you into the hand of . . . Nebuchadrezzar[20]. . . ." (22:24f.)

And again:

> Thus says the Lord:
> "Write this man down as childless,
>   a man who shall not succeed in his days;
> for none of his offspring shall succeed in sitting on the throne of David,
>   and ruling again in Judah." (v. 30)

---

19. The details are not given (cf. 2 Kgs. 24:2). The Chronicler notes that Nebuchadnezzar "bound him in fetters to take him to Babylon" (2 Chr. 36:6).

20. The form Nebuchadrezzar occurs 27 times in Jeremiah, Nebuchadnezzar 10 times. The two are dialectical variants of the Akkadian name, *Nabû-kudurri-uṣur* "Nabu protect my boundary stone."

Yet as bitter as the Exile was, it also carried the seeds of hope as Jeremiah learned in a vision just after Jehoiachin's deportation in 598. Two baskets of figs—one fresh, the other rotten—were the focal point of the vision. The Lord's interpretation reverberated with hope and judgment: the good figs were the exiles, to be preserved in the foreign land and returned to Judah to serve God in a new relationship of love and trust; the bad figs were the new king Zedekiah and his henchmen both in Judah and Egypt, to be destroyed by famine and pestilence (24:1-10).

Zedekiah. Zedekiah, Josiah's son and Jehoiachin's uncle, was Nebuchad-nezzar's puppet in every way. Only twenty-one years old, he was placed on the throne by the conqueror and his name changed from Mattaniah to Zedekiah to show his vassal status (2 Kgs. 24:17).

Zedekiah's task was monumental. His people had been stripped of political, religious, and economic leadership. His exiled predecessor, Jehoiachin, was still alive in Babylon, and many would view him as the rightful ruler. The climate was ripe for confusion, if not anarchy.

Zedekiah's reign was marked more by weakness than meanness. He was dominated by his spiritual and political counselors, who had neither skill nor stature. They pushed the king into conflict with Jeremiah, despite Zedekiah's general respect for the prophet, whose reputation had risen measurably since his prophecies of exile had proved true.

One area of conflict concerned the length of the Exile. Led by the prophet Hananiah, the king and his court expected a short captivity, perhaps only two years, after which Jehoiachin and the exiles would return (cf. 28:1-4). In con-trast, Jeremiah dispatched a letter encouraging the exiles to settle down in Babylonia and wait out the seventy-year captivity he had prophesied earlier (29:1-32).

A second area of conflict centered in Judah's relationship to Nebuchad-nezzar. Throughout the turmoil of Zedekiah's eleven-year reign, Jeremiah urged the young king to submit to the authority of Babylon. Four years after Zedekiah took the throne, when Egypt was forming a coalition among Edom, Moab, Ammon, Tyre, and Sidon to rebel against Babylon, Jeremiah dramatically urged him not to take part. To make plain the Lord's will, Jeremiah donned a wooden yoke as a symbol of the submission to Nebuchadnezzar which the Lord desired:

> "But if any nation or kingdom will not serve this Nebuchadrezzar king
> of Babylon, and put its neck under the yoke of the king of Babylon,
> I will punish that nation with the sword, with famine, and with pes-
> tilence, says the Lord, until I have consumed it by his hand." (27:8)

Jeremiah's words so outraged Hananiah that he snatched the yoke from Jere-miah's shoulders and broke it, hoping thereby to nullify the prophecy it sym-bolized. The Lord remained adamant: Judah was not to revolt. The broken wooden yoke was to be replaced by one of iron (28:12-16).

Jeremiah's words fell on deaf ears. Zedekiah sided with Egypt, and Nebuchadnezzar retaliated by invading Judah and laying siege to Jerusalem (588). Desperately the king sought some fresh word from God, but the response was a repetition of what he had heard for the past decade:

> "Behold, I will turn back the weapons of war . . . with which you are fighting against the . . . Chaldeans who are besieging you outside the walls. . . . I myself will fight against . . . the inhabitants of this city. . . ." (21:3-6)

The fall of Jerusalem (586), the looting of the temple, and the captivity of Zedekiah all came to pass as Jeremiah had prophesied (39:1-18; 52:1-30). Yet even while the capital was under heavy siege, Jeremiah was sent to Anathoth to redeem part of his ancestral land as a sign that God's final word would not be judgment. Exile would be followed by return (32:1–33:26).

Falsely deemed a traitor and wrongly accused of trying to desert to the Chaldeans, Jeremiah suffered harsh treatment from princes and priests, despite Zedekiah's respect for his prophetic gifts (37:1–38:28). Consequently, the bloody fall of Jerusalem brought some respite to Jeremiah, whose life the Babylonians spared (39:11f.).

The Governorship of Gedaliah. The long chain of Judah's judgment reached its final links when Nebuchadnezzar appointed Gedaliah governor (40:1-16). Jewish nationalists viewed their governor as a Babylonian puppet and savagely assassinated him. Fearing Nebuchadnezzar's wrath, a remnant of Jewish leaders under Johanan planned to flee to Egypt. Jeremiah urged them to remain in Judah and help restore the ravaged land. Rashly they spurned the prophet's word, and, in a final act of irony, spirited Jeremiah away with them to Egypt against his will (41:1–43:13). The last words from the aged prophet were spoken in Egypt promising judgment even there to the ragged band of Judean fugitives (44:1-30).

Jeremiah probably died in Egypt well before the return from exile. But the final editor of his book appended a story that gleams like light at the end of a tunnel: Jehoiachin, Judah's captive king, is shown mercy by Nebuchadnezzar's successor, Evil-merodach (52:31-34; see 2 Kgs. 25:27-30 and comments above; p. 287). This act of clemency appears to signal that the tide of judgment has been turned by the providence of God, and the waves of return and restoration which comforted Jeremiah's dark hours begin to rise.

LITERARY QUALITIES

No Old Testament prophet used a wider variety of literary forms or showed more artistic skill than Jeremiah. In its remarkable marriage of form and content, Jeremiah's poetry has both power and pathos. Given what Jeremiah was called to say—in his messages of doom and hope, his pleas for repentance, his confessions of personal struggle—it would be difficult to have said it better.

Like his fellow prophets, Jeremiah used literary patterns familiar to his hearers, but in fresh and striking combinations that gave his oracles a vitality, a vividness, and an urgency unsurpassed in the Bible. Only a sampling can be shown here.

Prose. More than in most prophetic writings, prose and poetry are interleaved in Jeremiah. The prose takes several forms:

(1) Prose oracles are not uncommon (7:1–8:3; 11:1-17; 17:19-27; 18:1-12; 23:1-8). Most are forms of judgment speech: indictment of sins, threat of judgment (often introduced by "therefore"), and messenger formula. A call to repentance or a command to act righteously may be included (7:5-7; 22:1-4). Frequently the oracle begins with divine instruction about where, when, and to whom the word is to be given (7:1f.). A poetic section may be included (e.g., 22:1-8, where vv. 6b-7 is poetry).

(2) One of Jeremiah's most famous salvation speeches is in prose—the prophecy of the "new covenant." The basic thrust is the contrast between the old covenant made at the Exodus and the new covenant to be written on the heart of God's people (31:31-34).

(3) Symbolic acts of prophecy usually are described in prose (13:1-11; 16:1-18; 19:1-15; 27:1-15). The form of these accounts is ordinarily as follows: the prophet is commanded by the Lord to perform an act; the prophet obediently does so; then the Lord interprets the act. These enacted prophecies are more than illustrative, for they are charged with divine power to accomplish what they symbolize.

(4) Autobiographical and biographical narratives form a large part of the book. The account of the prophet's call, told in the first person, is autobiographical narrative, even though some of God's words are poetic (1:4-19). The story of Jeremiah's suffering at the hands of Pashhur the priest is biographical narrative (20:1-6), as is the description of Jehoiakim's burning of Baruch's scroll (36:1-32). The distinction between prose biography and prose oracle is often blurred because judgment speeches and other prophecies sometimes occur within a narrative section (e.g., 35:1-19, where vv. 13-17 is a prose judgment speech).

(5) Historical narratives, which tell not Jeremiah's personal story but Judah's history, are found in 39:1-18 (fall of Jerusalem); and 52:1-34 (destruction of the temple and subsequent details of the Exile; cf. 2 Kgs. 24:18–25:30).

Poetry. (1) The judgment speech is frequent, but much more varied in form than in Amos. The indictment, for instance, may take the form of an admonition:

"Let every one beware of his neighbor,
    and put no trust in any brother;
for every brother is a supplanter,
    and every neighbor goes about as a slanderer." (9:4)

The threat of judgment may be a rhetorical question:

> "Shall I not punish them for these things?
>   says the Lord." (v. 9)

The oracles against the nations sometimes contain only the threat of judgment with no specific indictment of sin (46:1-12; 47:1-7). However, the speech against the Ammonites includes:

(a) an indictment:
> "Has Israel no sons?
>   Has he no heir?
> Why then has Milcom[21] dispossessed Gad,
>   and his people settled in its cities?" (49:1)

(b) a threat of judgment introduced by "therefore":
> "Therefore, behold, the days are coming,
>   says the Lord,
> when I will cause the battle cry to be heard
>   against Rabbah[22] of the Ammonites;
> it shall become a desolate mound. . . ." (v. 2)

(c) a promise of restoration:
> "But afterward I will restore the
> fortunes of the Ammonites, says the Lord." (v. 6)

(2) The "Book of Comfort" contains salvation speeches, promises of hope and deliverance for Judah (30:12-17, 18-22; 31:1-14, 15-22). Their form tends to be less stereotyped than that of the judgment speech. Sometimes Judah's plight is described in order to contrast what is and what will be:

> "For thus says the Lord:
> Your hurt is incurable,
>   and your wound is grievous.
> There is none to uphold your cause,
>   no medicine for your wound,
>   no healing for you.
>   . . . . . .
> For I will restore health to you,
>   and your wounds I will heal,
>   says the Lord." (30:12f., 17)

Frequently, a salvation speech contains elaborate descriptions of the restoration: rebuilding of cities, renewed fertility of crops, abundance of children, and a reestablished monarchy (vv. 18-21). Included in the promise may be the destruction of the enemies that have inflicted the suffering, usually in the form of a lex talionis, an exact equivalent of their crime:

---

21. The national god of the Ammonites, also called Molech or Moloch (see 32:35; Lev. 18:21), probably means "king."

22. Capital of Ammon, modern Amman.

"Therefore all who devour you shall be devoured,
and all your foes, every one of them, shall go into captivity;
those who despoil you shall become a spoil,
and all who prey on you I will make a prey." (v. 16)

A possible climax may be the renewal of the covenant, phrased in the language of wedding vows:

"And you shall be my people,
and I will be your God." (v. 22)

Portions of hymns may be included, as God not only proclaims deliverance but invites his people to sing about it:

For thus says the Lord:
"Sing aloud with gladness for Jacob,
and raise shouts for the chief of the nations;
proclaim, give praise, and say,
'The Lord has saved his people,
the remnant of Israel.' " (31:7)

Literary Techniques. Several of Jeremiah's literary techniques may be noted:
(1) His figures of speech are pungent, as is his description of Judah's sexual corruption:

"They are well-fed lusty stallions,
each neighing for his neighbor's wife." (5:8)

or his picture of the selfish greed of Judah's wealthy:

"For wicked men are found among my people;
they lurk like fowlers lying in wait.
They set a trap; they catch men.
Like a basket full of birds,
their houses are full of treachery." (vv. 26f.)

(2) Rhetorical questions are favorite devices. Jeremiah uses questions where the answer should be obvious, yet the people seem to disregard what they know to be right. The argument put in question form may be drawn from common custom:

"Can a maiden forget her ornaments,
or a bride her attire?
Yet my people have forgotten me
days without number." (2:32)

from the law:

"If a man divorces his wife
and she goes from him
and becomes another man's wife,

will he return to her?
    Would not that land be greatly polluted?
You have played the harlot with many lovers;
    and would you return to me?
        says the Lord." (3:1)

from nature:

"Does the snow of Lebanon leave the crags of Sirion?
    Do the mountain waters run dry,
    the cold flowing streams?
But my people have forgotten me,
    they burn incense to false gods." (18:14f.)

or from history:

"Has Israel no sons?
    . . . Why then has Milcom dispossessed Gad. . . ." (49:1)

A method of entrapment, these questions cause their hearers to condemn themselves. By giving the obvious answer, the hearer acknowledges that the proper line of conduct is equally obvious and yet he has done just the opposite.

(3) Like Isaiah and Amos, Jeremiah seems to have used literary forms usually associated with wisdom literature. Consider this illustration from nature:

"Even the stork in the heavens
    knows her times;
and the turtledove, swallow, and crane
    keep the time of their coming;
but my people know not
    the ordinance of the Lord." (8:7)

In addition, a popular proverb is used in a judgment speech in 13:12,[23] while the blessing-cursing pattern is found in 17:5-8 with an emphasis akin to Ps. 1.

(4) Psalmlike complaints are one literary form for Jeremiah's confessions. The "why" and "how long" of 12:1-4 and the ardent pleas for deliverance of 17:14-18; 18:19-23; 20:7-12 are examples of the complaint form.

(5) Jeremiah reached into many areas of Israel's life for literary ingredients to enrich his message. Often the form reinforced the content. The nuances would not have escaped his hearers, who would have recognized the forms as part of their everyday life. The courts of justice in the town gates furnished forms like the powerful indictment in 2:1-13, where the Lord argues his case against Judah. The watchtower, where the alert of impending battle was sounded, supplied these words:

---

23. Jer. 17:11 seems to be a proverb in the form of a familiar "like-so" comparison between animal and human behavior.

"Flee for safety, O people of Benjamin,
    from the midst of Jerusalem!
Blow the trumpet in Tekoa,
    and raise a signal on Beth-haccherem;[24]
for evil looms out of the north,
    and great destruction." (6:1)

From the battlefield are taken commands which signal an invasion of Egypt:

"Prepare buckler and shield,
    and advance for battle!
Harness the horses;
    mount, O horsemen!
Take your stations with your helmets,
    polish your spears,
        put on your coats of mail." (46:3f.)

This sampling shows the imaginative way in which Jeremiah employed familiar forms to stir his countrymen to respond to God's word.

JEREMIAH'S THEOLOGICAL CONTRIBUTION

The keystone of Jeremiah's theological insight is his emphasis on the Exodus as Israel's dominant spiritual experience. Included are deliverance from slavery in Egypt, the Sinai covenant with its detailed list of obligations, and settlement in Canaan by the guidance and power of the Lord. Most of the prophet's other theological themes lean, in varying degrees, on the Exodus.

Yahweh's Sovereignty in History. Israel's birth as a nation, Egypt's frustration in trying to prevent the Exodus, Canaan's surrender to Joshua were all seen as the direct result of divine intervention. As such, these monumental events gave shape to Israel's view of history as the arena where the Lord of Abraham, Isaac, and Jacob makes himself known.

Jeremiah strongly affirmed that events in Judah, Egypt, and Babylon were subject much more to divine sovereignty than to human politics. In other words, human politics could succeed only to the extent that they accorded with God's will. This was what Jeremiah persistently tried to impress on Jehoiakim and Zedekiah. Nebuchadnezzar's success was not due so much to political prowess or military strength as to God's command (cf. 27:6). Yahweh's sovereignty in history showed itself as he used nations to do his will.

This sovereign Lord also reserved the right to change his plans. In the midst of God's grand act of grace, Israel wandered in the wilderness forty years

---

24. Perhaps 'Ain Kârim ('En Kerem), west of Jerusalem; Bright, *Jeremiah*. Anchor Bible 21 (Garden City: 1965), p. 47.

in judgment.[25] Instead of remembering this stern lesson, Judah became complacent, presuming that the God of covenant grace would defend them and their capital from attack forever. But God is too sovereign for that, Jeremiah learned:

> "If at any time I declare concerning a nation or a kingdom, that I will
> . . . destroy it, and if that nation . . . turns from its evil, I will repent
> of the evil that I intended to do to it. And if at any time I declare
> concerning a nation or a kingdom that I will build and plant it, and
> if it does evil in my sight . . . then I will repent of the good which I
> had intended to do to it." (18:7-10)

Here Jeremiah takes the principle of blessing or judgment, applied to Israel in Deut. 27–28, and extends it to cover God's freedom in dealing with nations in general.

God's sovereignty in history was revealed in his judging nations directly and taking full responsibility, as Jeremiah's oracles against the foreign powers make clear (chs. 46–51). Time and again they picture judgment breaking forth with no word of the human agent responsible. This is not to say that only divine acts—earthquake, famine, plague, or flood—were involved. Usually the judgment came through military assault (cf. 51:1-4), but God claimed to have sent the armies just as he had breached the walls of Jericho (Josh. 6) and routed the troops of Midian (Judg. 6–7).

Old Torah and New. Neither Jeremiah's harsh indictments of Judah's sin nor his high hopes for future restoration can be understood apart from the Exodus. The idolatry so blatant in Manasseh's day (2 Kgs. 21) was all the more appalling in the light of God's magnificent rescue of his people from Egyptian bondage. In a telling argument God cites his early relationship with Israel, and then asks the condemning question:

> "What wrong did your fathers find in me
>   that they went far from me,
>   and went after worthlessness,[26]
>   and became worthless?" (Jer. 2:5)

Israel's defection was out of keeping with the actions of other peoples, even pagan nations:

> "Has a nation changed its gods,
>   even though they are no gods?" (v. 11)

---

25. What Num. 14:34 views as judgment, Jeremiah sees as part of Israel's devout past. Perhaps in comparison with Judah's rejection of the Lord in Jeremiah's day and the strong judgment yet to come, the wilderness wanderings were a period of grace.

26. "Worthlessness" is equivalent to "idols." The wording shows the emptiness of idolatry and its impact—people become what they worship.

Israel's defection was also out of keeping with their own past:

> "Yet I planted you a choice vine,
>   wholly of pure seed.
> How then have you turned degenerate
>   and become a wild vine?" (v. 21)

The personal as well as the national sins Jeremiah sees as violations of covenant law, which should have disciplined their lives as a yoke would an ox:

> "I will go to the great,
>   and will speak to them;
> for they know the way of the Lord,
>   the law of their God."
> But they all alike had broken the yoke,
>   they had burst the bonds. (5:5)

Whether commoners or leaders, the people of Judah had flaunted God's covenant with their fathers.

Nothing can account for this ungrateful rebellion except sin, as permanently stamped in human lives as a leopard's spots or the color of an Ethiopian's skin (13:23). When Jeremiah observes that the human heart—center of intellectual and moral decision—is deceitful and corrupt (17:9), he speaks not theoretically of human nature, but practically from years of observing how his countrymen have despised their covenant heritage while at the same time justifying their wicked conduct.

No superficial solution—not even as sweeping as Josiah's reforms—will remedy the flagrant idolatry and open corruption. To do so will take nothing less than a New Covenant—a binding relationship between a sovereign God and Israel his people: "And I will be their God, and they shall be my people" (31:33).[27] Like the Old Covenant, the New is initiated by the Lord (v. 31), an expression of his sovereignty.

The New Covenant is designed to meet the specific needs that made it necessary: (1) it is even more personal than the marital contract which Israel had so flagrantly violated ("my covenant which they broke, though I was their husband" [v. 32]); (2) it is written on the hearts of the people, whence their iniquity sprang—not stone tablets (v. 33); (3) it results in the true knowledge of God—the New Torah of full obedience and a rich fellowship without need of human teaching (v. 34); (4) it carries assurance of full forgiveness of the sins that called forth judgment (v. 34).[28]

---

27. The mention of both Israel and Judah (v. 31) indicates Jeremiah's idealism in looking to a time when God would countermand the rupture of Jeroboam's division and the ravage of Assyrian invasion. Jeremiah, like the other great prophets, could not picture a future that did not involve the unity of the whole house of Jacob.

28. This radical newness was seized upon by Jesus and the early Church to describe the transformation brought about by the Christian gospel (Mark 14:24; Heb. 8).

This need for and hope of total transformation beginning with the new law written in new hearts shapes Jeremiah's view of the future. It is expressed more in spiritual and personal terms than in political, as would be expected of a prophet who witnessed the tragic failure of a political system and sensed that no superficial reformation could provide lasting remedy.

Yet Jeremiah was not silent on the political future. True, he had renounced all hope that David's city and household would be spared. Yet a "righteous Branch" was to be raised up, a legitimate heir to David's throne. Justice within Israel's borders and security without would mark that reign (23:5f.). This would all be a gift of God's intervening grace, as the name of the promised king proclaimed: "The Lord is our righteousness," the One who looks out for the rights of his people.[29]

The New Covenant, with its New Torah, and the new king (the "Messiah," though Jeremiah did not use the term) combine to shape the prophet's picture of the future: a binding personal relationship with God and a bright national destiny.[30]

Strength of Personal Faith. This bright hope is further evidence of Jeremiah's deep dedication to God's will and strong confidence in his power. Nothing on the political horizon and nothing in the current religious situation—only his deep faith in the covenant Lord—would have prompted such optimism.

In a sense his whole ministry had been a spiritual preparation for his role as comforter as well as critic. His call and commissioning had assured him of God's personal interest: "Before I formed you in the womb I knew you," and "I am with you to deliver you" (vv. 5, 8; cf. 19). The encounter with God's word through the decades of his ministry must have convinced Jeremiah of the Lord's persistence and power to carry out his plans.

The word of God was "as it were a burning fire shut up" in Jeremiah's bones (20:9), and he could but declare it and watch it work.[31] The relentless drive of that word meant that God's future was assured.

Neither the persecution of political enemies nor the misunderstanding of familiar friends could persuade Jeremiah not to trust in God. Even his severe complaints about God's will seemed eventually to strengthen his faith, as did the doubts of false prophets like Hananiah (ch. 28).

Jeremiah's personal experiences cannot be separated from his message. His confidence in the grace of God to transform Israel's future was nurtured by God's gracious yet firm guidance of his own life. Jeremiah's own pilgrimage of judgment and grace became a paradigm whereby the character and will of the

---

29. The Hebrew (yhwh ṣidqēnû) suggests a pun on Zedekiah (ṣidqîyāhû). God's new king would be all that Zedekiah should have been and was not.

30. This combination, without mention of a messianic king, is found in 32:36-41.

31. See J.G.S.S. Thomson, *The Word of the Lord in Jeremiah* (London: 1959).

living God was conveyed to Israel and beyond.[32] If total obedience to the Lord of covenant grace is the major lesson of Scripture, no one in the Old Testament taught it better than Jeremiah.

FOR FURTHER READING

Berridge, J.M. *Prophet, People, and the Word of Yahweh*. Zurich: 1970. (Examines form and content of Jeremiah's proclamations.)

Blank, S.H. *Jeremiah, Man and Prophet*. Cincinnati: 1961.

Carroll, R.P. *From Chaos to Covenant: Prophecy in the Book of Jeremiah*. New York: 1981. (Takes view that Jeremiah is the product of the community rather than of the lone prophet.)

Harrison, R.K. *Jeremiah and Lamentations*. Tyndale Old Testament Commentaries. Downers Grove: 1973.

Hobbs, T.R. "Some Remarks on the Composition and Structure of the Book of Jeremiah." CBQ 34 (1972): 257-275. (Four "tradition complexes," the work of an individual theologian.)

Holladay, W.L. *Jeremiah: Spokesman Out of Time*. Philadelphia: 1974. (Includes contemporary applications.)

Hyatt, J.P. *Jeremiah, Prophet of Courage and Hope*. Nashville: 1958.

Thompson, J. Arthur. *The Book of Jeremiah*. NICOT. Grand Rapids: 1980.

Weinfeld, M. "Jeremiah and the Spiritual Metamorphosis of Israel." ZAW 88 (1976): 17-56.

---

32. See B.S. Childs, *Old Testament as Scripture*, p. 347: "The memory of his proclamation was treasured by a community of faith and consciously shaped by theological forces to serve as a witness for future Israel."

DATING OF JEREMIAH'S PROPHECIES AND EXPERIENCES

The dating of much of Jeremiah's material is controversial.
Passages which name the king or contain a chronological reference are noted with an asterisk.

King	Year(s)	Reference	Summary
Josiah	627 B.C.	1:1-19*	Jeremiah's call
	627-621	2:1-6:30	Indictments of Judah's sin; appeals to repentance; threats of judgment by invasion from north
	627-621	8:4-9:24 (MT 25)	Indictments of Judah's sin; Jeremiah's grief over failure of people to repent and his anticipation of their laments when judgment comes
	621	11:1-14	Jeremiah's support of Josiah's reform based on Book of the Covenant
	621	13:1-11	Symbolic act of burying waistcloth by Euphrates to show folly of dependence on other gods
	621	16:1-9	Lord commands Jeremiah not to marry in light of pending calamities
	621	30:1-31:40	Book of Consolation, which culminates in promise of New Covenant
Jehoahaz	609	22:10-12*	People exhorted to lament not Josiah's death but Jehoahaz' exile
Jehoiakim	608-605	7:1-8:3; 11:15-17; Ch. 26*	Prophecies of temple's destruction
	608-605	22:13-19*	Jeremiah indicts Jehoiakim for valuing splendor above righteousness
	608-605	17:1-27	Jeremiah chides Judah for idolatry and failure to keep sabbath, and laments over his own suffering
	608-605	21:11-22:9	King commanded to execute justice
	608-605	11:18-12:6 15:10-21 18:18-23 20:7-18	Complaints of Jeremiah as both opposition and God delay promised judgment

King	Year(s)	Reference	Summary
	605	25:1-26*	Summary of Jeremiah's message plus some oracles of judgment
	605	46:1–49:33*	Judgment speeches against Egypt and Judah's other neighbors
	605	19:1–20:6	Jeremiah's prophecies of doom provoke harsh opposition from Pashhur the priest
	605	45:1-5*	Lord promises to spare life of Baruch, Jeremiah's scribe
	601	12:7-17	Jeremiah laments ravages to Judah by invading tribes
	601-598	35:1-19*	Jeremiah brings Rechabites to temple as demonstration of obedience which people of Judah should have rendered to the Lord
	601-598	18:1-11	Jeremiah's visit to potter's house
Jehoiachin	598	15:5-9 9:10-11, 17-22 (MT 9-10, 16-21)	Lament over Nebuchadnezzar's attack on Jerusalem
	598	10:17-24 16:16-18	Jeremiah commands people to prepare for exile
	598	22:24-30* 13:18-19	Lord promises judgment to Jehoiachin
Zedekiah	597	24:1-10*	Good and bad figs, symbols of those God spares in exile and those he judges in Judah
	597	49:34-39*	Prophecy against Elam
	597	29:1-29*	Jeremiah's letter encouraging exiles to plan for long stay in Babylonia
	594	51:59-64*	Symbolic act of throwing scroll into Euphrates to prophesy destruction of Babylon
	594	27:1–28:16	Jeremiah's symbolic act of yoke of slavery and his contest with false prophet Hananiah

King	Year(s)	Reference	Summary
	595-590	23:1-40	Jeremiah's indictment of Judah's leaders (esp. the prophets) and his prophecy of David's Righteous Branch
	589	34:1-22*	Prophecy of Jerusalem's fall and indictment of Judah's aristocracy for failure to free their slaves
	588	21:1-10*	Jeremiah urges Zedekiah to surrender to Nebuchadnezzar
	588	37:1–38:28*	Siege of Jerusalem, Jeremiah's imprisonments, and his counsel that Zedekiah should surrender
	588	32:1-44*	Jeremiah buys field at Anathoth as symbol of hope for return from exile
	588	33:1-26*	Jeremiah assured that God will restore fortunes of his people after exile
	586	39:1-18*	Fall of Jerusalem, capture of Zedekiah, sparing of Jeremiah's life
	586	52:1-30*	Fall of Jerusalem, looting of temple, and tally of Nebuchadnezzar's captives
Gedaliah (Governor appointed by Babylon)	586	40:1-16	Jeremiah released to custody of Gedaliah, whom Nebuchadnezzar appointed governor of Judah
	586	41:1-18*	Assassination of Gedaliah; political confusion that followed
Johanan (Leader of Judean remnant)	586	42:1-22*	Jeremiah counsels Judah's remnant to stay in land and not seek asylum in Egypt
	585	43:1-13*	Judean remnant flees to Egypt to escape Nebuchadnezzar's wrath, takes Jeremiah with it against his will
	585	44:1-30*	Jeremiah's last speech to Jews in Egypt, reviewing people's sins and promising judgment even in Egypt
	560	52:31-34*	Evil-merodach succeeds Nebuchadnezzar, grants mercy to Jehoiachin after 37 years of captivity

CHAPTER 32

ZEPHANIAH
AND JOEL

ZEPHANIAH

If the prophetic books were placed in chronological order, Zephaniah would probably fit between Isaiah and Jeremiah. Zephaniah broke the half-century of prophetic silence in Judah during Manasseh's reign of violence and corruption.[1] He reshaped and applied the major themes of the great eighth-century prophets to the turbulent international and domestic scenes of the late seventh century. Certainly his preaching lent support to Jeremiah, as together they helped spark Josiah's reforms.

Personal Background. Nothing is known about Zephaniah except what is found in his writing. In the introduction (1:1) his family history is traced through four generations to Hezekiah. Two possible purposes may account for this unusually lengthy genealogy: Zephaniah may be seeking either to trace his lineage to Judah's great king to substantiate his intimate knowledge of the sins of Jerusalem's leaders (see vv. 11-13; 3:3-5) or to authenticate his true Jewish origin to overcome any questions raised by his father's name, Cushi ("Ethiopian"). If Hezekiah is the king by that name, as seems reasonable, then Zephaniah probably launched his prophetic career as a young man, perhaps age twenty-five. This suggestion arises because three generations (Cushi, Gedaliah, Amariah) are listed between Zephaniah and Hezekiah and only two (Amon, Manasseh) occur between Josiah (who gained power at a tender age) and Hezekiah.

The mention of Josiah's reign (1:1) provides the rough limits of Zephaniah's ministry (*ca.* 639-609 B.C.). Further attempts to pinpoint it are hazardous, but the graphic pictures of idolatrous practices in Judah and Jerusalem offer clues

---

1. Zephaniah's name may recall the suppression of prophetic activity under Manasseh: he had to be "hidden of the Lord" in order to survive the purges of the impious king.

431

that the prophecy dates from before Josiah's reforms and thus coincides approximately with the time of Jeremiah's call (*ca.* 626).[2]

Jerusalem lies at the heart of Zephaniah's concern. He indicts the city's religious degradation and social apathy (1:4-13; 3:1-7) and predicts its ultimate welfare (3:14-20). With an intimacy of detail born of firsthand acquaintance, Zephaniah describes the capital (1:10f.): the Fish Gate, probably in the northern wall near the Tyropoeon valley; the Second Quarter (Mishneh), apparently the northern section immediately west of the temple area; the Mortar (Maktesh), a natural basin (perhaps part of the Tyropoeon valley) just south of the Mishneh, used for a marketplace.[3] Zephaniah focuses on the northern sector because steep embankments on the other three sides encouraged attack from the north. The combination of detailed description and concern for the city's well-being suggests that Zephaniah was a resident of the capital.

Some scholars[4] have been even more specific in reconstructing Zephaniah's ministry, linking him with the temple prophets.[5] Indeed, both Isaiah and Jeremiah paid a good deal of attention to the temple. Joel is vitally concerned with the priests and their daily round of sacrifices. But saying that a prophet shows interest in the religious life of his temple is not the same as claiming that he was a temple prophet, a member of the temple staff whose task was to declare the word of God in connection with stated religious functions such as feast days. In Zephaniah's case the evidence is not strong enough to positively assert his relation to the temple.[6]

Historical and Religious Background. Judah never recovered from Manasseh's infamous half-century of rule. Hezekiah's son, despite token attempts at reformation (2 Chr. 33:12-19), left indelible blots on the nation's character. When Amon reverted to his father's worst traits, Judah's fate was sealed. Zephaniah shattered the prophetic silence not with hope but with impending doom:

---

2. J.P. Hyatt's argument ("The Date and Background of Zephaniah," *JNES* 7 [1948]: 25-29) that the oracles against the nation in ch. 2 harmonize better with the international picture in Jehoiakim's reign (*ca.* 609-597) generally has not been accepted (see F.C. Fensham, "Book of Zephaniah," *IDBS*, pp. 983f.).

3. For a full discussion of the geography, see W.S. LaSor, "Jerusalem," *ISBE* 2 (1982); also Y. Aharoni and M. Avi-Yonah, eds., *The Macmillan Bible Atlas*, map 114, p. 74. In contrast, H. Cazelles seems to identify the Mishneh of 2 Kgs. 22:14 with Zephaniah's Maktesh; "The History of Israel in the Pre-exilic Period," p. 311 in G.W. Anderson, ed., *Tradition and Interpretation*.

4. E.g., A. Bentzen, *Introduction* 2:153.

5. See A.R. Johnson, *The Cultic Prophet in Ancient Israel; The Cultic Prophet and Israel's Psalmody* (Cardiff: 1979); cf. W. McKane, "Prophecy and the Prophetic Literature," p. 166 in Anderson, *Tradition and Interpretation*.

6. On possible connections between Zephaniah and the political and religious establishments of Jerusalem, see R.R. Wilson, *Prophecy and Society in Ancient Israel* (Philadelphia: 1980), pp. 279-282. Recent emphasis on temple prophets has helped counter the extreme views of Wellhausen and followers that prophets and priests were almost continually at odds in ancient Israel. Yet it may be just as extreme to stress the connection too much; see E.J. Young, *My Servants the Prophets* (Grand Rapids: 1952), p. 103.

The great day of the Lord is near . . .
the sound of the day of the Lord is bitter. . . .
A day of wrath is that day,
a day of distress and anguish,
a day of ruin and devastation,
a day of darkness and gloom,
a day of clouds and thick darkness,
a day of trumpet blast and battle cry. . . . [7] (1:14f.)

What nation did Zephaniah see as the whip God would use to drive Judah to its knees? Some have found a clue in Herodotus' description of the waves of Scythian hordes that swept down from their mountain homes into western Asia and even as far as Egypt.[8] Modern scholars, however, shy away from this identification for lack of sufficient support from other ancient records. More probably Zephaniah sensed widespread restiveness produced by the foreboding of Assyria's imminent collapse and ominous rumblings from Babylon, seeking to recover its ancient splendor. Within two decades after Zephaniah's prophecy, proud Nineveh had been humbled (cf. 2:13-15) and Josiah killed at Megiddo (2 Kgs. 23:29), Nebuchadnezzar had roundly whipped the Egyptians at Carchemish, and Syria and Palestine were his. Within four decades Judah itself had been ravaged, and the cry and wail had risen desperately from the Fish Gate, Second Quarter, and Mortar. It was a day of wrath indeed!

Message. Two themes dominate this brief book: the threat of imminent judgment (1:2–3:7) and the hope of ultimate deliverance (3:8-20).

Apart from a brief call to repentance (2:1-3), 1:2–3:7 is unrelieved in its stress on God's wrath. The universal scope of God's judgment will have effects as cataclysmic as the flood in Noah's day (see Gen. 6):

"I will utterly sweep away everything
from the face of the earth. . . .
I will sweep away man and beast. . . ." (1:2f.)

The prophet first focuses on his own land and city (1:4–2:3), whose religious and social sins have made them objects of divine ire. They had sold themselves to the worship of Baal, the Canaanite fertility god; the sun, moon, and stars; and Milcom, king god of their Ammonite neighbors to the east. Their debilitating alliances with pagan nations, particularly Assyria, are symbolized in their aping foreign fashions which tended to compromise their identity as God's peculiar people. The social unsettledness hinted at in 1:9[9] is

---

7. Note the famous medieval Latin hymn, *Dies irae, dies illa.*
8. I.104-6.
9. The difficult phrase "who leaps over the threshold" may refer to the eagerness with which the servants of the rich descended upon the hovels of the poor to loot their scanty goods. An alternate interpretation sees a reflection of pagan superstition; see Hyatt, *JNES* 7 (1948): 25f.: "mount the podium" of an idol (see 1 Sam. 5:5).

Conical-topped tomb (second-first century B.C.) in the Kidron valley, traditional location of the valley of Jehoshaphat (Joel 3:32; cf. v. 14). (J. Finegan)

SEVENTH-CENTURY PROPHETS AND THEIR WORLD

Prophet	Judah	Egypt	Assyria	Babylonia	Notable events
700	Hezekiah 728-687		Sennacherib 705-681		
695	Manasseh 696-642				
690		Tarhaqa 690-664			
685					
680			Esarhaddon 681-669		
675					
670			Ashurbanipal 669-627		
665		Psamtik I 664-610		Šamaš-šum-ukin 668-648	Thebes sacked by Ashurbanipal
660					
655					Psamtik revolts ca. 655 Babylonian revolt fails
650				Kandalanu 647-627	
645	Amon 642-640				
640	Josiah 639-609				
635					
630			Sin-shar-iškun 629-612	Nabopolassar 626-605	
625 Zephaniah ca. 627 Jeremiah 627-					
620 Nahum 621-612(?)					
615					
			Fall of Nineveh 612		
610 Habakkuk	Jehoahaz 609 Jehoiakim 608-597	Neco II 610-595	Assur-uballit 612-609 last Assyrian king		Neco to Carchemish Josiah killed Neco deposes Jehoahaz
605 Obadiah(?)				Nebuchadnezzar 605-562	Battle of Carchemish
600 Joel(?)	Jehoiachin 597				Ashkelon submits Jehoiakim submits Jerusalem falls 597
595	Zedekiah 597-586				

amplified in 3:1-7, where the blame is placed squarely on the leaders. These sins, coupled with the spiritual and moral apathy of Jerusalem's citizenry, merit the fiercest kind of judgment, and Zephaniah describes God's wrath with sustained and white-hot fury almost unparalleled in Scripture.

In the finest prophetic tradition (see Isa. 13–23; Jer. 46–51; Ezek. 25–32; Amos 1–2) Zephaniah also includes oracles against Judah's neighbors (2:4-15). The Philistine coastal area, hotbed of opposition to Judah since the days of the Judges, receives special attention, with four key cities—Gaza, Ashkelon, Ashdod, Ekron—marked for judgment (vv. 4-7).[10] This territory, long accustomed to martial activities, felt the conqueror's boot before Judah: Nebuchadnezzar ravaged Ashkelon in 604 and used Philistia as a launching site for his abortive invasion of Egypt in 601. So blatant was the Philistines' paganism and so patent their opposition to God's purposes in Israel that the prophet feels no need to cite any ground for their judgment.

As for Israel's kinsmen, Moab and Ammon (see Gen. 19:36-38), familiarity apparently had bred contempt (vv. 8-11). Smarting for centuries from defeats at the hands of David (2 Sam. 8:2; 10:1-14) and Jehoshaphat (2 Chr. 20:22-30), they had goaded the Israelites and their God with barbed taunts. Moab and Ammon were absorbed into Nebuchadnezzar's network of nations and used to subdue Judah at the time of Jehoiakim's revolt, a task which they no doubt relished (2 Kgs. 24:2). The brief mention of the Ethiopians (2:12) demonstrates the geographical extent of God's sovereign sway (see 3:10).[11] Assyria and its proud capital, Nineveh, were earmarked for special judgment (2:13-15), which the ruthless coalition of Medes, Babylonians, and Scythians(?) unwittingly brought to pass in 612. Remember that these oracles were intended not for a foreign audience but for Judah alone, who frequently needed to be reminded that, though they belonged exclusively to God, God did not belong exclusively to them. He was Lord of all the earth, and ultimately both Judah and their friends and enemies had to reckon with him.

The indictment of Jerusalem (3:1-7) is more specific than those of the pagan nations: the city's greater privilege has issued in greater responsibility. The actions of the leaders had always been reflected in those of Israel's people. Now all normal channels for bringing God's instruction to the people—rulers, prophets, priests—were clogged with vice and greed (see Mic. 3). Even the tragic example of the northern kingdom could not brake Judah's race to self-destruction. The more God warned, the faster they plummeted toward calamity (Zeph. 3:6f.).

Turning from wrath to restoration the prophet makes clear that God's judgment is not only punitive but corrective. When the nations have been chas-

---

10. English translations are unable to convey the striking puns used in Zephaniah's incisive denunciation (v. 4).

11. Ethiopia may stand here in lieu of Eypt, because in the decades just prior Egypt had been under the sway of Ethiopian rulers (Twenty-fifth Dynasty); see Nah. 3:9.

tened, they will call on the Lord with "a pure speech" and serve him cordially (vv. 8-10). A lowly yet faithful remnant will survive in Judah to replace the leaders whose pride was their snare. Above all, God will dwell among his people and right past wrongs by giving prominence to the humble and renown to the lame and outcast (vv. 17-20), a theme at the heart of the Christian gospel (note the Magnificat sung by Mary in Luke 1:46-55).[12]

Theological Insights. Zephaniah elaborates on Amos' outline of the day of the Lord (cf. Amos 5:18-20), showing just how dark that "day of darkness not light" (v. 18) will be (see also Isa. 2:9-22). With a startlingly unique metaphor the day is likened to a banquet in which those who expect to be guests become victims (1:7f.; cf. the story of Isaac, Gen. 22:7). The point is clear. The people of Judah thought God would vindicate them before the nations. But his constant aim was to vindicate, on a universal scale (1:18; 2:4-15), his own righteousness, even though this proved costly to Judah, their neighbors, and their enemies.[13]

As interpreter of the covenant, Zephaniah saw that God's judgment of Judah was drastic but not final. Through restoration of the remnant his covenant love would triumph. This restoration is the positive, creative side of judgment, without which the purified remnant could not appear. If God's judgment means destruction of the wicked, it also means vindication of the righteous, who, refined by suffering, can render purer service.[14] Following Amos 3:12; Isa. 4:2f.; and Mic. 5:7f., Zephaniah viewed the remnant as the ruler of God's enemies (2:7), his humble, honest, sincere servant (3:12f.), and the victorious army whose success sprang from trust in the Lord (v. 17), not military prowess.

Like Isaiah, Zephaniah had seen God's greatness and was transformed by it. He saw that God cannot brook haughtiness and that people's only hope lay in recognizing their own frailty. Pride is a problem rooted in human nature, and neither Judah (2:3), Ammon, Moab (v. 10), nor Nineveh is exempt. Nineveh is made to epitomize insolence, boasting "I am and there is none else" (v. 15). Such rebellion, the declaration of spiritual independence from God, is the most heinous of sins. Those who escape God's fury are those who humbly "seek refuge in the name of the Lord" (3:12).

---

12. The day is past when scholars could relegate all such passages of hope to the postexilic period; see Fensham, *IDBS*, p. 984. Increasing appreciation of the nature of Israel's covenant-keeping God has confirmed that hand in hand with an emphasis on judgment was the hopeful expectation that the God who wounded would heal, or better, that he healed by wounding. His faithfulness is what shapes the future, not Israel's response. The judgment speeches against the foreign nations are one way of conveying hope: the nations' doom meant Judah's welfare (*šālôm*). See McKane, "Prophecy," pp. 172-75.

13. On the possible origins and meaning of the day of the Lord, see A.S. Kapelrud, *The Message of the Prophet Zephaniah* (Oslo: 1975), pp. 80-87; G. von Rad, *Old Testament Theology* 2:119-125.

14. On the positive aspects of judgment see L. Morris, *The Biblical Doctrine of Judgment*, pp. 22-24.

Picturing the Lord with lamp in hand searching Jerusalem and finding "men who are thickening upon their lees," he gives stern warning about the perils of complacency (1:12f.). These apathetic citizens are sluggish and lifeless like wine which has settled (see Jer. 48:11f.). Neither their own plight nor that of their fellows can prod them from their sedentary relaxation. Having refused both to advance God's program or stem the corruption, they share the punishment of the more active rebels:

> The great causes of God and Humanity are not defeated by the hot assaults of the Devil, but by the slow, crushing, glacierlike masses of thousands and thousands of indifferent nobodies. God's causes are never destroyed by being blown up, but by being sat upon.[15]

JOEL

Even less is known about Joel as a person than about Zephaniah. Apart from mentioning his father, Pethuel, he tells nothing of his personal history. His avid interest in Jerusalem, particularly the temple (1:9, 13f., 16; 2:14-17, 32 [MT 3:5]; 3 [MT 4]:1, 6, 16f.), suggests that he too was a resident. His stress on priestly ceremonies and religious festivities supports the theory that he was a temple prophet.

At least the first two chapters actually may have been used liturgically either during disasters like Joel's locust plague or in commemorating anniversaries of deliverance from them, just as was Lamentations on the anniversary of Nebuchadnezzar's destruction of the temple (586). The summons to witness to the events recorded here (1:3), calls to lament or complaint (vv. 5, 8, 11, 13f.), individual complaint (vv. 19f.), invitation to repentance (2:12-14), call to assemble in the temple (vv. 15-17a), fragment of a communal complaint (v. 17), and divine response promising salvation (vv. 18-27) all suggest possible liturgical use. If so this is again witness to the process by which the canon took shape. God's people not only heard the prophet's word but used it through the decades and centuries as part of their worship.

Date. The thorny question of date traditionally has been solved either by assigning the book to the period of the minority of Jehoash (Joash; ca. 835-796)[16] or by dating the prophet after the return from exile, near the end of the fifth

---

15. G.A. Smith, Book of the Twelve Prophets. Expositor's Bible (1956) 4:573.

16. E.g., K.A. Credner, Der Prophet Joel (Halle: 1831); A.F. Kirkpatrick, The Doctrine of the Prophets, 3rd ed. (London: 1901), pp. 57ff. More recently M. Bič has dated Joel as the earliest of the Minor Prophets because it supposedly reflects the struggle of Yahweh with Baalism, which goes back as far as Elijah; Das Buch Joel (Berlin: 1960), pp. 106-9.

century or even later.[17] Until recently E. König[18] stood virtually alone in support of a date between these extremes, i.e., ca. 609, just before or after Josiah's death, but A.S. Kapelrud has mustered weighty evidence for a date ca. 600 for Joel's ministry.[19] Recognizing that many arguments for either late or early dates were based on silence[20] or were inconclusive,[21] Kapelrud sought rather to show affinities between Joel, Zephaniah, and Jeremiah. An obvious example is the close similarity in Joel's and Zephaniah's views of the day of the Lord as a time of darkness. Such parallelism of thought plus the fact that a date between the two extremes may be the best explanation of some evidence[22] accounts for this survey's study of Joel in connection with Zephaniah.[23] Happily, Joel's message does not hinge on the date. Joel's message is important despite current inability to reconstruct his historical background with accuracy.[24]

Problem of Interpretation. Only slightly less troublesome than Joel's date have been the locusts in 1:4; 2:25. Many Christian interpreters have followed the Jewish Targum in viewing them as foreign armies which ravaged Judah in successive waves. This allegorical interpretation, based in part on the description of 2:4-11, is exemplified by E.B. Pusey, who identifies the four invaders as

---

17. E.g., W. Vatke, *Die Religion des Alten Testaments* (Berlin: 1835), and S.R. Driver, *The Books of Joel and Amos*, 2nd ed. Cambridge Bible (Cambridge: 1915). R.H. Pfeiffer suggests a date ca. 350; *Introduction*, p. 575. A. Robert and A. Feuillet reflect current scholarly consensus for a date ca. 400; *Introduction*, p. 359. See also H.W. Wolff, *Joel and Amos*. Hermeneia (Philadelphia: 1977), pp. 4-6.

18. *Einleitung in das Alte Testament* (Bonn: 1893).

19. *Joel Studies* (Uppsala: 1948), pp. 191f. Kapelrud stresses the oral transmission of prophetic messages, making the actual writing of the book some years (perhaps centuries) later. On somewhat different grounds, C.A. Keller (*Joël, Abdias, Jonas.* Commentaire de l'Ancien Testament 11a [Neuchatel: 1965], p. 103) and W. Rudolph (*Joel.* KAT 13/2 [1975]) have argued strongly for a late preexilic date: 630-600 and 597-587, respectively.

20. E.g., they lack mention of a king, the three major enemies (Assyria, Syria, Babylonia), or the northern kingdom.

21. E.g., they position Joel between Hosea and Amos in the Hebrew canon (while the LXX places Joel after Micah); stress the priesthood and temple services; mention Judah's traditional enemies—Tyre and Sidon, Philistia (3:4 [MT 4:4]), Egypt, and Edom (v. 19); and cite literary parallels between Joel and other prophets: compare 3:10 (MT 4:10) and Isa. 2:4; Mic. 4:3; compare 3:16 (MT 4:16) and Amos 1:2; compare 3:18 (MT 4:18) and Amos 9:13. See further J. Arthur Thompson, "The Book of Joel," *IB* 6 (1965): 731; O. Kaiser, *Introduction*, pp. 280f.

22. E.g., Joel's literary style resembles the earlier prophets rather than Haggai and Malachi, yet he uses an occasional word or phrase more characteristic of later Hebrew.

23. Recently attention has been given to the possibility of exilic and immediately postexilic dates. For exilic dates, see B. Reicke, "Joel und seine Zeit," in H.J. Stoebe, J.J. Stamm, and E. Jenni, eds., *Wort-Gebot-Glaube.* Festschrift W. Eichrodt. Abhandlungen zur Theologie des Alten und Neuen Tesaments 59 (1970): 133-141. J. Myers suggests a date ca. 520, making Joel a contemporary of Haggai and Zechariah; "Some Considerations Bearing on the Date of Joel," *ZAW* 74 (1962): 177-195. G.W. Ahlström dates the book 515-500; *Joel and the Temple Cult of Jerusalem.* VTS 21 (1971).

24. For thorough and recent discussion of Joel's date see L.C. Allen, *Joel*, pp. 19-25.

Assyria, Chaldea, Macedonia, and Rome.[25] Most modern commentators have found this approach too subjective. If the locusts are foreign armies, which foreign armies do they represent? Furthermore, it is unlikely that the locust waves actually are armies since they are compared to armies in ch. 2.

These figurative descriptions in 2:4-11 have prompted an apocalyptic interpretation which views the insects as unearthly creatures who will wreak havoc at the day of the Lord (cf. Rev. 9:3-11).[26] Regular use of the past tense, however, and the fact that the narrator seems to have been an eyewitness (see Joel 1:16) suggest that Joel is not forecasting the future but depicting divine judgment that has already taken place. This is not to overlook such apocalyptic features as the description of heavenly portents (2:30f. [MT 3:3f.]).

The literal approach seems to have prevailed.[27] The catastrophe in Joel is a series of locust invasions which strip the vegetation of Judah, bringing unprecedented damage. This devastation is conveyed powerfully by the chainlike poetic structure of 1:4:

> What the cutting locust left,
>   the swarming locust has eaten.
> What the swarming locust left,
>   the hopping locust has eaten.
> What the hopping locust left,
>   the destroying locust has eaten.

The thrust is not so much the various types of locusts as the thoroughness of their destruction. Judah's plight was made even worse because this marauding spanned more than one year (2:25). In powerful poetry sometimes approaching hyperbole the locusts are likened to a looting army, so relentless is their plundering, so terrible their sound and appearance. In the far-flung and all-encompassing judgment which they bring on Judah, the prophet cannot help but see a prototype of a future day (1:15).

Message. Joel consists of two almost equal parts: the locust plague and day of the Lord (1:1–2:17) and the victory to come (2:18–3:21 [MT 4:21]). In the first section the prophet speaks; in the second, the Lord. The turning point is 2:18 where the Lord, perhaps through a temple prophet, responds to the penitent overtures of his people and brings deliverance.

After stressing the unprecedented and unique nature of the calamity (1:2-4),

---

25. Pusey allegorizes even further by equating the four types of locusts with "four chief passions" which "desolate successively the human heart"; *The Minor Prophets* (1886; repr. Grand Rapids: 1950) 1:160.

26. The outstanding advocate of this approach was A. Merx, *Die Prophetie des Joel und ihre Auslegen* (Halle: 1879). J.A. Bewer, *Joel*. ICC (Edinburgh: 1911), and Pfeiffer, *Introduction*, combine the literal and apocalyptic interpretations by finding actual insects in ch. 1 and apocalyptic creatures in ch. 2.

27. E.g., Driver, *Joel and Amos*; G.W. Wade, *Joel*. Westminster Commentaries (London: 1925); Thompson, *IB*.

the prophet surveys various groups drastically affected by the plague—drunkards (vv. 5-7), farmers (vv. 11f.), priests (vv. 13f.)—and calls each to lament the tragedy. Particularly desperate, Joel feels, is the plight of the priests, who cannot maintain the daily round of sacrifices. The severity of God's judgment is sharp-ened by his having cut off his people's means of access to him. In the face of such death-dealing devastation, they have only one hope: to assemble in the temple and cry to the Lord (v. 14).

To Joel a disaster of such magnitude can mean only that the day of the Lord, God's final reckoning with his people and the nations, is near (1:15-20). In the insect invasions and drought (see vv. 19f.) which followed, the prophet sees the harbinger of the dreaded day of darkness forecast by both Amos (Amos 5:18-20) and Zephaniah (Zeph. 1:7, 14-18). In order to sense this connection, one must remember that the Hebrews were able to see the general in the particular. This is evident in their view of corporate personality, in which the entire nation may be treated as a single personality and a single person, partic-ularly a patriarch or king, may symbolize the nation. Similarly, each instance of God's judgment contained the facets of all judgment including the final one. B.S. Childs has perceived this close tie between the historical plague and the ultimate day:

> . . . the prophet can move freely from the threat of a past historical event to the coming eschatological judgment because he sees both as sharing the selfsame reality. To posit two totally separate and distinct historical events recorded in these two chapters not only misses the subtle literary manner of shifting from past to future but seriously threatens the theological understanding of prophetic eschatology which spans temporal differences.[28]

The thought of the day of the Lord prompts an even more vivid picture of the plague. Advancing like a relentless army the locusts besiege the land and terrorize its citizens (2:1-11). The sound is like rumbling chariots or crackling flames, and in huge clouds they hang shroudlike over the land and obscure the sun and moon. The literary form itself—a call to alarm (v. 1) followed by the description of destruction (vv. 2-10)—reinforces the military metaphors employed.

The situation is dire but not hopeless. The one way out is wholehearted repentance on the part of the entire nation (2:12-17). At times Joel has been criticized for undue interest in sacrifice and ritual. Indeed, he does favor the contemporary religious system more than do Amos, Hosea, or Jeremiah, but he has no more interest in ritual for ritual's sake than they. His ultimate appeal is not to the efficacy of offerings but to the gracious nature of the God of the covenant (vv. 13, 17). Joel also has been contrasted with Israel's great prophets because he makes no mention of the sins which precipitated the calamity.

---

28. *Old Testament as Scripture*, p. 391.

However, where they look forward to impending doom, Joel stands in the midst of it. Solution, not cause, is the pressing problem. That the Lord did answer his people's plea (2:18ff.) may indicate that in this case God's judgment brought the desired results: Judah turned from sin to God.

Judah's repentance is more than matched by God's full-scale restorations, announced in a powerful and extended oracle of salvation:[29] staple crops are restored (2:19, 22); insects and drought are withdrawn (vv. 20, 23); and the losses of the blighted years are repaid (vv. 24f.). On a larger scale, God's act of redemption becomes for the prophet a pattern of the final deliverance of his people, when both spiritual and material blessings are lavished on the remnant of Judah (2:28 [MT 3:1]-3 [MT 4]:1, 16-18, 20f.) while their enemies (3 [MT 4]:2-15, 19), overripe for judgment, are threshed in the valley of Jehoshaphat ("the Lord has judged").

As with judgment, the Hebrew also saw here the general in the particular: any single act of deliverance may have tremendous ramifications as it symbolizes God's power and willingness to perform full-scale redemption.[30] Deliverance from the plague damage (2:18-27) anticipates God's end-time rescue of his people (2:28–3:21 [MT 3:1–4:21]).

Theological Importance. In addition to striking portrayals of the day of the Lord and the compassionate nature of God, Joel teaches some valuable lessons about God's complete control of nature.[31] Nowhere does Joel hint that anyone or anything else is responsible for the locusts: they are God's army (2:11), dispatched and withdrawn by him (v. 20).[32] No dualism which would seek to attribute calamities to forces outside God's authority and no pantheism which would identify God with his creation find a niche here. God is Lord over all and yet active in all.

For the Hebrews God's creating and sustaining activity gave both unity and meaning to the reality around them. Shaped by God's touch and infused with

---

29. Elements characteristic of salvation speeches abound here: (1) God's promises are uttered in the first person; (2) God's creatures are commanded to "fear not" (2:21f.) and "be glad" (vv. 21, 23); (3) specific damages will be repaired (e.g., vv. 19f., 24-26); (4) the net result will be enlarged awareness of God's presence and uniqueness (v. 27), for which the people will praise him (v. 26).

30. See Ps. 22. The psalmist sees in his rescue cosmic significance: "All the ends of the earth shall remember and turn to the Lord" (v. 27 [MT 28]). Even generations yet unborn will feel the effects of what God has done for him.

31. Actually, Old Testament thought knows of no principle or order of natural reality but sees the entire universe as the creation under God's direct and immediate control.

32. "The northerner" (v. 20) apparently describes the locust army, which on this occasion may have invaded from the north. In general, the term is synonymous with enemy, since at this time the major military threats to Judah were posed by nations marching from the north or northeast (see Jer. 1:13-15; Zeph. 2:13). It may also connote Israel's apprehension about the north, where their neighbors thought their gods lived (see Isa. 14:13).

his power, the creation is both good and vital. Though appointed master over creation, humankind was not completely separated from it. Indeed, they enjoyed a certain kinship, for both were creatures of God. The sharp distinctions between animal and human, inanimate and animate were less rigidly maintained by the Hebrews; thus a poet like Joel could describe the plights of thirsty fields and famished animals in quasi-human terms (see 1:10, 18-20; 2:21f.). This close relationship within creation is seen even more clearly in that judgment for human sin takes its toll on nature while repentance and restoration bring not only forgiveness but prosperity and fertility (3:18 [MT 4:18]). Human beings and the rest of creation are so entwined that what touches one touches the other, whether in judgment or blessing (cf. Amos 4:6-10; 9:13-15).

Joel's picture of Israel's hopeful future contains an element of responsibility as well as privilege. The outpouring of God's spirit upon his people will lay upon the redeemed remnant the weighty obligations of the prophetic office. None will be exempt—young or old, slave or free, male or female (2:28f. [MT 3:1]). This prophecy looks forward to fulfillment of Moses' ancient wish:

"Would that all the Lord's people were prophets, that the Lord would put his spirit upon them!" (Num. 11:29)

Thus, the Israelites are to pledge themselves to the covenant in unswerving obedience (cf. Jer. 31:31-34; Ezek. 36:27) and to embody and proclaim God's sovereign love (cf. Isa. 61:1).

Under the inspiration of the Spirit, Peter found in the miracle of Pentecost God's announcement that what Joel had foreseen was coming to pass in the infant Church (Acts 2:17-21). The Messianic age discerned by Joel, Zephaniah, and their fellows was at hand. The Church has been recruited to carry on the prophetic ministry and longs for the restoration of Israel to that service (see Rom. 11:24). Then Joel's prophetic faith will have become sight, and the mission of both Israel and the Church fulfilled.

FOR FURTHER READING

Zephaniah
Smith, J.M.P. *Micah, Zephaniah, and Nahum*. ICC. Edinburgh: 1911. (Pp. 159-263.)
Watts, J.D.W. *The Books of Joel, Obadiah, Jonah, Nahum, Habakkuk and Zephaniah*. Cambridge Bible Commentary. New York: 1975.

Joel
Ahlström, G.W. *Joel and the Temple Cult of Jerusalem*. VTS 21 (1971).
Allen, L.C. *The Books of Joel, Obadiah, Jonah and Micah*. NICOT. Grand Rapids: 1976. Pp. 19-126. (Excellent commentary, devout and thorough.)

Kapelrud, A.S. *Joel Studies*. UUÅ 4. Uppsala: 1948. (Reflects Scandinavian school; thorough criticism of previous scholarship.)

Thompson, J.A. "Joel's Locusts in the Light of Near Eastern Parallels." *JNES* 14 (1955): 52-55.

Wolff, H.W. *Joel and Amos*. Hermeneia. Philadelphia: 1977. (Includes valuable excursuses on locusts, day of Yahweh, teacher of righteousness.)

CHAPTER 33

NAHUM AND HABAKKUK

NAHUM

THE personal background of Nahum (the name probably means "comforted by Yahweh") is difficult to reconstruct[1] apart from dating his prophecy between two events to which he alludes: the fall of the Egyptian city Thebes in 663 B.C. to the Assyrian armies of Ashurbanipal (3:8-10) and the destruction of Nineveh in 612 (1:1; 2:8 [MT 9]; 3:7). The tone of imminence throughout the book suggests a date shortly before the collapse of the Assyrian capital— perhaps *ca*. 615 when the coalition of Babylonians, Medes, and Scythians(?) that toppled the city was being formed.

More than a century of sporadic archaeological research in Nineveh has uncovered something of the splendor of Assyria's capital during the heyday of the empire under Sennacherib (*ca*. 705-681), Esarhaddon (*ca*. 681-669), and Ashurbanipal (*ca*. 669-633). Discoveries include the massive wall eight miles in circumference built by Sennacherib, his water system (including one of the most ancient aqueducts) and palace, and Ashurbanipal's palace and royal library which held more than 20,000 clay tablets, including the creation (Enuma Elish) and flood (Gilgamesh) epics.

The Babylonian Chronicle of the Fall of Nineveh,[2] a concise record of Nabopolassar's campaigns from 616 to 609, makes reasonably clear the circumstances surrounding Assyria's demise. Nabopolassar was not able to gain decisive victories over the Assyrians until joining forces with Cyaxares, king of the

---

1. Even his hometown, Elkosh (1:1), has defied identification, although sites in Assyria (north of Mosul), Galilee, and Judah have been suggested. That Nahum may have been the only prophet to have had a function within the framework of the cult has evoked strong debate; see G. von Rad, *Old Testament Theology*, 2:189. The view that the book was intended for liturgical use after Nineveh's fall rather than a prophecy written before that fall does not seem to have gained scholarly consensus; see B.S. Childs, *Old Testament as Scripture*, pp. 441f.

2. C.J. Gadd, *The Fall of Nineveh* (London: 1923).

Medes. Together they laid siege to Nineveh for about two months, apparently aided by the flooding river which ran through the city:

> The river gates are opened,
> > the palace is in dismay. (2:6)

Although Assyria did not vanish immediately, shorn of the fortress capital and the provinces which were necessary for support, the nation was in its death throes. Despite desperate attempts by Egyptian pharaoh Neco II to rally the Egyptian-Assyrian alliance against Cyaxares and Nabopolassar, Assyria could postpone the inevitable only until shortly after 609.

Literary Qualities. As a literary craftsman Nahum has no superior and few peers among the Old Testament poets.[3] His sense of the dramatic is felt throughout the book. In ch. 1, for instance, he simulates a court scene in which God as Judge directs alternating verdicts to Judah (1:12f., 15 [MT 2:1]; 2:2 [MT 3]) and Assyria (1:9-11, 14; 2:1 [MT 2]). Judah is encouraged to take comfort in the thought of imminent release after more than a century under the Assyrian yoke (1:9-11, 14). The passage becomes clear in light of Nahum's dramatic use of two audiences whom God addresses in turn—with judgment speeches to Assyria interleaved with salvation oracles to Judah. Whether the intent is liturgical or merely dramatic is not certain.[4] A number of scholars contend that the book was first composed as a New Year's liturgy for the autumn festival in 612, immediately after Nineveh's fall.[5]

As vividly as an eyewitness, Nahum describes, whether by vision or just imagination, the siege and frenzied activity of the armies of Nineveh as they try in vain to halt the invaders:

> The crack of whip, and rumble of wheel,
> > galloping horse and bounding chariot!
> Horsemen charging,
> > flashing sword and glittering spear,
> hosts of slain,
> > heaps of corpses,
> dead bodies without end—
> > they stumble over the bodies! (3:2f.; cf. 2:3f.)

No correspondent on the scene ever reported more graphically than Nahum does by prophetic foresight. Moreover, through his poetic genius he becomes a participant in the defense of Nineveh and, with subtle irony, barks out battle commands to the defenders:

---

3. Von Rad credits Nahum with "Poems of more than ordinary magnificence"; *Old Testament Theology* 2:188.

4. Further evidence of Nahum's conscious literary technique has allegedly been found in the imperfect acrostic pattern of 1:2-11. However, attempts to restore the original acrostic have not been successful.

5. O. Kaiser, *Introduction*, pp. 231f.

Man the ramparts;
  watch the road;
gird your loins;
  collect all your strength. (2:1)

And even more powerfully:

Draw water for the siege,
  strengthen your forts;
go into the clay,
  tread the mortar,
  take hold of the brick mold! (3:14)[6]

Linked to this flair for the dramatic is Nahum's gift for scintillating imagery, unexcelled in biblical literature. He sings of the majesty of God in a hymn which celebrates his coming to judge the nations (a theophany like Judg. 5:4f.; Ps. 18:7-15 [MT 8-16]; Hab. 3:3-15):

His way is in whirlwind and storm,
  and the clouds are the dust of his feet. (1:3)

He uses numerous metaphors or similes which are both apt and brief—palace maidens "moaning like doves, and beating their breasts" (2:7); Assyrian fortresses likened to trees laden with ripe figs: "if shaken they fall into the mouth of the eater" (3:12).[7] Nahum also employs at least two extended figures of speech. (1) Nineveh is compared to a lair where the lioness and her whelps pace restively while waiting for the lion to return with the prey (2:11f.)—which depicts the Assyrians sustaining themselves by annual foreign conquests. (2) No longer the seductive harlot who lured nations to their doom by her charm, Nineveh is now the gazing-stock of the world; her nakedness uncovered, she is pelted with garbage by passersby and no one cares (3:4-7).[8]

Yet despite his literary prowess, Nahum falls short of the greatest Old Testament writings because of the nature of his theme. A prophecy of destruction of an enemy capital cannot match the lofty themes of man's relationship to God which dominate Job, Habakkuk, and Isaiah (esp. ch. 40). But part of the beauty and strength of the Scriptures is that the various books augment and complement each other. Both Amos' note of God's universal sovereignty and Nahum's word of his special care for Judah are unique in value and contribution.

Theological Significance. The prophecy of Nahum, completely absorbed with the destruction and degradation of Israel's ancient enemy, presents some theo-

---

6. A. Parrot calls this "a remarkable touch of local colour," since in the region of Nineveh all walls were built of sun-dried brick; *Nineveh and the Old Testament*, trans. B.E. Hooke (New York: 1955), p. 84.
    7. Parrot refers this to the nearby fortresses of Tarbiṣu and Asshur, which fell before Nineveh and without as much resistance; *ibid.*, p. 79.
    8. These two images accord well with the fact that Nineveh was dedicated to Ishtar, goddess of war and love; see Parrot, *ibid.*, p. 26.

logical questions. Why, for instance, is he silent about the sins of his own people and their need for repentance? Only he and Obadiah, who also directs his ire at a hostile nation, neglect that message of spiritual and moral reform which lies at the heart of true prophetism. Yet, though loyal to Judah, these prophets are not narrow nationalists.[9] Nahum, particularly, senses the smarting wounds of many outraged nations. Like Amos (ch. 1) before and Habakkuk (ch. 1) after, he is insensed at human inhumanity. To have swerved from his central theme in order to censure Judah would have dissipated his attack and spoiled the unity of his message. Besides, Nahum's date coincides precisely with the reforms of Josiah (2 Kgs. 22:8–23:25), from which the king and some of the prophets took great hope.[10]

How can Nahum's vindictive, taunting lines be reconciled with the compassion and forgiveness in Hosea and Jonah and especially in Christ's teachings (e.g., Matt. 5:43f.)? Herein lies a more general Old Testament problem—the place of imprecatory writings in sacred Scripture. Both psalmists and prophets were at times relentless in insisting that God judge their enemies. This passion for retribution was part of the Hebrew (and general Semitic) emphasis on lex talionis, "an eye for an eye"—the punishment suits the crime.

Far from a savage call for blood, Nahum's prophecy testifies to his firm belief in the righteousness of God. The beginning hymn which describes God's character and action in judgment surely is the fount which waters the seeds of destruction sown in Nahum's speeches.[11]

The ruthlessness of the Assyrians was common knowledge: their policy of deporting masses of their victims—actually, brutal death marches—and their genocidal treatment of nations reckless enough to rebel against their iron yoke. Only a shriveled soul indeed would remain dispassionate in the face of such atrocities. As C.S. Lewis has forcefully demonstrated, the Jews cursed their enemies bitterly because they took right and wrong seriously.[12] More than the Assyrians' wickedness was involved; their imperialism offended the righteousness of God himself. If God is God, Nahum and his fellows held, he cannot allow unbridled wickedness to flourish indefinitely. Assyria, God's hired razor (Isa. 7:20), had eagerly shorn their neighbors, including Israel and Judah, and it was time for the razor to be broken: instruments of God's judgment are not exempt from judgment.[13]

If prophets like Nahum and Zephaniah seem to relish the prospect of an-

---

9. Bentzen numbers Nahum among the nationalistic prophets condemned by Jeremiah, but Nahum's sense of moral outrage differs considerably from the easy optimism of the false prophets; *Introduction* 2:150.

10. Von Rad, *Old Testament Theology* 2:189.

11. See Childs, *Old Testament as Scripture*, pp. 443f., on how the hymn (psalm) sets the theological tone for the book.

12. *Reflections on the Psalms* (New York: 1958), p. 30; his chapter on "The Cursings" contains many helpful observations.

13. The absence of a well-developed view of afterlife in this period forced the prophet to demand a temporal and public vindication of God's righteousness.

nihilation of their ancient enemy, it is because the suffering of their people had been acute. Their enthusiasm for such punishment may seem to outrun the bounds of propriety, for though they knew the law of neighbor love (Lev. 19:17f.), they had not seen it spelled out clearly in Christ. But the Christian revelation also has confirmed what the members of the old covenant knew well—that love has it sterner side. Its fires can sear as well as warm:

> A man who is deeply and truly religious is always a man of wrath. Because he loves God and his fellow men, he hates and despises inhumanity, cruelty and wickedness. Every good man sometimes prophesies like Nahum.[14]

In a sense Nineveh's doom epitomizes the fate of all nations whose ultimate trust is, as Kipling put it, "in reeking tube and iron shard." Military might does not preclude obligations of righteousness and justice. The crumbling rubble of the once arrogant city is a grim reminder that only those nations who rely firmly on the God who is the source of true peace will see "on the mountains the feet of him who brings good tidings, who proclaims peace" (1:15 [MT 2:1]).[15]

HABAKKUK

The absence of information concerning Habakkuk's personal background has provided ample opportunity for speculation concerning his message and times.[16] Dates ranging from 700 to 300 have been suggested, and enemies from the cohorts of Sennacherib to the phalanxes of Alexander have been identified in his writing. Current opinion, however, places him in the last quarter of the seventh century, roughly contemporary with Zephaniah, Jeremiah, Nahum, and perhaps Joel. The outstanding clue to his date is the reference to the imminent Chaldean (Babylonian) invasion of Judah (1:6). The earliest date would be ca. 625, when Nabopolassar seized the Babylonian throne and triggered· the rise of the Neo-Babylonian kingdom; the latest date would be ca. 598, just before Nebuchadnezzar's retaliatory attack on Judah in the days of Jehoiakim (ca. 609-598). The graphic descriptions of the Chaldean military exploits (vv. 6-11) may point to a date about 605, when at the battle of

---

14. R. Calkins, *The Modern Message of the Minor Prophets* (New York: 1947), p. 86. For observations on Nahum's belief in the "moral cohesiveness of history" and God's "righteous judgment of a morally offensive and inhuman empire," see N.K. Gottwald, *All the Kingdoms of the Earth*, pp. 231f.

15. This graphic announcement of the peace that Nineveh's collapse would bring (quoted from Isa. 52:7) is related by New Testament writers to the gospel of Christ, Prince of Peace (see Acts 10:36; Rom. 10:15).

16. A tradition preserved in the apocryphal Bel and the Dragon speaks of Ambakom (the Greek form of Habakkuk's name), son of Jesus of the tribe of Levi. No means exist either to substantiate or refute this tradition, which is not found in Theodotion's translation.

Carchemish Nebuchadnezzar's forces proved their power and prowess by routing the Egyptians.

Message. Like Haggai and Zechariah, Habakkuk is called "the prophet," possibly a technical title designating an official position in the religious community,[17] or perhaps merely indicating that this writing was worthy to be included among the canonical prophetic books. The close connection between prophetic vision and spoken message is expressed in the phrase "the oracle (KJV burden) of God which Habakkuk the prophet saw" (1:1), meaning that the prophets uttered what God showed them.

(1) Problem: God has not judged Judah's wickedness (1:2-4). God, not the people, is the first object of Habakkuk's censure. Judah's sin had become so flagrant and heinous that God's reputation was jeopardized by his reluctance to judge. Habakkuk's complaint about God's righteousness shapes the style of his book, a summary of his conversations with God. The judgment for which he pleads is twofold: vengeance on the wicked as well as vindication of the righteous.

The background of the violence, oppression, and lawlessness under which the prophet chafes seems to be the reign of the wretched Jehoiakim, who so vexed Jeremiah (Jer. 22:13-23).[18] Habakkuk, a theologian as well as a prophet, was baffled by the seemingly interminable delay in judgment, while whatever vitality remained in Judah from Josiah's reform was being sapped by the corruption of the national leaders.[19]

(2) God's answer: The Babylonians will judge Judah (1:5-11). Habakkuk did not have to wait long for God's response. The plural form of the pronoun "you" indicates that God's words are directed to a larger audience than just the prophet. The divine response rings with surprise. Ordinarily a complaint would be answered by a promise of deliverance, a salvation speech,[20] but here "deliverance" comes in the form of the Babylonian army ("Chaldeans," v. 6). The vivid description of their speed, maneuverability, and might captures something of the terror which Nebuchadnezzar's troops must have brought their victims. No fortress could withstand their battering rams, inclined planes, and sapping (tunneling under the walls), as the Ninevites had discovered; no king was clever

---

17. Habakkuk's interest in public worship is shown by the psalm-like nature of ch. 3 and its musical notation (v. 1). Whether he was a temple prophet, as Mowinckel and others have argued (see Bentzen, *Introduction* 2:151), is uncertain.

18. Some interpret the circumstances rather as the external pressure of the Assyrians, soon to be supplanted by the Babylonians. This view usually involves drastic rearrangement of the text (esp. 1:13); see Childs, *Old Testament as Scripture*, pp. 448-450, for various interpretations of the historical situation.

19. Habakkuk's plea has many parallels in the Psalms, particularly those of individual and communal lament (e.g., 7:9 [MT 10]; 13:1-4 [MT 2-5]; 22:1-5 [MT 2-6]; 44:23-26 [MT 24-27]; note especially the outcries of "how long?", "why?" See Lewis, *Reflections on the Psalms*, pp. 9-19, for some apt observations on judgment.

20. See, e.g., Ps. 12: complaint (vv. 1-4 [MT 2-5]); salvation speech (v. 5 [MT 6]); word of assurance (v. 6 [MT 7]); prayer for protection (vv. 7f. [MT 8f.]).

enough to outmaneuver them in open warfare, as Neco had learned at Carchemish. God was to employ this unholy alliance of skill and savagery to impose judgment on Judah.

(3) Problem: Can a righteous God use the wicked to punish those more righteous (1:12-17)? God's response posed an even more vexing question, again in the form of a complaint:

> Thou who art of purer eyes than to behold evil
>   and canst not look on wrong,
> why dost thou look on faithless men,
>   and art silent when the wicked swallows up
>   the man more righteous than he? (v. 13)

Habakkuk was well aware of Judah's faults, but by any standards his countrymen, particularly the righteous nucleus, were no match for the wickedness of the Babylonians. Apparently the fate of Babylon's enemies was common knowledge, and Habakkuk recoils at the thought of their ruthlessly ravaging Judah and Jerusalem. The sustained figure of speech in vv. 14-17, which compares the Babylonians to an unconscionable angler who fishes for the delight of killing his catch, is as impassioned a plea against inhumanity as the Old Testament contains.[21] Habakkuk did not doubt God's sovereignty over the enemy nation, but this sharpened the problem. How could a righteous God refrain from intervening?

(4) God's answer (ch. 2). Habakkuk's motive in posing these questions was neither idle curiosity nor a desire to dabble in divine affairs. He was an honest and devout seeker after truth, and God honored his quest. His watchtower (v. 1) was probably a place of solitude where he as one of God's watchmen (cf. Isa. 21:8; Ezek. 33:7-9) could listen for the voice of God without distraction.

The first part of God's answer, introduced by an announcement of a vision (vv. 2f.), allays the prophet's fears about God's judgment: the righteous remnant will be preserved (vv. 4f.). The precise meaning of these verses is difficult, but the basic thought is clear—the sharp contrast between the faithful righteous and the proud, debauched, and bloodthirsty Babylonians. The conduct of each group determines its fate: the Babylonians fail; the righteous live. "Faith" (Heb. *'emûnâ*) in v. 4 connotes faithfulness and dependability. The righteous rely on God, and, in turn, he can rely on them.

God's answer continues in the form of a taunt song with which the oppressed peoples will mock their oppressors (vv. 6-19). Five woes (vv. 6, 9, 12, 15, 19) punctuate this direful message: Babylon's doom is sealed.[22] Particular

---

21. In one Assyrian inscription Esarhaddon speaks of catching a king of Sidon like a fish and cutting off his head, while a stele found at Zinjirli in northern Syria depicts him holding Tirhakah of Egypt and an unnamed ruler on a leash with a ring through their lips; see Parrot, *Nineveh*, pp. 64f.

22. For a summary of the structure and proposed backgrounds of the woe oracles, see W.E. March, "Prophecy," pp. 164f. in J.H. Hayes, ed., *Old Testament Form Criticism* (San Antonio: 1974).

stress is given to God's law of retribution; the Babylonians are to be repaid measure for measure (vv. 6-8, 15-17). God is not mocked, and the Babylonians are not exempt from the law of sowing and reaping (Gal. 6:7). The poetic irony is remarkable, especially in the woe against the enemy's idolatry:

> Woe to him who says to a wooden thing, Awake;
> to a dumb stone, Arise!
> Can this give revelation?
> Behold it is overlaid with gold and silver,
> and there is no breath at all in it. (v. 19)

Babylon's cause is doomed not only because it was wicked but also because her gods are powerless. In contrast, the Lord of Israel rules the earth from his temple and bids all to stand in silence before him (v. 20). Perhaps this verse brought both comfort and rebuke to Habakkuk: comfort, as he was confronted personally by the sovereign of the universe; rebuke, because he, the protesting prophet, was included in "all the earth" which must yield to God's lordship.

(5) Habakkuk's response (ch. 3). The revelation of God's program for both righteous remnant and wicked oppressors and especially of God's person in all his sovereign greatness silences the protests. Like Job, Habakkuk can respond to God's answer only by prayer and confession of confidence.[23] He begins with a declaration of trust and a direct appeal that God repeat the redemptive work of the Exodus:

> O Lord, I have heard the report of thee,
> and thy work, O Lord, do I fear.
> In the midst of the years renew it;
> in the midst of the years make it known;
> in wrath remember mercy. (v. 2)

The prophet seems to stand between the times—looking back to the Exodus and ahead to the day of the Lord. But neither past nor future intervention will ease his problem: he longs for a display of God's power in his present circumstances. This prayer leads to an imaginatively vivid recital of the mighty acts of God (theophany; cf. Ps. 77:16-20 [MT 17-21]; 78:9-16). Using a battery of literary techniques including hyperbole (v. 6), irony (v. 8), personification (v. 10), and simile (v. 14), this hymn merges the various events into a highly

---

23. R.H. Pfeiffer (*Introduction*, p. 597) and many others view ch. 3 as an appendix taken from an ancient hymnal. The mention of Shigionoth (v. 1), probably a hymn tune (cf. Ps. 7:1), the occurrences of "*Selah*" (vv. 3, 9, 13), and the musical notations in v. 19 support such a theory. Though perhaps not connected with the prophecy originally, this hymn makes a fitting climax in its appeal for God's intervention and confidence in his righteousness. The title in v. 1, attributing the hymn to Habakkuk, need not be discredited; in fact, it would be difficult to discover reasons for adding this chapter if it were not his work. W.F. Albright finds "no valid reason why this book should not be treated as a substantial unit and dated between 605 and 589 B.C. . . ."; "The Psalm of Habakkuk," p. 2, in H.H. Rowley, ed., *Studies in Old Testament Prophecy*. His article is a careful study of the text and poetic structure.

stylized, emotion-charged description of God's redemptive activity which suggests cinematographic montage. Episode mounts upon episode—God's journey from the Sinai peninsula (vv. 3f.), the plagues (v. 5), wilderness march (v. 6), crossing of the Sea and Jordan (vv. 8-10), Joshua's long day (v. 11)—as the Exodus and Conquest are recreated before the prophet's eyes.

Habakkuk is both overwhelmed and encouraged as he relives the victories of the past. This fresh look at God's saving acts sparks his courage as he awaits the enemy's attack. Invasion may mean devastation and deprivation,[24] yet Habakkuk's staunch faith was untouched. Like Paul, he has learned the warmth of divine contentment in any state (Phil. 4:11), for he has seen the living God. Just as he had pleaded for God's mercy (3:2), he ends his book by confessng confidence in the God of the covenant, but with an enthusiasm sparked by the theophanic vision:

> Though the fig tree do not blossom,
> nor fruit be on the vines,
> the produce of the olive fail
> and the fields yield no food,
> the flock be cut off from the fold
> and there be no herd in the stalls,
> yet I will rejoice in the Lord,
> I will joy in the God of my salvation. (vv. 17f.)

Theological Insights. (1) Life for the faithful. God showed Habakkuk that the judgment of Judah, though sweeping, would not be total. He reaffirmed the promise that a remnant would be spared to carry on the redemptive mission and to serve as foundation for the renewed nation. Habakkuk's despair over the fate of the righteous (1:13) evoked God's promise that they would survive the awful day (2:4). The basis of their survival was their faithfulness, their total dependence and dependability.

This principle became the seed plot for Paul's key doctrine of justification by faith. The apostle's drastic reinterpretation of the Old Testament in the light of his own conversion caused him to focus on two passages: Gen. 15:6 and Hab. 2:4. The translation of Heb. *'emûnâ* "faithfulness" by Gk. *pistis* "faith" or "faithfulness" formed a useful bridge between Habakkuk's view of "life through faithfulness" and Paul's doctrine. What Habakkuk learned to be God's principle of operation in the Babylonian invasion, Paul with inspired insight saw to be God's universal principle of salvation. In this sense, Habakkuk's message gave strategic preparation for the New Testament evangel (see Rom. 1:17; Gal. 3:11; Heb. 10:38f.).

(2) Understanding through honest doubt. As Job's experience makes clear, honest doubt may be a truer religious attitude than superficial belief. Like Job,

---

24. A besieged nation must recruit farmers as soldiers. Furthermore, attacking armies live off the produce of their victims.

Habakkuk neither used his questions to shield himself from moral responsibilities nor shunned God's claims upon his life. He was genuinely perplexed by the unpredictable nature of God's dealings with him. He raised his protests actually because he thought so much of God, and hungered and thirsted to see God's righteousness vindicated as well as his own. God's revelation of himself laid the ghost of the prophet's doubts and gave birth to a finer faith; the redeeming God had used his questions as a means of grace to draw Habakkuk closer to himself.

FOR FURTHER READING

Nahum

Cathcart, K.J. *Nahum in the Light of Northwest Semitic*. Biblica et orientalia 26. Rome: 1973.

Haldar, A.O. *Studies in the Book of Nahum*. UUÅ 46-47. Uppsala: 1947.

Maier, W.A. *The Book of Nahum: A Commentary*. Grand Rapids: 1959. (Conservative Lutheran.)

Mihelic, J.L. "The Concept of God in the Book of Nahum." *Interp* 2 (1948): 199-207.

van der Woude, A.S. "The Book of Nahum: A Letter Written in Exile." *OTS* 20 (1977): 108-126. (Dates book 660-630; Nahum is from northern Galilee.)

Habakkuk

Brownlee, W.H. "The Historical Allusions of the Dead Sea Habakkuk Midrash." *BASOR* 126 (1952): 10-20. (Regarding Qumran commentary on chs. 1–2.)

Eaton, J.H. "The Origin and Meaning of Habakkuk 3." *ZAW* 76 (1964): 144-171. (Philological, mythological analysis.)

Gowan, D.E. *The Triumph of Faith in Habakkuk*. Atlanta: 1976. (Exegetical and expository.)

Irwin, W.A. "The Mythological Background of Hab. 3." *JNES* 1 (1942): 10-40. (Comparison with Canaanite mythological poetry.)

Lloyd-Jones, D.M. *From Fear to Faith: Studies in the Book of Habakkuk*. London: 1972. (Conservative exposition.)

CHAPTER 34

OBADIAH

OBADIAH is the shortest book in the Old Testament canon—twenty-one verses long. Next to nothing is known about the author, and scholars cannot agree on the date of the prophecy, making difficult identification of the historical situation that called it forth. Yet some scholars, pushing critical analysis to the extreme, have managed to divide this work into Proto- and Deutero-Obadiah, or even to find three or four sources for it.

Nevertheless, Obadiah is part of the word of God, which the believing community found to be divinely authoritative and included in the canonical prophets. The continuing believing community must therefore seek to hear God as he speaks through this prophet.

THE PROPHET AND THE PROPHECY

Obadiah is generally believed to be from Judah, but the ascription (v. 1) mentions neither his father's name nor his home region. The tradition that he was the steward of King Ahab (Talmud *Sanh.* 39b) and that of Pseudo-Epiphanius that he was a captain in the army of Ahaziah are without foundation and rejected by most scholars.

The "vision" concerns Edom (v. 1), Israel's ancient enemy. Analysis of the prophecy indicates two main parts:

Territory of the Edomites, "who live in the clefts of the rock" (Obad. 3). (W.S. LaSor)

Vision concerning Edom (vv. 1-14)
   Edom's fall pronounced (vv. 1-4)
   Completeness of the destruction (vv. 5-9)
   Reason: Cruelty against "brother" Judah (vv. 10-14)
Day of Yahweh (vv. 15-21)
   Judgment on the nations (vv. 15f.)
   Deliverance for Judah (vv. 17-20)
   Kingdom of Yahweh (v. 21)

Striking parallels exist between Obadiah and Jer. 49:7-22. J. Muilenburg says: "It is now quite generally agreed that the passage in Jeremiah is secondary."[1] O. Eissfeldt concurs, suggesting that the portions were a later addition to Jeremiah.[2] J.A. Soggin, however, contends that both accounts quote an earlier passage.[3] Parallels also exist between Obadiah and Joel; since the date

---

1. "Obadiah, Book of," *IDB* 3:579.
2. *Old Testament*, p. 403.
3. *Introduction*, p. 341.

of Joel (see Ch. 32) is so uncertain, there is no scholarly agreement as to which prophet may have influenced the other.[4]

This evidence seems to indicate that Obadiah was held in esteem by his people, especially by prophets. The utterance against Edom reflects other speeches common among the prophets of Yahweh (see Isa. 34; 63:1-6; Ezek. 25:12-14; 35; Amos 1:11f.; Mal. 1:2-5). Some scholars see such prophecies as extreme forms of nationalism, markedly inferior to other oracles in the classical prophets (see below).

Dates from 889 to 312 B.C. have been presented and defended by various scholars. Tension between Esau (Edom) and Jacob (Israel) appears at several points in the Old Testament, beginning with Gen. 25:23; 27:39f. During the Monarchy, Edom was often controlled by kings of Israel and Judah.[5] Sporadic wars are recorded (note 2 Sam. 8:13f., reading *'dm* for *'rm*; 1 Kgs. 11:14-17; 2 Kgs. 14:11; 16:5f.). When the Babylonians invaded the region, Edom quickly surrendered and assisted in the destruction of Jerusalem (Lam. 4:21; Ezek. 25:12; 35:10). The oracle in Obad. 11-14 is generally believed to refer to this event, hence requiring a date not long after that event. Subsequently the Edomites were pushed out of their territory by the Nabateans, and occupied the Negeb and Judah as far north as Hebron. Later they were known by the Greek equivalent, "Idumeans," the people of whom Herod the Great was an illustrious member.

Geographical Details. Mt. Esau (v. 19) is one of the highest mountains south-southeast of the Dead Sea, possibly Umm el-Bayyârah in the vicinity of Petra (Sela; cf. "the clefts of the rock," v. 3; RSV mg. "Sela"). Teman (v. 9) is

---

4. Parallels:

Obadiah	Jer. 49	Obadiah	Joel
v. 1	v. 14	v. 10	3:19 [MT 4:19]
v. 2	v. 15	v. 11	3:3 [MT 4:3]
v. 3a	v. 16a	v. 15	3:4, 7 [MT 4:4, 7]
v. 4	v. 16b	v. 15	1:15; 2:1; 3:14 [MT 4:14]
v. 6	v. 9	v. 17	2:32 [MT 3:5]
v. 6	v. 10a	v. 17	3:17 [MT 4:17]
v. 8	v. 7	v. 18	3:8f. [MT 4:8f.]
v. 9a	v. 22b		
v. 16	v. 12		

The parallel between vv. 1-9 and Jer. 49:7-22 is much closer than those with Joel. Jer. 49:14-16 is remarkably similar to vv. 1-4. Jer. 49:7-11 contains much of the same material as vv. 5-9, but the portions do not seem to be direct quotations, either of one another or both of an earlier source. The parallels with Joel are simply similar expressions, with no evidence of the use of a longer quotation. These parallels raise the question whether such materials were used in public worship and thus became part of common quotation. For the parallels with Jer. 49, see J.A. Selbie, "Obadiah, Book of," *HDB* 3 (1900): 578.

5. Judah's ability to keep Edom in check was viewed by the biblical historians as a test of the relative strength of Judah's kings.

identified with the ruins of Tawīlân, east of Petra.[6] Halah (v. 20, RSV, but Heb. *ḥēl* "army") may be a region of Assyria to which Israelites were taken (2 Kgs. 17:6; 18:11). Sepharad (v. 20) is traditionally taken to be "Spain," but other identifications are Sardis (in western Asia Minor; however, no "exiles" were located there) and Shaparda in southwest Media (cf. 2 Kgs. 18:11). Mention of the "exiles" (v. 20) is used to support a postexilic date.

MESSAGE AND RELEVANCE

To say that "Obadiah is of little theological interest and its presence in the canon can easily be explained as a result of the anti-Idumaean polemic which was in full flood at the beginning of the first century A.D."[7] is not sufficient to account for the preservation of this work or any other anti-Edomite prophecies. Nor is labelling Obadiah, or Esther and similar books, as mere chauvinism or a reaction against narrow nationalism satisfactory. Something deeper, more significant theologically, must be found to account for the preservation and canonization of the work, and its continuing effect on the believing community.

Edom. Oracles and prophecies against Edom, like those against other nations, were addressed primarily to Israel. The prophets did not travel to Edom to deliver their taunt songs, for who would have listened to them? What the prophets said about Edom was heard—as intended—by Israel, and evaluated, considered important, safeguarded, and canonized as the word of God.

Day of Yahweh. At least three points most frequently revealed by Yahweh through the prophets are pertinent here:
(1) Yahweh is a God who demands righteousness. Although longsuffering, he will not always tolerate behavior contrary to his revealed will. Since Israel is his particular people, whose destiny was to teach the nations about Yahweh and his Torah, he required of them a higher level of righteousness, and was determined to punish their disobedience. He would, of course, spare some and thus accomplish his will. Although not spelled out in Obadiah, this is in the background (see vv. 10-12, 17-21; also Amos 1–2).
(2) Yahweh is Ruler of heaven and earth, God of all nations. While not detailed, this is a strong undercurrent. If Yahweh were only the God of Israel, how could he punish Edom or even expect them to listen to his word? How could he hold Edom accountable for violence done to his brother Jacob? Far from a late idea in Israel, this underlies also the initial prophecies in Amos and

---

6. G.E. Wright and F.V. Filson, eds., *Westminster Historical Atlas to the Bible*, rev. ed. (Philadelphia: 1956), pl. X; Y. Aharoni and M. Avi-Yonah, *Macmillan Bible Atlas*, maps 52, 155; L.H. Grollenberg, *Shorter Atlas of the Bible*, puts Teman north of Petra; p. 164.
7. Soggin, *Introduction*, p. 341.

occurs in nearly all of the prophets. Moreover, it is basic to the Abrahamic covenant that Yahweh's blessing comes to the nations of the world through the elect Abraham and his descendants.

(3) But if Yahweh is holy and demands holiness of his people, while permitting all sorts of evil deeds by the nations of the world, how can he be the Ruler of the Nations? Obadiah answers first by citing the evil that Edom has done, and second by announcing the coming day of Yahweh: "As you have done, it shall be done to you, your deeds shall return on your own head" (v. 15). After this judgment upon all nations in the day of the Lord, then come restitution and restoration. "Saviors" ascend Mt. Zion and rule Mt. Esau. The result: "the kingdom shall be Yahweh's" (v. 21).

Relevance. Of what value today is a discourse on the internecine strife between Jacob and Esau? Must the message be relegated to a future time only, the "time of Jacob's trouble" (Jer. 30:7), or can it be applied today? If part of the eternal word of God, it must have relevance in all generations, despite its special importance in certain times and under certain conditions. If the message was addressed primarily to Israel and not to Edom, then those of the household of faith today will consider it addressed to them. It speaks of enemies of God's people, and the cruel and inhuman treatment they have carried out. But judgment begins at the house of God. How is treating one's brothers (v. 10) as the Edomites treated Judah different from the deeds of the pagan nations?

The wisdom of the Edomites was proverbial (cf. Jer. 49:7). The message against Edom was in part a condemnation of their wisdom (v. 8) and pride (v. 3). The prophetic message is always a judgment on purely human wisdom; even the "foolishness" of God is wiser than men (1 Cor. 1:25), while the wisdom of this world is foolishness with God (3:19). Obadiah is therefore particularly relevant in the modern age of secular humanism.

People still chafe and groan under injustices in this world, and long for a day when things will be "as they should be." This is acted out in election campaigns and political revolutions and contemplated in educational and philosophical theories. Human intervention, crucial though it is, is not the ultimate answer to this cry for justice. But God promises that his day will come. And when it does, he will right the wrongs, restore the just possessions (v. 19f.), and establish his rule on earth.

FOR FURTHER READING

Eaton, J.H. *Obadiah, Nahum, Habakkuk, Zephaniah.* Torch Bible Commentary. London: 1961.

Harrison, R.K. *Introduction.* Pp. 898-903. (Good discussion of date.)

Lillie, J.R. "Obadiah—A Celebration of God's Kingdom." *Currents in Theology and Mission* 6 (1969): 18-22.

Smith, G.A. *The Book of the Twelve Prophets*. Expositor's Bible (1956) 4:598-604.

Thompson, J.A. "Introduction and Exegesis of Obadiah." *IB* 6:857-867.

————. "Obadiah, Book of." *IBD*, pp. 1106-7. (Good survey.)

Watts, J.D.W. *Obadiah: A Critical and Exegetical Commentary*. Grand Rapids: 1969.

CHAPTER 35

EZEKIEL

Ezekiel is a prophecy from the Exile. According to the book itself, the prophet's message came from Yahweh during the first part of the Exile, between 593 and 571 B.C. Ezekiel is therefore the beginning of a new phase in Israelite prophecy, and its form and characteristics differ somewhat from the prophecies studied thus far. This is at least in part responsible for the difficulty critical scholars have had in trying to relate Ezekiel (as well as Zechariah and Daniel) to their accepted "norm" of Israelite prophecy.

EZEKIEL AND HIS TIMES

The Prophet. Ezekiel ben Buzi came from a priestly family (1:3). He grew up in Palestine, probably in Jerusalem, and was taken into exile in 597 (see 33:21; 2 Kgs. 24:11-16).[1] He was probably twenty-five years old at the time, for five years later, at thirty (see 1:1),[2] he was called to the prophetic office.

Ezekiel was happily married (24:16), and the sudden death of his wife, announced to him in advance by Yahweh, was used as a sign to Israel (vv. 15-24). He lived in his own house in exile, at Tel Abib on the Great Canal (3:15; cf. 1:1; *nᵉhar kᵉḇār* "river of Kebar," found only in Ezekiel); the location, if "the river Chebar" can be identified with Bab. *nāru kabari*, was between Babylon and Nippur. Elders came to Ezekiel's home for counsel (8:1), which agrees with the statement that he was "among the exiles" (1:1), living in one of the Jewish colonies that the Babylonians had transplanted from Judah. He dates certain revelations by "The Year of the Exile (YE) of King Jehoiachin"

---

1. J. Taylor-L.H. Brockington, "Ezekiel," *HDB* (1963), p. 295, date it in 586.
2. Several other interpretations of the "thirtieth year" have been given; see the commentaries. W. Eichrodt seems to have committed some oversight, for while he agrees that Ezekiel was thirty in 594, he suggests that the prophet was "profoundly impressed by the religious aspects of the reforms," referring to the cleansing of the temple in the days of Josiah—in 621, when Ezekiel was only three years old; *Ezekiel*, trans. C. Quin. OTL (Philadelphia: 1970), p. 1.

(597 = YE 1). His prophetic call came in YE 5 (593), and the last recorded date is YE 27 (571), indicating a ministry of at least twenty-three years.

Because of recorded visions, his strange behavior in acting out certain prophecies, the record of being transported from Babylon to Jerusalem and back (8:3; 11:24), and other details, Ezekiel has been called ecstatic, visionary, neurotic, psychotic, and schizophrenic.[3] Indeed, his behavior was "abnormal"— but what is "normal" with regard to a prophet on whom the Spirit of God has fallen?

Ezekiel has been described as priest and prophet, pastor and preacher, "the father of Judaism." C.R. Erdman suggests that the prophet taught the people to sing songs in the night.[4] Some have found his prose "woefully dull and

Western towers of the Ishtar gate constructed by Nebuchadnezzar II (605-562 B.C.), leading to the sacred processional way. (Oriental Institute, University of Chicago)

3. "The theological importance of the book of Ezekiel for the total biblical witness has often been jeopardized by the preoccupation of critical scholarship with the literary, historical, and psychological problems"; B.S. Childs, *Old Testament as Scripture*, p. 371.

4. *The Book of Ezekiel* (Westwood, N.J.: 1956), p. 9; see W.S. LaSor, *Great Personalities of the Old Testament*, p. 154.

repetitive,"[5] but others observe that his "powerful vision, bold imagery and stirring language can show itself confidently beside the poetry of other prophets."[6]

The Times. The Exile (597-538) was almost coterminous with the Babylonian empire (612-539).[7]

Physical conditions in exile apparently were acceptable to many Jews. The Babylonians were not bent on punishing conquered people, but merely were taking steps to prevent revolutions. The more cruel Assyrians carried out a policy of displacing populations, breaking up and scattering them, and leaving them to lose their national identity through intermarriage and other forms of absorption. By contrast, the Babylonians deported peoples in small groups and let them preserve their national identities. (Hence Judeans [or Jews] could return from exile, whereas the ten "Lost Tribes" had become absorbed.) Jeremiah had advised a policy of "business as usual" in captivity (Jer. 29:4-7), and this apparently was followed by the exiles. They built houses, planted vineyards, pursued their crafts, and grew to like their new existence. Before long, Jews were found in mercantile ventures.[8] When the opportunity came to return to Jerusalem, many preferred to stay in Babylonia, which marked the beginning of the Jewish center that later produced the Babylonian Talmud.[9]

Religious conditions in exile were mixed. Basing his conclusions in part on "exilic" additions to the preexilic prophecies, and to that extent not textually supported but essentially correct, J. Lindblom observes:

> It would be a great mistake to conclude from Isaiah's prophecies about the remnant, or Jeremiah's vision of the good figs, that those Jews who were deported to Babylonia were the moral elite of the Jewish people. The Babylonians did not select them for religious and moral reasons. As for the Isaianic idea of the remnant, its implication was simply that a part of the people would be saved from the general ruin and then turn to Yahweh.[10]

Note that the principle of sovereign election applies to the Exile as well as any other period of Israel's history. The exiles were not by that fact purified by fire

---

5. N.K. Gottwald, *A Light to the Nations* (New York: 1959), p. 381.
6. A. Weiser, *Old Testament*, p. 228.
7. For historical details, see M. Noth, *History*, pp. 280-299; J. Bright, *History*, pp. 324-339; R.K. Harrison, *History of Old Testament Times* (Grand Rapids: 1957), pp. 195-205; F.F. Bruce, *Israel and the Nations*, pp. 93-96.
8. See H. Gressmann, *Altorientalische Texte zum Alten Testament* (Berlin: 1926) 1:434f.
9. For an interesting picture of life in exile, see P. Heinisch, *History of the Old Testament*, trans. W. Heidt (Collegeville, Minn.: 1952), pp. 310-14.
10. *Prophecy in Ancient Israel*, pp. 386f. Biblical evidence indicates that criteria for deportation included nobility, youth, physical strength, and political and social acceptability.

and perfected in righteousness—only the elect could give such testimony. The postexilic picture of the Jewish people is still a picture of redemption incomplete.

Nevertheless, the Exile was a period of testing ideas about God—was he limited to Palestine? was he impotent against the gods of Babylon? could he be worshiped in a strange land?—and of faith. The theology of Ezekiel was suited to this new situation.

CANONICAL AND CRITICAL QUESTIONS

Canonicity. Obviously, Ezekiel was included in the canon, but proof of the book's canonicity lies mainly in a second fact, a lengthy discussion over whether it should be removed (or "hidden"). This is often presented in just the opposite form, suggesting that the debate concerned whether to admit Ezekiel into the canon. G.F. Moore states clearly: "The question was not, is this book sacred, or inspired, Scripture? but, assuming its prophetic authorship and inspiration, is it expedient to withdraw the book from public use lest the unlearned or the half-learned be stumbled by the apparent discrepancies between it and the Law?"[11] Hananiah ben Hezekiah of the school of Shammai burned three hundred jars of oil in his study while harmonizing the seeming conflicts between Ezekiel and the Pentateuch. Then, even though the prophecy was retained as canonical, reading of ch. 1 was not permitted in the synagogue, and private reading of the prophecy was forbidden to anyone under thirty.[12]

Criticism. In 1913, S.R. Driver wrote: "No critical question arises in connexion with the authorship of the book, the whole from beginning to end bearing unmistakably the stamp of a single mind."[13] But in 1924 G. Hölscher, who previously had held to unity of authorship, stated that Ezekiel had too long escaped the critic's knife; of the 1,273 verses in Ezekiel, he claimed 1,103 were additions to the original work.[14] Since then the theories have been numerous, citing ancient arguments and inventing new ones; many are mutually contradictory, and most have added nothing to religious knowledge. Some semblance of reason was restored by C.G. Howie.[15] W. Zimmerli has sought to understand the prophet, not just dissect him, with a theory of *Nachinterpretation* of the prophecy, by which process the original message influenced succeeding generations of readers who in turn left levels of growth in the accretions.[16]

A student of the critical process cannot be faulted for skepticism at the

---

11. *Judaism in the First Centuries of the Christian Era* (Cambridge, Mass.: 1927) 1:247.
12. *Ibid.*, pp. 246f.; Talmud *Shab*. 13b, *Ḥag*. 13a, *Men*. 45a.
13. *Introduction*, p. 297.
14. *Hesekiel: Der Dichter und das Buch*. BZAW 39 (1924).
15. *The Date and Composition of Ezekiel*. JBL Monograph 4 (Philadelphia: 1950).
16. *Ezekiel 1*, trans. R.E. Clements. Hermeneia (Philadelphia: 1979), pp. 69-74. The translator renders *Nachinterpretation* as "updating of tradition"; Childs, *Old Testament as Scripture*, pp. 359f., 369f., translates it "afterlife," which has a misleading connotation.

published results of such criticism. The "authentic" Ezekiel consists of only 170 verses (Hölscher), yet on this basis can be decided what is genuine and what is not? The prophet is preexilic and postexilic, even as late as the Greek period? He can be psychoanalyzed in absentia? He had no message of salvation, and any such element must be excluded from his prophecy? Childs' effort to return to Ezekiel's religious and theological contributions is certainly refreshing. The position of this survey is that Driver's 1913 conclusion has not been seriously shaken,[17] that subsequent efforts to dissect the book largely have cancelled each other, and that Ezekiel must be studied as the prophet who introduces a new stage in prophecy, resulting from the new situation in which the exiled people of God find themselves.[18]

CANONICAL FORM

Analysis. The prophecy consists of messages given at Yahweh's command, delivered orally (3:10; 14:4; 20:1, 27; 24:8; 43:10), and presumably gathered by the prophet or an editor at a later time. Thirteen dates are given, each connected with a revelation from Yahweh.

		day	mo.	yr.	YE (1=597/6)[19]
1:2	Opening vision	5	4	5	31 July 593
8:1	Vision in the temple	5	6	6	17 Sept. 592
20:1	Message to the elders	10	5	7	14 Aug. 591
24:1	Report of the siege of Jerusalem	10	10	9	15 Jan. 588
26:1	Prophecy against Tyre	1	(1)	11	(23 Apr.) 587
*29:1	Prophecy against Pharaoh	12	10	10	7 Jan. 587
*29:17	Prophecy to Babylon about Egypt	1	1	27	26 Apr. 571
30:20	Prophecy against Pharaoh	7	1	11	29 Apr. 587
31:1	Prophecy to Pharaoh	1	3	11	21 June 587
*32:1	Lamentation over Pharaoh	1	12	12	3 March 585
32:17	Lamentation over Egypt	15	1	12	27 Apr. 586
33:21	Report of Jerusalem's fall	5	10	12	8 Jan. 585
40:1	Vision of restored temple	10	1	25	28 Apr. 573

*Obviously not in chronological sequence.

---

17. See further the excellent remarks of H.G. May, who concludes that the data "make it improbable objectively to presume a multiplicity of authors"; "Introduction and Exegesis of Ezekiel," IB 6:50f.

18. C.C. Torrey, arguing for a date after 230, wrote: "The plain fact, as one day will be generally recognized, is that the author of the book had before him the complete Pentateuch, in the very form in which it lies before us at the present day"; *Pseudo-Ezekiel and the Original Prophecy* (1930; repr. 1970), p. 91. If this is accepted as an objective conclusion, independent of the date of Ezekiel, it has great significance for theories of postexilic compilation of the Pentateuch, for it could mean that the Pentateuch was taken into exile in its completed form.

19. Calculated from tables in R.A. Parker and W.H. Dubberstein, *Babylonian Chronology 626 B.C.–A.D. 75*, pp. 27f.

The prophecy divides into three parts:

Judgment on Israel (chs. 1–24)
   Prophet's call (1:1–3:21)
   Idolatry of the people (3:22–7:27)
   Visions of warning (chs. 8–11)
   Parables and allegories of judgment (chs. 12–19)
   Judgment on the nation (chs. 20–24)
Judgment on the (gentile) nations (chs. 25–32)
   [Ammon, Moab, Edom, Philistia, Tyre, Egypt]
Restoration of Israel (chs. 33–48)
   True shepherd (chs. 33–34)
   Land (chs. 35–36)
   People (chs. 37–39)
   Temple (chs. 40–43)
   Worship (chs. 44–46)
   River of life, holy city, holy land (chs. 47–48)

The third section could be divided into two parts, following 39:29, but since the temporal merges with the eternal throughout this portion, it seems better to consider it as a unit.

Allegories and Actions. Ezekiel includes a number of allegories: the vine (ch. 15), Yahweh's wife (16:1-43), eagles (17:1-21), lioness (19:1-9), vineyard (vv. 10-14), sword (21:1-17), Oholah and Oholibah (23:1-35), caldron (24:1-14). The prophecy also includes a number of prophetic actions: the brick with a map of Jerusalem (4:1-3), representing the coming siege of the city; the prophet lying on his left side 390 days and on his right for 40 (vv. 4-8), eating exiles' rations (vv. 9-17), representing the years of punishment for Israel and Judah, respectively (a day for a year, v. 6), and the starvation diet Jerusalem will be forced to endure; shaving his head with a sword, weighing and dividing the hair (5:1-12) representing the smallness of the remnant that shall escape, and only through fire; digging through the wall with an exile's baggage (12:1-12), so Ezekiel might tell the people of the coming exile; marking the route for the sword of the king of Babylon (21:18-23 [MT 23-28]), symbolizing the possible conclusions, either that he was led by false divination, or it was the doing of Yahweh. To these might be added the sign of the death of Ezekiel's wife (24:15-24), symbolizing how the delight of Yahweh's eyes also would be taken.

The distinction between symbolic act and symbolic word picture is sometimes difficult, so scholars do not agree completely in classifying the allegories and prophetic actions. The difficulty is increased because both forms are unusual among the prophets of Yahweh. Some scholars have attempted to distinguish sources.[20] However, it is not difficult to believe that in the turmoil of Jerusalem,

---

20. Childs' treatment is helpful; *Old Testament as Scripture*, pp. 363, 368f.

occupied by foreign forces, and in the midst of widespread unbelief, Ezekiel's means of presenting his messages—or rather, those that Yahweh imposed upon him—were designed to attract attention and make graphic representations that would be both self-explanatory and long remembered.

Ezekiel's Chronology. The date given for receiving the news of the fall of Jerusalem (33:21) corresponds to Jan. 8, 585 (see Table, p. 465). According to 2 Kgs. 25:1-3, the siege began on the tenth day of the tenth month of the ninth year of Zedekiah and ended on the ninth day of the fourth month, when the king fled. The span, as usually calculated, is about one and one-half years, and the fall of the city is often dated 587. But 2 Kgs. 25:8 clearly indicates that it was Nebuchadnezzar's nineteenth year—586. The problem is solved by understanding that Nebuchadnezzar's year was from Nisan to Nisan (spring), while Zedekiah's was from Tishri to Tishri (fall). Whichever system was used, Nisan was always "month 1" (see Ch. 21). The interval between the beginning of the siege and the fall of the city was two and one-half years—which agrees with the chronology in Ezek. 24:1f. and 33:21.[21]

Son of Man. This title is used some ninety times in Ezekiel,[22] always by Yahweh when addressing Ezekiel. As a form of address it appears elsewhere in the Old Testament only in Dan. 8:17.[23] The phrase occurs throughout Ezekiel (omitted only in chs. 1, 9, 10, 18, 19, 41, 42, 45, 46, 48), often preceded by the phrase, "The word of the Lord came to me." It occurs in messenger formulas (e.g., 2:3: "Son of man, I send you to the people of Israel . . ."; cf. 2:1; 3:4). Ezekiel describes the effect in 2:2: "And when he spoke to me, the Spirit entered into me and set me upon my feet; and I heard him speaking to me." Similar phenomena are found throughout the book, and Ezekiel implies that he was fully aware that Yahweh was conveying the very words or action that he was to use.

It is unlikely that the title "son of man" in Ezekiel is to be compared with the same title used by Jesus of himself (used for him elsewhere only by Stephen; Acts 7:56). It is questionable, also, that it has any relationship to the words "son of man" in Dan. 7:13 (Aram. *keḇar 'eᵊnāš*). Therefore Calvin's suggestion that Yahweh used the title to give Ezekiel stature, although he was an exile among exiles, misses the point.[24] More likely the title was used to stress the

---

21. See H.G. May, *IB* 6:59f.; J. Finegan, "The Chronology of Ezekiel," *JBL* 69 (1950): 61-66; Howie, *Date and Composition*, pp. 27-46; W.S. LaSor, "Jerusalem," *ISBE* 2 (1982): 1015-16.

22. BDB, p. 9, cites 87 occurrences; *Veteris Testamenti Concordantiae* (New York: 1955), p. 209, 93; G.V. Wegram, *The New Englishman's Hebrew and Chaldee Concordance* (Wilmington, Del.: 1972), 92.

23. Heb. *ben 'āḏām*. The plural, *beᵊnê hā'āḏām* "sons of man, human beings," occurs elsewhere, *ben 'āḏām* is found in parallel with *'eᵊnôš* in Job 25:6; Ps. 8:4 (MT 5). According to Eichrodt, the expression in Dan. 8:17 is derived from Ezekiel; *Ezekiel*, p. 61.

24. *Commentary on Ezekiel*, trans. T. Myers (Grand Rapids: 1948), s.v. 2:3.

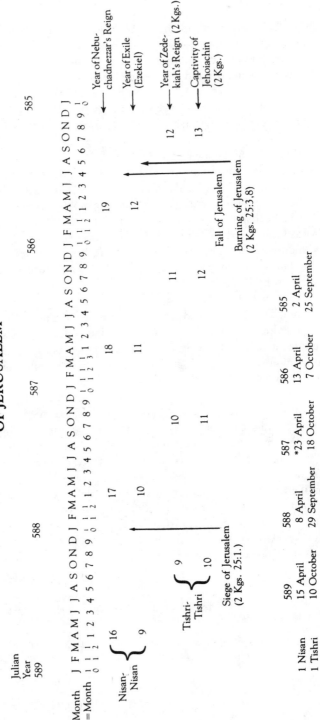

DATE OF THE SIEGE OF JERUSALEM

human nature of the agent over against the divine source of the message. Ezekiel had been commissioned to speak chiefly to Israelites already in exile (3:4, 11, 15). Even his Jerusalem experience (8:3–11:24) was designed to be related to these people (11:25), who might have looked upon him as a new religious leader with a message from a new deity. By insisting that it was "the word of Yahweh" that came unto him, and constantly repeating the title by which he was addressed, he removed any basis for such ideas. This was the same God, using the same method as before the Exile, namely speaking to and through his servants the prophets. From another viewpoint, Ezekiel himself must constantly be aware that he is but man, standing only by the power of the Spirit, and speaking as bidden by Yahweh.[25]

"Set Your Face Against." On nine occasions, the messenger formula takes the form, "son of man, set your face against . . ." (see 13:17). W.H. Brownlee suggests that this formula directed the prophet to go to the people or place mentioned in each instance.[26] The question remains, however, whether the formula has only such meaning. Does Ezekiel (or the editor) intend the audience to understand the statements so? Although much more study is needed, the text does not otherwise indicate that the prophet actually carried out such extensive travel assignments.[27]

This formula is used with messages to the mountains of Israel, "daughters of your people," the South, Jerusalem, the Ammonites, Sidon, Pharaoh king of Egypt, Mt. Seir, and Gog of the land of Magog. Careful study of the numerous commands to Ezekiel to prophesy, speak, say, make known to, or raise a lamentation against does not seem to indicate any special feature about these situations. Tentatively, this appears to be simply an alternate form of the messenger formula. In 3:8 Yahweh tells Ezekiel: "I have made your face hard against their faces"; the context indicates that the hearers will stubbornly resist the message. Thus, the formula may be intended to remind Ezekiel of this fact and strengthen his determination to carry out the order.[28]

"I Am Yahweh." This expression, which occurs many times in Ezekiel,[29]

---

25. See Eichrodt, *Ezekiel*, p. 61.

26. "Ezekiel," *ISBE* 2 (1982): 262. Evidence from extrabiblical sources lends support to his basic theory.

27. The clause *śîm pānêḵā* occurs in 6:2; 13:17; 20:46 (MT 21:2); 21:2 (MT 7); 25:2; 28:21; 29:2; 35:2; 38:2. It is followed by *'el* in all except 20:46 (MT 21:2, *derek*), and 29:2; 35:2 (*'al*). The instruction *lēḵ* "go" is found only in 3:1, 4, 11, always with reference to the exiles.

28. Note Luke 9:51 with reference to Jesus: "he set his face to go to Jerusalem," but careful exegesis does not support this as a messenger formula. It is elsewhere a common Semitic idiom meaning "to make up one's mind, determine."

29. Because of the extremely high frequency of the word Yahweh in the Old Testament, determining such expressions is difficult and open to error. According to BDB, the expression following some form of the verb "know" ("they shall know that," "you shall know that," occurs 49 times in Ezekiel and 9 elsewhere. Mandelkern cites some 60 in Ezekiel. In addition, other expressions, such as "I Yahweh have spoken," "I Yahweh shall speak," "they shall see that I am Yahweh," and "I (am) Yahweh," stand alone 6 times.

may be considered a hallmark of the book. It is reminiscent of use of the same expression in Leviticus. The purpose or result intended in messages to Ezekiel is often expressed in the "recognition" formula: "that you/they shall know that I am Yahweh." The meaning of this truth to Jews in exile and its significance as a testimony to pagan neighbors is obvious.

THEOLOGY

Visions of God. Ezekiel saw a wheel (1:15)—actually four wheels—not like those on Babylonian chariots, but "as it were a wheel within a wheel" (v. 16), and they "went in any of their four directions without turning as they went" (v. 17). The wheels were like the gleaming of a chrysolite, with rims "full of eyes" and spokes (v. 18). Wherever the living creatures went, the wheels went with them. Any artistic attempt to reproduce this vision is bound to end in frustration.

The four living creatures had the form of men, but each with four faces and four wings. Each had the human face in front, the face of a lion on the right side, an ox on the left side, and an eagle at the back.[30] "Each went straight forward; wherever the spirit would go, they went, without turning as they went" (v. 12; cf. v. 20). Then "they went in any of their four directions" (v. 17), or "darted to and fro, like a flash of lightning" (v. 14). Over their heads was something like a firmament, shining like crystal. The sound of their wings was like the sound of many waters, "the thunder of the Almighty" (v. 24). Above the firmament was something like a throne, and over this likeness of a throne a likeness as of a human form. Around him was rainbow brightness: "Such was the appearance of the likeness of the glory of Yahweh" (v. 28b; cf. 8:2; ch. 10).

At this point some readers would have nothing more to do with the book. But the believing community—first the postexilic Jews and then the Christians—has found here something symbolic of the presence of God. How can one portray his transcendence or providence? Ezekiel fell on his face before this vision of God, then found that God was not distant, but close to him; not unapproachable, but ready to talk. Yet the very form of address, "son of man," reminds Ezekiel of their difference. Ezekiel's doctrine of God, full and rich, begins by learning that God is the Other. One does not approach him until he so bids.

One day Ezekiel saw the glory of God[31] move from his accustomed place between the cherubim in the Holy of Holies to the threshold of the temple

---

30. In Christian symbolism, the lion represents Matthew, the ox Mark, the man Luke, and the eagle John; but this can hardly be drawn from Ezekiel's vision. The figures in Rev. 4:6f. are clearly derived from Ezek. 1.

31. Heb. *kᵉḇôḏ yhwh* "glory of Yahweh" (sometimes *kᵉḇôḏ ʾelōhîm* "glory of God") is another characteristic of the book. Only Isaiah and Psalms approach Ezekiel's usage.

(9:3), to the east gate (10:19), and finally from the midst of the city to the Mount of Olives on the east side (11:23). The glory of Yahweh had come down to fill the temple when Solomon dedicated it (2 Chr. 5:13f.), but now departed. God's warning to Solomon and the nation (7:19-22) now became reality. But on another day, Yahweh took Ezekiel to the east gate, where he saw the glory of the God of Israel coming from the east: "And the vision I saw was like the vision which I had seen when he came to destroy the city . . . and I fell on my face. As the glory of the Lord entered the temple by the gate facing east, the Spirit lifted me up, and brought me into the inner court; and behold, the glory of the Lord filled the temple" (Ezek. 43:1-5).

The departure of Yahweh from the Holy City and his return years later provide the outline of the prophecy. The reason is made clear: the stubborn sinfulness of the people caused him to leave; his promise led him to return. The people quickly rationalized their situation: they were suffering for what their fathers had done, and their God was not powerful enough to protect them. Ezekiel speaks to both of these doctrinal errors.

Idolatry. The basis of God's judgment on idolatry is given in Lev. 26:14-45: "if you will not hearken to me, and will not do all these commandments" (v. 14; cf. vv. 21, 23, 27). Ezekiel builds on this theme.[32] Note also Deut. 28:15-68, which enumerates the curses of disobedience. The central charge is "you did not serve the Lord your God with joyfulness and gladness of heart" (v. 47; cf. Ezek. 8:7-18). The threat of another period of captivity like that of Egypt (Deut. 28:20) is made because of the people's disobedience (v. 58).

Ezekiel's indictment of idolatry includes his challenge to the false gods (13:17-23).[33] His description of the sins and idolatries in ch. 16 is offensive to many readers, but it probably was so intended, for idolatry is offensive to Yahweh. In fact, it is the major sin in the Bible. All other sins start here.

Personal Responsibility. Both Jeremiah and Ezekiel quote what was probably a current proverb: "The fathers have eaten sour grapes, and the children's teeth are set on edge" (Jer. 31:29; Ezek. 18:2). Both prophets reject this disclaimer of personal responsibility, which blames the current situation on the older generation. Some mistakenly suggest that the concept of individual responsibility did not originate until the end of the seventh century. Only by completely reworking the entire Old Testament can this be substantiated. The commandment applying the sins of idolatrous parents to succeeding generations (Exod. 20:5) is not an attempt to shift the blame; quite the opposite—it points out how serious are the effects of one generation's sins of idolatry on their children and their children's children. Nevertheless, Ezekiel does mark a break with the

---

32. Driver, *Introduction*, p. 147, finds 27 similar expressions in Lev. 26 and Ezekiel, several "not occurring elsewhere in the Old Testament."
33. See E.L. Allen, "Exposition of Ezekiel," *IB* 6:132f.

dominant idea of the day: "In so far as it is a rejection of the philosophy of corporate responsibility, it represents a new current in Hebrew thought, although individualism was always prominent in the older Hebrew religion."[34] Ezekiel's concern for this matter may be studied in 3:16-21; 14:12-23; ch. 18; 33:1-20.[35]

Ezekiel sets forth the principle, "the soul (or person) that sins shall die." He illustrates this by three successive generations (18:5-9, 10-13, 14-17), each judged by its own deeds. As further illustration he describes a wicked man who converts and is spared (v. 21), and a righteous man who turns from righteousness and commits iniquity, and dies for the sin he committed (v. 24). Thus, Ezekiel shows that a son is not spared because his father is righteous, or punished because his father is wicked, but in every case is punished for his own sins.

On the other hand, children do suffer for the sins of their parents. A generation would be born in exile because of the sins of their parents. Such a truth as "corporate personality" and "believing community" does exist. The child of believing parents may belong to the community without becoming aware of it. Ezekiel is speaking of ultimate, eschatological responsibility, for every person must stand before God. Ezekiel is also addressing the generation going into exile, who want to avoid any personal responsibility: "The soul that sins shall die. . . . The righteousness of the righteous shall be upon himself, and the wickedness of the wicked shall be upon himself" (v. 20).

Sabbath. Ezekiel uses the expression "my sabbaths" twelve times, mostly in ch. 20. He has been accused of introducing an emphasis on cult (cultus, or formalized worship) contrary to the main prophetic position.[36] But an emphasis on the cult, particularly the Sabbaths, is found in the levitical legislation just prior to the entrance into the land of Canaan, and again in Ezekiel at the beginning of the Babylonian exile. In Leviticus the emphasis was upon "holiness," separation from the paganism that surrounded Israel. The cultic acts, particularly the Sabbaths and festivals, served to mark the Israelites as "a peculiar people" in the midst of Canaanite religion. The people's sin was summarized as "profaning my sabbaths" (cf. 20:12).

Jeremiah had introduced the idea that the Exile was directly related to Israel's failure to observe the Sabbaths (Jer. 17:21-27). The Chronicler associated Jeremiah's prophecy of seventy years of captivity (25:11f.; 29:10) with the keeping of the Sabbath: "All the days that [the land] lay desolate it kept sabbath, to fulfill seventy years" (2 Chr. 36:21).[37] After the Exile, led by Ezra's

---

34. May, *IB* 6:157.
35. See also H.H. Rowley, *The Faith of Israel*, pp. 101f.
36. See R.B.Y. Scott, *The Relevance of the Prophets* (New York: 1944), p. 209 and note 4.
37. In the form of the Ten Comandments as given in Deut. 5:6-21, the observance of the Sabbath is related to the deliverance from Egyptian bondage (v. 15). Failure to commemorate the Exodus by keeping the Sabbaths thus led to a reversal of the Exodus by means of exile.

reforms and then spurred on by the inroads of Hellenism, Judaism developed the Sabbath and other cultic requirements into a legalistic system.[38] Jesus, as the Gospels indicate, on occasion set out to "break" the Sabbath as so defined and replace it with a dynamic concept:[39] "The sabbath was made for man" (Mark 2:27f.). This has led Christians in many cases to read back into Ezekiel and Ezra a post-Pentecost view. But Christians must recognize that the cultic provisions of the Law were necessary to preserve the people of God, not only in the Exile but after their return. Until the law in the heart became a reality, the law as written had to be binding.[40]

The results of Ezekiel's prophecy can be seen in history. The faith of Israel survived the crucible of the Exile. The law became the great passion of the Jewish people, whether in Palestine or in the Diaspora. The very survival of Ezekiel's prophecy is one evidence of this fact.[41]

Tyre. The prophecy against Tyre (chs. 26–28) is a magnificent literary piece. Scholars who find Ezekiel prosaic and monotonous sometimes refer to this as the only imaginative bit of writing in the whole prophecy. Tyre, representing the Phoenician maritime mercantile confederacy, is portrayed as a ship (27:3-9), and the ports of call, along with the cargo, are described in detail. When news of Tyre's destruction reaches those who traded with them, they raise a lamentation (vv. 25-36).

Ch. 28 poses the most problems. Who is this "prince of Tyre" who said: "I am a god, I sit in the seat of the gods," yet was "but a man and no god" (v. 2)? Yahweh tells him: "You were the signet of perfection, full of wisdom and perfect in beauty. You were in Eden, the garden of God . . . blameless in your ways from the day you were created, till iniquity was found in you. . . . I cast you to the ground" (vv. 12-17). Like Isa. 14:12-21, this was often taken to refer to the Satan.

How can such an interpretation be held in the light of grammatico-historical exegesis?[42] In context the passage concerns Tyre, with immediate reference to its king (perhaps Ba'li II). Yet scholars have found both here and in Isa. 14 "reflections of Ugaritic mythology."[43] Even though the Ugaritic elements come from the fourteenth century or earlier, some scholars insist that these passages are "late," well into the postexilic period. Much more likely the mythological elements are very early, and survivals appeared in Israel prior to the Exile. After

---

38. See Talmud *Shab.*

39. See A.G. Hebert, *The Throne of David* (London: 1941), pp. 143-163; see also H.H. Rowley, *Worship in Ancient Israel*, pp. 144-175.

40. See Allen, *IB* 6:171.

41. See Howie, "Ezekiel," *IDB* 2:211.

42. The literary genre is the taunt song, a characteristic of which is hyperbolic ridicule.

43. May, *IB* 6:218; J. Morgenstern, "The Divine Triad in Biblical Mythology," *JBL* 64 (1945): 15-37.

the Exile, Canaanite (Phoenician) religious elements were no great problem in Judaism.

But a "satanic" element exists in the king of Tyre (Ezek. 28) just as in the king of Babylon (Isa. 14). "Satan" means "adversary"—originally not a proper name—and Tyre, with the Jezebel-Elijah confrontation and its determined effort to replace Yahwism with Baal worship, was satanic. Something Edenic, some existentialist "Adamic experience" that sought to be like God, is represented by these kings.[44] The principles inherent in all earthly rulers are essentially satanic. Like "Messiah," "Satan" as a technical term came into use later. Ezekiel, whose emphasis on eschatology runs like an undercurrent throughout his prophecy,[45] may have had in mind the Satan-Messiah confrontation of the end of the age when he spoke at length of Tyre.

Egypt. In rehearsing the history of Israel, the prophets often refer to the bondage in Egypt. In a sense there is a historical connection with the Exile, for the repeated efforts of Egyptian kings to use Judah as a foil in the struggle with Babylonia contributed to the Babylonian attacks upon Jerusalem, its siege, the removal of its kings, and finally its destruction. But in light of Ezekiel's eschatological overtones, something deeper may be involved, as in the case of Tyre. Detailed examination of the prophecy reveals problems of a historical nature. Egypt was not given into the hand of Nebuchadnezzar (cf. 29:19). The Nile was not dried up (30:12). Many of the details in ch. 30 can be checked off as "fulfilled"—but not by Babylon. The Egyptians were not scattered among the nations (v. 23). This is not to deny the validity of prophecy, but it does raise the question of interpretation. Ezekiel was living at the time, and certainly must have been aware that Babylon's efforts against Egypt had met with no great success, and had tapered off. In a few more years the king of Babylon would become more interested in his projects in Teima than in world conquest, and then the forces of Cyrus would overthrow Babylon. Ezekiel, it would seem, must have had in mind something more significant.

This becomes clearer in ch. 32, where Ezekiel is instructed to consign Egypt to "the nether world" (v. 18). There Pharaoh finds comfort upon seeing the other nations so condemned: Assyria (v. 22), Elam (v. 24), Meshech and Tubal (v. 26), Edom (v. 29), the princes of the north and the Sidonians (Phoenicians, v. 30). Ezekiel tells of the judgment to come on the cruel nations of the world, terror in the land of the living (v. 32). His God is not simply the Yahweh of defeated Israel in exile; he is Judge of all nations.

ESCHATOLOGY

According to some scholars, the subject of the end time is a later development in Israel, not only postexilic but late postexilic. To those who hold the Old

---

44. In both Babylonia and Canaan the king was often considered a deified human being. The concept of "sacral kingship" is built on such a belief.
45. See Childs, *Old Testament as Scripture*, pp. 366f.

Testament as divine revelation, this makes little sense, for the ultimate purpose of such acts is always in view. God's final triumph is set forth at the time of the Fall (Gen. 3), and is inherent in the call of Abram (12:3). The promise to David of an everlasting kingdom (2 Sam. 7:13) begins a series of promises of the kingdom. All of the eighth-century prophets, without radical emendation, have eschatological elements, as do their seventh-century counterparts Jeremiah and Zephaniah. Therefore, Ezekiel is hardly the first of the kind. On the other hand, with the end of the Davidic dynasty and the destruction of Jerusalem, the people of God needed a new emphasis, a more fully developed indoctrination, of what God's promises really mean. Ezekiel begins this new emphasis on eschatology.

Ezekiel often is looked upon as the first of the apocalypticists. If the term is used in the strict sense, namely the irruption into history of a divine savior, a "son of man"[46] as in the book of Enoch, then no such figure is portrayed here. But if it is taken to mean simply that Ezekiel used strange visions and figures, then he is, to that extent, apocalyptic.[47] Chs. 34–48 are the eschatological portions.

True Shepherd. Ch. 34 is a prophecy against the shepherds (v. 2), the spiritual and political leaders who have not fulfilled their God-given role (see v. 10). Yahweh identifies himself as the true shepherd: "I, I myself will search for my sheep, and will seek them out" (v. 11; cf. vv. 15f.; Luke 19:10). He will gather them from the countries, and bring them into their own land, and feed them (v. 13).

In v. 23, however, Yahweh says: "I will set up over them one shepherd, my servant David, and he shall feed them: he shall feed them and be their shepherd." Some compenetration seems to be present here, for the messianic king,[48] "David," is shepherd, yet so is Yahweh himself. This recalls Jesus' question to the Pharisees: "If David called him 'Lord,' how then is he his son?" (Matt. 22:45). The question must be faced: does Ezekiel lay the scriptural basis for identifying the Messiah with Yahweh (see John 10:1-18; Ezek. 37:24)?

New Heart and New Spirit. Like Jeremiah, Ezekiel makes clear that Yahweh's goal is not merely to punish his people and snatch a remnant to start over again with the same unredeemed humanity (see 36:24-27; cf. 11:19; 18:31; 37:14). Something new will be involved—a "new covenant," "new heart," "new spirit." Yet these figures of speech indicate that while it will be new it will not be

---

46. Curiously, but probably no more than a coincidence, "son of man" is used of both Ezekiel and the apocalyptic savior. The common denominator, most likely, is the fact that the term basically means "human being." In Daniel the one who is to come is "like a human being" (7:13, lit.).

47. See above, Ch. 30.

48. "Shepherd" is a Semitic term for "king, ruler." It is particularly appropriate here, for tending the sheep with tenderness and care is essential for flock and shepherd.

different. No new name replaces Israel, and no new figure replaces "David."
There is to be a law in the heart, but it is still the Torah. Ezekiel adds to the
central truth an additional element: "It is not for your sake, O house of Israel,
that I am about to act, but for the sake of my holy name, which you have
profaned among the nations to which you came" (36:22; cf. v. 32). God is not
defeated, and his plan is still in force.

The vindication of God's character is an important emphasis for Ezekiel,
as seen in his use of the expression "then they will know that I am the Lord."
The concept of a tragic deity, caught helplessly in the vortex of history, is
foreign to Ezekiel (and the entire Bible). Yahweh is Lord of history. His actions
will ultimately vindicate him, revealing his holiness, goodness, wisdom, and
power. When he has finished, his people will be like him in holiness.

Valley of Dry Bones. Ch. 37 does not portray the final resurrection, though
belief in the resurrection underlies the figures used. Rather, it is a prophecy of
the reestablishment of the single nation Israel: "These bones are the whole
house of Israel" (v. 11). "I am about to take the stick of Joseph" (the old
northern kingdom, Israel), "and I will join with it the stick of Judah, and make
them one stick" (vv. 19f.). Yahweh will gather Israel "from the nations among
which they have gone" and return them to their own land, with one king over
them all, and they shall be "no longer divided into two kingdoms" (vv. 21f.).
Certainly, this is the revival and reunion of the nation!

Yet, again the prophetic perspective is visible: "My servant David shall be
king over them; and they shall all have one shepherd" (v. 24). "They shall
dwell in the land where your fathers dwelt that I gave to my servant Jacob; they
and their children and their children's children shall dwell there for ever; and
David my servant shall be their prince for ever" (v. 25). By no legitimate kind
of exegesis can this be applied solely to postexilic Judaism. The postexilic regathering can only be a type, a foretaste, of the ultimate messianic kingdom.

A Second Exile? Chs. 38–39 appear to announce a second attack on the
nation (see Zech. 12:3). Ezekiel prophesies against Gog:

> "After many days you will be mustered; in the latter years you will go
> against the land that is restored from war, the land where people were
> gathered from many nations upon the mountains of Israel, which had
> been a continual waste; its people were brought out from the nations
> and now dwell securely, all of them." (38:8; cf. Rev. 20:8)

Straightforward exegesis indicates that this is after the postexilic reestablishment
of Judah; but only by tortured exegesis can it be made to apply to the Roman
destruction of Judah.[49] A power from the north comes against Israel "in the

---

49. Reference to New Testament passages is not intended to force the exegesis of
Ezekiel, but to show that New Testament authors seem to have had a similar understanding of the prophecies.

latter days" (vv. 14-16; cf. Rev. 19:17-21). "On that day there shall be a great shaking in the land of Israel" (38:19), but God "will summon every kind of terror against Gog" (v. 21). The battle against Gog is described in gory detail in ch. 39, and seems to represent the final judgment of the nations. It is a fitting introduction to the final section of the prophecy.

Will the Cult be Reestablished? One of the most difficult and vexing problems in interpreting Ezekiel is found in chs. 40–48. If the prophet was speaking as a fallible human, with no divine revelation, the problem disappears. If these chapters—even though they follow chs. 36–39, and although their figures do not fit the period—deal with postexilic Judah, the problem is less formidable. But everything in the passage seems to indicate that Ezekiel has the messianic age in view (see esp. 43:2-5, 7; 44:2; 47:7-12 [cf. Zech. 14:8; Rev. 22:1f.]; 48:35b).

At face value, Ezekiel seems to say that in the messianic age the temple will be rebuilt, the land apportioned by tribal inheritance (although on quite artificial lines), and the sacrificial system reestablished (see 45:18-25). This would appear contrary to the prophetic emphasis on the spiritual nature of the cult and of Yahweh as a God who does not delight in bloody offerings (e.g., Mic. 6:6-8; Isa. 1:11). It certainly is contrary to the New Testament view (esp. Heb. 8–10).

Only three interpretations seem possible:

(1) The literal reading would require establishment of the Israelite nation in the messianic age, with temple, ritual, and bloody sacrifices. This interpretation has been held by many "Chiliasts" and Premillennialists.[50]

(2) The typico-symbolical interpretation attempts to make the Christian era the messianic age. This view faces grave difficulties in attempting to explain the symbolism of chs. 40–48, but it runs into further difficulty with passages in both Testaments that foresee a future for Israel as distinct from the Church (see Rom. 9–11). However, it does seem to have some support from Heb. 8:13; 9:23–10:4.

(3) O. Piper sees the rebuilding of the temple and reinstitution of the sacrificial system as part of the "Jewish section of the Church." The sacrificial system would be memorial in character, similar to the Lord's Supper.[51]

---

50. For a strong argument against this position, see Keil-Delitzsch, *Commentary* 9 (repr. 1980), Ezekiel 2:382-434: reinstitution of bloody sacrifices is opposed to the teachings of Christ and the apostles; "glorification" of Canaan is not taught in the Old Testament; and "glorification" of Palestine is not taught in the New. Although based on numerous scriptural passages, the arguments seem more dogmatically controlled than exegetically derived—a factor present in all schools of interpretation on this subject.

51. See *God in History* (New York: 1939), p. 107: "Israel is prior historically to the church; but while the church has already taken possession of the whole heritage which God promised to His people, the Jews stand outside and have to wait. But they are not altogether rejected. As Abraham's children they will one day enter the Kingdom. That is to say: notwithstanding the fact that Christianity has become the church of the

Positive and negative values exist in each position. Any interpretation that denies the finality of the sacrifice of Christ must be rejected by those committed to the authority of the New Testament. Any view that fails to consider seriously the abundant scriptural material relevant to Israel (or the Jew) as a distinctive unit within the redeemed society, is deficient. Any approach which seeks to make the present age fully equivalent to the messianic age is not only unscriptural but unrealistic. Watering down the prophecies of the messianic age to make them describe the present era is hardly satisfactory exegesis of the Bible.

John's Use of Ezekiel. Comparison of the book of Revelation with Ezekiel indicates that the New Testament author drew heavily upon the figures and language of this prophecy, accounting for forty-eight of the sixty-five direct or indirect quotations from Ezekiel in the New Testament.

To the people in exile, Ezekiel brought a great message of hope. Yahweh had not forgotten them. Indeed, this was all part of his great plan. The restoration of his people, not merely to the old situation, but more importantly to a new and blessed life with Yahweh himself as their Shepherd, was the goal of his revelatory and redemptive activity. Therefore the people of God in all ages, both Jew and Gentile, synagogue and church, find hope and comfort in Ezekiel. Together, God's people long for the city whose name is "The Lord is there" (48:35).[52]

FOR FURTHER READING

Ellison, H.L. *Ezekiel: The Man and His Message*. Grand Rapids: 1956. (Noncritical; concerned with Ezekiel's message as directed to and interpreted by his contemporaries.)

Newsome, J.D., Jr. *By the Waters of Babylon: An Introduction to the History and Theology of the Exile*. Atlanta: John Knox, 1979.

Parunak, H.V.D. "The Literary Architecture of Ezekiel's MAR'ÔT 'ELŌHÎM." *JBL* 99 (1980): 61-74.

Power, E. "Ezechiel." *CCHS* §§ 477z–493k. (Good treatment, full bibliography.)

Rowley, H.H. "The Book of Ezekiel in Modern Study." Pp. 169-210 in *Men of God*. London: 1963. (Repr. from *BJRL* 36 [1953/54]: 146-190.)

Skinner, J. *The Book of Ezekiel*. Expositor's Bible. Grand Rapids: 1956. 4:213-350.

---

gentiles, the Jews will not be compelled to give up the belief and practice of their fathers when the hour comes for them fully to recognise Jesus Christ as their Messiah. They will then form a Jewish section of the church, Jewish in its tradition but enlightened by the spirit of Christ. But according to God's purpose this will happen only when all the gentiles have already entered the church."

52. For a comprehensive analysis of the religious ideas in chs. 40–48, see J.D. Levenson, *Theology of the Program of Restoration of Ezekiel 40–48*. HSM 10 (Missoula: 1976).

Taylor, J.B. *Ezekiel*. Tyndale Old Testament Commentaries. Downers Grove: 1969. (Introductory.)

Wevers, J.W. *Ezekiel*. NCBC. Grand Rapids: 1982.

Zimmerli, W. "The Message of the Prophet Ezekiel." *Interp* 23 (1969): 131-157.

CHAPTER 36

HAGGAI

ON 12 October 539 B.C., the army of Cyrus the Great entered Babylon and brought the Babylonian empire to an end. Dominion of the world thus passed from East to West,[1] for the empires of Assyria and Babylonia had been Semitic, but the new Medo-Persian empire was Indo-European. The Nabonidus chronicle says simply: "On the sixteenth day Ugbaru the governor of Gutium and the troops of Cyrus without fighting entered Babylon." Cyrus likewise records that the conquest was "peaceable": "Without any battle [Marduk] made [Cyrus] enter his town Babylon, sparing Babylon any calamity."[2]

Cyrus not only claimed to be invading at the invitation of Marduk, patron god of Babylon, but he also boasted that he was returning the gods of Sumer and Akkad, who had been brought to Babylon by the conquests of Nabonidus "to dwell in peace in their habitations."[3] Consistent with this attitude, in 538 Cyrus allowed the Jews to return to their own land and rebuild the temple at Jerusalem (see Ezra 1:1-4; 6:3-5).[4]

HISTORICAL SITUATION

The Return. One might suppose that the Jews, who had been in exile in Babylonia for fifty years or more (from 605 or 597 or 586 to 538), would be more than anxious to return "home." But following Jeremiah's advice, they had settled in Babylonia, built houses, planted gardens, married, and raised families.

---

1. See W.S. LaSor, *Great Personalities of the Old Testament*, p. 171.
2. See R.P. Dougherty, *Nabonidus and Belshazzar*. Yale Oriental Series (New Haven: 1929), pp. 170, 176. Cf. *ANET*, p. 315.
3. *DOTT*, p. 93.
4. It is objected sometimes that 538 was not "the first year of Cyrus," as Ezra dates it; see L.W. Batten, *Ezra and Nehemiah*. ICC (Edinburgh: 1949). However, Cyrus dates his reign from his conquest of Babylon. "From the seventh month of Cyrus' accession year (539) business texts dated to him continue without break to the twenty-seventh day of the fourth month (Du'uzu) of his ninth year, July, 530 B.C."; W.H. Dubberstein, "The Chronology of Cyrus and Cambyses," *AJSL* 55 (1938): 417.

Darius I (521-486 B.C.), seated, with Crown Prince Xerxes behind him; relief from Persepolis. (Oriental Institute, University of Chicago)

Some became very successful in business. Children born in exile were now more than fifty years old, with children and grandchildren of their own. Not all wanted to tear up established roots and return to a land they had never known. Some fifty thousand did return (Ezra 2:64; Neh. 7:66), with subsequent returns under Ezra (in 458)[5] and Nehemiah (445). A sizable Jewish community remained in Babylon for centuries, becoming a center of Jewish scholarship producing, among other things, the Babylonian Talmud. Therefore the return in 538 included only a fraction of the exiles.

A New "Exodus"? The prophets (especially Isaiah) had spoken of a deliverance by the Lord, often in terms reminiscent of the Exodus. But the regathering of the exiles was quite different. There had been no cruel bondage in Babylonia like that in Egypt. Sheshbazzar was no Moses with mighty power from God. Joshua son of Jehozadak was not Joshua son of Nun, empowered to dispossess those already settled in Palestine. Under Assyrian and Babylonian policies of displacing persons, only those least capable of revolt had been left in the land, and foreigners from other conquered lands had been brought in. Jerusalem had been destroyed and not rebuilt. The land had been ravaged, and little had been done to restore it.

Rebuilding the Temple. When the band of exiles under Sheshbazzar, who had been appointed governor, reached Jerusalem, they attempted to rebuild the

---

5. Others date this return in the days of Artaxerxes II (404-358) or Artaxerxes III (358-338) or by emending Ezra 7:7 to read "thirty-seven" (thus in the year 428). See Ch. 50.

temple (Ezra 5:14-16). But discouragements were many, including opposition from Samaritans—Israelites who had not gone into exile—and the work soon ceased. According to Ezra, they built the altar and instituted some cultic practices, but the foundation was not yet laid (3:2-6). Some, who recalled the glory of the former temple, were discouraged by the miserable building that was being constructed. But one must wonder how well a person who had been exiled perhaps as a child of ten in 586 would remember now the former temple. At any rate, this was the situation into which the prophet Haggai came.

HAGGAI AND HIS MESSAGE

The Prophet. Actually, very little is known about Haggai. He was a contemporary of Zechariah (Ezra 5:1), and largely through the work of these two prophets the temple was rebuilt (6:14). On the basis of Hag. 2:3 some have supposed that Haggai had seen the former temple, but the verse will not support this interpretation. More likely is the tradition from Epiphanius that he was a young man who had returned from Babylon with Sheshbazzar. His name, which may be compared with Lat. Festus or Gk. Hilary, suggests that he was born on one of the Israelite festivals (Heb. *hag*). The argument in vv. 11-14 should not be pressed as a proof that the prophet was also a priest.

His Message. The book of Haggai contains four prophecies, each precisely dated. These can be converted to the modern system of calendration[6] as follows:

1:1	= 1/6/YD (Year of Darius) 2	= 29 Aug. 520
2:1	= 21/7/YD 2	= 17 Oct. 520
2:10	= 24/9/YD 2	= 18 Dec. 520
2:20	=	= also 18 Dec. 520

All were given within a four-month period.

The first message (1:1-11) was addressed to Zerubbabel, the governor who had succeeded Sheshbazzar,[7] and to Joshua the high priest. Basically, it was a call to finish the temple (v. 2). According to Ezra, the building had been commenced immediately upon the return to Jerusalem, but the work had stopped (Ezra 5:16), partly because of discouragement (see Hag. 2:3) and partly because of opposition by those left in the land (see Ezra 5:3). Haggai, then, was calling the people to resume building the temple and thus to regain God's blessing.

---

6. Based on the tables in R.A. Parker and Dubberstein, *Babylonian Chronology 626 B.C.–A.D. 75.*

7. According to R.D. Wilson, Sheshbazzar was the Babylonian name equivalent to Zerubbabel; "Sheshbazzar," *ISBE* (1939) 4:2766. Some scholars have accepted this identification, but comparison of Ezra 5:14-16 with 5:2 suggests that Sheshbazzar no longer was alive when Zerubbabel began his work.

The message was obeyed by Zerubbabel, Joshua, and the remnant of the people (Hag. 1:12), and work was commenced on September 21, 520.

The second message (2:1-9) likewise was addressed to the governor, the high priest, and the remnant (v. 2). It appears that as work progressed, disappointment set in, and some compared it with the former temple (v. 3). The message can be summarized: "I am with you" (v. 4), but this is expanded by what seems to be an eschatological promise, namely that the Lord would shake the heavens and the earth, "and the desired of all nations will come, and I will fill this house with glory" (v. 7, NIV). Yahweh reminds his hearers that silver and gold are his, and promises that "the latter splendor of this house shall be greater than the former" (v. 9).[8]

The third message (2:10-19) is a dialogue between Yahweh and Haggai. Apparently Zechariah had recently called upon the people to repent (Zech. 1:1-6). Haggai's message, in the following month, appears to underscore this need. Following Haggai's argument carefully (actually, the Lord's basic question in 2:12), one gets the impression that the people seem to have felt that working on the holy place made them holy. Questioning the priests, one of whose tasks was to answer questions on the specific interpretation of the law, Haggai draws out the truth that contact of the unclean with the clean does not cleanse that which is defiled, but rather defiles that which is clean. In other words, work on the temple did not sanctify the people; rather, their sin desecrated the temple. For this reason, Yahweh had been inflicting the land with diminished produce. With the people's repentance, God would bless them (v. 19).

The fourth message (2:20-23) was addressed to Zerubbabel (v. 21). This message is clearly eschatological, for Yahweh declares that he is about "to overthrow the throne of kingdoms" and make Zerubbabel "like a signet ring; for I have chosen you" (vv. 22f.). The language concerns the end time, and the word "chosen" (or "elect") is often associated with the coming Redeemer. The prophecy of Zechariah provides further evidence of a distinct implication that the Messiah was about to be revealed, and indeed that Zerubbabel was accepted by some to be the Messiah. More detailed consideration of possible interpretations is needed before such identification can be accepted.

The total effect of these prophecies was to encourage the nation, its governor, its high priest, and the remnant of the people to finish rebuilding the temple. Known in Jewish terminology as "the Second Temple," this temple was never replaced by a third. The temple which Herod the Great rebuilt in the days of Jesus was considered to be simply a refurbishing.

---

8. The text does not indicate clearly an eschatological event. "The desired of all nations" occurs with a plural verb, hence the RSV translates "the treasures of all nations." Moreover, the text reads "the splendor of this the latter house," apparently meaning the temple then being built. No wonder the people thought that the messianic age was about to dawn!

DATED EVENTS OF THE YEARS 539-515

12 Oct.	539 (16 Teshritu)—Fall of Babylon; accession year of Cyrus[9]
24 Mar.	538 (1 Nisānu)—First year of reign of Cyrus (Dan. 5:31?)
	538—Edict permitting Jews to return to Jerusalem (Ezra 1:1)
? May	538—Departure of Sheshbazzar and group for Jerusalem[10]
Sept.	538 (7th month)—Arrival at Jerusalem (3:1)
10 Apr.	537 (2/–/Cyrus 2)—Work begun on altar (v. 8)
	537 (?)—Work on temple halted until days of Darius (4:5)
16 Jan.	535 (1/24/Cyrus 3)—Daniel's vision (Dan. 10:1)
29 Aug.	520 (6/1/Darius 2)—First message to Haggai (Hag. 1:1)
21 Sept.	520 (6/24/Darius 2)—Work resumed on temple (v. 15)
17 Oct.	520 (7/21/Darius 2)—Second message to Haggai (2:1)
27 Oct.	520 (8/1?/Darius 2)—Message to Zechariah (Zech. 1:1)
18 Dec.	520 (9/24/Darius 2)—Third, fourth messages to Haggai (Hag. 2:10, 20)
15 Feb.	519 (24 Shebat)—Message to Zechariah (Zech. 1:7)
7 Dec.	518 (9/4/Darius 4)—Message to Zechariah (7:1)
12 Mar.	515 (3 Adar/Darius 6)—Temple is finished (Ezra 6:15)
21 Apr.	515 (14 Nisan/Darius 6)—Passover is held (v. 19)

RELEVANCE FOR OTHER TIMES

The Problem. If the Old Testament is to be considered canonical, the authoritative and timeless word of God, how does the rebuilding of the temple concern any generation other than that engaged in the process? After it was built, certainly no other generation of Jews needed encouragement to build it. After it was destroyed again in A.D. 70, there is no reason to rebuild it again in the light of the teachings in the epistle to the Hebrews. Does the book, then, contain only "typical" or "spiritual" lessons? How can one draw a lesson from Haggai that is relevant today?

His Time. With the prophecies of Haggai, Zechariah, and Malachi, the prophetic section of the Jewish canon of Scripture closed. But faith was not dead. In fact, there was fervent hope that the Lord would fulfill the promises he had made through the prophets. Christians often refer to this time between the close of the Old Testament and the writing of the New as the "intertestamental period." To the Jew it is the "Second Commonwealth," the period when the foundations of Judaism were laid by Ezra and the men of the Great Syn-

---

9. D.J. Wiseman suggests that "Darius the Mede" is another name for Cyrus the Persian; *Notes on Some Problems in the Book of Daniel* (London: 1965), pp. 9-14.

10. Based on the fact that it took about four months to make the nine-hundred-mile journey (see Ezra 7:8f.; see also Ezek. 33:21, where news of Jerusalem's fall reached Babylon a little less than five months after the event).

agogue.[11] During this period Jewish authors produced a number of apocalyptic writings, and several Jewish sects arose which had distinctive messianic hopes and interpretations. At the time of Jesus' birth, according to the New Testament, devout Jews were looking for the Messiah, and some believed that the infant Jesus was this hoped-for One.

Haggai, along with Zechariah and Malachi, was to some degree responsible for this messianic expectation. The building of the temple was not merely to provide a cult center for establishing Judaism. The language of Haggai makes clear that the rebuilding was in some way to be related to the promise of the coming Redeemer. Some Jews of that period doubtless read more into Haggai's words than unfolding history would support. Zerubbabel was not the Messiah, nor was Joshua. In God's providence an interval existed—according to Christians, about 400 years; according to Jewish faith, it still continues—between the regathering of the exiles to Jerusalem and the coming of the Messiah. The rebuilding of the temple was an indication that God's promised redemption had not been forgotten and a sign of the people's faith in that promise. Haggai, then, has meaning for today and every age, until the promise becomes reality.

In addition to the messianic hope, which was important for the continued existence of Israel's faith, the reestablishment of the cult was also essential. Rebuilding the temple was only a part—yet a very important part—of the religion. Faithful transmission of the Torah to successive generations also was necessary. To a great extent that was the work of Ezra. But the law also is significant in Haggai. Some scholars find the legalism suggested by Haggai inferior to the ethical demands of the preexilic prophets. But both are required, for a sense of the divine origin of the Law, with its implied human responsibility, is necessary to enforce its ethical demands. Haggai was aware of the concept of the "Holy," and his lesson that human success and failure are related to awareness of the sanctity of God's law is necessary in every generation.

POSTEXILIC PERIOD

Formation of the Canon. During the period between the Testaments, the lengthy process that compiled the Old Testament canon was brought to completion. By the first century B.C. the Jews had a body of literature which they considered authoritative in matters of faith and morals. This same conviction is found in the New Testament. According to Jewish tradition, Ezra and the Great Synagogue (which included Haggai, Zechariah, and Malachi) were largely responsible for this final compilation of Scripture.[12]

Diaspora Judaism and the Synagogue. Jews lived not only in Babylon, but also

---

11. See G.F. Moore, *Judaism* 1:29-47.
12. The Great Synagogue lasted from the time of Ezra until Simeon the Just, who died *ca*. 270 B.C. (*Pirqe 'Abot* 1:2).

EXILIC AND POSTEXILIC PROPHETS AND THEIR WORLD

	Prophet	Judah	Babylonia	Egypt	Persia	Notable events
600	Jeremiah	Jehoiakim 608-597	Nebuchadnezzar 605-562	Neco II 610-595		Fall of Jerusalem 15/16 Mar. 597
595	Ezekiel	Jehoiachin 597		Psamtik II 595-589		Ration tablets of Jehoiachin, 10th-35th
590	Daniel	Zedekiah 597-586		Apries 589-570		yrs. of Nebuchadnezzar
585						Destruction of Jerusalem 12 Aug. 586
580						
575						
570				Amasis 570-525		Jehoiachin set free
565			Evil-merodach 562-560			
560			Neriglissar 560-556			Cyrus king of Anshan 559
555			Labashi-Marduk Nabonidus 556-539			
550						
545						
540		Zerubbabel returns 538	Last king of Babylon		Cyrus 539-530	Fall of Babylon Cyrus enters Babylon 12 Oct. 539, "Year 1" Rebuilding temple begins
535						537
530				Psamtik III	Cambyses	
525				Cambyses	530-522	
520	Haggai Zechariah			Darius I	Darius I 522-486	Work on temple resumed
515						Completed 10 Mar. 516
510						
500						
480				Xerxes I	Xerxes I 480-465	
465	Malachi			Artaxerxes I	Artaxerxes I 464-423	
458		Ezra				
445		Nehemiah 445-423				

in Egypt and quite likely other places. Reference to the Jews in Egypt occurs in Jeremiah, and the Aramaic papyri from Elephantine (on the Nile near the Aswan dam) indicate a sizable community there. During the next two or three centuries a large Jewish community developed at Alexandria, from which came the Greek translation of the Old Testament (the LXX). Synagogues developed as places of prayer and worship for Jews who no longer had access to the temple at Jerusalem, and by New Testament times they were located in Palestine, even in Jerusalem itself.

Political Scene. Under the Persians (539-331), Judah was part of the satrapy known as "Beyond the River," the region beyond the Euphrates. Standard Persian policy was to grant considerable home rule, but the Jews were under a governor, with no king of their own. With the conquest of Persia by Alexander the Great and the subsequent division of his empire among his successors (the Diadochoi), Palestine came under Seleucid rule, which was centered in Syria. During this period the Near East was considerably hellenized, and Judah was not exempt. Certain Seleucid rulers were zealous to extend this influence, and under Antiochus IV Epiphanes (175-164) efforts were made to destroy the Jewish religion by polluting the temple. Reaction was swift, led by the Hasmonean family (the Maccabees), and for about eighty years the Jews had "independence" under Hasmonean rule (142-63), until Pompey (106-48) claimed Palestine for Rome. A nominal Jewish kingdom was permitted by the Romans under Herod the Great (37-4), and to a greatly limited extent under other Herodian rulers. With the Jewish revolt and the destruction of the temple in A.D. 70, followed by the Bar Kochba revolt in 132-135,[13] the end came to Jerusalem Judaism.

Sectarian Judaism. Partly in reaction to hellenizing forces within Judaism, and partly, no doubt, as a result of the Assyrian and Babylonian conquests of Israel, Judaism developed a number of sects. At least seven can be named by the first century, and perhaps as many as twelve. What later developed into the Judaism of the Mishnah has been called "normative" Judaism, but the term is not entirely satisfactory for the formative period. Here need be mentioned only that Judaism was not monolithic (nor has it ever been). Sectarian literature was produced, some distinguished as "Apocrypha"[14] and "Pseudepigrapha,"[15] and some included among the Qumran literature.[16]

---

13. See Y. Yadin, "Bar Kochba," *IDBS*, pp. 89-92.

14. For background on the Apocrypha see B. Metzger, *An Introduction to the Apocrypha;* and Eissfeldt, *Old Testament*, pp. 571-603; for the text of the books, see *JB; The New English Bible with the Apocrypha* (Oxford and Cambridge: 1970); Metzger, ed., *The Oxford Annotated Apocrypha* [RSV] (New York: 1977).

15. For background on the Pseudepigrapha (Greek for books falsely ascribed to ancient writers), see Eissfeldt, *Old Testament*, pp. 603-637; for texts, see R.H. Charles, *The Apocrypha and Pseudepigrapha of the Old Testament*, 2 vols. (Oxford: 1913).

16. For background and text of the Qumran literature (Dead Sea scrolls), see A. Dupont-Sommer, *The Essene Writings from Qumran*, trans. G. Vermes (Gloucester, Mass.: 1973); G. Vermes, *The Dead Sea Scrolls in English* (Baltimore: 1962).

Summary of the Period. The postexilic period is considerably different from the preceding periods of the Old Testament. No king occupied the Davidic throne for most of the Second Commonwealth. No centralization characterized the cult at the Jerusalem temple which was at best a nominal central sanctuary, for the local synagogues served the needs of most Jews. No strong prophetic voice arose. Political and sociological pressures worked against the concept of national existence, countered in part by legalistic emphasis on the Torah and in part by apocalyptic hopes and expectations.

Haggai was the prophet to open this period of the foundations of Judaism. Others—the prophets Zechariah and Malachi, the scribe Ezra, the administrator Nehemiah—would make valuable contributions. Nevertheless in the postexilic period Israel indeed dwelled "many days without king or prince" (Hos. 3:4).

FOR FURTHER READING

Ackroyd, P.R. "The Book of Haggai and Zechariah 1–8." *JJS* 3 (1952): 151-56.

———. "Studies in the Book of Haggai." *JJS* 3 (1952): 163-176.

Baldwin, J.G. *Haggai, Zechariah, Malachi.* Tyndale Old Testament Commentaries. Downers Grove: 1972.

Bloomhardt, P.F. "The Poems of Haggai." *HUCA* 5 (1928): 153-195. (Translation and critical notes.)

Mason, R.A. "The Purpose of the 'Editorial Framework' of the Book of Haggai." *VT* 27 (1977): 413-421. (Hope for future outcome of Haggai's prophecy based on what had already been fulfilled.)

North, F.S. "Critical Analysis of the Book of Haggai." *ZAW* 68 (1956): 25-46. (Literary critical.)

Smith, G.A. *The Book of the Twelve Prophets.* Expositor's Bible (1956) 4:613-620. (Good discussion.)

Wright, J.S. *The Building of the Second Temple.* London: 1958.

CHAPTER 37

ZECHARIAH

THE dates given in Zechariah's prophecy[1] show it to be contemporary with the prophecy of Haggai. Chs. 9–14 are probably later, and no dates are given in that portion. The book is a postexilic prophecy, and distinctly different from the preexilic prophecies. These points are essential to a reliable picture of the historical nature of this revelatory work.

ZECHARIAH AND HIS PROPHECY

The Prophet. Zechariah ("Yah has remembered") is called "the son of" Berechiah, the son of Iddo (1:1), and also "the son of" Iddo (Ezra 5:1; 6:14; cf. Neh. 12:16). The Iddo in Nehemiah was the head of a "house," hence probably a more remote ancestor, and a priest. If this is the same Zechariah, he may be identified as a priest as well as a prophet—but this is not established. Zechariah was a very common name.[2] Iddo was also the name of an ancient prophet (e.g., 2 Chr. 13:22). Inclusion of the name of Berechiah has been suggested as an effort to identify Zechariah with the "son of Jeberechiah" in Isa. 8:2, but this seems contrived. Beyond these few facts, which are not without their own problems, little else is known. From Ezra 5:1; 6:14, it appears that the prophetic ministry of Haggai and Zechariah is what roused the elders under Zerubbabel and Joshua to complete the rebuilding of the temple.

According to one tradition, Zechariah was "already advanced in age" when he returned from Babylonia, and died at a "great age" and was buried beside Haggai. However, if Heb. *na'ar* is taken as an indication of age,[3] he was a

---

1. Month 8 of Year of Darius (YD) 2 began 27 Oct. 520 (1:1); the date in 1:7 converts to 15 Feb. 519, and that in 7:1 to 7 Dec. 518.
2. T.M. Mouch distinguishes thirty-three persons named Zechariah; "Zechariah," *IDB* 4:941-43.
3. The word can mean a young man from early childhood to marriageable age, as well as a "servant" of any age (much as "boy" has been used of servants regardless of age). In the context, "young man" is probably to be preferred.

"young man" (Zech. 2:4 [MT 9]). Therefore, some suggest that he was still prophesying in 470, possibly at age seventy or eighty. Jesus' words (Matt. 23:35; cf. Luke 11:51) sometimes are taken to mean that Zechariah suffered martyrdom, but more reasonably the statement brackets the record from Genesis to Chronicles (the first and last books of the Jewish canon), so the reference is to the Zechariah of 2 Chr. 24:22.

The Prophecy. The book divides clearly into two parts, regardless of authorship (see below). Chs. 1–8 are dated prophecies, largely in the form of visions. Chs. 9–14 contain no dated prophecies or "night visions" and exhibit a markedly different style. Of the first eight chapters W. Neil says: "There is every reason to believe that basically these are the authentic words of the prophet, possibly arranged in their present order by Zechariah himself, but more probably collected and edited shortly after his day."[4]

Chs. 1–8 may be analyzed as follows:

Call to repentance (1:1-6)
Night visions (1:8–6:8)
    Four horsemen; promise of restoration (vv. 8-17)
    Four horns, four smiths; judgment on nations (vv. 18-21 [MT 2:1-4])
    Man with measuring line; rebuilding of Jerusalem (2:1-13 [MT 5-17])
    Joshua and Satan; promise of "My servant the Branch" (ch. 3)
    Gold lampstand and two olive trees; "by My Spirit" (ch. 4)
    Flying scroll; curse over whole earth (5:1-4)
    Woman in ephah; Wickedness (vv. 5-11)
    Four chariots and their horses; patrolling the earth (ch. 6)
Real reason for fasting (7:1-14)
Result of Yahweh's promise: peace, prosperity for all (8:1-23)

The general outline, beginning with a call to repentance and ending with the fulfillment of God's purpose, is familiar. The night visions, however, introduce a new element in prophecy (see below).

Chs. 9–14 divide naturally into two parts (cf. 9:1; 12:1; note the heading "An Oracle" [Heb. *maśśāʾ*]):

Events leading to end of the age (chs. 9–11)
    Yahweh Lord of hostile cities (9:1-8)
    Zion's King comes (vv. 9-17)
    Shepherdless people gathered to the land (chs. 10–11)
Events of end of the age (chs. 12–14)
    Siege laid against Jerusalem (12:1-3)

---

4. "Zechariah, Book of," *IDB* 4:944.

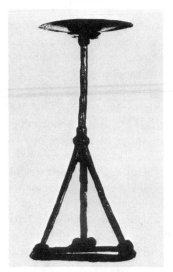

Tripod lampstand, an image related to Zerubbabel's completion of the temple in Zechariah's fifth vision (4:1-14); Megiddo. (Oriental Institute, University of Chicago)

Yahweh sustains Judah and destroys nations (vv. 4-9)
Yahweh pours out grace on his people (vv. 10-14)
Fountain of cleansing opened (13:1-6)
Judgment executed on the shepherd (vv. 7-9)
Day of the Lord described (ch. 14)

This portion offers great difficulty, both in analysis of the structure and interpretation of the parts. This can be seen in the wide variety of critical theories concerning composition of these chapters, and the many and great differences in interpretation, even among those with essentially the same view of composition.

Problems of Authorship. Neil says:

The latter part of the book of Zechariah presents vast, and in part, insoluble problems in respect of authorship, date, and interpretation. While it is not possible to establish beyond dispute whether one, two, three, or a variety of authors were responsible for chs. 9–14, it is almost universally agreed that on linguistic and stylistic grounds, as well as in theological ideas and historical background, the author of these chapters cannot be the prophet Zechariah.[5]

T. Henshaw argues that the two parts must be distinguished,[6] and O. Eissfeldt says that the two are from another hand and period.[7] G.L. Archer, who holds

---

5. *Ibid.*, 4:945.
6. *The Latter Prophets*, pp. 246f.
7. *Old Testament*, pp. 429, 434-37.

to unity of authorship, nevertheless gives the arguments against single author-ship in detail,[8] as does R.K. Harrison.[9] The arguments deserve careful consid-eration. J.S. Wright says: "It is not possible to prove the unity of the book, but one should not too readily abandon it."[10]

Arguments for dividing the book fall into three groups:

(1) Preexilic authorship for chs. 9–14. This may have originated because 11:12f. is quoted in Matt. 27:9f. as a prophecy of Jeremiah. The mention of Ephraim, of Assyria and Egypt as its enemies, of Aramean city-states and Phi-listine cities all suggest a preexilic date. However, the evidence is not uniform, part dating from before Tiglath-pileser's conquest of the Aramean states and portions of Israel, part suggesting a time just before the fall of Samaria, and part referring only to Judah and seeming to look back on Josiah's death. As a result, scholarship has become fragmented, with some dating chs. 9–11 and 13:7-9 before 721[11] and the balance of chs. 12–14 before 586. Although B. Otzen defends the preexilic date of chs. 9–10,[12] the preexilic theory has little support today.[13]

(2) Post-Zechariah authorship of chs. 9–14. Some assign these chapters to a single author, but again the view is fragmented. Eissfeldt prefers "the year 332, if only because of the allusion to be found here (v. 3) to the rampart heaped up by Tyre, and more precisely to the period of this year when Alexander made preparations for the siege of Tyre."[14] K. Marti and E. Sellin identify the shepherds of 9:8 as "Lysimachus, Jason, and Menelaus" or "Simon, Menelaus, and Lysimachus," thus bringing the date down to Maccabean times (ca. 160). Further, 11:4-17 is taken as reflecting events of the Maccabean war; the man who is killed in 12:10-14 is Onias III (murdered in 170; Sellin) or Simon (134; B. Duhm).[15]

(3) Two or more authors for chs. 9–14, rather than a single "Deutero-Zechariah." R.C. Dentan dates 9:1-12 to the siege of Tyre by Alexander (332); vv. 13-17 in the period of the Diadochoi or Ptolemaic rule, 10:3-12 in the period when the Ptolemies ruled over Palestine.[16] He rejects a Maccabean date based on the mention of the "Book of the Twelve" in Ben Sirach's apocryphal book of Ecclesiasticus (49:10; ca. 190): "It is hardly possible that any extensive additions could have been made to this collection after the book had attained what was evidently canonical status."[17]

---

8. *Survey*, pp. 411-15.
9. *Introduction*, pp. 952-56.
10. "Zechariah, Book of," *IBD*, p. 1679.
11. H.G.A. Ewald et al.
12. *Studien über Deuterosacharaja* (Copenhagen: 1964).
13. For a survey of the views, see Eissfeldt, *Old Testament*, pp. 434-440.
14. *Ibid.*, p. 437.
15. Cited in *ibid.*, pp. 438f.
16. "Introduction and Exegesis, Chapters 9–14 of Zechariah," *IB* 6:1090.
17. *Idem*. M. Treves, however, argues that this section is indeed Maccabean, written partly by Judas Maccabeus himself; "Conjectures Concerning the Date and Authorship of Zechariah IX–XIV," *VT* 13 (1963): 196-207.

H.L. Ellison[18] suggests that three anonymous prophecies, each beginning with the words *maśśā' dᵉḇar yhwh* "the burden of the word of Yahweh," are found at the end of the Book of the Twelve (Zech. 9:1; 12:1; Mal. 1:1). The first two came to be joined to Zechariah, and the third became the book of Malachi.[19] The theory is ingenious but has at least two difficulties. A. Bentzen pointed out earlier that the author of Malachi is "a person characteristically different from 'Deutero-Zechariah.' "[20] Therefore one cannot easily ascribe the three "burdens" to a single author. The second objection is related: the well-established tradition, found as early as Ben Sirach, refers to twelve, not thirteen or fourteen, prophets. No evidence exists that any of the three "burdens" ever circulated separately, except for Malachi.[21]

Among the various theories in defense of single authorship,[22] Archer holds to a date between 480 and 470 for chs. 9–14, and accounts for the differences in style to the three or four decades that separated the two parts of the prophecy. Particularly strong is his argument that the language throughout is more in keeping with that of Haggai and Malachi than with second-century writings from Qumran, and remarkably free of Aramaisms.[23] S. Bullough maintains that "the vision or dream writing of the first part, with all its hopes in a new era, is the work of a young man (of about thirty) in 520-518, while the more forbidding and remotely hopeful prophecies of the second part are the work of an older man (of about seventy), when the future of the Persian Empire had become less secure." He explains the difference in style and treatment between the two parts by the difference in the author's age and the changing political circumstances.[24]

All that scholarship has demonstrated positively is the difficulty of holding to a single author. Attempts to solve the problem find no clear direction and often cancel one another. Some are patently absurd.[25] B.S. Childs remarks: "It would seem that critical opinion has come full circle and the same issues are being as hotly debated today as in 1881."[26]

INTERPRETATION

Apocalyptic. A great confusion of ideas has been formed concerning apocalyptic. P.D. Hanson offers a useful approach: "Rather than describing an ideal

---

18. *Men Spake from God*, p. 123.
19. See also Eissfeldt, *Introduction*, p. 440; E. Sellin–G. Fohrer, *Introduction*, p. 469; and Dentan, IB 6:1089, 1117.
20. *Introduction* 2:161.
21. *Contra* Dentan.
22. Harrison, *Introduction*, pp. 953-56; Wright, *IBD*, pp. 1677-79; G.L. Robinson, "Zechariah, Book of," ISBE (1939) 5:3139f. See esp. A. von Hoonacker, *Les Douze petits Prophètes*. Etudes Bibliques (Paris: 1908), pp. 579-581.
23. *Survey*, pp. 415f.
24. "Zacharias," CCHS, §545k.
25. E.g., when were the Seleucids known as "Assyria"? Hence, how could "Assyria and Egypt" mean "the Seleucids and the Ptolemies"?
26. *Old Testament as Scripture*, p. 476.

type, . . . it is preferable to sketch the typical features of the work originally
designated 'apocalypse' in antiquity, the book of Revelation,"[27] and to measure
contemporary works against those features. He cites these elements in Rev.
1:1f.: a revelation given by God, through a mediator, to a seer, concerning
future events. Other elements are added from the following verses: indicating
that the seer in a vision is allowed to peer into the heavens to see events which
will determine future happenings; the seer is "in the Spirit" (an ecstatic state);
the interpretation is given by an angelic interpreter; the seer's response is awe,
followed by a word of comfort or admonition; and, however the vision is expressed, "it always has bearing on 'what is and what is to take place hereafter'
(1:19; cf. 1:1; 4:1)."[28]

On the basis of Hanson's criteria, Zechariah has elements of an apocalypse.
The prophet is given a series of eight "night visions" (1:7–6:15). The "angel
of Yahweh" explains the visions, acting as mediator (1:13f.). The present becomes a symbol of the future (vv. 16f.). No direct statement indicates that
Zechariah is given a vision of some event in heaven, but the reference to Joshua
standing before the angel of the Lord, and Satan "at his right hand to accuse
him" (3:1) may suggest a heavenly scene (cf. Job 1:6-12). Beyond doubt the
visions were given to reveal the future, including the announcement of "the
man whose name is the Branch" (see Jer. 23:5; 33:15; see also Isa. 11:1), a
term which becomes synonymous with "Messiah."[29]

One characteristic of apocalyptic is use of a present situation (or person)
as a type of the future. The message is sometimes difficult to interpret because
knowledge of the historical reference is lacking. At other times, even though
the historical situation is clear, the message is not always seen as concerning
the future. For example, a gold crown is set on the head of Joshua the high
priest, and he is ascribed a messianic role (6:12). But Zerubbabel was governor,
and, since the Messiah was to be of the Davidic line,[30] some scholars, failing
to understand the nature of apocalyptic, have tried to interpret this as an actual
attempt to crown Zerubbabel as Messiah. Since Zerubbabel's name is not in the
passage, they suggest that it has dropped out.[31] Zerubbabel turned out not to
be the Messiah, and the prophets were wrong. But the setting is apocalyptic:
Satan, a lampstand and two olive trees, four chariots with horses of most

---

27. "Apocalypse, Genre," *IDBS*, p. 27.

28. *Idem*.

29. Heb. *ṣemaḥ*. Isa. 11:1 uses Heb. *nēṣer*; by a process that is not strange in Judaism
and rabbinical exegesis, this gave rise to the belief that this prophecy claimed that the
Messiah "shall be called a Nazarene" (cf. Matt. 2:23), although no such prophecy can
be found in the canonical prophets. See J.G. Baldwin, "*ṣemaḥ* as a Technical Term in
the Prophets," *VT* 14 (1964): 93-97.

30. There was also belief in a Messiah of the priestly line, based on Deut. 18:18;
cf. T. Levi 8:14. The question became prominent in Qumran studies; see W.S. LaSor,
Bibliography of the Dead Sea Scrolls, 1948-1957 (Pasadena: 1958), pp. 88f.

31. See D.W. Thomas, "Introduction and Exegesis, Chapters 1–8 of Zechariah,"
IB 6:1080.

unearthly colors going forth to the winds of heaven. Surely the crowning of Joshua cannot be taken literally here! Such language is a typical way of presenting the future. Zerubbabel laid the foundation and also would complete the rebuilding of the temple (4:9), but the coming "Branch" is the one who will build the temple of the Lord (6:13).[32]

A number of interpreters attempt to reconstruct the historical situation. Henshaw, assuming that these chapters belong to the third or second century, concludes:

> they shed some light upon the political and religious conditions of Judah in the late post-exilic age. . . . Yahweh is revealed as the Lord of Creation . . . the universal ruler of mankind and the only true God. . . . When the day of the Lord came He would be king over all the earth and there would be 'one Lord and his name one' (xiv 9). But . . . the old idea of Yahweh as the God of war had been revived. Yahweh would encamp round Jerusalem like an army and no oppressor would ever again march through the land (ix 8). . . . These chapters show that at the time when they were written prophecy was practically dead and that its place had been taken by apocalyptic.[33]

Henshaw has completely failed to understand the nature of biblical apocalyptic.[34]

Recent emphasis has sought to reconstruct the socioreligious setting of the apocalyptic writings. Hanson analyzes the "several stages within the hierocratic (Zadokite) circles which supplied the impetus for the postexilic restoration."[35] The interrelationship between the historical situation and the language and figures of Scripture goes without question. Attempts of past generations of interpreters, devout believers in the Bible, to ignore almost completely the various aspects of the historical situation (sociological, religious, mythological) must be replaced by those who hold no less fervently to the inspiration and authority of the Scriptures, with interpretations that start where the particular Scripture started—with the people originally addressed. Still, this should not lead to a purely humanistic view of the word of God. Apocalyptic material, even if harder to understand, is no less the word of God and no less authoritative than other types of Scripture.[36]

Interpretation. Interpretation of apocalyptic writings is difficult for all who attempt it, and no less so for those who maintain belief in its divine authority.

---

32. On the use and interpretation of types in grammatico-historical exegesis, see LaSor, "Interpretation of Prophecy," *BDPT*, pp. 130-32; R.B. Laurin, "Typological Interpretation of the Old Testament," *BDPT*, pp. 136-39.
33. *Latter Prophets*, pp. 295f.
34. In contrast, cf. G.L. Robinson, *The Prophecies of Zechariah* (Chicago: 1896).
35. "Zechariah, Book of," *IDBS*, p. 982.
36. See further K. Koch, *The Rediscovery of Apocalyptic*. SBT, 2nd ser. 21 (Naperville: 1970); G.E. Ladd, "Apocalyptic Literature," *ISBE* 1 (1979): 151-161; L. Morris, *Apocalyptic* (Grand Rapids: 1972).

Indeed, it is probably more difficult, for they seek to understand the intention of the divine Author as well as recover the historical situation. Therefore the interpretation here is presented hesitantly and humbly, with no attempt to be exhaustive and no claim to be totally correct, in the interest of furthering the study of this and similar revelations.[37]

Chs. 1–8 begin in Jerusalem in 520, with the problems of getting the temple rebuilt, and end in an age to come when the gentile nations come to Jerusalem and plead: "Let us go with you, for we have heard that God is with you" (8:23). The apocalyptic visions must be fit into this framework, whether put there by the original author (highly probable) or by a canonical process. It is best to work from the clear to the unclear, the known to the unknown.

The first vision (see outline, above) raises the question about Yahweh's seventy-year indignation over Jerusalem and Judah (1:12). It concerns his determination to deal with Jerusalem in compassion (v. 16) and rebuild it (v. 17). He also expresses anger with the nations that, in carrying out his punishment on his people, "furthered the disaster" (v. 15). The total impact of this vision seems to set the stage for subsequent visions.

The "four horns" are nations that "scattered Judah, Israel, and Jerusalem" (v. 19 [MT 2:2]). The "four smiths" are avengers who will deal with the horns (v. 21 [MT 2:4]). The horns may be identified as four specific nations, and likewise the smiths. The third vision continues the theme, but moves on from the rebuilding of Jerusalem and judgment of the nations that plundered Yahweh's people, to the time when "many nations shall join themselves to the Lord in that day" (2:11 [MT 15]).

The next visions are more difficult to interpret, but the general theme can be found. Joshua the high priest is portrayed in rich apparel (3:4f.). The introduction of Satan is not explained, nor is he given further mention. Yahweh's servant "the Branch" is introduced as one who is to come (v. 8). The vision of the lampstand is related to Zerubbabel's completion of the temple (4:9), including the word of the Lord: "not by might, nor by power, but by my Spirit" (v. 6). The point seems to be that the future establishment of Jerusalem is not to come by human effort.[38] The two olive trees are the two "anointed ones"

---

37. Commentaries and theologies of scholars who hold basically this same view of Scripture sometimes show a reluctance to grapple with eschatological teachings. They maintain an eschatological agnosticism that is regrettable. Those areas of Scripture which elicit the widest divergence of interpretation are precisely the areas where the greatest cooperation in study is needed. If true in eschatological portions, it is even more so in apocalyptic (Ezek. 38–48; Zechariah [esp. 9–14]; Daniel; and Revelation).

38. The common apocalyptic view that the ultimate kingdom comes only by God's intervention is often called "pessimistic" and a repudiation of the prophetic attitude. But the prophets also taught that the ultimate achievement of God's purpose will be by God's action alone. The apocalyptic writers also believed in the ultimate triumph of God and establishment of his rule; H.H. Rowley, *The Relevance of Apocalyptic*, rev. ed. (New York: 1963), p. 36. The basic conflict is not between prophets and apocalyptists but between humanists and theists: Does man, by his own wisdom and power, bring in the Golden Age, or is this final achievement solely the work of God?

who stand by the Lord (v. 14).[39] They are identified sometimes as Joshua and Zerubbabel, but Joshua is not mentioned in the vision, and Zerubbabel seems to be distinguished from the olive trees in vv. 3-6.

The flying scroll (5:1) and the woman in the ephah (v. 7) are very difficult to interpret. The gist seems to be that a curse (vv. 3f.) is to be pronounced on the thief and the one who swears falsely (v. 4), and that the iniquity, "Wickedness" (vv. 6, 8), will be established in "the land of Shinar" (v. 11), interpreted to mean Babylonia.[40] If so, this is punishment on the nation that oppressed God's people.

Finally, the four chariots and horses from between the bronze mountains (6:1-8) go forth to patrol the earth. Interpretation is complicated by the portrayal of four horsemen in Rev. 6:2-8. However, Zechariah's vision is of chariots, not horsemen (but cf. 1:8). Moreover, while Zechariah may be the source of figures used in Revelation, Revelation is not the source of Zechariah's figures, and the meaning of Revelation must not be imposed on Zechariah. In 6:8, "those who go toward the north country [the chariot with the black horses, v. 6; possibly also the chariot with the red horses, 1:7; not otherwise included in the angel's answer] have set my Spirit at rest in the north country." Since in the previous prophets the "north country" is the source of invasions into Israel and Judah, this figure may imply that the patrols (v. 7) had made an end to such satanic aggression and set God's Spirit at rest.

This vision is followed by the crowning of Joshua and the pronouncement: "Behold, the man whose name is the Branch" (vv. 11f.). As a priest who would have known the Scriptures, Joshua was aware that the "Branch" was to be of the line of David—and he himself was not. Moreover, the crown was not left on his head, but was to be "in the temple of the Lord as a reminder . . ." (v. 14). The entire scene must therefore be taken as typical. The promise first given to preexilic prophets is being repeated. Moreover, the ambivalence in the original promise to David (2 Sam. 7:12f.) is found again in Zechariah. Having proclaimed that Zerubbabel would complete the house (4:9), Yahweh now announces that "the man whose name is the Branch" shall build it (6:12). Typological study of these passages, in the light of Jewish understanding before the advent of Christian interpretation, indicates that Solomon, Zerubbabel, Joshua, and the First and Second Temples were all typical or representative fulfillments of Yahweh's ultimate purpose. This is underscored by the closing words: "And those who are far off [cf. Eph. 2:13] shall come and help to build the temple of the Lord" (6:15).

Chs. 9–14 are even more difficult and precarious to interpret. The division into two "oracles" (9:1; 12:1) and the rule of working from the clear to the unclear are guides. In 9:1-8, judgment on the nations is in view, and is set over

---

39. The term for "anointed" is not the customary Heb. *māšîaḥ* "messiah" but *bᵉnê-hayyiṣhār* "sons of (anointing) oil."
40. See Gen. 10:10; 11:2; Isa. 11:11; BDB, p. 1042.

against the joy in Zion because of the coming of the king (v. 9). Then the note of judgment continues. Some scholars protest that Zechariah has rejected the God of mercy and gone back to the Yahweh of war.[41] But one element of apocalyptic, not yet fully developed but certainly present in Zechariah's time, is the concept of the satanic. A conflict rages above and beyond this earth between Yahweh and his Adversary. Zoroastrian influence sometimes developed this into a cosmic dualism, but the biblical position never looks upon the Adversary as coeval and coequal with Yahweh. He is one of the creatures, whether portrayed as a serpent (Gen. 3:1), king of Babylon (Isa. 14:4, 12-14), prince of Tyre (Ezek. 28:2-10), or Satan (Job 1:6-12; Zech. 3:1f.). He does maintain limited control on earth because some are willing to carry out his efforts to destroy God's people and God's redemptive work. It is against this satanic power that Yahweh Elohim directs his fierce wrath. To try to separate Yahweh of hosts from the God of mercy is to fail to recognize the relationship between satanic and redemptive. The satanic turns rulers into monsters and justice into mockery, tramples the rights of the widow and fatherless, corrupts human life at all levels, destroys or prostitutes the earth and its resources, and does everything it can to turn this world into hell. A God who is not opposed to the satanic, who cannot or will not one day end these demonic forces, is no God of mercy. Redemption means release from the bondage of the satanic, and Yahweh is a God who will redeem his people.

The following events are portrayed by Zechariah. No attempt is made here to interpret a scheme or program of events of the end of the age.

Advent of messianic king (9:9)
Universal dominion of messianic king (v. 10)
Appearance of Yahweh to protect his people (vv. 11-17)
Judgment on shepherds who misled the people (10:2f.)
Regathering of exiles, beyond that of Zechariah's day (v. 6)
(Regathering not merely from Assyria) (vv. 10f.)
Breaking of covenant, beyond that of 721 and 597 (ch. 11)
Siege of Jerusalem, beyond that of 586 (12:2)
Deliverance of Jerusalem, victory for Judah and Jerusalem (vv. 4-9)
Spirit of compassion in Jerusalem, mourning the one they have pierced
    (vv. 10-14)
Fountain for cleansing house of David and Jerusalem (13:1)
Striking of shepherd, scattering of sheep, destruction of two-thirds,
    refining of remaining third (vv. 7-9)
Gathering of nations against Jerusalem, exile of some inhabitants (14:2)
Advent of Yahweh to fight those nations (v. 3)
His presence on Mount of Olives (v. 4)
Day of no cold or frost, day or night (vv. 6f.)
Living waters flowing from Jerusalem (v. 8)

---

41. See Henshaw, p. 495 above.

Yahweh to become king over whole earth (v. 9)
Jerusalem to dwell in security (v. 11)
Element of rebellion yet remaining (vv. 17-19)
Everything in Jerusalem and Judah to be Holy to the Lord (vv. 20f.)

Efforts to systematize these events have resulted in divisions among the people of God. On the other hand, ignoring the Scripture has impoverished them.

Christians find fulfillment of the advent of the messianic king (9:9) in Jesus' Palm Sunday entry into Jerusalem. The presence of Yahweh on the Mount of Olives (14:4) is often taken to mean the Second Coming of Christ. This portion of Zechariah seems to indicate clearly an interval, probably of extended duration, between the two events. Some events in Zechariah may be equated with events in the present age, but the interpreter must take into account human fallibility. A satanic element seems to remain after Yahweh has become king—which some would equate with the release of Satan after the thousand years of Rev. 20:7-10.

Zechariah in the New Testament. Some seventy-one quotations of Zechariah appear in the New Testament (31 from chs. 1–8, 40 from chs. 9–14). Most are found in Revelation (31; 20 from chs. 1–8, 11 from chs. 9–14). Another twenty-seven are found in the Gospels (14 in Matthew, 7 in Mark, 3 each in Luke and John), twenty-two of which are from chs. 9–14. Many of these are found in the record of the last week of Jesus' ministry.

Modern Relevance. At present widespread interest focuses on the demonic, the "end of the world," "apocalypse now." Some intellectuals tend to denigrate such movements, and a large number of clergy avoid the subject. But historically, cults and schismatic movements seem to spring up to fill the void left by a lack of concern on the part of those responsible for teaching the laity. A healthy, fully scriptural presentation of the course of the present age, satanic opposition to God's redemptive program, spiritual wickedness in heavenly places, the Second Coming, the kingdom of righteousness and peace, and related subjects, could serve as a corrective for much of this fare. Zechariah is one prophet that should be studied in this connection.

FOR FURTHER READING

Baldwin, J.G. *Haggai, Zechariah, Malachi.*
Cook, J.M. *The Greeks in Ionia and the East.* London: 1962. (Esp. pp. 61-67, 98-110, 121-172.)
Culican, W. *The Medes and the Persians.* London: 1965. (Pp. 64-82, 156-167.)

Halpern, B. "The Ritual Background of Zechariah's Temple Song." CBQ 40 (1978): 167-190. (1:7–6:15 in light of extrabiblical literature.)

Jones, D.R. "A Fresh Interpretation of Zechariah IX–XI." VT 12 (1962): 241-259. (Dates book to first half of fifth century, by prophet in or near Damascus.)

Mason, R.A. The Books of Haggai, Zechariah and Malachi. Cambridge Bible Commentary. New York: 1977. Pp. 27-75 (chs. 1–8), 76-134 (chs. 9–14). (Useful on editing and expansion of prophetic works in general.)

Olmstead, A.T. History of the Persian Empire. Chicago: 1948. (Esp. pp. 107-161, 214-261, 495-524.)

The Persian Empire and the West. CAH 4 (1926). (Pp. 20-25, 173-193, 214-316.)

Smith, G.A. The Book of the Twelve Prophets. Expositor's Bible (1956). 4:620-639 (chs. 1–8), 668-679 (chs. 9–14).

CHAPTER 38

MALACHI

MALACHI is not only the last of the Book of the Twelve; the prophet himself is traditionally the end of prophetic activity (cf. Ps. 74:9; Zech. 13:2). In the days of the Maccabees it was written: "There was great distress in Israel, such as had not been since the time that prophets ceased to appear among them" (1 Macc. 9:27; cf. 4:46; 14:41). According to Jewish tradition, when the last prophets (Haggai, Zechariah, Malachi) died, the Holy Spirit departed from Israel (Tosefta *Soṭah* 13.2; *Sanh.* 11a). Josephus attributed the inferior nature of "the complete history" after the time of Artaxerxes to "the failure of the exact succession of the prophets" (*Apion* 1.8 §41).

The Anonymous Prophet. "Malachi" (Heb. *mal'āḵî*) "my messenger" (cf. 3:1, where the same word is used to describe the agent sent to prepare the way for God's future coming) may not be a personal name at all. The Targum adds a phrase to make the statement in 1:1 read: "by the hand of my messenger whose name is called Ezra the scribe."[1] Scholarship in general supports the view that Malachi is not a proper name, but does not agree in identifying Malachi with Ezra. G.L. Robinson observes: "If Ezra's name was originally associated with the book, it would hardly have been dropped by the collectors of the prophetic Canon."[2] Some have attempted to create a proper name by adding -*yā(h)*, thus *mal'āḵîyâ*, but such a name is not found elsewhere. The LXX reading, *aggélou autoú* "his messenger," indicates that the translators did not take it as a proper name; however, the change from "my" to "his" further complicates the problem.

Zech. 9:1; 12:1; Mal. 1:1 each begin with Heb. *maśśā'* "burden (of)." It has been suggested that these three "burdens" originally were written by one

---

1. Targum on Mal. 1:1; see 3:1; see also Talmud *Meg*. 15a. E.J. Young, by curious logic, understands the Targum to mean that Malachi was the author's name; "Malachi, Book of," *IBD*, p. 937.
2. "Malachi," *ISBE* (1939) 3:1969.

person.[3] B.S. Childs disposes of this theory convincingly.[4] Malachi and the passages in Zechariah differ markedly in style and structure.

No other prophecy is anonymous (including Obadiah). Anonymity, often said to be characteristic of Hebrew writings, is resisted in canonical prophecy as well as in rabbinic Judaism. In the light of these observations and the desire to avoid repeated reference to "the anonymous author of the twelfth Minor Prophecy," both book and author shall be referred to as Malachi.

The Times. The date of this prophecy receives broad scholarly consensus. The temple had been rebuilt, and was operating with cultic details already somewhat old and jaded (1:10, 13; 3:1, 10). The prophecy against mixed marriages (2:10-16) is similar to Nehemiah's view (see Neh. 13:23-27), which may suggest that Malachi was either contemporary with or slightly before Nehemiah. An approximate date of 450 B.C. is reasonable.

The conditions described imply that the return from exile had not brought anything like the messianic age. The people had lost heart. Some wept (2:13), but others had become skeptical (1:2; 2:17; 3:14f.). Adultery, perjury, oppression, and discrimination were characteristic (3:5). Organized religion was held in contempt (1:14; 3:7-12), underscored by widespread marriage with unbelievers (2:10). Anything was good enough for the service of Yahweh (1:9f.). The prophetic revelations that something new was necessary—a new heart, a new spirit, the law written on the heart, a shepherd who reflected perfectly the divine image—would be necessary if God's people were to walk in his ways.

The Prophecy. The book can be analyzed as follows:

Superscription (1:1)
Yahweh's love illustrated by Edom's fate (vv. 2-5)
Denunciation of clergy (1:6–2:9)
Idolatry and intermarriage (2:10-16)
God of justice (2:17–3:5)
Withholding tithes (3:6-12)
The righteous and the wicked (3:13–4:3 [MT 3:21])
Elijah and the day of Yahweh (4:4-6 [MT 3:22-24])

This general outline is framed in a question-and-answer format. "I have loved you," says Yahweh. "How have you loved us?" ask the people. The answer is given (1:2-5) and the vindication of God established. The people say: "Great

---

3. R.C. Dentan, "Introduction and Exegesis of Malachi," *IB* 6:1117.
4. *Old Testament as Scripture*, pp. 491f. However, Childs' observation that *maśśā'* in Mal. 1:1 is used in its absolute form, whereas the word in Zech. 9:1; 12:1 is in construct, does not have the support of the Masoretic accent, which is conjunctive in all three instances.

Bronze offering stand, showing worshiper or priest bringing gift to seated deity; Megiddo, tenth century B.C. (Oriental Institute, University of Chicago)

is the Lord, beyond the border of Israel!" (v. 5). The second topic is brought out by the question and answer in vv. 6f. The third part is highlighted by questions in 2:14f., 17. The fourth section is pointed up by the question in v. 17, the fifth by the questions in 3:7f., and the sixth by the question in v. 13.

This dialectical style (sometimes called "disputation-questions"), a characteristic of Malachi, points out the people's hostility. Whether expressed against the prophet or Yahweh is not stated, but Malachi's very use of the method indicates that the people were argumentative, questioning previously accepted beliefs and practices. They questioned Yahweh's love, which had been indicated by Israel's election. They failed to give him the respect due either a father or a master (1:6). The clergy rejected the requirement (e.g., Lev. 1:10) that only the best of the flock be presented as offerings (Mal. 1:7f.). The people profaned the covenant of the fathers by marrying women who served pagan deities, which act would yield children with diluted religious beliefs (2:15). The people had rejected the notion that all things come from God and the payment of tithes as recognition of this; in effect, they had "robbed God" (3:8). They had become arrogant, believing that evildoers who test God both prosper and escape punishment (vv. 13-15). Both priests and people had a low view indeed of the worship of Yahweh.

THEOLOGY

Yahweh of Hosts. The most common name of God in Malachi is Yahweh of Hosts (*yhwh ṣᵉḇā'ôṯ*), which is difficult to explain, both as to formation and significance.[5] Objecting to the standard translation, some suggest that Sabaoth is the name of a deity[6] and that "Yahweh, Sabaoth" is a compound name. Others think that the name is a shortened form of an original *yhwh 'ᵉlôhê ṣᵉḇā'ôṯ* "Yahweh, God of hosts." More important here than this particular problem is the term's significance and its usage.[7]

Three principal theories have been advanced for the meaning of "hosts": (1) Because the term is found in connection with the ark and its (limited) use in battle, some suggest that "Lord of hosts" means "Lord of the armies (of Israel)," or something like "warrior God." (2) S.R. Driver[8] and others suggest that it refers to the heavenly hosts, angels, or stars. (3) Rather than abandon altogether the attempt to find a meaning for the name, W. Eichrodt suggests that "the only remaining possibility is to assume that *ṣᵉḇā'ōt* does not refer to any particular 'hosts', but to all bodies, multitudes, masses in general, the content of all that exists in heaven and in earth." He contends that this insight into the prophetic usage of the word shows "a universalist tendency in the older Israelite conception of Yahweh, and proves that the primitive concept of the high God El had not been forgotten."[9]

Theodicy. Some scholars have found marks of a theodicy in Malachi. In the dialectic, the charge is made in various ways that Yahweh is not just, has not

---

5. Yahweh is a proper name and therefore supposedly not capable of standing in the construct state.

6. The name *Sabaoth* does occur in the LXX.

7. The expression occurs 267 times in the Old Testament, mostly in the prophets; B.W. Anderson, "Lord of Hosts," *IDB* 3:151. According to one count, it is found 63 times in Isaiah (57 in chs. 1–39), 83 in Jeremiah, 14 in Haggai, 53 in Zechariah (44 in chs. 1–8), and 24 in Malachi. It occurs only 5 times in all the rest of the prophets, and not at all in Ezekiel. Considering the relative sizes of the books, the term was used more frequently by the postexilic prophets, with remarkable "density" (i.e., the number of times it is used per page) in Malachi.

8. "Lord of Hosts," *HDB* 3 [1900]: 137f. However, W. Eichrodt argues that "the name *ṣᵉḇā'ôṯ* is never applied to the heavenly hosts"; *Theology* 1:192.

9. *Ibid*. 1:193. See also Anderson, "Hosts, Host of Heaven," *IDB* 2:654-56; BDB, p. 839.

maintained his love toward Israel, is not concerned about the quality of sacrifices, and actually delights in those who do evil in his sight. Yahweh's replies to these various attacks on his justice fall into three groups:

(1) Yahweh is God of all. The Lord of hosts is a great King, and his "name is feared among the nations" (1:14): "From the rising of the sun to its setting my name is great among the nations, and in every place incense is offered to my name, and a pure offering" (v. 11). The question, "Have we not all one father?" (2:10), probably should not be used to prove universality, for in context it almost certainly applies to Israel (i.e., Judah and Jerusalem). If the universality of God is a recent postexilic idea, it is a bit advanced for the time of Malachi. But as seen in earlier chapters, a considerable body of material indicates that this idea was early, then obscured by the influx of pagan ideas, and reemphasized by the prophets, notably Isaiah.

(2) Although Yahweh is God of all the world, Israel has a special place as a result of divine election. The choice of Jacob and the repudiation of Esau illustrates the point (1:2ff.). Israel was Yahweh's "son" and "servant," hence a debt of honor and fear exists (v. 6). The offerings should be choice, since they express gratitude for Yahweh's choice of Israel. The people's sacredness as a family of Yahweh must be safeguarded by the sanctity of marriage (2:10-16): "I hate divorce," says Yahweh the God of Israel (v. 16; the only time this title occurs in Malachi). His people owe him the recognition that everything is his, expressed by paying tithes (one-tenth of all produce or income; Deut. 14:22). Having failed to give him what was his, "those who feared the Lord" repented, and the basis for distinction between the righteous and the wicked was established (Mal. 3:16-18).

(3) The day of Yahweh, long known in Amos' day and talked about at length in Joel and Zephaniah, occurs again in the last of the Old Testament prophets. Indeed, the idea is found throughout the book, even where the term is not used. The vindication of God, the reply to the charges against his justice, will be found in this day (4:1 [MT 3:19]). "The Lord . . . will suddenly come to his temple" (3:1)—"but who can endure the day of his coming?" (v. 2). Like a refiner's fire and a fuller's soap (v. 2), he will refine and purify his priests, he judges the sorcerers, adulterers, those who swear falsely, who oppress the hireling, widow, or orphan—in a word, "those who do not fear me" (v. 5).

But the day is not all darkness and fire. The Lord has a "book of remembrance" in which are written the names of those who fear Yahweh.[10] "They shall be mine, says the Lord of hosts, my special possession on the day when I act" (3:17). The distinction will be made between the "righteous" and the "wicked," one who serves God and one who does not (v. 18). The day comes burning like an oven, "but for you who fear my name, the sun of righteousness shall rise, with healing in its wings" (4:2 [MT 3:20]).

---

10. This is a unique contribution of Malachi.

The Forerunner. Unique to Malachi is this doctrine concerning "Elijah the prophet" (4:5 [MT 3:23]). Isaiah had spoken of the "voice" that cries: "In the wilderness prepare the way of the Lord" (40:3). The somewhat vague idea that someone is to precede the messianic king and prepare for his coming develops into a rather full doctrine in the intertestamental period, and is found at Qumran and in the New Testament. Malachi names this forerunner "my messenger" in 3:1 and then, more specifically, "Elijah," an idea taken over in Judaism.[11] In the New Testament, John the Baptist is recognized as the forerunner, although that term is not used; he is asked: "Are you Elijah" (see John 1:21; see also Mark 1:2-8; Luke 7:27f.; and esp. Matt. 11:14).

So the prophetic period closes. Clearly the message says "Unfinished." The Exile was not the end, and the return was not the beginning of the new age. Malachi leaves an expectation—a fear of judgment and a hope of healing. Christians believe that fulfillment of this hope comes in at least two stages: the First Advent of Christ, providing salvation for all who believe God's revelation; and the Second Advent, the final judgment and ultimate salvation. Malachi, like the other prophets, does not make this distinction. Rather, he sees the near and the distant in a single view.

FOR FURTHER READING

Baldwin, J.G. *Haggai, Zechariah, Malachi.*
Braun, R. "Malachi—A Catechism for Times of Disappointment." *Currents in Theology and Mission* 4 (1977): 297-303. (Commentary on oracles and their format.)
Mason, R.A. *The Books of Haggai, Zechariah and Malachi.* (Pp. 135-162; book basically a unity, by levitical author closer to Haggai and Zech. 1–8 than to Zech. 9–14.)
Morgan, G.C. *Wherein Have We Robbed God? Malachi's Message to the Men of Today.* New York: 1898.
Neil, W. "Malachi." *IDB* 3:228-232. (A full discussion.)
Smith, G.A. *The Book of the Twelve Prophets.* Expositor's Bible (1956) 4:640-651. (Very helpful.)
Sutcliffe, E.F. "Malachias." *CCHS* §§555a–558g. (Some good material.)

---

11. In the Passover Seder, "Elijah's cup" remains untouched throughout the service. At last the door is opened and Elijah is not found, and the service concludes with the hope that the fulfillment will occur before the next year.

CHAPTER 39

THE WRITINGS

NAME

T HE third section of the Jewish canon is the Writings (Heb. $k^e\underline{t}\hat{u}\underline{b}\hat{i}m$). Apparently the Church Fathers minted the Greek term *hagiographa* "sacred writings" to describe this part of the Old Testament.[1]

Although a date for the completion of the Writings cannot be attested before *ca*. A.D. 100, ample evidence of a third section of the canon (in addition to the Law and the Prophets) does appear as early as 180 B.C., when Ben Sirach's grandson noted in the prologue to Ecclesiasticus that his distinguished grandfather "applied himself industriously to the study of the law, the prophets, and the other writings of our ancestors" (NEB). Jesus' words underscore such a tripartite canon: ". . . that everything written about me in the law of Moses and the prophets and the psalms must be fulfilled" (Luke 24:44). Most likely, "psalms" here is shorthand for all the Writings, since that book was the most significant liturgical work and may have stood first in the collection.

Uncertainty about the precise contents of the writings in the pre-Christian period should not suggest that the canon was in a complete state of flux. That Ben Sirach and the Wisdom of Solomon were not included must show that fairly clear boundaries had been drawn by at least 50 B.C. Furthermore, heated debates among the rabbis about the canonicity of Esther, the Song of Solomon, or Ecclesiastes indicate that these books had been well accepted by at least a strong sector of Judaism. It is doubtful that the Bible known to Jesus and the apostles varied at all in contents from the present Hebrew Scriptures.

ORDER

The order presently followed in the Hebrew Bible probably is no earlier than the twelfth century A.D.: Psalms, Job, Proverbs, Ruth, the Song of Solomon,

---

1. O. Kaiser, *Introduction*, p. 409.

Ecclesiastes, Lamentations, Esther, Daniel, Ezra, Nehemiah, 1–2 Chronicles.[2] Earlier Jewish traditions vary in the location of Chronicles—sometimes at the beginning, sometimes at the end of the collection—and the order of Job and Proverbs.[3] The five scrolls (Heb. m^egillôṭ) used for the feasts and fasts (Ruth–Esther) have appeared together since ca. the sixth century A.D., though the present order, which parallels approximately the liturgical events assigned, did not take shape until the twelfth century: the Song of Solomon (eighth day of Passover), Ruth (second day of Weeks, or Pentecost), Lamentations (ninth day of Ab, in mourning for the destruction of Solomon's temple), Ecclesiastes (third day of Tabernacles), Esther (Purim).

One puzzle has been why Chronicles follows Ezra and Nehemiah, when the material treated historically precedes those books. C.H. Gordon suggests one possible answer:

> The choice of Chronicles with which to close the Old Testament made for a happy ending [the edict of Cyrus signalling the end of the Exile] even though chronological considerations call for the order Chronicles-Ezra-Nehemiah.[4]

DATE AND PURPOSE

The date of the collection (300 B.C.–A.D. 100) must be distinguished from the dates of the individual books. As a collection, the Writings were preceded by the Pentateuch and the Prophets, although parts of Psalms and Proverbs undoubtedly were composed centuries before either of the earlier sections reached final form.

Consequently, other factors along with the historical process of collection caused these books to be lumped together as the Writings, although several (Ezra, Nehemiah, Chronicles, Esther, Song of Solomon, and Ecclesiastes) undoubtedly were composed, in their present form at least, after the time of Malachi, the last writing prophet. The unique character of the books has as much to do with their inclusion as does the date of composition or collection.[5]

An obvious purpose of several books in the Hagiographa (e.g., Psalms and the five scrolls) is their use in public worship. Another purpose which accounts for the grouping together of some books (Job, Proverbs, Ecclesiastes) is their use in practical instruction about the ways of God in human experience. A third purpose of books in the Writings (Esther, Nehemiah, Ezra) is to update covenantal history to cover a century or more after the return from exile.

---

2. O. Eissfeldt, *Old Testament*, p. 570.
3. *Ibid.*, p. 443. At times Ruth came just before Psalms to give the genealogy of David, the psalmist (see Talmud B. *Bat.* 14b).
4. *The World of the Old Testament*, p. 299.
5. Though many biblical books have an extended history of composition before being put in final form, in the case of Psalms and Proverbs one must consider the process of collection as well as composition of the various songs and sayings.

Chronicles is somewhat different: it aims at retelling Israel's history so the lessons of the past are brought directly to bear on the needs of the postexilic Jewish community.

The purpose of Daniel and its inclusion with the Writings and not the Prophets, where English versions put it, is discussed below (p. 659). It must have been included in the canon when the prophetic collection was complete. Happily the believing community heard God's voice in its examples of faith and courage and its visions of hope and victory.

Essentially, the purpose of the Writings as a whole was to collect those sacred books whose purpose, character, or date excluded them from the collections of law and prophecy.

Though the Writings do not contain specific commands of God like the Law or verbatim oracles like the Prophets, they are nonetheless essential for the edification of God's people: they give indispensable patterns for prayer and praise; they offer insight into God's work in history; they alert the reader to the lessons to be drawn from creation and the human social environment; they reflect the anxious and angry responses of believing people to the mystery of God's ways; and they model the courage and devotion his people are to maintain despite human frailty and hostile opposition.

In short, the Psalms, the wisdom literature, the Chronicler's history, the songs of love and lamentation, the visions of comfort, give startling expression to the depths of faith which God expects of his people. The impact of law, prophecy, and history on succeeding generations would have been less powerful had God not also inspired and preserved the emotions, the instructions, even the frustrations of the Writings. They are an essential part of "all Scripture . . . inspired by God and profitable for teaching, for reproof, for correction, and for training in righteousness . . ." (2 Tim. 3:16).

FOR FURTHER READING

Childs, B.S. *Old Testament as Scripture*. (Pp. 501-3.)
Henshaw, T. *The Writings: The Third Division of the Old Testament Canon*. London: 1963. (Historical background, summary, and analysis of individual books.)

CHAPTER 40

PSALMS

NAME

THE title "Psalms" reflects the book's name in the LXX (*Psalmoi*). The alternate Greek title, *Psaltērion*, frequently is used in its anglicized form, Psalter. Both terms probably entered English versions through the Latin Vulgate, which transliterated the Greek. The Greek words (from *psállō* "to pluck or twang") were used first for the playing of a stringed instrument or for the instrument itself. Later they were used to describe the song (*psalmós*) or collection of songs (*psaltērion*). Luke (20:42; Acts 1:20) used the full Greek title "Book of Psalms" (*bíblios psalmōn*).

Though the closest Hebrew word to "psalm" would be *mizmôr* "a song sung to instrumental accompaniment," the actual Hebrew title is *tᵉhillîm* "praises" or "songs of praise." The singular form (*tᵉhillâ*) is used in the title of Ps. 145 and occurs more than twenty times in various psalms (e.g., 9:14 [MT 15]; 22:25 [MT 26]; 33:1; 34:1 [MT 2]).[1]

In the Hebrew Bible, Psalms stands at the beginning of the Writings.[2] Rabbinic custom placed it before Proverbs and the rest of the wisdom literature, assuming that David's collection should precede that of his son, Solomon. The LXX puts Psalms at the beginning of the books of poetry. The Latin and English order, where Job precedes Psalms, probably is based on the supposed antiquity of Job.

STRUCTURE OF THE PSALTER

For at least two thousand years the Psalter has been divided into five books: Pss. 1–41; 42–72; 73–89; 90–106; 107–150. The best explanation of this

---

1. Heb. *tᵉhillîm* is masculine plural (the normal plural is *tᵉhillōt*; cf. 22:3 [MT 4]), which may indicate that it is a technical term for the collection. The use of that title is at least as old as Philo (*ca*. A.D. 40), who uses the literal Greek equivalent *hýmnoi*.

2. Luke 24:44 acknowledges the book's priority among the Writings and employs the title Psalms to describe the whole collection.

grouping is that the various sections may represent stages in the process of collection. That process stretched out over more than five hundred years. The earlier collections contained psalms attributed to David (3–41; 51–71), Korah (42–49), and Asaph (50, 73–83). To this were added some smaller collections like the Songs of Ascent (120–134) and the psalms which use "Hallelujah" (146–150).

Five books were formed, probably following the pattern of the Pentateuch. Indeed, the number of psalms (150) follows closely the number of sections into which the Pentateuch is divided for reading in the synagogue (153). Synagogue practice in the postbiblical period may have called for using a Psalm with each reading from the Pentateuch. Ps. 1, with its emphasis on the delights of the law, serves as a fitting introduction to that use of the Psalter. Each of the books ends with a doxology: 41:13 (MT 14); 72:18f.; 89:52 (MT 53); 106:48; and 150, which serves as a concluding doxology for the whole collection as well. The LXX contains a Ps. 151, purportedly related to David's combat with Goliath, but describes the poem as "outside the number [the traditional 150]."[3] Though both the Greek and the Hebrew contain 150 psalms in the received

Partially unrolled Thanksgiving scroll (1QH) from Qumran. (Israel Museum)

---

3. Qumran Cave 2 has yielded a Hebrew copy of Ps. 151. See J.A. Sanders, *The Psalms Scroll of Qumran Cave II*. Discoveries in the Judean Desert 4 (London: 1965), pp. 54-64.

collection, the actual numbering differs: the LXX combines Pss. 9 and 10 and divides Ps. 147 into 146 and 147. Thus, in the LXX all psalms from 10–147 are one number lower than their Masoretic counterparts.

LITERARY TYPES

The five books in the present Psalter seem to reflect the historical process of their collection. Each contains a range of literary types, which suggest different functions in Israel's private and public worship. Comparison of these literary forms makes possible a better grasp of both their meaning and their use.

The task of understanding a given psalm begins with certain questions: (1) What is happening in the psalm: complaint, praise, thanksgiving, instruction? (2) Who is speaking: an individual or the community? If an individual, is he a spokesman for a group: a king, a priest, or a prophet; or an individual complaining of suffering or giving thanks for deliverance? Are both singular and plural pronouns used, as though an individual and the congregation were both involved? (3) Is the king mentioned? Do words like "anointed," "son," or "shield" denote his relationship to God and Israel?

Only within the current century has the importance of such questions been learned. Until the early decades of the century, the standard scholarly approach to Psalms and other books was historical criticism (German *Zeitgeschichte*), which "sought to understand the books of the Bible by a critical analysis of their composition, their authorship, date, provenience, purpose, and sources."[4] For the Psalms, this method had proved highly inadequate for lack of specific data to help with dates and historical settings of the various poems. Even where a possible background is given in the titles of psalms (e.g., 7, 18, 30, 34, 51–52, 54, 56–57, 59–60, 63), neither the reliability of the tradition that produced the titles nor the psalm's use in the worship of Israel is certain. Invasions and battles may be mentioned, but nothing specific is said. Enemies loom large, but they are almost always nameless. Comparative study of the great nineteenth-century commentaries indicates no strong consensus as to the background, date, or use of the various psalms.

A new approach was needed, and H. Gunkel (1862-1932) more than anyone else provided it. Called form criticism (German *Formgeschichte*), this approach is based on three main premises: (1) Since the Bible contains religious literature, which by nature tends to resist change and maintain established patterns, literary materials may be categorized (German *Gattungen* "categories") according to formal similarities. (2) Similarity of form probably means similarity of use; presumably, therefore, similar forms were used in the same expressions of religious life (German *Sitze im Leben*). (3) Since similarities are found in forms of worship and liturgy among Israel and their neighbors, religious texts

---

4. J. Muilenburg, introduction to H. Gunkel, *The Psalms: A Form-critical Introduction*, trans. T.M. Horner (Philadelphia: 1967), p. iv.

from other Near Eastern cultures may help in understanding the use and meaning of Israel's literary forms. In other words, comparative literature and comparative religion may be useful in understanding the Old Testament.[5]

With Gunkel the emphasis in Psalm studies shifted from an attempt to pinpoint the time and setting of a given psalm's composition to an attempt to trace the psalm's use in public worship or private devotion. Concentration on authorship per se gave way to investigation of the religious setting in which the psalm may have arisen and of its oral transmission in living worship.[6]

Gunkel's analysis of literary categories remains the backbone of contemporary approaches to the Psalms, despite nearly six decades of scholarly amplification. The following list represents Gunkel's outline, as modified by later research:

Hymns. The hymns or psalms of praise ring with the enthusiasm of worshipers who sense that they are face to face with God. The hymns frequently contain three elements:

(1) A call to worship, where a leader urges the congregation to praise the Lord:

> O give thanks to the Lord,
>   call on his name. . . . (105:1)

Often the worshipers are called by name:

> O offspring of Abraham his servant,
>   sons of Jacob, his chosen ones! (v. 6)

The exhortations are in the plural, indicating that the whole congregation or a substantial group within it is involved.

(2) A description of God's acts or attributes, usually forming the body of the hymn, giving the motivation for praise:

> He is the Lord our God;
>   his judgments are in all the earth. (v. 7)
> So he led forth his people with joy,
>   his chosen ones with singing. (v. 43)[7]

---

5. In addition to the work cited in note 4, see Gunkel, *Einleitung in die Psalmen*, 3rd ed. HAT (Göttingen: 1975) [completed in 1933 by J. Begrich after Gunkel's death], as a ready source for his massive contribution to the study of the Psalms. See also A.R. Johnson, "The Psalms," pp. 166-181 in OTMS, for Gunkel's approach to form criticism.

6. For an analysis of the philosophical and cultural influences which prompted this shift from historical and literary criticism to form criticism, see E. Gerstenberger, "Psalms," pp. 179-183 in J.H. Hayes, ed., *Old Testament Form Criticism*.

7. This central section typically is expressed: (1) with Hebrew participles describing God's activity; usually translated as relative clauses (e.g., "who coverest thyself with light as with a garment, who hast stretched out the heavens like a tent"; 104:2); or (2) with "for" (Heb. *kî*) to introduce the reasons for praise (e.g., "For the Lord is good; his steadfast love endures forever . . ."; 100:5).

(3) A conclusion, calling for fresh praise or obedience:

Praise the Lord![8] (v. 45c)

Psalms which contain, in one way or another, most of these elements are 8, 19, 29, 33, 104–105, 111, 113–114, 117, 135–136, 145–150.

The life situations (*Sitze im Leben*) in which hymns were used and within which they developed must have been numerous: victory after battle, thanks for harvest, relief from drought and plague, commemoration of the Exodus, festive occasions like seasonal feasts, weddings, ordinations, and dedications.

A number of subcategories have been identified which seem to cluster around special events:

(1) Victory songs (e.g., Ps. 68) were patterned after the stirring hymn raised by Miriam:

"Sing to the Lord, for he has triumphed gloriously;
the horse and his rider he has thrown into the sea." (Exod. 15:21)[9]

(2) Processional hymns describe the longings and expectations of pilgrims and worshipers as they approach the temple. Some reflect the ardors of the journey as well as the anticipation of blessings (Pss. 84, 122). Others preserve a "liturgy of entrance," part of a ceremony by which pilgrims passed a test of loyalty to God before admittance to the temple court (15, 24). Others center in the processional that may have preceded worship. Songs like Ps. 132; 68:24-27 (MT 25-28) capture the scene of worshipers on the move, perhaps accompanied by the ark of the covenant, not unlike 2 Sam. 6:1-11, where David first brought the ark to the hills of Jerusalem. Descriptions of the glorious walls and buildings of the holy city are frequent (87).

(3) Zion Songs (Pss. 46, 48, 76) praise the Lord for his majestic presence in Zion:

His abode has been established in Salem,
his dwelling place in Zion. (76:2 [MT 3])

Just how these songs may have been used in worship is not certain. Biblical evidence is lacking for a possible Zion festival in Israel's seasonal calendar.[10]

(4) Enthronement songs (47, 93, 96–99) celebrate the reign of God as Lord of the nations. Two components are characteristic: an exhortation in the plural, calling the nations and creation to praise Yahweh; the reasons for the

---

8. The frequent use of "Hallelujah" at the beginning and/or end of a hymn lends credence to Gunkel's claim that the "basic form of the earliest hymn, as well as the primitive core of the singing of the hymn, is the word 'Hallelujah' "; *Psalms*, p. 11.

9 See Deborah's song after the victory over Sisera, Jabin, and their Canaanite army (Judg. 5:2-31). Israel's enemies could also lift their victory song, as in the Philistine reaction to Samson's capture (16:23f.).

10. Gerstenberger, "Psalms," pp. 216-18.

praise—God's coming (97:2-5), saving deeds to Israel (99:6f.), strength (97:4), glory (96:6), justice (99:4), and victory (47:3 [MT 4]).

S. Mowinckel focused attention on these psalms by reconstructing a "feast of Yahweh's enthronement." This alleged festival was connected with the autumn harvest and new year activities usually called the feast of Tabernacles (Lev. 23:33-36). Purportedly established early in the Monarchy, this feast enacted the enthronement of Yahweh as king of all creation, relived his victories over chaos at the first creation and his conquest of Pharaoh and others in the Exodus, reconsecrated the temple, and commemorated David's sovereignty over Israel and his settlement in Jerusalem. So important was this festival to Israel's cultic life that Mowinckel attached to it many psalms which are not strictly enthronement psalms (e.g., 47, 68, 81, 95, 132).[11]

A major challenge to Mowinckel's reconstruction has come from H.-J. Kraus, who questioned Mowinckel's interpretation (1) grammatically: Kraus argued against the translation of *yhwh mālak* as "Yahweh has become king," a pillar in Mowinckel's structure, by showing that the reference is to a state not an act, thus "Yahweh is king";[12] (2) cultically: How could God have been elevated to the throne when there was no image or representation as in the Babylonian and Canaanite cults from which Mowinckel drew his pattern? (3) theologically: Israel's view of the "living God" could not assume any mythic rhythm in which Yahweh dies annually or is weakened during the summer drought like pagan fertility gods; (4) exegetically: Kraus cites "the way in which the unchangeable and eternal kingship of Yahweh is extolled" in Ps. 93:2 as "subject to no variations."[13]

Both Mowinckel and Kraus note that the enthronement psalms have historical (remembering God's past deliverance) and eschatological (anticipating God's future victory) dimensions. Kraus stresses both their historical and eschatological character, whereas Mowinckel's chief concern was their use in the cult to express the present reality of God's exaltation as king.[14]

The debate will continue. This survey supports Kraus' criticisms of Mowinckel without necessarily accepting his (and Westermann's) conclusion that these psalms are postexilic, patterned after the "eschatological song of praise" in Isa. 52:7-10.[15] Yahweh's kingship is surely well attested in Israel's conscious-

---

11. *The Psalms in Israel's Worship*, trans. D.R. Ap-Thomas (Nashville: 1967) 1:106-192; see esp. pp. 129f.

12. Mowinckel rejects the contrast: "To the Israelite way of thinking there is no contradiction between [becoming king] and that he is king for ever; such a contradistinction is modern and rationalistic"; *ibid.* (1:115).

13. *Worship in Israel*, trans. G. Buswell (Richmond: 1966), pp. 205-7.

14. C. Westermann strongly supports Kraus, arguing that the eschatological hope expressed is the dominant characteristic; *The Praise of God in the Psalms*, trans. K.R. Crim (Richmond: 1961), pp. 145-151.

15. *Ibid.*, pp. 146f.

ness centuries before the Exile (Deut. 33:5), although how and when it became part of their faith is not yet agreed.[16]

Complaints of the People.[17] Psalms like 12, 44, 58, 60, 74, 79–80, 83, 85, 90, and 126 are prayers by the congregation in times of national emergency: invasion or defeat (44, 60, 74, 79–80; cf. Lam. 5); oppression by wicked enemies (58); danger of attack (88); plague, drought, famine, or other natural threat (85, 126; cf. Joel 2:15-17). Among the literary components in most psalms of communal complaint are:

(1) An address to God and a preliminary cry for help:

O God, why dost thou cast us off for ever? (74:1)

(2) A complaint describing the people's suffering, often in highly figurative terms. At times this focuses on the three parties involved—the enemies, the people themselves, and Yahweh:

(a) Thy foes have roared in the midst of thy holy place; (v. 4)
(b) We do not see our signs;
    there is no longer any prophet,
    and there is none among us who knows how long. (v. 9)
(c) Why dost thou hold back thy hand,
    why dost thou keep thy right hand in thy bosom? (v. 11)

(3) A confession of trust, frequently based on God's past deeds:

Yet God my king is from of old,
    working salvation in the midst of the earth. (v. 12)

(4) A petition for rescue, usually expressed in imperatives and often calling for punishment of the enemies:

Do not deliver the soul of thy dove to the wild beasts;
    do not forget the life of thy poor for ever. (74:19)
Do not forget the clamor of thy foes,
    the uproar of thy adversaries which goes up continually! (v. 23)

(5) An appeal to God's reputation or his covenant commitment:

Remember this, O Lord, how the enemy scoffs,
    and an impious people reviles thy name. (v. 18)

(6) A vow of praise in which the sufferers promise to celebrate their rescue with public praises:

---

16. Kraus, following W. Schmidt, connects the kingship of Yahweh with the building of the temple, on the analogy of Canaanite belief that a god was assured royal status when a temple for him had been built; *Worship in Israel*, pp. 203-5.

17. The term complaint is preferred to lament to describe the prayers for help in the Psalms. Lament better fits the *qînâ*, the dirge-like form used in Lam. 1–2, 4, where the tone is funereal and the tragedy irreversible.

Then we thy people, the flock of thy pasture,
will give thanks to thee for ever;
from generation to generation we will recount thy praise. (79:13; cf.
    74:21)[18]

The use of these complaints is clear. Solomon's dedicatory prayer included detailed descriptions of those occasions when God's people would gather at the temple and make supplication for his deliverance (1 Kgs. 8:33-40). More dramatically, the prophet Joel summoned the people to fast and to assemble with the priests to beg God to spare his people from the dreadful locusts (2:15-17).

The complaint in Joel is followed by a salvation speech, the promise of deliverance uttered in Yahweh's own words (vv. 19-29). Such speeches, delivered by a priest or temple prophet, may well have accompanied or interrupted the complaints and assured the people that their prayers had been answered.[19]

A few psalms may be complaints of the people even though in the "I form." In such cases a leader, probably the king, may have served as spokesman for the community (Pss. 89, 144).[20] Even psalms where the "we form" predominates sometimes use "I" or "my," as though the congregation was alternating with the spokesman in voicing the complaint (44:6, 15 [MT 7, 16]; 74:12; 83:13 [MT 14]).[21]

Whether these communal complaints were used at seasonal festive occasions (perhaps the Day of Atonement [Lev. 16]) as well as in emergencies is uncertain. Biblical evidence is lacking for any ceremony (akin to Babylonian rituals) where the king is subject to public humiliation and suffering during which he raises a complaint.[22]

Complaints of the Individual. More psalms fall into this category than any other.[23] The components of the individual complaints are virtually identical to those of the communal form.

---

18. This schema is adapted from Westermann's analysis; *The Praise of God in the Psalms*, pp. 53f. The "double wish" of rescue for Israel and destruction for the enemies is not included here because its form seems less certain (but see Ps. 79:9-12; 80:16b-17 [MT 17b-18]).

19. Ps. 12:5 (MT 6) is such a speech in the heart of what seems to be a communal complaint.

20. Ps. 89 begins like an individual song of thanksgiving with a strong confession of trust, a hymnlike account of God's might and majesty, and a reminder of God's covenant with David (89:1-37 [MT 2-38]). But vv. 38-51 (MT 39-52) are clearly a complaint, asking relief from enemy invasion. The references to "David," "thy servant," and "thy anointed" clearly mark the king as speaker (vv. 49-51 [MT 50-52]). Cf. 144:10 ("David"); and 144:12-15 (first person plural, as though the congregation added their wish for victory and prosperity).

21. Mowinckel's analysis of the national psalms in the I form (*Psalms* 1:225-246) is an important statement of the evidence, though his conclusion as to the number of such songs and their possible cultic uses is undoubtedly overstated.

22. See H.H. Guthrie, *Israel's Sacred Songs* (New York: 1966), pp. 135-145, for possible uses.

23. E.g., 3, 5–7, 13, 17, 22, 25–28, 31, 35–36, 38–40, 42–43, 51, 54–57, 59, 61, 64, 69–71, 86, 88, 102, 108–9, 120–130, 139–143.

(1) An address to God and cry for help:

> My God, my God, why hast thou forsaken me? (22:1 [MT 2])

(2) A highly poetic complaint:

> Many bulls encompass me,
>> strong bulls of Bashan surround me; (v. 12 [MT 13])
> I am poured out like water,
>> and all my bones are out of joint; (v. 14 [MT 15])
> Thou dost lay me in the dust of death. (v. 15c [MT 16c])

(3) A confession of trust:

> In thee our fathers trusted;
>> they trusted, and thou didst deliver them. (v. 4 [MT 5])

(4) A petition, sometimes expressed as a wish ("May the Lord . . ."), more frequently in the imperative, often with pleas like "hear," "remember," "save":

> But thou, O Lord, be not far off!
>> O thou my help, hasten to my aid!
> Deliver my soul from the sword,
>> my life from the power of the dog! (vv. 19f. [MT 20f.])

(5) An additional argument, such as an appeal to God's special care, a description of the rejoicing of God's enemies, a prayer of confession (51:3-5 [MT 5-7]), or a protest of innocence (26:3-8).[24]

> Yet thou art he who took me from the womb;
>> thou didst keep me safe upon my mother's breasts. (22:9 [MT 10])

(6) A vow of praise, promising public testimony and a thank offering (Lev. 7:11-18):

> I will tell of thy name to my brethren;
>> in the midst of the congregation I will praise thee. (22:22 [MT 23];
>> cf. vv. 25f. [MT 26f.])

The vow often had significance for the whole congregation, especially its poorer members, as the sacrifice was shared with the sufferer's friends and other worshipers[25]:

> The afflicted shall eat and be satisfied;
>> those who seek him shall praise the Lord! (v. 26 [MT 27])

(7) An assurance of being heard, where the sufferer expresses in advance his confidence in God's answer:

---

24. Westermann calls these "motifs designed to move God to intervene"; *The Praise of God in the Psalms*, p. 64.
25. See R. de Vaux, *Ancient Israel*, pp. 417f.

For he has not despised or abhorred
   the affliction of the afflicted;
and he has not hid his face from him,
   but has heard, when he cried to him. (v. 24 [MT 25])[26]

Perhaps the last stanza of Ps. 22 (vv. 27-31 [MT 28-32]) is also part of the assurance, describing the widespread impact of God's deliverance. In his own experience, the psalmist saw the possibility of a massive work of salvation. To the God who could rescue him, nothing was impossible. As in the communal complaint, the assurance may at times have been based on an oracle of salvation delivered by prophet or priest during the temple service in which the complaint was uttered.[27]

Three types of circumstances seem to have prompted prayers of individual complaint: (1) unjust accusations of crime or wrongdoing, in which false witnesses conspired with enemies of the sufferer to convict and punish the defendant falsely;[28] (2) penitence for personal sins (51, 130); (3) illness or incapacity (6, 39, 62, 88), which at times seems to have been combined with unjust accusations (13, 22, 28, 31:9-24 [MT 10-35], 35, 38, 41, 69, 71, 86, 102, 109). Whether the accusations made the sufferer ill or some illness led to accusations of sin (cf. Job 4), the sufferer is at once wracked with physical and emotional pain and abandoned by his loved ones.

Thanksgiving Songs of the Individual. In form these are often closely akin to that of the individual complaints. They were meant to be used when deliverance had been effected and the complaint had been answered. Among the thanksgiving songs are 23, 30, 32, 34, 40:1-10 [MT 2-11], 66, 92, 107, 116, 138–139, 146. The structural elements frequently found in these psalms include the following:

(1) A proclamation of love and praise:

I love the Lord . . . (116:1)

(2) An introductory summary:

. . . because he has heard my voice and my supplications. (v. 1; cf. v. 2)

---

26. In Ps. 22, the assurance comes in close connection with the vow of praise (v. 22 [MT 23]) and is actually part of a hymn fragment which the psalmist will urge the congregation to sing when deliverance takes place: "You who fear the Lord, praise him!" (v. 23 [MT 24]).

27. See W. Beyerlin, "Die *tôdā* der Heilsvergegenwärtigung in den Klageliedern des Einzelnen," ZAW 79 (1967): 208-224.

28. Among this type are listed Pss. 3–5, 7, 11, 17, 25–27, 31:1-8 [MT 2-9], 42–43, 52, 54–57, 59, 64, 70, 94:16-23, 120, 140–143. See E.A. Leslie, *The Psalms* [Nashville: 1949], p. 316), who follows the pioneering work of H. Schmidt, *Das Gebet der Angeklagten im Alten Testament.* BZAW 49 (1928). Such unjust accusations had been specifically outlawed in the Ten Commandments (Exod. 20:16; Deut. 5:20; cf. Exod. 23:1; Deut. 17:6f.).

(3) A poetic recollection of the time of need:

The snares of death encompassed me: (v. 3)

(4) A report of the petition and rescue:

Then I called on the name of the Lord:
"O Lord, I beseech thee, save my life!" (v. 4)

(5) A renewal of the vow of praise:

I will pay my vows to the Lord
in the presence of all his people. (v. 14; cf. vv. 12-19)

(6) An expression of praise:

Gracious is the Lord, and righteous;
our God is merciful. (v. 5; cf. vv. 6-8, 19c)

Two stories illustrate the use of the thanksgiving song: in the sanctuary at
Shiloh, Hannah, grateful for Samuel's birth, exulted in God's power to hear
her complaint (1 Sam. 2:1-10; cf. 1:9-18); Jonah, imprisoned within the great
fish, anticipated deliverance and gave thanks (Jonah 2:1-9). The two settings
point up the difficulties inherent in trying to define too precisely the connections between each type of psalm and Israel's public worship.[29]

Royal Psalms. Though not designating strictly a literary type, this term often
is used for a handful of psalms which refer to Israel's king. These shed light on
the role of the king in Israel's worship, the expectations and obligations which
the covenant laid upon the sons of David, and the quality of Judah's messianic
hope. They also show that attempts to call most psalms postexilic, when Judah
had no king, go against the evidence of the texts themselves.

Content and literary form permit reasonable guesses of occasions when
these royal psalms may have been used in public worship:

(1) Weddings. As father figure and religious leader of the people, the king
would necessarily celebrate his wedding in public ceremony. Parts of that ceremony are recorded in Ps. 45. Vv. 1-9 [MT 2-10] describe the groom and praise
his power, beauty, and devotion to righteousness; vv. 10-17 [MT 11-18] describe the bride, while pledging her to be loyal to the king and promising her
fame and fertility. The speaker ("I" in vv. 1, 17 [MT 2, 18]) seems to be a
priest or cultic prophet who addresses the royal couple in Yahweh's behalf. In
the wedding are repeated a number of exhortations and promises usually voiced
at the royal coronation (vv. 4, 6 [MT 5, 7]). The marriage gave opportunity

29. For the current status of the debate, begun by Gunkel and Mowinckel, over
which psalms were designed for cultic use, see Guthrie, *Israel's Sacred Songs*, pp. 14-25,
147-157; also Gerstenberger, "Psalms," pp. 200-205.

to stress the king's role as military leader and champion of justice, anointed by God himself (v. 7 [MT 8]).[30]

(2) Coronations. It is not certain whether psalms such as 2, 72, 101, and 110 were used at installation services, anniversaries of royal accession, or both. The fragmentary knowledge about such ceremonies comes from brief accounts of Solomon's hasty anointing (1 Kgs. 1:32-40) or Jehoash's bloody enthronement (2 Kgs. 11:9-21 [MT 12:1]), and portions of psalms that hark back to installation rites (e.g., Ps. 89:19-37 [MT 20-38]). It is tempting to piece together parts of a coronation ritual: Ps. 2 pits the king against gentile kings and affirms his power and authority as the anointed (v. 2) and adopted son of God (v. 7); Ps. 72 is a prayer by priest and/or people that God empower the king to fulfill his ordained role as guardian of justice (vv. 1-4), protector of peace (vv. 5-7), sovereign over vassal states (vv. 8-11), deliverer of the oppressed (vv. 12-14), and agent of prosperity (vv. 15-17); Ps. 101 sounds like the king's response, his oath of office pledging integrity—personally and on behalf of his household; Ps. 110 resembles Ps. 2 in its recitation of Yahweh's pledge of support to the new king, especially in times of foreign conflict. The drama or ritual accompanying these components of a coronation ceremony is unknown, but it must have been splendid to match the power of the poetry.

(3) Prayers before or after battle. Pss. 20–21, 89, and 144 were used to petition Yahweh for blessing and victory in battle. The king, as military leader, is mentioned specifically. An assurance of victory may at times have been uttered by an inspired priest or prophet during these prayers (note Jahaziel's word to Jehoshaphat; 2 Chr. 20:14-17). Indeed, some sort of divine assurance seems to have come between vv. 5 and 6 [MT 6 and 7] of Ps. 20 to account for the triumphant exclamation:

> Now I know that the Lord will help his anointed;
> he will answer him from his holy heaven
> with mighty victories by his right hand. (v. 6 [MT 7])[31]

Ps. 89 differs from other prayers before battle by taking the form of an individual complaint reminding Yahweh of past promises and his present absence.

Ps. 18 (found also as 2 Sam. 22) is a thanksgiving for an overwhelming victory. Of special interest is the poetic description of the divine intervention (theophany) that made the victory possible. The whole creation is involved in God's rescue of his king (18:7-19 [MT 8-20]).[32]

---

30. Other possible interpretations are listed in A.A. Anderson, *The Book of Psalms*. NCBC (Grand Rapids: 1981) 1:346f.

31. Ps. 21 has been catalogued variously as a coronation prayer and a prayer before or after battle. Vv. 8-12 (MT 9-13) seem future in tense supporting classification as a prayer before battle; these verses may well be an oracle of victory actually recorded during the prayer.

32. Ps. 132 often is classified as a royal psalm because of its stress on the ark of the covenant. Whether a procession of the ark was part of a coronation or its anniversary is not known.

All of these psalms reflect a unique tie between Yahweh and the king, although its precise nature is not readily discerned. D.J.A. Clines lists several possibilities: divine kingship (king is incarnation of God); sacral kingship (king is mediator of divine blessing); charismatic kingship (king rules by virtue of divine gift); sacerdotal kingship (king performs priestly functions); and divinely appointed kingship (king reigns by authority and choice of God). Though some evidence supports each of the interpretations, most emphasis should be on the last: Israel's kings received their authority by divine sanction carried out in human choices and activities like the ceremony of anointing and acclamation. The biblical narratives are as mindful of the human factors as of the divine in the making of a king.[33]

The early Church heard in the royal psalms the promises of the Messiah.[34] The poetic descriptions and ideal hopes did not find fulfillment in David's sons, from Solomon to Zedekiah, nor in the Maccabean heroes of the second century. The failure of earthly kings to bring the righteousness, justice, prosperity, and dominion heralded in these songs and prayers helped to lift the sights of God's people to a King yet to come. Peter expressed God's revelation of the King's true identity in language drawn from the royal psalms: "You are the Christ, the Son of the living God" (Matt. 16:16).

Wisdom Psalms. Virtually all students of the Psalms agree that a handful of psalms contain instruction for wise and responsible living. Disagreement comes over which are clearly wisdom psalms and how they were used.

To fit the category of wisdom, a psalm should: (1) reflect the literary techniques of wisdom—e.g., the use of proverbs, acrostics, numerical series, comparisons beginning with "better," admonitions addressed to sons, the use of 'ašrê "blessed (happy) is/are. . . ," figures of speech drawn from nature; (2) have an obvious intent to teach by direct instruction (e.g., Pss. 1, 127–128) or by grappling with a problem like the prosperity of the wicked (e.g., 37, 49, 73); (3) contain themes characteristic of wisdom—e.g., the doctrine of the two ways, the contrast between righteous and wicked, the importance of godliness in speech, work, use of wealth, and obedience to elders.

Applying these tests plus examining the use of "wisdom" vocabulary, J.K. Kuntz identifies three subtypes of wisdom psalms: (1) sentence wisdom psalms (127-128, 133), which describe exemplary conduct and its results, using expanded proverbs and similes; (2) acrostic wisdom psalms (34, 37, 112), in which each verse or line begins with the succeeding letter of the Hebrew al-

---

33. *Theological Students Fellowship Bulletin* 71 (1975): 1-8. The weakness of most other views of kingship is their imposing on the Scriptures patterns found elsewhere in Near Eastern societies.

34. For instance, 2:1f. is cited in Acts 4:25f.; 45:6f. (MT 7f.) in Heb. 1:8f.; 110:1 in Matt. 22:44; Acts 2:34f.; 110:4 in Heb. 5:6, 10. See R.T. France, *Jesus and the Old Testament* (London: 1971), pp. 163-69, for the argument that Ps. 110 is not just a royal psalm but also a direct messianic prophecy.

phabet; (3) integrative wisdom psalms (1, 32, 49), carefully planned compositions that center in significant wisdom themes, namely the relationship between wisdom and Torah (1), the certainty of just, if delayed, retribution (49), and the lessons to be learned from divine forgiveness (32).[35]

In addition to these wisdom psalms, others contain verses or stanzas that reflect the influence of wisdom literature. R.E. Murphy has isolated the following: Ps. 25:8-10, 12-14; 31:23f. (MT 24f.); 39:4f. (MT 5f.); 40:4f. (MT 5f.); 62:8-10 (MT 9-11); 92:6-8; 94:8-15.[36] That such ingredients are found in psalms of complaint and thanksgiving may indicate closer links, especially during later periods of psalm collecting (500 B.C. and after), between the temple and the wisdom movement than is often supposed.

The presence of wisdom materials has proved troublesome to those who view the psalms as basically the songs and prayers of public worship. Mowinckel, for instance, has developed definitions of psalms which do not include the didactic qualities of wisdom and, therefore, puzzles as to how "such private poetry was included in the collection of cult psalms transmitted to us, or was even used in the official worship of the Temple."[37]

Several possible solutions have been suggested by Mowinckel and others: (1) a fairly close connection must have existed between the wise men or scribes and the temple prophets and singers; the wise men may actually have helped compile and preserve the Psalter, including some of their own contributions; (2) the lines between various offices and services—priests, singers, prophets, scribes, wise men—should not be drawn too sharply; there is ample evidence of overlap in their activities;[38] (3) instruction and prayer may not have been clearly distinguished in Israel's worship; the thanksgiving songs, especially, gave opportunity for personal witness to God's guidance and personal exhortation, so that the line between wisdom psalms and psalms of personal thanksgiving is almost impossible to draw (see 32, 73, 78).[39]

THE PSALMS AND ISRAEL'S WORSHIP

The Jerusalem temple must have been a busy place. The laws prescribed daily services (Exod. 29:38-42; Num. 28:2-8) in the morning and at twilight, sabbath

---

35. "The Canonical Wisdom Psalms of Ancient Israel—Their Rhetorical, Thematic, and Formal Dimensions," pp. 186-222 in J.J. Jackson and M. Kessler, eds., *Rhetorical Criticism*.

36. "A Consideration of the Classification, 'Wisdom Psalms,'" *VTS* 9 (1962): 165-67.

37. "Psalms and Wisdom," *VTS* 3 (1955): 216.

38. Gerstenberger, "Psalms," p. 221, points out that the Babylonian Theodicy (*ANET*, pp. 601-4) is an acrostic written by a priest, probably for public, even cultic, use. This combination of wisdom form and theme with priestly activity may shed light on wisdom psalms and their possible cultic connection.

39. Murphy, *VTS* 9 (1962): 156-167, views the thanksgiving psalms as a bridge to tie psalmody and wisdom together within the cult: "It is clear that the psalmists found wisdom themes useful and that they exploited the wisdom style as an apt mode of expression"; p. 167.

rituals with extra sacrifices (Num. 28:9f.) and a greater number of participants (2 Kgs. 11:5-8), and special burnt offerings at the new moon (the beginning of each lunar month; Num. 28:11-15; cf. Hos. 2:11 [MT 13]). In addition, those with ready access may have used the temple to commemorate special family occasions. Public events also were observed in the temple: the coronation of the king, a victory in battle, relief from drought or plague, and experiences of national disaster.

Annual feasts lasted for several days and drew to Jerusalem pilgrims from throughout the land: Unleavened Bread and Passover, a combined feast in early spring (Exod. 23:15; Lev. 23:5); Weeks (a harvest festival in late spring, called Pentecost in the New Testament; Exod. 23:16; 34:22; Num. 28:26; Acts 2:1); Tabernacles in early fall (also called Booths or Ingathering; Exod. 23:16; 34:22; Deut. 16:16). Tabernacles, celebrating completion of the summer harvest as well as recalling Israel's wilderness days, apparently became the preeminent religious event of the year, though its precise role has been warmly debated.[40]

The variety of festive activities and the lack of specific mention of feasts in the Psalter necessitate caution against theories that try to integrate the Psalms around one particular feast. Just as criticism has been leveled against Mowinckel's reconstruction of an enthronement or new year festival,[41] A. Weiser's theory of a feast of covenant renewal coinciding with Tabernacles[42] likewise has drawn fire. His focus has several drawbacks: (1) he assumes a closer link between the account of God's theophany on Sinai and the theophanies or epiphanies of the Psalter than can be maintained;[43] (2) in highlighting the covenant ceremonies from the days of the Judges, he gives insufficient attention to the role of the Davidic covenant in the Psalms; (3) like Mowinckel, he neglects "the complexity of Israel's tradition and cultic life, sacrificing historical differentiation for an all-embracing 'lump' theory."[44]

More broad and balanced is Kraus' summary of the background of Israel's cult: (1) a tent festival commemorating the Exodus and wilderness wanderings was later incorporated in the feast of Tabernacles; (2) a covenant renewal ceremony, perhaps originally observed at Shechem (Josh. 24), also came to be part of the Tabernacles ritual; (3) David's election as king and Jerusalem's

---

40. For descriptions of the feasts and discussions of their history, development, and meaning, see de Vaux, *Ancient Israel*, pp. 71-110; Kraus, *Worship in Israel*, pp. 26-69.

41. See Kraus' criticism, summarized above. De Vaux cites the lack of biblical evidence to support Mowinckel's theory; *Ancient Israel*, pp. 502-6.

42. *The Psalms*, trans. H. Hartwell. OTL (Philadelphia: 1962), pp. 35-52.

43. Westermann distinguishes between theophany (divine appearance for revelation) and epiphany (divine appearance for rescue); *The Praise of God in the Psalms*, pp. 98-101. See Kraus, *Worship in Israel*, p. 216, for the view that theophany in the cult was not a "dramatic representation" akin to Babylonian myth and ritual but a characteristic Israelite declaration of a prophetic vision.

44. Guthrie, *Israel's Sacred Songs*, p. 19.

capture were remembered at Tabernacles along with the entry of the ark into the holy city (2 Sam. 6).[45]

Though the actual experience of worship in Israel and the use of the Psalms probably was even more varied and complex than Kraus' analysis admits, his approach does show ways in which earlier and later elements were combined, and it gives equal weight to wilderness/settlement components and later events of the Monarchy. Above all Kraus, with Weiser, has grounded Israel's public worship soundly in the events of their own history rather than in the myths and ceremonies of their neighbors as does Mowinckel.

Kraus' picture of a temple festival is worth noting, especially with regard to Tabernacles, the most important of the annual feasts before Passover (2 Kgs. 23:21-23), which assumed substantial importance in the time of Josiah (639-609). Possible components of the festival include:

(1) the pilgrimage to Zion, anticipated with joy (Ps. 42:1f. [MT 2f.]), pursued with patience (84:6 [MT 7]), and achieved with exultation (122:1f.);

(2) the ascent of the ark (perhaps from an area south of David's city), accompanied by hymns with a summons to enter the temple (95:1-6; 100), by memories of the recovery of the ark at Kiriath-jearim (132:6), and by recital of God's covenant with David (vv. 11f.);

(3) the entrance torah (15; 24:1-6), questioning the qualifications of true worshipers and answering (provided by the priests?) with a list of qualities like loyalty to God and integrity toward neighbor;

(4) the entrance liturgy (24:7-10), with antiphony between priests in the procession who beg for entry and priests within the temple who ask for a confession of faith in "Yahweh of hosts" as the password (v. 10);

(5) the adoration of Yahweh in the temple courts, expressed in hymns and instrumental accompaniment (150), punctuated with reminders of God's glorious deeds in creation (104) and history (105, 136), and climaxed, perhaps, in the expectation of a theophany (50:1-3; 80:1-3 [MT 2-4]), a special manifestation of God's presence and glory, longed for by the pilgrims even though they knew that God was always present in the sacred city (46:5 [MT 6]);

(6) the blessing of departure (91; 118:26; 121), assuring the pilgrims of God's protection and provision even though they could not stay permanently in the sanctuary as did the priests (84:10 [MT 11]).[46]

In their feasts and fasts, their daily worship, and their special celebrations, Israel remembered and relived God's past victories; committed themselves to present obedience of the covenant laws, which called for full loyalty to Yahweh; and anticipated future triumphs, especially the ultimate defeat of Yahweh's foes. Thanksgiving for the past, rededication for the present, and expectation for the future were the all-embracing components of Israel's worship as voiced in the

---

45. Kraus, *Worship in Israel*, pp. 131f., 136-141, 179-188.
46. *Ibid.*, pp. 208-218. For further comments on the "blessing of departure," see Westermann, "Book of Psalms," *IDBS*, p. 708.

HOLY DAYS AND HOLY SEASONS

Occasion	Date	Reference	Reason	Manner of Observance
New Moon (rō'š ḥōdeš)	First day of each month	Num. 10:10; 28:11-15	Appearance of new moon	Blowing of trumpets Solemn assembly
Sabbath (šabbāṭ)	Every seventh day regardless of lunar cycle	Exod. 16:22-30; 20:8-11; 23:12-16 Lev. 19:3; 23:2f. Num. 15:32-36; 28:9 Deut. 5:12-15	God's creation-rest (Exod. 20:8-11) Deliverance from Egyptian slavery (Deut. 5:12-15) Covenant-sign	Rest from all work Holy convocation (Isa. 1:13) Joy (Isa. 58:13)
Passover (pesaḥ) Unleavened Bread (ḥag hammaṣṣôt)	14-21 Nisan (First month) (either late Mar. or in Apr.) (also in second month; Num. 9:10f.)	Exod. 12:1–13:16; 23:15; 34:18-20, 25 Lev. 23:4-14 Num. 28:16-25 Deut. 16:1-8	Deliverance from Egyptian bondage	Holy convocations First and last days Removal of all leaven First of three annual pilgrimages (Deut. 16:16)
Weeks (šābu'ôt) Harvest Firstfruits Pentecost	6 Siwan (Third month) (May or June)	Exod. 23:16; 34:22 Lev. 23:15-21 Num. 28:26-31 Deut. 16:9-12	End of grain harvest [Giving of Law at Sinai]	Holy convocation No servile labor Offering of firstfruits Sin and peace offerings Second of three annual pilgrimages
[Ninth of Ab]	9 Ab (Fifth month) (July or August)	[Zech. 7:3-5]	Burning of Temple by Babylonians; burning of Second Temple by Romans	Fasting Deep mourning
Seventh New Moon [Rosh Hashanah]	1 Tishri (Seventh month) (Sept. or Oct.)	Lev. 23:24f.	[New Year]	Sacrifices (Num. 29:16) Blowing of trumpets No hard labor

Day of Atonement (yôm hakkippûrîm) [Yom Kippur]	10 Tishri (Sept. or Oct.)	Exod. 30:10; Lev. 16; Lev. 23:26-32; 25:9; Num. 29:7-11	Atonement for personal and national sins	Elaborate ritual (see Lev. 16); Sacrifice; Fasting; Holy convocation
Tabernacles (hag hassukkôt) Booths Ingathering	15-22 Tishri (Seventh month)	Exod. 23:16; 34:22; Lev. 23:33-36, 39-43; Num. 29:12-32; Deut. 16:13-16	Ingathering of fruit harvest	People dwell in booths (tabernacles); Holy convocations; First and last days; Third of three annual feasts
[Śimḥaṭ Tôrâ]	23 Tishri	[Neh. 8:9; 1 Esd. 9:50]	Completion of reading Torah; starting anew	Joyful assembly
[Hanukkah] Dedication Lights	25 Kislev (December)	1 Macc. 4:52-59; John 10:22	Recovering and cleansing of Temple by Judas Maccabeus, 164 B.C.	Eight-day festival; Giving of gifts
[Purim]	14(-15) Adar (Twelfth month) or Veadar* (Thirteenth month) (Feb. or Mar.)	Esth. 9:24-28	Deliverance from Haman's evil plot	Much rejoicing
Seventh (Sabbatical) Year	Every seventh year	Exod. 23:11; 21:1-6; Lev. 25:6; 26:32-35; Deut. 15:1-6; Jer. 34:8ff.	Rest for the land (Exile because the sabbath years had not been kept)	Festival; Release of slaves; Debts forgiven; Poor eat freely
Jubilee (Fiftieth year)	Every fiftieth year (7x7 years)	Lev. 25:8-58; Lev. 27:17-24	Rest for land	Release even of love slaves; Return of land to original owners; Influence on eschatology (Isa. 61:1f.; Lk. 4:18f.; Jubilees)

Festivals in [brackets] are modern occasions.

*Added seven times in nineteen years to keep calendar in phase with the seasons.

Psalms—a worship rooted in the healing, compelling, and hopeful revelation of God in their history.

TITLES AND TECHNICAL TERMS

No area of Psalm studies has produced less certainty than attempts to decipher the titles and notes at the beginning or end of individual poems. These cannot be defined or even dated with confidence. Though headings and notations of authorship are found in Mesopotamian and Egyptian psalms from well before David, evidence suggests that most biblical headings were added after the psalms began to be circulated and translated in the last two centuries B.C.[47]

A.A. Anderson's division of the notes into five categories will be followed here:

Collections, Compilers, or Authors. (1) "Of David" (*l^edāwiḍ*, 73 times), meaning, perhaps, "written by David," whose musicianship is well attested (1 Sam. 16:17-23; 18:10; 2 Sam. 1:17-27; 3:33f.; 23:1-7; Amos 6:5), "on behalf of David" (Ps. 20, a prayer for the Davidic king on the eve of battle), or "belonging to David," part of a royal collection, perhaps including David's compositions.

(2) "Of the Sons of Korah" (11 times; Pss. 42–49, 84–85, 87–88), probably connecting these psalms, by authorship, collection, or both, to a family of temple singers perhaps related to Levi's descendant in 1 Chr. 6:22 (MT 7).

(3) "Of Asaph" (12 times; Pss. 50, 73–83), linking them to one of David's musicians (1 Chr. 6:39 [MT 24]; 15:17; 2 Chr. 5:12) and his family of temple singers (Ezra 2:41).

(4) Other individuals named in connection with psalms: "of Solomon" (Pss. 72, 127); Heman the Ezrahite (88; a sage, 1 Kgs. 4:31; a temple singer of David's day, 1 Chr. 15:17-19; "the king's seer," 25:5); Ethan the Ezrahite (Ps. 89; associated with Heman in 1 Kgs. 4:31; 1 Chr. 15:17, 19); "of Moses" (Ps. 90); "to Jeduthun" (39) or "according to Jeduthun" (62, 77; listed with David's musicians, 1 Chr. 16:41).

Whether these titles attest to authorship is unclear, but they contain evidence for dating most psalms within the four centuries of the Monarchy rather than in the postexilic period. The description of the Psalter as the hymnbook of the Second Temple (Zerubbabel's temple, rebuilt in 516) has been extended in recent years to include Solomon's temple.

At least three factors have contributed to the recognition that the vast majority of the psalms were composed and used before the Exile: (1) Psalm forms were well known to prophets like Amos (hymn stanzas cited in 4:13;

---

47. For the possible antiquity of the headings, see K.A. Kitchen, "The Old Testament in its Context 3," *Tyndale Study Fellowship Bulletin* 61 (1971): 12. But O. Eissfeldt, *Old Testament*, p. 451, notes the lack of consensus on the headings in the Hebrew, Greek, and Syriac texts.

5:8f.; 9:5f.) and Jeremiah (hymn in 10:12-16; complaints in 15:15-18; 17:14-18). (2) The royal psalms together with their clues to the king's role in public worship best fit the Monarchy.[48] (3) Frequent parallels in vocabulary, grammar, and poetic structure between psalms and Ugaritic epic poetry (fourteenth century) are too numerous and striking to be accounted for unless the psalms stem from the earlier rather than later periods.[49]

Psalm Types. Most frequent is the Psalm (*mizmôr*), used more than fifty times in the Psalter and nowhere else in the Old Testament. It seems to be a technical term describing a cultic song accompanied by stringed instruments. Thirty psalms are called Song (*šîr*), perhaps originally secular in meaning. How it differs from *mizmôr* is unclear, though several songs (65, 75–76, 92) bear both titles. Heb. *miktām* describes six psalms (16, 56–60); there is no firm agreement as to its meaning, although "atonement" (Assyrian *katāmu*) is possible. Prayer (*tᵉpillâ*) seems to denote a psalm of complaint (17, 86, 90, 102, 142). *Maśkîl*, used with thirteen psalms (32, 42, 44), probably means "for instruction" or "for contemplation," though its precise use is obscure. The title Song of Ascents (120–136) most likely indicates that the psalm was used in the processional of ascent to the temple. Ps. 145 is called Praise (*tᵉhillâ*), from which comes the Hebrew title for the Psalter. Ps. 45 is fittingly called Song of Love (*šîr yᵉdîdōt*). *Šiggāyôn* (7) is uncertain.

Liturgical Aims and Usage. A handful of terms seem to indicate the occasion for use: *tôdâ* (100) may indicate either a psalm to be used for the thank offering (Lev. 7:12; 22:29) or a psalm of thanksgiving; *hazkîr* (Pss. 38, 70) has been variously explained as a psalm for the memorial sacrifice (*'azkārâ*; Lev. 24:7) or to remind Yahweh of the distress voiced in the complaint; Ps. 30 is labelled "A Song of the Dedication of the Temple"; *lᵉlammēd* (60) probably means "for instruction," though Mowinckel links it to the verb "to goad," suggesting David's attempt to goad his army to battle or the people's effort to goad Yahweh to intervene.[50] The notation to Ps. 92 calls it a "Song for the Day of the Sabbath"; the meaning of *lᵉ'annôt* (88) is uncertain, perhaps "for penance," "for singing," or some sort of musical instruction.

Technical Musical Expressions. Even less consensus occurs here. Words like *binᵉgînôt* "with stringed instruments" (4, 6, 54–55, 67, 76, and probably 61) and *'el-hannᵉhîlôt* (5) "for the flutes," specifying the kind of accompaniment,

---

48. Mowinckel, *Psalms* 1:46-48, argues this point cogently.
49. See Dahood, *Psalms*. Anchor Bible (Garden City) 1 (1965): xxix-xxx; 3 (1970): xxxiv-xxxvii. This massive work is distinguished by its use of Ugaritic and other Northwest Semitic texts to clarify the meaning of the psalms. The degree of Dahood's success is still under debate, but his research will affect every technical study of the psalms for the next generation.
50. *Psalms* 2:217.

are reasonably clear. However, terms like *higgāyôn* (9:16 [MT 17]), *haśśᵉmînît* (6, 12), *haggittît* (8, 81, 84), and *ʿᵃlāmôt* (46), *šôšannîm* ("lilies"; 45, 69, 80), *māhᵃlat* (53), and *ʾal-tašḥēt* (58–59, 75) await further study. Suggestions include names of tunes, instructions for accompaniment, or notes for use in temple rituals.

Even *lamᵉnaṣṣēaḥ*, used fifty-five times in the Psalter (cf. Hab. 3:19) and often rendered "to the choirmaster," has provoked numerous explanations: "for praise," "for the merciful disposition (of Yahweh)," "for propitiation," or designating a collection of psalms. Selah (*selâ*), used more than seventy times, continues to puzzle interpreters, who tend to see it as a musical notation indicating an increase in volume or an instrumental interlude, or instruction for some physical act of worship like falling prostrate in adoration.

Historical Notes. The chief value of the notes that link a psalm (e.g., 3, 7, 18, 34, 51–52, 54, 56–57, 59–60, 63, 142) to a historical event is their clues as to how postexilic Jewish interpreters understood the texts. Most of these headings are later additions and do not afford accurate information about the origin of the poems.

CONTRIBUTIONS TO BIBLICAL THEOLOGY

Like the windows and carvings of medieval cathedrals, the Psalms were pictures of biblical faith for a people who had no copies of the Scriptures in their homes and could not have read them. If the Jews had known only the Psalter (many must have memorized large numbers of psalms), they still would have had a profound understanding of their faith. Summaries of history (e.g., Pss. 78, 105–106, 136), instructions in piety (e.g., 1, 119), celebrations of creation (8, 19, 104), knowledge of God's judgment (37, 49, 73), assurances of his constant care (103), awareness of his sovereignty over all nations (2, 110) were built into the bone and marrow of their faith by the sustenance of the Psalter.

More than anything, the psalms were declarations of relationship between the people and their Lord. They assumed his covenant with them and its obligations to provision, protection, and preservation. Their songs of adoration, confessions of sin, protests of innocence, complaints about suffering, pleas for deliverance, assurances of being heard, petitions before battle, and thanksgivings afterwards were all expressions of their unique relationship to the one true God.

Awe and intimacy combined in Israel's appreciation of that relationship. They stood in awe of God's power and glory, his majesty and sovereignty. At the same time they pleaded before him with passion and vehemence; arguing with his decisions cogently and persistently, and begging for his intervention with vigor and tenacity. They revered him as Lord, and dealt with him as Father.

This sense of special relationship best accounts for the psalms that imprecate or curse Israel's enemies. The covenant was so binding that any foe of Israel was a foe of God and vice versa. Moreover, their relationship with God was expressed in a fierce hatred of evil that called for a judgment as severe as the crime (109; 137:7-9). Even that call for judgment was a product of the covenant, a conviction that the righteous Lord would protect his people and punish those who disdained his worship or his law. The judgment apparently would take place in the lifetime of the wicked.[51] Jesus' teachings about love for enemies (Matt. 5:43-48) may have made these psalms difficult for Christians to pray, but Christians must not lose the hatred of sin or the zeal for God's holiness that prompted them.[52]

G. von Rad subtitles the section of his *Old Testament Theology* on the Psalms and wisdom literature as "Israel's Answer."[53] Surely the Psalms are responses of the priests and people to God's acts of deliverance and revelation in their history.[54]

But they are revelation as well as response. Through them one learns what God's salvation in its varied fullness means to God's people, as well as the heights of adoration and the lengths of obedience which are their lot. No wonder Psalms, along with Isaiah, was the book most frequently cited by Jesus and his apostles. The early Church, like their Jewish forebears, heard God's word in these hymns, complaints, and instructions and made them a foundation for life and worship.[55]

FOR FURTHER READING

Allen, R.B. *Praise! A Matter of Life and Breath.* Nashville: 1980. (An introductory study of the Psalms with practical suggestions for their use.)

---

51. Dahood's work has recently reopened the question of whether the psalms raised intimations of hope for afterlife. His commentary and discussions of the theology of the Psalms will make it difficult for scholars to remain as dogmatic about the "this world-liness" of the psalms; *Psalms,* esp. 3 (1970): xli–lii.

52. C.S. Lewis, *Reflections on the Psalms,* pp. 20-33, has helpful comments on these cursings. See also H.H. Rowley, *Worship in Ancient Israel,* pp. 167-69, for a discussion of the imprecatory psalms which stresses the depths of suffering that gave rise to them.

53. 1:355-459.

54. B.S. Childs contends that Israel became increasingly aware of the value of these responses within a body of authoritative and sacred writings and that "they could be reworked and rearranged in a different situation without losing their meaning. . . . Far from being a sign of a loss of piety or an attachment to the past, this move testified to Israel's desire to articulate new praise to God through the mediation of older forms"; *Old Testament as Scripture,* p. 515.

55. Many helpful works attempt capsule summaries of the theological wealth in the Psalter. See G.S. Gunn, *God in the Psalms* (New York: 1956); Guthrie, *Israel's Sacred Songs;* H. Ringgren, *The Faith of the Psalmists* (Philadelphia: 1963); E. Routley, *Exploring the Psalms* (Philadelphia: 1975); Rowley, *Worship in Ancient Israel,* p. 246.

Eaton, J.H. "The Psalms and Israelite Worship." Pp. 238-273 in G.W. Anderson, ed., *Tradition and Interpretation*. (Survey of recent studies.)

Gray, J. *The Biblical Doctrine of the Reign of God*. Edinburgh: 1979. (Pp. 7-116 focus on the Psalms.)

Hayes, J.H. *Understanding the Psalms*. Valley Forge: 1976. (Good general introduction.)

Hunt, I. "Recent Psalm Study." *Worship* 49 (1975): 202-214.

Johnson, A.R. *The Cultic Prophet and Israel's Psalmody*. Cardiff: 1979.

O'Callaghan, R.T. "Echoes of Canaanite Literature in the Psalms." *VT* 4 (1954): 164-176.

Paterson, J. *The Praises of Israel*. New York: 1950. (Exegetical application of critical study.)

Perdue, L.G. *Wisdom and Cult*. SBL Dissertation Series 30. Missoula: 1977. ("A Critical Analysis of the Views of Cult in the Wisdom Literatures of Israel and the Ancient Near East.")

Ridderbos, N.H. "The Psalms: Style-Figures and Structure." *OTS* 13 (1963): 43-76.

Sabourin, L. *The Psalms: Their Origin and Meaning*. Staten Island: 1974.

Tsevat, M. *A Study of the Language of the Biblical Psalms*. JBL Monograph. Philadelphia: 1955. (Linguistic analysis of idiom of the Psalms as distinct from the whole of classical Hebrew.)

CHAPTER 41

WISDOM
LITERATURE

BIBLICAL wisdom literature is Israel's contribution to that vast body of written and oral sayings which made sage observations about life and set down in memorable form rules for success and happiness. Wisdom has roots deep in antiquity. The Egyptian Instructions of the Vizier Ptah-hotep was written about 2450 B.C., and Instruction for King Meri-ka-re[1] about 2180. Ancient Mesopotamia had a wealth and diversity of wisdom writings well before the time of Abraham. S.N. Kramer has distinguished five categories of Sumerian wisdom: proverbs; miniature essays; instructions and precepts; essays concerned with the Mesopotamian school and scribe; and disputes and debates.[2]

Thus, biblical wisdom literature, which had its formal beginnings in the tenth century, was preceded by a millennium and a half of written wisdom in the ancient Near East, plus countless centuries during which sage advice and observations on life had been passed orally from generation to generation. Since in form, if not always in content, biblical wisdom writings resemble their non-Israelite counterparts, it may be well to sketch briefly some main themes and forms of nonbiblical wisdom literature.

TYPES OF WISDOM LITERATURE

Customarily two main types of wisdom writings can be distinguished: proverbial wisdom—short, pithy sayings which state rules for personal happiness and wel-

---

1. This document shows the intensely religious form that wisdom could take in the First Intermediate Period: "Do not trust in length of years, for they regard a lifetime as (but) an hour. A man remains over after death, and his deeds are placed beside him in heaps. However, existence yonder is for eternity, and he who *complains of* it is a fool. (But) as for him who reaches it without wrongdoing, he shall exist yonder like a god, stepping out freely like the lords of eternity" (*ANET*, p. 415).

2. "Sumerian Wisdom Literature: A Preliminary Survey," BASOR 122 (1951): 28-31. See W. McKane, *Proverbs: A New Approach*. OTL (Philadelphia: 1970), pp. 51-208, for a very useful survey of Egyptian and Mesopotamian wisdom. See also R.J. Williams, "Wisdom in the Ancient Near East," *IDBS*, pp. 949-952.

fare or condense the wisdom of experience and make acute observations about life; and contemplative or speculative wisdom—monologues, dialogues, or essays which delve into basic problems of human existence such as the meaning of life and the problem of suffering. One should not read too much mysticism or philosophy into the terms "contemplative" or "speculative" here. The ancient sages did not deal in theory but were practical and empirical; they discussed not abstract problems but concrete examples: "There was a man in the land of Uz whose name was Job."

Proverbial Wisdom. From time immemorial people of wit and wisdom have coined and collected sage sayings about life. These wise men and women, the educated class of ancient societies, used these sayings as pegs on which to hang lessons for their pupils and as pointers for those who sought advice and counsel. One hallmark of a great person was the ability to dispense wisdom in proverbial form or to outwit a foe with clever sayings. For example, kings used wisdom techniques in official communiques (e.g., "Let not him that girds on his armor boast himself as he that puts it off," 1 Kgs. 20:11).[3]

The origin of the proverb is lost in the preliterary fog of antiquity, but many avenues of life must have contributed to its development. The earliest proverbs were designed for oral rather than written transmission, and much wisdom writing retained this oral emphasis. The book of Proverbs, for instance, puts far greater stress on hearing what is taught than on reading (see Prov. 1:8; 4:1, etc.). From earliest times wisdom sayings, especially in Mesopotamia, seem to have been connected with religious and magical practices. W.G. Lambert has pointed out that, rather than having a moral content, in Babylon "generally 'wisdom' refers to skill in cult and magic lore, and the wiseman is the initiate,"[4] the one who can get what he wants from the gods. Some trace the beginnings of wisdom sayings to cultic practices almost exclusively, but other factors like trade, commerce, and politics seem to have contributed as well.[5] In fact, with any phenomenon so widespread and ancient one should beware of such oversimplifications, for it seems to be a common human trait to attempt systematic observations about life.

The earliest literary documents reveal highly sophisticated forms of didactic sayings, especially in Egypt where the sages tended to use paragraphs dealing with one theme rather than brief, mutually independent and often metaphorical statements. Note the Instructions of Vizier Ptah-hotep:

---

3. Note Goliath's question to David: "Am I a dog, that you come to me with sticks?" (1 Sam. 17:43); and the sharp rebuke of Israel's Jehoash to Amaziah of Judah: "A thistle on Lebanon sent to a cedar on Lebanon saying, 'Give your daughter to my son for a wife'; and a wild beast of Lebanon passed by and trampled down the thistle" (2 Kgs. 14:9).

4. *Babylonian Wisdom Literature* (London: 1960), p. 1.

5. See A. Bentzen, *Introduction* 1:174-77.

Figure of Egyptian scribe from Sakkara, Fifth Dynasty (ca. *2494-2345* B.C.). (*W.S. LaSor*)

Let not thy heart be puffed-up because of thy knowledge; be not confident because thou art a wise man. Take counsel with the ignorant as well as the wise. The (full) limits of skill cannot be attained, and there is no skilled man equipped to his (full) advantage. Good speech is more hidden than the emerald, but it may be found with maidservants at the grindstones. . . .[6]

---

6. J.A. Wilson in *ANET*, p. 412.

These "instructions" probably should be classed among precepts and admonitions rather than proverbs, in the technical sense. A Babylonian counterpart, which Lambert dates in the Kassite period (1500-1100), is the *Counsels of Wisdom*, which advises on such subjects as avoidance of bad companions, kindness to those in need, the undesirability of marrying a slave girl, and the duties and benefits of religion:[7]

> Let your mouth be controlled and your speech guarded:
> Therein is a man's wealth—let your lips be very precious.
> Let insolence and blasphemy be your abomination;
> Speak nothing profane nor any untrue report.
> A talebearer is accursed.
> . . . . . .
> Do not return evil to the man who disputes with you;
> Requite with kindness your evil-doer,
> Maintain justice to your enemy,
> Smile on your adversary.
> . . . . . .
> "The house which a slave girl rules, she disrupts."
> . . . . . .
> Every day worship your god.
> Sacrifice and benediction are the proper accompaniment of incense.
> Present your free-will offering to your god.
> For this is proper toward the gods.[8]

These excerpts illustrate the practical, ethical, and religious character of Near Eastern wisdom literature at its best. To an extent they suggest the didactic essays in Prov. 1–9, and issue a warning against dating those longer and more unified chapters later than other parts of the book.

Brief, independent proverbs and popular sayings are found in lavish measure in Sumerian, Babylonian, and Assyrian texts. The popular sayings circulated among the common people and sometimes were designed more for entertainment than moral instruction. Many, apparently from the late Assyrian period (*ca.* 700), resemble fables, centered in the activity and conversation of animals and insects. For example:

> The spider spun a web for a fly.
> A lizard was caught
> On the web, to the spider's disadvantage![9]
> . . . . . .
> A *mosquito*, as it settled on an elephant,
> Said, "Brother, did I press your side? I will make [off] at the watering-
> place."

---

7. Lambert, *Babylonian Wisdom Literature*, pp. 96-107.
8. *Idem*.
9. *Ibid.*, p. 220. The point seems to be that people sometimes trip on snares they lay for others—a familiar motif in Proverbs (12:13; 29:6).

The elephant replied to the *mosquito*,
"I do not care whether you get on—what is it to have you?—
Nor do I care whether you get off."[10]

A longer, more highly developed Akkadian fable is the debate between the date palm and tamarisk (an evergreen shrub). Each claims to be more useful to the king: the palm for shade and fruit, the tamarisk for wood and foliage.[11]

The distinction between popular saying and proverb is not easy. Both may use observations from nature and contain an admonition or moral. "Proverb," as used here, refers to a brief, crisp maxim usually found in a series yet mutually independent. In Mesopotamian literature proverbs are usually in bilingual form, written in parallel columns in Sumerian and Akkadian. For example:

Whom you love—you bear (his) yoke.
. . . . . .
Seeing you have done evil to your friend,
    what will you do to your enemy?[12]
. . . . . .
A people without a king (is like) sheep without a shepherd.[13]
. . . . . .
Would you place a lump of clay in the hand of him who throws?[14]
. . . . . .
Has she become pregnant without intercourse? Has she become fat without eating?[15]
. . . . . .
Last year I ate garlic; this year my inside burns.[16]

These sayings from ancient Mesopotamia illustrate the concrete nature of Oriental thought. Observations about life are made in terms of down-to-earth objects, creatures, and experiences, with little abstracting or theorizing. The proverbs and popular sayings have an immediacy and vitality which drive their message home with vigor and directness. To illustrate this, contrast the English proverb "in union is strength" with the Arabic proverb "two dogs killed a lion," or "familiarity breeds contempt" with the Jewish saying "the poor man hungers and knows it not."[17] "Pretty is as pretty does" pales beside the much more pungent observation:

---

10. *Ibid.*, pp. 217, 219.
11. See R.H. Pfeiffer in *ANET*, pp. 410f.; see also Jotham's tale in Judg. 9:7-15, where the trees debate which of them should be king.
12. Lambert, *Babylonian Wisdom Literature*, pp. 230, 232. The latter anticipates the modern saying: "With friends like these, who needs enemies?"
13. *Ibid.*, p. 232; a favorite biblical analogy (e.g., Ezek. 34:5; Zech. 10:2; Matt. 9:36).
14. *Ibid.*, p. 235.
15. *Ibid.*, p. 247. This cause-and-effect proverb, a rhetorical question expecting the answer "of course not," is reminiscent of the sayings in Amos 3:3-6.
16. *Ibid.*, p. 249; cf. "you reap what you sow" or "your sins will find you out."
17. J. Paterson, *The Book That Is Alive* (New York: 1954), pp. 12ff.

A good wife is the crown of her husband,
> but she who brings shame is like rottenness in his bones. (Prov.
> 12:4)

or

Like a gold ring in a swine's snout
> Is a beautiful woman without discretion. (11:22)

The Hebrew equivalent of "a word to the wise is sufficient" is "a rebuke goes deeper into a man of understanding than a hundred blows into a fool!" (17:10). Indeed, English proverbs may be concrete ("a bird in the hand is worth two in the bush"; "people who live in glass houses should not throw stones"), but Hebrew and Semitic proverbs almost always are.

What makes an effective proverb? Why are some sayings cherished through the centuries and others cast aside? Archbishop R.C. Trench, eminent biblical scholar of the past century, lists several conditions for a successful proverb: (1) brevity—bulky sayings will not lodge well in the memory, and proverbs must be memorable; (2) intelligibility—its meaning must be grasped readily; (3) flavor—only the pungent proverb will stick in people's minds; and (4) popularity—even a good saying will die if not repeated frequently and passed along through the generations.[18]

Speculative Wisdom. The ancients were as vexed by some of the pressing problems of life as are modern people. Does life have any real purpose? Why do good people sometimes suffer, while the wicked go unscathed? Such questions are dealt with in the ancient wisdom writings of Mesopotamia and Egypt.

From the Kassite period in Mesopotamia comes a monologue of a sufferer who feels that all of life has turned in on him, a text named from its opening lines Ludlul Bēl Nēmeqi ("I will praise the Lord of wisdom"—Marduk, chief god of Babylon). The original poem seems to have been four to five hundred lines long, preserved in three tablets and possibly a fourth, whose material may or may not have been related to the original.[19] When the text first becomes legible the narrator is complaining about being forsaken by his gods:

My god has forsaken me and disappeared,
My goddess has failed me and keeps at a distance.
The benevolent angel who (walked) beside [me] has departed,
My protecting spirit has taken to flight, and is seeking someone else.
My strength is gone; my appearance has become gloomy;
My dignity has flown away, my protection made off. (I, 43-48)

Divine rejection is followed by the apathy or enmity of his friends, admirers, and slaves:

---

18. From *Proverbs, and Their Lessons*, 7th ed. (London: 1857), summarized by Paterson, *The Book That Is Alive*, p. 47. For a thorough study of proverbs in antiquity, see J.M. Thompson, *The Form and Function of Proverbs in Ancient Israel* (Hague: 1974).

19. Excerpts are from Lambert, *Babylonian Wisdom Literature*, pp. 33-61.

I, who strode along as a noble, have learned to slip by unnoticed.
Though a dignitary, I have become a slave.
To my many relations I am like a recluse.
If I walk the street, ears are pricked;
If I enter the palace, eyes blink.
. . . . . .
My friend has become foe,
My companion has become a wretch and a devil.
. . . . . .
My intimate friend has brought my life into danger;
My slave has publicly cursed me in the assembly.[20] (I, 77-81, 84f.,
  88f.)

Rejected by those he trusted both in heaven and on earth, the sufferer is further
plagued by a host of physical ailments. None of the traditional ritual or magic
cures provide relief, and he wonders why the gods have treated him like a
wrongdoer:

The diviner with his inspection has not got to the root of the matter,
Nor has the dream priest with his libation elucidated my case.
I sought the favour of the *zaqiqu*-spirit, but he did not enlighten me;
And the incantation priest with his ritual did not appease the divine
  wrath against me.
. . . . . .
Who knows the will of the gods in heaven?
Who understands the plans of the underworld gods?
Where have mortals learnt the way of a god?

He who was alive yesterday is dead today.
For a minute he was dejected, suddenly he is exuberant.

One moment people are singing in exaltation,
Another they groan like professional mourners.
. . . . . .
As for me, the exhausted one, a tempest is driving me!
Debilitating Disease is let loose upon me:
. . . . . .
My lofty statue they destroyed like a wall,
My robust figure they laid down like a bulrush,
I am thrown down like a bog plant and cast on my face. (II, 6-9,
  36-42, 49f., 68-70)

The text concludes with a series of dreams which reverse the sufferer's tragic
condition and show that Marduk's wrath has been appeased:

---

20. These couplets illustrate the use of synonymous parallelism in Akkadian poetry.
As in Hebrew writings, this parallelism marks off poetry from prose.

His hand was heavy upon me, I could not bear it.
My dread of him was alarming. . . .

. . . . . .

A third time I saw a dream,
And in my night dream which I saw—
. . . a young woman of shining countenance,
A queen of . . . , equal to a god.

. . . . . .

She said, "Be delivered from your very wretched state,
Whoever has seen a vision in the night time."

. . . . . .

After the mind of my Lord had quietened
And the heart of the merciful Marduk was appeased.

. . . . . .

He made the wind bear away my offences. (III, 1f., 29-32, 37f., 50f.,
60)

Although this work has often been called the "Babylonian Job," its author
makes little attempt to delve into why the righteous suffer. Furthermore, the
cultic and magical emphases, the stress on demons as instruments of affliction,
and the visionary messengers of healing are all a far cry from Job, where God
assumes full responsibility for both the suffering and its relief. Whereas Job
finally is confronted by the living God and thus learns to accept his plight, the
author of Ludlul describes at great length the stages of his healing. His actual
relationship with Marduk is left unexplored, while the relationship between
God and Job stands at the heart of the biblical work.

Ancient wisdom writings sometimes are also in dialogue form, such as the
Babylonian Theodicy, an acrostic poem of twenty-seven stanzas with eleven
lines each. Dated by Lambert *ca.* 1000, this poem is a conversation between
a sufferer who complains of social injustice and a friend who tries to harmonize
this with traditional views of divine justice.[21]

Orphaned at an early age, the sufferer wonders why the gods did not protect
him instead of giving inequitable support and protection to his parents' firstborn. The friend responds that piety will bring prosperity:

He who waits on his god has a protecting angel,
The humble man who fears his goddess accumulates wealth.

The sufferer counters with examples from both society and nature of violations
of this principle. But the friend is convinced that all abuses of justice will be
corrected and urges the sufferer to maintain piety and patience. The sufferer
continues his plea of injustice, even blaming his dire condition on religious
devotion:

I have looked around society, but the evidence is contrary.

---

21. Lambert, *Babylonian Wisdom Literature*, pp. 63-91.

The god does not impede the way of a devil.
A father drags a boat along the canal,
While his first-born lies in bed.

. . . . . .

The heir stalks along the road like a bully,
The younger son will give food to the destitute.

How have I profited that I have bowed down to my god?
I have to bow beneath the base fellow that meets me;
The dregs of humanity, like the rich and opulent, treat me with con-
    tempt. (243-46, 249-253)

The friend, now somewhat impressed by these arguments, takes refuge in the
thought that the ways of the gods are past knowing:

The divine mind, like the centre of the heavens, is remote;
Knowledge of it is difficult; the masses do not know it. (256f.)

Finally, both friend and sufferer seem to agree that the gods are ultimately
responsible for human injustice, since they fashioned people with a bent in this
direction. The friend acknowledges that the deities

Gave perverse speech to the human race.
With lies, and not truth, they endowed them forever.

Solemnly they speak in favour of a rich man,
"He is a king," they say, "riches go at his side."

But they harm a poor man like a thief,
They lavish slander upon him and plot his murder,

Making him suffer every evil like a criminal, because he has no *protection*.
Terrifyingly they bring him to his end, and extinguish him like a flame.
    (279-286)

The sufferer concludes by reaffirming his plight and pleading for respite.

In a real sense the dialogue ends by begging the question. Responsibility
for people's evil conduct is placed squarely on the gods. But some important
points are glossed over. Is the ultimate answer that the gods are unjust? If so,
what responsibilities are people to take for their actions? The differences from
Job's approach to the problem of suffering or injustice are apparent. In the
biblical account God's intervention provides the solution, and though his righteousness may be questioned, it is sustained at the end of the dialogue.

From a later period comes the Babylonian Dialogue of Pessimism, usually
dated to the first half of the first millennium. This dialogue between a master
and his slave follows a simple pattern: a nobleman tells his slave of his plans
to enjoy a certain recreation or pleasure. The slave replies by outlining the
merits of that proposition. Then abruptly the master decides not to carry out

his plans. Promptly and dutifully the slave gives cogent reasons for not following the plan:[22]

> "Slave, listen to me." "Here I am, sir, here I am."
> "Quickly, fetch me the chariot and hitch it up so that I can drive to
>   the open country."
> "Drive, sir, drive. A hunter gets his belly filled.
> The hunting dogs will break the (prey's) bones,
> The hunter's falcon will settle down,
> And the fleeting wild ass . . .(.)"
> "No, slave, I will by no means [drive] to the open country."
> "Do not drive, sir, do not drive.
> The hunter's luck changes:
> The hunting dog's teeth will get broken,
> The home of the hunter's falcon is in [. . .] wall,
> And the fleeting wild ass has the uplands for its lair." (17-28)
> . . . . . .
> "Slave, listen to me." "Here I am, sir, here I am."
> "I am going to love a woman." "So love, sir, love.
> The man who loves a woman forgets sorrow and fear."
> "No, slave, I will by no means love a woman."
> ["Do not] love, sir, do not love.
> Woman is a pitfall—a pitfall, a hole, a ditch.
> Woman is a sharp iron dagger that cuts a man's throat." (46-52)

Somewhat like in Ecclesiastes, various possibilities for pleasure and public service are suggested and then discarded. None seems worthwhile to the master, who has lost his appetite for life. The conclusion, however, is poles apart from that of the skeptical Old Testament Preacher:

> "Slave, listen to me," "Here I am, sir, here I am."
> "What, then, is good?"
> "To have my neck and your neck broken
> And to be thrown into the river is good.
> 'Who is so tall as to ascend to the heavens?
> Who is so broad as to compass the underworld?' "
> "No, slave, I will kill you and send you first."
> "And my master would certainly not outlive me by even three days."
>   (79-86)

SCOPE OF BIBLICAL WISDOM LITERATURE

Role of the Wise Man. Like their Babylonian, Canaanite, Edomite, and Egyptian neighbors, Israel had, from the beginnings of national consciousness,

---

22. This analysis follows the more serious interpretation of the text rather than Speiser's satirical interpretation, evaluated by Lambert, *Babylonian Wisdom Literature*, pp. 139-141; the quotations are from pp. 145-49. See also T. Jacobsen in H. Frankfort et al., *The Intellectual Adventure of Ancient Man* (Chicago: 1946), pp. 216-18 and W.S. LaSor, pp. 104-6 in G. Rendsburg et al., eds., *The Bible World*.

people famed for wisdom. Skill in dispensing advice was not limited to men, for early in Israel's history are several references to wise women. The song of Deborah mentions the answer of the "wisest ladies" on whom Sisera's mother depended for advice (Judg. 5:29). Similarly, 2 Sam. 14:2-20 cites the "wise woman" of Tekoa, who was apparently more than a professional mourner. Her words in v. 14 suggest that she was familiar with the proverbial sayings of the wisdom circles: "We must all die, we are like water spilt on the ground, which cannot be gathered up again." Other early examples include David's counselor, Ahithophel: "Now in those days the counsel which Ahithophel gave was as if one consulted the oracle of God; so was all the counsel of Ahithophel esteemed, both by David and by Absalom" (2 Sam. 16:23); and the wise woman of Abel (a place famous for its wise counsel), who "went to all the people in her wisdom" (20:22).[23]

Israel's wisdom movement undoubtedly began in clan life, where it was used to prepare each generation to assume responsibilities of family, land, and social leadership.[24] However, wisdom took on new significance under Solomon, whose court offered support and prestige. The literary aspects are rooted in this period, when Solomon's wealth, international contacts, and cultural pursuits combined to launch the movement that produced the biblical wisdom writings. Solomon's stellar role in the development of this official wisdom is attested in 1 Kgs. 4:29-34 (MT 5:9-14):

> And God gave Solomon wisdom and understanding beyond measure, and largeness of mind like the sand on the seashore, so that Solomon's wisdom surpassed the wisdom of all the people of the east, and all the wisdom of Egypt. . . . He also uttered three thousand proverbs; and his songs were a thousand and five. . . . And men came from all peoples to hear the wisdom of Solomon, and from all the kings of the earth, who had heard of his wisdom.

(See also Prov. 1:1; 10:1; 25:1.)

The precise setting within which the movement flourished is a matter of question. The general consensus is that Solomon and his successors established schools, modeled after those in Egypt, to train administrators, scribes, and other officials for the tasks of the centralized government. Though sensible, this supposition lacks much biblical support. The first actual mention of a school in Jewish literature is in the time of Sirach (ca. 180; Sir. 51:23). Thus despite the traditional interpretation of Jer. 18:18, which seems to point to the existence of three offices—prophet, priest, wise man—R.N. Whybray has raised

---

23. The use of other wisdom techniques, like fables (e.g., Judg. 9:8-15) and riddles (e.g., 14:12-19), is further evidence of the role of the wise in Israel. See E. Jones, *Proverbs and Ecclesiastes*. Torch Bible Commentary (Naperville: 1961), pp. 28-31.

24. On clan life as a setting for the development of both wisdom and legal sayings, see E. Gerstenberger, "The Woe-Oracles of the Prophets," *JBL* 81 (1962): 249-263; and H.W. Wolff, *Amos the Prophet: The Man and His Background*, trans. F. McCorley, ed. J. Reumann (Philadelphia: 1973).

strong doubt that the wise in Israel occupied a special office or constituted a separate class. Rather, he has concluded, they were the intelligentia, regardless of their vocation or profession.[25]

Prov. 25:1 indicates that Hezekiah also served as patron of the sages. By the time of Jeremiah (*ca.* 600) the wise man on occasion could be compared in prestige and influence to the prophets and priests. Like other religious leaders, the sages drew the prophet's fire for failing to discharge their duties in obedience to God and his word:

> The wise men shall be put to shame,
>   they shall be dismayed and taken;
> lo, they have rejected the word of the Lord,
>   and what wisdom is in them? (Jer. 8:9)

Again, Jeremiah's enemies acknowledge the prominence of the wise men when they seek to refute Jeremiah's prophecy that the law would perish from the priest, counsel from the wise, and the word from the prophet (18:18). Perhaps the clearest testimony to the prestigious position of sages during this period is the extent to which the prophets used wisdom sayings and techniques in their writings. Amos' writings are laced with wisdom motifs, e.g., the three-four pattern of chs. 1–2 (see Prov. 30:15, 18, 21, 24, 29; cf. Job 5:19) and disputation questions of 3:3-8; 6:12. Prophetic use of wisdom forms also indicates that divisions of office should not be considered ironclad.[26]

The wise were obligated to counsel people who faced difficult decisions or needed advice as to the proper course of action, including leaders of government.[27] Much of this advice probably was dispensed in proverbial form. The truly wise person had ready access to sayings which would speak pungently and clearly to an inquirer's problem (note Eccl. 12:9: "Besides being wise, the Preacher also taught the people knowledge, weighing and studying and arranging proverbs with great care"; also v. 11: "The sayings of the wise are like goads, and like nails firmly fixed are the collected sayings which are given by one Shepherd"). Also, the sages were to contemplate the perplexing issues of life and make appropriate pronouncements or observations. Job and Ecclesiastes are the most notable examples. This phase of wisdom is as close as the Hebrews came to what the Greeks called "Philosophy," though the differences are marked.

Characteristics of Biblical Wisdom. In garnering their wise sayings, the sages knew no limitations of culture or nationality. In fact, one distinctive of wisdom literature is its international character. Proverbs of one society can be borrowed

---

25. *The Intellectual Tradition in the Old Testament.* BZAW 135 (1974).

26. See J. Lindblom, "Wisdom in the Old Testament Prophets" in M. Noth and D. W. Thomas, eds., *Wisdom in Israel and in the Ancient Near East.* VTS 3 (1955): 192-204; also Wolff, *Amos the Prophet*; J. W. Whedbee, *Isaiah and Wisdom* (Nashville: 1970).

27. The role of the wise as statesmen has been stressed, perhaps overly, by McKane, *Prophets and Wise Men.*

easily by another, because their very character as observations based on study or reflection upon life gives them a universality not always found in epic or historical writings.

Accordingly, wisdom in the ancient Orient and the Old Testament tends to emphasize the success and well-being of the individual. This individualism contrasts with the prophets' marked emphasis on national and corporate religious life. The great themes of Israel's faith—election from Egypt, the covenant relationship with Yahweh, official worship, the day of the Lord—play little part in wisdom writings. Further, almost no references to Israel's history are found. This, however, should not be interpreted as meaning that wisdom in Israel was a secular matter or that Israel's wisdom writings did not differ from those of their neighbors. Far from it! No one can read Job, Proverbs, or Ecclesiastes without hearing overtones of Israel's distinctive faith.[28] For the true Israelite all wisdom stemmed from God and was available to human beings only because they were creatures of God, capable of receiving his revelation. But more than this, only the devout worshiper, who feared God, could really begin to be wise. Wisdom based on human skill or ingenuity was a gift of God, part of his order in creation. But without awe of God and obedience to him, wisdom was doomed to defeat because of pride and presumption. Part of the fear of God for Israel's wise men was their reverence for the divine order in creation that governed all of life, rewarding sound judgment and behavior and inflicting harmful consequences on foolishness.[29]

Biblical Wisdom Writings. In the broadest sense of "wisdom" as "didactic or instructive literature," Job, Proverbs, and Ecclesiastes are clearly the three great contributions of Israel's sages to the Old Testament. In addition, certain Psalms reflect wisdom themes (see 1, 32, 34, 37, 49, 73, 112, 127–28, 133; see above, Ch. 40, p. 522). They either contain precepts or admonitions (rather than hymns or prayers) or deal with perplexing questions like prosperity of the wicked and adversity of the righteous. Both Song of Solomon and Lamentations reflect considerable wisdom influence in their graphic figures of speech and highly stylized forms, particularly the acrostic patterns of Lamentations. Moreover, both Job and Ecclesiastes, though examples of speculative wisdom, contain numerous proverbs.

---

28. See D.A. Hubbard, "The Wisdom Movement and Israel's Covenant Faith," *Tyndale Bulletin* 17 (1966): 3-33.

29. On order as foundational to wisdom thinking, see W. Zimmerli, "Concerning the Structure of Old Testament Wisdom," pp. 175-199 in J.L. Crenshaw, ed., *Studies in Ancient Israelite Wisdom* (New York: 1976): "God's claims need not be called into conflict with those of man. Rather, it is his belief that man's requirements in life are best cared for within the divine order of the world, and that man's real claim on advantage will be entirely satisfied through willing participation in the world's divine ordering" (p. 198); G. von Rad, *Wisdom in Israel*, trans. J.D. Martin (Nashville: 1972): "One becomes competent and expert as far as the orders in life are concerned only if one begins from knowledge about God" (p. 67); H.H. Schmid, *Wesen und Geschichte der Weisheit*. BZAW 101 (1966): 21.

In the New Testament the wisdom school is reflected in many of Christ's teachings, particularly his proverbs and parables drawn from nature, and in his ability to pose and solve puzzling questions. As the "greater than Solomon" (Matt. 12:42), Christ was the master sage, fulfilling this Old Testament office as well as those of prophet, priest, and king. The epistle of James, which stresses the wisdom from above (3:15) and uses analogies from nature and proverbs, is an outstanding example of New Testament wisdom literature.[30]

FOR FURTHER READING

Crenshaw, J.L. *Old Testament Wisdom: an Introduction*. Atlanta: 1981. (A fine survey of the whole field.)

Emerton, J.A. "Wisdom." Pp. 214-237 in G.W. Anderson, ed., *Tradition and Interpretation*. (Esp. pp. 221-231, "The Wisdom Literature and Other Parts of the Old Testament.")

Gammie, J.G. et al., eds. *Israelite Wisdom*. Festschrift S.L. Terrien. New York: 1978. (Theological and literary essays.)

Hubbard, D.A. "Wisdom." *IBD*, pp. 1650f. (Parts of the preceding discussion were adapted from this article.)

———. "Wisdom Literature." *IBD*, pp. 1651f. (Parts of the preceding discussion were adapted from this article.)

Mack, B.L. "Wisdom Myth and Mythology." *Interp* 24 (1970): 46-60. (Depicts creativity of wisdom schools in interpreting postexilic situation.)

Morgan, D.F. *Wisdom in the Old Testament Traditions*. Atlanta: 1981. (A review of the role of wisdom in the various periods of biblical literature.)

Murphy, R.E. *Wisdom Literature*. Forms of the Old Testament Literature 13. Grand Rapids: 1981.

Scott, R.B.Y. *The Way of Wisdom in the Old Testament*. New York: 1971. (Particularly insightful on differences between Old Testament and ancient Near Eastern wisdom.)

Wilken, R.L. *Aspects of Wisdom in Judaism and Early Christianity*. Notre Dame: 1975. (Cross cultural essays on wisdom in late antiquity.)

---

30. For the contribution of wisdom literature to the New Testament, see H. Conzelmann, "Wisdom in the NT," *IDBS*, pp. 956-960.

CHAPTER 42

PROVERBS

THE book of Proverbs is actually a collection of collections. The variety in literary style illustrates the wide range of the Hebrew *māšāl*, apparently derived from a root meaning "to be like" or "compared with."[1] Thus, a proverb originally may have been a comparison of a type found frequently in the Old Testament:

> Pleasant words are like a honeycomb,
> sweetness to the soul and health to the body. (Prov. 16:24)

or:

> Better is a dinner of herbs where love is
> than a fatted ox and hatred with it. (15:17)

Frequently, however, no comparison appears even in the oldest proverbs (e.g., "Out of the wicked comes forth wickedness"; 1 Sam. 24:13). Rather these sayings comprise pithy, succinct phrases which condense the wisdom of experience. In Prov. 1–9 *māšāl* also describes the longer, sermonlike passages which are not strictly proverbs (cf. Job's speeches, 27:1; 29:1). Elsewhere it may denote a byword (Deut. 28:37; Jer. 24:9; Ezek. 14:8) or a taunt song (Isa. 14:4ff.), in which apparently the sufferer becomes an object lesson.[2]

PURPOSE

Hebrew wisdom is the art of success, and Proverbs is a guidebook for successful living. By citing and illustrating both negative and positive rules of life, Proverbs

---

1. Some scholars connect *māšāl* with the root "to rule," so a proverb was originally a word spoken by a ruler and therefore filled with special power and meaning; see A. Bentzen, *Introduction* 1:168.
2. See A.R. Johnson, "מָשָׁל," VTS 3 (1955): 162-69. See W. McKane, *Proverbs: A New Approach*, p. 26, for the assumption that *māšāl* "has some such meaning as 'model,' 'exemplar,' 'paradigm.' "

Wisdom of Amenemope, Egyptian proverbs which bear resemblance to Prov. 22:17–23:11. (British Museum)

clarifies right and wrong conduct in a host of situations. The absence of allusions to Israel's history and the great prophetic themes (e.g., the covenant) does not mean that the authors were unaware of them. Rather, their aim was to apply the principles of Israel's covenant faith to everyday attitudes and experiences. The laws of love (Lev. 19:18; Deut. 6:5; cf. Mark 12:29-31) are central Old Testament emphases, and Proverbs serves as an extended commentary on them. Every true Israelite was bound to view God's law as an unconditional obligation demanding full allegiance and total obedience.[3]

This lies very close to the concept of the fear of the Lord which is the beginning of wisdom (Prov. 1:7; 2:5; 9:10; Job 28:28; Ps. 111:10). Akin to the knowledge of God as stressed in the great prophets, this obligation is the conscious concern with pleasing God in every aspect of living. The prime mission of Proverbs is to spell out strikingly, memorably, and concisely just what it means to be fully at God's disposal.

CONTENTS

Proverbs seems to contain at least eight separate collections, distinguishable by either an introductory subtitle or a striking change in literary style. Prov. 1:1-6

---

3. See W. Eichrodt, *Man in the Old Testament*, trans. K. and R.G. Smith. SBT 4 (London: 1951).

is a general introduction or superscription, clarifying both the book's purpose and its connection with Solomon, Israel's master sage.[4]

Importance of Wisdom (1:7–9:18). Chs. 1–9 illustrate the techniques of wisdom at the height of the movement in Israel. The teacher addresses the pupil as his son (e.g., 1:8; 2:1; 3:1) and maintains a paternalistic tone throughout. Oral instruction dominates, as the frequent references to hearing and memorizing indicate; writing scarcely is mentioned. The teacher would repeat the lessons for the student to memorize and quote verbatim. Although not so easy to remember as the shorter, disconnected sayings of chs. 10–22, these chapters contain numerous figures of speech and graphic expressions which aid the hearer's memory. Constant use of parallelism, the genius of Semitic poetry, was itself a help in memorizing.

The writer's purpose here is to draw the strongest possible contrast between the results of seeking and finding wisdom and those of pursuing a life of folly. Both wisdom and folly are intensely religious and extremely practical concepts. Wisdom begins with the fear of God and moves out into the whole range of life. Folly is not ignorance, but the deliberate disdain of moral and pious principles. The combination of moral depravity, spiritual irresponsibility, and social insensitivity described in Isa. 32:6 is an apt summary of Proverbs' view of the fool:[5]

For the fool speaks folly, and his mind plots iniquity:
to practice ungodliness, to utter error concerning the Lord,
to leave the craving of the hungry unsatisfied,
and to deprive the thirsty of drink.

Although by no means devoid of specific instructions, chs. 1–9 serve largely to clarify the issues involved in the choice of wisdom or folly, righteousness or wickedness, and to prepare for the several hundred specific proverbs which follow. While praising the virtues of true wisdom, the teacher sternly warns the pupil against certain prevalent temptations: crimes of violence (1:10-19; 4:14-19), binding oneself by a rash or hasty pledge (6:1-5), laziness (vv. 6-11), dishonesty (vv. 12-15), and especially sexual immorality (2:16-19; 5:3-20; 6:23-35; 7:4-27; 9:13-18). The vivid descriptions of the lurid charms of wanton women may refer not only to the dangers of physical unchastity but also to the menace of spiritual impurity—worship of false gods, often described by the prophets (particularly Hosea: 1:2; 2:13; 4:12-15; and Jeremiah: 3:1-13; 5:7f.) as adultery or harlotry. Because the Canaanite and other Near Eastern religions involved

4. B.S. Childs discusses the significance of this introduction in setting Proverbs in the international context of wisdom which Solomon represented (1 Kgs. 4:29-34; 10:1-29) and anchoring the wisdom movement to the beginnings of the Monarchy rather than the postexillic period; *Old Testament as Scripture*, pp. 551f.

5. Christ's warning in Matt. 5:22 against branding anybody a fool likely is based on these connotations of the word.

ritual cult prostitution the sage could issue both warnings at once. The profoundly religious character of these chapters (e.g., 1:7; 3:5-12), their moral and social concern, and the hortatory, sermonlike style are reminiscent of the speeches in Deuteronomy.[6]

The personification of wisdom in ch. 8 is of special importance. Here Wisdom is pictured as a woman calling the human family to follow her instruction and find the meaning of life. This personalization is not without precedent in the Old Testament. Job 28, for instance, describes Wisdom as a mystery which human beings in spite of all technological achievements (e.g., skill in mining, vv. 1-11) cannot discover. God alone knows the answer to wisdom's puzzle (vv. 23-28). In Prov. 1:20-33 Wisdom is a woman ranging through the streets and marketplaces pleading with persons to turn from their foolish ways and find instruction and security in her. Long life is in her right hand and wealth and honor in her left; and all her paths are peace (3:16f.).

This personalization peaks in 8:22-36, where Wisdom claims to have been created before all else, even suggesting that she assisted God in creation (v. 30; cf. 3:19).[7] These claims are more practical than theological: Wisdom presents her credentials so as to attract cordial allegiance (8:32-36). Thus it is somewhat hazardous to find here hypostatization, the view that wisdom has an independent existence. The Hebrews thought and wrote in concrete, not theoretical, terms. This resistance to speculation often led their poets to treat inanimate objects or ideas as though they had personality.[8]

This personification, which became even more intense during the intertestamental period (e.g., Sir. 24:1-34), has made significant contributions to New Testament christology. The doctrine of the *Lógos* "Word" in John 1:1-14 is based, in part at least, on Prov. 8: both wisdom and the Logos exist from the beginning (8:22; John 1:1); are active in creation (8:30; John 1:3); and have a life-giving influence (8:35; John 1:4).[9] Similarly, Paul's description of the

---

6. M. Weinfeld has argued strongly that the text of Deuteronomy was influenced deeply by the scribes and wise men of the Jerusalem court in Hezekiah's time and later; "The Origins of the Humanism in Deuteronomy," *JBL* 80 (1961): 241-47.

7. Heb. *'āmôn*, translated "as one brought up" in the KJV, probably should be read "craftsman" or "master workman" (RV, RSV). See W.F. Albright, "Some Canaanite-Phoenician Sources of Hebrew Wisdom," *VTS* 3 (1955): 8.

8. See H.W. Robinson, *Inspiration and Revelation in the Old Testament*, p. 260: "Clearly this is a strong and remarkable personification of Wisdom. . . . Wisdom is not an entity in its own right, though this poetical description depicts it as having an independent existence." Note G. von Rad, *Wisdom in Israel*, p. 153: Wisdom in Prov. 8 "has no divine status, nor is it a hypostatized attribute of Yahweh; it is, rather, something created by Yahweh and assigned to its proper function." For a review of alleged Canaanite and Egyptian backgrounds of this personification, see J.A. Emerton, "Wisdom," pp. 231-33 in G.W. Anderson, ed., *Tradition and Interpretation*.

9. C.H. Dodd, *The Interpretation of the Fourth Gospel* (Cambridge: 1953), p. 275: "It is difficult to resist the conclusion that, while the Logos . . . has many of the traits of the Word of God in the Old Testament, it is on the other side a concept closely similar to that of Wisdom, that is to say, the hypostatized thought of God projected in creation, and remaining as an immanent power within the world and in man." See also H. Ringgren, *Word and Wisdom* (Lund: 1947), for a survey of the personification of wisdom in the ancient Near East.

lordship of Christ in Col. 1:15-20 contains overtones of Prov. 8, and the specific references to Christ as the source of true wisdom (1 Cor. 1:24, 30) are deeply rooted in Proverbs.[10]

The question of the authorship of these chapters may never be answered conclusively. The superscription (1:1-6) seems to credit the entire book to Solomon. Since he is mentioned again specifically as author of the collection which begins at 10:1, chs. 1–9 are probably the product of anonymous sages. Usually considered among the latest sections of the book, these essays may have been included as late as 600 B.C., although much of the material seems to stem from an earlier age. Noting a number of parallels in thought and structure between this section (especially chs. 8–9) and Ugaritic and Phoenician literature, W.F. Albright concludes that "it is entirely possible that aphorisms and even longer sections go back into the Bronze Age in substantially their present form."[11] In sharp contrast with the tendency of some recent studies to date wisdom materials by length, placing shorter sayings earlier and longer speeches later,[12] the existence of longer wisdom speeches in Egypt and Mesopotamia well before Solomon's time witnesses to the antiquity of this literary form. "Length can therefore no longer be regarded as a criterion for dating the various parts of the book."[13]

Proverbs of Solomon (10:1–22:16). This section of some 375 proverbs generally is considered the oldest in the book. Increased understanding of ancient Near Eastern wisdom literature and fresh light on the splendors of Solomon's reign have brought renewed appreciation for his role as patron of Israel's wisdom movement. Intimate contacts with the Egyptian court, access to foreign learning afforded by a far-flung empire, the comparative peace of his reign, administrative innovations calling for a highly trained bureaucracy, and fabulous wealth which could support companies of scribes and recorders enabled Solomon to pursue cultural interests on a scale impossible to his heirs. Coupled with his God-given wisdom (1 Kgs. 3:9-28), these factors strongly support biblical claims concerning his activities as a wise man (1 Kgs. 4:29ff. [MT 5:9ff.]; Prov. 1:1; 10:1; 25:1).[14]

---

10. See W.D. Davies, "The Old and the New Torah: Christ the Wisdom of God," pp. 147-176 in *Paul and Rabbinic Judaism* (New York: 1967). For a thorough discussion of the contribution of wisdom thought to christology, especially regarding the preexistence of Christ, see R.G. Hamerton-Kelly, *Pre-existence, Wisdom, and the Son of Man*. Society for New Testament Studies Monograph 21 (Cambridge: 1973).

11. VTS 3 (1955): 5.

12. See O. Kaiser, *Introduction*, p. 379.

13. R.N. Whybray, "Book of Proverbs," *IDBS*, p. 702. Whybray (*Wisdom in Proverbs*. SBT 45 [London: 1965]) and C. Kayatz (*Studien zu Proverbien 1–9*. WMANT 22 [1966]) have sought connections between the longer wisdom speeches of chs. 1–9 and their Egyptian counterparts.

14. For the impetus given wisdom literature and history writing during the reigns of David and Solomon, see M. Noth, *History*, pp. 216-224. The bleaker side of Solomon's reign was its oppressive financial burden and consequent loss of freedom for Israel's citizenry; see W. Brueggemann, *In Man We Trust* (Richmond: 1972), pp. 64-77.

These proverbs usually consist of two stichs (lines). In chs. 10–15 the poetic structure is largely antithetic: the second line of the parallelism states an idea opposite to that of the first:

A son who gathers in summer is prudent,
> but a son who sleeps in harvest brings shame. (10:5)

or:

The memory of the righteous is a blessing . . .
> but the name of the wicked will rot. (v. 7)

This structure is admirably suited to wisdom teaching because it makes clear both the negative and the positive courses of attitude or conduct. Furthermore, it depicts in graphic form the conviction of the sages that ultimately people have only two ways to walk—the way of the righteous (wise) or that of the wicked (foolish), of blessing or dire judgment (cf. Ps. 1).

Chs. 16–22 use antithetic parallelism sparingly. The predominant patterns are synthetic parallelism, in which the second line completes the first:

The Lord has made everything for its purpose,
> even the wicked for the day of trouble. (16:4)

and synonymous parallelism, in which the second line restates the first:

Pride goes before destruction,
> and a haughty spirit before a fall. (v. 18)

The sayings in chs. 10–22 show little continuity, and no system of grouping is discernible. All but a handful are classified as statements or affirmations (German *Aussagen*), with verbs in the indicative mood. They contain concisely summarized observations from experience:

A friend loves at all times,
> and a brother is born for adversity. (17:17)

or:

A cheerful heart is a good medicine,
> but a downcast spirit dries up the bones. (v. 22)

The lesson in each is implied; no direct exhortation is given to the student.[15]
An alternate form is the "better" proverb:

Better is a little with righteousness
> than great revenues with injustice. (16:8; cf. 12:9; 15:16f.; 16:19; 17:1)

---

15. This type is "self-confirming, commending itself to empirical validation or to disconfirmation": J. Crenshaw, "Wisdom," p. 231 in J.H. Hayes, ed., *Old Testament Form Criticism*.

This comparison contrasts righteousness as so infinitely preferable to injustice that no amount of wealth can compensate for its absence.

Another form of comparison is based on "like" or "as":

Like vinegar to the teeth, and smoke to the eyes,
  so is the sluggard to those who send him. (10:26; cf. 11:22; 16:24;
  17:8)

At times the comparison is implied, with no connecting word:

The crucible is for silver, and the furnace is for gold,
  and the Lord tries hearts. (17:3)

Such comparisons demonstrate the Hebrew belief in "visible connections which point to an all-embracing order in which both phenomena [in the comparison] are linked with each other."[16] This order is what the wise men sought to understand and express in their proverbs.

Despite some religious emphasis (see 15:3, 8, 9, 11; 16:1-9), most of these proverbs are not related explicitly to Israel's faith but are based on practical observations of everyday life. Their point is intensely practical, frequently stressing the profits or rewards of wise living (see 11:18, 25-31). Some biblical scholars, believing that pure religion should involve worship of God for what he is and not for what he gives, have criticized this concern.[17] But since God had not yet revealed the mystery of life after death or the role of suffering in his redemptive program, how could a practical scribe have made his point without highlighting the blessings of the wise and the pitfalls of the fool?[18]

Words of the Wise (22:17–24:22). The title of this section has been concealed in 22:17 by the Masoretic text and English versions:

Incline your ear, and hear the words of the wise,
  and apply your mind to my knowledge.

---

16. Von Rad, *Wisdom in Israel*, p. 120.

17. See. N.K. Gottwald, *A Light to the Nations*, (New York: 1959), p. 472: "As the book of Proverbs now appears it is a potpourri of sayings and short poems, generally mediocre as literature, tedious as ethics, banal as religion. . . . In their obviousness the [religio-ethical] principles render God necessary only as the Guardian of the system." Von Rad is much more positive in judging the quality of the proverbs: "Only the man who has allowed his senses to be dulled in his dealing with the materials or who does not know the real purpose of this poetic wisdom can be deceived as to the magnitude of the intellectual achievement of our wisdom teachers"; *Wisdom in Israel*, p. 50.

18. How that doctrine of reward and retribution worked has been the subject of sharp debate. K. Koch sees the punishment meted out to the foolish as not the work of God directly but the inevitable result of their wicked acts—an almost automatic form of retribution (26:27), only occasionally aided by Yahweh. H. Gese also affirms a connection between an act and its consequences but allows for a greater degree of divine freedom and intervention (cf. 21:31). For a summary of these arguments, see Emerton, "Wisdom," pp. 216-18.

The more obvious heading, "These also are sayings of the wise" (24:23), implies that this is a separate collection. The identity of those who composed, collected, polished, and arranged the sayings is unknown. They may have been royal scribes commissioned to build a collection of useful maxims and sage observations (like Hezekiah's men, 25:1).

These proverbs, in contrast with the previous section, are generally longer (many being two or more verses in length), more closely related, and sustained in theme. Antithetic parallelism is rare (see 24:16), while synonymous and, especially, synthetic parallelism are frequent. The topics show considerable variety: concern for the poor (22:22, 27), respect for the king (23:1-3; 24:21f.), discipline of children (23:13f.), moderation in drinking (vv. 19-21, 29-35), obedience to parents (vv. 22-25), and moral purity (vv. 26-28). Here also a religious emphasis (22:19, 23; 24:18, 21) is present, although the proverbs are predominantly practical and the influence of Israel's faith is implicit rather than explicit.

The characteristic form of proverb here is the admonition or exhortation (German *Mahnwort*). These verbs are imperative or jussive (a third-person command, usually translated with "Let . . ."), either negative or positive:

Hearken to your father who begot you,
     and do not despise your mother when she is old. (23:22)

The exhortation carries the authority of the teachers and the experiences on which they drew but frequently is reinforced by explanatory clauses:

Be not among winebibbers, or among gluttonous eaters of meat;
     for the drunkard and the glutton will come to poverty,
     and drowsiness will clothe a man with rage. (vv. 20f.)

In these admonitions also, the idea of a divine order which governs the outcome of obedience and disobedience is implicit.

The sayings of 22:17–23:11 bear remarkable resemblance to a section of the Egyptian proverbs of Amenemope (Amenophis), probably *ca.* 1000 or somewhat earlier. For decades scholars have debated as to which collection influenced the other, although widespread agreement now favors Amenemope as the original.[19] Whatever their source, these proverbs have been shaped and molded by Israelite sages in terms of Israel's historic faith, and thus have become part of God's inspired message. For instance, Amenemope warns:

Guard thyself against robbing the oppressed
     And against overbearing the disabled. (ch. II)

---

19. See W. Baumgartner, p. 212 in *OTMS*. For a thorough review of the possible relationships between the two works, see G.E. Bryce, *A Legacy of Wisdom: The Egyptian Contribution to the Wisdom of Israel* (Lewisburg, Pa.: 1979).

while Proverbs adds a significant reason for abstaining from such robbery:

> Do not rob the poor, because he is poor,
> or crush the afflicted at the gate;
> for the Lord will plead their cause. . . . (22:22f.)

The following passages illustrate parallels between Proverbs and the Instruction of Amenemope:[20]

Amenemope	*Proverbs*
Give thy ears, hear what is said,	Incline your ear, and hear the words
Give thy heart to understand them.	of the wise,
To put them in thy heart is worth	and apply your mind to my
while. . . . (ch. I)	knowledge;
	for it will be pleasant if you keep
	them within you. . . . (22:17f.)
Do not carry off the landmark at the	Do not remove an ancient landmark
boundaries of the arable land,	or enter the fields of the fatherless;
Nor disturb the position of the	(23:10)
measuring-cord;	
Be not greedy after a cubit of land,	
Nor encroach upon the boundaries of	
a widow. (ch. VI)	
...they [riches] have made	For suddenly it takes to itself wings,
themselves wings like geese	flying like an eagle toward heaven.
And are flown away to the heavens.	(v. 5b)
(ch. VIII)	
Do not eat bread before a noble,	When you sit down to eat with a
Nor lay on thy mouth at first.	ruler,
If thou art satisfied with false	observe carefully what is before you;
chewings,	and put a knife to your throat if you
They are a pastime for thy spittle.	are a man given to appetite.
Look at the cup which is before	Do not desire his delicacies, for they
thee,	are deceptive food. (vv. 1-3)[21]
And let it serve thy needs.	
(ch. XXIII)	

Additional Sayings (24:23-34). This brief collection contains both concise proverbs (v. 26) and longer maxims (vv. 30-34; cf. 6:6-11). The keen sense of moral and social responsibility characteristic of Proverbs is much in evidence here (24:28f.), although with little stress on religion. This section also is the product of an anonymous company of wise men.

---

20. Trans. J. Wilson, *ANET*, pp. 421-25.
21. Some scholars connect *šilšôm* (read by the rabbis *šālîšîm* [AV, ASV "excellent things"]) in 22:20 with *šᵉlōšîm* (RSV "thirty") and suggest an allusion to the thirty chapters of Amenemope.

Proverbs of Solomon Copied by Hezekiah's Men (25:1–29:27). Both in style and content this section bears a number of similarities to 10:1–22:16 (e.g., compare 25:24 with 21:9; 26:13 with 22:13; 26:15 with 19:24). However, the proverbs here tend to vary in length. Antithetic parallelism is less frequent (although chs. 28–29 contain numerous examples), while comparison appears repeatedly here (25:3, 11-14, 18-20).

As with the proverbs in 10:1–22:16, there is no reason to doubt the Solomonic origin of this collection. The Jewish tradition[22] that Hezekiah and his company wrote Proverbs is based on 25:1. This reference accords well with the eighth-century king's interest in literature, implied by his restoration of patterns of worship instituted by David, including the singing of Davidic and Asaphic psalms (see 2 Chr. 29:25-30). His interest in these hymns and his concern for the Hebrew prophets (see Isa. 37) may well have been paralleled by his patronage of Israel's wisdom movement. Perhaps his scribes copied the proverbs in these chapters from an older manuscript specifically for this collection. Or they may have written down maxims which had been preserved in oral form from the early days of the Monarchy.[23] While it is not impossible that something of the turbulence of the eighth century is reflected here,[24] most of the allusions to kings or officials are general enough to fit the Solomonic period as well.

Words of Agur (30:1-33). Both Agur and his father Jakeh defy identification. They were probably from the tribe of Massa, descendants of Ishmael, who settled in northern Arabia.[25] If Agur and Lemuel (ch. 31) are Massaites, their collections of maxims are further examples of this international character of Hebrew wisdom, adopted and molded to the Israelites' covenant ideals.[26]

The precise thought of vv. 2-4 is difficult to discern. A slight sarcasm is detectable as the writer apparently quotes a skeptic who claims that little can be known about God, especially his role in the universe. The doubter chides the wise man to tell him about his God. The sage shuns argument and affirms the truthfulness of God's word and the security to be found in him (vv. 5f.; cf. Job 38–40, where Job is silenced when confronted personally by the Lord of the universe). Agur concludes this section by a brief but moving prayer that God supply only his real needs, lest either in poverty or self-sufficiency he be tempted to sin (vv. 7-9).

---

22. Talmud B. *Bat.* 15a.
23. See Bentzen, *Introduction* 2:173.
24. S.R. Driver senses an uneasiness about the Monarchy in this section in contrast with 10:1–22:16 (cf. 28:2, 12, 15ff., 28; 29:2, 4, 16); *Introduction*, p. 401.
25. This tribe (see Gen. 25:14; 1 Chr. 1:30) seems to be the Mas'a who paid tribute with Tema to Tiglath-pileser III. See also the Masanoi located by Ptolemy (*Geography* v.19.2) northeast of Duma. The proper name Massa in 30:1 (RSV) is translated "prophecy," "oracle" in AV, ASV.
26. Ithiel and Ucal (v. 1) have not been identified. A change in the division of the Hebrew words eliminates the names: "I have wearied myself, O God, I have wearied myself, O God, and am consumed" (cf. ASV mg., BDB).

The remainder of the chapter is largely observations from nature or social relationships which contain implicit lessons for successful living. A characteristic feature is the use of numerical patterns in the organization of the statements, particularly the x, x + 1 pattern ("three things . . . four . . .") well-attested in the Old Testament (Amos 1–2; Mic. 5:5) and Semitic (esp. Ugaritic[27]) literature. In wisdom literature this pattern creates a feeling of anticipation by building to a climax and is an aid to the hearer's memory. At times the numerical proverbs exhibit a gamelike quality which may bear some ancient connection to the riddle.[28]

Words of Lemuel (31:1-9). Like Agur, this king of Massa is unknown. His brief collection consists of sage advice by his mother to prepare him for office. She warns him to avoid excess with women and wine and encourages him to protect the rights of the poor and underprivileged. The rabbinic tradition that Lemuel and the names in 30:1 are epithets of Solomon is an obvious attempt to attribute the whole book to him and generally is not accepted.[29]

Description of a Virtuous Wife (31:10-31). Even though it has no separate title, this carefully polished anonymous poem is separated from the sayings of Lemuel by its alphabetical acrostic form. The highly self-conscious techniques involved in this form, a late development in Hebrew literature (see. Ps. 119), not only aided memorization but served to affirm the sense of wholeness embodied in this picture of the perfect wife and mother. This portrait of an industrious, competent, conscientious, pious woman is a conclusion well-suited to a book which teaches the nature and importance of a life lived in obedience to God in every detail.[30]

Limits of Wisdom. In seeking to interpret the various proverbs and apply them to life, one must bear in mind that they are generalizations. Though stated as absolutes—as their literary form requires—they are meant to be applied in specific situations and not indiscriminately. Knowing the right time to use a proverb was part of being wise:

---

27. See C.H. Gordon, *Ugaritic Textbook*. Analecta Orientalia 38 (Rome: 1965), §§7.7, 17.3.

28. On the numerical form, see von Rad, *Wisdom in Israel*, pp. 36f., 122f.; Crenshaw, "Wisdom," pp. 236-38. See also Ch. 23, p. 315.

29. One reason is the Aramaic influence here (e.g., *bar* "son," *mᵉlāḵîn* "kings").

30. For an interesting example of the light shed on Proverbs by Ugaritic studies, see G.R. Driver, "On a Passage in the Baal Epic (IV AB iii 24) and Proverbs xxxi 21," *BASOR* 105 (1947): 11. Driver suggests that v. 21 should read "clothed in double garments" (instead of "clothed in scarlet"), following the LXX (v. 22) and Vulgate and confirmed by a passage in the Baal epic; see M. Dahood, *Proverbs and Northwest Semitic Philology* (Rome: 1963), p. 620.

A word fitly spoken
  is like apples of gold in a setting of silver. (25:11)

Implicit, then, to a correct understanding of wisdom was the awareness of
its limits.[31] As effective as the proverbs were as a guide to success, they could
be misleading if viewed as magical sayings which would always and automatically
bring results. The best spirits among the wise warned against such presumptive
self-confidence and made room for God to work his sovereign surprises:

A man's mind plans his way,
  but the Lord directs his steps. (16:9; cf. vv. 1f.; 21:31)

In part at least, the failure of the wisdom circles to follow their own convictions about these limits led to the sharp reactions of Job and Ecclesiastes.

DATE OF THE COLLECTION

Prov. 25:1 makes clear that the book could not have been completed before
Hezekiah's time (ca. 715-686). The last two chapters may well have been added
during or shortly after the Exile (ca. 500). Most likely chs. 10–29 were edited
during Hezekiah's time and the introductory and concluding chapters were
added during the two following centuries. The fifth century is a reasonable date
for the final editing, although most of the contents are much earlier, with most
individual proverbs and even longer speeches stemming from long before the
Exile.[32]

Attempts to date various sayings within the book as later than others
because they are overtly religious[33] should be disregarded. The entire background of the sayings so clearly implies a faith in Yahweh that no distinction
can be made in dating between verses that mention his work and those that do
not. His presence in the order which he created and sustains is presumed in
every saying: "The experiences of the world were for [Israel] always divine
experiences as well, and the experiences of God were for her experiences of the
world."[34]

PROVERBS AND THE NEW TESTAMENT

New Testament writers have drawn freely from Proverbs to support their teachings. For instance, a number of quotations and allusions are embedded in the
New Testament: e.g., 3:7a, Rom. 12:16, KJV; 3:11f., Heb. 12:5f.; 3:34, Jas.

---

31. See von Rad, *Wisdom in Israel*, pp. 97-110; also W. Zimmerli, "The Place and
Limit of Wisdom in the Framework of the Old Testament Theology," *SJT* 17 (1964):
146-158.
32. On literary grounds, Albright dates the contents of Proverbs before the seventh-
century Aramaic sayings of Ahiqar; *VTS* 3 (1955): 6.
33. McKane, *Proverbs*, pp. 17-21.
34. von Rad, *Wisdom in Israel*, p. 62; see Kaiser, *Introduction*, p. 383.

4:6 and 1 Pet. 5:5b; 4:26, Heb. 12:13a; 10:12, Jas. 5:20 and 1 Pet. 4:8; 25:21f., Rom. 12:20; 26:11, 2 Pet. 2:22. The Christ who came to fulfill the law and the prophets (Matt. 5:17) also fulfilled the wisdom writings by revealing the fullness of God's wisdom (Matt. 12:42; 1 Cor. 1:24, 30; Col. 2:3). As the "greater than Solomon," he used the techniques of the sages—proverbs, parables, illustrations from nature, puzzling questions—to gain his hearers' attention and fix his words in their hearts. If Proverbs is an extensive commentary on the law of love, then it is also part of the Old Testament preparation for the coming of the One in whom divine love took on human form.[35]

FOR FURTHER READING

Fox, M.V. "Aspects of the Religion of the Book of Proverbs." *HUCA* 39 (1968): 55-69. (*ḥokmâ*, in the sense of ethical-religious wisdom, viewed as a bridge to Hellenistic thought.)

Hubbard, D.A. "Proverbs, Book of." *IBD*, pp. 1290f. (Parts of the preceding discussion were adapted from this article.)

Kitchen, K.A. "Proverbs and Wisdom Books of the Ancient Near East: The Factual History of a Literary Form." *Tyndale Bulletin* 28 (1977): 69-114. (Prov. 1–24 is of second-millennium origin, formed into literary unity in early first millennium.)

Murphy, R.E. "Assumptions and Problems in Old Testament Wisdom Research." *CBQ* 29 (1967): 101-12 [407-18].

Scott, R.B.Y. *Proverbs–Ecclesiastes*. Anchor Bible 18. Garden City: 1965.

Thompson, J.M. *The Form and Function of Proverbs in Ancient Israel*. Hague: 1974. (Includes examination of skeptical element in Hebrew wisdom.)

Whybray, R.N. *The Book of Proverbs*. Cambridge Bible Commentary. New York: 1972.

Williams, J.G. *Those Who Ponder Proverbs: Aphoristic Thinking and Biblical Literature*. Sheffield: 1981. (The use of proverbial forms and themes throughout the Bible.)

---

35. See C.T. Fritsch, "The Gospel in the Book of Proverbs," *Theology Today* 7 (1950): 169-183; R.E. Murphy, "The Kerygma of the Book of Proverbs," *Interp* 20 (1966): 3-14. A list of "subject-studies" has been compiled by D. Kidner, *The Proverbs*. Tyndale Old Testament Commentary (Chicago: 1964), pp. 31-56.

CHAPTER 43

JOB

"**H**AVE you considered my servant Job?"—the pointed question that Yahweh put to Satan (1:8; 2:3)—triggered the forty-two chapters of suffering, complaint, argument, and response that comprise the book of Job. Few stories in the literature of human experience have such power to stretch minds, tax consciences, and expand vision as does Job's. No one who witnesses the disaster in the land of Uz, eavesdrops on the conversations in Yahweh's court, arbitrates the debate between Job and his friends, or shivers at the voice from the whirlwind can be the same again. One's view of divine sovereignty and freedom as well as one's picture of human suffering and arrogance and integrity will be altered forever. That is both the danger and the blessing of the book.

NAME AND PLACE IN CANON

The name Job (Heb. *'iyyôḇ*), which W.F. Albright has interpreted as "Where is (my) Father?", is attested in the Amarna letters (*ca.* 1350 B.C.) and the Egyptian Execration texts (*ca.* 2000). In both cases it is applied to tribal leaders in Palestine and its environs.[1] These occurrences lend weight to the possibility that the book recorded the ancient experience of an actual sufferer whose story was given its present setting by a later poet. However, the value of the story is in no way affected by the inability to determine whether it has a historical basis.

Two less likely interpretations of the name, which seek to find in it symbolic significance in keeping with the book's message, link it (1) to the root *'yb* "be an enemy," interpreted as either an active form (opponent of Yahweh) or a passive form (one whom Yahweh has treated as an enemy); or (2) to Arab. *'wb*, thus "one who repents."

---

1. M.H. Pope, *Job*. Anchor Bible, 3rd ed. (Garden City, N.Y.: 1979), pp. 5f. Another possible parallel is found in Akkadian texts from Mari and Alalakh; see W.F. Albright, "Northwest-Semitic Names in a List of Egyptian Slaves from the Eighteenth Century B.C.," JAOS 74 (1954): 222-233.

The book's presence in the canon has not been questioned,[2] but its location within that canon has been subject to debate. In the Hebrew tradition, Psalms, Job, and Proverbs almost always were linked, with Psalms first and the order of Job and Proverbs varying. The LXX differed widely in the placement of Job—one text put it at the end of the Old Testament, following Ecclesiasticus. The Latin versions established an order which the English tradition has followed primarily: Job, Psalms, Proverbs. Because of the story's alleged patriarchal setting and the belief that Moses was the author, the Syriac Bible inserts the book between the Pentateuch and Joshua. Uncertainty as to both date and literary genre accounts for this wide range.[3]

BACKGROUND

Date. Neither the ancient rabbis nor modern scholars exhibit a consensus as to the date of Job. The marks of antiquity are apparent in the prose prologue (1:1–2:13) and epilogue (42:7-17): (1) without priesthood or shrine, Job performed his own sacrifices (1:5); (2) his possessions, like Abraham's and Jacob's, were measured in sheep, camels, oxen, asses, and servants (1:3; cf. Gen. 12:16; 32:5; (3) his land was subject to raids of pillaging tribes (1:15-17); (4) Job's life span of 140 years is matched only in the Pentateuch (42:16); (5) the epic character of the prose story has its closest parallels in Genesis and Ugaritic literature; (6) an ancient, righteous hero named Job was cited by Ezekiel in connection with Noah and Daniel[4] (Ezek. 14:14, 20). Though the author deliberately may have coined such characteristics, most likely the prose story was indeed ancient and handed down by tradition from its original setting prior to 1000.[5]

Few scholars would date the poetic sections (3:1–42:6) so early. The affinities of Job to Jeremiah (compare 3:3-26 with Jer. 20:14-18), the latter half of Isaiah (especially the song of righteous suffering, 52:13–53:12), Ps. 8 (compare Job 7:17f. with Ps. 8:5f. [MT 6f.]), and Prov. 8 (compare 15:7f. with Prov. 8:22, 25) point to the seventh century or later.[6] Though it is fashionable to propose an exilic or postexilic date for final compilation, no compelling reason

---

2. Except by the famous exegete of the Antiochian school, Theodore of Mopsuestia (*ca.* A.D. 350-428).

3. For this and other technical matters, see. E. Dhorme, *A Commentary on the Book of Job*, trans. H. Knight (London: 1967), pp. vii-xii.

4. Daniel here is usually connected to the Ugaritic hero Dan'el rather than the biblical figure whose book is included among the Major Prophets. The Aqht legend describes Dan'el as a king who dispenses justice to the widow and fatherless. See S.B. Frost, "Daniel," *IDB* 1:761.

5. Evidences for the story's antiquity are discussed by Pope, "Book of Job," *IDB* 2:913f.; cf. Albright, *VTS* 3 (1955): 13 note 3.

6. Albright notes differences in poetic style and structure between Job and Ugaritic poetry and concludes that the author of Job probably lived in the sixth or fifth century; *ibid.*, p. 14.

to do so exists. The book concerns personal, not national, suffering. It is about God's freedom to impose unmerited pain and human willingness to accept it without losing faith. It does not concern the nature and limits of divine retribution as do Lamentations and Habakkuk. Its questioning of conventional wisdom need not mean that it was composed after the book of Proverbs; the points with which Job collided surely were prevalent long before final codification in Proverbs. All in all, completion of the work between 700 and 600 seems reasonable.[7]

Near Eastern Parallels. Additional support for a preexilic date is the presence from antiquity of stories of righteous sufferers. Such stories belong "to the category of higher Wisdom, which was speculative in temper, unconventional in approach, and concerned with ultimate issues."[8] None of these ancient tales (see Ch. 41) is a true parallel to Job. At most they show that, from the dawn of literature, people have been puzzled at the ways of the gods, especially when they entailed human suffering. Job's puzzlement, then, has a lengthy chain of precedent but no sign of direct ancestry. The differences in theology, ethics, tone, and mood between Job and alleged parallels (e.g., the Indian legend of Hariscandra, Sumerian Man and his God, Akkadian Ludlul Bēl Nēmeqi, Babylonian Theodicy, Egyptian Protests of the Eloquent Peasant, or Admonitions of Ipu-wer) are so striking as to highlight not Job's dependence on earlier documents but the uniqueness of the work:[9]

> Job stands far above its nearest competitors, in the coherence of its sustained treatment of the theme of human misery, in the scope of its many-sided examination of the problem, in the strength and clarity of its defiant moral monotheism, in the characterization of its protagonists, in the heights of its lyrical poetry, in its dramatic impact, and in the intellectual integrity with which it faces the 'unintelligible burden' of human existence.[10]

Authorship. The author of Job hides nameless in the background of his work while demonstrating overwhelming sensitivity to the human plight, capacity for massive theological understanding, grasp of vast areas of culture and learning, insight into deep struggles among opinionated persons, and skill in literary craftsmanship. Rarely in the history of artistic endeavor has anyone left such a noble legacy yet so little evidence of his identity, circumstances, or motive.

---

7. If Job is to be connected with any preexilic event, it would be the death of Josiah in 609 (2 Kgs. 23:29f.). Undoubtedly his tragic demise at the hands of the Egyptians so soon after his godly reforms would have shaken the standard beliefs in divine punishment and reward.

8. R. Gordis, *The Book of God and Man* (Chicago: 1965), p. 53.

9. For summaries see Pope, *Job*, pp. LVI-LXXI; F.I. Andersen, *Job*. Tyndale Old Testament Commentary (Downers Grove: 1976), pp. 23-32.

10. Andersen, *ibid*., p. 32.

Bedouin encampment similar to the pastoral setting of the story of Job. (W. S. LaSor)

Despite the author's personal reticence, a few assumptions seem reasonable: (1) He must have experienced something of Job's suffering himself, so authentic is his empathy. (2) He must have found release from his pain in some encounter with God akin to that so powerfully described in Yahweh's speeches from the whirlwind (38:1–41:34 [MT 26]; cf. Ps. 73:17). (3) He must have been thoroughly steeped in the wisdom techniques and tradition, as both the theme and the literary devices suggest. (4) His suffering must have set him at odds with the conventional wisdom, which taught absolute patterns of retribution within the divine order—blessing is always the fruit of righteousness, suffering ever the wage of sin. (5) He must have been an Israelite, as his view of divine sovereignty, call for divine justice, and impeccable code of ethical behavior (31:1-40) intimate. (6) He must have used the non-Israelite setting of Uz (whether south in Edom or east in Gilead) both because it was the source of the ancient story and because such suffering is a universal human woe. (7) In good Hebrew fashion, he must have wanted to share his experience to fortify friends and/or students against future suffering, even more skillfully than did his fellow wisemen in Pss. 37, 49, and 73.

STRUCTURE

Movement of the Book. While debate continues about the unity of Job (see below) and possible sources and backgrounds of the various parts, the thrust and movement of the work in its finished form must be sought. O. Kaiser cites K. Budde's analogy between the development of such a masterwork and the construction, often over centuries, of medieval cathedrals. Those massive sanctuaries arouse deep appreciation in their final architectural form, to which each stage contributed, and "to restore the original plans . . . would be an act of barbarism."[11] Dissecting Job into component parts actually may diminish one's understanding of its message. A glance at the book's literary structure reveals:

Prologue (prose)	chs. 1–2
Job's lament (poetry)	3
Dialogue between Job and Friends	4–27
(Poetry) in three cycles:	
Eliphaz [Job replies to each]	
Bildad	
Zophar	
Poem on Wisdom (poetry)	28
Job's complaint (poetry)	29–31
Elihu's speeches (poetry)	32–37
Yahweh's speeches (poetry)	38–42:6
Epilogue (prose)	42:7–17

The over-all form is A-B-A (prose-poetry-prose). The central dialogue, the heart of the work, is framed by Job's lament and complaint, giving him the first and last word in relation to his friends. The speeches of Elihu and Yahweh, which seek to resolve the matter, deliberately unbalance the symmetry to call attention to their intrusions and, thereby, to underscore the inability of the major participants to achieve a solution.

A more detailed look at the role of each section and its relation to the whole shows:

(1) A drama on a double stage: Job's prosperity and Yahweh's test (prose prologue, chs. 1–2). The narrative alternates between the land of Uz, where Job lives with integrity and piety, in prosperity (1:1-5) or in disaster (vv. 13-22; 2:7-13), and the court of Yahweh, where the Satan (see below) challenges Yahweh to test Job (1:6-12; 2:1-6). Dramatic contrast (tragic reversal) sharpens the pathos and spotlights Job's plight—the radical change from life with an ideal family and vast possessions to poverty, pain, and loneliness (1:1-5; 2:7f.). Repetition, delicate yet powerful, deepens the poignancy and increases the suspense—the standard description of Job's uprightness (1:1, 8; 2:3), the stereotyped account of the Satan's coming and going and conversation with Yahweh (1:6-8; 2:1-6; cf. 1:12b; 2:7a), the tragic report of the messenger (1:16f., 19), and the summary of Job's passing of the test (1:22; 2:10b).

The contribution of the prologue to the movement of the book is generous. It sets the stage for all conversation that follows and reveals to all readers the book's purpose, while veiling it from Job who sees only the scenes in Uz and remains utterly unaware of the tests in heaven. It shows that God's honor is on

---

11. Kaiser, *Introduction*, p. 391.

the line along with Job's—his trust in Job is the ultimate risk—and shows that God's interest lies more in Job's response of trust than in his personal comfort. It depicts God's sovereignty over the Satan, who can not harm Job beyond God's limits (1:12; 2:6), and sets up a deliberate tension with the conversations that follow by honoring Job's strong trust in Yahweh (1:21f.; 2:9f.). It introduces the three friends as sympathetic comforters, thus preparing for the sharp conflict that ensues.

(2) A fate worse than death: Job's despair and Yahweh's silence (poetic lament, ch. 3). With a despair matched only by Jeremiah's shorter lament (Jer. 20:14-18), Job both curses his birth (Job 3:1-10) and wails his complaint (vv. 11-26). This contrast with his controlled piety in the prologue is startling and deliberate. The author refuses to soften the shock with explanation or transition. Using characteristic Semitic hyperbole (emphasis by over-statement), he lays bare Job's full humanity. The trauma of loss has eased off, and the full horror of his plight has hit him. Job sees his life stripped of all signs of divine blessing and, therefore, all sources of joy.

Clearly, though implicitly, God has become his enemy: who else is responsible for the very survival which he questions? This attack on God's creative power, timing, and providence sets the tone for the dialogue that follows. No comfort is found in Israel's cult or history—realities on which the author is consciously silent: "it is in an existence totally without community or saving history that Job in steely isolation carries on his struggle with God."[12]

(3) A comfort more painful than censure: three accusers and one defender (poetic dialogue, chs. 4–27). Here the author's genius shines through both in detail and over-all execution. The conversational form, with each friend given two or three times to speak, enriches the debate both through repetition and variety. Each friend speaks from a different perspective—Eliphaz as a gentle mystic (chs. 4–5, 15, 27; esp. 4:12-31), Bildad as a firm traditionalist (chs. 8, 18, 25; esp. 8:8-10), Zophar as a rash dogmatist (chs. 11, 20; esp. 11:5f.).[13] The basic message of each is the same: unaware of the prologue's heavenly test, each calls Job to repent of the sin that must have caused his suffering (Eliphaz, 4:7-11; 15:12-16; 22:21-30; Bildad, 8:3-7; Zophar, 11:13-15).

Job's responses relentlessly affirm his innocence (6:24f.; 9:15, 20f.; 13:18, 23; 23:7, 10-12; 27:2-6), though he variously wishes to die (6:8-13), chides his friends' treachery (vv. 14-23), laments his demeaned status (7:1-6), berates God for his suffering (vv. 11-21), despairs of his ability to win an argument with God (ch. 9), reflects on the power and mystery of God's ways (12:7-25), begs for opportunity to put his case before God without the friends' intervention (13:3-28), depicts the ruthlessness of God which ought to be avenged (16:6-22; ch. 19), argues that God does not always follow established patterns of justice

---

12. G. von Rad, *Old Testament Theology*, I:412.
13. On the structure of the third cycle (chs. 22–27), which in its present form has no speech credited to Zophar, see below.

but allows the wicked to thrive (chs. 21, 24), and cowers in terror at the thought of God's elusive yet awesome presence (23:3-17). The repetition heats the argument to boiling and thus both tautens the suspense and rivets the reader to the issues. The conversational (dialogue) pattern indicates the interpersonal character of suffering—understanding can make it bearable, but rejection can turn it intolerable. Job's responses, often in the form of psalmlike complaints (e.g., 9:15-35; 13:23-28; 16:6-17), show that while he is at odds with his friends' dogma, his more substantial quarrel is with God, who he knows is responsible. Job's protest is not that he is sinless but that his suffering far exceeds any sin he may have committed. His responses are not always directed at the preceding speech but may reach back to earlier questions or arguments (e.g., Job in 9:3f., 15-24 speaks after Bildad, but he is actually answering Eliphaz's question "Can a mortal man be righteous before God?" [4:17]).[14]

The exquisite character of the poetry, with its balance, parallelism, compactness, sensitivity to sound, and fertile imagery, gives the dialogue power yet restraint. Despite the rounds of repetition, the intensified attacks of the friends, and Job's fortified attempts at defense, the dialogues reach no solution; the gulf is wider at the end than at the beginning, and further help from outside is the only hope.

(4) An interlude with a message: musings on the mystery of wisdom (poetic paean, ch. 28). This magnificent description of the wonders of wisdom and its inaccessibility to human enterprise seems to be the author's intervention. If part of Job's speech which began in 27:1, it probably is to be interpreted ironically. Job had feared God (28:28; cf. 1:1, 8; 2:3), but to no avail![15] If this is a purposeful interlude, it should be credited to the final author, who uses it to bring one phase of the book to a close and prepare for the next. As though reflecting on the stalemate to which the windy dialogue has led, he muses on the human inability to discover, buy, or discern true wisdom without divine help. Indeed, that is his summary of the book thus far: neither Job nor the friends have found the key. By pointing to the need for divine help ("God understands the way to [wisdom], and he knows its place," 28:23), he sparks anticipation for the speeches from the whirlwind (ch. 38).

(5) A protest against heaven: Job's calamitous fall and demonstrated innocence (poetic complaint, chs. 29–31). Skillfully prolonging the suspense, the author gives Job one more chance to state his case. Job does so in three ways that virtually summarize the book thus far. First, he reviews the scenes in the land of Uz by recounting his tragic reversal from blessing and prestige (ch. 29) to mockery and anguish (ch. 30). Next, he swears an oath of innocence, in which the ethical and religious virtues expressed in capsule form in the prose story (1:1, 8; 2:3) are amplified in expansive detail (31:1-34). Finally,

---

14. D. Robertson, *The Old Testament and the Literary Critic* (Philadelphia: 1977), p. 41.
15. This sarcastic interpretation of ch. 28 is developed by Robertson, *ibid.*, p. 46.

he restates his wish for a hearing with God, sealing that wish with a curse that he would be ready to endure if his guilt were proven (vv. 35-40). At the crucial point, when the author reaches out to resolve the issue. Job reaffirms his driving theme: he has done nothing to warrant his suffering; the next move is up to God—either to vindicate Job or destroy him.

(6) A rebuke and a lesson: Elihu's attempt to correct both Job and his friends (poetic discourse, chs. 32–37, with prose introduction, 32:1-5). The whole movement of the story thus far indicates that only if God appears can the matter find solution. The friends have shot their bolt; the dust of Job's final sally has begun to settle; the reader is ready to hear from God himself. Instead, with a surprise and suspense surely intended, a new figure is introduced. More than a little irony is expressed: even Elihu's name ("he is God") contributes to the humor. The name may be divine, but the approach is as human as those of the others.

Despite strong scholarly consensus that Elihu's speeches were inserted after the basic work had been completed, they play a significant role in the movement of the book. They enhance the suspense by postponing the climax. They reinforce understanding of the issues by reviewing Job's arguments (33:8-13) and repeating the friends' answer or trying new ones.[16] The speeches show that the younger wisdom[17] was essentially no more effective than the older, despite its great verbosity. They amplify the theme stated briefly by Eliphaz (5:17) that suffering may have a disciplinary and refining role in God's providence (33:14-30; 36:8-12).[18] These passages prepare for the voice of God, both by chiding Job's arrogant ignorance of God's ways (35:16; cf. 38:2) and by placarding God's majestic sovereignty over the whole creation as evidence of his trustworthiness in matters of justice (34:12-15; 36:24–37:24).[19] They give final evidence of earthly inability to fathom heaven's mysteries; like the others, Elihu had no knowledge of the test between Yahweh and the Satan.

(7) A voice that silences debate: Yahweh's revelation of his power and glory (poetic discourse, 38:1–42:6). Throughout the book, Job's problem has been with God, though his friends' dogmatic and astringent arguments increase

---

16. Gordis, *The Book of God and Man*, p. 105, notes that Job's major complaints against God—innocent suffering, unjust persecution, and refusal to hear—are answered in reverse order: refusal to hear (vv. 11-30), unjust persecution (34:1-30), innocent suffering (vv. 31-37).

17. Elihu's youth, vv. 6-10, may explain why he was not mentioned in the prologue; perhaps he tagged along as a student of the others and was treated as part of the entourage not worthy of being named.

18. According to Gordis, Elihu holds that suffering is in part a "warning to the righteous, not only against sins both actual and patent, but against offenses potential and latent"; *The Book of God and Man*, pp. 113f. Though this interpretation may be theologically sound, Elihu's words seem to assume actual sin—especially arrogance, as Gordis also stresses (p. 114).

19. Even in literary form Elihu's discussion of the glories of divine power resembles the speeches of Yahweh, especially in the use of disputational rhetorical questions (see 37:15-20; 38:31-35).

his aggravation. Eliphaz, Bildad, Zophar, and Elihu all seek to speak on God's behalf to clear Job's doubts and ease his struggle. To a man, they failed. Finally, it is Yahweh's turn.

The divine presence blasts the silence of Uz with all the force of a whirlwind (38:1). It is as though God himself is impatient with the author's tactics of surprise and suspense and brushes past him to confront Job with incredible power and directness. That confrontation merits several observations: (a) The style hurls at Job a seemingly inexhaustible stockpile of rhetorical questions carrying their own answers in a manner which renders Job defenseless. (b) Yahweh faces Job with the wonders of creation (38:4-11), the cycles, seasons, and order of the universe (vv. 12-38), the life patterns of animals and birds (38:39–39:30) as a cosmic and conclusive demonstration of the divine sovereignty governing all reality, presumably including Job's life. (c) Partial application of this power to Job's own history is implied only when God challenges whether Job also can effect righteous judgments in history (40:10-14). (d) Yahweh gives no direct answer to Job's quandary, disclosing neither its reason nor the Satan's test. (e) Yahweh's battery of arguments confirms Job's worst predictions of what would happen if they met: "If one wished to contend with him, one could not answer him once in a thousand times. . . . If it is a contest of strength, behold him!" (9:3, 19). (f) Repetition is used characteristically to heighten the intensity of the theophany and to overwhelm Job doubly, reducing him almost to speechless submission (40:3-5; 42:1-6): Yahweh's second speech focuses sharply on two creatures—Behemoth (hippopotamus? 40:15-24) and Leviathan (crocodile? 41:1-34 [MT 40:25–41:26])—whose habits are beyond human reckoning; the first speech sweeps broadly around the universe, without lingering on the details of any one aspect. (g) Job's last word is the one he has resisted throughout the tense and tedious debate with his friends: "therefore I despise myself, and repent in dust and ashes" (42:6).[20] (h) Job's contrition is not an admission that his suffering is deserved because of sin, but rather that his complaints against God stem from his not having known God well enough (vv. 3-6). (i) The answer comes not so much in the flood of new information as in a new relationship with the Lord of the universe: "but now my eye sees thee" (v. 5). (j) Much of what the friends and Elihu have said about God may be true, but hearing about him and encountering the King of heaven are not the same—the "why" of suffering is a lesser matter than the "Who."

(8) A vindication scarcely needed: God restores Job's reputation, wealth, and family (prose epilogue, 42:7-17). For Job to recognize the vast difference between God's wisdom and power and his own ignorance and frailty is what

---

20. J.B. Curtis suggests a contrary interpretation of 42:2-6, concluding that, far from repenting, Job expresses contempt and revulsion toward the God whose power has all but crushed him without answering his call for justice. This interpretation is so utterly out of harmony with the epilogue that follows that it is hard to conceive how Job's answer and the epilogue could have been combined; "On Job's Response to Yahweh," *JBL* 98 (1979): 497-511.

God wanted. The test has been passed, the wager with the Satan won—but only after monumental struggle and massive pain. Job's faith, strong at the beginning, has been refined like gold through the fires of adversity, misunderstanding, and doubt. In the epilogue the author lets that golden character glisten in the light of God's blessings: Job's vindication begins with the repeated rebuke of the three friends (vv. 7f.),[21] a rebuke ringing with irony, especially when God brands as "folly" the friends' view of the very essence of pious wisdom (v. 8). Moreover, God assigns to Job the priestly or prophetic role in intercession reminiscent of his original dutiful service to his children (v. 8; cf. 1:5). This vindication is a magnanimous display of grace: God forgives the friends, restores Job's possessions and family (42:10, 12-15), prolongs his life, and multiplies his posterity (vv. 16f.);[22] Job in turn emulates God's grace by praying for the friends whose arguments had bludgeoned him (v. 10) and by his generosity to his daughters (v. 15).[23] The vindication is affirmed in the honor and sympathy accorded by Job's kin, who come to fulfill the role intended for the friends (compare v. 11 with 2:11). It completes the book's movement by describing God's restoration of Job's possessions even beyond their initial state, by noting God's integrity in acknowledging that Job had passed the test and in disproving the friends' contention that Job's deprivation was linked to sin, and by stressing that poverty is not necessarily a more righteous state than prosperity. It centers in the power of God,[24] who was responsible for both the calamity and the restoration, and it shouts its word of grace in both its setting and its content. God leaves the courts of heaven and comes to the ash heap of Uz to forgive the doctrinaire sages and restore the fortunes of the beleaguered Job, whom he affectionately and affirmingly calls his servant (vv. 7f.; cf. 1:8; 2:3).

Unity of the Book. If this analysis of the story's movement and the intricate connections between its parts is substantially correct, the question of unity already has been answered affirmatively. Some brief comment, nevertheless,

---

21. For the implications of this rebuke, see below.

22. The twofold restoration of Job's possessions, especially his livestock (vv. 10, 12), may show wry humor—Israelite law required thieves to pay double for stealing an ox, ass, or sheep (Exod. 22:4 [MT 3]). Some versions, following the Targum (11QtgJob), read *šiḇ'ānâ* (42:13) as a dual form ("twice seven") and credit Job with fourteen sons in the restoration (cf. Dhorme, Gordis).

23. Inclusion of daughters in the inheritance seems remarkable in view of Israelite law (Num. 27:8), where a daughter inherited her father's property only if no son existed to serve as heir. Furthermore, recent studies on nomadism in the ancient Near East have modified the older view which was based largely on Arabic models of camel nomadism. New theories posit a villager-pastoralist symbiosis between the settled agricultural community and the pastoralists moving seasonally into the steppe with the flocks seeking pasturage. Villagers and pastoralists were integrated parts of one tribal community. For a brief but thorough resume of the theory and its evidence, see W.G. Dever, "The Patriarchal Traditions," pp. 102-117 in J.H. Hayes and J.M. Miller, eds., *Israelite and Judaean History.*

24. That the Satan is not mentioned in the epilogue writes volumes about God's sovereignty even in human adversity.

may help point up some problems in the book's composition and their possible solutions:

(1) The relationship of the prose prologue and epilogue to the poetic sections has been explained in a number of ways. Most scholars reject the idea that the poem was written first and the prose sections added later. The dialogues are hard to understand without the story as their setting, and lead nowhere without the epilogue to complete them. More likely is the theory, sketched earlier, that the author adapted the prose story by recounting his own theological and, perhaps, personal struggle in the poetic sections.[25]

Though some aspects of the prologue and epilogue seem in conflict with the tone of the poetry, this need not mar the book's integrity: (a) the semi-nomadic life depicted in the prologue can be reconciled with the agricultural (31:8, 38-40) or even urban setting (19:15; 29:7) if Job is seen to winter in a city not far from his farm land and follow his flocks in other seasons;[26] (b) the difference in Job's mood and response between the prologue and dialogue can be accredited to passage of time and the sharp aggravation prompted by his friends' easy answers.

(2) The third cycle of the dialogue (chs. 22–27) appears incomplete: Bildad's speech is strangely short (25:1-6); part of Job's response sounds more like Bildad (26:5-14); and the final verses of Job's response, describing the terrible fate of a wealthy wicked person and his family (27:13-23), may originally have belonged to Zophar. The problem here is not multiple authorship. Rather, this portion of the manuscript was probably damaged and inadequately reconstructed at an early date.[27] An alternate explanation sees the truncated cycle as possibly "the author's way of showing that the debate had collapsed,"[28] whether out of a sense of defeat by Job's logic or from frustration at his resistance.

(3) The poem on wisdom (ch. 28) has often been identified as a later addition.[29] As the text now stands it is assigned to Job, but it represents such a change from his irritated mood that it would have to be interpreted sarcastically (see above). Nevertheless, both this poem and Yahweh's final speeches speak of human inability to discern the mysteries of God. Since the tone and content do not fit well with the speeches of either Job or his comforters, it is

---

25. The prose-poetry-prose (A-B-A) sequence is not in itself a sign of disunity. Note the Code of Hammurabi with the poetry-prose-poetry order of prologue-laws-epilogue and the linguistic pattern of the book of Daniel: Hebrew-Aramaic-Hebrew.

26. S. Terrien, *IB* 3:886.

27. Gordis, *The Book of Job* (New York: 1978), pp. 534f., discusses this cycle and the most likely reconstruction; see p. 547 for his view on the damaged text.

28. Andersen, *Job*, p. 34.

29. E.g., A. Robert and A. Feuillet, *Introduction*, pp. 425f.: "The invocation of wisdom seems to be an interpolation. . . . One might even say that the theme does not seem to be occasioned at all by the statements of Job and his friends." See H.H. Rowley, *Job*. NCBC (Grand Rapids: 1980), pp. 13f.

best to see the poem as the author's own interlude, designed to ease the tension and reflect on the inadequacy of both sides of the argument.[30]

(4) Yahweh's second speech (40:15–41:34 [MT 26]) frequently has been considered a later addition, because it supposedly lacks brilliance, is redundant (Job has already ceased to argue; 40:3-5), and concentrates on just two animals.[31] In defense of the unity of the two speeches of Yahweh and their role in the book, P. Skehan argues that the first speech (chs. 38–39) is designed deliberately to speak to the first section of Job's final monologue (chs. 29–30), while the second speech (40:7–41:26) is calculated in content and length to overmatch the second section of Job's monologue (ch. 31).[32] Gordis affirms the unity of the two speeches, arguing that the descriptions of the hippopotamus and the crocodile, in whom God delights despite their repulsiveness to humans, strongly support "the contention that the universe and its Maker cannot be judged by man in anthropocentric terms."[33] The second speech may seem redundant to western ears only because we do not recognize the Hebrew use of repetition to heighten the suspense.[34] The increasing length of the descriptions of animals (horse, 39:19-25; hippopotamus, 40:15-24; crocodile, 41:1-34 [MT 40:25–41:26]) is part of the artistry; the multiplication of details is designed to overwhelm Job and evoke the desired surrender.[35]

(5) The speeches of Elihu (32:1–37:24) have provoked more controversy among scholars than any other portion of Job. O. Eissfeldt's view is typical: "The speeches violently disturb the artistic structure of the original book."[36] Among the arguments usually adduced in support of such a verdict is the observation that Elihu is not mentioned in the prologue or prior to his appearance. Two explanations of this omission are possible: as part of the comforters' retinue or one of their pupils, he was not singled out for special mention;[37] or mention is delayed deliberately to enhance the surprise and increase the suspense which these speeches produce.

Admittedly remarkable given the length and intensity of the speeches, the epilogue says nothing about Elihu's intervention. Perhaps because Elihu's words

---

30. Andersen, *Job*, p. 53; Dhorme, *A Commentary on the Book of Job*, pp. xcvii-xcviii; and Gordis, *The Book of Job*, pp. 536-38. Dhorme suggests that the author composed this poem and Yahweh's speeches later and inserted them, while Gordis holds that the author wrote the poem at an earlier stage in his career and then included it in the book.

31. Rowley, *Job*, p. 13.

32. "Job's Final Plea (Job 29–31) and the Lord's Reply (Job 38–41)," *Bibl* 45 (1964): 51-62.

33. *The Book of Job*, p. 558.

34. Note that Job's response, which promises silence (40:3-5), is not yet the full-fledged confession which God seeks, therefore calling for the second speech.

35. Andersen, *Job*, p. 49.

36. *Old Testament*, p. 457.

37. The prologue indicates that the three friends came from a distance and had to set a time and place (2:11) of rendezvous before they visited Job.

both celebrated God's wondrous mysteries and rebuked Job with less venom than did the friends' dogmatism, he required no direct censure. Elihu's speeches may have been added by the author at a later date without calling for a har-monizing of the details by adding his name to the epilogue, which already had been written.[38]

The style of Elihu is said to differ significantly from that of the dialogue. Arguments based on the use of divine names (e.g., El, Yahweh, Eloah, El Shaddai) or the alleged presence of Aramaic words are noteworthy, but not conclusive. Different subjects and circumstances can call for different wording even from the same author. One key similarity in style with the rest of the book is Elihu's use of quotations as background for his own remarks (e.g., 33:8-11; 34:5f.; cf. 42:3-4a). This may spotlight one of the author's purposes here: to summarize and restate key positions in Job's stance in order to prepare for Yahweh's conclusive speeches.

Though discussion of the unity and integrity of Job will persist, increasingly scholars have concluded that the book is best understood not when dissected into separate parts, each with its own history, but when its final form is studied with a commitment to grasping the message as it now stands. Gordis' summary is fitting: "The book thus emerges [from the various stages of the author's work] as a superbly structured unity, the work of a single author of transcendental genius, both as a literary artist and as a religious thinker, with few peers, if any, in the history of mankind."[39]

Neither the inspiration of the work nor its authority as Scripture depends on its unity. The Holy Spirit can as readily supervise an editorial process as he can an original author's composition. The product of that inspiration is what commands attention and obedience, even though the process may be veiled in the mists of antiquity.

LITERARY CONSIDERATIONS

Genre. What kind of book is Job? The question has defied conclusive answer, as seen from a sampling of proposed genres:

(1) "Complaint and reconciliation" has sometimes been identified as a distinct genre, following the pattern of the Babylonian Ludlul Bēl Nēmeqi. H. Gese has identified three components in this genre: account of suffering; lamentation; divine intervention to heal the sufferer.[40] The major weakness is

---

38. So Gordis, The Book of God and Man, pp. 110f. D.N. Freedman credits the Elihu speeches to the author but their insertion to a later editor; "The Elihu Speeches in the Book of Job," HTR 61 (1968): 51-59.

39. The Book of Job, p. 581.

40. Lehre und Wirtlichkeit in der alten Weisheit (Tübingen: 1958). N.H. Snaith also has used this pattern to reconstruct the development of the text in three stages: (a) prologue and epilogue (without mention to friends), Job's monologues (chs. 3, 29–31) and apology (40:3-5), and Yahweh's speeches (chs. 38–41); (b) account of the friends (2:10-13; 42:7-10) and dialogue (chs. 4–28); and (c) Elihu speeches (chs. 32–37); The Book of Job: Its Origin and Purpose. SBT, 2nd ser. 11 (Naperville: 1968).

that this suggestion does not account for the heart of the present book—the controversy with the friends.

(2) C. Westermann[41] and others have thought the psalmlike laments (complaints) to be the backbone of Job. This theory contends that Job is not the typical discussion of suffering expected in wisdom literature but a more poignant and personal exploration.[42] Westermann has rendered yeoman service in stressing the numerous parallels between Job's speeches and psalms of individual complaint. But the role of the prologue and epilogue as well as the friends' counsel distinguish the book markedly from the simpler, more stereotyped psalm forms.[43]

(3) B. Gemser and others suggest legal disputation as the key to the book's form:

> Formally it cannot be better understood than as the record of the proceedings of a *rîb* [legal controversy or indictment] between Job and God Almighty in which Job is the plaintiff and prosecutor, the friends of Job are witnesses as well as co-defendants and judges, while God is the accused and defendant, but in the background and finally the ultimate judge of both Job and his friends.[44]

Gemser's insight into possible legal innuendoes and terms is useful, but a disputation category is insufficient to describe the structure and thrust of the work as a whole.

(4) As a school lecture the book would represent attempts by a master teacher to deal forcefully with students' questions about "God's supervision of the righteous and the wicked."[45] This approach seems much more appropriate to the didactic style of Ps. 37 than the spirited debate of Job. Moreover, so little direct evidence exists for the presence of schools in Israel that caution is required in accepting this view, which builds a theory on the unsure foundation of another theory.[46]

(5) As a philosophic debate, Job could be modeled after the dialogues of

---

41. *The Structure of the Book of Job: A Form-Critical Analysis*, trans. C.A. Muenchow (Philadelphia: 1981).

42. Von Rad finds the dialogues not "contentious debates" but "complaints from the one side and pastoral words of comfort from the other"; *Wisdom in Israel*, p. 209. Note J.A. Soggin: "As well as being a piece of wisdom literature, the book of Job is a dramatic representation of the literary genre of the 'individual lament' in a dramatic form"; *Introduction*, p. 389.

43. See G. Fohrer, review of Westermann, *Der Aufbau des Buches Hiob*, VT 7 (1957): 107-111.

44. B. Gemser, "The *Rîb-* or Controversy-Pattern in Hebrew Mentality," VTS 3 (1955): 135. This view is based in part on L. Köhler, *Hebrew Man*, trans. P.R. Ackroyd (Nashville: 1956), which reconstructs ancient Israelite court procedures partly on the basis of Job.

45. M.B. Crook, *The Cruel God: Job's Search for the Meaning of Suffering* (Boston: 1959), p. 5.

46. See R.N. Whybray, BZAW 135 (1974): 33-43, for a discussion of evidence for and against the existence of schools.

Plato,[47] but the subtle reasonings and theoretical arguments of the Greek symposium seem a continent away from the intense personal and theological debate on the ash heap at Uz.

(6) Tragedy in the Greek pattern has often been suggested.[48] At least two factors militate against any comparison with Greek drama: the virtual absence of any dramatic presentation in worship or entertainment in Jewish life before the second century B.C., and vast differences in content between the impassive yet often malicious fates and moral flaws that comprise Greek tragedy and the tension between God's freedom and Job's integrity that governs that book.

(7) Job can be defined as comedy in light of "its perception of incongruity and irony; and . . . its basic plot line that leads ultimately to the happiness of the hero."[49] Though this is attractive, it remains to be proven that such comedic components were prevalent in the Middle East during the first millennium.

(8) Parable form (Heb. *māšāl*) was suggested as early as Rabbi Simeon ben-Laqish (second century A.D.), who believed that Job was a fictional character whose story was written to convey a spiritual lesson.[50] Indeed, Job's speeches sometimes are called *māšāl* (27:1; 29:1), and his experiences obviously are intended as spiritual instruction.[51] Parable, however, may be misleading as a genre for such a complicated story as Job's, because it is generally associated with brief, pertinent stories having just one specific point to make.

(9) Epic history is another frequent suggestion. Andersen likens Job to the stories of the patriarchs, Moses, David, or Ruth, and assigns to it four characteristics: economy in relating facts; objectivity in describing the characters' actions without plumbing their emotions; restraint by the author in making moral judgments; and focus on the speeches which reveal the plight and faith of the characters.[52] But none of these other "epics" contains speeches of the length, power, and intensity of those in Job.

Each of these approaches may have something to contribute to an understanding of Job. The matter of genre is more than an item of intellectual curiosity; it is an essential clue to the book's meaning. Form and content are inextricably intertwined.

So important, in fact, is Job's genre that the book must not be fit into any preconceived mold. It does weep with complaint, argue with disputation, teach

---

47. E.g., C. Fries, *Das philosophische Gespräch vom Hiob bis Platon* (Tübingen: 1904).

48. H.M. Kallen, *The Book of Job as a Greek Tragedy Restored* (New York: 1918); cf. R.B. Sewall, *The Vision of Tragedy*, 2nd ed. (New Haven: 1980), pp. 9-24.

49. J.W. Whedbee, "The Comedy of Job," *Semeia* 7 (1977): 1; see J.A. Holland, "On the Form of the Book of Job," *Australian Journal of Biblical Archaeology* 2 (1972): 160-177. For a view akin to this but denying the happy ending, see Robertson: "Irony pervades the entire book and provides the decisive key to understanding its complicated theme"; *The Old Testament and the Literary Critic*, p. 34.

50. Midrash *Gen. Rab.* 67; Talmud B. *Bat.* 15a.

51. For the possible range of meaning for *māšāl*, see D.A. Hubbard, "Proverb," *IBD*, pp. 1289f.

52. *Job*, pp. 36f.

with didactic accuracy, excite with comedy, sting with irony, and relate human experience with epic majesty. But above all, Job is unique—the literary gift of an inspired genius.[53]

Literary Characteristics. Students of literature lavish superlatives when describing the artistry of Job. For example, the varieties of poetic parallelism, including the exquisite use of complete triplets and even longer units, alone reveal considerable literary prowess. The present survey must be content with a brief look at the metaphors and similes, the vivid descriptions of the creation, and the quotations which are hallmarks of the author's style:

(1) Metaphors and similes abound in startling numbers and quality fully deserving of A.S. Peake's accolade: "The poet is a master of metaphors, taken from many spheres of life."[54] For example:

My days are swifter than a weaver's shuttle, (7:6)

My days are swifter than a runner;
   they flee away, they see no good.
They go by like skiffs of reed,
   like an eagle swooping on the prey. (9:25f.)

He breaks me down on every side,
   and I am gone,
and my hope has he pulled up like a tree. (19:10)

They waited for me as for the rain;
   and they opened their mouths as for the spring rain. (29:23)

Even more impressive are the extended metaphors, so intricately detailed that they border on allegory:

My brethren are treacherous as a torrent-bed,
   as freshets that pass away,
which are dark with ice,
   and where the snow hides itself.
In time of heat they disappear;
   when it is hot, they vanish from their place.
The caravans turn aside from their course;
   they go up into the waste, and perish.
The caravans of Tema look,
   the travelers of Sheba hope.
They are disappointed because they were confident;
   they come thither and are confounded.
Such you have now become to me;
   you see my calamity, and are afraid. (6:15-21)

---

53. So also Pope: "The book viewed as a unit is *sui generis* and no single term or combination of terms is adequate to describe it"; *Job*, p. XXXI.
54. *Job*. Century Bible (Edinburgh: 1905), p. 41.

For there is hope for a tree,
if it be cut down, that it will sprout again,
and that its shoots will not cease.
Though its root grow old in the earth,
and its stump die in the ground,
yet at the scent of water it will bud
and put forth branches like a young plant.
But man dies, and is laid low;
man breathes his last, and where is he? (14:7-10)

(2) Descriptions of the creation are virtually unrivaled in poetic power:

Has the rain a father,
or who has begotten the drops of dew?
From whose womb did the ice come forth,
and who has given birth to the hoarfrost of heaven? (38:28f.)

Do you give the horse his might?
Do you clothe his neck with strength?
Do you make him leap like a locust?
His majestic snorting is terrible.
. . . . . .
He laughs at fear, and is not dismayed;
he does not turn back from the sword.
Upon him rattle the quiver,
the flashing spear and the javelin. (39:19f., 22f.)

(3) Quotations play a significant role in the argument, though they are sometimes hard to identify. Gordis divides them into a number of categories:[55]

Citations from folk wisdom: "Then Satan answered the Lord, 'Skin for skin![56] All that a man has he will give for his life' " (2:4). Proverbs may also be quoted in 11:12; 17:5.

Direct quotations of the speaker's thoughts:

When I lie down, I ask, "When shall I arise?"
But the night is long, and I say,
"I have had my fill of tossing till daybreak." (7:4)[57]

Quotation of a speaker's previous viewpoint:

I have made a covenant with my eyes;
how then could I look upon a virgin?
What would be my portion from God above,
and my heritage from the Almighty on high? (31:1f.)

---

55. *The Book of God and Man*, pp. 174-189; see also *Poets, Prophets and Sages* (Bloomington: 1971), pp. 104-159.

56. Gordis, *The Book of Job*, p. 20, reviews various interpretations and settles on this: "a man will give anyone else's skin on behalf of, i.e., to save his own skin."

57. Translation from Gordis, *The Book of God and Man*, p. 179.

Gordis captures the full meaning of v. 2 by adding an introductory line to clarify its relationship to v. 1: "*For I thought*, if I sinned [by that lustful look], What would be my portion from God above. . . ?[58]

Quotation of a proverb as a text:

> I am young in years,
>   and you are aged;
> therefore I was timid and afraid
>   to declare my opinion to you.
> I said, "Let days speak,
>   and many years teach wisdom."
> But it is the spirit in a man,
>   the breath of the Almighty,
>   that makes him understand. (32:6-8)

Elihu used the proverb in order to refute it and justify his right to intervene, despite his youth.

Quotation of a proverb to correct a proverb:

> Wisdom is with the aged,
>   and understanding in length of days.
> With God are wisdom and might;
>   he has counsel and understanding. (12:12f.)

Adding "You say" to the first verse and "But I say" to the second[59] clarifies the debate.

Quotations of another person's views:

> You say, "God stores up their iniquity for their sons."
> Let him recompense it to themselves, that they may know it. (21:19)

The RSV rightly adds "You say" as Job summarizes views expressed by the friends in 5:4; 18:12; 20:10, 26.

The following quotation, which should be introduced by "You say," seems to summarize the argument of the comforters that God's ways are incomprehensible (4:17; 11:7-12; 15:8, 14):

> Will any teach God knowledge,
>   seeing that he judges those that are on high? (21:22)

Job answers that question in vv. 23-26.

Sometimes the text itself uses an introductory phrase to make clear that what follows is a quotation:

---

58. *Ibid.*, p. 181. He extends the quotation to include vv. 3f.
59. *Ibid.*, p. 184. Illustrations of these last two uses of quotations also can be found in Ecclesiastes (see p. 595), suggesting that this was a standard technique of unconventional wisdom.

For you say, "Where is the house of the prince?
Where is the tent in which the wicked dwell?" (v. 28)[60]

One could write an essay on a biblical approach to aesthetics by citing Job alone. The combination of sublime reflection on the ways of God with the human family and consummate literary achievement place Job in a class by itself within world literature.

Forms. "The book of Job is an astonishing mixture of almost every kind of literature to be found in the Old Testament."[61] Indeed, the forty-two chapters are a gold mine for the study of form criticism. With incredible ingenuity the author has woven several dozen readily distinguishable literary forms into the texture of the work. The sampling here will not only document this impressive literary display, but also give clues as to the mood and intent of the author, who used the forms not so much to impress the audience as to convey the nuances of the message:

(1) The prose narrative (1:1–2:13; 32:1-5; 42:7-17) tells the basic story, serves as a setting for the poem, and introduces Elihu. Most of the characteristics have been discussed above (pp. 564f.).[62]

(2) The laments over his birth (ch. 3; cf. 10:18f.) represent the strongest literary form available to Job to express the depths of his depression (cf. Jer. 20:14-18). Actually two kindred forms are combined here: (a) the curse on one's birthday—a way of calling for death or contemplating suicide in order to reserve and counteract all the consequences of that day (3:3-10); and (b) the complaining questions, which begin with "why" and call for no specific answer but introduce explanatory descriptions of suffering (vv. 11-26; cf. 10:18f., where the question is followed by a wish that he had been born dead). The author intends to picture Job in the depths of defeat in order to set the stage for the friends' counsel and Job's response.

(3) The complaint form is that which Job himself most frequently employs (chs. 6–7; 9:25–10:22; 13:23–14:22; 16:6–17:9; ch. 23; 29:1–31:37).[63] The use of this form has several purposes. It keeps the book from being a didactic discourse on the reasons for suffering, and allows for fulsome descriptions of the suffering in poignant and figurative poetry (e.g., 16:6-17), one of its chief characteristics in the Psalms. The form embraces other components such as implied pleas for rescue (13:24f.) and oaths of innocence (31:3-40). It can be directed to the friends whom Job now counts as enemies (e.g., 6:14-23), or to God (e.g., 10:2-22), leaving room for all three participants in a complaint—

---

60. On ch. 21, see *ibid.*, pp. 185f.
61. Andersen, *Job*, p. 33.
62. Pope points out the similarities between this story and the book of Ruth; *Job*, p. LXXI.
63. *Idem.* Though one could quibble over details, this list is generally accurate and gives an idea of the part such complaints play in the book.

God, foes, and sufferer. It hovers above total despair, implying confidence in God's willingness to hear and his ability to rescue (e.g., 19:23-29).

(4) The hymn celebrates the acts and attributes of God (e.g., 9:4-10; 12:13-25; 26:5-14; 36:24–37:13).[64] Both Job (9:4-10; 12:13-25) and the friends (Bildad [?], 26:5-14; Elihu, 36:24–37:13) use the hymn to describe divine majesty—the friends, to silence Job; Job, to demonstrate his understanding of God's greatness, despite his desire to put his case before God. The hymns in the dialogue anticipate God's revelation from the whirlwind—and recall the contrast between human grasp of God's glory and God's own self-understanding and self-revelation.

(5) The vision description of Eliphaz (4:12-21) has no close parallel in the Old Testament. Like some prophetic visions it also contains an audition, but the detailed account of the apparition and the physical reaction it sparked are unique here. The description is a reminder that the wise men were not restricted to natural observations but were open to mystical experiences as well.

(6) Personal observations (4:8; 5:3-5) were a common form of wisdom instruction (see Prov. 7:6-23; 24:30-34; Eccl. 1:13f.; 3:10). These first person singular accounts argue not from well-proven generalities as in a proverb but from judgments based on what Job himself has seen and learned:

> As I have seen, those who plow iniquity
> and sow trouble reap the same. (4:8)

(7) Proverbs are abundant throughout Job. Both Job (e.g., 6:14, 25a; 12:5f., 12; 13:28; 17:5) and the friends (Eliphaz, 5:2, 6f.; 22:2, 21f.; Zophar, 20:5; Elihu, 32:7) cite them liberally. Most are descriptive sayings, with verbs in the indicative mood. The hearers are left to make their own applications:

> Surely vexation kills the fool,
> and jealousy slays the simple. (5:2)

> For affliction does not come from the dust,
> nor does trouble sprout from the ground;
> but man is born to trouble
> as the sparks fly upward. (vv. 6f.)

Job may use a proverb and then refute it:

> How forceful are honest words! (proverb)
> But what does reproof from you reprove? (6:25)

or counter a proverb with a proverb (12:12f.), as does Qoheleth (see above, p. 595). Exhortation (admonition), a form familiar from Proverbs, with im-

---

64. Pope also notes parallels between hymn fragments in Job and Ps. 104 (compare Ps. 104:6-9 with Job 38:8-11; Ps. 104:21, 27 with Job 38:39-41; Ps. 104:30 with Job 12:10; Ps. 104:32 with Job 9:5; 26:11); *ibid.*, p. LXXII.

perative verbs and frequently with a reason given for the command, is also found:

> Agree with God, and be at peace;
>   thereby good will come to you.
> Receive instruction from his mouth,
>   and lay up his words in your heart. (22:21f.)

This was a standard form of instruction, implying that the teacher had the right by experience and authority to issue these exhortations. Inclusion of a reason indicated that the teacher's authority was not arbitrary but was backed by sound evidence.

(8) Rhetorical questions (sometimes called disputation-questions) are a dominant part of the argumentation. Each participant in the dialogue makes generous use of them: Eliphaz, 4:7; 15:2f., 7-9, 11-14; 25:3f.; Bildad, 8:3, 11; 18:4; 25:3f.; Zophar, 11:2f., 7f., 10f.; Job, 6:5f., 11f., 22f.; 7:12; 9:12; 12:9; 13:7-9; 27:8-10; Elihu, 34:13, 17-19, 31-33; 36:19, 22f.; 37:15-18, 20. Scarcely any literary form is more useful in debate, because the questioner can determine the answer by the way he casts the question. The listener is lured into debate because he has to answer. Usually the required answer is "No!" or "By no means!" or "Of course not!" or "No one!":

> Think now, who that was innocent ever perished?
>   Or where were the upright cut off? (Eliphaz, 4:7)

> Should a multitude of words go unanswered,
>   and a man full of talk be vindicated? (Zophar, 11:2)

> Is my strength the strength of stones,
>   or is my flesh bronze? (Job, 6:12)

> Who gave him charge over the earth
>   and who laid on him the whole world? (Elihu, 34:13)

Note that the bite of the question is sharpened by the poetic parallelism—in these cases synonymous—which states the question in two closely related forms, doubling the intensity.

The question forms in the divine speeches need special mention. They may call for the answer "I do not know" or "I was not there":

> Where were you when I laid the
>   foundation of the earth?
> Who determined its measurements—
>   surely you know!
> Or who stretched the line upon it? (38:4a, 5)

or for the answer "No!" as in rhetorical questions:

> Have the gates of death been revealed to you,
>   Or have you seen the gates of deep darkness? (v. 17)

or for an admission of weakness, "No, I cannot!"

> Can you lift up your voice to the clouds,
>   that a flood of waters may cover you? (v. 34)

Designed to force Job to admit his ignorance ("I do not know!") and power-lessness ("Of course, I cannot!"), these questions are reinforced in at least two ways: (a) by the injection of imperatives needling Job to respond—"Tell me, if you have understanding" (38:4b), "Declare, if you know all this" (v. 18); and (b) by the use of irony in which God chides Job as sharply as Job chided the friends: "You know, for you were born then, and the number of your days is great!" (v. 21; cf. 12:2). The questions, thus fortified, weigh on Job like a leaden mantle until he sinks to his knees in speechless humility.

(9) Onomastica, catalogues or encyclopaedias containing organized lists of natural phenomena, may furnish partial literary background to the speeches from the whirlwind.[65] Scientific lists of stars, constellations, types of precipitation, and other data were compiled both in Egypt and Israel as a means of training students to understand the realities around them. Such lists may also have influenced other biblical passages (see Ps. 148, which names a catalogue of natural entities and urges them to praise Yahweh). Solomon may have used such onomastica to organize his vast knowledge of God's creatures, so admired by his biographer (1 Kgs. 4:33).[66] The question form which dominated Job 38 also has Egyptian parallels in the thirteenth-century Papyrus Anastasi I, in which a scribe, Hori, attacks with a barrage of questions the alleged ignorance of another scribe, Amenemope.[67] Possibly then, Job 38 follows an earlier form, perhaps pioneered in Egypt, in which such lists were couched in questions and used either for debate or instruction.[68] These parallels in form do not, of course, account for the theological power of the whirlwind speeches. The magnificent questions on creation (vv. 4-11) have no Egyptian parallel.

(10) A number of characteristic wisdom forms deserve mention: (a) The 'ašrê ("blessed" or "happy"; cf. Ps. 1:1) formula spells out the pattern of life that leads to happiness (5:17-27). (b) The numerical proverb (here combined with the 'ašrê saying, 5:19-22) highlights a series of threats from which God will deliver the happy person whom he reproves (see Prov. 30 for the x, x + 1 pattern). (c) The summary appraisal concludes a statement with a summation of its significance (8:13; 18:21; 20:29):

---

65. Von Rad, "Job XXXVIII and Ancient Egyptian Wisdom," pp. 281-291 in *The Problem of the Hexateuch*, trans. E.W.T. Dicken (Edinburgh: 1966); cf. A.H. Gardiner, *Ancient Egyptian Onomastica*, 3 vols. (London: 1947).

66. G.E. Bryce, *A Legacy of Wisdom*, pp. 164f. Similarly perhaps the detailed description of Behemoth (40:15-24) and Leviathan (ch. 41) reflect forms in which sages set their scientific study of the animal world.

67. *ANET*, pp. 477f.

68. Von Rad, *The Problem of the Hexateuch*, pp. 290f.

Such you have now become to me;
  you see my calamity, and are afraid. (6:21)[69]

(d) Sarcastic overstatement (6:27; 11:12; 12:2; 15:7; 26:2-4) was often used in ancient contests (e.g., Goliath, 1 Sam. 17:43; Jehoash, 2 Kgs. 14:9). (e) Parody is close to sarcasm, as Job's rendition of Ps. 8:4 (MT 5) suggests:

What is man, that thou dost make so much of him,
  and that thou dost set thy mind upon him,
dost visit him every morning,
  and test him every moment? (7:17f.)

(f) The wish (6:2-4, 8-10; 11:5; 13:5; 19:23f.; 23:3; 29:2-6) was particularly effective in both complaint and debate, expressing a powerful desire for change either in circumstances (e.g., 6:2-4) or in the opponent's response (e.g., 13:5).[70]

(11) Eliphaz seems to have applied the prophetic judgment speech to Job in the third cycle (22:5-11):
  indictment or accusation (vv. 5-9)
  therefore (typical transition) (v. 10)
  announcement or threat of judgment (vv. 10f.)
So enraged had Eliphaz become that he resorted to the form used by prophets to denounce Israel's wicked leaders (e.g., 2 Kgs. 1:16) or the nation as a whole (e.g., Amos 3:10f.).[71]

THEOLOGICAL CONTRIBUTION

All biblical books must be studied as a whole, with their parts seen in relationship to the author's overall intent. This is particularly true of Job. Its full message cannot be discerned short of the final page.[72] To a large extent, the tracing of the book's movement has been an exposition of its message.

In essence, the story is the message. Its parts must not be snatched from the whole, nor its thrust hardened into rigid principles or fine-tuned into narrow

---

69. Similar in form is 27:13, actually an "introductory appraisal" because it precedes the section it summarizes (vv. 14-23).
70. For a survey of wisdom forms in Job and elsewhere, see J.L. Crenshaw, "Wisdom," pp. 225-264 in J.H. Hayes, ed., *Old Testament Form Criticism*.
71. Other prophetic forms may be found in 5:23-27, reminiscent of a salvation speech with its extended promise of peace, safety, and prosperity (cf. Amos 9:14f.), and 11:13-20; 22:21-30, where Zophar and Eliphaz offer what resemble oracles of invitation to Job, urging him to return to the Lord (cf. Hos. 14:1-3; Isa. 55:6-9).
72. Note B.S. Childs: "The present shape of the book seeks to address a wide range of different questions about wisdom which vary in accordance with the battle being fought. The contours of both the outer and inner limits of wisdom are carefully drawn, and any attempt to cut the tension is to sacrifice the specific canonical role of this remarkable book"; *Old Testament as Scripture*, p. 543; see also p. 544 on the book's function with respect to the larger canon, particularly in supplying "a critical corrective to the reading of the other wisdom books, especially Proverbs and Ecclesiastes."

propositions. To do so would violate what the book teaches about the mysteries of God's workings in the lives of his people.

Freedom of God. This, if any, doctrine should be singled out. Both Job and his friends were utterly baffled by God's freedom. The friends assumed that suffering was always and only the sign of God's retribution. Job could imagine no worthy divine purpose to his unmerited suffering.

To the purveyors of conventional wisdom, the book introduces a God who is free to work his surprises, correct human distortions, and revise the books written about him. He was free to enter into the Satan's test and tell none of the participants about it, to time his intervention and determine its agenda. He was free not to answer Job's goading questions nor agree with the friends' high-sounding doctrines. Above all, he was free to care enough to confront Job and to forgive the friends.

As with the whole of Scripture, Job's author pictured God as neither bound by human agendas nor beholden to human concepts of him. What he does springs freely from his own will and character, with no guidelines to which he must conform. He chose to create and sustain the universe, to inaugurate and govern history's march, to work by the order and pattern spelled out in Deuteronomy and Proverbs, and to transcend those bounds in Job. That he is Lord and those choices are his to make is one lesson from Job. Another is that people find freedom only to the degree that they acknowledge God's. Nothing is more frustrating and restricting than to set up rules for God and then wonder why he does not follow them.

Testing of the Satan. One of the earliest Old Testament references to this adversary is his appearance in the prologue (cf. 1 Chr. 21:1; Zech. 3:1). The Satan has access to the presence of Yahweh, yet is governed by his sovereignty. While nothing suggests that the Satan is not God's creature—the biblical doctrine of creation rules out any true form of dualism—every indication is that the Satan's intentions are harmful. He represents conflict and ill will. His purposes are contrary to God's will and hostile to Job's welfare.

The absence of the Satan from the epilogue is not "to be regretted as a flaw in the harmony of the prologue and epilogue,"[73] but a deliberate factor in the book's message. God, not the Satan, is sovereign; the test has been passed; the story points to Job's future not his past. The Satan is but an interloper in the relationship of God and Job as depicted in the book's beginning and ending.

In a sense the role of the Satan in Job anticipates his role in the rest of the Bible. He is a creature of God, yet an enemy of God's will (cf. Matt. 4:1-11; Luke 4:1-13). He seeks to plague God's people both physically (2 Cor. 12:7) and spiritually (11:14). He has been defeated by Christ's obedience and will disappear from the story at the end (Rev. 20:2, 7, 10).

---

73. Robert and Feuillet, *Introduction*, p. 425.

The thrust of the Satan's strategy was not to lure Job into acts of sin—immorality, dishonesty, violence—but to tempt him to *the* sin—disloyalty to God. Loyalty, trust, and allegiance are the essence of biblical piety and the roots from which all fruits of righteousness stem. The Satan, as is ever his pattern, sought the root of the matter: Job's relationship to God. Job passed this test of loyalty and earned full marks, despite his protests, doubts, and challenges along the way.

Strength for Suffering. Not every life will bear afflictions of the magnitude of Job's, yet suffering, intense and prolonged, will be the lot of virtually every human being. Surely one of Job's purposes is to help in bearing them.

The book does this by preparing the reader to accept God's freedom. Job shatters idols in people's minds and leaves a realistic picture of God. The view of the free God opens people to mysterious purposes, to righteous goals in the suffering that he may allow. He is seen as mighty but not mean, victorious but not vindictive. The reader can believe that he will work good through suffering, even though one rightly may hate every bit of the pain.

Job also teaches the importance of friendship in suffering, and especially the dangers of simplistic advice, naive counsel, or false comfort. In a sense, the greatest tragedy of the book is that of failed friendship, made worse by sensible theology badly applied.

Job did not suffer in silence, but argued with his friends and complained to God. In the end, God overrode those complaints, but he did not judge Job for them. Whatever else a biblical relationship with God includes, it surely has room for an honesty built on trust in God and the security of his love. Some of the Bible's noblest—Jeremiah, the Psalmists, Habakkuk, even Jesus Christ (Mark 14:36; 15:34)—complained of their lot and thus found respite from suffering.

A final lesson about dealing with suffering comes from Job's sense of loyalty to God. His conscience was clear. Although it was extraordinary, his pain was not aggravated by the burden of guilt. Open rebellion, flagrant disloyalty, refusal of forgiveness all can make suffering unbearable for anyone, adding to the pain the worry of blame. But Job knew that his commitment to God was clear, and he trusted in that commitment to sustain him until death and beyond (19:23-29).[74]

"Have you considered my servant Job?" (1:8; 2:3) is a fitting question for all. James uses Job as an example of those who learn happiness from the school of suffering: "Behold, we call those happy who were steadfast. You have heard of the steadfastness of Job, and you have seen the purpose of the Lord, how the Lord is compassionate and merciful" (Jas. 5:11). Is there a better summary of

---

74. For further background on a biblical approach to suffering, see H.W. Robinson, *The Cross in the Old Testament* (London: 1955); E.S. Gerstenberger and W. Schrage, *Suffering*, trans. J.E. Steely (Nashville: 1980).

the book's message—a steadfast sufferer held in the arms of a God of purpose and compassion?

FOR FURTHER READING

Andersen, F.I. *Job*. Downers Grove: 1976

Baab, O.J. "The Book of Job." *Interp* 5 (1951): 329-343. (Form and content.)

Glatzer, N. "The Book of Job and Its Interpreters." Pp. 197-221 in A. Altmann, ed., *Biblical Motifs*. Cambridge, Mass.: 1966. (Survey of rabbinic interpretation through Middle Ages.)

Guillaume, A. *Studies in the Book of Job*. Leiden: 1968. (Sees book as product of "Arabian milieu.")

King, A.R. *The Problem of Evil: Christian Concepts and the Book of Job*. New York: 1952. (Contemporary applications.)

Kraeling, E.G. *The Book of the Ways of God*. New York: 1939. (Exegetical.)

MacKenzie, R.A.F. "The Transformation of Job." *Biblical Theology Bulletin* 9 (1979): 51-57. (Identifies "transformation theme" akin to classical Greek tragedies.)

Polzin, R. *Biblical Structuralism: Method and Subjectivity in the Study of Ancient Texts*. Philadelphia: 1977. (Includes study of the framework, code, and message of Job, pp. 54-121.)

Rowley, H.H. "The Book of Job and Its Meaning." *BJRL* 41 (1958): 167-207.

Sanders, P., ed. *Twentieth Century Interpretations of the Book of Job*. Englewood Cliffs: 1968. (Reprinted essays on meaning, method by G.B. Gray, A.S. Peake, A. Toynbee, G. Murray, K. Rexroth, and others.)

Terrien, S.L. *Job: Poet of Existence*. Indianapolis: 1957. (Christian-existentialist interpretation.)

Zerafa, P.P. *The Wisdom of God in the Book of Job*. Rome: 1978. (Restoration from Exile is act of God's mercy, not result of human obedience to wisdom.)

CHAPTER 44

ECCLESIASTES

NAME

Ecclesiastes is a Greek translation of Heb. *qohelet* "one who convenes a congregation," presumably to preach to it.[1] "Preacher," then, is not an inaccurate translation of either the Greek or Hebrew, although Qoheleth (sometimes spelled Koheleth) would hardly meet the Christian meaning, since his texts were taken more from his own observations of life than from the Law or the Prophets.

PLACE IN CANON

Some Hebrew tradition placed Qoheleth among the five scrolls (Megilloth) used on official festive occasions, assigning it to Tabernacles. This practice is attested in documents from the eleventh century A.D.

Other Hebrew groupings link Qoheleth to Proverbs and the Song of Solomon, as established in the LXX and preserved in the Vulgate and English versions. The reasons are clear: the implied reference to Solomon in 1:1, 12, 16; and their obvious connection as examples of wisdom literature attached to Solomon's name.[2] This group was placed after Psalms because it was thought that the writings linked to Solomon should follow those attributed to his father David.

The tie between Solomon and Qoheleth probably helped the book find its

---

1. *Qôhelet* (1:1f., 12; 7:27; 12:8-10) is a feminine participle of a verb derived from *qāhāl* "congregation" or "assembly." This form apparently denoted an office and secondarily was used to describe the one who held the office. Ezra 2:55-57 contains similar cases of feminine participles which once designated offices but became proper names: Hassophereth "scribe" and Pochereth-hazzebaim "tender of gazelles." Cf. English names like Penman and Fowler.

2. The Talmud (*B. Bat.* 15a) also included the opinion that these books, along with Isaiah, were put in written form by King Hezekiah and his colleagues; see Prov. 25:1.

way into the Scriptures, but not without difficulty. The rabbis and early Christian sages were aware both of the book's seeming contradictions and its humanistic, almost skeptical, perspective. The positive verdict of Hillel (*ca.* 15 B.C.) triumphed over the negative opinion of Shammai, and the book was preserved in the canon. Doubts about its inspiration and authority survived among Christians at least until the time of Theodore of Mopsuestia (*ca.* A.D. 400), the great exegete of the school of Antioch, who questioned Qoheleth's right to stand among the holy books.

AUTHOR AND DATE

Protestant scholars since Luther's time have tended to date Qoheleth substantially later than Solomon, despite the almost unanimous tradition of the rabbis. The rabbis' view is based on their literal interpretation of 1:1 and their tendency to link Solomon's name with all wisdom literature, since he was viewed as master sage just as his father was associated with the Psalter as master singer.

A variety of evidence exists for a date much later than the tenth century. Solomon's name is not mentioned in the text, where only veiled allusions occur ("the son of David, king in Jerusalem," 1:1; "king over Israel in Jerusalem," v. 12; "surpassing all who were over Jerusalem before me," v. 16; cf. 2:9). Even these veiled allusions disappear after ch. 2, and some later statements do not fit well in a king's mouth (e.g., 4:13; 7:19; 8:2-4; 9:14f.; 10:4-7). Furthermore,

Pool of Solomon (south of Bethlehem), "from which to water the forest of growing trees" (Eccl. 2:8). (W.S. LaSor)

much of what Qoheleth says presupposes the highly developed wisdom movement reflected in Proverbs, a movement which, in Israel, began with Solomon
but only reached its height after Hezekiah's time (seventh century). The serious
questioning of the beliefs and values of ancient Israel points to a time when
prophetic activity had crested and vital hope in God's active presence and
power had waned. Finally, both vocabulary and sentence structure are postexilic, more closely akin to Mishnaic style than any other Old Testament book.[3]

For a century or more now this linguistic argument has been the most
cogent line of evidence for a date between 400 and 200.[4] A date later than
200 is ruled out, both by Ecclesiasticus (Sirach; ca. 180), which refers to Qoheleth, and by fragments of Qoheleth among the Qumran scrolls.[5]

Efforts to buttress this dating with parallels to Greek philosophy have not
proved fruitful. Despite superficial resemblances to Aristotle, Theogonis, Epi-
cureans, and Stoics, Qoheleth was a Semitic wise man, not a Greek philoso-
pher, and his mood and approach reflect a very different world. Somewhat more
valid are similarities to the thought and style of Egyptian wisdom writings,
especially more pessimistic works like the Song of the Harper.[6] This is not to
say that Qoheleth consciously borrowed from foreign sources. Rather, he followed an ancient train of wisdom writers in questioning his colleagues' conclusions. Because he and they were Israelites steeped in Israel's peculiar faith and
culture, the book is unique and ought not be seen as the literary offspring of
Egyptian or Mesopotamian parents.

It is far easier to say that King Solomon did not write Ecclesiastes than to
say who did. To be sure, the author was a wise man eager to challenge the
opinions and values of other wise men. But who he was or where he lived is
unknown. Suggestions that he was a Phoenician or Alexandrian Jew have not
received wide acceptance,[7] and Qoheleth's reference to Jerusalem, the hub of
political and commercial activities, should be taken at face value.

---

3. The Mishnah ("second law") contains the earliest rabbinic commentary on
various biblical commandments, organized by subjects. It was compiled early in the
Christian era.

4. Though W.F. Albright posited a slightly earlier (fifth century) date (*Yahweh and
the Gods of Canaan*), Franz Delitzsch's verdict still stands: "If the Book of Koheleth were
of old Solomonic origin, then there is no history of the Hebrew language. . . . the Book
of Koheleth bears the stamp of the postexilian form of the language"; Keil-Delitzsch,
Commentary 6:190.

5. J. Muilenburg has dated these fragments late in the second century B.C.; "A
Qoheleth Scroll from Qumran," *BASOR* 135 (1954): 20-28.

6. See R.K. Harrison, *Introduction*, pp. 1075-77, for a helpful summary of the
debate over possible foreign influences. O. Eissfeldt acknowledges that Qoheleth's Hellenistic environment may have made a modest contribution in thought and language,
but "there is nothing more than casual contact" with any particular Greek school or
writings; *Old Testament*, pp. 498f.

7. Albright, *VTS* 3 (1955): 15. M. Dahood's arguments for a Phoenician linguistic
background have not carried the day; "Canaanite-Phoenician Influence in Qoheleth,"
Bibl 33 (1952): 30-52, 191-221; "The Phoenician Background of Qoheleth," 47 (1966):
264-282. A. Weiser, citing supposed Egyptian influence on thought and Greek impact
on language, argues for an Alexandrian origin; *Old Testament*, pp. 309f.

If Solomon is not the actual author, why does Qoheleth seek to link himself with the great king? The simplest answer is for literary effect. The words of the honored head of Israel's wisdom movement would carry weight with the sages whose views Qoheleth aimed to correct. Moreover, Solomon himself could serve as a model of the life Qoheleth was striving to evaluate. Wisdom, pleasure, wealth, influence, accomplishment were attributes touted by the wise men. The author could offer no better illustration of their limitations than Solomon's own case.[8]

The author does not pretend to be Solomon so as to deceive his audience. His literary intent is plain. He does not mention Solomon nor carry the disguise beyond the first two chapters. His strategies are to capture his readers' attention and to use the circumstances of Solomon to probe ironically the weaknesses in his fellow sages' teachings; he then sets aside Solomon's garb and presses his arguments home. Effectively he uses the master's name to judge the thoughts of those who claimed to be his true followers.

THEME AND CONTENTS

The mention of Solomon and the conventional sages who counted him their mentor gets to the heart of Qoheleth's purpose and theme. In a word, he sought to use traditional tools of wisdom to refute and revise its traditional conclusions. Like Job, he protested the easy generalizations with which his fellow teachers taught their pupils to be successful. They had oversimplified life and its rules so as to mislead and frustrate their followers. Their observations seemed superficial and their counsel thin in a world beset by injustice, toil, and death.

Theme. For Qoheleth, conventional wisdom was not only inadequate, but close to blasphemous. At stake was the difference between God and humankind. The sages trespassed on territory belonging to God when they tried to predict infallibly the outcome of conduct both wise and foolish. The freedom of God and the mystery of his ways were realities that Qoheleth understood better than his countrymen, who did not always recognize the limits divine sovereignty has placed on human understanding. Two of his main emphases speak to this point:

> For who knows what is good for man while he lives the few days of his vain life, which he passes like a shadow? For who can tell man what will be after him under the sun? (6:12)

These rhetorical questions point out the vast gulf between what God knows and what human beings can know.[9]

---

8. Qoheleth's context and audience must have been affluent. Otherwise his denunciations of wealth, pleasure, and fame would have fallen on deaf ears. See R. Gordis, "The Social Background of Wisdom Literature," pp. 196f. in *Poets, Prophets and Sages*.

9. For the development of these themes and their role in the book's structure, see A.G. Wright, "The Riddle of the Sphinx: The Structure of the Book of Qoheleth," CBQ 30 (1968): 313-334.

Failure to recognize human limits has caused humankind to value their accomplishments in wisdom, pleasure, prestige, wealth, and justice far too much. This false confidence is what Qoheleth attacks in his main theme:

> Vanity of vanities, says the Preacher,
>   vanity of vanities: All is vanity. (1:2)

The literary form adds to the intensity: (1) the pattern "x of x" is a superlative (as in "Kings of Kings" or "Song of Songs"), meaning the vainest vanity, the most futile futility; (2) repetition of the phrase is a standard Hebrew means of emphasis; (3) the blanket conclusion "All is vanity" makes the point as sweeping as possible. "Vanity" (Heb. *hebel*) may mean "breath" or "vapor" (Isa. 57:13), thus something without substance, "nothingness," "emptiness," "futility."[10]

The bulk of the Preacher's words demonstrate and explain this theme. He begins with his conclusion and then spends twelve chapters to show how he reached it. Actually, "all is vanity" is only the negative half of his conclusion. He continues to drive it home (1:14; 2:11, 17, 19, 21, 23, 26; 4:4, 7f., 16; 5:10 [MT 9]; 6:9; 8:14; 12:8) because his brashly optimistic countrymen needed to hear it. But interwoven with it is his positive conclusion about what is good and meaningful in life:

> There is nothing better for a man than that he should eat and drink,
> and find enjoyment in his toil. This also, I saw, is from the hand of
> God. (2:24)

This point is reaffirmed periodically (3:12f., 22; 5:18-20 [MT 17-19]; 8:15; 9:7-10) and underscored in the conclusion: "Fear God, and keep his commandments" (12:13), meaning not the laws of Moses but the counsels of Qoheleth to enjoy the simple things of life as God gives them.

Structure. Qoheleth's unique method of argumentation makes a coherent outline of this work almost impossible. It seems to be more a collection of separate thoughts than a unified argument which can be systematically followed from beginning to end. Part of the problem may be in imposing a modern definition of a "book" as "a unified, logically argued and constructed whole."[11]

Of the many ways in which the book has been analyzed, the form chosen here recognizes two essential points in Qoheleth's method: the typically Semitic repetitive nature of his arguments to demonstrate his theme; and the use of clusters of proverbs, "words of advice" to clarity or reinforce the argument, a device particularly telling in light of Qoheleth's desire to correct the more conventional wise men.[12]

---

10. For a discussion of possible meanings for *hebel*, see E.M. Good, *Irony in the Old Testament* (Philadelphia: 1965), pp. 176-183, in which he finds "irony" a useful translation.
11. *Ibid.*, p. 171.
12. The variety of contemporary analyses is noted by Wright, *CBQ* 30 (1968): 314-320. Wright's own construction offers a commendable alternative which has the merit of pointing out the book's subtle inner unity.

Introduction (1:1-3)
  Title (v. 1)
  Theme (vv. 2f.)
Theme demonstrated—I (1:4–2:26)
  by human life in general (1:4-11)
  by knowledge (vv. 12-18)
  by pleasure (2:1-11)
  by the fate of all persons (vv. 12-17)
  by human toil (vv. 18-23)
    Conclusion: Enjoy life now as God gives it (vv. 24-26)
Theme demonstrated—II (3:1–4:16)
  by God's control of all events (3:1-11)
    Conclusion: Enjoy life now as God gives it (vv. 12-15)
  by the lack of immortality (vv. 16-21)
    Conclusion: Enjoy life now as God gives it (v. 22)
  by evil oppression (4:1-3)
  by work (vv. 4-6)
  by miserly hoarding of wealth (vv. 7-12)
  by the transient nature of popularity (vv. 13-16)
Words of Advice—A (5:1-12 [MT 4:17–5:11])
  Honor God in your worship (5:1-3 [MT 4:17–5 :2])
  Pay your vows (vv. 4-7 [MT 3-6])
  Expect injustice in government (5:5f. [MT 7f.])
  Do not overvalue wealth (5:10-12 [MT 9-11])
Theme demonstrated—III (5:13–6:12 [MT 5:12–6:12])
  by wealth lost in business (5:13-17 [MT 12-16])
    Conclusion: Enjoy life now as God gives it (vv. 18-20 [MT 17-19])
  by wealth that cannot be enjoyed (6:1-9)
  by the fixity of fate (6:10-12)
Words of Advice—B (7:1–8:9)
  Honor is better than luxury (7:1)
  Sobriety is better than levity (vv. 2-7)
  Caution is better than rashness (vv. 8-10)
  Wisdom with wealth is better than wisdom alone (vv. 11f.)
  Resignation is better than indignation (vv. 13f.)
  Moderation is better than intemperance (vv. 15-22)
  Men are better than women (vv. 23-29)
  Compromise is sometimes better than being right (8:1-9)
Theme demonstrated—IV (8:10–9:12)
  by the inconsistencies in justice (8:10-14)
    Conclusion: Enjoy life now as God gives it (v. 15)
  by the mystery of God's ways (vv. 16f.)
  by death, common fate of wise and foolish alike (9:1-6)
    Conclusion: Enjoy life now as God gives it (vv. 7-10)
  by the uncertainty of life (vv. 11f.)

Words of Advice—C (9:13–12:8)
  Introduction: a story on the value of wisdom (9:13-16)
  Wisdom and folly (9:17–10:15)
  Rule of kings (vv. 16-20)
  Sound business practices (11:1-8)
  Enjoying life before old age comes (11:9–12:8)
Epilogue
  Aim of the Preacher (12:9f.)
  Commendation of his teachings (vv. 11f.)
  Conclusion of the matter (vv. 13f.)[13]

Unity. Such outlines as the above or those of H.L. Ginsberg[14] and A.G. Wright[15] presume a unity to Qoheleth's work that would have been rejected out of hand or at least seriously questioned a generation ago. G.A. Barton's approach, by no means most extreme in assigning parts of Qoheleth to other authors, is typical. He saw at work beside the original author: "an editor deeply interested in the Wisdom Literature" (responsible for "wisdom glosses" in 4:15; 5:3, 7a; 7:1a, 3, 5-9, 11f., 19; 8:1; 9:17f.; 10:1-3, 8-14a, 15, 18f.) and a later editor "deeply imbued with the spirit of the Pharisees" (responsible for pious glosses that "support the orthodox doctrines of the time," e.g., 2:26; 3:17; 7:18b, 26b, 29; 8:2b, 3a, 5-6a, 11-13; 11:9b; 12:1a, 13f.).[16]

More than anything, a fresh understanding of Semitic literature and its manner of argumentation has prompted the recent emphasis on the unity of Qoheleth. R. Gordis has made a substantial contribution to the newer scholarly consensus, noting parallels between Babylonian and Egyptian wisdom literature and Qoheleth in the tendency to combine conventional and unconventional wisdom and to imbed traditional proverbs in original material. Further, he argues that many apparent contradictions (recognized by the rabbis who debated the book's canonicity) result from the author's struggle with life's complexities, not an editor's attempts at patchwork.

One of Gordis' best contributions is the suggestion that other apparent contradictions can readily be resolved when it is seen that Qoheleth often quoted material in order to refute it. For example, the comment on work in

---

13. Adapted from an outline privately circulated by R.B. Laurin; see Laurin, *The Layman's Introduction to the Old Testament* (Valley Forge: 1970), pp. 104f. The adaptation highlights the conclusions about enjoying life now. A great pioneer in the study of Ecclesiastes, C.D. Ginsburg recognized the importance of these passages as boundary markers for the major divisions of the book; *Coheleth* (London: 1861).
14. "The Structure and Contents of the Book of Koheleth," *VTS* 3 (1955): 138-149.
15. *CBQ* 30 (1968): 313f.
16. *The Book of Ecclesiastes*. ICC (Edinburgh: 1908), pp. 43-46. E. Jones takes an almost identical approach; *Proverbs and Ecclesiastes*, pp. 259-262. K. Siegfried, *Prediger und Hoheslied*. HKAT (Göttingen: 1898), is often cited as the most intricate theory of composition, finding comments by three main editors in addition to the author, plus glosses by a half dozen others.

4:5 ("The fool folds his hands, and eats his own flesh") is a piece of conventional wisdom aimed to condemn laziness. To point out its inadequacy, Qoheleth cites his own proverb: "Better is a handful of quietness than two hands full of toil and a striving after wind" (v. 6).

Undoubtedly the strongest argument against multiple authorship is the question of motive. If Qoheleth caused so many problems to the wise and pious among the Jews, why did they bother to rework the book with a multitude of glosses? Gordis remarks: "None of these scholars seeks to explain why the book was deemed worthy of this effort to 'legitimize' it, when it could so easily have been suppressed."[17]

Generally, it is recognized, even by Gordis, that the title (1:1) and epilogue (12:9-14) may have been added by a disciple of Qoheleth, speaking of his master in the third person. But the work itself remains intact with all its puzzling perplexities.

Form-critical studies during the past forty years have divided the book into segments of various lengths and number. A growing tendency is to view the book "as a *cahier* or notebook," rather than a debate, dialogue, or philosophical treatise.[18] Of the unity of these notes, von Rad remarks:

> There is, to be precise, an inner unity which can find expression otherwise than through a linear development of thought or through a logical progression in the thought process, namely through the unity of style and topic and theme, a unity which can make a work of literature into a whole and which can in fact give it the rank of a self-contained work of art.[19]

LITERARY CHARACTERISTICS

Reflections. The backbone of Qoheleth's literary style is a series of first-person prose narratives in which the Preacher relates his observations about the futility of life. These reflections (Zimmerli calls them "confessions")[20] begin with such phrases as: "And I applied my mind" (1:13, 17), "I have seen everything" (v. 14), "I said to myself" (v. 16; 2:1), "Moreover I saw" (3:16), "Again I saw" (4:1, 7; 9:11). The role of observation is key, reflected by repeated use of the verb "to see." J.G. Williams, following Zimmerli, found in this "confes-

---

17. *Koheleth—The Man and His World*, 3rd ed. (New York: 1968), p. 71. Weiser (*Old Testament*, p. 309) and Eissfeldt (*Old Testament*, p. 499) agree to the basic unity of the book, yet admit that a pious redactor may have added a few verses in the name of doctrinal orthodoxy.

18. Gordis, *Koheleth*, p. 110. For a summary of the efforts of W. Zimmerli, K. Galling, and F. Ellermeier to divide the book into literary units (usually more than thirty), virtually all attributed to Qoheleth, see O. Kaiser, *Introduction*, p. 398.

19. *Wisdom in Israel*, p. 227.

20. *Die Weisheit des Predigers Salomo* (Berlin: 1936), p. 26. J.L. Crenshaw cites the stylistic affinity of these confessions to the Egyptian royal confessions (German *Bekenntnis*); "Wisdom," p. 257 in J.H. Hayes, ed., *Old Testament Form Criticism*.

sion style" a "departure from the security and self-certainty of the wise."[21] Questioning whether clear-cut conclusions about the human place in God's cosmos can be affirmed, as other wise men taught, Qoheleth can only rehearse what he has searched, seen, and concluded. The reflective literary form matches precisely his understanding of reality: empirical yet personal.

Frequent in these reflections is the summary conclusion, usually one closing sentence completing the argument: "I perceived that this also is but a striving after wind" (1:17); "Then I considered all that my hands had done . . . and behold, all was vanity and a striving after wind . . ." (2:11); "This also is vanity" (v. 23); "This also is vanity and a striving after wind" (v. 26; 4:4, 16; 6:9).[22]

Proverbs. Qoheleth used proverbs in both conventional and nonconventional ways. Like his fellow sages, he used two main types: (1) Statements (called "truth sayings" by Ellermeier) simply affirm what reality is like: "He who loves money will not be satisfied with money; nor he who loves wealth, with gain" (5:10 [MT 9]). (2) Admonitions (or "counsels") are commands, sometimes positive: "Cast your bread upon the waters, for you will find it after many days" (11:1); sometimes negative: "Be not quick to anger, for anger lodges in the bosom of fools" (7:9). The variety of expansions and modification is almost endless.

A favorite form of Qoheleth's is the comparison of two forms of conduct, one "better" than the other (4:6, 9, 13; 5:5 [MT 4]; 7:1-3, 5, 8; 9:17f.). The literary form is a hedge against pessimism and nihilism: things may not be all good or bad; but some are surely better than others.

The proverbs occur at two main points: (1) imbedded in the reflections, where they reinforce or summarize the conclusion (1:15, 18; 4:5f.; vv. 9-12 is almost a numerical proverb like Prov. 30:5, 18, 21, 24, 29); and (2) clustered in the "words of advice" sections (5:1-12 [MT 4:17–5:11]; 7:1–8:9; 9:13–12:8).

Most important is their role in the argument. Frequently, Qoheleth uses proverbs to help his hearers cope with life's difficulties. Such proverbs become a kind of commentary on his positive conclusion calling his followers to enjoy life now as God gave it (note the "words of advice" in 5:1-12 [MT 4:17–5:11]; 9:13–12:8, which are filled with sound counsel on how to make the best of life).

---

21. "What Does It Profit a Man?: The Wisdom of Koheleth," *Judaism* 20 (1971): 179.

22. Ellermeier finds three subgroups: (1) unitary critical reflection: the observation begins with a negative and consistently criticizes an optimistic understanding of life (3:16-22; 6:1-6); (2) critical broken reflection: the starting observation is positive, then criticizes false optimism (3:1-15; 4:13-16); and (3) critical reverse broken reflection: the thought begins negatively, then progresses to something of value, though the initial reservation remains (4:4-6; 5:13-20 [MT 12-19]); *Qohelet* 1 (Herzberg: 1967): 88ff. For a summary of Ellermeier's analysis, which is based on the direction of the argument more than the precise literary form, see Kaiser, *Introduction*, p. 399.

Qoheleth quotes other proverbs so he can argue against them. He sometimes cites conventional wisdom, then counters it with his own statements
(2:14; 4:5f.). In 9:18, the first line represents the traditional value put on
wisdom: "Wisdom is better than weapons of war." This may be true, Qoheleth
says, but it should not be overvalued because "one sinner destroys much good."[23]

A clever device is the Preacher's use of antiproverbs, sayings coined in
wisdom style but with a message opposite that of the tradition:

For in much wisdom is much vexation,
and he who increases knowledge increases sorrow. (1:18)

The contrast between these statements and the happiness promised by wisdom
in passages like Prov. 2:10; 3:13; 8:34-36 is striking and must have cut Qoheleth's wise opponents to the quick. Small wonder that his admiring disciple
noted the master's skill in the use of proverbs (12:9).

Rhetorical Questions. To draw his audience into his argument and force the
desired response, Qoheleth frequently uses rhetorical questions. Since they
often occur toward the end of a section, they are a clue to his point: "What
has a man from all the toil and strain with which he toils beneath the sun?"
(2:22); "What gain has the worker from his toil?" (3:9). The questions lure the
reader into Qoheleth's net, in which he wants to capture assent to his verdict
of futility.[24]

Allegory. "Enjoy life now as God gives it" is the Preacher's positive conclusion. At the end of the book, he reinforces it graphically with an allegory or
extended cluster of metaphors (12:2-7). His main point, made in an admonition
("Remember also your Creator in the days of your youth"; v. 1), is driven home
in a picture of the toll of old age on human vitality. An estate, which falls into
disrepair and ultimately abandonment, is likened to members of the human
body: fading light is the loss of vitality (v. 2); keepers of the house, the arms;
strong men, the back; grinders, the teeth; those that look through the windows,
the eyes (v. 3); shut doors, the ears; rising at the voice of a bird may be the
inability to sleep; daughters of song are the strength of the voice (v. 4); the
blossoming almond tree speaks of gray hair, and dragging grasshoppers of crip-
pling frailty (v. 5); silver cord, golden bowl, pitcher, and wheel are all figures
of life functions snapped at death (v. 6). The allegory is introduced by a proverb
to make its meaning and purpose clear; similarly, it closes with a literal descrip-

---

23. Ampler treatment of the use of proverbs in various forms of argumentation may
be found in Gordis, *Koheleth*, pp. 95-108; and in his "Quotations in Biblical, Oriental,
and Rabbinic Literature," pp. 104-159 in *Poets, Prophets and Sages.*

24. Other rhetorical questions are found in 1:3; 2:2, 12, 15, 19, 25; 3:21; 5:6, 11
[MT 5, 10]; 6:6-8, 11f.; 7:16f.; 8:1, 4, 7. The answers they insist on are almost always
negative: "nothing," "none," "no one."

tion of death (v. 7) that rules out speculation as to its general thrust, even though interpretation of the details may vary.[25]

CONTRIBUTIONS TO BIBLICAL THEOLOGY

Freedom of God and Limits of Wisdom. Far from a mere skeptic or pessimist, Qoheleth sought to contribute positively to the lives of his contemporaries and their relationship to God. He did so by stressing the limits to human understanding and ability. Thus, even his verdict about the vanity of much of what is viewed as dependable he would have considered a positive contribution to human insight.

(1) People are limited by the way in which God has determined the events of their lives. Thus they have little power to change the course of history:

> What is crooked cannot be made straight,
> and what is lacking cannot be numbered. (1:15)

That antiproverb is echoed in the rhetorical questions:

> Consider the work of God;
> who can make straight what he has made crooked? (7:13)

Even the times for life's experiences are set in place in such a way that human toil cannot alter them (3:1-9).[26]

"Under the sun" (1:3, 9, 14; 2:11, 17-20, 22; 3:16; 4:1, 3, 7, 15; 5:13, 18 [MT 12, 17]; 6:1, 12; 8:9, 15, 17; 9:3, 6, 9, 11, 13; 10:5) is an almost nagging reminder of the earthbound life of perplexed humanity. At base, it means that people are in the world, not in heaven where God dwells. In many contexts, it

> suggests also that the sun relentlessly makes *labour* and *toil* hard, as relentlessly exposes everything to view, showing how 'empty' it is, and just as relentlessly measures the passage of ceaseless days and nights.[27]

(2) Human creatures are limited by their inability to discover God's ways. They may understand, says Qoheleth, that their lives are determined by God's sovereignty, but they cannot understand how or why. This was especially vexing to Israel's wise men, who sought to know the proper time for each of life's tasks:

---

25. For a discussion of allegory, including the possibility that 12:2-7 may have developed from a riddle, see von Rad, *Wisdom in Israel*, pp. 45f.; Crenshaw, "Wisdom," pp. 246f.

26. The opposites "born–die," "plant–pluck," etc. are examples of merismus, a literary device in which extremes are mentioned so as to cover them and everything in between.

27. W.J. Fuerst, *The Books of Ruth, Esther, Ecclesiastes, The Song of Songs, Lamentations*. Cambridge Bible Commentary (Cambridge: 1975), p. 103.

To make an apt answer is a joy to a man,
>and a word in season [lit. "in its time"], how good it is! (Prov. 15:23)[28]

The problem is not God's, but humankind's:

He has made everything beautiful in its time; also he has put eternity[29] into man's mind, yet so that he cannot find out what God has done from the beginning to the end. (3:11)

As A.G. Wright has shown, the phrases "not find out" ("who can find out?") or "do not know" ("no knowledge") dominate chs. 7–11.[30] No wonder Qoheleth counsels against rashness in prayer: ". . . for God is in heaven, and you upon earth; therefore let your words be few" (5:2 [MT 1]).

The wise men of Proverbs recognized the limits of human wisdom and the sovereignty of God's ways:

A man's mind plans his ways,
>but the Lord directs his steps. (Prov. 16:9)

Many are the plans in the mind of a man,
>but it is the purpose of the Lord that will be established. (19:21)

But Qoheleth's neighbors apparently had underplayed these truths in their over-confidence about their human ability to effect their own destinies. Why Qoheleth chose to stress those limitations has sparked sharp debate.

Von Rad credits this to a loss of trust in God, accompanied by a radical desire to find more systematic order in life and to discern the future more clearly than the older wise men dared.[31]

In contrast Zimmerli views Qoheleth as a "frontier guard" who refused to allow the sages to claim an all-embracing skill in controlling life. Qoheleth knew that a true "fear of God never allows man in his 'art of directing' to hold the helm in his own hands."[32] Also, according to Zimmerli, Qoheleth's silence about Israel's election served as a negative reminder that a doctrine of creation by itself is incomplete until "it dares to believe that the creator is the God who in free goodness promised Himself to His people."[33]

---

28. See von Rad, "The Doctrine of the Proper Time," pp. 138-143 in *Wisdom in Israel*.

29. "Eternity" is probably the best translation of '*ōlām* here, provided it is not taken in quantitative terms alone, the mere extension of time into the distant future. In this context, it must stand for "God's ways in the world," "the course of worldly events as God alone shapes and understands them." He has granted the consciousness that he is at work but not the power to grasp what he is doing. See Gordis, *Koheleth*, pp. 221f.; Williams, *Judaism* 20 (1971): 182-85.

30. *CBQ* 30 (1968): 325f.

31. *Wisdom in Israel*, pp. 226-237.

32. *SJT* 17 (1964): 158.

33. *Idem*.

Facing Life's Realities. (1) Grace. Though Qoheleth indicates no concern for Israel's experience of covenant or redemption, he certainly was aware of God's grace. For him, grace showed itself in God's provision of the good things of creation. His positive conclusion ("There is nothing better for a man than that he should eat and drink, and find enjoyment in his toil") is rooted in God's goodness: "This also . . . is from the hand of God; for apart from him who can eat or who can have enjoyment?" (2:24f.). Elsewhere (3:13), this is all described as "God's gift to man." A dozen times the root $n\bar{a}tan$ "give" is used with God as subject. Whatever else may have baffled him about the inscrutable ways of God, Qoheleth had no doubt that his grace appears daily in provisions of the Creator who "has made everything beautiful in its time" (v. 11).

The realities of grace and human limitation converge in Qoheleth's use of "portion" (Heb. $h\bar{e}leq$; 2:10, 21; 3:22; 5:18f. [MT 17f.]; 9:6, 9). Translated "lot" or "all" (2:21), the term signifies the partial, and limited, nature of God's gifts. He does not give mankind everything, yet these simple pleasures are gifts, which the Preacher urges his fellows to make the most of. To an extent "portion" is contrasted with "profit" ($yitr\hat{o}n$), another favorite word (1:3; 2:11, 13; 3:9; 5:9, 16 [MT 8, 15]; 7:12; 10:10f.; cf. the cognate $m\hat{o}tar$ "advantage," 3:19). Profit describes the surplus that human labor can generate; portion depicts the lot which God's grace bestows. Mankind can earn nothing; God sees that they have enough.[34]

(2) Death. Prominent in the verdict that "all is futility," death's coming is sure, but its timing is not. It is the one fate that comes to all—wise and foolish (2:14f.; 9:2f.), man and beast (3:19). Death confronts people most drastically with their limitations, reminding them continually that the future is beyond their control. It strips them naked, whether they have toiled with wisdom only to leave their goods to the undeserving (2:21) or whether they have wanted to leave them to an heir but lost them first (5:13-17 [MT 12-16]). Qoheleth's description of death seems based on the creation narrative of Gen. 2, where divine breath and earthly dust combined to make the human self. In death the process seems reversed: "and the dust returns to the earth as it was, and the spirit returns to God who gave it" (12:7), although Qoheleth questioned just how dogmatic one could be (3:20f.). For him, death was the great discourager of false optimism.[35]

(3) Enjoyment. If "toil" (Heb. $'\bar{a}m\bar{a}l$) dominated Qoheleth's view of the harshness and rigors of life (2:10, 21, 24; 3:13; 4:4, 6, 8f.; 5:15, 19 [MT 14, 18]; 6:7; 8:15; 10:15; verb form $'\bar{a}mal$: 1:3; 2:11, 19f.; 5:16 [MT 15]; 8:17), so he used "joy" or "enjoyment" (from $\acute{s}mh$) frequently, especially in stating his positive conclusion (2:24f.; 3:12, 22; 5:18-20 [MT 17-19]; 7:14; 8:15; 9:7-9;

---

34. See Williams, *Judaism* 10 (1971): 185-190, on these terms.
35. Note Zimmerli's summation, *SJT* 17 (1964): 156: "In a manner hitherto unheard-of in the Old Testament, Ecclesiastes sees death as the power that takes away the power of the whole creation and even of man's Wisdom."

11:8f.). As grim as are life's painful present and precarious future, joy is possible when sought in the right place: gratitude for and appreciation of God's simple gifts of food, drink, work, and love. Writing to a society preoccupied with the need to succeed, achieve, produce, control,[36] Qoheleth warned of the joylessness and futility of such endeavors. Joy was not to be found in human achievement, as elusive as chasing the wind (2:11, 17, etc.), but in the everyday gifts apportioned by the Creator.[37]

Preparation for the Gospel. Though Qoheleth contains no recognizable prophetic or typological material, it does prepare for the Christian gospel. This does not mean that was the book's central purpose or the reason for its inclusion in the canon. As a critique of the extremes of wisdom, a window on the tragedies and injustices of life, and a pointer to the joys of existence, it stands on its own as a word from God to all humankind.[38]

Yet its Christian value should not be ignored. Its realism in depicting the ironies of suffering and death helps explain the crucial importance of Jesus' crucifixion and resurrection. Qoheleth's insistence on the inscrutability of God's ways underscores the magnificent breakthrough in divine and human communication which the Incarnation effected. His dreary pictures of wearying toil paved the way for the Master's call from taxing labor to gracious rest (Matt. 11:28-30). His command to enjoy God's simple gifts without anxiety found echo in Jesus' exhortations to trust the God of the lily and the sparrow (6:25-33).

With burning eye and biting pen, Qoheleth challenged the overconfidence of the older wisdom and its misapplication in his culture. Thereby, he prepared for the "greater than Solomon," "in whom are hid all the treasures of wisdom and knowledge" (12:42; Col. 2:3).[39]

FOR FURTHER READING

Ginsberg, H.L. *Studies in Koheleth*. New York: 1950.
Loader, J.A. *Polar Structures in the Book of Qoheleth*. BZAW 152 (1979). Form-critical analysis finding "intended polar structures" rather than "contradictions.")

---

36. Dahood notes the frequency of commercial terms like profit (*yiṭrôn, môṭār*), toil (*'āmāl*), business (*'inyān*), money (*kesep*), portion (*ḥēleq*), success (*kišrôn*), riches (*'ōšer*), owner (*ba'al*), and deficit (*ḥesrôn*).

37. J.S. Wright has captured well this dominant note of joy; "The Interpretation of Ecclesiastes," *Evangelical Quarterly* 18 (1946): 18-34. See also R.E. Murphy, "Qohélet le sceptique," *Concilium* 119 (1976): 60; R.K. Johnston, " 'Confessions of a Workaholic': A Reappraisal of Qoheleth," CBQ 38 (1976): 14-28.

38. Note B.S. Childs: "By being set in the eschatological framework of a coming divine judgment, Koheleth's message is not only limited to present human activity, but sharply relativized in the light of the new and fuller dimension of divine wisdom. When later Jews and Christians contrasted the wisdom of this world (I Cor. 1.20) with the wisdom of God, they were interpreting the Hebrew scriptures according to their canonical shaping"; *Old Testament as Scripture*, pp. 588f.

39. For a Christian application of Qoheleth's main themes, see D.A. Hubbard, *Beyond Futility: Messages of Hope from the Book of Ecclesiastes* (Grand Rapids: 1976).

Ogden, G.S. "The 'Better'-Proverb (Tôb-Spruch), Rhetorical Criticism, and Qoheleth."
    JBL 96 (1977): 489-505.
Whitley, C.F. *Koheleth*. BZAW 148 (1979). (Detailed study of the language; argues for
    post-Maccabean composition.)

CHAPTER 45

THE SONG
OF SONGS

TAKING its name from 1:1, "The Song of Songs [i.e., the finest song], which is Solomon's" (an alternate name, Canticles, is derived from the Vulgate), this book is placed first among the five scrolls (Megilloth) in the Jewish canon used on festive occasions; it is assigned to be read at Passover.

CANONICITY

Acceptance in the Jewish canon apparently did not come easily, as the Mishnah more than hints. Rabbi Akiba's strong affirmation (ca. A.D. 100) undoubtedly was calculated to quell opposition and settle forever the book's place: "The whole world is not worth the day on which the Song of Songs was given to Israel; all the Writings are holy, and the Song of Songs is the holy of holies."[1]

Without doubt the erotic nature of the Song provoked opposition. Eventually this objection was outweighed by the poems' connection with Solomon and by rabbinic and Christian allegorical interpretations, which helped to mitigate the sensual tone. As the Jews began to find within the book a picture of God's matchless love for Israel they did not hesitate to count it with those writings so holy that they "defile the hands."[2]

AUTHORSHIP AND DATE

Traditional Solomonic authorship is based on references to him throughout the book (1:5; 3:7, 9, 11), especially in the title (1:1). Heb. lišlōmōh (1:1), literally "to Solomon," may indicate authorship but other interpretations are possible: "for" or "in the style of Solomon." Solomon's skill as a songwriter is known

---

1. Mishnah Yad. 3:5.
2. B.S. Childs rejects this view: "Instead, the Song entered the canon in essentially the same role as it had played in Israel's institutional life. It celebrated the mysteries of human love expressed in the marriage festival"; Old Testament as Scripture, p. 578.

from 1 Kgs. 4:32 (cf. Ps. 72; 127), but his relationship to these love poems is obscure.[3] Attempts to fit the love and loyalty expressed here into Solomon's pattern of political marriage and excessive concubinage (see 1 Kgs. 2) have not been successful.

Alleged Persian and Greek loanwords,[4] almost uniform employment of the relative pronoun form characteristic of later Hebrew,[5] and words and phrases reflecting Aramaic influence[6] indicate that final editing, if not the actual composition, was probably later than Solomon. However, the book need not be dated in the Hellenistic period (after 330). Ample evidence exists both for intercourse between Ionia and Canaan and for Aramaic impact on Hebrew literature from the early centuries of the Monarchy. Attempts to prove, on the basis of geographical references as well as language, that the Song originated

"Like Lebanon, choice as the cedars" is the beloved in the Song of Songs (Cant. 5:15). (W.S. LaSor)

----

3. Talmud B. Bat. 15a attributes the song to Hezekiah and his scribes, undoubtedly following Prov. 25:1.

4. Pardēs "orchard," 4:13; appiryôn, from Greek phoreíon, AV "chariot," but better RSV "palanquin," 3:9.

5. še instead of 'ªšer, except in 1:1.

6. See S.R. Driver, Introduction, p. 448.

in the northern kingdom have not been successful. Many of the place names are in the north (e.g., Sharon, 2:1; Lebanon, 3:9; 4:8, 11, 15, etc.; Amana, Senir, Hermon, 4:8; Tirzah,[7] Damascus, 7:4 [MT 5]; Carmel, v. 5 [MT 6]), yet no provincialism can be shown. The poet has a ready knowledge of the geography of Palestine and Syria from En-gedi (1:14) to Lebanon.

The lack of historical references in the Song makes dating difficult. H.J. Schonfield argues for the Persian period, more precisely between Nehemiah's time and 350. Following in part linguistic arguments and geographical data (no evidence for a divided kingdom), he finds in the descriptions of Solomon's fabulous glory reflections of "the pomp and circumstances of the Persian Empire and the luxurious palaces of the Great King at Susa (Shushan) and Persepolis."[8] But the witness of archaeology to Solomon's splendid reign seems to render Persian influence unnecessary. Hebrew writers familiar with the traditions concerning Israel's golden age needed no Persian prototypes. The Song's lavish setting accurately reflects Solomon's glory, just as the luxury, wealth, and wisdom of Ecclesiastes carefully record his regal circumstances.

In sum, though Solomon himself probably was not the author, much of the setting and tone reflect his age. As with Proverbs, the nucleus or core of Canticles may have been transmitted (perhaps orally), added to, and then given its present setting by a nameless, inspired poet around the time of the Exile.[9]

LITERARY QUALITIES

Strictly speaking, the Song should not be classified as wisdom literature, since its dominant form is love poetry, not instruction or debate. But because it is connected with Solomon and probably was copied, preserved, and published by wisdom circles, it can be studied alongside that corpus.[10] Moreover, by celebrating the glories of marriage as a gift of the Creator and a norm for human life, its poets are close kin to the wise men.[11]

Most of the Song is stylized conversation between the lover and beloved

---

7. Mention of Tirzah may argue against an exilic or postexilic date for at least this part of the Song. This ancient Canaanite city (Josh. 12:24), the first capital of the northern kingdom (1 Kgs. 14:17; 15:21; 16:6ff.), is not mentioned after *ca.* 750 (2 Kgs. 15:14, 16). A strong argument for an early date for at least some of the poetry is its obvious similarities with the Egyptian love poetry of the Eighteenth Dynasty (*ca.* 1250); see J.B. White, *A Study of the Language of Love in the Song of Songs and Ancient Egyptian Poetry.* SBL Dissertation Series 38 (Missoula: 1978), pp. 91-159; R.E. Murphy, "Song of Songs," *IDBS,* p. 837.

8. *The Song of Songs* (New York: 1959), pp. 75-83.

9. O. Kaiser, *Introduction,* p. 366: "It should be assumed then that in Canticles we have a later collection of wedding and love songs from different periods."

10. Murphy, *idem*.

11. Childs, *Old Testament as Scripture,* pp. 574-78.

(e.g., 1:9ff.; 4:1ff.; 6:2ff.), though much may be imagined speech, uttered when the partner was absent. Various forms of love poetry have been identified.[12]

Descriptive Songs. In this ancient form, well attested in Babylonian, Egyptian, and modern Arabic (where it is called *wasf*) literature, each lover describes the other's beauty in highly figurative language (he describes her, 4:1-7; 6:4-7; 7:1-9 [MT 2-10]; she describes him, 5:10-16). These descriptions salute the partner, while stimulating both to ready themselves for love (see 1:15f., where each in turn admires the other's beauty).

Self-descriptions. Only the woman used this form, usually to disclaim modestly the beauty ascribed to her (1:5f.; 2:1). Her self-description in 8:10 seems to take pride in her virginity and maturity; she had passed her brothers' test (vv. 8f.).

Songs of Admiration. This form differs from the descriptive song in calling attention to the loved one's dress or ornamentation (e.g., the jewelry in 1:9-11; 4:9-11). Cant. 7:7-9 shows the passion that such admiration aroused, as the lover longs to possess the one he so admired.

Songs of Yearning. The lovers' ardent desire, especially when apart, is voiced in such songs (e.g., 1:2-4; 2:5f.; 8:1-4, 6f.). The characteristic form is a wish for love or a call to love. This form of song is a reminder that absence can make the heart grow fonder.

Search Narratives. Twice the woman recounts her impassioned searches for her lover. Unable to sleep, she wanders through the city looking for him—once with satisfaction (3:1-4), once with frustration (5:2-7). These narratives show her openness in expressing desire: vigorously and persistently she takes initiative in love.

Game of Love. The second search narrative begins a "game" between the woman and her friends, the "daughters of Jerusalem":

She: search narrative (unsuccessful)	5:2-7
She: oath placed on friends to help find the lover	v. 8
Friends: teasing question about lover's worth	v. 9
She: answer song describing his beauty	vv. 10-16
Friends: teasing question about accompanying her to find him	6:1

---

12. See White, *Language of Love*, pp. 50-55, which combines the insights of F. Horst, "Die Formen des althebräischen Liebesliedes," pp. 176-187 in H.W. Wolff, ed., *Gottes Recht* (Munich: 1961), with those of W. Staerk, *Lyrik. Die Schriften das Alten Testaments* 3/1 (Göttingen: 1920), and E. Würthwein, *Die fünf Megilloth*, 2nd ed. HAT 18 (Tübingen: 1969).

She: erotic account of where he is; formula of belonging (cf. 2:16; 7:10a)
(indicates that she will not share him) 6:2f.

This game illustrates the playfulness which was part of ancient wisdom, and also shows how numbers of literary forms can combine in a larger unit. Even more, it is a reminder of the exclusive, covenantal relationship that the partners enjoyed.

Other Literary Forms. The Song contains several other forms, such as: (1) formula imposing an oath (2:7; 3:5; 5:8; 8:4), showing how strongly the woman's friends support her commitment and how earnestly she wants freedom to be with her lover undisturbed; (2) teasing song (1:7f.), catching the banter between the lovers in their desire to be together (see 2:14f.; 5:2f.); (3) boasting song (6:8-10; 8:11f.), expressing the lover's delight in her uniqueness, a delight shared by the friends, who join in praising her (6:10); (4) invitation to love (2:5, 17; 4:16; 7:11-13; 8:14), offered by the woman, usually with the urgency of an imperative.

Apart from the lovers, the participants are identified only with great difficulty. Brief responses (1:8; 5:9; 6:1, etc.) have been credited to "daughters of Jerusalem," perhaps friends or "bridesmaids" (1:5; 2:7; 3:5, 35, etc.); citizens of Jerusalem, who describe the royal entourage as it approaches the city (3:6-11); and citizens of Shulam (8:5). In this highly figurative, lyrical poetry the central characters may be recreating the speeches of others. For instance, the Shulammite[13] seems to be quoting her brothers in 8:8f. Schonfield attributes these short responses, regardless of context, to a chorus. This simple approach is a welcome relief from attempts (especially in the last century) to treat the Song as a highly complex drama.

The book's impact lies in the warmth and intensity of the love depicted, especially in the rich and graphic imagery. These very qualities which are the poem's source of strength present problems to western tastes. The vividly detailed descriptions of the lovers' bodies and their frankly acknowledged, passionate desire seem too highly spiced. But they are the product of a distant time and place. They are vivid but not lurid, and the open honesty of their approach may put them a cut above the innuendo sometimes found in their contemporary western counterparts. Frequently the similes or metaphors sound strange or even uncomplimentary:

---

13. The only name given the heroine (6:13), its derivation and meaning are problematic. It has been linked to an unknown town of Shulam or considered a variant of Shunammite. Some identify her as Abishag, the Shunammite (1 Kgs. 1:3ff.). H.H. Rowley rejects these views, contending that the term is a feminine form of Solomon, "the Solomoness"; "The Meaning of the Shulammite," *AJSL* 56 (1939): 84-91.

Your hair is like a flock of goats,
    moving down the slopes of Gilead; (4:1)

or:

Your neck is like the tower of David,
    built for an arsenal,
Whereon hang a thousand bucklers,
    all of them shields of warriors. (v. 4)

A. Bentzen's suggestion is helpful: "Orientals fix the eye on one single striking point, which according to our conceptions is perhaps not characteristic."[14] Thus, in the wavelike motion of a flock of goats moving down a distant slope the poet finds an image of the grace and beauty of the beloved's tresses falling in gentle waves upon her shoulders. Similarly, the strength and erectness of her neck, ornamented with jewelry, remind him of David's tower-fortress bedecked with warriors' shields.[15]

SUGGESTED INTERPRETATIONS

Scholars probably agree less about the origin, meaning, and purpose of the Song than about those of any other Old Testament book. Erotic lyrics, absence of a religious note, and opaqueness of plot baffle scholars and tempt their imaginative ingenuity. Not only is the history of interpretation full of conflicting theories, but all the resources of modern scholarship—archaeological discoveries, recovery of huge bodies of ancient literature, insights into oriental psychology and sociology—have produced no uniform approach to the book.[16]

Allegorical. Perhaps (within the providence of God) the allegorical interpretation, along with the tradition of Solomonic authorship, is responsible for the Song's presence in the canon. The earliest recorded Jewish interpretations (in the Mishnah, Talmud, and Targum) find in it a portrait of God's love for

---

14. *Introduction* 1:130. T. Boman offers helpful suggestions regarding the figures of speech: e.g., comparisons between the maiden and a tower (4:4; 7:4f.), a wall (8:10), or Mt. Carmel (7:5) are expressions of her purity, her inaccessibility as a chaste and sheltered virgin aloof from the temptations of those who would seek to defile her. References to the dovelike qualities of the Shulammite (1:15; 2:14; 4:1) are also descriptive of her purity; *Hebrew Thought Compared with Greek*, trans. J.L. Moreau (Philadelphia: 1960), pp. 77-89.

15. Some passages are illuminated by an understanding of Semitic custom. E.g., the Shulammite's wish that her lover were her brother "that nursed at my mother's breast" in order that they might have ready access to each other probably refers not to a uterine brother (from the same womb) but a "milk brother," nursed by her mother. Rather than incest, such love could be enjoyed without shame or the normal social restrictions which prevented easy access between lovers. See R. Patai, *Sex and Family in the Bible and the Middle East*, pp. 194f.

16. This section is heavily indebted to H.H. Rowley, "The Interpretation of the Song of Songs," pp. 195-245 in *The Servant of the Lord*. For a massive compendium on the history of interpretation, see M. Pope, *Song of Songs*. Anchor Bible 7C (Garden City: 1977), pp. 89-229.

Israel. This accounts for the book's use at Passover, which celebrates God's covenant love. Not content with general allusions to God's relationship with Israel, the rabbis vied to discover specific references to Israel's history.

The Church Fathers set the pace for much subsequent Christian interpretation by baptizing the Song into Christ, seeing in it Christ's love for the Church or the individual believer.[17] Christians also have contributed detailed and imaginative interpretations, as attested by headings traditionally found in the KJV containing such interpretative summaries as "The mutual love of Christ and his Church" or "The Church professeth her faith in Christ." The place of allegory in modern Roman Catholic understanding of the Song is illustrated in the important commentary of A. Robert, R. Tournay, and A. Feuillet.[18]

Typical. Seeking to avoid the subjectivity of the allegorical approach and preserve the literal sense of the poem, this method stresses the major themes of love and devotion rather than the details of the story. In the warmth and strength of the lovers' mutual affection, typological interpreters hear overtones of the relationship between Christ and his Church. Justification for this view has been based on parallels with Arabic love poems, which may have esoteric or mystical meanings; on Christ's use of the story of Jonah (Matt. 12:40) or the serpent in the wilderness (John 3:14); and on the well-known biblical analogies of spiritual marriage (e.g., Jer. 2:2; 3:1ff.; Ezek. 16:6ff.; Hos. 1–3; Eph. 5:22-33; Rev. 19:9).

That generations of Christians and Jews have gained devotional benefits from allegorical or typical approaches to the Song cannot be denied. The question, however, is what the author intended. The allegorical interpretation is questionable because scholarly control is impossible. The possibilities for variety in the interpretation of details are limitless, with no valid means of confirming or disproving the conflicting viewpoints. One is more apt to find his or her own ideas than to discern the author's intent. A further weakness of the allegorical and typical interpretations is the complete absence of any hint that the Song is to be interpreted in other than its natural sense.[19]

Dramatic. The presence of dialogue, soliloquy, and choruses (see above) has led students of literature, both ancient (e.g., Origen, *ca.* A.D. 240) and

---

17. In the beauty and purity of the Shulammite, some Roman Catholic interpreters (e.g., St. Ambrose) see the Virgin Mary; see F.X. Curley, "The Lady of the Canticle," *American Ecclesiastical Review* 133 (1955): 289-299.

18. *Le Cantique des Cantiques.* Études Bibliques (Paris: 1973).

19. The works of J. Fischer (*Das Hohe Lied.* Echter Bibel 10 [Würzburg: 1950]) and of L. Krinetski (*Das Hohe Lied.* Kommentare und Beiträge zum Alten und Neuen Testament [Düsseldorf: 1964]) illustrate the strengths and weaknesses of a typological approach; cf. White, *Language of Love,* pp. 20f. A variation is the "parabolic" interpretation ventured by T.R.D. Buzy, *Le Cantique des Cantiques,* 3rd ed. (Paris: 1953), and H. Schneider, *Das Hohelied.* Herders Bibel Kommentar (Freiburg im Breisgau: 1962); both find in the Song a parable of a renewed covenant between Israel and Yahweh.

modern (e.g., Milton), to treat it as a drama. In the nineteenth century two forms of dramatic analysis were in vogue. Franz Delitzsch's commentary found two main characters, Solomon and the Shulammite, identified by some scholars (quite incorrectly in the view of this survey) with Pharaoh's daughter, whom Solomon wed in a marriage of convenience (1 Kgs. 3:1). The two-character theory usually sees the Song as a drama celebrating the more-than-physical affection which bound Solomon to the Shulammite above the others of his harem. An alternate dramatic theory involved three characters. First detailed by H. Ewald and adapted by S.R. Driver, it includes the maiden's shepherd lover as well as Solomon and the Shulammite. The plot turns on the Shulammite's faithfulness to her rustic lover despite Solomon's luxurious attempts to woo and win her.

The three-character theory (or "shepherd hypothesis") may help to explain why the lover sometimes is pictured as a shepherd (e.g., 1:7f.) and why the poem ends not in Jerusalem but in a northern pastoral setting. Yet it is not without weaknesses: the absence of any dramatic instructions, and the complexity introduced if the Shulammite responds to Solomon's overtures by reminiscing of her shepherd sweetheart. A major difficulty for dramatic interpretations is the paucity of evidence of dramatic literature among the Semites, particularly the Hebrews.

Nuptial Songs. J.G. Wetzstein's study of Syrian wedding rites fostered a fresh view of the Song at the end of the last century.[20] Some scholars[21] found in such week-long festivities a number of parallels to elements within the Song: bride and groom are treated like king and queen; descriptions of the beauties and virtues of the lovers are sung; the bride performs a sword dance (see 6:13; 7:1); March is the preferred month (see 2:11); the couple are mounted on a beautifully decorated threshing table which becomes a royal throne (see 3:7-10).

These and other parallels have aided measurably, but this approach is probably not the whole answer. Even if Schonfield's contention that similar wedding customs can be traced in Jewish antiquity is accepted,[22] problems remain: the Song as it stands cannot easily be divided into parts corresponding to the seven days, and the Shulammite is nowhere called a queen. Würthwein modifies Budde's approach considerably while still holding to a strong connection between most poems in the Song and Israelite wedding ceremonies.[23] Not far from this view, J.-P. Audet understands the Song as an engagement pact.[24]

Liturgical Rites. As new light has been shed on ancient Near Eastern life,

---

20. Appendix to Keil-Delitzsch, *Commentary* 6, trans. M.G. Easton (repr. 1976), pp. 162-176.
21. Esp. K. Budde, *Das Hohelied*. HSAT (Tübingen: 1923).
22. *The Song of Songs*, pp. 32-34.
23. *Die fünf Megilloth*, pp. 25-71.
24. "The meaning of the Canticle of Canticles," *Theology Digest* 5 (1957): 88-92.

scholars have sought to illuminate obscure Old Testament passages by comparison with the religious customs of Mesopotamia, Egypt, or Canaan. An illustration is the theory (usually associated with T.J. Meek)[25] that Canticles is derived from liturgical rites of the cult of Tammuz (cf. Ezek. 8:14), Babylonian god of fertility. The combination of passionate conversation and pastoral setting has been taken as support, inasmuch as the rites celebrated the sacred marriage (Gk. *hieròs gámos*) of Tammuz and his consort Ishtar (Ashtarte) which produced the annual spring fertility.[26] Modern western culture shows that pagan religion may leave a legacy of terminology without influencing religious beliefs (e.g., names of days and months); still, it seems highly questionable that the Hebrews would have accepted a pagan liturgy, smacking of idolatry and immorality, without thorough revision in terms of Israel's distinctive faith.[27] Canticles bears the marks of no such revision. Any pagan influence must be so indirect as to be virtually negligible.

Love Song. In recent decades some scholars have viewed the Song as a poem or collection of love poems, perhaps but not necessarily connected with wedding celebrations or other specific occasions.[28] Despite attempts to divide the Song into several independent poems, an overriding air of unity[29] is evidenced in the continuity of theme, refrainlike repetitions (e.g., 2:7; 3:5; 8:4), and chainlike structure binding one part to the preceding.[30]

In the tone of the lyric poetry one can feel the Song's message. Though movement is evident, there is only a shadowy sketch of a plot. The couple's love is as intense at the beginning as at the end; thus, the poem's power lies not in a lofty climax but in the creative and delicate repetitions of the themes of love—a love longed for when apart (e.g., 3:1-5) and enjoyed to the full when together (e.g., ch. 7), relished amid the splendor of the palace (e.g., 1:2-4) or in the serenity of the countryside (7:11ff.), and reserved exclusively

---

25. E.g., "The Song of Songs," *IB* 5:98-148.

26. See H. Schmökel, *Heilige Hochzeit und Hoheslied*. Abhandlungen für die Künde des Morgenlandes 32/1 (Wiesbaden: 1956); S.N. Kramer, *The Sacred Marriage Rite* (Bloomington: 1969). White, *Language of Love*, p. 24, notes the imprecise nature of the supposed parallels and the vast differences in tone from the Song.

27. See White, *ibid.*, p. 24: "It is difficult to believe that sacred marriage could have been deeply rooted in Israel to the extent that a part of the ritual could have achieved inclusion into the Hebrew canon."

28. E.g., W. Rudolph, *Das Hohelied*. KAT 17/2 (Gütersloh: 1962); G. Gerlemann, *Das Hohelied*. BKAT 18 (Neukirchen: 1965).

29. See Rowley, *The Servant of the Lord*, p. 212. For a strong argument that the Song is an anthology rather than a unified poem, see White, *Language of Love*, pp. 28-34; also R. Gordis, *The Song of Songs and Lamentations*, rev. ed. (New York: 1974), p. 16: "If the Song of Songs be approached without any preconceptions, it reveals itself as a collection of lyrics."

30. Each succeeding poem stems from a word, phrase, or thought in the previous section: F. Landsberger, "Poetic Units within the Song of Songs," *JBL* 73 (1954): 203-216. Another approach finds six poems unified by repetition of key terms; J.C. Exum, "A Literary and Structural Analysis of the Song of Songs," *ZAW* 85 (1973): 47-79.

for the covenant partner (2:16; 6:3; 7:10).[31] It is a love strong as death, which water cannot quench nor floods drown, freely given yet beyond price (8:6f.).[32]

PURPOSE

What place does such love poetry have in Scripture, especially if not originally intended as an allegorical or typical message of God's love? The book is an object lesson, an extended proverb or parable (māšāl) illustrating the rich wonders of human love, itself a gift of God's love. Though expressed in bold language, the Song provides a wholesome, biblical balance between the extremes of sexual excess or perversion and an asceticism, too often taken as a Christian view of sex, which denies the essential goodness and rightness of physical love within the divinely prescribed framework of marriage. E.J. Young suggests going a step further: "Not only does it speak of the purity of human love; but, by its very inclusion in the canon, it reminds us of a love that is purer than our own."[33]

FOR FURTHER READING

Albright, W.F. "Archaic Survivals in the Text of Canticles." Pp. 1-7 in D.W. Thomas and W.D. McHardy, eds., *Hebrew and Semitic Studies Presented to Godfrey Rolles Driver*. Oxford: 1963. (Alleged Canaanite elements.)

Gaster, T.H. "What 'The Song of Songs' Means." *Commentary* 13 (1952): 316-322. (Background and interpretation.)

Gollwitzer, H. *Song of Love: A Biblical Understanding of Sex*. Trans. K. Crim. Philadelphia: 1979. (An affirmation of a positive approach to sex in the Bible.)

Hubbard, D.A. "Song of Solomon." *IBD*, pp. 1472-74. (Parts of the preceding discussion were adapted from this article.)

Kessler, R. *Some Poetical and Structural Features of the Song of Songs*. Ed. J. Macdonald. Leeds University Oriental Society Monograph 8. Leeds: 1957.

Landy, F. "Beauty and the Enigma: An Inquiry into Some Interrelated Episodes of the Song of Songs." *JSOT* 17 (1980): 55-106. (Examines 1:5f., 7f.; 8:8-10, 11f.)

---

31. See White, *Language of Love*, p. 27: "Although the Israelite social ethos did not exclude eroticism, the social morality did exclude adultery and emphasized the necessity of virginity before marriage. . . . The Song . . . cannot, therefore, be understood as a tract justifying pre-marital sexual intercourse." S.C. Glickman stresses both the Song's unity and its marital setting by noting a chronological sequence from courtship (1:1–3:5), to wedding procession (3:6-11), to consummation (4:1–5:1), and beyond; *A Song for Lovers* (Downers Grove: 1976).

32. For a more detailed analysis with explanatory notes, see G. Verkuyl, ed., *New Berkeley Version of the Holy Bible in Modern English* (London: 1963).

33. *Introduction*, p. 354.

CHAPTER 46

RUTH

JEWISH tradition places the book of Ruth among the Writings, but the LXX, followed by the Vulgate and English Bible, places it immediately after Judges, since both are set in the same age.

NAME AND CONTENTS

The book is named from its principal character, Ruth the Moabitess, who had married into the family of Elimelech, a Judahite from Bethlehem. Because of famine Elimelech had gone to dwell in Moab, together with his wife, Naomi, and their two sons. In the course of time all three men die, and Naomi is left alone with her daughters-in-law, Ruth and Orpah. Resolving to return to Judah, where the famine has ended, Naomi seeks to send the two back to their families. Orpah complies reluctantly, but Ruth resolutely refuses in language that has become the paradigm of the love and devotion that one woman can give to another (1:16f.). She and Naomi return to Bethlehem, where Ruth, having gone out to glean, chances on the fields of Boaz, a distant kinsman of Elimelech. At the end of the harvest, Naomi sends Ruth to the threshing floor to request that Boaz fulfill the levirate responsibility of the next of kin to marry the widow and raise a son to bear her dead husband's name. He is willing, but a nearer kinsman has prior right. In the climax of the story Boaz skillfully persuades the nearer kinsman to give up that right and then marries Ruth. The son born of this marriage is celebrated as a "son . . . born to Naomi." This preservation of the family line is of no small moment, for the child Obed becomes the father of Jesse, father of David.

DATE AND AUTHORSHIP

Like so many Old Testament narratives, the book of Ruth is anonymous and without a single clue to suggest its author. The Talmud records the tradition that Samuel was the author, but the book must have been written after David

(4:17b) and sufficiently long after the events related to warrant the comment of v. 7 explaining a long-forgotten custom. No scholarly consensus has been reached as to date, with estimates ranging from the early Monarchy to the postexilic era. Most of the pertinent evidence can be accounted for best by assuming that it is preexilic, and, for lack of more precise criteria, a date somewhere in the period of the Monarchy (tenth-seventh centuries B.C.) seems best.[1]

SOCIAL FEATURES

One difficulty facing the modern reader is that interpretation of the story involves two social customs of ancient Israel which have no modern western exemplars: the levirate and redemption of land. The levirate,[2] described in legal form in Deut. 25:5-10, refers to the fact that if a man in ancient Israel died without a son the obligation fell upon the next-of-kin[3] to marry the widow and produce a son, "that his [the deceased's] name may not be blotted out in Israel" (v. 6). Although the data in Ruth, Deut. 25:5-10, and the story of Judah and Tamar in Gen. 38 present such differences in details that a coherent view of the levirate in Israel is exceedingly difficult,[4] unquestionably the major turning point in the book is Naomi's stratagem to induce Boaz to accept this obligation, even though he apparently is so distantly related that neither he nor others thought it immediately incumbent upon him. In a most human and exquisitely told portion of the story, the scene at the threshing floor in ch. 3, Naomi achieves this by using the young and attractive Ruth to motivate Boaz. Her stratagem is most successful (vv. 10f.), but at that juncture a complication is introduced: another kinsman nearer than Boaz has not only prior obligations but prior right. Since Boaz may not safely ignore that prior right, he assembles the elders at the city gate,[5] invites the nearer kinsman to attend, and then informs him that Naomi is "selling the parcel of land which belonged to our

---

1. Note S.R. Driver: "The general Hebrew style (the idioms and the syntax) shows no marks of deterioration; it is palpably different, not merely from that of Esther and Chronicles, but even from Nehemiah's memoirs or Jonah, and stands on a level with the best parts of Samuel"; *Introduction*, p. 454.

2. From Latin *levir* "brother-in-law," thus "marriage with the brother-in-law."

3. The legal form in Deut. 25 mentions only brothers living together in connection with the levirate obligation. However, both Gen. 38 and Ruth extend the obligation. It is attractive to hypothesize that the order of obligation was the same for the levirate as for inheritance (Num. 27:8-11) and the redemption of the relative who has been forced to indenture himself (Lev. 24:47-55), i.e., brother, paternal uncle, paternal uncle's son, and "the member of his clan who is most nearly related" (Num. 27:11).

4. For excellent summaries of the main arguments and problems, see H.H. Rowley, "The Marriage of Ruth," pp. 169-194 in *The Servant of the Lord*; also T. and D. Thompson, "Some Legal Problems in the Book of Ruth," *VT* 18 (1968): 79-99.

5. The gate is where business and legal transactions were carried on in ancient cities. For its broader significance, see E.A. Speiser, " 'Coming' and 'Going' at the 'City' Gate," *BASOR* 144 (1956): 20-23.

kinsman Elimelech. So I thought I would tell you of it, and say, Buy it . . ."
(4:3f.).

This surprising development in the story is the first inkling of property
belonging to Elimelech and points to another obligation binding on the next
of kin: redemption of land. Land was inalienable; it could not be sold outside
the family. If poverty forced such an action, the next of kin was obligated to
purchase the land and so keep it within the family.[6] An example of the principle
in action may be found in Jer. 32:6-15.

Thinking himself faced with this obligation alone, the nearer kinsman
responds affirmatively (4:4). Boaz then prompts him to give up his right by
informing him: "The day you buy the field from the hand of Naomi, you are
also buying Ruth the Moabitess, the widow of the dead, in order to restore the
name of the dead to his inheritance" (v. 5). The kinsman then responds that
to do so would impair his own inheritance (v. 6), so he is forced to withdraw.
Were he responsible for only the levirate, his own estate would not have been
in jeopardy. The child of the levirate marriage would have been supported by
Elimelech's property until old enough to inherit it. And if he faced only the
redemption obligation, the price of the land would have been compensated for
by the land itself. But when the land he must buy must then go to the child
of his levirate marriage with Ruth, the kinsman is unable to accept such a dual

*Threshing floor such as the one where Ruth persuaded Boaz to fulfill his responsibility
as next of kin (Ruth 3). (W.S. LaSor)*

6. See Lev. 25:25ff.; no order of obligation is specified, but perhaps the order
would conform to that established for inheritance; cf. note 3 above.

obligation. He voluntarily cedes his rights in the matter to Boaz (v. 6). Apparently Boaz was sufficiently wealthy that this dual obligation presented no problem. Better still, since the genealogy of David in vv. 18-22 names Boaz as ancestor instead of Mahlon and Elimelech, Boaz may have had no sons. The child born of his marriage to Ruth, although the child of Mahlon by a legal fiction, also would have been Boaz's by actual paternity and thus heir of both Boaz and the line of Elimelech.

LITERARY NATURE AND THEOLOGY

Ever since the foundational article of H. Gunkel,[7] scholarship generally has agreed that the genre of Ruth is a novella, a short story, highly artistic in both style and construction, which develops a plot through several episodes until reaching a denouement. It is also a story with a purpose, seeking to edify and instruct. As such Ruth is comparable to the Joseph story (Gen. 37, 39–50), the marriage of Isaac (ch. 24), Judah and Tamar (ch. 38), and the Court History of David (2 Sam. 9–20). These integrated narratives contrast markedly with collections of traditions such as the Abrahamic or Jacob cycles in Gen. 12–36. The genre is marked by an elevated, almost poetic and rhythmic prose style. The stories are both entertaining and instructive, focusing on God's providential activity in the lives of the participants. The reader is expected, and subtly importuned, to participate in these experiences and learn by emulating or avoiding these examples.[8]

As an example of this short story form, Ruth is a literary masterpiece.[9] The author, with consummate artistry, great delicacy, obvious enjoyment, yet a bare minimum of words, has depicted people who, although magnanimous, are believable. At one level this is what the story teaches: its characters live, love, and relate so as to be the enfleshment of the Hebrew concept of $ṣ^edāqâ$ "righteousness," "integrity," illustrating in concrete terms life under God's covenant. The story has no villain. Orpah does leave her mother-in-law, but only after a second appeal, and the nearer kinsman is perfectly willing to redeem the land until his own patrimony is jeopardized by the concomitant requirement of marrying Ruth. Against this background the unusual kindness and fidelity of Boaz, the faithfulness and commitment of Ruth, and the sagacity and perseverance of Naomi can be seen in their true perspective. They are almost fully the personification of ḥesed "loving-faithfulness." The story is told with such skill that they evoke naught but admiration.

At another level, the book centers on the lineage of David (4:17b). The

---

7. "Ruth," pp. 65-92 in *Reden und Aufsätze* (Göttingen: 1913).

8. See particularly E.F. Campbell, "The Hebrew Short Story: Its Form, Style and Provenance," pp. 83-101 in H.N. Bream, R.D. Heim, and C.A. Moore, eds., *A Light Unto My Path* (Philadelphia: 1974).

9. For the literary devices with which the author skillfully crafts his story, see the introduction to Campbell, *Ruth*. Anchor Bible 7 (Garden City: 1975), pp. 3-23.

genealogy in vv. 18-22, clearly a later addition, also makes that clear. Here this narrative of mundane events in the lives of quite ordinary people has been placed in the context of the larger divine economy. The original point of the narrative thus is extended beyond showing God's providence and care in the life of one family. It concerns the entire life of the nation, for in the son born to Naomi the history of God's rule under David has begun.[10] In this way the book relates to the Bible's main theme of redemptive history. Thus it is striking to note that the author identifies Ruth as "the Moabitess" in several places where her ethnic origin is uncalled for and even superfluous.[11]

Although anything but a polemic,[12] the book certainly bears witness to the fact, stressed elsewhere in the Old Testament (e.g., Jonah), that God's mercy was not limited exclusively to Israel. The ideal king, David, and ultimately the Messiah sprang from such a line.[13]

However, the primary purpose of the narrative is to show the gracious guidance of God in the life of this family.[14] In fact, the major actor in the drama is God, whose presence in the story leads from Naomi's bitter complaint in 1:20f.:

> "Do not call me Naomi ['Pleasant'], call me Mara ['Bitter'], for the Almighty has dealt very bitterly with me. I went away full, and the Lord has brought me back empty."

to the glad cry of the women of Bethlehem in 4:17: "A son has been born to Naomi." God's gracious guidance is made especially clear through the prayers of the principals, including Boaz's fervent blessing for Ruth in 2:12; 3:10 and the sudden return of Naomi's hope in 2:20, each of which is answered in the book's denouement. This is a book about God's ruling over the events of the lives of those who trust him. It is a divinely granted "rest" (KJV 1:9; 3:1) that "a scheming old lady and a nicely perfumed young woman can bring about with a little strategy."[15]

And yet the book of Ruth stresses God's "all-causality" differently from much other Old Testament literature.[16] No guidance comes through dreams, visions, angelic visitations, or voices from heaven, and no prophet is sent with his "thus saith the Lord." God works behind the scenes through the ordinary motivations and events of the story. He "is everywhere—but totally hidden in

---

10. See B.S. Childs, *Old Testament as Scripture*, p. 566.
11. 1:22; 2:2; 4:5, 10; in addition, her foreign origin is stressed in 2:6, 10.
12. A number of scholars have forced this as the book's major purpose, interpreting it as a postexilic counter to the exclusivism of Ezra and Nehemiah. For bibliography see Rowley, *The Servant of the Lord*, p. 173.
13. See Matt. 1:5. While a strong separation existed in Israelite society and faith (and so also in Judaism), Ruth and Jonah show that a significant segment of Old Testament society recognized the genuine universal element in her life and purpose.
14. See Childs, *Old Testament as Scripture*, p. 565.
15. Campbell, "The Hebrew Short Story," p. 98.
16. See M. Hals, *The Theology of the Book of Ruth* (Philadelphia: 1969), pp. 18f.

purely human coincidences and schemes, such as a young girl's accidental steps and an old woman's risky plan."[17] The author stresses thus one particular aspect of God's providence—its hiddenness. He conceals God's guidance in normal human causality[18] simply because he believes it is by nature hidden. This theology of absolute but hidden causality is not unique to Ruth, however. The Court History of David (2 Sam. 9–20) and the story of Joseph (Gen. 37, 39–50), among others, also stress God's complete and continuous control of events, not overtly or supernaturally, but imperceptibly and naturally, through the mundane course of life. At times God does intervene directly in the court of human affairs to effect the purposes of redemption. But in the book of Ruth he acts much more subtly—through the everyday events and motivations of ordinary people, the ripples of whose lives stirred little beyond the pool of their own community. Through their faithfulness and God's hidden guidance, this family was preserved for Israel—a matter of no small moment, for from it stemmed great David and, many generations later, great David's greater Son.

FOR FURTHER READING

Anderson, A.A. "The Marriage of Ruth." *JSS* 23 (1978): 171-183. (Disputes identification of levirate union in Ruth.)

Beattie, D.R.G. "The Book of Ruth as Evidence for Israelite Legal Practice." *VT* 24 (1974): 251-267. (Includes summary of medieval rabbinic and contemporary critical scholarship.)

Burrows, M. "The Ancient Oriental Background of Hebrew Levirate Marriage." *BASOR* 77 (1940): 2-15.

Knight, G.A.F. *Ruth and Jonah*. 2nd ed. Torch Bible Commentary. London: 1966. (Book concerned with "right relation between Church and community.")

Leggett, D. *The Levirate and Goel Institutions in the Old Testament*. Cherry Hill, N.J.: 1974. (Conservative.)

Loretz, O. "The Theme of the Ruth Story." *CBQ* 22 (1960): 391-99. (Book is "gestalte Geschichte.")

Myers, J.M. *The Linguistic and Literary Form of the Book of Ruth*. Leiden: 1955. (Argues for poetic nucleus underlying book.)

Prinsloo, W.S. "The Theology of the Book of Ruth." *VT* 30 (1980): 330-341.

Rauber, D.F. "Literary Values in the Bible: The Book of Ruth." *JBL* 89 (1970): 27-37. (Analysis by specialist in literary studies.)

Sasson, J.M. *Ruth: A New Translation with a Philological Commentary and a Formalist-Folklorist Interpretation*. Baltimore: 1979.

---

17. Hals, "Book of Ruth," *IDBS*, p. 759.

18. This guidance occurs not only in the conscious acts of the participants. In 2:3 Ruth "happened to come to the part of the field belonging to Boaz. . . ." In a book so full of God's guidance, the author's attributing to chance the meeting of Ruth and Boaz obviously intends the reverse; for Ruth it was pure chance, but not for God.

CHAPTER 47

LAMENTATIONS

THE English title aptly describes this little book's contents. Its five chapters contain Judah's lamentations mourning the destruction of Jerusalem and its temple (586 B.C.). The historical narratives of 2 Kgs. 25 and Jer. 52 give the facts; the five poems of Lamentations capture the emotions.

The LXX and Vulgate use a similar title: "Wailings" or "Dirges" (*Threnoi*; Lat. *Threni*). The Vulgate subtitle, *Id est Lamentationes Jeremiae Prophetae*, became the basis for the English name. The usual Hebrew name is '*êkâ*, from the characteristic word of lament ("how!") with which chs. 1–2, 4 begin.[1]

In the Hebrew Bible, Lamentations is usually third among the five scrolls (Megilloth) used in the Jewish annual feasts or fasts. On the Ninth of Ab (mid-July), Jews traditionally have mourned the destruction of Solomon's temple by Nebuchadnezzar and also of the Second Temple by the Roman Titus (A.D. 70). The reading of Lamentations as part of such observances seems to date to the early years of the Exile, immediately after the tragic events which the book commemorates. Jeremiah describes a company of eighty men from Shechem, Shiloh, and Samaria that made a pilgrimage to the temple's site in 585 (Jer. 41:4f.). Moreoover, Zechariah (518) mentions a seventy-year-old custom of fasting in the fifth (Ab) and seventh (Tishri) months (7:1-7).

Date and Authorship. Lamentations is a fruit of Judah's disastrous defeat and painful exile. Its contents establish the range of possible dating (586-530). The vivid impressions of chs. 1–4 suggest that their woeful strains were composed shortly after Jerusalem's fall. Ch. 5 may be from somewhat later in the Exile, when the sharp pains of defeat had dulled into the chronic ache of captivity.

Lamentations is anonymous. The text itself says nothing of authorship. A tradition took form in pre-Christian times attributing the book to Jeremiah.[2]

---

1. Some rabbis also used the name *Qînôt*, meaning "funeral dirges" or "lamentations."
2. Targum at Jer. 1:1; Talmud B. Bat. 15a; LXX and Vulgate headings. Note the LXX introduction: "And it came to pass after Israel was taken captive and Jerusalem laid waste that Jeremiah sat weeping and raised this lament over Jerusalem. . . ."

The arguments for and against Jeremiah's authorship are a stand-off. The traditional view gains support from similarities in tone between the books, especially sensitivity to Judah's suffering; Lamentations' profound theological insight, which combines the themes of judgment and grace in a manner worthy of Jeremiah; and certain parallels in style (e.g., both describe Judah as a smitten virgin; Jer. 14:17; Lam. 1:15). Arguments against Jeremiah's authorship usually follow these lines: (1) Would Jeremiah have led in lamentation rather than calling the survivors to repentance and pointing to God's new day? (2) Can passages that speak of the failure of prophetic vision (2:9) or seem to imply policies that Jeremiah had opposed (4:12, 17) be attributed to him? (3) Do the variations in poetic style and in the alphabetic order of the acrostic poems suggest multiple rather than single authorship?[3]

Inasmuch as the book itself is anonymous, it may be well to leave the matter there. Though the traditional view cannot be given irrefutable proof, it does have the advantage of pointing to the kind of person whom the Spirit inspired to write the book: (1) an eyewitness to the tragic events described in minute detail; (2) a profound theologian who grasped the deeper causes of the terrible judgment as well as their painful symptoms; (3) a poet of great skill; (4) a true patriot who mourned his country's passing and yet knew that such death was the only hope for new life.

No known person combined all those characteristics better than Jeremiah, whom the Chronicler remembers to have uttered laments over Josiah's death (2 Chr. 35:25). If not Jeremiah, Judah was fortunate indeed to have another person of such remarkable gifts to help deal with their losses just as Jeremiah had prepared them to expect them. In this discussion the singular "author" is used to reflect the conviction that the poems in Lamentations are not a collection of diverse materials but reflect the insight and skill of one person.

POETIC STYLE

Acrostic Form. The first four chapters are acrostics with stylistic variations: chs. 1–2 contain twenty-two verses of three lines each, and the first word of each verse begins with the successive Hebrew letter; ch. 4 does the same, but the verses are two lines; ch. 3 is the most tightly constructed, for its sixty-six verses are divided into twenty-two clusters of three verses each, and each of the three begins with the appropriate letter. Even ch. 5, which is not in alphabet form, seems to have been affected somewhat by the acrostic pattern: it too has twenty-two verses of one line each.

Why the alphabetic acrostic? In some situations it may be an aid to mem-

---

3. The question is the order of ayin and pe: ch. 1 has ayin before pe; chs. 2–4 have pe before ayin. On alphabetical order in biblical acrostics, see R. Gordis, *Poets, Prophets and Sages*, pp. 82f. The reversal of ayin and pe is found in the alphabet from Izbet Sartah (twelfth century); see W.S. LaSor, *Handbook of Biblical Hebrew* 2:58.

ory. By remembering the order one may be helped to recall the content of each verse. This mnemonic purpose probably does not account for the alphabetic structure of Lam. 1–4: the series of acrostics might confuse the memory as well as help. How would one know which verse beginning with gimel or daledh belonged in which chapter? As a piece of artistry the acrostic was an act of devotion by the poet.

In Lamentations the acrostic form seems to serve at least two other purposes: (1) it signals a full expression of anguish and contrition, by covering the subject from aleph to tau (i.e., A to Z); (2) it places artistic constraints on the lament, thus keeping it from deteriorating to an uncontrolled wail, howl, or whine.[4]

Dirges. The use of the exclamation "how!" (Heb. *'êkâ*) and the short, sobbing lines with parallel structure mark parts of Lamentations (esp. sections of chs. 1–2, 4) as dirges or laments over a great tragedy.[5] Though often used at funerals to lament the loss of a loved one (2 Sam. 1:19-27), the dirge (*qînâ*) was not necessarily restricted to that use but could highlight any tragedy, particularly one that seemed difficult to reverse.[6]

The dirge form in Lamentations has too much variety to be labeled strictly a funeral song. The city of Jerusalem is not described as a dead body, but a lonely widow (1:1). More important, the city itself at times joins in the lamenting (e.g., vv. 12-16, 18-22). At other times the poet addresses the city directly:

What can I say to you, to what compare you,
O daughter of Jerusalem? (2:13)[7]

An effective device in the Hebrew dirge is the dramatic contrast, which describes the previous state of the deceased or bereaved in glowing terms (see 2 Sam. 1:19, 23), making the present tragedy all the more pathetic:

How lonely sits the city
that was full of people!

---

4. For the conceptual meaning of the acrostic pattern, see N.K. Gottwald, *Studies in the Book of Lamentations*, 2nd ed. SBT 14 (London: 1962), pp. 23-32.

5. For a brief discussion of rhythmic patterns that the dirge may use, see Gordis, *Poets, Prophets and Sages*, p. 68.

6. Sumerians used a lament form to mourn the loss of a city to a foreign invader. Apparent parallels with the biblical book have raised questions about possible Sumerian influence. Direct influence does not seem likely. It is safer to say that Lamentations is an example of a literary-liturgical pattern with early antecedents in Mesopotamia. For an account of the supposed parallels, see D.R. Hillers, *Lamentations*. Anchor Bible 7A (Garden City: 1972), pp. XXVIII–XXX.

7. The Hebrew construction is an appositive, to be understood as "daughter which is Jerusalem" (likewise the frequent "daughter of Zion," e.g., 2:8, 10, 13). "Daughter" is a term of endearment, and the phrases could be translated "Cherished Jerusalem" or "Fair Zion."

How like a widow she has become,
    she that was great among the nations!
She that was a princess among the cities
    has become a vassal. (Lam. 1:1)

Individual and Communal Complaints. Alternating with the dirge forms are complaint patterns akin to those in Psalms and Jeremiah. Lamentations uses both an individual form (ch. 3), where one person (probably the poet) speaks on behalf of the community, and a communal form (ch. 5), where the congregation lifts its voice in unison before the Lord to complain of suffering.[8]

The individual complaint in ch. 3 begins with a description of suffering in which God is not appealed to directly but his judgment is described in the third person (vv. 1-18). Only toward the end does the poet consistently address God in the second person (vv. 55-66). Still, many standard elements of the complaint are present: (1) description of suffering in highly figurative terms: darkness, illness, chains, animal attack, assault with arrows (vv. 1-18); (2) plea for relief (v. 19); (3) expression of trust (vv. 21-36); (4) certainty of being heard (vv. 55-63); (5) plea for vengeance on the enemies used to inflict punishment on Judah (vv. 64-66).[9]

The communal complaint in ch. 5 focuses almost exclusively on the poignant description of suffering (vv. 2-18). It begins and ends with a plea for restoration (vv. 1, 20-22) and reflects a brief glint of hope or confidence (v. 19).

Use of the complaint form does more than merely add to the varieties of expression. It goes beyond the dirge by: allowing the poet or congregation to address the Lord directly, while the dirge usually is voiced to those present at the mourning rites; providing opportunity for personal confession of sin, while the dirge may only describe the sin that caused the calamity (compare 3:40-42 with 1:18); and making room for hope by expressing trust and the certainty of being heard.

Lamentations is a precise and delicate blend of form and content. Acrostics, dirges, complaints, and vivid descriptions of suffering all combine to voice in terms most memorable the doom and hope of a people for whom dire judgment was the necessary prelude to grace.

THEOLOGICAL CONTRIBUTION

What Jeremiah prophesied, Lamentations experienced in tragic vividness—the destruction of Jerusalem and decimation of its populace. Beyond the physical suffering, in itself shattering, lay the spiritual torment of the question, "Why?"

---

8. Sometimes "lament" is used to describe these prayers. It seems less confusing to reserve that term for the dirge, with its description of a virtually hopeless situation like death, and to use "complaint" for the prayers which plead for God's rescue from unhappy circumstances. Cf. Job's complaints discussed above (p. 578).

9. The poet's flair for variety led him to use elements of a communal complaint in the middle of the chapter (vv. 40-47).

God's judgment was not viewed as wrong by those who strolled through Jerusalem's ashes. Indeed the poet holds him to be right in judging rebellion (1:18), punishing sin (vv. 5, 8f., 18, 22; 2:14; 3:40-42; 4:13, 22; 5:7), and revealing his wrath (1:12ff.; 2:1-9, 20-22; 3:1-18; 4:6, 11).

Yet the final disaster must have caused a crisis of faith, with which Lamentations' theology of doom and hope tries to cope. The people of Judah must have been thoroughly puzzled because Josiah's reforms were brushed aside so lightly by the harsh hand of God, who within a mere score of years allowed the righteous king to fall in battle (609) and the sacred city to be breached and violated (586). Did not God's action in history run contrary to the clear pattern taught in Deuteronomy and followed throughout the Monarchy—righteousness of a ruler leads to blessing on God's people?[10]

Another aspect of the crisis in Judah's faith was caused by the firm belief that Zion was inviolable. The Davidic monarchy survived for four centuries in Judah despite the dynastic upheavals in the northern kingdom and its conquest by Assyria in 721. This stability coupled with the assurance that God had entered into special covenant with David's son (2 Sam. 7) led to a belief that Jerusalem could never be humbled by enemy attack. After all, it was the dwelling place of God himself. He would never tolerate enemy invasion of his own home. This sublime confidence was unassailably reinforced by Sennacherib's mysterious defeat in the days of Hezekiah (701).

Then Nebuchadnezzar breached the inviolable walls and burned the im-

Lamentation scene, Eighteenth-Dynasty (late fourteenth century B.C.) relief from Memphis. (Foto Marburg)

10. Gottwald points up the sharp tension between Deuteronomic faith and historical adversity; *Studies in the Book of Lamentations*, pp. 47-53. Cf. B.S. Childs, *Old Testament as Scripture*, p. 593.

pregnable temple. What was God doing? What were his people to believe? How could they handle this reversal of a policy they deemed unshakeable?[11]

Lamentations was written to express these tensions through the catharsis of confession, aided by the completeness symbolized in the acrostic form. It was written also to encourage acceptance of God's judgment while affirming hope beyond that judgment.[12] Though history, at God's hands, has trapped them in tragic surprise, Israel is urged not to doubt that his sovereignty ultimately will do what is good for them and all creation.

The tragic reversal from height of favor to depth of despair dominates Lamentations as it does Job. In both God's purposes are shrouded in mystery. Yet hope and faith are made possible by the revelation of the character of the God who has allowed such pain.

The poet's strong faith must have heartened generations of his countrymen. To find hope in the midst of disaster and lead others to it takes the deepest knowledge of God.

In Lamentations the three great strands of Israel's literature and faith are woven together: the prophets' insights into the judgment and grace of the covenant Lord; the priests' liturgical expressions of contrition and hope; the wise men's wrestlings with the mysteries of suffering. The poet of Lamentations is heir to them all, but not as mere scribe or recorder. The texture and pattern of the weaving are his own, adding a subtlety and beauty that make the book a treasured tapestry of biblical revelation.

FOR FURTHER READING

Ackroyd, P.R. *Exile and Restoration: A Study of Hebrew Thought of the Sixth Century B.C.* OTL. Philadelphia: 1968.

Cannon, W.W. "The Authorship of Lamentations." *Bibliotheca Sacra* 18 (1924): 42-58.

Gordis, R. "A Commentary on the Text of Lamentations." Pp. 267-286 in A.A. Newman and S. Zeitlin, eds., *The Seventy-fifth Anniversary Volume of the Jewish Quarterly Review*. Philadelphia: 1967.

_____. "Commentary on the Text of Lamentations (Part Two)." *JQR* 58 (1967-68): 14-33. (Critical notes.)

Habel, N.C. *Jeremiah, Lamentations*. Concordia Commentary. St. Louis: 1968.

---

11. A detailed presentation of this tension is found in Albrektson, *Studies in the Text and Theology of the Book of Lamentations* (Lund: 1963), pp. 219ff.

12. "One of the results of incorporating the events of the city's destruction into Israel's traditional terminology of worship was to establish a semantic bridge between the historical situation of the early sixth century and the language of faith which struggles with divine judgment. For this reason the book of Lamentations serves every successive generation of the suffering faithful for whom history has become unbearable"; Childs, *Old Testament as Scripture*, p. 596.

Hubbard, D.A. "Lamentations, Book of." *IBD*, pp. 869-871. (Parts of the preceding discussion were adapted from this article.)

McDaniel, T.F. "The Alleged Sumerian Influence upon Lamentations." *VT* 18 (1968): 198-209.

————. "Philological Studies in Lamentations." *Bibl* 49 (1968): 27-53, 199-220. (Comparative study using Northwest Semitic materials.)

Shea, W.H. "The *qinah* Structure of the Book of Lamentations." *Bibl* 60 (1979): 103-7. (Acrostics define precise structure of the work as a whole.)

CHAPTER 48

THE SCROLL
OF ESTHER[1]

Eᴤᴛʜᴇʀ is a remarkably different biblical book: neither the word for God nor the name Yahweh occurs in the Hebrew text;[2] the scene is Susa, winter capital of Persia, not Israel; the book concerns the marriage of its Jewish heroine with a gentile king; it solves the problem of an incipient anti-Semitism (actually, anti-Jewish action) by a bloody self-defense, which—even worse—is so enjoyable that it is repeated by Esther's request on the following day! Nevertheless, the scroll belongs in the canon, as Jewish scholars recognized after long discussion, and commands consideration.

THE STORY AND ITS BACKGROUND

Plot. From a literary viewpoint, the story of Esther is wonderfully constructed. It begins in the court of Ahasuerus (probably Xerxes I, 485-465 B.C.), at a banquet where "the splendor and pomp of his majesty" are on display. Heady with wine, the king orders Vashti the queen brought in to exhibit her beauty. She refuses and is banished, and a new queen sought. Hadassah (Esther), in the care of her cousin Mordecai, a Jew, is taken along with many others to the palace to join the royal harem. She pleases the king and becomes his queen.

Haman is promoted to a place of honor, but Mordecai will not bow down to him. Hatred develops into a furious desire to destroy Mordecai, but, considering a vendetta against one man as beneath him (v. 6), Haman determines to eliminate all the Jews because of their different ways. The king approves his suggestion and signs an edict condemning all Jews to death on 13 Adar (twelfth

---

1. Heb. *mᵉgillaṭ 'estēr*, often referred to simply as *Megillah* "Scroll." It is doubtless the most widely published Old Testament book, because of its festive use at Purim.
2. The LXX text contains 107 additional verses, "Additions to Esther," found before 1:1; after 3:13; 4:17; 8:12; 10:3; and at the end. They add the missing religious elements and are obviously a later effort to secure canonicity.

month). Mordecai learns of the plot, and calls on Esther to plead before the king.

By a curious twist of events, Haman, who thinks himself about to be honored, is caught in a compromising situation and hanged on the very gallows he had erected for Mordecai's execution. The plot to kill the Jews is explained to the king. Because of the immutability of Persian law he cannot countermand his edict, but arranges for the Jews to be made aware of the plan and given permission to defend themselves. On the appointed day, the Jews slay a large number of those who had sought to destroy them. Esther asks the king to repeat the event the next day, and many thousands of the enemies of the Jews are slain. The event is celebrated with feasting and exchanging of gifts; this celebration, Purim,[3] is to be observed by Jews throughout all generations. Mordecai is made "next in rank" to the king.

Historicity. Scholars long have been divided on this question, some insisting that the book is an accurate historical record (see 10:2), and others that it is fiction. The current trend seems to be a retraction from extreme positions, and

Reconstructed palace at Susa, winter capital of Persia. (W.S. LaSor)

---

3. From *pûr* (in Akkadian, a four-sided die), the lot which Haman cast (3:7). According to one interpretation, it was cast until it indicated the day on which the pogrom was to be carried out. If so, the casting took place in Nisan (April/May) 474, and the date selected was 5 April 473 (cf. v. 13).

a willingness to admit that, while the story as such may not be historical, the background is so full of accurate Persian detail that it must be based on history. Hence it is perhaps a historical novella or short story.[4] If Ahasuerus was Xerxes I, his "third year" (1:3) would have been 483/2, and Tebeth of his seventh year (2:16) either December 479 or early January 478. Between 483 and 480 Xerxes carried out a campaign against the Greeks, which ended in the disastrous naval battle of Salamis. According to Herodotus (vii.114; ix.108f.), his queen was Amestris, which cannot be equated with Vashti, and only with great difficulty with Esther. The story, however, indicates that the king had a large harem and probably a sequence of favorite queens.

The argument against historicity based on 2:5f. hardly deserves mention. By taking the relative pronoun "who" to refer to Mordecai rather than its immediate antecedent, some argue that Mordecai would have been about 120 years old. Esther, "the daughter of his uncle" (v. 7), could hardly have been of the same generation. Reading the clause normally, Mordecai and Esther appear at least four generations removed from the captivity; assuming an average of thirty-five years to a generation, this would not be unreasonable.[5]

The argument that the book is based on Babylonian mythology, with Esther equal to Ishtar and Mordecai to Marduk, was a product of the pan-Babylonian period of scholarship (ca. 1880-1930, before discovery of the Ugaritic tablets) and has lost much popularity. Quite possibly, even children of Jewish parents in the Diaspora could have been given names of popular persons (although hardly of pagan deities), and Esther and Mordecai could be Persian (not Babylonian) names.[6]

Is Historicity Essential? To suggest that Esther is without historical or factual basis will at once raise objection. Some argue that if the Bible is allowed to be considered unhistorical in any part, ultimately it loses all historicity. But this logic does not necessarily follow. The same argument could be raised against the parables of Jesus. The prior question to be answered is: Does the event have significance in the revelatory and/or redemptive actions of God? To move at once to the ultimate point in the argument, if the Crucifixion and Resurrection did not happen, then the redemptive work revealed by them did not take place and the Christian's "faith is in vain" (see 1 Cor. 15:12-17). Though Esther's revelatory significance is indicated by its inclusion in the canon, that its events

---

4. See B.S. Childs, *Old Testament as Scripture*, p. 601.
5. To interpret "Agagite" (3:1) as a reference to Agag (cf. 1 Sam. 15:8) and to link Mordecai (a descendant of Kish, hence related to Saul) and Haman with the Saul-Agag story is not necessary. Haman (Humman) is known to be a Persian or Elamite name. Susa was in the portion of Persia that was originally Elam.
6. The name Mardukâ is attested by archaeological discovery; see D.W. Harvey, "Esther, Book of," *IDB* 2:151, with reference to A. Ungnad, "Keilinschriftliche Beiträge zum Buch Esra und Ester," *ZAW* 58 (1940-41): 240-44; 59 (1942-43): 219. For a full discussion of objections to the book's historicity and replies, see R.K. Harrison, *Introduction*, pp. 1087-1097.

were necessary for God's redemptive purpose would be most difficult to show. God's work of redemption could have continued, even if Haman had exterminated "all" the Jews, by the providential preservation (as in the case of Joash, 2 Kgs. 11) of some Jew or Jews to carry on the line.[7]

RELIGIOUS SIGNIFICANCE

To Authenticate Purim? Some scholars see Esther as an etiological story composed to explain and authenticate the feast of Purim.[8] Today Purim is an almost totally secular celebration, usually ending with drinking *"adloyada"* (i.e., *'aḏ lôʼ yāḏaʻ* "until he doesn't know"), based on the Talmudic instruction: "Drink wine until you can no longer distinguish between 'Blessed be Mordecai' and 'Cursed be Haman' " (*Meg.* 7b).[9] The question must be asked, especially in light of 9:11-16, whether such a book has religious value. The Rabbis elevated it to a place equal with or possibly above the Torah (Jer. Talmud *Meg.* 70d), and Maimonides asserted that when the rest of the Bible passed away in the days of the Messiah, Esther and the Torah would remain.[10] But was this because of its religious and ethical teachings, or because it held out to a persecuted people a promise of survival? The strong affirmations of rabbinical hyperbole at least served to counter the many and bitter criticisms levelled against Jews.

Which came First—Purim or Esther? The view that Esther was written to give religious authority for the feast of Purim must be challenged. The feast has no known origin in Persian, Babylonian, or other lore. If it did not originate in a historical event, such as described in Esther, it must have originated as a result of the (fictional) story of Esther. The book commonly is dated to the second century, because the first apparent reference to it is in 2 Macc. 15:36, which mentions "Mordecai's day."[11] The earliest reference to the whole story of Esther is found in Josephus (*Apion* i.8 §40; *Ant.* xi.6 §§184-296).[12]

---

7. Attacks on the book's value have been strong and sometimes bitter. Luther wished it "did not exist at all"; No. 3391f., *Tischreden* (Weimar: 1914) 3:302. H.G.A. Ewald felt that on coming to Esther "we fall as if from heaven to earth"; *The History of Israel,* ed. R. Martineau (Göttingen: 1869) 1:197. The book's right to canonicity was challenged (Jer. Talmud *Meg.* 70d), chiefly because it inaugurated a new feast, thus implying that Moses was incomplete. This objection was answered by the theory that Esther was revealed to Moses at Sinai but was not to be put into writing until the Persian period; see G.F. Moore, *Judaism* 1:245. Christians also debated the canonicity, and it was not officially recognized as Scripture until the council of Carthage in A.D. 397.

8. See J.A. Soggin, *Introduction*, p. 403.

9. See Moore, *Judaism* 2:53.

10. Cited in B.W. Anderson, "Introduction and Exegesis of Esther," *IB* 3:830; J.A. McClymont, "Esther, Book of," *HDB* 1 (1889): 773, cites J.G. Carpzov, *Introduction in libris Veteris Testamenti* (Leipzig: 1714) 20:6.

11. See R.H. Pfeiffer, *Introduction*, pp. 740f.

12. The entire story is recounted in *Ant.* xi.6. Josephus identifies Ahasuerus as Artaxerxes (successor to Xerxes) and follows rabbinic tradition in making Haman a descendant of King Agag and the destruction of the Amalekites the basis of Haman's hatred of the Jews. He seems to have used the LXX text.

But whether such a late date can be supported is questionable for several reasons: (1) the Greek additions were already in the LXX (second century at the latest), and they clearly do not belong to the original Hebrew text; (2) nascent Judaism of that period was becoming legalistic, and Esther shows no evidence of regard for the Torah, prayer, Jewish feasts, or anything else that might be related to the Judaism of that period; (3) the Hebrew of Esther is unlike that of the Dead Sea scrolls;[13] (4) the book is devoid of apocalyptic elements. The Jews' problem was not solved by Michael or any other angelic being. No idea of Satan is present. Elements commonly found in second-century Palestine—dualism, angelology, and satanology, commonly attributed to Persian influence—are not even hinted at in this work which shows so many indications that it originated in, or was at least thoroughly familiar with, Persia.

In this light, a more reasonable conclusion is that the story of Esther, whether historical fact or historical novel, and the observance of Purim came from the Persian Diaspora. Their arrival in Palestine may have been considerably later, depending on interpretation of 9:20-22, 29-32.

Doctrine of Providence. If Esther does not contain a reference to God, it certainly proclaims faith in God's protection of his people. Haman sought to destroy all Jews throughout the kingdom (3:6). Since the Persian empire extended from India to Ethiopia (1:1; Nubia, modern Sudan), including most of Asia Minor, Syria, Palestine, and other lands, this would have meant extermination of almost all living Jews. When Mordecai learned of the edict, he put on sackcloth and ashes, and publicly wept (4:1), going to the very entrance of the king's gate. Likewise there was great mourning among the Jews, with fasting, weeping, and lamenting.

Learning of this, Esther sought the reason, and Mordecai sent her a copy of the decree (4:8) and a charge to intercede with the king for her people. She had not told the king that she was a Jew (2:20).[14] But Mordecai knew that this fact would come out, and Esther could not hope to escape, even in the palace (v. 13). At that point Mordecai expressed his firm faith in Providence: "For if you keep silence at such a time as this, relief and deliverance will rise for the Jews from another quarter, but you and your father's house will perish" (v. 14).

Anti-Semitism. Animosity toward Jews when fully developed results in genocide: the attempt to exterminate Jews. This satanic scheme is probably much older than the time of Haman. In Moses' day, Pharaoh attempted to exterminate (or drastically limit the population growth) of the Hebrew slaves. Edom's

---

13. Esther is the only canonical book not found at Qumran.
14. Perhaps the custom of *kitmân* "guarded secret" or *taqiyyä* "piety," acceptance of a pretension to be of a race, culture, or religious belief for the sake of peaceful coexistence, was practiced in Persia at that time; see W.S. LaSor, *Handbook of Biblical Hebrew* 1:66f. In modern times, this custom has made it possible for Sunni and Shi'ite Muslims, normally bitter enemies, to make the pilgrimage to Mecca together.

centuries-long hostility toward Judah can probably be explained as a kind of anti-Semitism. Ultimately, as brought out in the New Testament, this is not merely anti-Jewish hostility, but hatred of the people of God (John 15:18). Its source is satanic: the attempt to defeat God in his redemptive purpose. Its historic outworking involves all of God's people, Christians as well as Jews. In its final form it is anti-Messiah or anti-Christ (personified as "Antichrist"). The divine revelation here can be summarized, at least in part: "Let my people alone. If you attempt to harm them, the harm will return on you" (see 9:1).

The Jews included the scroll of Esther in their canon. Because of the enduring nature of its message, they came to find the book as age-long as the Torah itself, continuing even into the age of the Messiah. Christians also included it in their Scriptures, recognizing its divine authority. Esther says to the Christian that anti-Jewish hostility is not God's will, and he cannot tolerate it. It also says that as God's people, Christians can and will become the object of the world's hatred and persecution (see John 15:18-20). Likewise, they can also have faith that "relief and deliverance" will arise, as it did for Mordecai and Esther and the Jews in the Persian empire.

The method used by the Jews in Susa and the kingdom of Ahasuerus is not commended in Scripture. Later, a Jewish Teacher would say: "All who take the sword will perish by the sword" (Matt. 26:52). Perhaps the event in Esther never happened. Many would prefer that way of avoiding ch. 9. But among those who know the horrors of the Crusades, or the terror of the Holocaust, who would dare deny that such acts happen? But they should not. Vengeance is the Lord's prerogative, and belongs to him alone (Deut. 32:35; Rom. 12:19; Heb. 10:30).

FOR FURTHER READING

Anderson, B.W. "The Place of the Book of Esther in the Christian Bible." *Journal of Religion* 30 (1950): 32-43.

Berg, S.B. *The Book of Esther: Motifs, Themes and Structure.* SBL Dissertation 44. Missoula: 1979. (Jewish people shares with Yahweh responsibility for its fate.)

Bettan, I. *The Five Scrolls.* Jewish Commentary. New York: 1950. Pp. 195-247.

Gordis, R. "Religion, Wisdom and History in the Book of Esther—a New Solution to an Ancient Crux." *JBL* 100 (1981): 359-388. (Argues that genre is a Persian chronicle and stresses its basic historic character.)

Humphries, W.L. "Esther, Book of." *IDBS*, pp. 279-281.

Jones, B.W. "Two Misconceptions About the Book of Esther." *CBQ* 39 (1977): 171-181. (Intent is to reconcile Jews to their status as a minority; cites humorous aspects of book.)

Loader, J.A. "Esther as a Novel with Different Levels of Meaning." *ZAW* 90 (1978): 417-421.

Moore, C.A. *Esther.* Anchor Bible 7B. Garden City: 1971. (Comprehensive.)

Talmon, S. " 'Wisdom' in the Book of Esther." *VT* 13 (1963): 419-455.

CHAPTER 49

THE CHRONICLER'S
PERSPECTIVE

W HEN turning in the English Bible from 2 Kings to 1 Chronicles,[1] one senses familiar terrain. It may seem curious that the narrative of redemptive history, progressing from Genesis through the Exodus, Conquest and Settlement, Monarchy, and Captivity, should be sidetracked by a return to "Adam, Seth, Enosh" (1 Chr. 1:1) and a repetition of the familiar stories of David, Solomon, and their successors. Indeed, about one-half of the material in Chronicles[2] is repeated virtually word for word from earlier Old Testament books.

The viewpoint or perspective of the Chronicler is what sets this work off from that of his predecessors and justifies its inclusion in the canon. Far from being Samuel and Kings warmed over, Chronicles has a freshness and flavor all its own and, when its purposes are understood, furnishes rich nourishment for theological thought. Four main parts comprise the history recorded in 1–2 Chronicles:

---

1. The name Chronicles stems from Jerome's suggestion (*ca* A.D. 400) that the book be called a "Chronicle of the Entire Sacred History." The Hebrew title (*dibrê hayyāmim*) means "The Events of the Days," while the LXX *paraleipomena* "The Omitted" may refer to material omitted from either 1–2 Samuel and 1–2 Kings or an earlier Greek translation. In the Hebrew canon Chronicles is the last book of the Writings, following Ezra and Nehemiah.
2. The division into 1–2 Chronicles is found in the LXX but not in Hebrew manuscripts before the Middle Ages. This division is dictated by practical considerations (such as the book's unwieldy size) rather than anything inherent in the writings. Therefore, the term Chronicles refers to both books as a whole, and their writer, who was possibly the author or editor of Ezra and Nehemiah, is called the Chronicler. Recent research has looked more to "a Chronistic school whose activity . . . extended over a period from about 515 B.C. to some time after the work of Ezra or Nehemiah" than to a single author for all three works; J.R. Porter, "Old Testament Historiography," p. 154 in G.W. Anderson, ed., *Tradition and Interpretation*; see also S. Japhet, "The Supposed Common Authorship of Chronicles and Ezra-Nehemiah Investigated Anew," *VT* 18 (1968): 330-371. For convenience' sake the term Chronicler here will describe the work of the editor(s).

Genealogies from Adam to David	1 Chr. 1–9
Reign of David	10–29
Reign of Solomon	2 Chr. 1–9
Reign of David's sons to the Exile	10–36

Continuity and selectivity are twin considerations for a historian. Continuity is necessary because of the interrelatedness of history. Each event bears a definite relationship to others—like a thread in a fabric—and cannot be understood in isolation. Selectivity is mandatory because no one could record (and who would want to read?) everything that happened in any given era. The historian, therefore, singles out and highlights what is significant. Both considerations involve subjectivity: the historian makes decisions on the basis of what seems important, influenced, in part at least, by his or her interests—whether economics, sociology, politics, religion, military encounters, or some combination.[3]

The Hebrew Chronicler is not a historian in the strict western sense. To him Israel's history was pregnant with spiritual and moral lessons, which he brought to birth through a kind of historical midwifery. He is not concerned

Reconstruction of Herodian temple at Jerusalem. (W. S. LaSor)

3. The various approaches to history employed in Israel and her neighbors are surveyed in R.C. Dentan, ed., *The Idea of History in the Ancient Near East* (New Haven: 1955).

so much with the bare facts of Israel's history as with their meaning. If all valid historical writing is interpretative, the Chronicler's is highly interpretative.

All this is not to say that the Chronicler's account is inaccurate when he departs from his main source of information—the books of Samuel and Kings.[4] The essential accuracy of many of the episodes gleaned from other sources, especially the book of the Kings of Israel and Judah (e.g., 1 Chr. 9:1; 2 Chr. 27:7; 35:27; 36:8),[5] has been demonstrated by recent archaeological findings. W.F. Albright notes that the preexilic documentary material found in Chronicles but not in Kings "has repeatedly been shown to be original and important. . . ."[6]

The Chronicler frequently has been accused of irresponsibility with numbers,[7] particularly regarding the size of combatting armies. According to 1 Chr. 21:5 Israel's army numbered 1,100,000 and Judah's, 470,000; while 2 Sam. 24:9 lists armies of 800,000 for Israel and 500,000 for Judah. But even here the Chronicler's figures are not always higher than those in Samuel-Kings. In fact, in five of the seventeen cases of apparent discrepancies, the numbers in Chronicles are lower. It is sometimes suggested that numbers are easily miscopied, particularly where Hebrew may have symbolized figures by giving numerical values to letters of the alphabet. While manuscript evidence of this practice is lacking, it may well be that some discrepancies may be due to scribal errors, and others to different methods of reckoning.

Again, the Chronicler may have reproduced accurately numbers in sources which varied from those used by the editors of 1–2 Kings. Numbers are frequently round approximations with symbolic significance: forty years may mean a generation, or the thousand thousand (RSV "million") of Zerah's Egyptian forces (2 Chr. 14:9) may connote a huge army. It is hazardous to impugn the Chronicler's accuracy when such inadequate tools are available for gauging his work.

---

4. Which text of Samuel-Kings the Chronicler used is not certain. That he seems sometimes to reproduce the MT almost verbatim and at other times to range away from it suggests either that he worked from an old Palestinian text different at points from the MT or that he used an interpretation or commentary (Heb. *midrāš*) on Samuel-Kings (2 Chr. 24:27). See W.E. Lemke, "The Synoptic Problem in the Chronicler's History," *HTR* 58 (1965): 349-363; also Porter, "Old Testament Historiography," p. 156.

5. The Chronicler mentions a number of other writings, usually credited to prophets, e.g., Samuel, Nathan, Gad (1 Chr. 29:29), Ahijah, Iddo (2 Chr. 9:29), Shemaiah (12:15), Jehu (20:34), Isaiah (32:32). Twice these bear the name "midrash"—"story" or "commentary" (13:22; 24:27). Most likely these indicate various parts of the same work, a midrash on the book of the Kings of Israel and Judah, with the sections cited attributed specifically to the prophets. R.H. Pfeiffer claims that the midrash is the work of the Chronicler himself, but this view has not gained general acceptance; *Introduction*, p. 805. Midrash here should not be understood in the sense of "imaginative interpretation," as in later Jewish use, but as "book" or "writing," as translated by the LXX; see M.P. Miller, "Midrash," *IDBS*, p. 594.

6. *From the Stone Age to Christianity*, p. 273. Cf. J.M. Myers, *I Chronicles*. Anchor Bible 12 (Garden City: 1965), p. LXIII: "within the limits of its purpose, the Chronicler's story is accurate wherever it can be checked, though the method of presentation is homiletical."

7. See Myers, *idem*.

HISTORICAL PERSPECTIVE

Some differences between Chronicles and Samuel-Kings may be accredited to the Chronicler's chronological distance from the events recounted. Though scholars share no precise agreement as to his date, it seems quite certain that the Chronicler could not have compiled his work much before 400 B.C., especially if he is also responsible for the books of Ezra and Nehemiah.[8] Thus removed by more than a century from even the latest events that he records, the author is able to single out those episodes whose significance he finds of lasting value, particularly with regard to his own circumstances. The Chronicler is keenly sensitive to the way the past illustrates the present and seeks to learn for himself and to teach his fellows the weighty lessons of grace and judgment in Israel's history.

Those lessons were crucial to the survival and stability of the Chronicler's people. They had been battered by the harshness of the Exile and beleaguered by the circumstances of their resettlement. The Chronicler's concern was to recount the history in such a way as to assure the people that Yahweh was ruling and to urge their full loyalty to him.[9]

The good kings of Judah—David (1 Chr. 10–29), Solomon (2 Chr. 1–9), Jehoshaphat (17:1–21:1), Hezekiah (chs. 29–32), and Josiah (chs. 34–35)—loom large in his sight, and he describes their exploits at length while omitting mention of their faults, which from his distant vantage point appear insignificant by contrast. Rather than try to whitewash them—for the stories of their shortcomings recorded in Samuel and Kings would remain firmly lodged in the readers' memories—he focuses on their sterling qualities and stresses the fruits of their obedience to God.

POLITICAL PERSPECTIVE

The northern kingdom had drawn prophetic censure from the beginning, for the combination of non-Davidic kings and syncretistic worship had been more than the prophets could tolerate. Ezekiel (36:24), Hosea (3:5), Amos (9:11), Micah (5:2-4 [MT 1-3]), and others look forward to a reuniting of the two kingdoms under a son of David. Since this was the prophetic ideal and the disruption of the northern kingdom had been a mistake in the first place, the Chronicler expends little effort recounting its history. Whereas the authors of

---

8. Albright gives substantial reasons for attributing all of these books to Ezra, as Jewish tradition contends (Talmud B. Bat. 15a); "The Date and Personality of the Chronicler," JBL 40 (1921): 104-124. However, D.N. Freedman dates the Chronicler's work ca. 515 and connects it with the ministries of Haggai and Zechariah; he attributes the memoirs of Ezra and Nehemiah to a later hand which stressed the religious patterns of Moses rather than the religious contributions of David as stressed in Chronicles; "The Chronicler's Purpose," CBQ 23 (1961): 441.

9. Specifics about the Chronicler's historical and social circumstances are difficult, especially if dated to the late fifth or early fourth century; see P.R. Ackroyd, I & II Chronicles, Ezra, Nehemiah. Torch Bible Commentary (London: 1973), p. 27.

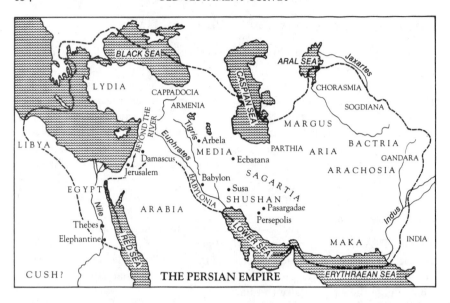

THE PERSIAN EMPIRE

Kings survey the members of each northern dynasty, the Chronicler mentions them only when their paths cross Judah's (e.g., Ahab's alliance with Jehoshaphat, 2 Chr. 18). That the northern kingdom had no measurable renaissance after the Exile undoubtedly was interpreted as the seal of God's judgment upon them. Therefore, he turns full attention to Judah, which had survived the Exile and was carrying on the spiritual and ethical ministry once entrusted to all Israel.[10] Some scholars detect in this neglect of the northern kingdom an anti-Samaritan bias in Chronicles (and especially Ezra-Nehemiah).[11] While hostile feelings did exist, they certainly did not originate with the Chronicler,[12] who in this regard stands in the prophetic tradition reflected in Amos and passages such as 2 Kgs. 17.

The glorification of David and his family is noteworthy. Both the struggles of Jesse's son with Saul (who merits only one brief chapter—1 Chr. 10) and his gross sins with Bathsheba and Uriah (see 2 Sam. 11–12) are bypassed. Similarly, the ill-fated attempts of Absalom (chs. 14–19) and Adonijah (1 Kgs. 1–2) to seize the throne from David and Solomon escape mention. The divinely-chosen Davidic family had surmounted these difficulties, and to retell

---

10. This emphasis probably accounts for the sparseness of material prior to David (1 Chr. 1–9). The Chronicler is content with very brief family histories, mostly genealogies from Adam to David, with whose ascent to power Judah came into its own. Though largely a catalogue of names, these genealogies have a theological purpose: to remind the restored community of its deep roots and strong continuity in God's program for redemption from creation on.

11. E.g., M. Noth, *History*, p. 296; J.A. Soggin, *Introduction*, p. 418.

12. Ackroyd brands the attempt to relate the Chronicler's purpose to the Samaritan schism "ill-founded, not least because of the chronological uncertainties"; "I and II Chronicles," *IDBS*, p. 158.

them would only have detracted from the Chronicler's chief purposes.[13] The statement that, for the Chronicler, David replaces Moses as Israel's religious patron[14] is probably excessive, but it does point up his central role in Israel's religious life. The spiritual vitality of the people stemmed from him. What he was they became, whether for good or ill.[15]

THEOLOGICAL PERSPECTIVE

With some justification Chronicles has been called an example of dogmatic historiography,[16] history written from a theological point of view. The Chronicler's theology has many facets. For example, he stresses the direct activity of God. Battles are won or lost not according to warriors' prowess or the size of opposing forces but according to God's will and, at times, miraculous intervention (e.g., 2 Chr. 13:15-18; 17:10; 20:22-25). The Chronicler testifies to Israel's time-tested belief that they won their battles in the strength of the Lord (Exod. 15; Pss. 2; 20; 21; Prov. 21:31).

The Chronicler's conviction that righteousness exalts a nation is matched by his emphasis on individual retribution, whether of judgment or reward. Like Ezekiel, he saw that a person (not his children) will be rewarded for his actions (Ezek. 18:2ff.; cf. Jer. 31:29). Although this principle is part of the Chronicler's theology (e.g., his moralizing on the death of Saul where 1 Samuel is silent; cf. 1 Sam. 31:8ff.; 1 Chr. 10:13f.),[17] it certainly did not originate with him. Actually, in his own sermonic fashion, he merely applies the principles announced in Deuteronomy (e.g., Deut. 27–28) and tested in Judges, Samuel, and Kings.[18]

The Chronicler's use of citations and stories from earlier books underscores

---

13. See Freedman, CBQ 23 (1961): 437: ". . . the principal objective of the Chronicler was to write a history of the dynasty of David, not primarily in terms of its historical and political achievements (though these form the framework, appropriated from Samuel-Kings), but its accomplishments in the religious and specifically cultic areas. . . ." City and ruler, temple and priest appear to be the fixed points around which he constructs his history and theology.

14. See E. Jacob, cited by N.H. Snaith, OTMS, p. 111.

15. For the tensions between the ideal view of the kings' duties and their less than ideal practices, see K.W. Whitelam, The Just King.

16. E.g., A. Bentzen, Introduction 2:213.

17. For comparisons of Samuel-Kings and Chronicles, see W.D. Crockett, A Harmony of the Books of Samuel, Kings, and Chronicles (repr. Grand Rapids: 1951).

18. Note B.S. Childs, Old Testament as Scripture, p. 652: "By emphasizing the verifiable consequences of disobedience, the Chronicler simply drew forth the truth of a lesson which history itself had confirmed." Assuredly, the stories of Manasseh's repentance (2 Chr. 33:12ff.) and Josiah's fatal defiance of the divine oracle (35:22) were not manufactured so the Chronicler could force the facts of history to fit his theory of retribution (see Bentzen, Introduction 2:214): Manasseh's penitence is made to account for his lengthy reign and Josiah's disobedience, for his untimely death. The details in both Kings and Chronicles are too sketchy to contrast. A partial, ineffective reform by Manasseh, the results of which were totally undone by Amon (2 Kgs. 21:19-26; 2 Chr. 33:21-25), is certainly possible.

his theological emphasis on the authority of the Scriptures. One facet of his style is the so-called "Levitical Sermon,"[19] which uses snatches of the prophets, law, or historical books as texts (e.g., 2 Chr. 19:6f. draws from Deut. 1:17; Zeph. 3:5; 2 Chr. 20:15-17 quotes from Exod. 14:13; 1 Sam. 17:47). But, as Childs notes, the Chronicler reaches beyond mere quotations to include the "entire corpus of prophetic writing."[20] The stories from Samuel-Kings, for instance, were read not as mere history but as a revelation of God's will and plan for his people in their present circumstances. Jewish tradition builds on this view of revelation by calling Joshua, Judges, Samuel, and Kings the "Former Prophets."

Perhaps the dominant theological emphasis of Chronicles is the constant concern for the temple, its worship, and its officials, the Levites. Comparison of the accounts of the inauguration of worship in Jerusalem under David (2 Sam. 6:12-19; 1 Chr. 15:1–16:3) or Hezekiah's reform (2 Kgs. 18:4-7; 2 Chr. 29–31) reveals the Chronicler's avid interest in the structure and personnel of Israel's religion. Though he is by no means disinterested in the Hebrew prophets,[21] the Levites, who assisted the priests in preparing sacrifices and who served as temple attendants, singers, and gatekeepers, are particularly dear to his heart. No doubt this priestly interest, along with lack of concern for the northern kingdom, accounts for his nearly complete silence (cf. 2 Chr. 21:12-15) on Elijah and Elisha, who are so important in Kings.

Although his priestly perspective cannot be doubted, one need not hold that "the Chronicler gave the Levites a higher place than they ever actually had."[22] The complex history of the relationship between priests and Levites brooks no sweeping generalities of any kind. Just as likely the Levites, either through their own ambition or through default of the priests (perhaps too few to serve efficiently the growing populace), had usurped some priestly functions. Ezekiel seems concerned to correct such abuses by reinstating the Mosaic law (see Ezek. 44:10-14).

The Chronicler's overarching concern is the theocratic character of the community. God's direct activity, the pattern of retribution, scriptural authority, and centrality of the temple are all components in the rule of God over his people. The Chronicler longs for and seeks to contribute to a recovery of the glorious days of David and Solomon—not by reestablishment of the monarchy but by a return to obedient worship. To a people stripped of kings and forced to obey Persian law, he preaches the word of hope: belief in the Lord and the

---

19. G. von Rad, "The Levitical Sermon in I and II Chronicles," pp. 267-280 in *The Problem of the Hexateuch*.

20. *Old Testament as Scripture*, p. 653.

21. See Freedman, *CBQ* 23 (1961): 440: "For the Chronicler monarchy and prophecy go hand in hand; his emphasis on the function of the prophet as adviser to the king is distinctive of his work."

22. Snaith, *OTMS*, p. 111.

message of his prophets would restore to Judah an epoch of glory akin to the nation's golden age (2 Chr. 20:20).

Just as the authors of Kings selected, edited, compiled, and interpreted Israel's history from their own perspectives, so does the Chronicler from his. If he accords the temple and its staff greater glory than his prophetic counterparts, perhaps he discerns in the patterns of the past the importance of keeping the nation's heart sound by ample attention to the consequences of correct worship. Never embarrassed by the "foolishness of preaching," the Chronicler seeks to distill from the successes and failures of the leaders of old the catalysts which would produce a constant moral and spiritual concern in the baffling chemistry of postexilic society.

FOR FURTHER READING

Ackroyd, P.R. "The Chronicler as Exegete." *JSOT* 2 (1977): 2-32.

——. "History and Theology in the Writings of the Chronicler." *CTM* 38 (1967): 501-515.

Coggins, R.J. *The First and Second Books of the Chronicles*. Cambridge Bible Commentary. New York: 1976. (Introductory level.)

Richardson, H.N. "The Historical Reliability of the Chronicler." *Journal of Bible and Religion* 26 (1958): 9-12.

Torrey, C.C. *The Chronicler's History of Israel*. 1954; repr. Port Washington, N.Y.: 1973. ("Restores the original unity of Chronicles-Ezra-Nehemiah.")

Williamson, H.G.M. *Israel in the Books of Chronicles*. Cambridge: 1977. (Theme that faithful nucleus need not be exclusive.)

CHAPTER 50

EZRA-NEHEMIAH

IN the English Bible, Ezra and Nehemiah are placed with the "historical" books following 1–2 Chronicles. In the Hebrew canon, however, they are part of the third division, the Writings, and are placed before Chronicles, even though their contents chronologically follow those books.[1] Furthermore, the two books probably formed a single work in the Hebrew canon. Indeed, the final Masoretic notes are lacking at the end of Ezra, the total of verses given at the end of Nehemiah is that for both books, and the middle verse given is that for the combined works. The contents also support this, for the "memoirs" of Ezra, begun in Ezra 7–10, are completed in Neh. 8–10. The division into two books did not take place in the Hebrew Bible until the fifteenth century A.D., and apparently originated in Christian circles.[2] However, the portion of Nehemiah that comprises Nehemiah's memoirs (1:1–7:73a; chs. 11–13) may have circulated initially as a separate corpus before being incorporated into the book as it now stands. Indeed, the Nehemiah corpus is introduced by a heading: "The words of Nehemiah the son of Hacaliah." Also, it differs significantly in literary style and form from the Ezra corpus, and at least one major section is duplicated, the list of returning exiles (Ezra 2 = Neh. 7).

NAME AND CONTENTS

The names of the two books are taken from the principal character of each, although it is important to stress that the second half of the so-called memoirs of Ezra is set forth in Neh. 7:73b–10:39. Since two works among the apocryphal books also are entitled Ezra or use the Greek form Esdras, and there is no

---

1. Although by far the most frequent order, this is not the only one extant among Hebrew manuscripts. Some Spanish manuscripts, one Masoretic treatise (thirteenth century), and, most notably, the famous Aleppo codex (tenth century) place Chronicles at the beginning of the Writings with Ezra-Nehemiah at the end.

2. It is first attested in Origen (third century).

consistency in the use of these names in the LXX and Vulgate, great confusion results. (For the more common of these names, see Table.)

Ezra-Nehemiah sets forth the events of two distinct periods in Israel's restoration to the land after the Exile: the return of the exiles and rebuilding of the temple, 538-516 B.C. (Ezra 1–6); and the work of the leaders in establishing the community religiously (Ezra) and physically (Nehemiah), 458–ca. 420 (Ezra 7–Neh. 13).

Return of the Exiles and Rebuilding of the Temple. With the authority of a decree from Cyrus king of Persia (Ezra 1:1-4), Sheshbazzar prince of Judah returned to Jerusalem with the temple vessels taken by Nebuchadnezzar (chs. 1–2). The account includes a list of the returnees who "came with Zerubbabel, Jeshua . . ." (2:2). 3:1-6 records that Jeshua the son of Jozadak, the priest, and Zerubbabel the son of Shealtiel rebuilt the altar and established regular sacrifices. The rest of ch. 3 recounts the preparations for rebuilding the temple and laying the foundation (vv. 7-13).

When the local populace offered to help (4:1f.), they were turned down by Zerubbabel (v. 3), and for spite seriously hindered the project "all the days of Cyrus king of Persia, even until the reign of Darius king of Persia" (vv. 4f.). The rest of ch. 4 summarizes the opposition to the work, including not only Zerubbabel's rebuilding of the temple but also Nehemiah's rebuilding of the city walls in the middle of the following century.[3] Beginning with v. 8, the account is in Aramaic, which continues in use until 6:18. Ch. 4 concludes by reporting that the work "ceased until the second year of the reign of Darius king of Persia"

	1	2	3	4
MT	Ezra	Nehemiah	(lacking)	(lacking)
KJV, RSV	Ezra	Nehemiah	1 Esdras	2 Esdras*
LXX	Esdras B		Esdras A	(lacking)
Vulgate	1 Esdras	2 Esdras	3 Esdras	4 Esdras

1—Old Testament book of Ezra
2—Old Testament book of Nehemiah
3—Greek work containing 2 Chr. 35–36, Ezra, and Neh. 8:1-12, with some difference in order, plus an account not in the Old Testament.
4—Composite apocalyptic work originally in Greek but now extant only in a Latin text

*The Ezra Apocalypse in English translation is sometimes called 4 Ezra.

---

3. Lack of chronological concern by the author or editor has caused modern scholars to question the integrity of the account (see below).

Cyrus cylinder (536 B.C.), permitting release of the Jewish exiles and restoration of the temple. (British Museum)

(v. 24). Chs. 5–6 tell of the final rebuilding of the temple under the leadership of Zerubbabel and Jeshua and the constant prodding of the prophets Haggai and Zechariah (vv. 1f.). The account recalls the initial opposition of Tattenai, Persian governor of the province Beyond the River,[4] who wrote to Darius to verify the Jews' report that their construction was in compliance with an edict of Cyrus. Darius ordered a search of the royal archives, in which the decree was discovered. Darius responded to Tattenai not only to permit the construction but to pay the cost in full from the royal revenues and to provide materials for sacrifice (5:3–6:12). The temple was finished on the third of Adar in the sixth year of Darius (12 March 515; v. 15). A festival of dedication was celebrated (vv. 16-18) then, and a Passover feast on the fourteenth day of the following month (21 April 515).

Work of Ezra and Nehemiah. No record of events has been preserved for the period after completion of the temple until the time of Ezra some fifty-seven years later, except for the brief notice in Ezra 4:6 that "they"[5] wrote an accusation against the Jews at the beginning of the reign of Ahasuerus (486-465; better known by his Greek name Xerxes).

---

4. Aram. *ʿᵃbar-nahᵃrâ*, lit. "the other side of the river," a technical term for that province of the Persian empire that stretched from the Euphrates down the Syrian and Palestinian littoral to the borders of Egypt. Obviously the point of orientation for the name is Persia and Mesopotamia.

5. Apparently the "people of the land" (v. 4), who effectively stopped work on the temple until the days of Darius. These were the remnants of the northern tribes mixed with other groups whom the Assyrians deported to Palestine. Two such deportations are mentioned here, one under Esarhaddon (680-669; v. 2) and one under "the great and noble Osnappar" (v. 10), usually identified with Assurbanipal (668-627).

(1) Return of Ezra; problem of mixed marriages (Ezra 7–10). In the fifth month of the seventh year of Artaxerxes (7:8), Ezra, "the priest, the scribe" (v. 11), and "a scribe skilled in the law of Moses" (v. 6), returned from Babylonia to Jerusalem, commissioned by the king to "make inquiries about Judah and Jerusalem according to the law of your God" (v. 14) and to appoint magistrates and judges to govern all who knew that law and to teach those who did not (v. 25). The story of the return is told in detail in the first person (ch. 8), including a list of the families who accompanied Ezra. Ch. 8 concludes with a third-person summary of the offerings by the returned exiles and the delivery of the king's commission to the Persian authorities (vv. 35f.). The narrative resumes in the first person, relating the report of the Jewish officials that many of the people, including priests and Levites, had intermarried with peoples of the land (9:1f.). After Ezra's fast (vv. 3-5) and long prayer (vv. 6-15), a large assembly gathered round him and in great remorse offered to divorce their foreign wives, summoning Ezra to supervise the task according to the law (10:1-5). So the men of Judah and Benjamin assembled at Jerusalem, on the twentieth day of the ninth month (v. 9), and agreed to call a commission of elders to investigate the matter (vv. 13-17). The commission met for two months (10:17) to examine the matter. The account closes with the list of offenders (vv. 18-44).

(2) Return of Nehemiah (Neh. 1–2); building of the walls (chs. 3–7). At this point the memoirs of Ezra break off and are not resumed until 7:73b. Instead the narrative takes up the story of Nehemiah's return. Since large portions are in the first person, it is often called Nehemiah's memoirs.[6] In the month of Chislev in the twentieth year (1:1) of Artaxerxes (2:1), Hanani, Nehemiah's brother, arrived from Jerusalem with a delegation of Judeans to inform him that the inhabitants of Judea were in dire straits and the walls of Jerusalem still lay in ruins (1:2f.). Nehemiah, who was cupbearer to the king (v. 11), then wept and prayed fervently (vv. 4-11). Some four months later,[7] as Nehemiah was serving Artaxerxes, opportunity arose to inform the king of the city's deplorable condition and to request permission to return and rebuild it (2:1-5). Permission was granted, along with authority to requisition timber for the walls (vv. 6-8), and Nehemiah returned (vv. 9-11).

After a three-day stay he secretly surveyed the ruined walls at night (vv. 11-16) and then informed his fellow Jews of his commission, urging them on to the task (vv. 17f.). Ch. 2 concludes with the derision of Sanballat the

6. The account begins with the editorial heading "The words of Nehemiah the son of Hacaliah."

7. The date is given as Nisan in the twentieth year of Artaxerxes (2:1). Since Chislev, the month the report came from Judea, is the ninth month and Nisan the first, it would seem as if 1:1 should read the nineteenth year or 2:1 the twenty-first. The editor may simply be using the alternate practice, in use in preexilic Israel, of beginning the year in the autumn with the seventh month, Tishri. If so, Chislev is the third month of the twentieth year of Artaxerxes and Nisan, the seventh. This is preferable to positing a mistake by editor or copyists. For a summary of the Hebrew calendar, see Ch. 21.

Horonite, Tobiah the king's official in Ammon, and Geshem the Arabian (vv. 19f.).

The narrative then recounts the successful completion of the wall. A summary of the groups involved and the portion each constructed is given (3:1-32). A detailed report follows citing the opposition of Sanballat and Tobiah, beginning with mockery (4:1-6 [MT 3:33-38]) and then the threat of armed attack (vv. 7-9 [MT 4:1-3]). Nehemiah responded by arming the workers and organizing half the force to labor and half to stand guard (vv. 10-23 [MT 4:17]). Economic hardships plagued the work force, made worse by the additional burden of work on the walls (5:1-5). Nehemiah instituted emergency measures, pledging to take no interest or pledges for loans to the needy and requiring the same from the nobles and upper classes, who returned all previous exactions (vv. 6-13). Ch. 5 concludes with a summary of Nehemiah's beneficence in not drawing on the governor's allowances from the local taxes, even to support the common table he maintained (vv. 14-19). Opposition continued with personal attacks, enticing Nehemiah to leave the city so they might attack him (6:1-4) and threatening to report to the king that he planned to rebel (vv. 5-9). Finally the opponents commissioned oracles that would cause Nehemiah to barricade himself in the temple through fear of his life (vv. 10-14). All of these he resisted and the wall was completed on 25 Elul after fifty-two days' work (v. 15).[8]

Ch. 7 includes Nehemiah's ordinances for the safety of the city (7:1-3) and the observation that the population was very small (v. 4). This prompted Nehemiah to take a census, but he found the list of the first returnees (vv. 6-73a, a repetition of Ezra 2:2-70 except for minor differences). Nehemiah's memoirs then are interrupted by the resumption of the story of Ezra and are not concluded until ch. 11.

---

8. Many consider this figure, which represents about nine weeks (assuming that they did not work on the Sabbath), as far too short a time for so monumental a task. They prefer the figure given by Josephus (*Ant.* xi.5.8) of two years and four months (e.g., J. Bright, *History*, p. 381). However, it must be remembered that the city of Nehemiah's time comprised only the very limited extent of the Ophel ridge south of the Temple Mount. Recent excavations in the Jewish Quarter of the Old City make this "minimalist position" quite certain. These excavations, carried out at more than a dozen sites, have found clear evidence of occupation of the western hill in the late Judean Monarchy (eighth or seventh century), but none of these sites revealed any occupation levels whatsoever for the Persian period or even the early Hellenistic era. This shows that the area was abandoned during the period of the return and the rebuilding of the temple and walls by Zerubbabel and Nehemiah. For a succinct report see the statement of the excavator, N. Avigad, "Excavations in the Jewish Quarter of the Old City, 1969-1971," pp. 41-51 in Y. Yadin, ed., *Jerusalem Revealed* (New Haven: 1976). Furthermore, in this period the wall on the eastern side of the city, above the Kidron valley, ran along the crest of the ridge rather than further down the slope as did the preexilic wall, further reducing the area walled in; see K.M. Kenyon, *Jerusalem* (New York: 1967), pp. 107-111. For a succinct statement and a map, see B. Mazar, *The Mountain of the Lord* (Garden City: 1975), p. 193. For a persuasive and detailed argument to the contrary, see W.S. LaSor, "Jerusalem," *ISBE* 2 (1982). Quite possibly Nehemiah found significant sections of the wall still extant, so part of the work involved filling in the breaches and completing the height, rather than starting anew.

(3) Ezra's reading of the law; feast of Booths, fast and covenant (Neh. 7:73b–10:39 [MT 40]). On the first day of the seventh month (8:2), upon invitation of the assembled people, Ezra read aloud from the "book of the law of Moses which the Lord had given to Israel" (v. 1), from dawn until midday, standing on a wooden pulpit facing the square before the Water Gate (v. 3). At the same time, the Levites also read and interpreted "so that the people understood the reading" (v. 8). At Ezra's instructions, the initial sorrow of the people at hearing the law was changed into a joyous festival (vv. 9-12).

On the second day, the prescriptions for the feast of Booths in the seventh month were encountered, so the people brought branches, built booths, and celebrated the festival for eight days (vv. 13-18).

Ch. 9 records that on the twenty-fourth day of that month, the people held a solemn fast and assembled for worship (vv. 1-5), while Ezra publicly uttered a long prayer of confession (vv. 6-37). A first-person account follows, reporting the decision to make a firm covenant (v. 38 [MT 10:1]). This account continues in 10:29, but is interrupted by the insertion of the list of those who signed the covenant, given in the third person (10:1-27 [MT 2-28]). The terms of the covenant are then set forth, namely, to keep the law, strictly observe the marriage rules, keep the Sabbath, and pay the tithes and temple dues regularly (vv. 28-39 [MT 29-40]).

(4) Repopulation of Jerusalem; dedication of the walls; Nehemiah's social and religious reforms during his second governorship; statistical lists (chs. 11–13). This section concludes the account of Nehemiah and very clearly continues the narrative that left off at 7:4. It begins with a brief summary of the repopulation of Jerusalem by lot (11:2f.), to which is attached a series of lists: those dwelling in Jerusalem (vv. 3-24) and the villages of Judah and Benjamin (vv. 25-36); priests and Levites who returned with Zerubbabel (12:1-9); genealogy of high priests from Jeshua to Jaddua (vv. 10f.); heads of priestly and levitical houses (vv. 12-26). Then follows the account of the dedication of the walls, celebrated by two processions which proceeded around the walls in opposite directions, meeting at the temple (vv. 27-43). The section concludes with the appointment of officials for collection of the levitical tithes and offerings (vv. 44-47), and the exclusion of foreigners from the community (13:1-3).

The book concludes with brief summaries of reforms carried out during Nehemiah's second governorship, which began ca. 432.[9] These reforms include the expulsion of Tobiah the Ammonite from a room in the temple granted him by the high priest Eliashib (vv. 4-9); and measures to provide the tithes due the Levites (vv. 10-14); and to prevent profanation of the Sabbath (vv. 15-22); and mixed marriages (vv. 23-29). The chapter concludes with a summary of Nehemiah's good works (vv. 30f.).

---

9. The text records that he returned briefly to Persia in Artaxerxes' thirty-second year (433; 13:6).

HISTORICAL BACKGROUND

Judah in the period of the restoration was but a small part of a vast Persian province, and its political and even religious fortunes were dependent on Persian power and policy. When Nebuchadnezzar, the captor of Jerusalem, died in 562, Babylonian power rapidly declined under ineffectual rulers. Babylon's end came at the hands of Persia, a new power destined for the dominant role in the ancient Near East for the next two centuries. The founder of this empire was Cyrus, king of Anshan in southern Iran, who rebelled against his Median overlords and by 550 succeeded in taking control of their vast empire. He extended its domain from the Aegean Sea to the border of Afghanistan. Babylon then stood alone and in 539 fell to the Persians after a single battle on the frontier. By 539 Cyrus controlled all western Asia to the borders of Egypt.

Cyrus was an enlightened ruler whose general policy was to permit peoples deported by the Babylonians to return to their homelands. He also carefully respected the religious sensibilities of his subject peoples and governed by permitting considerable local autonomy. He kept firm control, however, through the Persian army and a complex governmental system. In keeping with his policy of repatriation, Cyrus permitted a group of Jewish exiles to return to Judah in 538 and provided funds for rebuilding the temple.

Judah remained relatively unaffected by the major historical movements and events of the empire. It will suffice to review the rest of Persian history, particularly that period pertinent to the era of Ezra-Nehemiah, in tabular form:[10]

Ruler	Major Events
Cambyses (530-522)	Conquered Egypt in 525
Darius I (522-486)	Defeated and executed the usurper Gaumata to gain the throne. Faced massive revolt from east to west for two full years. Empire achieved its definitive organization and greatest stability and extent. Only failure was the attack on Greece.
Xerxes I (Ashasuerus) (486-465)	Destroyed Babylon in 482. Invaded Greece but was repulsed in 479 and completely driven out in 466.
Artaxerxes I (Longimanus) (465-424)	Faced rebellion in Egypt for six years. Signed the peace of Callias (449), giving the Greek cities independence and excluding the Persian fleet from the Aegean.
Darius II (Nothus) (423-404)	As a result of Peloponnesian War, gained firm control of Asia Minor.

---

10. For a succinct but excellent overview, see Bright, *History*, pp. 360-375. See also P.R. Ackroyd, "The History of Israel in the Exilic and Post-exilic Periods," pp. 328-342 in G.W. Anderson, ed., *Tradition and Interpretation*.

| Artaxerxes II (Mnemon) (404-358) | Egypt gained independence in 401. Major western rebellion barely put down. |
| Artaxerxes III (Ochus) (358-338) to Darius III (336-331) | Artaxerxes III was ruthless and reconquered Egypt. Empire dissipated in gory intrigues and internal weakness, falling to Alexander the Great in 331. |

This turbulent and momentous period in ancient Near Eastern history is the setting for the events of the return from exile and establishment of the Jewish community under Ezra and Nehemiah.

LITERARY NATURE

Even the short summary of Ezra-Nehemiah presented above reveals the wide variety of sources and types of literary units employed in its construction. Three main blocks of material may be distinguished: the Sheshbazzar and Zerubbabel narrative (Ezra 1–6); the Ezra narrative, largely in the first person (bulk of Ezra 7:1–10:44 and Neh. 7:73b–10:39); and the Nehemiah narrative, also largely first-person (major part of Neh. 1:1–7:73a and 11:1–13:31). Within these three major sections various sources may be distinguished:

(1) Memoirs of Ezra and Nehemiah, both doubtless taken from the auto-biographical accounts themselves. The first-person portion of the Ezra material is found in Ezra 7:27–9:15 (except 8:35f., a third-person summary); the rest is third-person narrative, except for the covenant section in Neh. 9:38–10:39 [MT 10:1-40]. In the Nehemiah material the first-person narrative extends from Neh. 1:1–7:5 and 12:31–13:31.

(2) Documents and letters. The edict of Cyrus allowing the exiles to return is given in Aramaic in Ezra 6:3-5; the Hebrew variant in 1:2-4 is an adaptation addressed to the Jews in exile. The letter from Artaxerxes authorizing Ezra's return is set forth in 7:12-26, also adapted for the exiles. Other Aramaic letters between officials in Palestine and the Persian court include the letter from Rehum and Shimshai to Artaxerxes (4:8-22) and the exchange between Tattenai and Darius (5:7-17; 6:6-12). These ultimately must have come from the Persian state archives.

(3) Lists of various kinds. A representative sample includes: list of exiles who returned with Zerubbabel (Ezra 2:1-70, repeated in Neh. 7:7-72a); list of heads of families who returned with Ezra (Ezra 8:1-14); inventory of temple vessels returned to Sheshbazzar by the Persian court (1:9-11); list of those who married foreign wives (10:18-44); list of builders of the wall (Neh. 3:1-32). The closing section of the account of Nehemiah's first governorship (ch. 11) sets forth a series of lists, including the new inhabitants of Jerusalem (vv. 3-19); other villages occupied by Jews (vv. 25-36); list of high priests from Jeshua to Jaddua (12:10f.); and a list of the heads of priestly and levitical houses (vv.

12-26). All of these lists must have come from the temple archives or records of the Jewish governor's office.

A very striking feature is the manner in which the memoirs of Ezra and Nehemiah are cut in half and interleaved with one another as follows:

(1) Ezra 7:1–10:44   First half of Ezra's memoirs: his arrival; problem of mixed marriages

(2) Neh. 1:1–7:73a   First half of Nehemiah's memoirs: his arrival; building of the wall

(3) 7:73b–10:39 [MT 40] Second half of Ezra's memoirs: reading of the law; feast of Booths; covenant

(4) 11:1–13:31   Second half of Nehemiah's memoirs: dedication of the wall; second governorship

Since Ezra's arrival is dated in the seventh year of Artaxerxes and Nehemiah's in the twentieth year, this order clearly means that Ezra spent thirteen years in Jerusalem (about which nothing is preserved) before reading and establishing the law, the major task for which he had been commissioned.

Further evidence of the author's literary methods and procedures may be seen in Ezra 4, in the Sheshbazzar-Zerubbabel narrative. After relating how the returned exiles refused to allow the people of the land to participate in rebuilding the temple (vv. 1-3), the narrator summarizes their opposition (vv. 4f.) and observes that they frustrated the rebuilding attempt all the days of Cyrus (538-530), until the reign of Darius I (522-486). At this point he inserts a brief mention of an accusation against the Jews in the reign of Ahasuerus (Xerxes I, 486-465; v. 6). This is followed by a brief note about an Aramaic letter to Artaxerxes I (465-424; v. 7), and the text of another letter to Artaxerxes is given in full (vv. 8-16) with his reply ordering the rebuilding to cease (vv. 17-22). As a result the work was stopped by force (v. 23). Since the temple was completed in 515, the last three accounts must relate to the building of the walls. The narrator obviously is not interested in giving a chronologically determined report, but bases the contents on topical association, accusations against returning exiles.

AUTHORSHIP AND DATE

As is common with ancient Near Eastern literature in general and Old Testament writings in particular, no direct indication of authorship has been preserved in Ezra-Nehemiah. The Talmud attributes 1–2 Chronicles as well as Ezra-Nehemiah to Ezra, but adds that the work was completed by Nehemiah.[11]

The similar view that all of this material, excluding the Nehemiah memoirs, was written by the same author-compiler, usually identified as "the Chron-

---

11. B. Bat. 15a.

icler," has been accepted almost without question by the overwhelming majority of modern scholars.[12] The point has been argued persuasively by C.C. Torrey[13] and A.S. Kapelrud.[14] In addition, several scholars also have argued that the Chronicler was Ezra himself, or a close disciple.[15] However, the view that Chronicles-Ezra-Nehemiah is one work has never been without opponents. Recently it has been challenged seriously on the grounds of a systematic investigation of linguistic and stylistic differences between Chronicles and Ezra-Nehemiah,[16] and on the basis of significant differences of purpose and ideology[17] as well as literary and theological features.[18]

For the most part, recent assessments of date assume the unity of Chronicles-Ezra-Nehemiah, and are based principally on the lists of Davidides in 1 Chr. 3:10-24 and high priests in Neh. 12:10f., 22.[19] Albright has shown these to carry down to 400 at the latest.[20] No person or event later than this date is mentioned in the work. In marked contrast, the LXX list of Davidides in 1 Chr. 3:10-24 extends the list for eleven generations instead of seven. On this evidence the most plausible date for the writing-compiling[21] is 400 or shortly thereafter. Later dates have been proposed, arguing that the Aramaic of Ezra (4:8–6:18; 7:12-26) is late, or assuming that the order of the events is

---

12. See H.H. Rowley, "The Chronological Order of Ezra and Nehemiah," p. 138 in *The Servant of the Lord*. Recent commentaries and histories accept the conclusion, frequently without documentation; e.g., J.M. Myers, *1 Chronicles*, p. XVIII; *Ezra-Nehemiah*. Anchor Bible (Garden City: 1965), p. LXVIII; Bright, *History*, p. 395; R.H. Pfeiffer, "Ezra and Nehemiah," *IDB* 2:219.

13. "There is no portion of the whole work Chron.-Ezr.-Neh. in which the Chronicler's literary peculiarities are more strongly marked, more abundant, more evenly and continuously distributed, and more easily recognizable, than in the Hebrew narrative of Ezr. 7–10 and Neh. 8–10"; *Ezra Studies* (1910; repr. New York: 1970), p. 241.

14. *The Question of Authorship in the Ezra-Narrative* (Oslo: 1944).

15. W.F. Albright, *JBL* 40 (1921): 104-124; Myers, *Ezra-Nehemiah*, p. LXVIII; Bright, *History*, p. 398.

16. S. Japhet, *VT* 18 (1968): 330-371. Japhet observes three categories in which the two bodies of material differ markedly: linguistic opposition, specific technical terms, and stylistic peculiarities. Klein, however, challenges the validity of her conclusions on the grounds that she takes inadequate account of the fact that the Nehemiah memoirs per se are irrelevant to the Chronicler's style, and that significant sections of Nehemiah are added later; "Ezra and Nehemiah in Recent Studies," p. 375 note 34 in Cross-Lemke-Miller, *Magnalia Dei*.

17. D.N. Freedman, *CBQ* 22 (1961): 436-442. F.M. Cross, Jr., seeking to account for these differences in purpose and linguistic features as well as the acknowledged similarities that led to the view of common authorship, has posited a theory of three successive editors of the composite work, the first in the time of Zerubbabel, ca. 520, supporting building the temple and emphasizing the royal Davidic ideology; the second after the work of Ezra, 458; and the third, including Nehemiah's memoirs, ca. 400; "A Reconstruction of the Judean Restoration," *JBL* 34 (1975): 4-18, esp. 14f.

18. J.D. Newsome, Jr., "Toward a New Understanding of the Chronicler and His Purpose," *JBL* 94 (1975): 201-217.

19. See Bright, *History*, pp. 396f.; Myers, *Ezra-Nehemiah*, pp. LXVIII ff.

20. *JBL* 40 (1921): 104-124.

21. This designation is chosen since the author both composed material himself (e.g., the third-person introduction to the Ezra block, Ezra 7:1-10) and used a variety of materials from other sources (see above).

confused and therefore the author must have lived long enough after the events for their true order to have been forgotten. None of these reasons is compelling, especially since the Aramaic of Ezra is clearly earlier than that found at Qumran.

HISTORICAL AND CHRONOLOGICAL CONSIDERATIONS

Relationship between Sheshbazzar and Zerubbabel. As noted concerning the literary nature of ch. 4, detailed chronology is not a major criterion of the narrator for ordering this work. This is also apparent in the relationship between Sheshbazzar and Zerubbabel. The book of Ezra clearly states that the first return was led by Sheshbazzar "the prince of Judah" (1:8), who brought back to Jerusalem the temple vessels taken by Nebuchadnezzar (v. 11b).[22] He is designated governor in 5:14, and in v. 16 is reported to have laid the temple's foundation. No other information is given in Ezra about Sheshbazzar, not even his ancestry.

Ch. 2 seems intended as a continuation of ch. 1, for it sets forth the names of the returning exiles mentioned in the first chapter. However, Zerubbabel heads the list and Sheshbazzar does not appear at all! In the rest of the narrative Zerubbabel, together with Jeshua the priest, first sets up an altar and a cultus (ch. 3), then takes the lead in rebuilding the temple, both laying the foundation (v. 10; cf. v. 6, which explicitly states that it was not yet laid) and rebuilding the temple itself (5:1f.). Zerubbabel is identified as the son of Shealtiel (3:2, 8; 5:2; cf. Hag. 1:1, 12), who, according to the genealogy in 1 Chr. 3:17,[23] was the eldest son of Jehoiachin (the last king of Judah, exiled in 597). He is designated governor of Judah throughout the book of Haggai. Whether Zerubbabel returned with the first group of exiles in 538 or sometime later is not certain, although the juxtaposition of chs. 1–2 implies the former. At any rate, he led the rebuilding of the temple beginning in 520, instigated by the preaching of Haggai and Zechariah.

A plausible case can be made that Sheshbazzar was Zerubbabel's uncle if he can be identified with the Shenazzer given as the fourth son of Jehoiachin in the Davidic genealogy (1 Chr. 3:18).[24] Resolution of the conflict over when and by whom the foundation of the temple was laid is not readily apparent. At best it may be surmised that the start made by Sheshbazzar was so inconsequential that, when later taken up by Zerubbabel, the work could be attributed

---

22. Hiphil *he'elâ* must be understood as "took up" rather than "sent up," since the Aramaic source in 5:15f. unequivocally states that Sheshbazzar returned to Jerusalem. Further, this would then be the only clear instance in the Old Testament where the causative stem of *'ālâ* has the factitive rather than causative force.

23. In v. 19, however, the father of Zerubbabel is given as Pedaiah, a younger son of Shealtiel.

24. Albright very plausibly argues that both names are corruptions of the Hebrew rendering of the Babylonian name *Sin-ab-uṣur*, a common name of the period. This is strongly supported by the Greek version of the name in 1 Esdras, *Sanabassaros*. See *JBL* 40 (1921): 109f.

to both, or that Zerubbabel returned early enough to play a major role in laying the foundation under the authority of Sheshbazzar.[25] A considerable number of scholars long have held that, in spite of the evidence in Ezra for an independent province,[26] Judah was under the jurisdiction of Samaria until the time of Nehemiah.[27] Recently discovered evidence has given far greater credence to the obvious and natural implications of the biblical statements that Judah was an independent province with its own governor from the time of Sheshbazzar to Nehemiah. This evidence includes a series of more than seventy bullae[28] and two seals of unknown origin,[29] obviously part of an archive preserving official documents,[30] and a number of stamped jar handles from excavations at Ramat Raḥel with the inscription "Judah" and the names of governors and their officers.[31] These inscriptions have been dated to the very late sixth century and preserve the names of governors of Judah after Zerubbabel, with a high probability that some represent members of his immediate family.[32]

Date and Chronological Order of Ezra and Nehemiah. The clear and unmistakable implication of the biblical presentation of events is that Ezra preceded

---

25. Both harmonizations must contend, however, with the explicit statement of Ezra 3:6 that, when Zerubbabel built an altar and instituted sacrificial worship (why was this not done by Sheshbazzar if he returned earlier?), the foundations of the temple were not yet laid.

26. Note the title of "governor" given to Sheshbazzar and Zerubbabel, the reference to "the province of Judah" (5:8), "governor of the Jews" (6:7), and Nehemiah's statement about "the former governors who were before me" (Neh. 5:15).

27. E.g., Myers, *Ezra-Nehemiah*, p. 133. Bright observes: ". . . it is not clear what Sheshbazzar's official position was: whether governor of a reconstituted and separate province of Judah, or deputy governor of the district of Judah under the governor of Samaria, or merely a royal commissioner in charge of a specific project"; *History*, p. 363. For a clear statement supporting the independence of Judah, see G. Widengren, "The Persian Period," pp. 510f. in J.H. Hayes and J.M. Miller, eds., *Israelite and Judaean History*.

28. Small lumps of clay used to seal letters and other documents. The clay was pressed on the knotted cord or string with which the papyrus or leather roll was tied. Frequently in wet areas the papyrus or leather has completely disintegrated, leaving only the bulla. Very often the bullae have been stamped with an embossed oval seal, leaving an inscription in the wet clay. These usually contain the name of the owner, or of the official if not the document of a private individual.

29. The only information about their provenience is that they were found "in the Jerusalem region."

30. See Avigad, *Bullae and Seals from a Post-Exilic Judean Archive*. Qedem 4 (Jerusalem: 1976), pp. 30ff.

31. See Y. Aharoni et al., *Excavations at Ramat Raḥel* I (Rome: 1962); II (1964): "Beth-haccherem," pp. 174-76 in D.W. Thomas, ed., *Archaeology and Old Testament Study* (London: 1967); Avigad, *Bullae and Seals*, pp. 6f., 21f., 35f.

32. So S. Talmon, "Ezra and Nehemiah," *IDBS*, p. 321. Avigad has been able to reconstruct tentatively the names and approximate order of governors succeeding Zerubbabel to fill the seventy-year gap between Zerubbabel and Nehemiah. One very interesting seal is that of a woman, "Shelomit, the 'maidservant' of the governor," obviously one of high standing who filled some important role in the administration of the province of Judah; *Bullae and Seals*, pp. 11-13, 31f. It is tempting to identify her with the Shelomith mentioned as a daughter of Zerubbabel in 1 Chr. 3:19.

Nehemiah, arriving in the seventh year of Artaxerxes (458; Ezra 7:7). Nehemiah arrived thirteen years later in the twentieth year (445; Neh. 2:1). He returned to Persia after a governorship of twelve years, in Artaxerxes' thirty-second year (433; 13:6), and subsequently returned to Judah a short time later for a second term of unknown length. From the evidence of the Elephantine texts,[33] it is reasonably certain that the Artaxerxes mentioned in connection with Nehemiah is Artaxerxes I Longimanus (465-424), hence the dates given above. As yet no extrabiblical correlation exists for any person or event mentioned in the Ezra material.

In spite of these facts, the view of the vast majority of modern scholars is that this biblical order is seriously in error. This is based on the following literary data and alleged problems: (1) the memoirs of Ezra and Nehemiah are cut in half and interleaved with one another; (2) this arrangement posits an interval of thirteen years between Ezra's arrival (seventh year of Artaxerxes; Ezra 7:7) and his reading of the law after Nehemiah's arrival (twentieth year; Neh. 2:1), even though this was the major task commissioned by the king; (3) Ezra's memoirs do not mention Nehemiah at all in the first-person sections,[34] and Nehemiah's memoirs mention Ezra only at Neh. 12:36, where he leads a procession at the dedication of the wall;[35] (4) the biblical order allegedly implies that Ezra's mission failed, since Nehemiah's reforms, carried out in his second governorship (ch. 13), cover the same ground as those abuses Ezra was commissioned to correct; (5) both Josephus and 1 Esdras know a different order of events (although Josephus may have been using 1 Esdras). Recent studies on 1 Esdras have demonstrated increasingly its value as an independent recension of the Ezra material, originally composed in Hebrew.[36] Here the account follows

---

33. See *ANET*, pp. 491f. These business documents and letters were found on the island of Elephantine, north of the first cataract of the Nile and opposite Aswan. They belonged to a Jewish military colony established at least as early as the fall of Jerusalem in 586. The texts throw brilliant light on the affairs of the Jewish colony in Upper Egypt, especially for the period 425-400. In 410 these Jews wrote a letter to Johanan, high priest at Jerusalem (Neh. 12:22), regarding the rebuilding of their temple. In 407 they sent a long appeal in the same regard to Bagoas, governor of Judah, in which they mentioned a similar letter to "Delaiah and Shelemiah, the sons of Sanballat the governor of Samaria." Assuming this is the same Sanballat who was the inveterate enemy of Nehemiah (2:19; 4:1 [MT 3:33]), the Artaxerxes referred to in 2:1 must be Artaxerxes I.

34. In the third-person sections Nehemiah is mentioned only at Neh. 8:9 (at the reading of the law), omitted by 1 Esdras (see below), and 10:1, as a signatory of the covenant. These are considered secondary interpretations by those who hold to another order than that implied by the biblical account.

35. Since Ezra is mentioned at the end of the long list of the members of this procession, this also is often considered a later insertion.

36. A generation ago H.H. Howorth, Torrey, and esp. S. Mowinckel posited that 1 Esdras represents the original Alexandrian translation of the second century B.C., while the present text of the LXX Esdras A stems from a Palestinian translation by one of the precursors of Theodotion. With the discovery of the Qumran scrolls, the independence, textual reliability, and Alexandrian origin of 1 Esdras have been established. See Klein, "Old Readings in I Esdras: The List of Returnees from Babylon (Ezra 2/Nehemiah 7)," *HTR* 62 (1969): 99-107. For a brief but comprehensive statement, see Cross, *JBL* 94 (1975): 7f.

Ezra 1–6,[37] gives the first half of Ezra's memoirs (Ezra 7:1–10:44), but then passes directly to Neh. 7:73, the continuation of the Ezra account. The text then proceeds to 8:12, where, unfortunately, it breaks off. At Neh. 8:9, where the biblical text reads "And Nehemiah, who was the governor, and Ezra the priest . . . said . . ." (thus placing Nehemiah on the scene when Ezra read the law), 1 Esdras simply reads "And the governor and Ezra the priest . . . said. . . ." Josephus follows this same order, telling the whole story of Ezra before turning to the story of Nehemiah (*Ant.* xi.5.4-6).

These facts and problems, along with others of less importance, have occasioned a voluminous scholarly debate over the order of Ezra and Nehemiah, and a number of other options have been argued. Basically these can be reduced to two (with infinite variety in detail), each of which places Ezra after Nehemiah:[38] (1) the Artaxerxes mentioned in Ezra 7:7 is Artaxerxes II Mnemon (404-358), so that Ezra returned in 398, long after Nehemiah's work was completed;[39] (2) desiring to give credence to the biblical evidence that Ezra and Nehemiah were contemporaries but to avoid the problems alleged in the biblical order, an error is posited in the text at Ezra 7:7 and the text is emended to read the *thirty*-seventh year of Artaxerxes. Thus Ezra returned in 428 during Nehemiah's second governorship.[40]

None of the facts presented nor the problems alleged present either compelling reasons for doubting the contemporaneity of Ezra and Nehemiah or valid objections to the order clearly presupposed by the biblical text. The view that would place Ezra in Jerusalem in 428 is based upon an emendation which is totally without textual evidence. Without the supposed need to place Ezra after Nehemiah no such an emendation ever would have been suggested. The failure of either of the memoirs to mention the other figure[41] proves nothing regarding contemporaneity. Neither Haggai nor Zechariah mentions the other, although both preached in Jerusalem at the same time regarding the building of the temple. Still, this is no argument for chronologically separating them.[42] That Nehemiah's reforms had to cover the same areas as Ezra's can just as plausibly be attributed to the seriousness and intractability of the problems addressed, particularly mixed marriages, and the stubbornness of Israel's will—fully attested by her earlier history—rather than to the failure of Ezra's efforts. No tangible evidence necessitates dating Ezra after Nehemiah.

---

37. Except for a major change of order (Ezra 4:7-24 is placed between 1:11 and 2:1) and one long addition not in the biblical text.

38. A few scholars (e.g., Torrey, *Ezra Studies*) have questioned whether Ezra even existed at all, making him an invention of the Chronicler! With very few exceptions, this radical view has been abandoned.

39. Systematically presented first by A. van Hoonacker ("Néhémie et Esras, nouvelle hypothèse sur la chronologie de l'époque de la restauration," *Muséon* 9 [1890]: 151-184; 317-351; 389-401) and held since by many scholars, if not a majority. Cogently presented, with exhaustive bibliography, in Rowley, *The Servant of the Lord*, pp. 137-168.

40. Persuasively argued in Bright, *History*, pp. 391-402.

41. Assuming the few references present can be treated as secondary. However, this is a tendentious argument!

42. Talmon, *IDBS*, p. 320.

Archaeological evidence now exists which, fragmentary and partial though it may be, speaks to the reliability of Ezra-Nehemiah. The Samarian papyri from the Wâdī Dâliyeh[43] have made it possible to establish the sequence of governors of Samaria from Sanballat the Horonite in the time of Nehemiah to Alexander the Great in 332.[44] The papyri also distinguish the biblical account of Nehemiah's expulsion of the son of Jehoiada the high priest (Neh. 13:28) from the very similar story by Josephus set in the period of Sanballat III, a contemporary of Alexander the Great.[45]

A silver bowl found in the northeastern delta of Egypt, inscribed "Qaynu son of Gašm king of Qedar," and dated no later than 400,[46] places Geshem the Arab, ally of Sanballat and enemy of Nehemiah (Neh. 2:19; 6:1-6), in the first half of the fifth century.

All of these considerations and new evidence make radical surgery unnecessary to give the biblical narrative historical credibility.[47]

ACHIEVEMENTS AND SIGNIFICANCE

Context—Israel in the Restoration Period. Before estimating the achievements of Ezra and Nehemiah, it is necessary to sketch briefly the situation in Israel's life as the people of God against which the significance of their work must be understood. The fall of Jerusalem and the Exile had brought to an end the hopes placed in the nation-state and the national destiny, hopes shaped by the secure confidence that God had chosen Zion eternally as his earthly seat and promised David unconditionally an eternal dynasty. This theology, isolated from the demand for obedience to the covenant stipulations, had led the nation to the end of its existence.[48] The prophetic interpretation of this awful end as

---

43. Found in a cave in the wadi about nine miles north of Jericho and some 1470 feet above the Jordan, twenty legal and administrative documents were uncovered along with the skeletons of some two hundred people. The documents and the jewelry, seals, and rings found with them indicate that these people were influential and wealthy. References to Antiochus II (404-359) and Darius III (335-330) and the coins found date the texts to *ca.* 375-335. The circumstances and date suggest that the find documents the sad conclusion to an event recorded by Josephus. Samaria, at first favorable to Alexander the Great, later burned alive Andromachus, Alexander's prefect over Syria. Alexander returned to Samaria and destroyed the city. The leaders of the revolt apparently fled to the cave where they were discovered and killed. See Cross, "Papyri of the Fourth Century B.C. from Daliyeh," pp. 41-62 in Freedman and J.C. Greenfield, eds., *New Directions in Biblical Archaeology* (Garden City: 1969).

44. See Cross, *JBL* 94 (1975): 4-18 and the genealogical chart on p. 17.

45. See Cross, "Papyri," pp. 59-62.

46. See I. Rabinowitz, "Aramaic Inscriptions of the Fifth Century B.C.E. from a North-Arab Shrine in Egypt," *JNES* 15 (1956): 1-9.

47. See also E.M. Yamauchi, "The Reverse Order of Ezra/Nehemiah Reconsidered," *Themelios* 5 (1980): 7-13.

48. For an excellent summary, see Bright, *History*, pp. 347-351.

God's judgment for the nation's sin and dereliction of covenant obligations, together with the prophets' equally strong faith in and proclamation of God's ultimate redemption, provided a coherent explanation of the tragedy. It portrayed the catastrophe not as the contradiction but as the vindication of Israel's historic faith. Out of this theological understanding and hope, and the beneficent policy of the Persians, the restoration was born, and a new community began to take shape in Palestine after Cyrus' decree in 538. By the time Ezra and Nehemiah had completed their work toward the end of the third quarter of the following century, this community was firmly established both physically and religiously.

But no revival of the old national institutions was possible.[49] Israel was no longer a nation but a minor portion of one vast province of an empire reaching from the borders of India to the Danube in northern Greece and from south-central Russia to Libya. Prior to the fall of Jerusalem, a Judahite's identity came from being part of the nation-state of Judah, with its Davidic institutions and theology, boundaries, court, temple, and capital city. Now all that was gone, irrevocably. What kept Israel from becoming so socially and culturally assimilated to their neighbors as to disappear into the ethnic fabric and background as did all the other small peoples?

Through the work of Ezra and Nehemiah Israel's new identity became centered around the law and temple. At this crucial juncture, through the providence of God's redemptive acts, the identity of the people of God was created by the very religious forms and content that, prior to the Exile, never successfully became the center of their life.[50] This accomplishment was the work of Ezra and Nehemiah.

Achievements and Significance of Ezra. The primary architect of Israel's new identity was Ezra the priest, the "scribe skilled in the law of Moses" (Ezra 7:6). Ezra's royal commission authorized him "to make inquiries about Judah and Jerusalem according to the law of your God" (v. 14). Besides bringing offerings from the court (vv. 15-20), Ezra had authority to appoint magistrates and judges (v. 25) and to invoke punishment on those who failed to comply (v. 26). Many scholars feel that the title "scribe of the law of the God of Heaven" (v. 12) was

---

49. Such a possibility was briefly entertained in the early stages of the restoration. Begun under the leadership of Davidides Sheshbazzar and Zerubbabel, the new community looked for renewal of the old order when, at the accession of Darius I in 520, the Persian empire seemed to be distintegrating. Both Haggai and Zechariah spoke of Zerubbabel in messianic terms. But such hopes soon were seen to be futile. Darius became firmly ensconced upon the throne of an empire whose stability and extent exceeded that of his predecessor.

50. How peripheral the law actually was to Israel's life before the Exile is revealed by the fact that in Josiah's eighteenth year (621) a copy of "the book of the law" was found during renovation of the temple, so long in disuse that its discovery provided the major impetus for Josiah's reform. Such an event would have been utterly impossible in the postexilic period.

the official Persian title for the secretary of the government in charge of Jewish affairs.[51] Thus Ezra arrived in Jerusalem with both the power and zeal to reorganize the Jewish community around the law and to bring its life into conformity with this norm.

Ezra 7:10 records that he "had set his heart to study the law of the Lord, and to do it, and to teach his statutes and ordinances in Israel." This implies that he had spent a long time in preparation for the task, and supports the tradition which makes of him almost a second Moses. Ezra's primary identity in the titles accorded him in the introduction to his memoirs (vv. 1-10) is "scribe," which as the new designation for the spiritual leader of the community signals a new era in its life. This era is determined by the Torah, the law, as its central reality, and the scribe (Heb. *sôpēr*) as primary religious leader became the interpreter and expositor of the law.[52] In preexilic use, scribe was the title of a high-ranking officer of the state, at one time a kind of minister of finance (2 Kgs. 22:3ff.) or secretary of state (Isa. 36:3; cf. 22:15), or a person in charge of legal documents with a special chamber in the royal palace (2 Kgs. 18:18; Jer. 36:12). Scribes were never priests. But in the restoration, beginning with Ezra, all that changed. Ezra was both priest and scribe, but his primary identity and task was the study and exposition of the law. This is seen in the public reading of the law (Neh. 8). Here Ezra led the reading while the Levites associated with him expounded and interpreted, possibly in Aramaic translation (v. 8).[53] As time passed the study of the law became more and more separated from the priesthood, especially as the higher strata of priests became willing tools of the hellenization promoted by the secular rulers and forsook their priestly duties in quest of political power. Since membership in the community was measured by conformity to the law, all were students of the law. A professional class of scribes grew up alongside the priesthood, eventually displacing it as spiritual leaders of the people. This process was completed fully by the time of the New Testament, when the scribes were the most influential leaders in religious matters.

Although the exact contents of the law that Ezra brought back are open to question, most scholars feel that it must have been substantially the Penta-

---

51. H.H. Schaeder, *Esra, der Schreiber*. Beiträge zur historischen Theologie (Tübingen: 1930), pp. 48ff.; cf. G. von Rad, *Old Testament Theology* 1:88f.

52. This choice of terms also might have been influenced by Persian terminology. The imperial Aramaic equivalent *sâpᵉrā'* was a common expression for an official of the Persian empire. The official's particular sphere of responsibility was usually described with a following genitive, as in Ezra's title in the Aramaic edict: "scribe of the law of the God of Heaven" (7:12). However, any such influence quickly became secondary to the development of the term within Israel itself.

53. The meaning here is unclear and disputed. The word involved means lit. "divided, split up," which has been understood to mean "clearly," "in sections," or "in translation."

teuch as known today.[54] It is highly probable that Ezra primarily was responsible for its collection and editing.

Ezra towered above his contemporaries, "realizing as perhaps no one else had since Moses and the prophets, that man cannot live by bread alone, only by and through the words that proceed from the mouth of God."[55]

ROLE AND SIGNIFICANCE OF NEHEMIAH

If Ezra accomplished the spiritual establishment of the new community, Nehemiah succeeded in giving it physical stability. Having learned, while in the high position of cupbearer to the king, that the community in Judah was "in great trouble and shame" (Neh. 1:3), he succeeded in having himself appointed governor in Judah with authority and resources to rebuild the city walls. Nehemiah acted with skill and daring. After surveying the walls at night to avoid detection by those who might oppose the work, he assembled a labor force and, dividing the walls into sections, supervised the building process, which was accomplished in the remarkably short time of fifty-two days. He faced determined opposition: mockery (2:19; 4:1-3 [MT 3:33-35]); armed raids (vv. 7-12 [MT 4:1-5]); a ruse to draw him outside the city, without doubt to murder him (6:1-4); threatened blackmail (vv. 5-9); and finally a prophet hired to foretell his death so he would retreat to the temple in fear of his life. All of these he met with courage, wisdom, and an invincible determination to complete the task.

With the wall completed he then took measures to increase the population of Jerusalem and to correct social, economic, and religious abuses. His prayers and piety reveal a man of strong religious conviction. Nehemiah thus provided the physical structure and social and economic stability within which the religious community, formed by the zeal and erudition of Ezra, could grow. Their combined work was a most judicious uniting of Israel's identity with its religious life and forms in such a way as to preserve the people of God, the oracles of God, and the promises of redemption against that day when God would fulfill all the old covenant yearnings and hopes in the person and work of Jesus Christ.

THEOLOGY OF EZRA-NEHEMIAH

For all the new elements in the institution and identity of the restoration community, no new theology informs and creates them. Although nothing specific is said in Neh. 8–10 about the contents of the book of the law which Ezra read, it was unmistakably the ancient Mosaic law known from time immemorial and preached by the prophets. This is made abundantly clear in the

---

54. See Myers, *Ezra-Nehemiah*, pp. LIX–LXII.
55. *Ibid.*, p. LXXIV.

long prayer attributed to Ezra (Neh. 9:6-37, esp. vv. 12ff.). According to the arrangement of the book's author-compiler, this promulgation of the law was not what Ezra first set out to do upon arrival in Jerusalem. Whether the present arrangement is understood as indicating an actual chronology, so that Ezra waited thirteen years before reading the law, or whether it is viewed as topical and, when chronology matters, the chapters must be rearranged so Ezra's work is accomplished in a shorter space of time,[56] the present structuring does not picture Ezra as introducing a new, more legalistic system. The public reading of the law occurs *after* the repentance and reform regarding mixed marriages, a repentance instigated by invoking the ancient Mosaic law (see Ezra 10:3). The law is not read to reform the people but is read to a reformed people.[57]

This reaffirmation of the law and its centrality, however, did stress an almost xenophobic exclusivism, a separatism that went to the wrenching extent of compelling divorce in a large number of families. This seems to reflect an ungenerous and altogether unloving repudiation of foreigners.[58] But the text must be viewed in its context. The restoration community was a tiny island in a vast ocean of pagan peoples, without clear boundaries. Unchecked assimilation would mean the end of the community, and along with it the precious heritage it preserved for the world. Harsh realities called for stern measures, which rarely enjoy the clear-cut alternatives of moral opposites. The real error lay with those who perpetuated these measures and attitudes long after they were needed, thus producing that prejudice against gentiles which the New Testament exposes and which the early Church had difficulty in overcoming. The same error is perpetuated today by those who disregard the context of Ezra's stern measures and use them to justify a legalistic and exclusivistic lifestyle which all too readily succumbs to the pride of external observance. This was not the purpose of the law in all its detail, but rather

> the recognition that there is no part of life which is outside the concern
> of God, and that the completely fit community is one in which all life
> is brought under control.[59]

This new era in the life of the people of God is understood as a continuation of God's redemptive acts on their behalf. Ezra's long prayer (Neh. 9) at the

---

56. E.g., placing Neh. 8–9 after Ezra 8, etc. See Bright, *History*, p. 396; Talmon, *IDBS*, pp. 325f.

57. See B.S. Childs, *Old Testament as Scripture*, p. 636: "The observation to be made is that the reading of the law in Neh. 8 is a part of the liturgical celebration by the people of God. The attempt to shift the reading of the law to Ezra 8 derives from a typical Protestant misunderstanding of Old Testament law. Far from being a legalistic system which seeks to dictate a religious behaviour by rules, the tradition assigned the law a liturgical function which had been reserved for the restored and forgiven community."

58. Contrast, e.g., the message of Jonah, with its ringing challenge that Israel take up their mission to the world and that God cares not just for foreigners but even Ninevites (Jonah 4:11)!

59. P.R. Ackroyd, *Exile and Restoration*, p. 255.

public reading of the law shows this most clearly. Here Ezra rehearses redemptive history, beginning with Abraham's call (vv. 7f.) and centering in the great redemptive act of Exodus (vv. 9-15), wilderness wanderings (vv. 16-21), and conquest of Canaan (vv. 22-25). The restoration is grouped with these and seen as a new exodus, worthy to be taken as similar testimony to God's saving power and covenant faithfulness. This can be seen especially when one recognizes that in the background of the restoration period lie the words of Isa. 40–66. Again and again this prophet affirms that the "new thing" (42:9; 43:19; 48:3) which Yahweh will do will be a new exodus, with a highway through the desert that blossoms and flows with water (40:3-5; 41:18f.; 49:9-11). It is no coincidence that upon completion of the temple this new beginning is celebrated by observance of Passover (Ezra 6:19-22), and upon conclusion of the reading of the law, the feast of Booths, commemorating the wilderness experience, is celebrated (Neh. 8:14-18). These acts emphasize the similarity and continuity between this new exodus and that of centuries before (see v. 17).

Israel's new situation was a return to a covenant people rather than a nation-state. Although the realities of the political situation did force them to this identity, it was no soul-shattering wrench for Israel to divest themselves of the garment of statehood, for they were the "people of God" before they became a state. As von Rad notes:

> . . . Israel threw off the vestment of her statehood together with her monarchy with surprising ease and without apparent internal crisis. This must be connected with the fact that the state as such was somewhat of a borrowed garment for Israel; for long before she became a state, she had belonged to Jahweh.[60]

Surely this divorce of Israel's life and identity from their political and national forms can be seen as preparation for the New Testament transition to that form of the people of God in which the ethnic, physical, and geographical aspects are left behind fully and finally in the New Israel, the Body of Christ, the Church—multinational, multiracial, and determined by spiritual not physical or geographical criteria.

The importance of the temple in postexilic thought must be stressed. Because of the new unity between Israel's religious forms and cultus and their identity, postexilic thought moved toward a right understanding of the nature of God's presence which the temple symbolized. It was the symbol of that presence which God chooses to give[61] in a way that never could be achieved in the preexilic age with its divided allegiance to political and national concerns. Here again is a development toward the preparation for the New Testament conception of the presence of God in a Person in whom his glory was revealed and who "tabernacled among us, full of grace and truth" (John 1:14).[62]

---

60. *Old Testament Theology*, 1:90.
61. Ackroyd, *Exile and Restoration*, p. 248.
62. *Ibid.*, pp. 250f.

FOR FURTHER READING

Bickermann, E. *From Ezra to the Last of the Maccabees*. New York: 1947. (Foundations of the Jewish community.)

Bossman, D. "Ezra's Marriage Reform: Israel Redefined." *Biblical Theology Bulletin* 9 (1979): 32-38. (Purification of the cultic community.)

Cook, S.A. "The Age of Zerubbabel." Pp. 19-36 in H.H. Rowley, ed., *Studies in Old Testament Prophecy*.

Kidner, D. *Ezra and Nehemiah: An Introduction and Commentary*. Tyndale Old Testament Commentaries. Downers Grove: 1979. (Evangelical and strongly apologetic, yet aware of critical problems and study.)

Klein, R.W. *Israel in Exile: A Theological Interpretation*. Overtures to Biblical Theology 6. Philadelphia: 1979.

Leeseberg, M.W. "Ezra and Nehemiah: A Review of the Return and Reform." *CTM* 33 (1962): 79-90.

Rowley, H.H. "Nehemiah's Mission and Its Background." *BJRL* 37 (1954/55): 528-561.

Wright, J.S. *The Building of the Second Temple*.

————. *The Date of Ezra's Coming to Jerusalem*. London: 1958. (Lecture.)

Yamauchi, E.M. "The Archaeological Background of Nehemiah." *Bibliotheca Sacra* 137 (1980): 291-309.

CHAPTER 51

DANIEL

$\mathbf{T}$HE book of Daniel is an apocalypse.[1] As such, it has one of the greatest messages in the Old Testament: the kingdoms of this world will be replaced by the kingdom of God. Other prophets have given glimpses of this future, but in Daniel the message is sustained, revealed in a number of visions throughout the book. It is pitiful that a work of such grandeur has been trivialized, considered ridiculous or fantastic and not to be taken seriously, or used as the vehicle for all sorts of speculation, systems of the end time, and date setting.

DANIEL AS APOCALYPTIC PROPHECY

Even though Daniel is clearly apocalyptic, most scholars insist on dealing with it as history. Some (e.g., E.J. Young, R.K. Harrison) argue for the historicity of the book, and others (e.g., H.H. Rowley, J.A. Montgomery) either argue against sixth-century historicity or present details of second-century Palestine supposedly recorded in it.[2] But just as with the book of Revelation, perhaps in Daniel exact historical accuracy is not the book's primary intent when it mentions "Nebuchadnezzar,"[3] "Belshazzar," and "Darius the Mede," but rather its intent is the revelation that is being presented symbolically.

Prophecy. Daniel is not included among the Prophets in the Hebrew canon. Some argue that its late date meant that that section of the canon had already been closed. Others hold that the book is not true prophecy but another form

---

1. See pp. 493-95 above.
2. See P.D. Hanson, *IDBS*, p. 27; and pp. 493-95 above.
3. The form Nebuchadnezzar occurs regularly in Daniel, as in all other places in the Bible except Jeremiah (Nebuchadnezzar 10 times, Nebuchadrezzar 27) and Ezekiel. BDB has no more reason to say that the spelling Nebuchadnezzar is used "incorrectly" (p. 613) than for an American to say that "colour" is incorrect. The differences are regional or dialectal.

which does not condemn sinful behavior or commend a high ethical system. Such views suggest a misunderstanding of the book's purpose.

One basic purpose is to reveal events to take place as the covenant God unfolds the future. God gave Daniel and his companions "learning and skill in all letters and wisdom; and Daniel had understanding in all visions and dreams" (Dan. 1:17). When called to interpret Nebuchadnezzar's dream, he states that God "has made known to King Nebuchadnezzar what will be in the latter days" (2:28; cf. vv. 44f.). Nebuchadnezzar's dream of the tree cut down foretells what would happen to him until he recognized that "the Most High rules the kingdom of men" (4:25 [MT 22]). The interpretation of the words Belshazzar saw on the wall concern the end of his kingdom (5:26). Daniel's dream of the four beasts

Statue of he-goat (Ur, ca. 2500 B.C.), which in Daniel's vision of ch. 8 represents "the king of Greece" (v. 21). (British Museum)

is a revelation of the end of human kingdoms and the coming of the kingdom which the saints of the Most High are to inherit (7:17, 27). The vision of the Ram and the He-goat is "for the time of the end" (8:17; cf. v. 19). The vision of the evenings and mornings is to be sealed up, "for it pertains to many days hence" (8:26). Daniel's concern over the seventy years of Jeremiah's prophecy is interpreted as touching not only the restoring and building up of Jerusalem, but also "the coming of an anointed one, a prince," and then one who "makes desolate" (9:25-27). The prophecy of conflict between Persia and Greece is deemphasized, and "the man" tells Daniel that he came "to make you understand what is to befall your people in the latter days" (10:14). The prophecy concerning future kings in Persia, the victory of Greece (a reasonable inference, but not specifically stated), and the breaking of that kingdom into four parts (an inference; cf. 11:3f.) appears to detail the end of the Persian empire, Alexander's victory, the division of his kingdom among his generals ("successors" or Diadochoi), and the rise of the Ptolemies in Egypt and Seleucids in Syria, all leading to "the abomination that makes desolate" (11:31; cf. 9:27; 12:11; see also Matt. 24:15; Mark 13:14). But this is not the main purpose of the revelation. The prophecy proceeds until the time that "Michael" shall arise, "that great prince who has charge of your people," when "your people shall be delivered" (12:1) and the resurrection of the dead will take place (v. 2, clearly indicating a still-distant future). When Daniel wants to know more, he is reminded that "the words are shut up and sealed until the time of the end" (v. 9; cf. v. 4).

Apocalyptic Prophecy. Daniel is a different kind of prophecy, in many respects, from that seen in the Prophets. Nevertheless it is prophecy. As indicated, the purpose of the prophets of Israel was to make known Yahweh's will, which includes the future, at least to the extent that punishment and restoration are involved. The element of foretelling is present in all the prophets, but it is secondary to what God requires of his people. Nevertheless, God's ultimate purpose (teleology) was always a part of true prophecy.

In apocalyptic prophecy, the stress is clearly on future events. It begins with the present situation—Daniel in the Babylonian court, dealing with Babylonian or Persian kings. His visions include Persia, Greece, kings of the north and south, rulers that make trouble for the people of God, an anointed one cut off, and the cessation of sacrifices. The reader, if not encouraged to fit these prophecies into exact historical situations, can—as the people of God repeatedly have been able—fit the message to a current historical need.

Apocalyptic prophecy is given in forms that are timeless. Knowledge of the time of the end is sealed up, but the people of God are called into circumstances where they ask, as did Daniel: "How long shall it be till the end of these wonders?" (12:6); "What shall be the issue of these things?" (v. 8). The message is perseverance and hope. Only when one loses sight of the purpose and attempts to unseal the book, or to fit apocalyptic visions into historical details (or vice versa), does the message become obscure. The book of Daniel was not intended to exhaust itself in the days of Antiochus Epiphanes, or the Roman destruction of Jerusalem, in A.D. 100, 1844, or even 1984. It was intended "for the time of the end," and to proclaim to any who believe that theirs is such a time of dire persecution that "the Most High rules," and that the saints of the Most High will inherit a kingdom which shall never be destroyed.

DANIEL AND THE BOOK

The Person. According to 1:6, Daniel was one of the "youths" taken from Jerusalem to Babylon by Nebuchadnezzar to be trained for service in the king's palace. Nothing is told about his lineage, and the only known details of his later life are those recorded in the book itself.

A Daniel[4] is mentioned in Ezek. 14:14, 20; 28:3 as exemplary in wisdom and righteousness. Because this Daniel is mentioned with Noah and Job, some argue that Ezekiel must be referring to the Daniel of the apocalyptic prophecy. However, a "Dan'el" (written with the consonants *dn'l* as in Ezekiel) is mentioned in Ugaritic writings.[5] It can be argued that, since Daniel was only a boy at the time of Ezekiel, it is unlikely for Ezekiel to have grouped him with Noah and Job. Yet Daniel's extraordinary experiences (as recorded in the book) may well have become known outside Babylon.[6] The question will be left open.

According to dates given in the book, Nebuchadnezzar took the youths to Babylon in 605 (probably on a campaign just before he succeeded to the throne).[7] His dream, which Daniel interpreted, was in 603. Daniel continued in royal service "until the first year of King Cyrus" (538; 1:21), and received a revelation in the third year of Cyrus (10:1; the date in v. 4 is equivalent to 23 April 536).

---

4. The Hebrew consonants of the name in Daniel are *dny'l*; in Ezekiel *dn'l*, hence some would read "Danel."

5. E.g., 1 Aqht 19; see C.H. Gordon, *Ugaritic Textbook* 1:245-250; *ANET*, pp. 149-155, with bibliography; J. Day, "The Daniel of Ugarit and Ezekiel and the Hero of the Book of Daniel," *VT* 30 (1980): 174-184. S.B. Frost's thesis that the biblical story was built on stories of the Ugaritic (Phoenician) Dan'el, is without foundation, as Frost concedes: "The older traditions make no reference to the other outstanding characteristics of the hero of the book Daniel"; *IDB* 1:762. These characteristics are wisdom and righteousness (p. 761), which comes from Dan'el of Ezekiel, and not the Ugaritic Dan'il.

6. Nippur, in the vicinity of Tel Abib, where Ezekiel lived, was only about 80 km. (50 mi.) from Babylon.

7. In May/June 605 Nebuchadnezzar "conquered the whole area of the Hatti-country" (which would include Palestine). Nabopolassar died on 8 Ab of his twenty-first year (15 Aug. 605) and on 1 Elul (7 Sept.) Nebuchadnezzar "sat on the royal throne in Babylon," but did not "take the hands of Bel" until the month of Nisan (2 Apr. 604). The preceding period he called his "accession year," and returned to Hatti-land until Shebat (Feb. 604) and "took the heavy tribute of the Hatti-territory to Babylon." See D.J. Wiseman, *Chronicles of the Chaldean Kings* (626-556 B.C.), p. 69. Dates are calculated from R.A. Parker and W.H. Dubberstein, *Babylonian Chronology, 626 B.C.-A.D. 75*, p. 27. The "third year of the reign of Jehoiakim" (1:1) would end on 6 Oct. 605 (using a Tishri-Tishri year), which would fit Nebuchadnezzar's invasion of summer 605.

If Daniel was in his early teens in 603,[8] he would have been about seventy-five in 536.

Contents. The book divides obviously in two parts: stories (chs. 1–6) and visions (chs. 7–12). However, a second division is possible, based on language, which does not correspond with the first. From 2:4b to 7:28 is in Aramaic,[9] the rest in Hebrew. This must be considered when discussing the date or unity of the book.

The book may be outlined as follows:

Daniel and the kings of Babylon and Persia (chs. 1–6)
    Daniel and companions brought to Babylon (ch. 1)
    King's dream of the image (2:1-16)
        Daniel's interpretation (vv. 17-45)
        Nebuchadnezzar's response (vv. 46-59)
    Golden image (3:1-7)
        Daniel's companions refuse to worship; cast into the furnace (vv. 8-23)
        Delivered from fire (vv. 24-30)
        Nebuchadnezzar responds (4:1-3 [MT 3:31-33])
    Nebuchadnezzar's tree dream (vv. 4-18 [MT 4:1-15])
        Interpretation and fulfillment (vv. 19-33 [MT 16-30])
        Nebuchadnezzar's response (vv. 34-37 [MT 31-34])
    Belshazzar's feast; writing on wall (5:1-12)
        Daniel's interpretation (vv. 13-28)
        Belshazzar's response (vv. 29-31 [MT 1])
    Daniel in lions' den (6:1-18 [MT 2-19])
        Daniel delivered (vv. 19-24 [MT 20-25])
        Darius' response (vv. 25-28 [MT 26-29])
Dreams and visions of Daniel (chs. 7–12)
    Four beasts from the sea (7:1-18)
        Interpretation (vv. 19-28)
    Ram, he-goat, and horn (8:1-14)
        Interpretation (vv. 15-27)
    Daniel and Jeremiah's seventy years (9:1f.)
        Daniel's prayer for his people (vv. 3-19)
        Gabriel's interpretation (vv. 20-27)

---

8. The royal captives are called Heb. *yᵉlāḏîm* "children" (1:4), which can be used for "offspring" of any age. Since these captives were to be trained for court service, they must have been quite young.

9. Arguments concerning the date of the Aramaic in R.D. Wilson, *The Aramaic of Daniel* (New York: 1912), and esp. H.H. Rowley, *The Aramaic of the Old Testament* (1929), are linguistically outdated. See now J.A. Fitzmyer, *The Aramaic Inscriptions of Sefire* (Rome: 1967); *A Wandering Aramean* (Missoula: 1979); "The Aramaic Language and the Study of the New Testament," *JBL* 99 (1980): 5-21; D.W. Gooding, "The Literary Structure of the Book of Daniel and Its Implications," *Tyndale Bulletin* 32 (1981): 43-79; J. Greenfield, "Aramaic," *IDBS*, pp. 39-44; W.S. LaSor, "Aramaic," *ISBE* 1 (1979): 229-233.

Vision by the Tigris (10:1-14)
   Interpretation (vv. 15-21)
King of the south and king of the north (11:1-28)
   Profaning of temple (vv. 29-35)
   King exalts himself (vv. 36-45)
Time of trouble; resurrection (12:1-4)
   Book sealed, time hidden (vv. 5-10)
   "Blessed is he who waits" (vv. 11-13)

Daniel and the Kings. Chs. 1–6 sometimes are called the "historical" chapters. Without denying that they may be historical, one must ask whether they are intended to be such. Was the purpose of the divine Author to give a (partial) history of Babylon from 605 to 538? Or were historical names and places simply the media in which the revelation was given?

A clear pattern is evident in this section. An event occurs—a dream, a fiery furnace, handwriting on the wall—and, if necessary, an interpretation is given. A reaction occurs, in which the king expresses faith in Daniel's God as "God of gods" (2:47), "Most High" (4:34), "the living God, enduring forever" (6:26 [MT 27]), or issues a decree that no one speak against this God (3:29), or that all shall tremble and fear "before the God of Daniel" (6:26).

Certain questions arise with regard to this structure. Why would God give a revelation concerning "what will be in the latter days" (2:28) to these gentile (thus pagan) rulers rather than to the people of his covenant? Is it not more reasonable to assume that such revelations were given to the Jews (Israelites) through this apocalyptic medium? If the effect of the various events was so great on the kings, why does no historical evidence exist? Particularly in the case of "Darius the Mede," whose laws could not be altered, why was not his decree (6:26f. [MT 27f.]) carried out by succeeding kings?

By way of reply it may be said that here lies a watershed in God's revelatory and redemptive process. When the Medo-Persians defeated the Babylonians, the power passed from the Semitic peoples to the Indo-Europeans, and remains so to the present.[10] Christians believe that with the First Advent of Christ, the Crucifixion and Resurrection, and the subsequent destruction of Jerusalem in A.D. 70, the old era ended and the present era began. With the momentous decision of the Jerusalem conference (Acts 15), gentiles were admitted to the Church as people of God, and distinction between Jew and gentile ended (Rom. 9:24-26; cf. Hos. 2:23 [MT 25]; Eph. 2:11-15). The revelation to gentile kings of certain details of "what shall be hereafter" and expressions of condescension before—if not actual faith in—the God of Israel by these kings in Daniel may be a revelatory way of saying that an age is ending and another about to begin, that henceforth even gentiles will serve the God of Daniel.

---

10. See LaSor, *Great Personalities of the Old Testament*, pp. 171f.

This revelation may well have taken place through the events as described in Daniel. Or perhaps the revelation to Daniel, and through Daniel to the people of God, was given only in dreams and visions. In either event, the message is that the God of Daniel, and of Israel, is supreme over all kings and gods. He alone is worthy to be worshiped, for the times are in his hands.

Daniel's Dreams. A distinct change occurs in chs. 7–12. Whereas in chs. 1–6 Daniel's events are told in the third person, here the account is in the first person (with very few exceptions, e.g., 7:1; 10:1). Chs. 1–6 focus on historical kings: Nebuchadnezzar, Belshazzar, and Darius the Mede.[11] Chs. 7–12 concern "four great beasts" emerging from the sea (7:3), one "with the clouds of heaven" (v. 13), another with ten horns on its head and "the other horn" (v. 20), a "ram" charging to the west, north, and south (8:3f.), a he-goat from the west (v. 5) with a great horn that is broken and replaced by four horns, one of which "grows exceedingly great" (vv. 8f.); and two beings, "Gabriel" (v. 16; 9:21) and "Michael" (10:13, 21; 12:1). These chapters are distinguished as "apocalyptic" on account of their unnatural or even grotesque nature. But both parts of Daniel have the same purpose: to reveal things to come in the future. Therefore, on the basis of the root meaning of the word, both are apocalypses. Only the media are different. Indeed, Daniel's visions are mentioned also in chs. 1–6 (1:17; 2:19), as are Nebuchadnezzar's (4:5, 10, 13 [MT 2, 7, 10]); and other prophets of Israel received revelations in "visions."

According to the date formulas, the visions of chs. 7–12 are intermixed chronologically with the events of chs. 1–6. Nebuchadnezzar's first dream is dated in the second year of his reign (603/2; 2:1). Belshazzar's feast and the handwriting on the wall (5:30) must be dated to the day that Babylon fell to the Medo-Persian power, 12 October 539. His first year (7:1) is dated *ca.* 554, and the third year (8:1) *ca.* 552. The first year of Darius the Mede (see 9:1)—however the name is interpreted—is to be placed in the first year of the Persian hegemony (538). If he is taken to be Darius I in 11:1, the first year would be 520. The third year of Cyrus (10:1) would be 536.[12] These dates generally are disregarded in interpreting or commenting on the text.

DATE AND AUTHORSHIP

Probably no date for a biblical book has been so positively asserted and so bitterly denied as that of Daniel. Traditionally the book has been accepted as

---

11. For problems of identification, see D.J.A. Clines, "Belshazzar," *ISBE* 1 (1979): 455f.; "Darius," *ibid.*, pp. 867f.; R.P. Dougherty, *Nabonidus and Belshazzar*; Wiseman, *Notes on Some Problems in the Book of Daniel*, pp. 9-16.

12. The date in v. 4 converts to 23 April 536. In spite of charges that the Scripture writers were ignorant of the fact that Cyrus had reigned already since 559, all extant documents of Cyrus date his reign from the capture of Babylon. See Ch. 36 note 3 above.

written toward the end of the sixth century. But because of the detailed prophecies concerning the Persians and Greeks (ch. 10), the "mighty king" (probably
of Greece; 11:3) and the division of his kingdom into four parts "but not to his
posterity" (taken to be Alexander the Great and his successors; v. 4), the kings
of the south and north (taken to be the Ptolemies and Seleucids; vv. 5f.), and
particularly the details of the profaning of the temple and "the abomination
that makes desolate" (taken to be Antiochus IV Epiphanes' desecration of the
temple in 168; v. 31), a large number of scholars (liberal and conservative[13])
contend that Daniel was written later, *ca*. 164.[14] To some conservative scholars,
such a date would make the prophecies "after the event" and therefore fraud-
ulent; the book would be deceptive, and not divine revelation. The discussion
has been long, and sometimes heated.[15]

Language. The linguistic evidence has not always been given its proper
weight in dating the book. Scholars have long been aware that the language
of Daniel is earlier than the second century.[16] The consensus was that the
Hebrew resembled that of the Chronicler and was earlier than that of the
Mishnah; it is noticeably closer to Chronicles than to Qumran (second-first
centuries). Similarly, the Aramaic (2:4b–7:28) is closer to that of Ezra and the
fifth-century papyri than to that from Qumran. Thus, some scholars (e.g.,
Childs) have tended to date chs. 1–6 earlier, and suggest that a later author
built on this material for chs. 7–12. This overlooks two facts: the Aramaic
section continues through ch. 7, which is of the same age as the Aramaic of
chs. 2–6; and the Hebrew of chs. 7–12 is identical with that of chs. 1–2.

All evidence (except the inference that Antiochus Epiphanes and other
historical data are in the author's view) points to a date earlier than the second
century. The historical data of all chapters, from Babylonian to Ptolemaic and
Seleucid, indicate an earlier date. The linguistic evidence, both Hebrew and
Aramaic, suggests a date possibly in the fourth or even fifth century. The

---

13. F.F. Bruce, *Israel and the Nations*, while not specifically dating Daniel, seems to
indicate that the writing was after the events; see pp. 124, 133, 141 note 1.

14. Frost dates it "between December 17 (?), 167 (1 Macc. 1:54), and the corresponding date in 164 (1 Macc. 4:52)," and narrows this to "*ca*. 166-165 B.C."; *IDB* 1:
767.

15. See R.K. Harrison, *Introduction*, pp. 1105-1134; "Daniel, Book of," *ISBE* 1
(1979): 861-65; Wilson, "Daniel, Book of," *ISBE* (1939) 2:783-87; C. Boutflower, *In
and Around the Book of Daniel* (1923; repr. Grand Rapids: 1963), pp. 1-12; E.J. Young,
The Prophecy of Daniel (Grand Rapids: 1949), pp. 15-26, 223-253; E.B. Pusey, *Daniel the
Prophet* (New York: 1885), pp. 1-57, 232-461; B.S. Childs, *Old Testament as Scripture*,
pp. 611-621 and bibliography, pp. 608-611; O. Eissfeldt, *Old Testament*, pp. 517-529
and bibliography, pp. 512f.; A. Jeffrey, "Introduction and Exegesis of Daniel," *IB* 6:
341-352; G.L. Archer, Jr., *Survey*, pp. 365-388; J.G. Baldwin, *Daniel*. Tyndale Commentaries (Downers Grove: 1978). J.B. Payne calls late date views "a deception and a
fraud"; "Daniel, Book of," *ZPBD*, p. 199.

16. See F. Delitzsch, "Daniel," in J.J. Herzog, ed., *Realenzyklopädie für protestantische
Theologie und Kirche* 3 (Hamburg: 1855): 273; J.A. Montgomery, *The Book of Daniel*.
ICC (Edinburgh: 1927), pp. 13-22.

evidence of the LXX and Qumran[17] indicates that Daniel was in existence in its full form, and had been distributed over a relatively wide area, prior to the time of Antiochus Epiphanes.

Author. Other than the statement that Daniel "wrote down the dream" (7:1), no claim of authorship is made in the book. Chs. 1–6, expressed in the third person, may well have been written by someone else about Daniel. Chs. 7–12, largely in the first person, may have been accounts told by Daniel to another person or persons, or perhaps written down following the dreams and visions (see 7:1) and subsequently passed on. It sometimes is argued that Daniel himself wrote the book, with Matt. 24:15 offered in support,[18] but Jesus says "spoken of by the prophet Daniel," which does not in fact assert that he recorded those words in writing. According to the Talmud, a Jewish tradition placed some sort of editorial responsibility for Daniel on the men of the Great Synagogue,[19] sometime between Ezra (*ca*. 450) and Simeon the Just (270). It is not unreasonable, then, to attribute the dreams and visions to Daniel, who passed them on (in written form or otherwise), and that they finally were put in canonical form in the fourth or third century.

Daniel is called a "prophet" in a Florilegium (collection of scriptural proof-texts) from Qumran (4QFlor), by Jesus (Matt. 24:15), and Josephus (*Ant*. x.11.4 §249). But the book is not in the canon of the Prophets, and therefore it is questioned whether Daniel actually was one. The suggestion has been made that Daniel was, strictly speaking, a "seer" (Heb. *ḥôzēh, rō'ēh*), since he received revelations in dreams and visions, but this distinction will not hold up, for the canonical prophets also received revelations in this way (see Isa. 1:1). Young, among others, proposes that Daniel had the prophetic gift but did not occupy that office.[20] But this appears to be a distinction without biblical warrant. More reasonable is the view that Daniel was sent not to Israel, but to the Babylonian court.[21] But even this suggestion falls short, for Daniel indeed was sent to Israel. His message was intended primarily for the people of God, who canonized it. The book has served both synagogue and church, but no permanent effect on the gentiles is evident other than through the mediation of God's people. On the basis of the book's genre, it was understood as concerning the end time by those who used it in the pre-Christian period (Enoch, the Sibylline Oracles, 1 Maccabees) and by Jesus (see Matt. 13:41f.; 24:10, 21) and John the Revelator (Rev. 12:14; 13:1, 5, 7). It has no immediate reference to Israel or the Jews (except in Daniel's prayer for his people [ch. 9] and in accusations against them [3:8, 12]). It therefore stands in a category different from the canonical

---

17. Fragments of Daniel from Qumran prove that the Aramaic section at that date began and ended where it does in the Hebrew Bible as it now stands.

18. See Young, *Daniel the Prophet*, pp. 19f.

19. B. *Bat*. 15a; see note 10 above.

20. *The Prophecy of Daniel*, p. 20.

21. *Idem*.

prophets, even the apocalyptic portions of such prophets as Isaiah, Ezekiel, and Zechariah.

INTERPRETATION OF THE PROPHECY

Interpretation of the dreams and visions in Daniel is most difficult. This may be partly because many commentators begin with Antiochus Epiphanes and chs. 10–11, and force all other interpretation to culminate at that point.[22] In certain schools of interpretation, much of the problem derives from the attempt to convert the "times," "weeks" (or heptads), and "days" into chronological systems. For those who take the work to be a divine revelation, the difficulty lies partly in its use of forms and figures that are intentionally obscure; the book is shut up and sealed "until the time of the end" (12:4).

The Kingdoms and the Kingdom. In ch. 2 Daniel interprets Nebuchadnezzar's dream image of "what shall be hereafter" (v. 45). The four parts of the image represent four successive kingdoms, beginning with that of Nebuchadnezzar (vv. 38-40). As the fourth deteriorates (vv. 41-43), a "stone cut out by no human hand" (v. 34) smashes the entire image, striking its feet, so that no trace is left (v. 35). But the stone "became a great mountain and filled the earth" (v. 35), interpreted by Daniel to be a kingdom, set up by God, which shatters all others and stands forever (vv. 44f.).

Most view this dream and its interpretation as the basis for the vision of the four beasts in ch. 7. Those who argue for two authors, or at least an earlier and a later part of the book, look upon ch. 7 as picking up the theme of ch. 2. In any event, the two must be considered together. In ch. 7, four great beasts rise from the sea (v. 3). The following verses suggest that these did not arise together, but each was succeeded by another (see vv. 5-7). The fourth beast put forth horns, the fourth of which was speaking "great words" (v. 11). But then the beast was slain, and Daniel saw in a vision "with the clouds of heaven . . . one like a son of man" (v. 13). To him was given "dominion and glory and kingdom" that included "all peoples, nations, and languages" and would never pass away (v. 14). The beasts "are four kings who shall arise out of the earth. But the saints of the Most High shall receive the kingdom," and possess it forever (vv. 17f.).

This is the theme of the book. The goal is not the Hellenistic age, but the kingdom of God. True, when Daniel wanted to know more about the "fourth beast" (8:15)—obviously, the last kingdom before God's kingdom was to be established—the details given seem to fit the period from the end of the Persian empire (cf. v. 20), through the time of Alexander (v. 21) and his four succes-

---

22. See Montgomery: "The historical objective of the bk., whether it is understood as contemporaneous to the writer or as prophetically foreseen, is the Hellenistic age"; *Daniel*, p. 59. He supports this position by chs. 10–12.

sors (v. 22), to a king of great power and destruction (vv. 23-25). He is to be broken "by no human hand" (v. 25).

Prophecies that concern the future often have "prophetic perspective" (or compenetration), so that the near-at-hand and the distant future are merged. In Isa. 9, for example, what starts out as a message of brightness and joy for Zebulun and Naphtali (representative portions of the land taken captive by Assyria), moves on to "the latter time" (9:1 [MT 8:23]), and climaxes with the "Prince of Peace" on the throne of David, of whose government "there will be no end" (vv. 6f. [MT 5f.]). Daniel's vision must be understood in just such a way. Certainly no one will claim that the kingdom "not made with hands" historically replaced that of Antiochus Epiphanes.[23] No one familiar with the prophets can possibly evaluate either the present Christian age or the preceding Maccabean period as fulfilling Daniel's description of the everlasting kingdom, much less that described, for example, by Isaiah, Jeremiah, or Ezekiel.

The interpretation systems commonly presented may be diagrammed as follows:[24]

Head of gold (First beast) >	Babylonian empire	Babylonian empire	Babylonian empire
Breast of silver (Second beast) >	Medo-Persian empire	Median kingdom	Medo-Persian empire
Belly of brass (Third beast) >	Greek empire	Persian empire	Alexander the Great
Legs of iron (Fourth beast) >	Roman empire	Greek empire	Alexander's successors

Unless content to suspend judgment, one is forced into a choice of difficulties. The Persian empire cannot be split into two successive kingdoms, as required by those who make the second and third kingdoms the Medes and Persians. But it is equally difficult to draw the Roman empire from Daniel's dreams and visions. Whatever system of interpretation is chosen, exegesis of the text shows that the spotlight is on the kingdom of God which replaces all earthly kingdoms.

Fourth Beast. In response to Daniel's desire to know more about the fourth beast (7:19), he is given a further vision. A beast with ten horns, and another

---

23. Some who follow the Antiochus Epiphanes interpretation simply say that the author of this part of the book was mistaken; see Frost, *IDB* 1:768.

24. See Boutflower, *In and Around the Book of Daniel*, pp. 13-23; Young, *The Prophecy of Daniel*, pp. 274-294; Montgomery, *Daniel*, pp. 59-62; Jeffery, *IB* 6:382-390, 452-467; G.F. Hasel, "The Four World Empires of Daniel 2 against its Near Eastern Environment," *JSOT* 12 (1979): 17-30.

coming up, makes war with the saints and prevails over them "until the Ancient of Days came" (vv. 20-22). "One of those who stood there" (v. 16; cf. v. 23) explains the vision: the fourth kingdom will be different from the others (v. 23), and will be exceedingly cruel and destructive. One of its kings is blasphemous, and persecutes "the saints of the Most High" (v. 27). This continues "for a time, two times, and half a time" (v. 25). Then his dominion is taken and given to the saints of the Most High (vv. 26f.).

One easily can be lost in details and miss the clear message. Is this time span three and one-half years, and is it half of the Great Tribulation? Is this blasphemous king the Antichrist, or "666"? When the final fulfillment takes place, the meaning will be clear. Meanwhile, the message is one of great hope to all "the saints of the Most High." Whenever any earthly ruler persecutes the people of God, his times are limited and his destruction assured. Saints of every age have found comfort in their own interpretations, and still the vision retains its age-long message of hope and assurance.

Ram, He-goat, and Horn. The horn is symbolic of power (1 Kgs. 22:11; Zech. 1:18ff. [MT 2:1ff.]), particularly that of the reigning house (Ps. 132:17; Ezek. 29:21). In chs. 7–8 and Rev. 13 and 17, the horns symbolize rulers of empires. The ram with two horns standing on the banks of the river Ulai in Elam seemingly represents the Medo-Persian empire. A he-goat comes from the west with amazing speed (8:5), destroying the ram. It has a great horn, which is broken and replaced by four conspicuous horns (v. 8). This is usually interpreted as Alexander the Great, who died shortly after conquering Persia and the east, and was succeeded by four generals. Out of one horn comes "a little horn" which becomes very great (v. 11), easily identified with Antiochus Epiphanes who profaned the temple on 25 Chislev (27 Dec.) 168 (see 1 Macc. 1:54; 2 Macc. 6:2; Josephus *Ant.* xii.5.4 §§248-256). Daniel asks how long this will continue, and is told: "For two thousand and three hundred evenings and mornings; then the sanctuary shall be restored to its rightful state" (v. 14).[25]

The interpretation given by "Gabriel" is a vision "for the time of the end" (v. 17), and supports the identifications of the kings of Media and Persia (v. 20), the king of Greece (v. 21), Alexander the Great, and his four successors (v. 22). At the end "a king of bold countenance" (v. 23) shall arise and cause fearful destruction (v. 24), "but, by no human hand, he shall be broken" (v. 25). Here again one-on-one identification is hazardous. If Antiochus Epiphanes is intended, was he broken "by no human hand"? It is better to leave the message in its timeless form. The ultimate fulfillment "pertains to many days hence" (v. 26), but its application belongs to the people of God in any age. Their enemies are God's enemies, and God's kingdom is eternal.

---

25. Often taken to mean 2,300 evening and morning sacrifices, hence 1,150 days. But Jeffrey observes that "from data in 1 Maccabees, the actual number of days between the defilement of the altar in 168 B.C. and its rededication in 165 was, on any calculation, somewhat less than 1,150 days" (*IB* 6:476)—actually 1,094 days.

Daniel's Prayer for His People. Daniel believed, from his knowledge of Jeremiah's prophecy, that a period of seventy years was decreed for the desolation of Jerusalem (9:2; cf. Jer. 25:11f.). He was aware that the time was nearly up, and prayed to God, confessing his sin and those of his people, asking God to act without further delay (v. 19). Once again Gabriel (in Luke 1:26, an angel; in intertestamental literature, an archangel) speaks to Daniel of "the coming of an anointed one" (v. 25). The exegesis of vv. 25-27 is extensive. Calculations of the "seven weeks," "sixty-two weeks," and the remaining "one week," which is divided in half (v. 27), have concerned many scholars. Lack of a common result raises doubts about the methods used.

"An anointed one" (vv. 25f.) is expressed by Heb. *māšîah*. The KJV, NASB, and others translate "Messiah" here, although the definite article is lacking. Indeed, the term seems to refer to a messianic prince, to rule over the coming kingdom. Later "Messiah" became a technical term (see above, p. 396). Efforts to convert the seven weeks to forty-nine years, and to demonstrate that this prophecy was fulfilled when the temple was rebuilt, or to calculate from the sixty-two weeks the date of the coming of the Messiah or the Crucifixion (cf. v. 26) have yielded much confusion. Moreover, the order in the passage is: (1) the going forth of the word to restore Jerusalem; (2) the coming of an anointed one, a prince; (3) Jerusalem rebuilt "with squares and moat, but in a troubled time"; (4) the anointed one cut off, city and sanctuary destroyed; and (5) the coming prince destroys the city, makes a covenant for "one week," and for "half of the week" halts sacrifice and offering (v. 27). Frankly, very grave difficulties arise in attempting to fit this order into most reconstructions.[26]

Actually, Gabriel has taken Jeremiah's prophecy of seventy years, then understood to apply to the period of the Exile, and turned it into an end-time prophecy of "seventy weeks of years" (v. 24). This complex picture includes restoration of the city, a troubled time, the cutting off of an anointed prince (who seems to have ruled during the sixty-two "weeks"), a coming prince, and people bent on destroying the city and sanctuary, "until the decreed end is poured out on the desolator" (v. 27). Those who, in any age, long for the restoration of Jerusalem find here a message of hope. Those who seek the messianic prince are assured that he will come. Those living in days of trouble, wars, and desolations know that this is only for "one week" and that in the end the "one who makes desolate" meets his ordained end. Truly, Gabriel's reply far exceeds Daniel's original request.

Desolating Abomination. In a precisely dated vision (23 Apr. 536; 10:4), Daniel is told what is to befall his people in the latter days (v. 14). The very fact that Michael, one of the chief princes (v. 13), also described as "your prince" (v. 21), and the speaker ("a man clothed in linen," v. 5; probably the

---

26. For careful exegesis, see Montgomery, *Daniel*, pp. 377-401; Young, *The Prophecy of Daniel*, pp. 191-221.

Gabriel mentioned in 9:21) are involved should indicate that the circumstances transcend the historical. The ruler of Persia had withstood this speaker "twenty-one days," but Michael came to aid the offensive (v. 13) and was left to do battle while the speaker left to tell Daniel of future events (v. 14). However, he would return "to fight against the prince of Persia" (v. 20).[27]

The message appears to continue in ch. 11.[28] "Three more kings" are to arise in Persia, then a fourth who moves against Greece (v. 2). Then "a mighty king shall arise"—not identified with Greece in the biblical text, although usually so interpreted—who rules "with great dominion" (v. 3). His kingdom is divided "toward the four winds of heaven, but not to his posterity" (v. 4).

Interpreters take this mighty king to be Alexander the Great, who made no provision for a succession and so four generals divided his kingdom. Most commentators take the details of this vision quite specifically: the "king of the south" is the Lagide or Ptolemaic line, which ruled from Egypt ca. 323-30, and the "king of the north" is the Seleucid line, which ruled from Syria for approximately the same period. However, these details are not historically precise. The book of Daniel is neither "history written in advance" nor "prophecy after the event." It is apocalyptic, which is always transhistorical; it seems to spring from history, but its purpose goes beyond history and provides a timeless message. For this reason, Daniel's prophecies have served God's people not only under the Ptolemies and Seleucids, but in the first century B.C., the first century A.D., and succeeding periods.[29]

The king of the north, turning back from a thwarted attempt on the south, focuses on "those who forsake the holy covenant" (v. 30), and his forces profane the temple, taking away the continual burnt offering and setting up "the abomination that makes desolate" (vv. 29-31; cf. 12:11; Matt. 24:15; Mark 13:14). With few exceptions, modern commentators have made this portion of Daniel nothing but a review of history.[30] Jesus, on the other hand, along with many Jews of his time, saw here a message that could apply to an indefinite future, whether the destruction of Jerusalem in A.D. 70 or the coming of the Son of Man (Matt. 24:15; cf. v. 3; Mark 13:2, 4). A great and powerful ruler would come to "seduce with flattery" those who claim to belong to the household of faith yet "violate the covenant." This happened when the Hellenizers sought to turn Jews into gentiles in the pre-Maccabean period. It has happened many

---

27. Apparently the beginning of doctrines and theories about angelic Princes of the nations; see Montgomery, *Daniel*, pp. 419f.

28. The date formula in v. 1 seems to be a gloss, added to clarify the chronological sequence, but it may be a "flashback" spoken by the same speaker in ch. 10.

29. This is supported by the use of Daniel in Enoch, the Qumran literature, the New Testament, and other writings.

30. See Montgomery, *Daniel*, pp. 420-468: "There appears to be an utter lack of allusion to this chap. in early Jewish and Christian literature. And subsequently the Jewish comm. with their characteristic lack of historical sense make the chap. a phantasmagoria of fanciful allusions . . ."; p. 468. Perhaps early Jewish and Christian commentators better understood the nature of apocalyptic.

times since, and will happen to a much greater extent at the end of the age. "But the people who know their God shall stand firm and take action" (Dan. 11:32).

At that time, Michael will take charge (12:1). "A time of trouble" will ensue (see Matt. 24:21; Mark 13:19; Rev. 12:7; 16:18), but "your people shall be delivered." Dan. 12:2 is a clear reference to the resurrection at the end of the age. Among these secrets that are "sealed until the time of the end" (v. 9) are the "times" (v. 7) and the "days" (vv. 11f.).

One Like a Son of Man. In 7:13, when the beasts are slain, "one like a son of man"—note the contrast with "beasts"—comes "with the clouds of heaven." As the title of address used by Ezekiel (see above, p. 467), the designation "son of man" means "human being, man." Jesus often referred to himself by this title. Some scholars claim that he thus was claiming to be the Messiah, but this seems quite unlikely.[31] Rather, Jesus was using a term that had a deeper meaning, which, when the time came, could be expanded to include fulfillment of Daniel's prophecy (Matt. 24:30; 26:64 and par.; cf. Rev. 1:7, 13; 14:14).[32]

To understand this development, it is necessary to look at the history of the term. Book II of Enoch, the "parables" or "similitudes," contains a rather full doctrine of the "son of man." He is depicted not as a human being, but as a preexistent heavenly being who rules over a universal kingdom. In early Judaism two doctrines developed separately: the Messiah, a human king from the line of David; and a divine or semidivine being, a "son of man," who came from heaven to bring to a close this age and to inaugurate the age to come. The Qumran community held to a purely Son-of-David messiah. No part of Enoch Book II has been found there, although many fragments of other parts of the book were recovered. Some would date Book II as later, possibly post-Christian. At any rate, whereas in Judaism the ideas were kept distinct, the New Testament blends them into one doctrine (see Matt 26:63f.), in explanation of the uniqueness of Jesus.

The Christian Church has always been intrigued by the book of Daniel. At times its scholars have developed fanciful interpretations, some of which have proven false; but most have been a source of hope in times of great stress. Attempts either to establish historical details or to determine the times and seasons may miss the book's timeless message. Yet if that message is sought first, the details need not be lost, for they will become clearer as the time of the end approaches. A healthy, biblical apocalyptic that seeks first to hear what the

---

31. Rowley points out that it would have been meaningless for Jesus to charge his disciples to tell no one that he was the Christ if "son of man" was an equivalent term; *The Relevance of Apocalyptic*, pp. 30f. See M. Casey, "The Corporate Interpretation of 'One like a Son of Man' (Dan. VII 13) at the Time of Jesus," *Novum Testamentum* 18 (1976): 167-180.

32. See LaSor, *Great Personalities of the New Testament* (Westwood, N.J.: 1961), p. 42.

Spirit is saying, is greatly to be desired—particularly in times of trouble. "He who has an ear to hear, let him hear what the Spirit is saying to the churches" (Rev. 3:22).

FOR FURTHER READING

Baldwin, J.G. *Daniel.* Downers Grove: 1978.

Borsch, F.H. *The Son of Man in Myth and History.* Philadelphia: 1967.

Brekelmans, C.H.W. "The Saints of the Most High and Their Kingdom." OTS 14 (1965): 309-329.

Clifford, R.J. "History and Myth in Daniel 10–12." BASOR 220 (1975): 23-26. (Ultimate enemy is Death.)

Collins, J.J. *The Apocalyptic Vision of the Book of Daniel.* HSM 16. Missoula: 1977. (Book is collection of traditional writings; difficulties of apocalyptic imagery.)

Davies, P.R. "Eschatology in the Book of Daniel." JSOT 17 (1980): 33-53. (Opposes apocalyptic interpretation.)

Hartman, L.F., and Di Lella, A.A. *The Book of Daniel.* Anchor Bible 23. Garden City: 1978. (Edited in Maccabean period.)

Jones, B.W. "The Prayer of Daniel IX." VT 18 (1968): 488-493. (Apocalyptic used to answer problem of suffering.)

Lacocque, A. *The Book of Daniel.* Trans. D. Pellauer. Atlanta: 1979. (Chs. 1–6 are midrashim; 8–12, apocalypses; 7, both.)

Millard, A.R. "Daniel 1–6 and History." *Evangelical Quarterly* 49 (1977): 67-73. ("Probably accurate as to its details.")

Nicholson, E.W. "Apocalyptic." Pp. 189-213 in G.W. Anderson, ed., *Tradition and Interpretation.* (Survey of modern opinion on nature and purpose of apocalyptic literature.)

Rowley, H.H. *Darius the Mede and the Four World Empires in the Book of Daniel.* 2nd ed. Cardiff: 1959.

Saydon, P.-P. "Daniel." CCHS §§ 494a–513r.

Wallace, R.S. *The Lord Is King: The Message of Daniel.* Downers Grove: 1979. (Contemporary applications.)

Whitcomb, J.C. *Darius the Mede: A Study in Historical Identification.* Grand Rapids: 1959.

Wilson, R.D. *Studies in the Book of Daniel: A Classic Defense of the Historicity and Integrity of Daniel's Prophecies.* 1917; repr. Grand Rapids: 1979.

Wood, L. *Commentary of Daniel.* Grand Rapids: 1973. (Dispensationalist.)

GENERAL BIBLIOGRAPHY

Aharoni, Y. *The Land of the Bible*. 2nd. ed. Philadelphia: 1979.

————and Avi-Yonah, M. *The Macmillan Bible Atlas*. Rev. ed. New York: 1977.

Albright, W.F. *The Archaeology of Palestine*. Rev. ed. Baltimore: 1960.

————. *From the Stone Age of Christianity*. 2nd ed. Garden City: 1957.

————. *Yahweh and the Gods of Canaan*. 1968; repr. Winona Lake: 1978.

Alt, A. *Essays on Old Testament History and Religion*. Trans. R.A. Wilson. Oxford: 1966; Garden City: 1968.

Anderson, G.W. *A Critical Introduction to the Old Testament*. 2nd ed. Naperville: 1960.

————, ed. *Tradition and Interpretation*. Oxford: 1979.

Archer, G.L., Jr. *A Survey of Old Testament Introduction*. Chicago: 1964.

Baly, D. *The Geography of the Bible*. Rev. ed. New York: 1974.

Bentzen, A. *Introduction to the Old Testament*. 2 vols. Copenhagen: 1948.

Bright, J. *Early Israel in Recent History Writing*. London: 1956.

Bright, J. *A History of Israel*. 3rd ed. Philadelphia: 1981.

Bruce, F.F. *Israel and the Nations*. Grand Rapids: 1969.

Childs, B.S. *Introduction to the Old Testament as Scripture*. Philadelphia: 1979.

Clements, R.E. *Prophecy and Covenant*. London: 1965.

————. *Old Testament Theology: A Fresh Approach*. London: 1978.

Cross, F.M., Jr. *Canaanite Myth and Hebrew Epic*. Cambridge, Mass.: 1973.

————, Lemke, W.E., and Miller, P.D., Jr., eds. *Magnalia Dei: The Mighty Acts of God*. Festschrift G.E. Wright. Garden City: 1976.

Driver, S.R. *Introduction to the Literature of the Old Testament*. 9th ed.; repr. Magnolia, Mass.: 1972.

Dyrness, W. *Themes of the Old Testament*. Downers Grove: 1979.

Eichrodt, W. *Theology of the Old Testament*. Trans. J.A. Baker. 2 vols. OTL. Philadelphia: 1961.

Eissfeldt, O. *The Old Testament: An Introduction*. Trans. P.R. Ackroyd. New York: 1965.

Frankfort, H., et al. *Before Philosophy*. Baltimore: 1949.

Goldingay, J. *Approaches to Old Testament Interpretation*. Downers Grove: 1981.

Gordon, C.H. *The World of the Old Testament*. Garden City: 1958.

Gottwald, N.K. *A Light to the Nations*. New York: 1959.

Grollenberg, L.H. *Shorter Atlas of the Bible*. Trans. M.F. Hedlund. New York: 1959.

Guthrie, D., and Motyer, J.A., eds. *New Bible Commentary Revised*. Grand Rapids: 1970.

Hahn, H.F. *The Old Testament in Modern Research*. 1954; repr. Philadelphia: 1966.

Harrison, R.K. *Introduction to the Old Testament*. Grand Rapids: 1969.

Hayes, J.H., ed. *Old Testament Form Criticism*. San Antonio: 1974.

————and Miller, J.M., eds. *Israelite and Judaean History*. OTL. Philadelphia: 1977.

Kaiser, O. *Introduction to the Old Testament*. Trans. J. Sturdy, Minneapolis: 1975.

Kaiser, W.C., Jr. *Toward an Old Testament Theology*. Grand Rapids: 1978.

Keil, C.F., and Delitzsch, F. *Commentary on the Old Testament*. Repr. 10 vols.; Grand Rapids: 1973.

Kuhl, C. *The Old Testament, Its Origins and Composition*. Trans. C.T.M. Herriott. Richmond: 1961.

LaSor, W.S. *Great Personalities of the Old Testament*. Westwood, N.J.: 1959.

McKenzie, J.L. *Dictionary of the Bible*. Milwaukee: 1965.

Martens, E.A. *God's Design: A Focus on Old Testament Theology*. Grand Rapids: 1981.

Noth, M. *The History of Israel*. Trans. P.R. Ackroyd. 2nd ed. New York: 1960.

Orchard, B., ed. *A Catholic Commentary on Holy Scripture*. New York: 1953.

Parker, R.A., and Dubberstein, W.H. *Babylonian Chronology, 626 B.C.–A.D. 75.* Providence, R.I.: 1971.

Pfeiffer, R.H. *Introduction to the Old Testament.* Rev. ed. New York: 1948.

Pritchard, J.B., ed. *Ancient Near Eastern Texts Relating to the Old Testament.* 3rd ed. Princeton: 1969.

von Rad, G. *Old Testament Theology.* Trans D.M.G. Stalker. 2 vols. New York: 1962-65.

————. *The Problem of the Hexateuch and Other Essays.* Trans. E.W.T. Dicken. Edinburgh: 1966.

Robert, A., and Feuillet, A. *Introduction to the Old Testament.* New York: 1968.

Rowley, H.H. *The Faith of Israel.* London: 1956.

————. *From Joseph to Joshua.* London: 1950.

————. *The Servant of the Lord and Other Essays on the Old Testament.* 2nd ed. Oxford: 1965.

————. *Worship in Ancient Israel.* Philadelphia: 1967.

————, ed. *The Old Testament and Modern Study.* Oxford: 1951.

————, ed. *Studies in Old Testament Prophecy.* Edinburgh: 1950.

Sellin, E., and Fohrer, G. *Introduction to the Old Testament.* Trans. D.E. Green. Nashville: 1968.

Soggin, J.A. *Introduction to the Old Testament.* Trans. J. Bowden. OTL. Philadelphia: 1976.

Thomas, D.W., ed. *Documents from Old Testament Times.* New York: 1961.

de Vaux, R. *Ancient Israel.* Trans. J. McHugh. 2 vols. New York: 1965.

————. *The Early History of Israel.* Trans. D. Smith. 2 vols. Philadelphia: 1978.

Weiser, A. *The Old Testament: Its Formation and Development.* Trans. D.M. Barton. New York: 1961.

Wellhausen, J. *Prolegoma to the History of Ancient Israel.* Trans. J.S. Smith and C.A. Menzies. 1885; repr. Magnolia, Mass.: 1973.

Wright, G.E., ed. *The Bible and the Ancient Near East.* Festschrift W.F. Albright. 1961; repr. Winona Lake: 1979.

Young, E.J. *An Introduction to the Old Testament.* Rev. ed. Grand Rapids: 1958.

Zimmerli, W. *Old Testament Theology in Outline.* Trans. D.E. Green. Atlanta: 1978.

SUBJECT INDEX

AUTHOR INDEX

689

FOREIGN TERMS

Greek and Latin

'aggélou autoú 501
apokálypsis 9
apokalýptō 9
christós 396
dies irae 433
'éxodos 131
hieros gamos 609
pentáteuchos 54
pistis 453
prophētēs 298
theópneustos 12
týpos 161

Hebrew and Aramaic

'āḏām 7, 72
'ªllûp̄îm 169
'āmāl 598
'āmôn 550
'āśâ 71
'ašrê 522, 581
'āzal 157

ba'al 32
bāḥar 182
bārā' 71, 77
ben-'āḏām 467
bᵉnê hayyiśhar 497
bᵉrēšîṯ 68
bōšeṯ 32

dᵉmûṯ 78
dn'l 662
dny'l 662

'eḇeḏ 392
'eḇeḏ yhwh 392
'eḇer hayyarḏēn 47
'ēḏ 73

'elep 169
'ᵉmûnâ 451, 453
'ᵉnôš 467

gā'al 384
gālâ 9
gēr 104, 113
gᵉ'ûlîm 385
gō'ēl 384

ḥag hamaṣṣôṯ 526
ḥag hassukkôṯ 527
Ḥanukkāh 527
ḥaṭōm 375
ḥawwâ 72
ḥāyâ 136
hazkîr 529
ḥeḇel 590
ḥēl 458
ḥeleq 598
ḥerem 207
ḥeseḏ 340. 614
ḥōzeh 667

'îš 72
'iššâ 79
'iyyôḇ 560

kᵉḇar 'ᵉnāš 467
kᵉḇôḏ 'ᵉlōhîm 470
kᵉḇôḏ yhwh 470
kipper 156, 384

lᵉ'annôṯ 529
lēḵ 469
lᵉlammēḏ 529

mal'aḵî 501
māšāl 547
māšîaḥ 396, 497, 671
maśkîl 529

maśśā' 490, 492, 493,
501
maśśā' dᵉḇar
yhwh 493
mazkîr 191
miškān 146
mišpāṭ 390, 391, 392
mizmôr 510, 529

na'ar 489
nāḇî 298
nᵉhar kᵉḇār 461
nepeš ḥayyâ 79
nēṣer 494

'ôlām 597

pāḏâ 384
pesaḥ 526
pûr 625

qāḏôš 151, 381
qḏš 381
qᵉḏēšâ 336
qᵉḏēšîm 152
qᵉḏēšôṯ 152
qînâ 516, 617, 619
qôḏeš 151
qôheleṯ 586

rîḇ 573
rō'ēh 667
rō'š ḥōḏeš 526
rûaḥ 385, 387
rûaḥ yhwh 388

šabbāṯ 526
šāḇû'ôṯ 526
šāliš̌im 555
šālôm 437
ṣārar 375

695

This book is due for return on or before the last date shown below.